MI'KMAQ TREATIES ON TRIAL

History, Land, and Donald Marshall Junior

In 1725–6 the British colonial government of Nova Scotia signed a treaty of friendship and peace with the local Mi'kmaq people. This treaty explicitly acknowledged the co-existence of Mi'kmaq and British law – but much of its meaning stemmed from its complex negotiation, which was influenced by the history of aboriginal-European relations in Acadia prior to 1726. William Wicken argues that after 1749 a more forceful British military presence led officials to re-interpret the treaty in the light of their own interests.

From 1994 to 1996, the author was an expert witness for the defence at the *Marshall* trial, during which the Supreme Court of Canada integrated aboriginal perspectives on treaty making into current interpretations. Dr Wicken was one of the historians who gathered and presented the historical evidence to the court.

This timely and original work intersperses close analysis of the 1726 treaty with discussions of the *Marshall* case, and shows how the intercultural relationships and power dynamics of the past have shaped both the law and the social climate of the present. The author argues that the treaties must be viewed in their historical context, and that of the oral tradition of Mi'kmaq people, to be properly understood.

Current high-profile legal cases involving aboriginal rights lend this work a special significance among the legal and academic communities, where it is destined to spark debate. It is of particular relevance to history and native studies students.

WILLIAM WICKEN is an associate professor in the department of history at York University. He co-authored a report in 1993 on Mi'kmaq treaties for the Royal Commission on Aboriginal Peoples, and from 1993–5 was a researcher and employee for the thirteen reserves of Nova Scotia investigating their aboriginal title claim. He frequently testifies as an expert witness in court cases involving aboriginal and treaty rights in Atlantic Canada. In 1998, he co-edited *New Faces of the Fur Trade* with Jo-Anne Fiske and Susan Sleeper-Smith.

Mi'kmaq Treaties on Trial

History, Land, and Donald Marshall Junior

WILLIAM C. WICKEN

UNIVERSITY OF TORONTO PRESS
Toronto Buffalo London

© University of Toronto Press 2002
Toronto Buffalo London
Printed in Canada

Reprinted 2008, 2011

ISBN 0-8020-0718-X (cloth)
ISBN 0-8020-7665-3 (paper)

Printed on acid-free paper

National Library of Canada Cataloguing in Publication Data

Wicken, William Craig, 1955–
    Mi'kmaq treaties on trial : history, land, and Donald Marshall
Junior

Includes bibliographical references and index.
ISBN 0-8020-0718-X (bound)   ISBN 0-8020-7665-3 (pbk.)

    1. Micmac Indians – Fishing – Law and legislation.   2. Micmac
Indians – Treaties.   3. Marshall, Donald, 1953– – Trials, litigation, etc.
4. Treaties – Language.   I. Title.

KE7709.W52 2002   343.71507′692′089973   C2001-902298-0

University of Toronto Press acknowledges the financial assistance to its
publishing program of the Canada Council for the Arts and the Ontario Arts
Council.

This book has been published with the help of a grant from the Humanities
and Social Sciences Federation of Canada, using funds provided by the Social
Sciences and Humanities Research Council of Canada.

University of Toronto Press acknowledges the financial support for its
publishing activities of the Government of Canada through the Book
Publishing Industry Development Program (BPIDP).

To John H. Wicken
(1924–   )
who taught me about history
and to
Florence M. Wicken (née Clause)
(1924–73)
who taught me about justice

Contents

Illustrations through Text:

Illustration section follows page 146

Acknowledgments

It is normal for authors to turn PhD dissertations into books. I chose not to do so and instead, soon after arriving at York University, embarked on the rather foolhardy project of writing an entirely new manuscript. My thesis and this book share a common subject – the Mi'kmaq. But the similarities end there.

Even so, I owe a great deal to the people who guided me through my graduate degrees. I benefited at McGill from the assistance of Pierre Boulle, Catherine Desbarats, Ella Laffey, Stephen Randall, and John Herd Thompson. For my PhD I worked with two consummate scholars – Toby Morantz and the late Louise Dechêne. Professor Morantz provided me with a grounding in social and political anthropology that has deeply influenced my scholarship. Professor Dechêne helped me appreciate the difficulties of understanding the past and the sources that illuminate it.

I could not have conducted my research without the help of the archivists at the National Archives of Canada in Ottawa, the Archives nationales de Québec and Archives du séminaire de Québec in Quebec City, the New Brunswick Museum in Saint John, and the Public Archives of New Brunswick in Frederiction. However, I did most of my research at the Public Archives of Nova Scotia in Halifax. Over the years I have benefited from the friendly and scholarly atmosphere the archive's staff have created. I would especially like to thank Barry Cahill, John McLeod, Julie Morris, and Gary Shutlack for their assistance over the years. My thanks also to David Christianson of the Nova Scotia Museum and Judy Deetz and Diane O'Neill of the Art Gallery of Nova Scotia, each of whom helped me locate the artwork and photographs for this book.

In the final stages of my dissertation, I moved to Halifax, where I began working as a researcher for the Aboriginal Title Project, an initiative overseen by the thirteen Mi'kmaq communities of Nova Scotia. Over the next two years I learned more about Mi'kmaq history than I had during my years in graduate school. At the Treaty Rights and Aboriginal Research Centre at Indian Brook, I was fortunate to work with Gillian Allen, Bob Beal, Laverne Copage, Denise MacDonald, Jim Michael, and Wallace Nevin, each of whom was involved in some way in the Marshall case as well as later cases.

I would also like to thank James Youngblood Henderson and Don Julian, who at various times shared with me their thoughts on Mi'kmaq history.

While I was working for the Mi'kmaq community, and later while I was a post-doctoral student, the Gorsebrook Research Institute of Saint Mary's University provided me with much-needed office space, a computer, access to university libraries, and much else. Jackie Logan facilitated my entry to Saint Mary's, and throughout the years of the Marshall trial provided the defence team with a convenient meeting place. Thérèse Arseneau, Colin Howell, and Madine Vanderplatt also deserve special mention for their assistance.

In 1996 I left Nova Scotia for York University. Over the past five years I have been lucky to work alongside some of the finest scholars in the country. I owe my greatest debt to my co-instructors in History 1050, a first-year course that introduces students to the social history of Western Europe and North America from 1700 to 1920. I have learned much from Stephen Brooke, Douglas Hay, Kathryn McPherson, H.V. Nelles, Adrian Shubert, and Marc Stein. Each of them, in very different ways, has contributed to my understanding of the past.

Though the research for this book was conducted for the most part at universities, it is based on events that took place in court rooms. Since 1993 I have spent much of my time either testifying as an expert witness or preparing to do so. Stephen Augustine, a member of the Mi'kmaq Grand Council and a researcher with the Canadian Museum of Civilization, John Reid from Saint Mary's University, and Stephen Patterson from the University of New Brunswick contributed in different ways to my understanding of the treaties between the Mi'kmaq and the British. Though Professor Patterson and I have often disagreed in the courts about how the treaties should be interpreted, I have learned much about the eighteenth century by listening to his testimony. I expect that Patterson will also disagree with much of this book. Perhaps he and I have opposed each other too long to make mutual comprehension possible. Or perhaps, the courtroom has allowed us to see our differences so clearly. Regardless, I hope that Professor Patterson will sometime soon write his own book-length interpretation of the treaties.

I have benefited as well from the persistent questioning of lawyers in various court cases over the past seven years: lawyers including Juli Abouchar, Don Burrage, Paul Carver, James Clarke, Ed Hearn, Peter Leslie, Shayne McDonald, Bob Matthews, and Michael Paré. My special thanks to Keith McCormick of the New Brunswick Prosecution Office for his engaging cross-examination of my evidence in *R. v. Bernard* and for later, in September 2000, sharing his understanding of New Brunswick's history during a drive from Fredericton to Newcastle. But I owe my greatest debt to Bruce Wildsmith and Eric Zscheile. Throughout the Marshall trial, Eric's intelligence, diplomatic skills, and wonderful midwestern humour were a source of strength for us all. Bruce deserves special mention, as much for his collegiality as for his brilliance. Over the years he has demonstrated both his skill as a trial lawyer and his uncanny ability to fit history and the law together. At no time did he reveal all of this more brilliantly than during the oral arguments before the Supreme Court in November 1998.

I would also like to thank those judges who sat through my often lengthy testimony and then tried to make sense of it: Justice Leo Barry of the Supreme Court of Newfoundland, Justice E.A. Bowie of the Tax Court of Canada, Justice Patrick Curran of the Nova Scotia Provincial Court, Justice John D. Embree, also of the Nova Scotia Provincial Court, and Justice Denis Lordon of the New Brunswick Provincial Court. I promise to never again bring York's library into the courtroom.

I have also benefited from the comments of a number of scholars who read earlier versons of the manuscript. Both Kathryn MacPherson and John Reid read my very earliest attempts to make sense of the treaties. My thanks also to Marc Egnal for reading two earlier chapters and for his advice that I should start again. His honesty saved me both time and energy. Finally, Robert Sweeny of Memorial University undertook, as always, to read whatever I gave him and then provided cogent and pointed comments. Robert may not agree with the final product; even so, the book is much better than it was when first delivered into his hands.

At University of Toronto Press, I was assisted by Jill McConkey and Frances Mundy. Thank you, Jill, for putting up with my queries and for your enthusiasm. I also would like to thank Matthew Kudelka, whose careful copy editing has much improved the book. My ego, Matthew, is not bruised.

I owe the most to Donald Marshall Jr and to my family. My thanks to Marshall for deciding to sell the fish he caught in August 1993, and for the strength of his belief that he had a right to do so.

Books are often created from discussions within the family. Before, during, and after the *Marshall* trial, I talked about this book with Jane Greenlaw far too often. Indelibly this book has assumed its present form because of those discussions. Our children, Keelin and Marcus, lived through the *Marshall* trial and afterwards with a father who was more often absent than present. This, above all, has been my greatest sorrow. However, I hope that in some way this book will assist in their own understanding of the past – and of their father's.

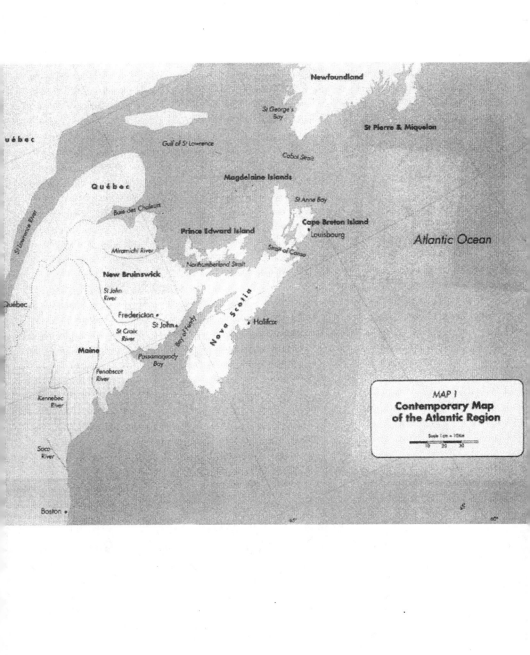

Newfoundland

St George's
Bay

St Pierre & Miquelon

Gulf of St Lawrence

Cabot Strait

Québec

Magdelaine Islands

St Anne Bay

Baie des Chaleurs

Prince Edward Island

Cape Breton Island

Louisbourg

Atlantic Ocean

Miramichi River

Northumberland Strait

Strait of Canso

New Bruinswick

St John
River

Nova Scotia

Québec

Fredericton

St John

Halifax

St Croix
River

Bay of Fundy

Maine

Passamaquody
Bay

Penobscot
River

Kennebec
River

MAP 1
**Contemporary Map
of the Atlantic Region**

Scale 1 cm = 100km
10   20   30

Saco
River

Boston

St Lawrence River

MI'KMAQ TREATIES ON TRIAL

History, Land, and Donald Marshall Junior

Introduction

In 1994 and 1995 I was one of three historians who testified at the trial of Donald Marshall Jr, a Mi'kmaq resident of Nova Scotia. The Canadian government had charged Marshall with fishing for eels and selling them without a licence. Marshall argued that a treaty his ancestors signed with Great Britain in 1761 superseded federal fisheries legislation. According to the federal government, the 1761 treaty had made Marshall's ancestors subject to British law, and therefore he was subject to federal fisheries law. Other Mi'kmaq living in Newfoundland, Nova Scotia, Prince Edward Island, New Brunswick, and the Gaspé region of Quebec disagreed. According to these communities even though it does not refer to fishing, the 1761 treaty nevertheless expresses the basis of their relationship with the non-Mi'kmaq population of Atlantic Canada. The Mi'kmaq also argue that their oral understanding of the treaties is different from its written text.

This book explores the historical basis of the Mi'kmaq's claim by analysing the context in which an earlier treaty, signed in 1726, was first confirmed, and later renegotiated in 1749, 1752, and 1760–1. The 1726 treaty was the first treaty signed between the Mi'kmaq and the British; as such, it became the foundation for all later treaties between them. I argue that while the 1726 treaty explicitly acknowledged the co-existence of Mi'kmaq and British law in interactions between the two communities, after 1749 a more forceful British military presence led officials to reinterpret the treaty, de-emphasizing its original oral meanings and stressing the primacy of the English text in the treaty's interpretation.

This contradiction between 'text' (of the treaties) and oral 'context' has been a source of continuing disagreement between the Mi'kmaq of

Atlantic Canada and federal and provincial governments. This disagreement arises mainly from how each party has historically understood the treaty relationship. Donald Marshall Jr's trial, which began in the latter months of 1994, is a case in point. At that trial, I testified on Marshall's behalf. I will begin with a brief account of that trial, for the purpose of situating my view of the treaties in a historical context.

On 24 August 1993, Donald Marshall Jr, Jane McMillan, and Peter Martin were observed by a federal Department of Fisheries and Oceans (DFO) officer fishing for eels in Pomquet Harbour. Pomquet Harbour is located on the northeastern shore of mainland Nova Scotia near the town of Antigonish. The eels Marshall and his companions caught were later transferred from a small outboard motorboat to a holding pen located on the Afton Mi'kmaq reserve. Marshall helped 'weigh and load his eels onto a truck belonging to the South Shore Trading Company Limited of Port Elgin, New Brunswick. South Shore is engaged in the purchase and sale of fish. Marshall sold 463 pounds of his eels to South Shore at $1.70 per pound.' Later that day the truck was stopped by a DFO official and Marshall, McMillan, and Martin were charged with violating federal fishing regulations. Specifically, they were charged with fishing and retaining fish 'without being authorized to do so under the authority of a license issued pursuant to Maritime provinces Fishery Regulations, the Fishery (General) Regulations, or the Aboriginal Communal Fishing Licenses Regulations.' They were also charged with fishing for eels during a closed period of the fishery, and with selling eels without having obtained 'a license issued for the purpose of commercial fishing.'[1] All charges were later dropped against McMillan, though not against Marshall and Martin. Martin, however, did not retain legal counsel. In the end, the federal government proceeded to trial only against Marshall.[2]

Marshall's defence was funded by the Union of Nova Scotia Indians (UNSI) and the Confederacy of Mainland Micmacs (CMM), the two political organizations representing the 'status' Mi'kmaq of Nova Scotia. Status Mi'kmaq are those people of aboriginal descent who are recognized as 'Indian' under the definitions set out in the Indian Act. According to that act, individual Indians can lose their 'status' in a number of ways; as a result, many people of aboriginal descent are no longer considered to be Mi'kmaq by the Canadian government. All of the status Mi'kmaq in Nova Scotia are associated with one or another of the province's thirteen reserve communities. In 1997 there were 11,208 status Mi'kmaq in Nova Scotia.[3]

The reserve communities are politically distinct from UNSI and CMM, though both organizations help coordinate reserve programs. Between 1969 and 1984, all thirteen reserves were associated with UNSI. Political disagreements between mainland and Cape Breton bands led to the formation of CMM in 1984. In 1993 the confederacy represented six mainland bands, while the union continued to represent all five Cape Breton bands as well as two mainland reserves, Indian Brook and Acadia. Both organizations would not normally have involved themselves in defending Marshall. However, Marshall was registered at Membertou, a Cape Breton community associated with UNSI, but was fishing at Afton, a mainland reserve represented by CMM, so both organizations cooperated in his defence. They also cooperated because they were upset with how the federal government was allocating commercial fishing licences.

Before 1990 the Mi'kmaq did not have any special right to the commercial fishery; this meant they were forced to buy commercial licences. Licences were expensive and only a limited number of them were available, so few Mi'kmaq were in a position to acquire them.[4] However, in 1990 in *R. v. Sparrow,* the Supreme Court of Canada ruled that aboriginal people had a right to fish for subsistence or ceremonial purposes, a right that superseded the right of all other members of society. This right, said the court, could be restricted, but the onus was on the government to demonstrate why such a limitation was necessary. Conservation, for instance, was a legitimate reason to restrict aboriginal peoples' right to fish.[5] In response to *Sparrow,* the federal government initiated the Aboriginal Fisheries Strategy (AFS). Under this program, communal fishing licences were distributed to aboriginal communities in Atlantic Canada and British Columbia. Each community was to harvest a specified amount of fish, with the amount to be established through negotiation. Where an agreement could not be reached, the federal government reserved the right to unilaterally impose harvest allocations. These licences were mainly for food, social, and ceremonial fishing, but in a limited number of situations fish could also be caught for sale.[6]

As of August 1993, two Mi'kmaq communities had refused to sign licensing agreements under the AFS program. These were Membertou, Marshall's 'official' residence, and Afton, where he, McMillan, and Martin had sold their fish to a New Brunswick company. People in Afton and Membertou feared that by signing a licensing agreement and accepting federal jurisdiction, they would be undermining their treaty and aboriginal rights. They believed that any agreement they reached with the government would later be used by DFO in future negotiations regarding the fishery.[7]

To the people of Afton and Membertou, and to CMM and UNSI, the *Sparrow* decision had demonstrated that the government was unwilling to implement further changes to an aboriginal fisheries program without direction from the Supreme Court. Indeed, *Sparrow* provided hope that the court might rule favourably on a case involving the commercial fishery. In 1993 a court case in British Columbia focusing on this issue was on appeal to the Supreme Court, though the defendant there was not covered by treaty and had based her claim on an aboriginal right.[8]

There are significant differences between a treaty right and an aboriginal right. A *treaty right* stems from the words used in an agreement between an aboriginal community and a European government. Treaties were signed at various times in Canada's history. The British signed treaties with aboriginal communities in eastern Canada during the 1700s, and with communities in Ontario in the late 1700s and early 1800s. Later, between 1871 and 1921, aboriginal people in western and northern Canada signed treaties with the Canadian government. An *aboriginal right*, in contrast, stems from the fact that aboriginal people were the first inhabitants of North America. Prior occupations of aboriginal communities are thought to provide them with certain rights that non-aboriginal people do not enjoy. Since the Supreme Court of Canada's decision in 1973 in *R. v. Calder*, the federal government has recognized that Canada's aboriginal people have 'aboriginal rights.'

Today the treaty and aboriginal rights of Canada's aboriginal peoples are protected under Canada's 1982 Constitution. Section 35(c) of the Constitution reads: 'The existing aboriginal and treaty rights of the aboriginal peoples of Canada, are hereby recognized and affirmed.'[9] What does this mean? That's a question that many people, including aboriginal leaders, academics, lawyers, judges, journalists – not to mention the general public – have been asking since 1982. Many of these same people have their own answers, but rarely do they agree.

Part of the problem has been that the intergovernmental conferences that were to define 'treaty and aboriginal rights' never did so. As a result, since 1982 the job of outlining section 35(c) of Canada's Constitution has been left to judges. Their decisions have been controversial, and some cases have gone all the way up to the Supreme Court of Canada. Witness, for instance, the storm of protest from aboriginal communities that greeted Chief Justice MacEachern's 1991 decision in *R. v. Delgamuukw*, and the Supreme Court's own pronouncement on that case in December 1997.[10] The Supreme Court's decisions in *R. v. Donald Marshall Jr.*, issued on 17 September and 17 November 1999, would also be controversial, eliciting sharp and protracted responses from aboriginal and non-aboriginal communities, from politicians and media commentators, and from the general public.[11]

The question posed by the *Marshall* case was relatively simple. Did he have a right to engage in the commercial fishery, irrespective of federal regulatory legislation that made selling fish without a licence a criminal offence? If he didn't, then he was guilty, since the defence did not dispute the facts presented by the Crown. But if he did have such a right to sell fish, then how was this right to be regulated? Did he have an open-ended right? Or could his right to fish and to sell fish be restricted by the federal government? What kind of right did he have? Was the selling of fish an aboriginal right? That is, was it a right he enjoyed because of his ancestors' prior occupation of Atlantic Canada? Or was selling fish a treaty right, a right that stemmed from treaties his ancestors had signed in the 1700s? And if the latter was the case, then what treaty gave Marshall a twentieth-century right to sell fish? Was it possible that a treaty could give him the right to sell fish, even though it did not mention fish?

In 1993 the lawyers representing Marshall concluded that a defence strategy focusing solely on proving the Mi'kmaq community's aboriginal right to the commercial fishery would be a difficult sell in the courtroom. It would require them to demonstrate conclusively that selling fish was integral to Mi'kmaq society prior to European contact. Finding such evidence would be difficult, since the archaeological record does not yield the kind of proof that courts demand. For this reason, the lawyers representing Marshall decided that a defence focusing on a treaty right would be a far better strategy.

CMM and UNSI were asking the court to reverse more than two centuries of colonization. During the eighteenth century, aboriginals had experienced little difficulty in fishing and providing for their families. This reflected the scattered nature of European settlement in Nova Scotia and the fact that most Mi'kmaq lived in coastal areas. In 1761 there were about 8,000 people of European descent living on mainland Nova Scotia, and the Mi'kmaq population was perhaps half that number.[12] By the 1990s, the relationship between the two populations had shifted dramatically: in 1996 there were 909,288 people living in Nova

Scotia, of whom only 10,333 were officially recognized by the federal government as Mi'kmaq.[13] In other words, in 1761 the Mi'kmaq had formed between 30 and 35 per cent of the population of Nova Scotia, yet 245 years later they comprised only 1.19 per cent.

The Mi'kmaq community's economic situation had also changed. In the 1760s they were living in coastal villages between April and November, and then migrating inland during winter to hunt for moose and caribou. By 1993 each community had found itself confined to a small reserve. Few of these reserves were in coastal areas. Take the case of Indian Brook, the largest of the mainland communities, with 1,909 inhabitants in 1997. Located in central Nova Scotia halfway between Halifax and Truro, the reserve is between 40 and 50 miles from the coast. In 1708 these same people had lived near Musquodoboit, a forty-five minute drive north of Halifax. Between 1708 and 1997, something had indeed changed for the Mi'kmaq of this region.

Both CMM and UNSI wanted more commercial fishing licences distributed to their communities. This would provide more employment and release many people from a dependency on welfare. But in 1993 this demand met with resistance from the federal government because of the growing crisis in the Atlantic groundfish industry.[14] By 1993 the decline in groundfish stocks had led to the virtual shutdown of the Newfoundland fishery. Though this crisis had less impact on Nova Scotia's fishery,[15] some Cape Breton and northern mainland communities were dependent on cod, leading some local fishermen to begin harvesting other types of fish. The resulting economic and political situation meant that DFO was unwilling to implement more changes to the aboriginal fishery – a position that was apparently supported by the federal Cabinet. Not surprisingly, UNSI and CMM requests for greater access to the commercial fishery were unsuccessful.

The government's inability to conclude an agreement with UNSI and CMM resulted in the charges against Marshall proceeding to trial. Both the Mi'kmaq and the federal government understood that policy on the aboriginal fishery would be decided by the courts. Both also understood that the trial judge's decision would be appealed to the higher courts. This understanding was expressed early in the trial by the federal Crown prosecutor, Michael Paré, in his remarks to Mr. Justice John D. Embree on 24 November 1994: 'It is probably inevitable, however this case resolves itself, that this case will be on its way to the Nova Scotia Court of Appeal and perhaps, in all likelihood, on its way to the Supreme Court of Canada.'[16] Paré's forecast was correct. The trial judge's decision of

27 June 1996 was appealed to the Nova Scotia Court of Appeal. Its decision was issued on 26 March 1997.[17] That decision was appealed to the Supreme Court, where oral arguments were presented to seven justices on 5 November 1998. Their decision was released on 17 September 1999.

The trial of Donald Marshall Jr took place intermittently from 21 November 1994, when the examination of the first witness began, to mid-February 1996, when the lawyers representing Marshall and the federal government made their closing arguments. Since Marshall admitted that he had been fishing and selling fish without a licence, the onus was on him to prove why he should not be subject to federal legislation. During pretrial negotiations, Bruce Wildsmith, appearing on behalf of UNSI, and Eric Zscheile, representing CMM, voiced their client's intent to argue that the eighteenth-century treaties superseded federal legislation. Because this defence strategy focused on historical issues, both the defence and the prosecution relied exclusively on professional historians to lead their evidence.

The government's only witness was Stephen E. Patterson, a historian from the University of New Brunswick. Though mainly a specialist in eighteenth-century New England, Patterson had begun researching the British–Mi'kmaq treaties in 1988. His interest had been sparked by a request from the office of Nova Scotia's Attorney-General that he testify in a treaty-related case.[18] By November 1994, Patterson had written two articles about the treaties.[19] In *Marshall*, Patterson testified for eleven days. This included ten days of direct examination by the government's lawyer, Paré, and one day of cross-examination by Wildsmith. Because of scheduling difficulties, Patterson's direct testimony only ended on 19 April 1995. After the defence completed its evidence, he again testified in mid-October 1995. Patterson testified a second time because the Crown had presented its evidence first and therefore had the right to rebut any new evidence introduced by the defence.[20] Though the defence could have called back its two witnesses to rebut Patterson's new testimony – called surrebuttal – Wildsmith and Zscheile chose not to do so.

The defence relied on two historians: John G. Reid from Saint Mary's University, and me. Reid was the first to testify, in early May 1995. His academic research focuses on European and native peoples inhabiting the Maritime region prior to 1710.[21] In 1993 the Royal Commission on Aboriginal Peoples asked him to prepare a report on the treaties signed between Great Britain and the Abenaki between 1676 and 1726.[22] This is what sparked his interest in the Nova Scotia treaties. In total, Reid testified for seven days, which included five days of direct examination and two days of cross-examination.

After Reid finished his testimony, I took the stand, testifying for fourteen and a half days – ten days of direct examination and four-and-a-half days of cross-examination. At the time, I was employed as a researcher with the Aboriginal Title Project, a joint initiative of the thirteen Mi'kmaq reserve communities in Nova Scotia. As was not the case with Patterson and Reid, my research in 1993 was solely on the Mi'kmaq. My doctoral dissertation, defended in June 1994, had analysed the evolution of the Mi'kmaq communities found in present-day Nova Scotia.[23] This dissertation, however, had not discussed the treaties. Like Reid, I got interested in the treaties after the Royal Commission on Aboriginal Peoples hired me to write a report. Unlike Reid, however, I examined the Mi'kmaq treaties in my report. In sum, each of the historians who testified in *R. v. Marshall* had done archival research on the history of the northeast, but none had analysed the treaties until requested to do so by a government agency.

Each historian who testified in *Marshall* submitted to the court the primary documents used to support his opinions. The prosecution's historical evidence was prepared by Patterson and consisted of six bound volumes containing 153 documents.[24] These documents were copies of government correspondence from the eighteenth century. They had been taken mainly from three archival collections: the records of the Nova Scotia government, housed in Halifax at the Public Archives of Nova Scotia; the correspondence of British colonial officials in Nova Scotia with their superiors in Great Britain, housed at the Public Record Office in England; and, to a more limited extent, letters sent to Versailles by French officials in New France, housed at the Archives nationales in Paris. For the most part, these documents focused the court's attention on events between 1752 and 1761. Patterson's decision to centre his testimony on these dates stemmed from the defence team's declared intention to use the 1752 and 1760–1 treaties as the basis of their defence.

Thematically, the documents submitted by Patterson showed the gradual integration of Mi'kmaq society into European norms of behaviour. A critical part of his testimony was his account of the growing dependence of Mi'kmaq communities on European manufactured goods, particularly guns, powder, shot, and other items used for hunting and fishing. With the defeat of the French forces at Louisbourg in July

1758, Patterson argued, Mi'kmaq communities had few other choices but to trade with British merchants. This, according to him, was the context in which the 1760–1 treaties should be read. He acknowledged that the Mi'kmaq would have had an imperfect cultural understanding of the treaties, but contended that the long period of contact with Europeans before 1761 would have minimized this factor. Patterson conceded that there were some problems in translating English legal terms into Mi'kmaq, but emphasized that the Mi'kmaq understood that once the treaties were signed, they would be subject to British law. In sum, Patterson argued that the Mi'kmaq negotiated the best possible deal they could under very difficult circumstances.

The defence team also submitted documents to the Court. An initial set was delivered to the Crown's lawyers on 20 March 1995. After Patterson completed his testimony on 19 April, some documents were deleted from the original submission. This was because the two lawyers representing Marshall – Wildsmith and Zscheile – had decided to rely solely on the 1760–1 treaties, and not to resort to the 1752 treaty. During the first week of May, nine bound volumes containing 231 documents were given to Paré.

The defence documents spanned a broader time frame than those of the Crown. For instance, Reid and I both argued that the 1760–1 treaties cannot be understood in isolation from the treaties made before then. Reid contended that the Mi'kmaq treaties evolved from treaties signed between the colony of Massachusetts and the Abenaki between 1678 and 1725. For this reason, the first two defence volumes were almost exclusively composed of materials relating to the Abenaki. Indeed, these two volumes would form the core of Reid's testimony.

The rest of the defence documents provided additional material for evaluating the 1760–1 treaties. Part of that documentation provided insights into the oral discussions preceding and antedating the signing of the treaties. These materials gave fuller meaning to the treaties' English words and suggested strongly how the Mi'kmaq would have understood them. In Reid's interpretation and my own, this documentation showed that the Mi'kmaq and the British had different understandings of certain conceptual issues discussed in the treaties.

The historical evidence in the trial of Donald Marshall Jr posited two different understandings of the 1761 treaty. One interpretation, offered by Patterson, saw the treaty texts as reflecting a political order imposed on the Mi'kmaq. In Patterson's opinion, the political and military forces arrayed against the Mi'kmaq in the late 1750s – and especially the demise of French power in North America – minimized their ability to influence the treaty process. For our part, Reid and I argued that the 1761 treaty was the result of a consensual agreement made between the Mi'kmaq and British. We stressed that British power was less omnipotent and more tenuous than Patterson suggested. We argued that the British wanted a treaty to neutralize the Mi'kmaq during the war with France so that British settlement of the region could proceed peacefully. For these two reasons, we argued that the treaty's language was less reflective of British power than Patterson supposed.

Judge Embree delivered his decision on 27 June 1996 to a packed Antigonish courtroom.[25] For Embree, the central issue was what the English text of the treaty said. The defence was asking him to override federal fishing statutes. If he was to find in Marshall's favour, he needed a solid evidential basis that would support such a judgment and one that the public and his judicial colleagues would perceive as conclusive and incontrovertible. In examining the historical documents placed before him, he searched for the facts needed to determine Marshall's guilt or innocence. The problem was determining what was a fact and what was not, and how these 'facts' should be employed in understanding the written treaty texts – a difficulty that judges, lawyers, and historians have struggled with in other litigation.[26]

This contradiction between the written text of the treaties and the oral context in which they were created forms the central focus of this book. This approach is based on Jack Goody's analysis of how the development of writing systems has minimized the contribution of oral communication in formulating legal relationships. Written law, he argues, is concerned mainly with adopting a universal language that supersedes local circumstances. In addressing broader societal concerns, the law becomes divorced from the 'context of speech.' Words can afterwards be abstracted without regard to their original context, since the words in which they were first voiced are gradually lost. This process is furthered by the compilation of additional written documentation, which then becomes an interpretative framework for understanding the original law.[27]

If we adopt Goody's approach to analyse how the treaties were negotiated, then we must conclude that the treaty texts were instruments employed by the British to establish a general legal framework for mediating relations with the Mi'kmaq. As products of a large imperial bureaucracy, the treaties were drafted in a manner consistent with British colonial policies. Any concerns expressed by Mi'kmaq delegates stemming from local matters were not formally included in the written English text, though they were considered to form part of the treaty's oral meanings. Thereafter, the written text became the principal avenue for understanding the treaty's meanings. Any words spoken when the treaty was negotiated became less important in its later interpretations. Two social acts – the writing of the treaty and later accounts of it – were embodied within the written culture of the colonizer. This simplified future understanding of the treaties by privileging British interpretation while marginalizing Mi'kmaq participation in creating the treaty.

This book reflects my experience as an expert witness in the continuing legal wrangle between the Mi'kmaq of Atlantic Canada and the federal and provincial governments regarding treaty interpretation. My involvement began while I was an employee of the UNSI and the CMM during the Marshall case in 1994 and 1995, and has continued since then. In the following pages, I discuss issues that first emerged during the trial of Donald Marshall Jr and that have been examined more fully in subsequent litigation. Since September 1995, when my testimony ended in *Marshall*, I have testified in five other cases: *Vaughan Pictou, et al. v. R* (1997 in the Federal Tax Court of Canada), *R. v. Bernard* (1999 in New Brunswick Provincial Court), *R. v. Stephen Frederick Marshall, et al.* (1999 in the Nova Scotia Provincial Court), *R. v. Duthie and Paul* (2000 in New Brunswick Provincial Court), and *R. v. Drew* (2000–01 in Supreme Court of Newfoundland). At this writing, I am preparing to testify in what may eventually become known as Marshall #3: *Shubenacadie v. the Attorney-General of Canada*, in which the UNSI is seeking clarification from the Federal Court regarding the implementation of the Supreme Court's ruling in *Marshall*.

This book is based both on my historical research and on my experience as an expert witness. While this book is based on eighteenth-century documents, my analysis has been shaped by the litigation process. I have learned much from the men who stood across from the witness box: Bruce Wildsmith, senior counsel for the UNSI; Eric Zscheile, legal counsel for the CMM; Michael Paré and Ian MacRae, federal lawyers in *Marshall*; Peter Leslie of the Federal Tax Office of Canada; Keith McCormick and Pierre Charbonneau of the New Brunswick Attorney-General's Office; James Clarke and Paul Carver of Nova Scotia's Public Prosecution Office; Don Burrage and Edward Hearn, who represented the Newfoundland government in *Drew*; and Bob Mattews and Shayne MacDonald, who represented the Conne River band in the same case. These lawyers, who questioned my conclusions, searched for inconsistencies, and looked for alternative explanations, have helped me frame my own ideas. This book therefore incorporates the practices of the historian and, in a more limited manner, the precepts of the lawyer attempting to understand the past. The adversarial process has led perhaps to a more complete understanding of the treaties than if we had not been so engaged.

Perhaps this book is a 'regional history'; any history of the early eighteenth century must be regional to a large extent. As Geoffrey Plank writes: 'Examined in detail, imperial history is always local history.'[28] In contrast, historians of the nineteenth and twentieth centuries must move beyond the local community to consider how industrialization affected ordinary people's lives. A study of the Mi'kmaq of Nova Scotia during the twentieth century would be very different from this one, as it would have to evaluate how the national state and an emerging national economy affected individual communities. The world of the early eighteenth century, however, was far less integrated and far more dispersed than the world of the centuries that followed. Though historians now believe that the industrialization of Great Britain began in the mid-eighteenth century, the changes it precipitated did not substantially affect either Nova Scotia or the treaties the British signed with the Mi'kmaq.

But it is also true that Nova Scotia was part of a North Atlantic world, in which trade and politics linked Nova Scotia with the New England colonies, with the Caribbean, and with Europe.[29] The Mi'kmaq treaties of 1726 and 1761 were a creation of this North Atlantic world. Rivalry between the British and French for control over trade spurred the treaty signings, in the sense that Great Britain believed that the French–Mi'kmaq alliance threatened its commercial and political aspirations in the North Atlantic. The treaties provided Great Britain with more secure access to the Nova Scotia fishery and facilitated the defeat of French forces in North America. Thus, the treaties arose out of a regional interaction with transatlantic economic forces.

Yet a study centred mainly on the European side of this North Atlantic world would tend to downplay the Mi'kmaq as historical actors. My purpose in this book is to centre the reader's attention on the Mi'kmaq and to emphasize their agency in the making of a 'new world.' This focus, I hope, will allow the reader to better understand the current political and legal struggle between the Mi'kmaq of Atlantic Canada and federal and provincial governments. This struggle, I contend, is not a creation of the 1982 Constitution, nor the work of clever lawyers. Quite the contrary. The *Marshall* case could not have happened had the Mi'kmaq community not believed that the treaties signed with the British between 1726 and 1761 meant something different from what a literal reading of them suggests.

This book focuses on the 1726 treaty as a historical and legal document. It is divided into three parts, each of which discusses the 1726 treaty. In the two chapters of Part I, I examine the seventy-seven aboriginal individuals whose names are on the treaty. When combined with other sources, these names help us analyse how individual Mi'kmaq identified themselves in relation to one other and to the lands they occupied. These two chapters are the starting point for my analysis of the 1726 treaty. In Part II, I examine sequentially each article of that treaty. Chapters 3 to 6 analyse the written text and develop the central thesis of the book – that the treaty should be understood as an oral text that has been written in an English format. It flows from this that there are often multiple meanings to the treaty – meanings that can be understood only by examining the historical context of each treaty article. Chapter 7 analyses the social and economic interests of British officials who were directly or indirectly involved in making the treaty. This chapter acts as a counterpoint to Chapters 1 and 2, by considering the clash between the cultural and economic interests of the Mi'kmaq and the British. Part III is a marked departure from the earlier chapters, in that it focuses on how the 1726 treaty was interpreted by later generations of British and Mi'kmaq officials. Chapters 8 and 9 explore how changes in British policy, signified by the founding of Halifax in 1749, altered the oral meanings that had been attached to the written text of the 1726 treaty. Chapter 8 examines the signing of the 1749 and 1752 treaties, while Chapter 9 analyses the 1760–1 treaties.

As much as possible, I have considered both British and Mi'kmaq understandings of the treaty. The treaty would not have existed if there had not been an agreement. Nor would later British officials and Mi'kmaq chiefs have renewed it. However, British interpretations of the treaty are far easier to discern than Mi'kmaq ones. If there is less of a Mi'kmaq world in these pages than one would hope, it is because that world was too often constrained by the spaces created by British and French pens and by my own.

Interspersed throughout the book are extended comments regarding the *Marshall* case. These comments are organized chronologically, beginning with November 1993 and ending with November 1999. My purpose in discussing the *Marshall* case while concurrently analysing the 1726 treaty is to enable the reader to evaluate how history is interpreted in the courts by historians, by lawyers, and by judges. For the most part, my comments on this process are less analytical than perhaps some might hope. However, my silence is a deliberate one; I have attempted as much as possible to separate myself from the history in which I was an actor. Only at the very end of the discussion on *Marshall* do I assume a more analytical tone and attempt to merge the history of the treaties with the history of the *Marshall* case. I have left a number of issues unresolved, in part because I stand too close to the events I examine and because the *Marshall* case is still unfolding. In any case, this book should be read both as a history of the 1726 treaty and as a historical document. Whether these two readings are one and the same, I leave for the reader to judge.

I have used the term 'Mi'kma'ki' to describe the geographical area inhabited by the Mi'kmaq both at the time of contact and afterward. This land surface encompasses southern Newfoundland, Cape Breton, mainland Nova Scotia, Prince Edward Island, the eastern coast of New Brunswick from the headwaters of the rivers flowing into the Gulf of St Lawrence to the coast, and the Gaspé peninsula of present-day Quebec. This area is often referred to as Eastern Canada, since it encompasses the easternmost parts of Canada. Throughout the book, I also refer to 'mainland Mi'kma'ki.' By this I mean the present-day provincial boundaries of mainland Nova Scotia. In contrast, I use 'British Nova Scotia' to describe the area occupied by British forces after 1710. I also use the Mi'kmaq word 'Unimaki' in referring to Cape Breton Island and southern Newfoundland, and 'French Île Royale' when discussing areas occupied by French-speaking peoples on Cape Breton after 1713.

PART ONE
The Mi'kmaq in 1726

We belong on this land, we're going to live on this land and we're going to stay on this land.

Donald Marshall Jr., quoted in *Toronto Globe and Mail*, 28 October 1999

The first time I heard that charges had been laid against Donald Marshall Jr was Thursday, 25 November 1993, at a meeting of the Treaty Working Group. The Treaty Working Group was composed of people working for the Mi'kmaq community who had a direct interest in the treaties. I had just begun working for the Aboriginal Title Project and so was new to the group's workings. This was the first and only meeting I would be asked to attend.

Various people were present. Representing the Mi'kmaq community were Ben Sylliboy, the Grand Chief of the Grand Council, Dan Christmas, the executive director of the Union of Nova Scotia Indians, and Reg Maloney, vice-president of UNSI and chief of the Shubenacadie reserve, which is about forty-five miles inland from Halifax. Three lawyers were present: Bruce Wildsmith, a professor of law at Dalhousie University who also acts as legal counsel for the Union, Eric Zscheile, a lawyer and full-time employee of the Confederacy of Mainland Micmacs, and D. Bruce Clarke, a Halifax-based lawyer with the firm Burchell MacAdam & Hayman, who provides legal advice to the Native Council of Nova Scotia Indians. The native council represents the province's non-status Indians. Its president in 1993 was Dwight Dorey, who claimed that his group had some 30,000 members – a claim disputed by the chiefs from the thirteen reserves representing the province's status Indians. Three others were also present: Olive Dickason, a recently retired history professor from the University of Alberta, Bob Beal, then director of the Treaty and Aboriginal Rights Research Centre (TARR) at Shubenacadie, and me. Dickason had been invited to give a short presentation on treaties. Beal was present because as head of TARR and coordinator of the Aboriginal Title Project, he would be able to harness the manpower necessary to assemble the historical documentation to be used in Marshall's defence. During the afternoon, Wildsmith briefly presented the details regarding the charges against Marshall.

One of the historical issues discussed that day was the economic and political character of Mi'kmaq society in the 1700s. The first thing Wildsmith wanted to know about was eels. If evidence could be found that eels had been an important component of the Mi'kmaq economy at the time the treaties were signed, the defence's case would be bolstered, as a direct link could then be made between the commercial provisions of the treaty and the selling of eels. Although the main focus of his query was eels, any evidence showing Mi'kmaq selling fish to Europeans before and after 1760 would be good enough.

The second historical issue raised by Wildsmith was the identity of Jean Baptiste-Cope, a Mi'kmaq who had signed the 1752 treaty. Both Wildsmith and Zscheile would have liked nothing better than to use the 1752 treaty as their principal historical defence. This was because the fourth article of that treaty seemed to provide an open-ended historical right of the Mi'kmaq to engage in a commercial fishery. But there was a problem: Cope was identified in the treaty as the chief of Shubenacadie, a community well inland on the Nova Scotia mainland. Mr. Marshall was from Cape Breton and had been fishing at Pomquet, a reserve on the northern coast of the mainland. However, at an earlier trial in 1989–90, experts testifying on behalf of the Mi'kmaq community had argued that in 1752 Cope had been the Grand Chief of the Grand Council. These experts had contended that Cope had signed the treaty on behalf of all Mi'kmaq. If the courts accepted this historical argument, Marshall would be a beneficiary of the 1752 treaty, and his defence would be substantially easier than if the 1761 treaty was relied upon.

Wildsmith raised the issue on 25 November because he understood how hard it would be to convince a judge that Cope was the Grand Chief in 1752. That had been the problem in 1989–90 when the provincial prosecutor for Nova Scotia, Alison Scott, had introduced evidence through Stephen Patterson that Cope was nothing more and nothing less than what the treaty said he was, chief of Shubenacadie. I was the new kid on the block, and among other things, Wildsmith likely wanted to know what I thought.

Both then and afterwards, I argued that there was no direct historical evidence demonstrating that Cope was Grand Chief in 1752. Likewise, I said that there was no evidence that the Grand Council existed in the 1700s. I stressed, however, that the lack of evidence did not mean that Cope had not been Grand Chief, nor did it mean that the Grand Council did not exist. It only meant that there was no historical documentation to make a definitive statement. I would be pressed on this issue by Michael Paré in his cross-examination of my evidence in *R. v. Donald Marshall Junior,* and later still by James Clarke in *R. v. Stephen Frederick Marshall, et al.* Both Paré and Clarke would have preferred that I referred to Cope as the Grand Chief. Since they had been briefed well by Patterson regarding the lack of direct evidence regarding Cope's identity, a response from me that Cope had been Grand Chief would have allowed them to diminish my credibility before the court, by pointing out that my opinions were not supported by the historical record. In other words, they could argue that I was acting as an advocate for the defence and not as an objective witness.

These issues regarding the economic and political character of

Mi'kmaq society in the 1700s illustrate the difficulty of providing expert historical evidence to the courts. In demonstrating that Marshall had a commercial right to sell the eels he had caught, the defence lawyers would have preferred evidence showing that eels were integral to Mi'kmaq society in the 1700s. If this evidence could not be found, the case wouldn't have been lost, although its existence would have made the defence's work easier. In later cases – notably *R. v. Bernard* (New Brunswick Provincial court) and *R. v. Stephen Frederick Marshall* (Nova Scotia Provincial Court) – Crown lawyers would stress the difference between the right that the Mi'kmaq defendants were asking to be estab-lished and the historical economy of their ancestors. In both these more recent cases, a number of Mi'kmaq loggers had been cutting timber from Crown land and then selling the timber to pulp mills. They did so without proper authorization from provincial regulatory bodies. In these two logging cases, the Crown lawyers attempted to demonstrate the incompatibility between this twentieth-century practice and the eighteenth-century Mi'kmaq economy. In their cross-examination of my evidence, both Keith McCormick from New Brunswick and James Clarke from the Nova Scotia Prosecution Office wanted to know if there was any evidence that before the treaties with the British were signed, the Mi'kmaq had cut logs in order to sell them. While there was no such evidence, there was historical documentation showing that the Mi'kmaq used wood products and plants for their own subsistence, and that they used timber in making the birchbark canoes they sold to the British. So, although the documents did not directly support the cutting and selling of timber, there was evidence that the Mi'kmaq had cut timber. Simi-larly, in *R. v. Marshall,* though there was only one document showing a Mi'kmaq selling eels, there was more evidence regarding the sale of fish.

Similarly, even though there was no direct evidence that the Grand Council functioned in the 1700s, there were records showing intervil-lage councils meeting with the governor of French Île Royale. Were these intervillage councils actually meetings of the Grand Council? If they were, there was no document that said so, and this made it difficult to focus the defence's historical evidence on the 1752 treaty. To make matters worse, both British and French sources showed that Cope's influence within the Mi'kmaq community in 1752 was much contested, suggesting that he really wasn't anything more than a local leader.

In sum, there are difficulties in presenting historical evidence to the courts: first, in directing the historical evidence to the specific act for which the defendant is claiming a constitutional right, and second, in presenting conclusions without a strong evidential basis. Both these evidential problems would figure at the trial of Donald Marshall Jr.

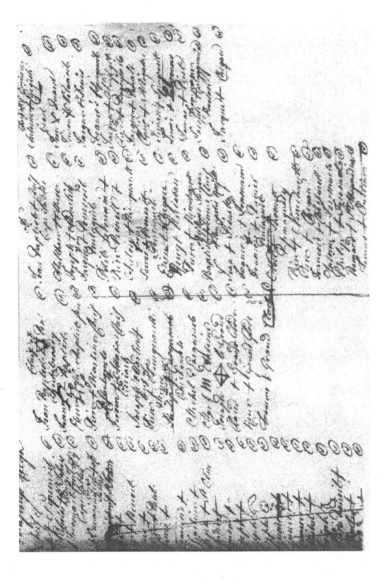

Treaty of 1726, dated 4 June 1726, showing aboriginal signatures. This copy accompanied Lt.-Gov. Armstrong's dispatch to London on 27 November 1726.

Province & the Deputies of the ffrench Inhabitants of Sᵗ Province hereunto Sett our Hands & Seals att Annapolis Royall this 4ᵗʰ Day of June 1726 & in the twelveth Year of His Majestys Reign.

Chief of
(?) Nipitmoit
Nicholas X Sᵗ. Johns
  Chiefs of
Paul Tecumart X one of yᵉ
  Cape Sables
Joseph Ounaginitish X of
  Sables
Marquis X of St. Johns
Obin' X
Piere X Benoit
Denis X
Puize X Paul
Louis X
Francois X
Sᵗ Castine X
Joseph X Sᵗ Obin
Andre X
Simon X
Joseph X
Joseph [totem]
Joseph [totem]
Francois X
Francois X
Francois X
Michel X
Joseph [totem]
Piere Benoit X
Charles X
Andre X

  Chief of
Jean Baptist [totem] Pon
  Chachabanuly
Jean [totem] Baptist
Etienne fils de Baptist Pon
  of
Piere X Martine Chief
  Re/fmbuezo
Jirom Xᵉˢ Attanas Chief
  Gislaux
Joseph Martine X
  Chief of
Piere X Armquarett
  Mizis
  Chief of
Philip X Eargomot
  Onekanito
Michel [tm] Eargamet
Mark [tm] Antoine
Joseph [totem] le Grand
Claud X Ornud Glode
Rene X Grand Glode
Francois X Grand Glode

  of
Jean Baptist X Chief
  Cape Sables
Matthew X Muse
Joseph X Miductuk
  from
Jacque X Pemeriot
  Pemaquit
Petit Jermain X
Piere Pirnett X
Antoin X Nimaquarett
  from
Lewis X Pemeroit
  Pemquit
Eden X Chegau
Reny X Nectabau
Piere X Nimcharett
  of yᵉ River Indians
Baptist X Tomns Chief
  of Annapolis Royall
Jean X Pisnett
Francois X Jermain
  from
Francois X Xavier
  Pemquit
Noel X Shomitt
  Paᵒmawody
Piere X Nimcharett
Piere X Chegau
Francois X Chickanett
Antoine X Tecumart
Philip X Tecumart
Bernard X Sᵗ Abommadin
Tomas X Outine

  Chief of Kwara
Antoine X Eglish
  Coust
Jean X Quaret
Simon X Nehmoit
Jacque X Denis
Francois X Spugomoit
Jacque X Nughiquit
Claud X Begamonit
Jacque X Penall
Claud X Migaion
Simon X Spugomoit
Louis X Lavoinst
Jean X Pinet
  from yᵉ Cape
Joseph X Chigagniata
  Breton
Jacque X Chegan

Typescript copy of the Aboriginal signatures to the 4 June 1726 treaty that accompanied Armstrong's dispatch of 27 November 1726. The typescript comes from evidence books in *R. v. Stephen Frederick Marshall, et al.*

Chapter One

The Mi'kmaq and Land

In fishing for eels, Donald Marshall Jr was doing what his ancestors had always done. But he was not fishing with his family or with other members of his home community, and though he likely kept some eels, most of the catch he sold. For Marshall's ancestors, fishing was part of a way of life that included hunting moose, gathering berries, growing corn and tobacco, making canoes, and repairing firearms. If we had asked Marshall in 1993 what his occupation was, he probably would have described himself as a self-employed fisherman – a response his eighteenth-century ancestors would not have understood. For them, fishing was not an occupation or a skill; rather, it was something they did. But in 1993, the economy of which the Mi'kmaq were part was dramatically different than it had been two hundred years before. To live, Marshall needed an occupation. In 1993 he was fishing, and selling the fish he caught to purchase things he did not make, including items for his personal use such as food and clothing. Though Marshall is Mi'kmaq, he was fishing within an economic and political system based on different precepts than had held during his ancestors' time.

This does not mean that Marshall does not think of himself as Mi'kmaq, or that we should not think of him as Mi'kmaq, simply because he is not living as his ancestors did. Rather, Mi'kmaq society has evolved over the centuries, and so too has the Mi'kmaq identity. But it is hard to understand that evolution, in part because we know so little about the Mi'kmaq before 1500.

Mi'kmaq history began long before the arrival of European fishing fleets off the Nova Scotia coast in the early 1500s. Describing that early history, however, is not so easily done. The Mi'kmaq, like other aboriginal communities, did not leave written records, so historians have been forced to adopt other means to understand Mi'kmaq history. One favoured method is to use the classificatory systems developed by anthropologists for understanding non-European societies – an approach that stresses understanding a community's linguistic affiliation, economy, kinship system, and political organization. By adopting this approach, and folding in the earliest written descriptions made of Mi'kmaq society by French traders, travellers, and missionaries, we can describe Mi'kmaq society before the 1500s. For instance, we can say that the Mi'kmaq were an 'Algonquian'-speaking people, that their economy was centred on hunting and gathering, and that they tended to live in large communities during the summer months. Of course, such statements are cursory, even simplistic when compared with the sophisticated analyses that have been made of contemporaneous Houdenosaunee and Huron communities. But for the Huron and the Houdenosaunee, an abundance of pre-1500 archaeological sites exist that have yielded valuable information about those peoples.

The same cannot be said for the Mi'kmaq. Quite simply, far less archaeological material is available to help us understand their pre-1500 past. Because of this, we do not know how and when these people came to think of themselves as Mi'kmaq. What we can say is that people have lived in the present-day Maritimes since at least 11,000 BP and that over the centuries, community identities have been shaped and reshaped, as much through internal events as through outside influences.[1] For much of the period before 1500, we are unable to determine the cultural identity of the communities that inhabited the Atlantic region.[2] We cannot say, for instance, that the people who lived in the region 11,000 BP are the ancestors of the Mi'kmaq. What we do know is that beginning around 2500 BP, the people living in the Maritime region of Atlantic Canada began slowly to develop an identity distinct from other people to the west of them.[3] By the early 1600s, these people were inhabiting much of coastal Atlantic Canada and sharing a common language and culture. This identity was recognized by both themselves and others. These people called themselves, L'nuk, or the People. Europeans called them 'Mi'kmaq.'[4]

Europeans began settling in Mi'kma'ki in the early 1600s, and the first extensive descriptions of the region date from that time. Yet these provide little information that we can use to analyse Mi'kmaq history. Though the sources improve for the 1700s in both quantity and variety, the information they provide about the Mi'kmaq is still not extensive. For the most part, the Mi'kmaq lived their lives outside the purview of the European fishermen, traders, farmers, soldiers and colonial officials who came to Mi'kma'ki. Little was written about the Mi'kmaq, if only because little was known.

I do not pretend that the following portrait of Mi'kmaq society between 1726 and 1761 is exact. Such precision is impossible, as the written sources are far too few to even attempt a painstaking examination of the sort that we can make, for instance, of Montreal in 1830. We do not have maps showing where each and every Mi'kmaq household was located. We do not have censuses that list each resident. We do not have notarial records. And though there are some parish registers that mention Mi'kmaq births, marriages, and deaths, these are the exception, not the norm. In sum, we lack almost all of the most basic sources of information that historians of the early modern period use in examining the past.

But as other historians have shown, certain events sometimes lead to the creation of a document that allows more to be said about a community's history.[5] On 4 June 1726, British officials and Mi'kmaq delegates signed a treaty. It was written on parchment and measured about two feet wide by three feet long, and comprised eight clauses, which were intended to govern British–Mi'kmaq relations. What makes this treaty special, aside from what it says, is that it bears the names of seventy-seven aboriginal people. At no other time in the 1700s would so many Mi'kmaq be identified as meeting with British officials. This chapter uses the 1726 treaty to explore the economic and social identity of the Mi'kmaq identity in 1726.

Affixed to the treaty are the signatures of fifty Mi'kmaq men, who are identified with nine separate villages on mainland Mi'kma'ki, Unimaki, and the east coast of New Brunswick (see pp. 22–3). The presence of their signatures points strongly to a political unity among Mi'kmaq villages with clearly defined territories. Cape Sable, La Hève, Richibucto, Shediac, and Chignecto are examples. The families that inhabited each of these territories shared a common identity that was shaped by marriage, by cooperative labour, by political structures that mediated internal and external relationships, and by a common historical experience. This identity was reinforced by customs that regulated both community actions and the resources on which those actions depended. The delegates who signed the treaty represented each community's interest in preserving the customs governing their territory and its inhabitants. Close attention to the Mi'kmaq who signed the treaty reveals these social and political institutions.

This chapter and the following one describe Mi'kmaq society in 1726, using the treaty as the focal point for analysis. These chapters do not attempt to chart the evolution of Mi'kmaq society from first contact to 1726. Rather, the goal here is to understand the society at the time its members first entered into a treaty relationship with the British. I will not be considering issues that are often examined in accounts of aboriginal–European relations during the colonial period. For instance, I will not be discussing the impact of European diseases, or the influence (if any) of French missionaries on Mi'kmaq cosmology.

The 1726 treaty was the first the Mi'kmaq made with the British. It is composed of two parts: the articles of peace and agreement signed by the Mi'kmaq, and the reciprocal promises made to the Mi'kmaq and signed by colonial officials.

The Mi'kmaq and the British signed the treaty differently. The British officials, including John Doucett, the Lieutenant-Governor of Annapolis Royal, and William Shirreff, secretary of the Nova Scotia Council, wrote their names using an alphabetic script. Doucett and Shirreff were natural-born subjects of the British Crown stationed at Annapolis Royal, where they served as representatives of George I. Using this information, we can discover more about each of them, by referring to the correspondence of the Board of Trade, the records of the War Office, and the documents of the Fortieth Regiment of Foot, which was the unit stationed at Annapolis Royal from 1717 to 1749.

Identifying the aboriginal people listed on the treaty is more difficult. In total, there are seventy-seven signatures. Fifty-nine signatures include both a family and a personal name; the other eighteen consist of a personal name only. Eight individuals signed using a totemic emblem; the other sixty-nine marked an 'X' beside their name, which indicates that they were unable to write in alphabetic script.[6] These delegates in some respects resembled the peasants, artisans, soldiers, and vagrants of early modern Europe, who also marked an 'X' beside their names (written for them by parish priests) on marriage or baptismal certificates. Because of these peoples' social status and illiteracy, only limited written information is available to explain their lives. Even fewer sources exist for understanding aboriginal people. This is because aboriginal people (including the Mi'kmaq) were not integrated into the European economy. The

Mi'kmaq were not farmers. They did not work as labourers or artisans and did not live in any of the principal French or English settlements of either French Acadia or British Nova Scotia. Because most Mi'kmaq rarely interacted with Europeans, few Europeans wrote about them. Thus, the seventy-seven aboriginal names at the bottom of the 1726 treaty reflect a past more illusory than real. Names mean little if the people they belong to cannot be located within the community that shaped them.

But if it is not possible to recount the personal histories of the aboriginal signers of the 1726 treaty, some things can be said about them. The first relates to their cultural identity. Though the cultural identity of each signer is not given, the treaty does identify fifteen people with one of five geographical regions: present-day Nova Scotia, the eastern coast of New Brunswick, the St John River valley, the St Croix River, and the Penobscot River (see map on page xiii). For Nova Scotia, the communities listed in the treaty are Annapolis, Cape Sable, the Eastern Coast, Minas, Chebenacadie, and Cape Breton. For the eastern coast of New Brunswick, Chignecto, Shediac, and Richibucto are listed; while for central New Brunswick, the St John River is given. Also listed are Passamaquoddy along the Maine–New Brunswick border, and Pentagoet, which refers to an area near the mouth of the Penobscot River.

Analyses of censuses made by French missionaries and British officials before and after 1726 indicate the cultural identity for each community mentioned in the treaty. The nine communities situated in mainland Mi'kma'ki, Unimaki, and southeastern New Brunswick were inhabited by Mi'kmaq speakers. The people living along the St John River[7] were called 'Maliseet.' The British called them the St John River Indians, though they called themselves the Wuastukwiuk, meaning 'people of the Wulastuk River.'[8] Immediately to the west of them were the Passamaquoddy, who lived along Passamaquoddy Bay in summer and migrated up the St Croix River in winter. Finally, there were the 'Penobscot,' who are usually grouped with the 'Abenaki' and who lived along the Penobscot River. 'Abenaki' refers to culturally similar communities living between the Penobscot and Saco rivers. In total, the treaty identifies delegates from four distinct cultural communities: Mi'kmaq, Maliseet, Passamaquoddy, and Penobscot.[9] At times, these four societies are referred to collectively as the Wabanaki, or the People of the Dawn.

We might easily conclude that the Mi'kmaq speakers lived in fixed settlements, just as we would suppose that the British officers who signed the treaty lived at a place called Annapolis Royal. What we know about the Mi'kmaq economy in the 1700s suggests otherwise. The Mi'kmaq of

1726 differed from other aboriginal peoples in the Northeast.[10] The Houdenosaunee [Iroquois], for example, tilled the soil and lived in palisaded villages that often numbered between 500 and 1,000 inhabitants. Mi'kmaq communities were smaller and more nomadic, as their region was less conducive to growing maize, pumpkins, beans, and other cultigens. Though they grew corn in small garden plots, they depended mainly on fishing and hunting. This meant that communities did not live in one place for long periods. Rather, families moved as was necessary.[11] The ten people identified with a specific place in the treaty therefore were not part of a community that lived in a fixed settlement; rather, they moved from place to place throughout the year.

Then how would these individuals have thought of themselves? Did those who were identified as from Cape Sable think themselves as 'Cape Sable Indians'? Or did they conceptualize their identity in a different manner, one that emphasized a smaller, more localized community?

In Mi'kmaq society, identity was closely associated with the family. Families were composed of a man, a woman, and their children. As in most preindustrial societies, households also included relatives who were not living with their immediate relations. Analysis of the 1708 nominal census, made by the French missionary Abbé Gaulin of seven communities on mainland Mi'kma'ki and Unimaki, shows that this household extended to include elderly parents, single or widowed siblings, and orphaned nephews and nieces. Within these seven communities, the average household size was between five and six people – a size similar to eighteenth-century James Bay Cree families.[12]

Between November and March, small groups of two or more households wintered inland together, hunting for moose, caribou, beaver, and other fur-bearing animals. Called hunting groups, these households were usually related by marriage through a parent, a brother, a sister, an aunt, or an uncle.[13] Co-residency among male relatives was common. For instance, at least seven of the sixteen male household heads listed in the 1708 census of Port Royal had a direct familial relationship with one other male household head in the same community.[14] However, similar linkages among females cannot be made, since their family names are not given in the census.

The migration patterns of Mi'kmaq hunting groups varied for reasons of climate and topography. Villages of the southern mainland likely moved into their winter hunting groups later than families living farther north, and returned earlier in the spring to the coast – perhaps by as much as two or three weeks. On mainland Mi'kma'ki, winter life differed in more northern areas for two additional reasons. First, families living on the southern mainland hunted grey seals, which bred in coastal areas in January and February.[15] Second, mainland Mi'kma'ki has a number of harbours that make coastal areas accessible. One need only think, for instance, of the elongated tentacles of the Halifax Harbour stretching some five miles inland from the coast to the Bedford Basin. In contrast, Unimaki and the northeast shore of the mainland are more rugged.

These environmental differences between south and north affected the size of winter hunting groups. On the northern mainland and on Unimaki, hunting groups comprised three to five households (i.e., between sixteen and twenty-seven people).[16] In southern regions, hunting groups were larger, reflecting a shorter winter and more moderate temperatures. This conclusion is suggested by a census recorded on 20 December 1763 of two Mi'kmaq hunting groups living near the Minas Basin. This census lists thirty-six people hunting along the Cornwallis River and forty-two people hunting west of the Checunectock River (Kennetcook River).[17] In sum, the environment influenced the timing of a community's migration and the size of the migrating groups.

Generally, more people lived on mainland Mi'kma'ki than on Unimaki, and in the case of the mainland, most lived south of the Shubenacadie River. These conclusions are supported by Abbé Gaulin's 1721 census, which shows 838 Mi'kmaq living in nine mainland communities and one Unimaki community. The nine mainland communities formed 87 per cent of the total Mi'kmaq population – a figure, however, that does not include east coast New Brunswick villages. Of the nine villages listed by Gaulin, six were situated on or below the Shubenacadie River and accounted for three-quarters of the total mainland population (543 people).

The men who signed the 1726 treaty therefore would have identified with a specific group of people with whom they shared familial as well as social and economic ties. For instance, among those signing the 1726 treaty were men who hunted together during the winter. Paul Tecumart (column one of the 1726 treaty), aged sixty-three, and his two adult sons (column three) likely lived together for most of the winter, even though by this time Antoine (thirty-two) and Phillipe (twenty-six) were probably married and had children of their own. This was also likely to be true of the four Grand brothers, Joseph, Claud, René, and François (column two). Indeed, the joint appearance of each of these family members at the treaty signing reflected personal and social bonds.

Other factors influenced the size of household groups and the duration of the winter hunt. By 1726, one factor was peoples' need to acquire European goods.[18] In winter, the Mi'kmaq trapped furs to trade for European goods.[19] By 1726, trading had become a regular feature of the Mi'kmaq economy. Families thought of the winter as the time for trapping furs and skins and for preparing them for the spring trade.

There are no financial records of Mi'kmaq–European trade. There are, however, some port records from Boston and Louisbourg noting fur exports from British Nova Scotia during the early 1700s. For instance, of the fifteen vessels arriving at Boston from Annapolis Royal in 1718 and 1719, six carried beaver furs, eight 'furs,' and five 'peltry.'[20] Similarly, port records dating from 1740 to 1743 show that Acadian traders from mainland Mi'kma'ki arrived at Louisbourg laden with furs and skins. On 1 July 1742, Jacques Pobomcoup, 'captain of the vessel named "la marie" weighing twenty-five tons arrived at Louisbourg ... who said that he had left from Cape Sable six days before to come to Louisbourg to trade.' On board his vessel he carried 66 caribou skins, 800 rabbit furs, 80 hundredweight of dried cod, as well as a barrel of oil.[21]

Families produced furs for exchange because hatchets, knives, guns, powder, shot, kettles, cloth, blankets, and needles and thread had practical value. Some items, such as guns, made hunting easier. Before 1600, families had depended exclusively on projectiles such as spears and bows and arrows, and on hand-held weapons like clubs, to hunt moose and deer.[22] Though easily portable, these weapons had many drawbacks. As Nicolas Denys noted in the late 1600s, at least three arrows were required to kill an adult moose.[23] Guns had too many advantages for Mi'kmaq hunters to ignore them. By the 1720s, the Mi'kmaq had integrated guns into their household economy. Other European goods were also useful. Hatchets, for instance, were used for cutting firewood, stripping bark, and butchering animals, while knives were employed for cleaning and tanning furs and skins. Items like these enhanced a family's ability to exploit the region's resources by reducing the time that had to be spent hunting and trapping.

The trade in furs created new exchange systems within the Mi'kmaq family economy. Before 1500, families likely produced an annual surplus of furs and skins to trade with other communities. For instance, exchange systems had developed linking the Mi'kmaq with communities in southern New England. Trade with the Pokanoket, who obtained copper from Nova Scotia via coastal trading routes, is one example of this.[24] But such trade was limited, as the Mi'kmaq did not accumulate goods but consumed them. This meant that there was a practical limit on the number of furs they traded. With the arrival of European fishermen and traders in the 1500s, new systems of exchange were created as the Mi'kmaq consciously chose both to trade the bulk of their furs to Europeans, and to trade a far greater number of them. This decision, made individually by communities scattered throughout the eastern seaboard, precipitated a new economic conjuncture in Mi'kmaq history. From that time on, families would have less influence over the prices attached to individual furs and goods than had been the case in their trade with aboriginal communities.

Some changes must have occurred in families' winter migration patterns after 1500, considering that they now had less control over how many furs they needed. For example, they must have wintered for longer periods of time in areas where the animals could be trapped and hunted. These changes required adjustments in how the land was used.

How did this system of land use work? Did it predate contact, or did it evolve in response to the trade in furs with Europeans? Anthropologists have debated these questions since the early twentieth century, when Frank Speck began investigating land use patterns among northeastern Algonquian-speaking people. Speck conducted fieldwork during the early 1900s under the auspices of the Canadian Geological Survey in Newfoundland, Nova Scotia, the southern Labrador coast, Quebec, and northern Ontario – a broad territory that included Mi'kmaq, Cree, and Anishinabe (Ojibwa) communities. He contended that the basic social unit in these communities was the family hunting group, which was composed of people related through marriage who held exclusive hunting, trapping, and fishing rights over a clearly defined territory. In principle, these territories were transmitted to later generations through the oldest male. This form of social organization, said Speck, developed because of the region's highly localized and constant faunal population, which made it possible to exploit fur-bearing animals and herbivores. Similar territorial divisions did not evolve where there was a reliance on migratory animals, such as barrenland caribou and buffalo, since they roamed over larger areas than moose and deer. Barrenland caribou and buffalo were more efficiently hunted by many families working together. Territorial division made it easier for families to survive the hardships of winter, as their inherited knowledge of a territory made hunting easier. According to Speck, hunting territories were likeliest to develop in an environment that promoted family isolation, and also where a degree of permanency was possible, such as along river systems.[25]

Speck spent part of the summer of 1914 visiting Mi'kmaq communities in Nova Scotia, Cape Breton, and Newfoundland. After interviewing the local inhabitants, he concluded that the Mi'kmaq – like the Montagnais, Mistassini, and Algonquin of northern Quebec, the Anishinabe (Ojibwa) of northern Ontario, and the Penobscot of eastern Maine – divided their lands 'into more or less well recognized districts in which certain individual proprietors or families enjoyed the inherited privilege of hunting.' However, among the Mi'kmaq, hunting territories seemed to be 'less permanent, less hereditary, than elsewhere.' According to Speck, there was a flexibility regarding how territories were allotted, inherited, and loaned that was not found among other northeastern Algonquian-speaking people. Though Speck did not assign a date to when Mi'kmaq families began dividing their lands into hunting territories, he implicitly suggested that this practice dated from at least the late 1600s.

Historical documentation confirms Speck's analysis. Writing in the late 1690s, the Recollet missionary Chrestien Le Clercq commented on the hunting practices of Mi'kmaq inhabiting the Gaspé: 'It is the right of the head of the nation, according to the customs of the country, which serve as laws and regulations to the Gaspesians, to distribute the places of hunting to each individual.'[26] Le Clercq was discussing a political council that allocated hunting grounds to individual family groups. Similar patterns existed on mainland Mi'kma'ki, though in this instance, the information dates from 1801, when Nova Scotia's surveyor-general, Titus Smith, made notes of his three-year trek across the colony. According to Smith, by the end of the American Revolution in 1783, the Mi'kmaq had 'divided all the Hunting grounds among their families.'[27] Though Smith did not suggest why they did so, it is quite possible that the influx of Loyalist refugees beginning in the late 1770s forced Mi'kmaq families into the interior, which in turn compelled them to manage the moose and beaver populations more carefully. To the extent this argument is plausible, however, one would expect that families would have made such adaptations before then, in response to the burgeoning fur trade, increasing European settlement, and/or the need to conserve resources.

Territoriality set in place a formal mechanism regulating economic relationships among families. By establishing where groups of related households would hunt during winter, the Mi'kmaq privileged the customary rights of families living in each territory. This is implied in both Le Clercq's and Smith's comments. Le Clercq wrote that individuals could not trespass into another territory.[28] Smith was more explanatory:

They did not kill more Moose than was necessary to supply themselves with provisions as they considered them as their own property and Indians travelling through the Hunting ground of another might kill any game he met with if he was in want of provisions but he usually informed the proprietor of what he had done and offered him the skin; which the proprietor usually refused of this acknowledgement of his right. If an Indian found a trap set upon his land he put a stone in it and sprang it, and if he found any Indian who were camped upon his land, without his permission he took away all the undried skins he found in their camp whils't they said not a word to oppose his right.[29]

According to Smith, each hunting group was responsible for administering its own territory. This included regulating both the size of the animal population and the use of the territory by outsiders. Outsiders could travel through another group's territory, but there were protocols governing their movement. Travellers had to recognize the proprietor group's rights. Smith also wrote that people could hunt outside their own territory, but only in times of need. Since family groups managed the land's animal population, any unwarranted intrusion undermined a group's ability to maintain a material and spiritual balance between its own needs and those of the animal population. When travellers did not inform the proprietor group of their presence, the latter could confiscate their goods in compensation for violating its rights. In sum, the territorial division of lands for the winter hunt created boundaries within Mi'kmaq society as well as customary laws governing the land and each family's relationship to it. What is critical is that this relationship identified individual groups of families as inhabiting defined areas, where they enjoyed specific rights and obligations.

It follows that the men who signed the 1726 treaty were not just individuals; they were members of hunting groups that lived together each winter. Familial relationships were important, but so was each family's relationship to its hunting territory. This relationship between a family and its hunting territory was recognized by other Mi'kmaq families.

Had these families lived in isolation from one another for the entire year, we would have few grounds to suspect that they saw themselves as belonging to a larger people. We might conclude that the men who signed the treaty did so only as representatives of their hunting group. Such a conclusion would be wrong, since we know that from March to November, families that had lived separately in winter congregated again in larger numbers at three sites: in riverine areas in the early spring, along the coast in the summer, and again at riverine sites in the late fall. This annual migration was neither haphazard nor anarchistic; rather, it was a pattern of life that year after year brought together the same families who occupied adjacent lands. There were some variations in this migration; even so, it created a shared sense of identity among people occupying a defined territory. This identity can be described in relation to two interrelated processes: the shared use of resources, and the social act of marriage.

In the early spring, families moved toward the coast, to known fishing sites. In the following weeks they harvested first eels and then other species, such as smelt, gaspereau, and salmon. Since spawning is influenced by water temperature, fish runs began in the south earlier than in the north,[30] so families would move toward the coast earlier in southern regions. These spring villages may have held as many as seventy people.[31]

The size of fish migrations was one factor influencing families to pool their labour. Fishing was a community task involving men and women, the young and the old. In 1770 the Englishman William Owen described how one Passamaquoddy community, living near present-day St Andrew's in southern coastal New Brunswick, coordinated the labour of men, women, and children to kill more than 700 sea-fowl in a two-hour period. Though Owen's account describes the Passamaquoddy and concerns the harvesting of ducks and murres, his description shows the importance of coordinating community labour:

At this season the Sea fowl cast their pinion feathers and cannot fly; the Indians had, agreeable to annual custom assembled all their Canoes and 'drove' (as they call it) the great bay, closing in by degrees and at length towards high water had forced them all into this large pond, or lagoon, which has but a very narrow entrance, and at low water the greatest part of it is left dry. About ½ past 3 most of the water being ebbed out of the pond, the Indians drove the birds by degrees into a Creek of it to the Northwd where I with a party of men, Woman, and children lay in ambush, and sallied out with paddles and bludgeons; a generall massacre ensued, and what escaped us afforded about two hours excellent diversion to the Gunmen and Indian Squaws, who seemed to excel their husbands in dexterity and certainty of hitting their object. About ½ past 5, the action ceased, and the dead being numbered amounted to 700 ducks, murrs, coots, &c. which after we had taken a few of the ducks were divided out by the Chief in equal proportions to the twelve families.[32]

Wildfowl were not the only game more easily hunted by many people working together. Typically, fishing also required the cooperation of many families. Cooperation made it easier to build weirs, increased the size of the catch, and reduced the time spent cleaning, splitting, and preserving the meat for future use. While very much a response to the region's ecology, the pooling of labour during periods of bird and fish migrations also fostered social and economic relationships among individuals and families – relationships that implicitly emphasized the community values of cooperation and reciprocity. Fishing produced sustenance, but it also reproduced social values and enhanced each individual's sense of community. These bonds were formed among families over time. They involved specific activities and were forged in specific places. Culture and place were inextricably linked together.

These relationships, which linked community and history together, came to be reflected in the names the Mi'kmaq gave to the places they inhabited. This toponymy was recorded in the nineteenth and twentieth centuries by white missionaries. Some of these place names referred to the fish or animals that frequented the area. In the Cape Sable region of the southwestern mainland there was Pogomgog, 'where holes are made for fishing' – that is, a place where people came in winter to fish. There was also Oipgomegageneg, 'place fishing,' where people fished in spring and autumn. On the eastern shore were found Aasugadich (Clam Harbour, N.S.), 'clam-ground,' and Anukwakade (Country Harbour, N.S.), 'flounder ground.' However, not all names referred to a region's resources. Some referred to community tasks, for example, Kakagwek (Hantsport, N.S.), 'where meat is sliced up and dried,' Sgogeneg, 'weir place,' the location of a weir to trap salmon and other fish moving upriver to spawn, and Nooloktoochk (Cow Bay, N.S.), 'bivouacking place.'[33] Some names referred to an event in a community's history and became embedded in the language as a mnemonic device.[34] Thus, there was Plotageneg, 'Bloody Creek Lake,' as well as Aglasieoegatig, 'English settlement.'[35] These names were a means for communities to remember their history.

Mi'kmaq place names had more than a functional use; they also strengthened a community's identity with the surrounding landscape.[36] As Richard Basso has pointed out, place names in aboriginal cultures have a symbolic importance, in that they enable people to remember through words the cultural meanings that have become embedded in the community's collective memory, and so become a way to convey moral meanings to later generations.[37] Place names in Mi'kmaq society of the 1700s played a similar function, which testifies to how language forms a cultural framework in which identity supersedes the individual and becomes part of a shared understanding and knowledge.

In the late spring, families living near one another moved toward the coast, where they formed with other families what some anthropologists have called the summer village. The geographical areas noted by Gaulin in his 1721 census reflect the principal summer villages on mainland Mi'kma'ki and Unimaki. These were Annapolis, Cape Sable, La Hève, Shubenacadie, the River St Mary, Cape Breton, Antigonish, Pictou/ Tatamagouche, and Chignecto. The exact size of these summer villages varied from region to region. Summer villages might total three hundred people – a number that approximates the size of the community that the French explorer Jacques Cartier met at Pasepebiac Point along the eastern coast of New Brunswick in July 1534.[38]

The summer village was where young women and men formed relatonships. Young people renewed friendships, and parents evaluated prospective partners for their children. For the Mi'kmaq, these times when young people and parents socialized were important social events, since youth living within the same hunting group were considered to be too closely related to marry.[39] Though young people often married individuals from outside the geographical area, it was quite common for them to marry within their summer village. Data on these marriages are few. For instance, two of the five marriages involving individuals from Cape Sable recorded by French priests between 1725 and 1735 were endogamous, as was one of the three marriages recorded for Annapolis couples.[40] The significance for a community's sense of identity lay in how marriage fostered social and economic relationships. Each new marriage linked the spouses' families together, and so added to the number of people who perceived their interests to be intertwined.

The 1726 treaty helps us conceptualize how Mi'kmaq society was organized at the time. Though some of the Mi'kmaq who signed cannot be identified, others are associated with specific places and named as 'chiefs' of their communities. We can assume that the others present were also from these communities. This shows that though they lived in small groups during winter, individuals also identified with a broader geographical grouping of families that anthropologists have termed the summer village. The Mi'kmaq who assembled at Annapolis Royal in the summer of 1726 recognized an affiliation that superseded their family and hunting group. It was this relationship to this territory that formed how individual Mi'kmaq conceptualized the world.

Chapter Two

The Mi'kmaq Polity

In analysing the treaties, it is critical to determine the nature of Mi'kmaq political life. Since the Mi'kmaq participated in treaty negotiations, they must have had the political capacity to do so. They must have had an explicit political order and a common political will or they could not have exerted any influence on the treaty-making process. Without such a political order the treaties would have been redundant, as the British could have simply forced themselves on the Mi'kmaq through military means. That the British did not, and recognized that they could not, and were worried even as late as 1808 about the dangers the Mi'kmaq posed to British Nova Scotia's security, indicates that such an order did exist.[1] There is no more telling proof of this than that the British signed not just one treaty with the Mi'kmaq but five separate agreements over fifty-three years between 1726 and 1779.

The existence of a political order in Mi'kmaq life is clear to see in the 1726 treaty. In that treaty, ten individuals are identified as chiefs for nine separate villages. These ten men had been appointed to represent their village's interests to the British. They also shared a common political interest. If they had not, many of them would not have arrived at Annapolis Royal together. They also shared a common political affiliation with the Maliseet, Passamquoddy, and Abenaki communities, each of which sent delegates to sign the 1726 treaty. Thus, the treaty provides a summary of the principal political relationships within Mi'kmaq society in 1726.

Among the seventy-seven names appearing at the bottom of the articles of peace and agreement are ten men identified as chiefs of their villages: Paul Tecumart and Jean Baptist of Cape Sable, Jean Baptist

Pon and Tomas Outine of Shubenacadie (Chebenakady), Piere Martine of Richibucto, Jirom Attanas of Shediac, Pierre Amquaret (Piere Armquarett) of Minas, Philip Eargomot of Chignecto (Chickanicto), Baptist Tomus of Annapolis Royal, and Antoine Egigish from the eastern coast. Each of these individuals had been appointed to represent their villages' interests at the treaty negotiations.

That conclusion, however, is not immediately supported by the treaty. While some villages, such as 'the eastern Coast,' are represented by one individual, others are represented by two. Two chiefs are listed for Shubenacadie (Chebenakady), while other records show that in 1726 both La Hève and Chignecto had additional leaders besides those identified in the treaty.[2] While these inconsistencies may reflect British misapprehensions, a more likely explanation is that village leadership was shared. This scenario seems plausible, since in winter families lived in small hunting groups.

Evidence for multiple local leaders comes from census data collected in 1722 and 1763. Abbé Gaulin in his 1722 census recorded Jacques Necoute as the chief of Minas. Though Necoute's name does appear in the 1726 treaty – as 'Jacque Nughquit' – he is not identified as a chief. Rather, another man is recorded as chief – Pierre Amquaret. Thus, two separate documents made within a span of four years, record two different individuals – Jacques Necoute and Pierre Amquaret – as the 'chief' of Minas.

We can clarify the relationship between Necoute and Amquaret by analysing a nominal census of local Mi'kmaq hunting groups made by Isaac Deschamps in December 1763. There were two hunting groups living near Fort Edward (Windsor). For each, Deschamps recorded the family names of the male family head. He described each hunting group by its 'tribal name.' Hunting between the Cornwallis and Gaspereau rivers was the 'Amquaret tribe'; hunting to the south of them was the Necout 'tribe.' This use of family names reflects the predominance of these families in each group. The 'Amquaret tribe' comprised thirty-six people: fourteen men, six married women, two aged women, eight boys, and six girls. Though only men's names were listed, the presence of six married women suggests there were at least six households. Of the fourteen adult men recorded by Deschamps, seven bore the name Amquaret, indicating the importance of this family in the hunting group's political life. The predominance of 'Necoute' in the other hunting group enumerated by Deschamps is even more pronounced: eleven of the fourteen adult males bore that name. Both Deschamps's method of identifying each hunting group and the predominance in sheer numbers of the Necoute and Amquaret family members suggests the political importance of those families.[3]

Deschamps's census helps explain the political identity of the two 'chiefs' present at Annapolis Royal in 1726. Both Pierre Amquaret and Jacques Necoute came from families living near Minas. Lands there were divided into two hunting territories in winter. The Amquaret and Necoute families were each associated with one of these territories, and leadership in each area was exercised by one of their family members. It follows that Amquaret and Necoute were at the 1726 treaty negotiations to represent the interests of their family hunting groups.

All of this suggests that certain families tended to dominate local leadership positions from one generation to the next. Another example of this relates to the Mi'kmaq living near Chignecto. In 1684 and 1685 the French priest Claude Moireau recorded in his parish registers the baptism of the children of 'Argiumeau, capitaine de sauvage.' This same family continued to provide leaders over the next century: Argimeau (Eargomot) is the name of the chief of Chignecto recorded in the 1726 treaty, of an individual who set out for Halifax from Chignecto to negotiate the terms of an agreement with the British in 1755, and of the chief from Chignecto who signed the July 1761 treaty.[4] These three Argimeaux need not have been direct descendants; nonetheless, their common residency strongly suggests that they were all members of a family line that exercised continuous leadership at Chignecto from the mid-1680s to 1761.

Additional evidence regarding the inheritance of leadership comes from examining the family relationships of the men who signed the 1726 treaty. If the sons of chiefs were expected to inherit the leadership, then some provision must have been made to instruct them as to their future responsibilities. In the present context, they would have to remember what promises their forefathers made to the British, and what promises the British made in return.

Three chiefs' sons were at the treaty-signing ceremony. Paul Tecumart (Tecounemac in the 1708 census) noted as a chief from Cape Sable in column one, was present with two of his adult sons, Antoine and Philip (column three). Similarly, the chief of Shubenacadie, 'Jean Baptist Pon,' was accompanied by one of his sons, 'Etiene fils de Baptist Pon,' and possibly by another son identified as 'Jean Baptist' (column 2). Since Jean Baptist affixed his assent using a totemic symbol similar to the one used by Etiene, some lineal relationship likely existed between the two. Michel Argimeau, the twenty-two-year-old descendent of Philip Argimeau, chief of Chignecto (column two), was also present.

The ten chiefs listed on the 1726 treaty were associated mainly with their hunting groups, but each was also a member of a summer village. For instance, Pierre Amquaret and Jacques Necoute were leaders of hunting groups but were also members of the same summer village. As this case illustrates, some summer villages sent more than one representative to sign the treaty. Others did not. Antoine Egigish, for instance, was the only individual from La Hève, a summer village on the eastern coast of mainland Mi'kma'ki.

In 1722, La Hève's population was 157. Presumably, this village would have comprised four or five hunting groups. What political relationship existed between these hunting groups and the summer village? How much influence did chiefs associated with hunting groups have over other chiefs in the village? And if leadership was localized, how was it possible for the village of La Hève to delegate one person, Antoine Egigish, to represent its interests at Annapolis Royal?

Had the interests of local hunting groups dominated the Mi'kmaq polity, none of the treaties – either in 1726 or afterwards – would have been possible. Instead, representations would have later been made to the British that the individuals signing on behalf of these villages did not have the consent of other family heads to conclude an agreement. That such remonstrations were not made would show that in 1726, individual leaders were delegated to represent the interests of a broader political entity, the summer village. As shown in Chapter 1, summer villages were composed of families who lived in a common geographic and social space and who shared a common historical consciousness. To take just one example, Antoine Egigish was delegated to speak for all those hunting groups who lived together at La Hève during the summer.

In accepting that responsibility, Egigish would have received specific instructions. In 1736, for instance, the Penobscot *sakamaw* (chief), Arexes, said that after receiving a letter from the Governor of Massachusetts, 'we had a Council at Our Village in order to appoint Delegates to represent our Grievances.'[5] Two years later, Wiwurna, an Abenaki sakamaw, said that before his arrival in Boston, 'all the Gentlemen Councillors of the Norridgewalk tribe sat round and told me what I should say, as the Gentlemen of the Council sit here.'[6] A similar situation existed for the Mi'kmaq. When Jean-Baptiste Cope from Shubenacadie arrived in Halifax in mid-September 1752 to treat for peace, he informed the Nova Scotia Council that his people had 'empowered him to treat in behalf of them all.'[7]

What process did villages use to delegate authority to their chief? Of this, there is no direct evidence, though the size of summer villages – 100 to 300 people – suggests that affairs were governed through a collective decision-making process involving adult village members.[8] While time-consuming, these discussions enhanced social cohesion and so minimized any ill will. Economically and socially, cohesion was highly valued, since major political disagreements might undermine village stability.

The importance of consultation in village life is illustrated by the number of people at Annapolis Royal. Fifty Mi'kmaq men signed the treaty, forty more than the number designated in the treaty as village 'chiefs.' The ratification therefore was an occasion for others to participate in negotiating the treaty with the British. Not surprisingly, representation was greatest from villages closest to the British fort. Twenty-seven of the forty people not designated as 'chiefs' can be identified with specific villages. Of this number, twelve came from Cape Sable, seven from the Annapolis region, another three from Minas, and one each from La Hève and Chignecto.

Who participated in village discussions? Again, there is no direct evidence, but clues are provided by the size and economic structure of communities. The maximum size for summer villages was about 300 people; many had fewer. In the 1708 census of Cape Sable, twenty separate households are listed, containing twenty adult men and twenty adult women. That all household males would have been involved in discussions seems clear – a facet of Mi'kmaq life evident in the fact that all the individuals who signed the 1726 treaty were men. The participation of women is less clear.

Two factors suggest that women participated. First, adult women generally formed more than half of each village's adult population. Here, 'adult' is defined as someone who is married or has been married, and so includes both married and widowed individuals. In 1708, adult women accounted for twenty-four of the forty married or widowed adults living at Cape Sable. Women were also the majority of adults in the other six communities enumerated in 1708. Probably, there were more female than male adults because so many men died in the wars of the late 1600s and 1700s. Of the 842 people recorded in 1708, forty-five were widows. Significantly, one widow was eighteen years old, seven were under thirty, and five more were under forty. Second, women were responsible for most of the important aspects of village life – that is, household production, reproduction, and consumption. As the household was principally the domain of women, they also must have played an important role in village life, since any political decision would directly affect their ability to manage the household economy.[9] For these two reasons, it seems likely that women actively participated in village discussions.

Women's participation in public discussions with the British is also invisible. No women's names appear on the 1726 treaty. Nor do any women appear in the later treaties, either as signatories or as participants in the treaty negotiations. The absence of women at treaty conferences may reflect the bias of European male writers, who were members of a society in which women were considered unfit to assume a role equal to men in public life, and so were prone to ignore women's participation in Mi'kmaq political life. While this is possible, it is more likely that women did not assume public positions in interactions with European communities.

Women, however, would have influenced treaty discussions with the British in less visible ways. As Karen Anderson has suggested in her study of seventeenth-century Huron society, there was a fluidity between public and private spheres in most aboriginal societies. Men may have dominated the public decisions, but women would have influenced the political process either by refusing to comply with men's decisions or by seeking the removal of those who did not comply with their expressed interests.[10] Though Huron society was founded on different organizational principles than that of the Mi'kmaq, Anderson's approach is useful for conceptualizing the role of Mi'kmaq women in treaty discussions with the British in 1726.

Even though women are not mentioned in the treaty discussions at Annapolis Royal, they would have been involved in the private discussions about the negotiations. For instance, we know from the registers for Saint-Jean-Baptiste parish that some women journeyed with their families to Annapolis in June 1726. On 4 June 1726 (15 June N.S.), for instance, Pierre Pisnet from Cape Sable 'signed' the treaty. Three days later, on 7 June (18 June N.S.) he and his wife Anne witnessed the baptism of their two-year-old son, François, by René Charles de Breslay, the parish priest at Annapolis Royal. Similarly, Pierre Chegau, also of Cape Sable, 'signed' the treaty and ten days later was officially married to Marguerite, the seventeen-year-old daughter of the chief of Cape Sable.[11] The British records do not refer to any women at the negotiations; even so, as these two examples illustrate, at least two women had travelled from Cape Sable to Annapolis with their families. It follows that although women did not participate directly in the public negotiations with British officials, they would have been aware of the issues and would have contributed to the ongoing private discussions taking place away from the sight, sound, and pen of British officials.

Decision making at the village level was less formal than we might suppose. Village councils would have been unusual except to decide important issues, such as peace and war, or to determine areas to be hunted during winter. After all, summer villages were composed of families who knew one another. Decisions were likely to be made informally as people engaged in their daily tasks. However, it is likely that some structure existed, for otherwise certain decisions could not have been made. Chiefs likely assumed a role in provoking discussion and seeking agreement. Though we don't know precisely how this process operated, it seems logical to assume that issues would have been discussed first by chiefs within their own hunting group, and afterwards with the other adult villagers.

Some individuals were more influential than others. Gender, age, status, and knowledge were all factors that gave some opinions more weight than others. Extra value was placed on elders' opinions. Elders were men and women who, though not holding positions of leadership, were recognized for their knowledge and for their ability to act in the village's interest.[12] In most preindustrial societies, people often died before their grandchildren were born, so a long life was considered to be a mark of prestige and individual worthiness. In 1767 the British surveyor Samuel Holland encountered sixty Mi'kmaq on Unimaki, who told him they were waiting to meet 'an old man more than 120 years of age who they say is the Eldest of the Tribe upon whose counsel they set great value.'[13] Similarly, in intervillage councils in the second quarter of the eighteenth century, elders were always present during public discussions with the French governor of Île Royale.[14]

But the European presence in Mi'kma'ki introduced changes to village life, so it must have altered people's expectations of their leaders. L.F.S. Upton has argued that Mi'kmaq reliance on the French regime, especially after a garrison was stationed on Île Royale (Cape Breton) in 1713, resulted in changes to how villagers evaluated their leaders. According to Upton, the children of French–Mi'kmaq marriages were especially valued, since French officials preferred dealing with them.[15]

Intermarriage between Mi'kmaq and French did occur, as the 1726 treaty makes clear. Among the fifty Mi'kmaq names on the treaty are seven men whose surnames suggest that their ancestors intermarried with European men. In this group are Piere Martine, chief of Richibucto

(Column 2), Joseph Martine (Column 2) Matthew Muse, (Column 3), Pierre and Jean Pinet (Pisnett, Column 3), Tomus Pinet (mistranscribed as Jean Pinet, Column 4), and Jacque Denis (Column 4).

We can trace the heritage of only one of these men, Matthew Muse. Muse's grandfather was Philippe Mius (later changed to Muse), who arrived from France in 1651. Soon afterwards, Louis XIV granted Philippe the seigneury of Pobomcoup on the Tusket River on the south-western mainland. In 1678, Philippe's fourth child, d'Azit, married Marie, a Mi'kmaq woman. The couple later moved to La Hève and lived there as members of the Mi'kmaq community. This living situation was acknowledged by Abbé Gaulin, who included the couple as members of the Mi'kmaq community of La Hève, thereby making a clear distinction between them and the French community living nearby. While three of d'Azit's sons, Matthew (Mathieu), Maurice, and François, married Mi'kmaq women, three daughters and one other son opted to marry with people of French heritage. Matthew Muse's cultural identity therefore was a mix of Mi'kmaq and French, not only in terms of his parent's heritage, but also in terms of his siblings.

Whatever his heritage, in 1726 Muse was Mi'kmaq. This cultural identification is demonstrated by the fact that both British and French officials described him as such. He was, as the Nova Scotia Council recorded on 4 June 1726, one of those 'Indians' who had come to ratify the treaty.[16] Similarly, when the French priest René de Breslay recorded the birth of Matthew's daughter Marie on 18 June 1728, he identified him as a 'sauvage du cap de sable.'[17]

When Doucett identified Muse as 'Mi'kmaq,' it must have been at least partly because his appearance and attire set him apart from the French-speaking Acadians who also were present at the treaty negotiations. Muse's hair was probably long, and mixed with bear grease to ward off insects.[18] Probably, bits of cloth of various colours dangled from tiny holes pierced in his earlobes. To mark the solemnity of the occasion, he would also have painted his face black. Muse's clothing would also have been distinctive. He would have worn a breechcloth, a piece of material about a 'quarter of a yard long' wrapped around his waist and between his legs, and from his shoulders would have hung a blanket, and he would have worn sealskin shoes.[19] Thus Muse, and the other Mi'kmaq men with French blood in their veins, would have been dressed so that little doubt as to their identity could be left in Doucett's mind.

So Muse, Denis, and Martine were Mi'kmaq. But they were also physically and culturally different from the other Mi'kmaq present at Annapolis Royal. Each was lighter-skinned than his Mi'kmaq relatives, and spoke some French and possibly English as well. Their facility with language is evident from an incident of August 1726: two of Matthew Muse's Mi'kmaq nephews, James and Philippe, captured a New England fishing vessel off the coast of La Hève. In a deposition made later in Boston, one fisherman claimed that James had threatened him with a knife 'saying God Dam your Blood, you shall not live a Minute longer.'[20] Matthew Muse probably learned French as a child, like his nephew James, and would have spoken it when visiting the homes of siblings who had married into Acadian families. Though two of his sisters were living in small east coast communities, another sister and a brother were in Acadian communities along the Annapolis River. These familial ties distinguished Muse from other Mi'kmaq, and provided him with access to information and European goods that others of his village would not have enjoyed. His mixed cultural heritage also made him more welcome in neighbouring French-speaking communities than he would have been otherwise. Language, an understanding of European ways learned from siblings, and appearance all would have distinguished Muse from other Mi'kmaq men.

As the points of contact between Mi'kmaq and Europeans multiplied, the influence of men like Muse increased. These men had unique skills. For example, they could act as interpreters. During the summer of 1701 a French nun, Sister Chauson, encountered a 'French man who had married an Indian who served them and us as an interpreter.'[21] Similarly, in the late 1600s the French missionary Abbé Thury met a French man who had lived among the Mi'kmaq since his youth. As Thury later recounted, this 'gave me an occasion to speak to them (the Mi'kmaq) with more advantage, of the fall of the angels and of man by their sins, of the mystery of incarnation.'[22] As interpreters, men like Matthew Muse also mediated relations between European and Mi'kmaq societies. Certainly, Muse's presence at Annapolis Royal in 1726 indicates that he was a man of influence. Otherwise he would not have been there. His presence at the signing of the 1726 treaty therefore illustrates that individuals of mixed parentage were valued for their ability to move back and forth between the Mi'kmaq and European worlds.

But men like Muse may have been less influential than Upton supposed. An analysis of the surnames of the fifty Mi'kmaq men who are identified in the treaty provides some clues as to the importance of individuals of Mi'kmaq heritage in village politics relative to their French cohabitants. Forty individuals were present at Annapolis Royal who were not identified by British officials as village chiefs. Though these men's status is unknown, each must have been respected by his peers. If they hadn't been, they would not have been there. These fifty men represent a microcosm of the Mi'kmaq polity.

The surnames of the fifty Mi'kmaq men can be divided into four categories: Mi'kmaq, French, Christian, and unknown. Seven of the fifty men bear surnames suggesting French heritage. Another nine are identified by French baptismal names such as Antoine or Jermain. Two names are of unknown origin,[23] and twenty-eight are Mi'kmaq.

Regarding those with French surnames, we can conclude that their names came from fathers, grandfathers, or even great-grandfathers, since sons adopted their father's surname. The same cannot be said of the nine men using French baptismal names as surnames. Though these men's heritage is not clear, the fact that they deliberately used baptismal names as a personal means of identification suggests that they leaned more toward Catholicism than did other Mi'kmaq. Mi'kmaq living near Annapolis tended to be 'better' Catholics – a result of missionary activity, which was more extensive there than elsewhere.

More than half the surnames on the treaty (twenty-eight of forty-nine) are Mi'kmaq. Though all twenty-eight of these men had been baptized, the fact that all of them kept their Mi'kmaq surnames strongly suggests that their families had not intermarried with people of French descent.

Of course, this analysis of male surnames hides children who were born to an Acadian woman and a Mi'kmaq man. The heritage of these children would have been disguised when the woman's cultural identity was subsumed by her spouse's surname. However, no such intermarriages can be found in parish registers, which reflects the fact that Acadian women had neither the skills nor the inclination to pursue a way of life so different from the pastoral pursuits of their parents. No doubt marriages like this did occur, though they would have been uncommon except during periods of crisis in Acadian society. Such a crisis arose in 1755, when the Nova Scotia government expelled the Acadians from the colony. Some Acadians managed to elude British patrols by moving closer to Mi'kmaq villages, a social setting that led to more mixed marriages than had occurred since the early 1600s. In sum, the Mi'kmaq at the treaty negotiations of 1726 were less integrated into French society than Upton and others have suggested. This was as true for the chiefs who signed the treaty as for the other forty individuals present.

The 1726 treaty tells us the political and cultural makeup of the Mi'kmaq men present at Annapolis. It also shows that they considered themselves part of the same people. Otherwise, the various villages would not have negotiated in common. This alliance will be clearer when we consider the social ties among those villages that signed the 1726 treaty.

Nine summer villages were represented at Annapolis Royal: Cape Sable, the Annapolis River, Minas, the eastern coast (La Hève), Shubenacadie, Cape Breton, Chignecto, Shediac, and Richibucto. The first five were located on the southern mainland of Mi'kma'ki, the remaining four in what is now eastern New Brunswick and Unimaki.

The first five villages were geographically close to one another, which fostered close political and social cooperation among them. Mi'kma'ki's river system allowed easy communication between villages (the Mi'kmaq were expert canoeists). In 1686, New France's intendant, Jacques de Meulles, was able to travel through the interior of the southern mainland from the Annapolis Basin to Port Rossignol (Liverpool) on the Atlantic coast with the assistance of two Mi'kmaq guides.[24] Later generations of Mi'kmaq would surely not have forgotten their ancestors' knowledge of river routes. From this, it is obvious that there was constant movement between villages.[25]

Villages were also linked by marriage. The strongest evidence of such social ties among southern mainland villages comes from Saint-Jean-Baptiste parish, where eleven marriages of Mi'kmaq couples were recorded between 1726 and 1735. Of these eleven marriages, five involved individuals from different villages on the southern mainland. In 1726, for instance, Etienne Chegeou, a native of Cape Sable, married Anne of Port Royal. Nine years later, Pierre Ceiller, also of Port Royal, married Françoise Muse of La Heve.

These exogamous marriages strengthened the social and political relationships between villages. In summer, sisters, brothers, and parents journeyed to neighbouring villages, reaffirming family ties, coddling infants born over the winter, and caring for elderly parents. This social behaviour is reflected in the parish registers. In April 1734, the baptism of the daughter of Madeline Mius (Muse) and Baptiste Perrot of Cape Sable was attended by Françoise, the wife of Jean Baptiste of Annapolis. Françoise's presence was more than just a symbolic gesture of good will, for she was there to formally agree to become the child's godmother – a commitment that involved caring for the child's spiritual and physical welfare. As this example illustrates, the biological and emotional ties created by marriage and childbirth fostered continuing social interaction between villages on the southern mainland.

There were fewer familial ties between southern mainland villages and more distant villages in Unimaki and the east coast of New Brunswick. Geography created physical and emotional barriers that most families were reluctant to cross. It also made for fewer opportunities for young people to meet. Also, parents may have posed obstacles: mothers would have been unwilling to see their daughters and sons living so far from them, among people less familiar. Even so, some marriages did occur between individuals from distant villages. Of the eleven marriages for which residency was noted, two involved individuals from villages far from mainland Mi'kma'ki. In 1726, Noel Sunnepas from the Miramichi married Françoise Tannietch from La Hève. Later baptismal records show a marriage between a Unimaki woman and a Cape Sable man. Though we cannot judge how representative these data are, geography was undoubtedly one factor working against strong social ties between southern mainland villages and those in Unimaki and along New Brunswick's eastern coast.

In the matter of social and familial ties, the southern mainland villages and the villages of the Northumberland Strait and east coast New Brunswick tended to form separate constellations. The limited evidence from the parish registers of Île Saint-Jean (Prince Edward Island) bears this out. For example, in June 1722 the French priest de Metvier recorded a Mi'kmaq couple from the eastern coast of New Brunswick as the godparents of a child whose parents lived near Antigonish.[26]

The parish registers suggest that marriages influenced social relations among villages, but they do not tell us much about these communities' political connections. If the 1726 treaty were the only evidence of some affiliation among Mi'kmaq villages, then we might interpret it as a new political conjuncture in Mi'kmaq political life. But it isn't the only evidence: we also have the correspondence of the governor of French Île Royale, Joseph de Saint-Ovide.

Saint-Ovide was governor of Île Royale between 1717 and 1739. During these years, he met annually with Mi'kmaq village leaders. His notes of these meetings, later incorporated into his letters to the Minister of the Marine in Versailles, constitute the most complete written account of Mi'kmaq intervillage councils in the first half of the 1700s.

The letters show that from at least 1719, Mi'kmaq from various villages came together every year.[27] On these occasions, usually in late June or July, Saint-Ovide would meet with village leaders.[28] These meetings took place at two separate locations. Saint-Ovide met villagers from the Gaspé, the east coast of New Brunswick, and the northern shore of mainland Mi'kma'ki at Port La Joye on Île Saint-Jean (P.E.I). He met villagers from the southern and eastern mainland and Unimaki at Port Toulouse on the southeastern coast of Cape Breton Island. This arrangement may have been the result of geography, as villagers from eastern New Brunswick were reluctant to travel through the Strait of Canso.[29] But it may also have reflected social and political divisions.

At each location, families gathered annually. In 1732 there were roughly 200 people at Port Toulouse when Saint-Ovide arrived. A similar number of people greeted him at Port La Joye.[30] The number of Mi'kmaq chiefs and elders varied. In 1732, Saint-Ovide met thirty-two chiefs and elders from Unimaki and the northeastern mainland.[31] His accounts suggest that meetings with the governor included eight individuals from each village. In his 1734 meetings at Port La Joye, around six representatives from each village were present – a total of fifty-two people.[32]

In their discussions with Saint-Ovide, the Mi'kmaq delegated one individual to speak on their behalf.[33] This suggests that prior to the meeting, representatives from each village had met in council and appointed one person to voice their common concerns. That intervillage councils existed is also suggested by the fact that speakers would only respond to Saint-Ovide's queries after privately discussing the issue with other delegates.[34]

Some scholars have suggested that this intervillage council was a formal political structure called the Grand Council, an organization that united all Mi'kmaq villages in Atlantic Canada. This council, called the Sante Mawiomi (Grand Council or Holy Gathering), divided Mi'kma'ki into seven districts.[35] These seven districts were first identified by the Baptist missionary Silas T. Rand in 1875:[36]

The Indian name for the whole country, is Megüumaage, MICMAC-LAND, or Country of the Micmacs. They divided it into seven districts, each district having its own chief, but the chief of Cape Breton, which comprised one district, was looked upon as head of the whole. As marked on the 'wampum belt', C.B. is at the head. To his right stretch away three districts with their chiefs, viz. Pictou, Memramcook, and Restigouche; and the same number to the left, viz: Eskegāwaage (from Canso to Halifax,) Shubenakadie, and Annapolis, which reaches to Yarmouth. These two arms of the country are named from two prominent points, viz., Cape Chignecto, and Cape Negro Sĭgŭnĭkt, and Kĕspoogwĭt. All the inhabitants of the former are designated, Sĭgŭnĭktawâk, Sĭgŭnĭktians: and those of the later, Kespoogwĭtĭnak, Kespoogwitians. The meaning of these two names is sufficiently plain. Kespoogwĭt means: The land's end. Sĭgŭnĭkt is a sock, or cloth for the foot, and reason for its application is a Legend too long for insertion here.[37]

Within each district there could be more than one village. The titular head of the council was the Grand Chief, who was elected by male family heads and was assisted by the Grand Captain. The *putus*, or wampum keeper, safeguarded treaties of friendship and alliance made by the council and may also have been designated as a speaker in intertribal discussions.[38]

There is considerable debate regarding when the Grand Council was formed. According to one interpretation, which is based on the contemporary community's oral understanding of its history, the council emerged sometime before 1600.[39] Other researchers disagree, and contend that the Grand Council formed in response to an expanding imperial presence[40] or as a result of the collapse of French authority after 1763.[41] Both these arguments assume that since a pan-Mi'kmaq political structure is first mentioned in the eighteenth century, it did not exist before then. The suggesiton here is that if the council had existed, some European would have mentioned it.

Five Mi'kmaq men signed the 1726 treaty using totemic symbols, and this may be evidence of a Grand Council. The other forty-five Mi'kmaq simply marked an 'X.' The five who signed using totems are listed in column two. At the top of this column is 'Jean Baptist Pon,' Chief of Shubenacadie, who signed using a six-pointed star. Below him are the names of his two sons, both of whom drew the picture of an animal, possibly a beaver. And farther down the column, Mark Antoine marked what looks like an 'M,' while Joseph le Grand drew a cross enclosed by a square or rectangle.

Each of these men signed his name with a totem because these 'words' had some meaning. This use of symbols is revealing. Each of Jean-Baptist's sons drew an animal beside his name, a signature sometimes used by Mi'kmaq to identify themselves as members of a particular village. In the early part of the twentieth century, a Mi'kmaq resident of the Miramichi River related the importance of these symbols:

When I was a little boy, I was one day helping my father with a canoe and I

saw him put a mark on it that mark was on the end of the canoe and represented sturgeon; I asked him at the time what it was for, and he told me
there were three district bands on the Miramichi and that in order to distinguish their boats and apart, they used a mark. The mark of his people of
the Southwest Miramichi was the sturgeon. I went down to Burnt Church
and saw an old man down there, he was 88 years of age, who belonged to
the Little South West Miramichi and he told me that the chief of their
band used the mark of a beaver on their stone pipes and that he did not
know just where they had any mark of their canoe or not, but that they
used to adorn the canoe with flowers made with wicker then he said, the
chief of the band on the main Northwest River used the mark of a man
with a bow and arrow drawn done in work on the clothes and marked into
the clothes.'[42]

If the beavers drawn by Jean-Baptist's two sons represented the village
to which they belonged, this renders even more curious the symbols
used by their father, Jean-Baptist Pon, and by Marc Antoine and Joseph
Le Grand. The symbols these three men drew do not resemble animals.
Rather, they are similar to the hieroglyphics adopted by French missionaries in the 1600 and 1700s to instruct their Mi'kmaq parishioners
in the Catholic faith. Some research has suggested that these hieroglyphics predated the Europeans' arrival in Mi'kma'ki.[43] Hieroglyphs
were used mainly after 1600 as mnemonic symbols to remember articles
of the Catholic faith, but they were also used for secular purposes – to
inscribe maps, to keep tribal records, and in at least one instance to
record the terms of an agreement with the French governor of Île Royale.[44] However, the meanings attached to the symbols used by these
three men are unclear. Jean-Baptist Pon, for instance, signed the 1726
treaty using a six-pointed star. In the hieroglyphs, an eight-pointed star
represented 'the sun' – an important cultural symbol in Mi'kmaq
society.[45] A five-pointed star was used in religious texts to depict
'heaven.'

Do these symbols represent more than just personal or local symbols
of identification? Do they refer to a political alliance among many villages? Though we cannot answer these questions, the fact that five individuals made a point of identifying themselves using hieroglyphs
suggests that both they and others recognized that they occupied a special political position both within their own villages and among other
Mi'kmaq. But we don't know whether these symbols refer to a Grand
Council.

This debate over whether the Grand Council existed illustrates the difficulties of reconciling community-based oral information with empirically focused European historical traditions.[46] Both approaches have weaknesses. Europeans, including French-speaking missionaries, were not privy to internal village and intervillage meetings, and therefore would have known little about the Mi'kmaq polity. For example, the French governor of Île Royale, Saint-Ovide, referred to Mi'kmaq councils in 1726, 1727, and 1728 at which neither he nor other French officials were welcomed.[47] At the same time, arguments positing that the council existed before 1700 are premised on an oral consciousness and should be evaluated in the same critical manner as those European documents which purport to describe aspects of Mi'kmaq society.

The 1726 treaty suggests that there was some formal alliance uniting Mi'kmaq villages. This unity encompassed the southern mainland, Unimaki, and coastal New Brunswick, and reflected social and cultural ties that had developed prior to 1726. This unity assumed a definite shape, as is suggested by the meetings among several Mi'kmaq villages and Saint-Ovide before and after 1726. But Saint-Ovide's correspondence does not make any reference to the existence of the Grand Council.

The Mi'kmaq villages listed in the 1726 treaty were allied with three other aboriginal societies: the Maliseet, the Passamaquoddy, and the Penobscot. Five men from these communities are identified in the treaty: Marquis from the St John River, Jacque Pemeroit, Lewis Pemeroit, and Francois Xavier from Penobscot (Pentagoet, Pentaquit), and Noel Stromett from Passamaquoddy.

The presence of these five men at Annapolis Royal reflected an economic and political alliance among the Wabanaki. This alliance emerged before 1600. Though we lack written documentation from this time, materials unearthed by archaeologists show that before European contact, there were commercial links between northeastern coastal communities. A focal point of their trade was the mouth of the Penobscot River in eastern Maine. A great many exotic materials have been found there, which strongly suggests that the area was used for interregional trade and may have been the site of a trading fair bringing together people from neighbouring communities.[48]

The arrival of European traders and settlers in the early 1600s triggered substantive changes in many communities to the west of the Mi'kmaq. These changes cannot be documented with any real precision. In particular, little information is available for 1600 to 1675. Even

so, we can say that from at least the 1670s there were pockets of culturally similar communities living along the major river systems from the
Saco River to Passamaquoddy Bay. The French referred to the people
living along the Saco, Androscoggin, Kennebec, and Penobscot rivers as
the Abenaki,[49] the people along the St Croix as the Passamaquoddy, and
the people along the St John as the Maliseet. Passamaquoddy territory
included much of the land around what is now the southern section
of the Maine–New Brunswick border; the Maliseet occupied the central part of present-day New Brunswick and the south shore of the
St Lawrence River. Significantly, seventeenth- and eighteenth-century
French and English observers considered each of these societies to be
culturally distinct from the Mi'kmaq.

The post-Contact period brought the Abenaki, Passamaquoddy, Maliseet, and Mi'kmaq into more frequent contact with one another. This
led to alliances but also to war. These wars were mainly over access to
furs and to the valued European goods they purchased.[50] This was as
true for Mi'kmaq relations with the Abenaki as it was for their relations
with the Montagnais and the Inuit; both these groups lived along
Mi'kma'ki's northern borders, across the St Lawrence River.

Instability in Mi'kmaq–Abenaki relations ended in the mid-1600s, as a
result of two related processes. First, the French-Houdenosaunee wars
of the 1640s reinforced existing relations between the French and their
aboriginal neighbours, who included the Mi'kmaq and Abenaki.[51] The
Houdenosaunee are often referred to as the Iroquois, and during the
1600s were living in large palisaded villages between Lake Champlain,
just south of Montreal, and Niagara Falls to the west. French merchandise was a crucial component of the alliance, in that the French provided the Mi'kmaq and Abenaki with unfettered access to European
goods. Both communities would have viewed access to such goods and
to French military support as an important counterweight to the
Houdenosaunee (Iroquois), with whom the Mi'kmaq and the Abenaki
had been intermittently at war since the 1500s. In forming a commercial
and political alliance with the French king, both communities also
accepted missionaries into their midst. Though they likely understood
the precepts of the Catholic Church differently than the missionaries
had hoped, being 'Catholic' reinforced the cultural bonds that linked
the Mi'kmaq to their Abenaki neighbours.[52]

The second factor strengthening the alliance between the Mi'kmaq
and their western neighbours was New England expansionism. This

expansion took two forms: an aggressive extension of Massachusetts into Abenaki lands after 1675, and the movement of fishing boats into Nova Scotia waters beginning in the 1660s. As this expansion occurred in the context of a rivalry between New England and New France, it reinforced the Abenaki–Mi'kmaq alliance in opposition to New England expansionism and in support of French sovereignty. Opposition to New England was expressed for the first time during King William's War between 1689 and 1697, when Mi'kmaq, Maliseet, Passamaquoddy, and Abenaki warriors joined with French militiamen and officers in attacking New England settlements and forts on Abenaki lands.[53] Thereafter, this alliance was a means for articulating a united opposition to the English colonies.

The Mi'kmaq–Abenaki alliance is expressed in the 1726 treaty. By signing the treaty together, the Mi'kmaq, Maliseet, Passamaquoddy, and Penobscot were expressing in very clear terms a common political will. Each of these communities was distinct, yet their common interest had led them to negotiate and sign a treaty together. The British well realized all of this, and knew they were forming a common political relationship with all those communities signing the treaty. The unique political identity of the Wabanaki was recognized by both parties. Had it not been, the treaty might also have been signed by other residents of the region – in this case, French-speaking Acadians. Clearly, the Mi'kmaq, Maliseet, and Abenaki conceptualized their identity as distinct from that of the Acadians. This identity was acknowledged by the British officials who signed the treaty, including John Doucett.

The 1726 treaty offers a brief but revealing window onto the social and political networks linking individual communities inhabiting the Atlantic region. The aboriginal names affixed to the 1726 treaty express a political unity among villages who thought of themselves as Mi'kmaq, and between them and the Passamaquoddy, Maliseet, and Abenaki people living to the west.

In the treaty are people who were long part of an enigmatic past. In 1726 they emerge from the fog that often surrounds them to show us they are a people with a surprisingly complex pattern of life. From this date forward, they remain fixed in our minds as a product of their own making. But often, these aboriginal delegates will disappear from view. They will disappear from the documents that grace our world, and from our rational mode of thought, which stresses that we can only know what can be proven by rules we ourselves invent. As we journey on, through the paths that lead to Annapolis Royal in 1726, and to Halifax in 1752 and in 1761, we must keep reminding ourselves that the Mi'kmaq delegates who had signed the 1726 treaty live and breathe, shape and reshape their world in ways that will also form the world that the British live within.

PART TWO
The 1726 Treaty

It is one of their customs to write in books what they have done and seen, instead of telling them in their villages where the lie can be given to the face of a cowardly boaster, and the brave soldier can call on his comrades to witness for the truth of his words.

James Fenimore Cooper, *The Last of the Mohicans: A Narrative of 1757*, 1826

Whereas by the Articles of Peace and agreement Made & concluded upon att Boston in New England the Fifteenth Day of Decr: One Thousand Seven Hundred & twenty five by our Delegates & Representatives Sanguarum (allias Loron) Alexis Francois Xavier & Meganumbe as appears by the Instruments then Sign'd Seal'd & Exchanged in the Presence of the Great & Generall Court or Assembly of ye Massachusetts Bay by our Said Delegates in behalf of us the Said Indians of Penobscott, Norridgewolk, St. Johns, Cape Sable, and the other Indian Tribes belonging to & inhabiting within these His Majesty of Great Britain's Territories of Nova Scotia & New England & by Majr Paul Mascarene Comissioner from this said Province in behalf of His Majesty by which Agreement itt being requir'd tht the Said Articles Shoul'd be ratified with Full Power & Authority by an Unanimous Consent & desire of the Said Indian Tribes are Come in Complyance with ye Articles Stipulated by our Delegates as aforesaid and do in Obedience thereunto Solemnly Confirm & ratifie ye Same & in Testimony thereof with Hearts full of Sincerity. Wee have Sign'd & Seal'd the Following Articles being Conform to what was requir'd by the Said Majr Paul Mascarene & Promise to be perform'd by our Said Delegates.

Whereas His Majesty King George by the Concession of the Most Christian King made att the Treaty of Utrecht is become ye Rightfull Possessor of the Province of Nova Scotia or Acadia According it its ancient Boundaries, wee the Said Chiefs & Representatives of ye Penobscott, Norridgewalk, St. Johns, Cape Sables & of the Other Indian Tribes Belonging to & Inhabiting within This His Majesties Province of Nova Scotia Or Acadia & New England do for our Selves & the said Tribes Wee represent acknowledge His Said Majesty King George's Jurisdiction & Dominion Over The Territories of the said Province of Nova Scotia or Acadia & make our Submission to His said Majesty in as Ample a Manner as wee have formerly done to the Most Christian King.

That the Indians shall not molest any of His Majesty's Subjects or their Dependants in their Settlements already made or Lawfully to be made or in their carrying on their Trade or other affairs within the said Province.

That if there Happens any Robbery or outrage Comitted by any of our Indians the Tribe or Tribes they belong to shall Cause satisfaction to be made to ye partys Injured.

That the Indians shall not help to convey away any Soldiers belonging to His Majesty's forts, but on the contrary shall bring back any soldier they shall find endeavouring to run away.

That in case of any misunderstanding, Quarrel or Injury between the English and the Indians no private revenge shall be taken, but Application shall be made for redress according to His Majesty's Laws.

That if there any English Prisoners amongst any of our aforesaid. Tribes, wee faithfully promise that the said Prisoners shall be releasd & Carefully Conducted & delivered up to this Government or that of New England

That in testimony of our Sincerity wee have for ourselves and in behalf of our Selves & in behalf of Our Said Indian Tribes Conforme to what was Stipulated by our Delegates at Boston or aforesaid, this day Solemnly Confirmd & ratified each & every one of the aforegoing Articles which shall be punctually observed and duly performed by Each & all of us the Said Indians. In Witness Whereof wee have before the Honourable John Doucett & Councill for this His Majesty and the Deputies of the french Inhabitants of Sd Province hereunto Sett our Hands & Seals att Annapolis Royall this 4th day of June 1726 in the twelvth year of His Majesty's Reign.

Reciprocal Promises Made by Captain John Doucett: 1726
London, England, Public Record Office, Colonial Office Series 217/4: doc. 321

Whereas Maj. Paul Macarene one of the Council for this his Majesty's Province of Nova Scotia Commissioned and Appointed By the Hon.ble Lieutenant-Coll. Lawrence Armstrong, Lt. Govr and Commander in Chief of this his Majesty's said province to Negotiate and treat about a peace with the Indians Engaged in the Late Warr hath by and with the Desire of his Majesty's said Council in Conjunction with his Majesty's province of New England, Concluded and Effected the Same for this His Majesty's said province as well as for that of New England with Sangauraum (alias) Laurent, Alexis, Francois Xavier and Maganumbe, Delegates of the Penobscott, Norrigwock, St. John's & of the Cape Sable Indians & of the other Indian Tribes Belonging to and Inhabiting within this his Majesty's said province of Nova Scotia & that of New England as appears by the Instruments Sign'd Seal'd and Exchang'd by the Said Maj. Paul Mascarene Commissioner for this His Majesty's said province and the Said Indian Delegates in presence of the great and general Court or Assembly of the Province of the Massachusetts Bay Bearing date at the Council Chambers in Boston New England the Fifteenth day of December one thousand Seven hundred and twenty Five, Whereof the Following Articles being Exactly the Same as is required by the said Delegates to be performed on his Majesty's Part by this his said Government

I do therefore in the Name of the Honble Lawrence Armstrong Esq the Lt. Gov & Commander in Chief as aforesaid By with the Advice of the Council of this his Majesty's said province for and in the name of my master his most Sacred Majesty George of great Brittain, France & Ireland King Defender of the Faith &c The Chiefs of the Said Indian Tribes having Conforme to the said Articles Stipulated by their said Delegates come here and first performed their parts Ratify & Confirme the same and in Testimony thereof I Have to the Following Articles Sett my hand & Seal:

Whereas the Chiefs of the Penobscott, Norrigwock, St. Johns Cape Sable Indians and of the other Indian Tribes & their Representatives Belonging to and Inhabiting within this his Majesty's Province of Nova Scotia Conforme to the Articles Stipulated by their Delegates, Sangarumn (alias) Laurens, Alexis, Francois Xavier, & Meganumbe, at Boston in New England The Fifteenth day of December one thousand Seven hundred & twenty five have come to this His Majesty's Fort of Annapolis Royal and Ratifyed said Articles and made their Submission to his Majesty George By the grace of god of great Brittain France & Ireland King Defender of the Faith &c and Acknowledged his said Majesty's Just Title to this his said province of Nova Scotia or Acadia & promised to Live peaceably with all his Majesty's Subjects & their Dependants & to performe what Further is

Contained in the Severall articles of their Instruments. I do therefore in His Majesty's name for and in Behalf of this his said Government of Nova Scotia or Acadia Promise the Said Chiefs & their Respective Tribes all marks of Favour, Protection & Friendship

And I do Further promise & in the absence of the honble the Lt. Govr of the Province in behalf of the this said Government, That the Said Indians shall not be Molested in their Persons, Hunting Fishing and Shooting & planting on their planting Ground nor in any other their Lawfull occasions, By his Majesty's Subjects or Their Dependants in the Exercise of their Religion Provided the Missionarys Residing amongst them have Leave from the Government for So Doing

That if any Indians are Injured By any of his Majesty's Subjects or their Dependants They shall have Satisfaction and Reparation made to them According to his Majesty's Laws whereof the Indians shall have the Benefit Equall with his Majesty's other Subjects

That upon the Indians Bringing back any Soldier Endeavouring to run away from any of His Majesty's Forts or Garrisons, the Said Indians for this good Office Shall be handsomely rewarded.

That as a Mark and token of a true Observation & Faithfull Performance of all and Every Article promised on his Majesty's part by the Government I have by and with the Advice of the Council for said Government Releas'd and Sett att Liberty the Indian Prisoners

Given under my hand and Seal at his Majesty's Fort of Annapolis Royall this 4th day of June in the Twelvth year of his Majesty's Reign

By Order of his hon the Lt Gov   *John Doucett*
by and with the Advice of the Council   *Lieu Govt of Annapolis Royall*
W. Shirreff Secy

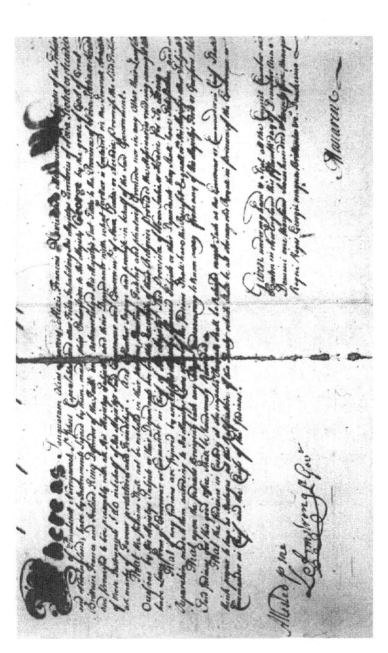

Reciprocal promises made by the British to the Mi'kmaq on 4 June 1726. Enclosed in Doucett's letter to the Duke of New-castle, 16 August 1726.

On Monday, 21 November 1994, the trial of Donald Marshall Jr began. Since Marshall had been fishing from the Afton reserve on the northern mainland of Nova Scotia, the case was heard in the nearby town of Antigonish. Later, after representations were made to the Judge regarding the expense of hearing the case in Antigonish, the venue was changed to Halifax. Beginning in early April, all evidence and arguments were heard in the federal court building on Lower Water Street.

The case was heard before Mr. Justice John D. Embree, a provincial court judge. Though Marshall was charged with violating a federal statute, minor criminal offences are usually heard by provincial judges. The prosecution, however, was handled by federal government lawyers. Leading the prosecution team was Michael Paré from the Halifax office of the Department of Justice. He was assisted by Ian McRae, a lawyer with the Department of Fisheries and Oceans in Ottawa.

Central to the historical evidence presented and to the legal arguments made before Judge Embree was how the treaties should be read and interpreted. Thus, the treaty documents were formally submitted to the court. The first witness to explain their significance was the Crown's only witness, Professor Stephen Patterson, who began his testimony on 21 November 1994.

An expert witness occupies a paradoxical position in the courtroom. He or she is there as a friend of the court, offering expert opinion on matters in which the court lacks knowledge. Expert witnesses are not advocates for one side or the other. That said, in *Marshall* and other cases, Patterson testified as a Crown witness and Reid and I testified for the Mi'kmaq. A historian one hundred years from now might conclude from this 'fact' that Patterson was an advocate for the Crown whereas Reid and I were advocates for the Mi'kmaq.

Such a conclusion would be wrong, and shows how difficult it is to make 'facts' into history. None of the witnesses in *Marshall* or later cases saw themselves as advocates. To be sure, our testimony differed regarding how the treaties should be interpreted. But – and this is the important point – those differences reflected contrasting approaches to the study of history. Patterson tended to stress the political power of the British Empire over the Mi'kmaq in the eighteenth century, while Reid and I emphasized the agency of the Mi'kmaq in making the treaties. Expert witnesses, however, sometimes act like advocates and forget their role in the courtroom. For instance, they tend to stress those historical documents and analyses that support a particular legal position.

There is nothing that prepares them for the adversarial nature of cross-examination. Opposing counsel has no inherent interest in the witness – indeed, the reverse is true. The opposing counsel's job is to inflict as much damage on the expert witness's testimony as possible. If this means undermining the witness's credibility, so be it. Moreover, what the witness assumes to be a given – for example, the importance of human agency – opposing counsel does not. For the witness, this presents an enormous difficulty – how to reduce into a few choice and convincing words what has been the work of an entire generation of social historians. Faced with such a daunting task, and faced with a lawyer who doesn't quite seem to understand the authority with which the witness speaks, the witness may become irritated, rattled, uneasy, even angry. All the time, the judge watches and takes notes.

There are added problems. From the time the expert enters the witness box, he or she is not allowed to talk with counsel about any aspect of the testimony. As Judge Embree told Patterson on the first day of the Marshall trial: 'Dr Patterson, any break that we take in this matter, I direct you not to discuss your evidence or your testimony with anybody while we're in recess or on any breaks.'[1] The witness enters the courtroom alone and leaves the courtroom alone. Indeed, the witness says very little to the lawyers outside the witness box – at most, 'good morning' and 'see you tomorrow.' The witness is cut off from discussing any part of the case so as to ensure that no one tampers with the testimony.

During cross-examination, the witness's isolation becomes more important. It is at this time that defence lawyers get their first glimpse of the government's legal argument. This argument is first made through the cross-examination of the defence witness. However, the witness is a historian and not a lawyer, and so cannot decipher the legal reasoning underlying the prosecutor's questions. The witness's inadequacies are not necessarily liabilities. Indeed, sometimes the less a historian understands the law the better. If they understood it too well, they would run the risk of confusing history with the law, and of telescoping their answers to fit the law. This is what historians must avoid. A historian must answer the questions as a historian. This means, above all else, admitting that historical documents are ambiguous and that there are inconsistencies and contradictions in how the past is interpreted. To do otherwise would be to risk conflating the past with the present. All of this is simple in theory but difficult in practice. Because the witness is isolated, and uncertain regarding the arguments underlying the prosecutor's questions, cross-examination is an especially tense time.

In the courtroom, the political and financial implications of an academic's testimony are great. As a result, these people tend to steer their evidence in a way they normally wouldn't in the classroom. For instance, as a result of the Supreme Court's decision, the federal government decided to spend $500 million on issues relating to the *Marshall* decision.[2] None of us who were involved in *Marshall* knew just how much money was at stake, but we recognized that the stakes were high, and I had to consciously force myself not to let this fact influence my testimony. In sum, expert witnesses face the difficult task of balancing the demands of their 'client' with the demands of their profession.

Other problems confront the expert witness in the courtroom. The courtroom is an unforgiving place; there are no second chances, and no colleagues to correct one's errors. Every word is painstakingly transcribed. This transcript afterwards becomes the basis for the legal arguments made before the judge. Witnesses must choose their words carefully and strive to ensure that their explanations cannot be interpreted in any other way except the way they intended. The trial judge's decision may be appealed to a higher court; in contrast, the witness will not have another opportunity to testify. Whatever the witness says at trial becomes the basis of legal argument in the superior courts. So it is absolutely critical that witnesses not offer opposing counsel the opportunity to twist their words. For a good example, just what Patterson meant when he referred to the 'right to sell fish' while being cross-examined by Wildsmith at trial was a matter of some dispute when the case reached the Supreme Court.

Before Patterson began his testimony, the Crown sought the Court's permission to qualify him as an expert witness. After Patterson took the stand, Mr. Paré told Judge Embree that he would be asking the court to qualify Patterson as 'a Historian, with expertise in British Colonial Administration, and British Colonial Development in North America, and British Colonial Indian Policy, including British–Indian Relations, Treaty and otherwise, in New England and Nova Scotia.' Then began a lengthy examination by Paré of Patterson's qualifications. This examination was conducted mainly through reference to the witness's curriculum vitae, which was entered as a Crown exhibit. Paré's questioning of Patterson took almost two hours. After Paré completed his examination, one of Marshall's lawyers, Bruce Wildsmith, cross-examined the witness.[3] Usually, the point of such a cross-examination is to restrict the expert's ability to speak to certain issues. Wildsmith attempted to restrict Patterson's evidence to issues relating to British colonial policy, including British Indian policy and 'the British perspective on the British Micmac relationship.' Wildsmith did not want Patterson to speak to the Mi'kmaq perspective on their relationship with the British.[4] For the defence lawyers, this was a key issue, since they were familiar with Patterson's interpretation of the eighteenth-century treaties. If Patterson was only allowed to speak about British perspectives on treaty-making, the Crown would be unable to introduce evidence through him regarding how the Mi'kmaq understood the treaties. The Supreme Court of Canada had already said in earlier judgments that both parties' understandings should figure in how courts interpret an Indian treaty. Had the Crown been prevented from addressing how the Mi'kmaq understood the treaties, its ability to make a plausible legal argument would have been undermined.

However, Judge Embree was not about to make a ruling that would make it difficult for the Crown to make its case, and adopted a liberal interpretation of the rules for qualifying expert witnesses. Judge Embree stated that 'an expert is ... someone who has specialized knowledge, whether that be gained from study, or research, or experience, or some combination of all of those, which knowledge is relevant to some aspect of the case before the court, and which is outside the normal expected knowledge of the trier of fact.' In other words, an expert was someone who knew more about an issue than the judge. Based on this reasoning, the Judge granted Paré's submission to qualify Patterson as an expert on the historical development of the northeastern British colonies, including Mi'kmaq perspectives of treaty-making.[5]

Judge Embree reserved the right to determine how much weight he would give to each expert's testimony (which was to include, for the defence, John Reid's and my own). Here, the credibility of each witness would be critical. What criteria would Judge Embree use in evaluating the three witnesses? Certainly, the demeanour of the witnesses would be crucial. How would they present themselves? Would they demonstrate an extensive knowledge of the documents they presented to the court? Equally important would be the judge's view of each witness's objectivity. Would the witness be willing to recognize the problems and contradictions implicit in the documentation? Or would he be interpreting the documents as if he was an advocate and not an objective scholar? Ultimately, the trial judge is exclusively responsible for determining the credibility of witnesses, and can make if he so chooses disparaging remarks about a witness's testimony. Such remarks can do a great deal of damage, by making an appeal to a higher court difficult. This is because a higher court cannot contradict the trial judge's opinion of a witness.

After the judge's remarks, Paré began his examination-in-chief of Patterson, asking him various questions about Nova Scotia history. Paré focused mainly on the eighteenth-century treaties. Indeed, Paré's first question to Patterson concerned the treaties: 'Professor Patterson, perhaps as a preliminary matter, it might be helpful for us if you could provide us with a broad outline of the treaties that were signed by the Government of Nova Scotia with the native people of the Province.'[6] Patterson replied by first describing each of the treaties, beginning with the 1726 treaty and continuing chronologically through the 1749, 1752, 1760–1, and 1779 treaties.

Paré's line of questioning to Patterson was carefully thought out. Critical in the judge's decision would be the legal text used by the defence to argue that the Mi'kmaq enjoyed constitutional protection from the application of a federal statute. From the court's perspective, the treaty text was the starting point of any analysis. This approach is different from that of a historian, who is more likely to examine the broader historical context in which a treaty was created before talking about the treaty itself.

In the Donald Marshall trial, the treaties were examined to determine whether they provided the Mi'kmaq with a right to trade fish to the British, and to what degree, if any, this right was restricted. In later cases – *R. v. Bernard* and *R. v. Stephen Frederick Marshall, et al.* – the emphasis would be different. In those cases, the legal argument would be that the Mi'kmaq had not surrendered their land by treaty or by other means and therefore should have a right to cut timber on Crown land. In both instances, I would be examined to determine whether the Mi'kmaq had surrendered any portion of their lands to the British, and whether the treaties had in some way restricted the areas that could be used by the Mi'kmaq.

In the following four chapters, I will attempt to incorporate the arguments made in each court case in which I have been involved. I am less interested in the historical context than in the text that elucidates that history. When this approach is taken, more emphasis can be placed on examining the oral meanings attached to each article of the treaty by British and Mi'kmaq negotiators.

Chapter Three

The Genesis of the 1726 Treaty: The Wabanaki–New England War of 1722–1725

The 1726 treaty was signed by the three northernmost New England colonies – Massachusetts, New Hampshire, and Nova Scotia – and the Abenaki, Passamaquoddy, Maliseet, and Mi'kmaq people. Treaty discussions began in Boston in the summer of 1725, the Mi'kmaq and Maliseet having delegated four Penobscot Abenaki to negotiate for them. On 15 December 1725, an agreement was signed, though the terms stipulated that each village would have to ratify the treaty. Abenaki villages, which would have included peoples living along the Penobscot River and farther west, were to ratify the treaty at Casco Bay at the mouth of the Kennebec River. The Mi'kmaq, Maliseet, and Passamaquoddy were to ratify the treaty at Annapolis Royal in British Nova Scotia. (Typescripts of the Annapolis Royal treaty are on pages 61–4.)

The 1726 treaty ended a period of intermittent conflict between the British colonies and the Wabanaki. Between 1689 and 1697, and again from 1702 to 1713, the Mi'kmaq and their allies had been at war with Massachusetts. In 1722 the region was again plunged into conflict. This war, which would end with the signing of the 1726 treaty, was different from the earlier conflicts. The earlier wars in the colonies had been sideshows in a greater conflict between Great Britain and France. In contrast, the conflict between Massachusetts and Nova Scotia and the Wabanaki in 1722–5 occurred during a period of peace between France and Great Britain.

Peace having been made in Europe, New France disclaimed any official interest in New England's conflict with the Wabanaki. French and aboriginal warriors did not fight side by side, as they had before. Nor did French privateers cruise the Massachusetts shoreline, capturing fishing and trading vessels. But even though French militiamen and privateers were not directly involved in the Wabanaki conflict, Versailles was concerned about the war's implications for New France. Fearing that a New England victory might undermine France's historic alliance with the Wabanaki and expose the St Lawrence River valley and Île Royale to British attack, officials in Quebec and Louisbourg fanned Abenaki and Mi'kmaq distaste for the New Englanders, and supplied guns, ammunition, and other support to the Wabanaki. Thus, though the war of the 1720s did not officially involve France and its North American colonies, French material support for the Wabanaki signified that this was more than just a local conflict between the New England colonies and the region's indigenous inhabitants.

By 1725, the Mi'kmaq's Wabanaki allies had all signed treaties of peace and friendship with the British. The Mi'kmaq themselves had not. The Abenaki had signed their first treaty with Massachusetts in 1678, and had renewed their friendship in 1686, 1693, 1698, 1713, and 1714. These treaties had focused on problems stemming from New England settlement on Abenaki lands, mainly along the Saco, Kennebec, and Penobscot rivers.[1] None of these treaties dealt specifically with lands inhabited by the Maliseet or the Passamaquoddy; nonetheless, those communities' close social and political ties with the Abenaki led to their signing the 1713 treaty.[2]

For the Mi'kmaq, the 1726 treaty represented a new political conjuncture in their relations with European people. French traders had settled permanently in Mi'kma'ki in 1610. Over the following century, French settlers would continue to arrive. Their numbers, however, were always small, which may have been why Versailles did not dispatch a contingent of officials and soldiers until 1670. Mi'kmaq relations with these French-speaking settlers developed over a long period of intermittent contact and were based not on written treaties but on informal agreements that often did not involve French colonial officials. With the signing of the 1726 treaty, all this changed: the Mi'kmaq had entered into a new type of relationship with a European nation, and were forced to conceptualize their relations with European people in a different way than they had with the French.

The same treaty marked a change in Britain's relations with North America's aboriginal peoples. In Great Britain's other colonies, the settlers justified in various ways their occupation of lands once inhabited by aboriginal peoples. They contended, as did the early settlers of Plymouth and Massachusetts, that they were living on lands vacated by the original inhabitants. Or they contended that settlement stemmed from the purchase of land from neighbouring aboriginal communities. Or they contended that their occupation came by right of conquest – that they had been forced to launch a defensive war to protect themselves from aggression by local communities.[3] None of these situations applied to Nova Scotia, since British occupation there stemmed not from settlement or conquest but from the Treaty of Utrecht, which had ended a war fought with France between 1702 and 1713.

By Article 12 of the Treaty of Utrecht, France had surrendered its dominion over Acadia to Great Britain.

> The most Christian King shall take care to have delivered to the Queen of Great Britain ... solemn and authentic letters, or instruments, by virtue whereof it shall appear, that the island of St. Christophers is to be possessed alone hereafter by British subjects, likewise all Nova Scotia or Acadia, with its ancient boundaries, as also the city of Port Royal, now called Annapolis Royal, and all other things in those parts, which depend on the said lands and islands, together with the dominion, propriety, and possession of the said islands, lands and places, and all right whatsoever, by treaties, or by any other way obtained, which the most Christian King, the crown of France, or any other subjects therefore, have hitherto had to the said islands, lands and place, and the inhabitants of the same.[4]

The Treaty of Utrecht did not discuss Great Britain's relationship with the Mi'kmaq. The 1726 treaty did. Great Britain had obtained from France the right to occupy Acadia 'with its ancient boundaries'; at the same time, by signing the 1726 treaty with the Mi'kmaq, Great Britain was acknowledging that its dominion in Nova Scotia would thereafter be exercised through the framework negotiated with the region's indigenous inhabitants, the Mi'kmaq and Maliseet. The discussions that led to the signing of the 1726 treaty were thus the result of a complex intermingling of three separate but interrelated political claims to the region: British, French, and Wabanaki.

In the two previous chapters, I used the aboriginal names listed in the 1726 treaty to examine Mi'kmaq society. I made the argument that the treaty was signed by Mi'kmaq delegates whose identity was based mainly on their association with the lands their families inhabited. However, more than a century of contact with Europeans had resulted in a political alliance among Mi'kmaq villages, and between those villages and neighbouring aboriginal societies. This context sets the stage for understanding the 1726 treaty that ended the 1722–5 war.

The war of 1722–5 erupted because of disputes between the Abenaki and the Massachusetts government over British activity in the region. This disagreement went back to the 1600s, when New England merchants first purchased lands from the Abenaki. The persistent disagreement between the Abenaki and the New Englanders regarding the validity of those purchases highlights the dissonance between the British intent to enclose lands and Abenaki attempts to mark the limits of English settlement. The 1726 New England–Abenaki treaty was yet another attempt to resolve this nettlesome difficulty. Even after it was signed, problems lingered that reflected different conceptions of land use. Similar problems would surface again in British–Mi'kmaq discussions.

This background of the 1722–5 war, and its repercussions, provide one context for evaluating the treaty signed at Boston on 15 December 1725. Because the New England colonies failed to win the 1722–5 war decisively, they had no choice but to deal with Wabanaki concerns regarding the scope of British and New England activity in the region.

The treaty ratified by the Mi'kmaq at Annapolis Royal was an exact copy of the agreement signed at Boston in December 1725 by four Penobscot delegates and by Paul Mascarene, who represented Nova Scotia at the negotiations. The first part comprises the articles of peace and agreement signed by the Mi'kmaq, Maliseet, Passamaquoddy, and Penobscot delegates. These articles are the terms that the aboriginal delegates agreed to uphold in their future relations with the British colonies. The second part of the treaty comprises the reciprocal promises made to the aboriginal communities by Nova Scotia officials. This document was signed by the lieutenant-governor of the garrison, John Doucett, and consists of the terms the government agreed to abide by in their relations with the aboriginal communities signing the treaty. I will now begin discussing the treaty's eight articles sequentially.

The Articles of Peace and Agreement: Clause 1, Part 1
Whereas by the Articles of Peace and agreement Made & concluded upon att Boston in New England the Fifteenth Day of Decr: One Thousand Seven Hundred & twenty five by our Delegates & Representatives Sanguarum (alias) Laurens, Alexis Francois Xavier & Meganumbe as appears by the Instruments then Sign'd Seal'd & Exchanged in the Presence of the Great & Generall Court or Assembly of ye Massachusetts Bay by our Said Delegates in behalf of us the Said Indians of Penobscott, Norridgewolk, St. Johns, Cape Sable, and the other Indian Tribes

belonging to & inhabiting within these his Majesty of Great Britains Territories of Nova Scotia & New England & by Majr Paul Mascarene Comissioner from this said Province in behalf of His Majesty ...

The first clause of the 1726 treaty referred to an earlier agreement, signed in Boston on 15 December 1725, that had ended three years of war between the colonies of Massachusetts, New Hampshire, and Nova Scotia and the 'eastern Indians.' New England officials often used the term 'eastern Indians' in reference to the aboriginal communities to the north and east of Massachusetts, namely the Abenaki, Passamaquoddy, Maliseet, and Mi'kmaq. The 1726 treaty did more than end the conflict between the Mi'kmaq and the British of Nova Scotia; it also ended a more general war that had enveloped northeastern North America.

The origin of the war was a dispute between Massachusetts and the Abenaki living along the Kennebec River. The former claimed that private merchants had bought lands at the mouth of the Kennebec between 1639 and 1686.[5] These purchases, officials argued, had been affirmed in treaties signed after 1686. For instance, the terms of the 1693 treaty included the provision 'that their Majesties Subjects the English shall and may peaceably and quietly enter upon improve and for ever enjoy all and singular their Rights of Land and former Settlements and Possessions within the Eastern parts of the sd Province of the Massachusetts Bay without any pretensions or claimes by us or any other Indians.'[6] British claims to 'former possessions' also were included in the 1699 treaty; in 1713 these claims were modified to include 'all islands, Islets, Shores, Beaches & Fishery within the same without any Molestation or Claime by us or any Indians & be in no waies molested interrupted or Disturbed therein, Saveing unto the Said Indians their own Grounds & free liberty of Hunting, Fishing, Fowling and all other theire lawfull liberties & Priveledges.'[7]

Some Abenaki did not accept Massachusetts's claims, questioning the legality of the purchases and wondering how it was possible for one individual to sell lands when the land belonged not to one person but to the whole community.[8] Consider here Wiwurna's words to Samuel Shute, governor of Massachusetts, in 1717: 'We can't understand how our Lands have been purchased, what has been Alienated was by our Gift.'[9] Other leaders sought clarifications from Massachusetts officials regarding the boundary between the purchased lands and the lands the colonists considered as still belonging to the Abenaki. Massachusetts officials used vague language to describe the limits of British settlement, and constantly expanded that area's boundaries. This soon led to complaints by the Abenaki that the settlers were overreaching the terms of former agreements. In 1718 the governor of New France, Philippe de Vaudreuil, reported that some New Englanders had requested permission to build a small house at the mouth of the Kennebec to trade with the Abenaki, and then had proceeded to build several houses, including a fort. These actions, said Vaudreuil, 'had opened the eyes of the Indians who had asked the English to leave.'[10] Despite repeated discussions, Abenaki disgruntlement continued, which led to several disputes with local settlers.[11]

A contemporary account discusses the chilly relationship between the English and the Abenaki, which would lead to Massachusetts declaring war on the 'eastern Indians':

> The Indians took Umbrage at these Settlements, pretending their Ancestors had no Right to alienate those Lands; And, Accordingly, gave frequent Disturbances to the English, Threatening to drive them off from Kennebeck River and Killing their Creatures & taking Provisions & other Things out of their Houses. At first these Insults were confined to that River, The Indians pretending that they were very well Satisfied with the more Western Settlemts; But at Length, they proceeded to deny the english Right to any Lands to the Eastward of Wells, threatening the People & Killing the Creatures & Pulling down their Fences, even up to Wells.[12]

The spark that ignited the 1722–5 war was the killing of some livestock belonging to settlers living at the mouth of the Kennebec. In retaliation, the Massachusetts government imprisoned several Abenaki men, whom they intended to keep until suitable compensation had been paid for the slaughtered livestock. The government later argued that these hostages had been given freely; Abenaki accounts dispute this claim.[13] Regardless, once the agreed sum of 200 beaver furs had been paid, the government refused to release the prisoners. This elicited a sharp response from the Abenaki and their allies.[14] The Norridgewalk Abenaki, who lived along the Kennebec River, summoned their allies to pressure the British to release the prisoners.[15] This council met at Norridgewalk in late July of 1721, and included delegates from the Mi'kmaq, Maliseet, and Passamaquoddy, as well as from aboriginal communities along the St Lawrence River, such as the Huron, Montagnais, and Houdenosaunee from Kahnewake and Kahneseteke. The Huron came from near Quebec and the Houdenosaunee from the Montreal area. The council delivered a letter to Samuel Penhallow, the commander of the British fort on Arrowsick Island at the Kennebec's mouth:

Grand Capitaine des Anglois,
    These are the words of the entire Abanaquis nation scattered over this continent and over Canada and of all the other Christian savages their allies who have gathered together on my land for the purpose of speaking to thee in this manner and who, after having waited for thee for more than fifty days and after having waited for my people whom I am surprised thou art not sending back according to thy word, are now all together summoning thee to withdraw from the land of the Abanaquis which thou unjustly wantest to usurp and which has for boundaries the Kenibege River which separates it from the land of the Iroquois. I would have the right to ask thee to return the whole territory which lies between that River and mine, since thou ownest none of it but by seizure, but I am willing to let thee have that territory on the absolute condition that no Englishman may dwell within a league of my Peggakki River, nor from that boundary along the seashore which parallels the entire stretch of my land nor along the estuaries of my Rivers, nor on any of the off-shore islands which belong to my land where I can go by canoe.[16]

Though the council threatened that failure to respond would result in further destruction of English property, the letter writer's purpose was to goad the New Englanders to build a border between their people and the Abenaki. The proposals were intended to resolve the conflict. As the Penobscot said to the Reverend Joseph Baxter in late August 1721, 'It is now seven years since we have lived in peace with ye English, and we desire to do so always. The King of England, and the King of France are brothers, and we desire ye the English and Indians may live as Brothers and we will never hurt them if They do not break the Peace first.'[17]

Tempers simmered through the autumn and winter of 1721. The Abenaki were irritated by the government's attempt to capture Sébastien Rale from their village in January 1722, and by the five-month imprisonment of Mr Casteen, a Penobscot leader. In the spring of 1722 the Norridgewalk decided to attack New England settlements along the Kennebec, and sent messages asking their allies for assistance. Some settlers' houses were burned, and five prisoners were taken in lieu of Abenaki hostages held in Boston. However, as the Jesuit missionary

Father Rale wrote in a later account of these events, care was taken not to harm the settlers. English retaliation followed swiftly: some militiamen attacked a group of Abenaki, killing five and wounding three. That attack, wrote Rale, sparked a more general conflict, which the Norridgewalk had not wanted to start.[18]

Though a peaceful resolution to the conflict might have been possible, some Massachusetts leaders were enraged by the actions of the Abenaki. Officials were also concerned that the French were supporting the Abenaki. Indeed, an unsuccessful attempt to capture Rale in January 1722 had yielded a cache of private letters between the missionary and the governor of New France, Philippe Rigaud de Vaudreuil; in the Massachusetts government's estimation, these letters confirmed that the French were involved. The *New England Courant* reported in February 1722 that among Rale's papers 'was a letter from the Governor of Canada directing the Indians to use their utmost Force, to keep the English from settling at the Eastward and promising to supply them with Powder and Ball for that End.'[19] Vaudreuil's words raised the spectre of French settlers appearing on New England's doorstep. To New England officials, this was unthinkable, even heretical. After all, in the last war, which had pitted New France against Massachusetts, both the French and the Indians had committed countless unchristian actions. In every English colonist's memory were the horrific events of 29 February 1704, when a force of French, Mohawk, and Abenaki had destroyed the village of Deerfield, killing 40, capturing 112, and burning 'seventeen houses with barns.'[20] Would not making Wells the northern limit of English settlement make similar attacks easier to execute? Without the New Englanders living among them, would not the Abenaki sell their lands to the French?[21] The English colonists must have been thinking along these lines in the summer of 1722. For Massachusetts officials, the continued harassment of English settlers living along the Kennebec River warranted swift retaliation.

Why the Mi'kmaq involved themselves in the war that followed is more difficult to establish, as so few records from that time are available. The Mi'kmaq were close allies of the Abenaki and would have been kept informed of their feud with Massachusetts. But they did not join the conflict rashly; this is strongly suggested by comments that Mi'kmaq elders made to the governor of Île Royale, Joseph Saint-Ovide, in July 1721: they would not go in aid of their Abenaki brethren 'until they had more news [and] until they had first consulted among themselves.'[22]

The following summer, these consultations among Mi'kmaq villagers resulted in a consensus to aid the Norridgewalk. This is suggested by events that took place along the Bay of Fundy in June 1722, when two New England trading vessels were seized: one at Otter Harbour in Passamquoddy Bay, and the other near Chignecto. The crews of the New England vessels were not injured, though ransoms were demanded and the master of George Lapham's sloop was kept as a hostage.[23]

The treatment of these vessels' crews shows that the Mi'kmaq, Maliseet, and Passamaquoddy were adopting a strategy similar to the one employed by the Norridgewalk Abenaki in their attack on the Kennebec settlers. In none of these incidents were Englishmen killed, which suggests that the actions were meant to limit the scope of English commercial activity in the region rather than to initiate a full-scale war.[24] The coordinated character of the Abenaki, Maliseet, and Mi'kmaq actions reflected an effort to demark clearly the lands that English traders and settlers would be allowed to use, at a time when such boundaries either had not been established or – as in the case of the Abenaki – had been established but were subject to conflicting interpretations.

If this was the intent of the Mi'kmaq and Maliseet actions, the British officials at Annapolis Royal didn't realize it. One of the captured vessels was released, and docked at Annapolis. Soon after, the lieutenant-governor of the garrison, John Doucett, ordered the imprisonment of twenty-two Mi'kmaq men, women, and children, whom he had learned were in 'town and up the Cape.'[25] Doucett's actions were intended to halt further seizures of New England vessels and to forestall any forays against the garrison. The possibility of such an attack had been suggested by a released captive, Hibbert Newton, who told Doucett that the Mi'kmaq from Chignecto, Minas, and Cape Sable were gathering to 'destroy all the English at Annapolis and burn their houses.' Considering that Mi'kmaq families were present at Annapolis Royal, any fears of this were almost certainly groundless. Regardless, Doucett's action escalated the conflict.[26]

There is no need to chronicle the events of the war that followed. By July 1722, Massachusetts, New Hampshire, and Nova Scotia had mobilized their military forces. Meanwhile, the Wabanaki had mobilized themselves. The Mi'kmaq and Maliseet would not have participated had they not themselves been angry with the British. (The sources of their anger will be examined in due course.) Suffice to say that after 1722, the Mi'kmaq were responding as much to their own concerns about British policy as they were to Abenaki conflicts with New England settlers along the Kennebec.

The 1722–5 conflict was unlike any war the Wabanaki had fought before. There were no prolonged sieges of Annapolis Royal or Boston. Nor were there any pitched battles on open fields. Neither the Mi'kmaq nor the Abenaki would have used such foolhardy tactics, considering how few of them there were relative to the colonists. Censuses from this era estimate that there were only 2,500 Abenaki, Maliseet, and Passamaquoddy, and another 1,500 Mi'kmaq.[27] These figures certainly underrepresent the actual population, though by how much is not known. The population of Massachusetts was possibly fifteen times larger – some 62,390 in 1710. In contrast, New Hampshire had only 5,681 inhabitants, and Nova Scotia perhaps 400 English.[28] In 1720, Penobscot and Norridgewalk delegates had visited Boston, which had 12,000 inhabitants, so they would have known full well that they would be vastly outnumbered in a war.[29] The Wabanaki made the rational choices they could, and launched occasional forays against English settlers and occasional raids on New England fishermen along the eastern coast of mainland Mi'kma'ki.[30]

The New England colonies could afford to do more, as they had both the population and the firepower. So they launched an aggressive campaign, moving up the Kennebec and Penobscot rivers and attacking Abenaki villages. Never before had the New Englanders been so successful in penetrating Abenaki lands. The strategy had telling effects.

In early August 1724, a militia company led by Captain Johnson Harmon attacked Norridgewalk, the main Abenaki village on the Kennebec; 160 Abenaki found themselves confronting 200 militiamen. Most of the Abenaki chose to flee rather than fight. At least thirty-one did not, which allowed the others to escape. Most of the defenders were killed, among them seven of the village's headmen as well as Sébastien Rale, the French Jesuit whom the New Englanders had long accused of fermenting Abenaki hostility toward them.[31]

The loss of thirty kinsmen was catastrophic for the Abenaki of Norridgewalk; so were the subsequent actions of Harmon's men. Harmon later described the day's actions: 'After which we destroyed all their corn and about Forty canoes and took about three barrels of gunpowder and about 25 small arms, together with other plunder, as Blankets, Kettles, etc.'[32] Harmon and his men had done more than kill a few of the village's headmen; they had also made the survivors' existence tenuous, by destroying their village and its cornfields.

The Abenaki were farmers who depended heavily on corn in autumn and winter. Though they supplemented their diet with wild game, fish, and berries, the destruction of Norridgewalk's corn only a month before harvest would have left its inhabitants with few options but to flee northward to Odanak, an Abenaki village seventy miles east of Montreal, to which some of their kin had fled years before.[33] Attacks like the one on Norridgewalk, and constant fear of new ones, could only have wearied the Abenaki, goading some families to move north, where they could live in relative peace and security.[34]

But if the Abenaki were weary of the war, so too were the New Englanders. They had been at war with the northeastern tribes since the late 1600s. The 1722–5 conflict was yet another financial burden on them, which they would not have borne lightly. Samuel Sewall, a former member of the colonial assembly, wrote in September 1721: 'Many thousands of pounds have been already expended on this Controversy.'[35] These costs took various forms. There was the cost of housing and feeding the Kennebec settlers who had fled in fear of the Abenaki.[36] There was the cost of housing and feeding native prisoners.[37] There was the cost of maintaining an armed militia. There were rewards to be paid for prisoners captured and scalps taken. As in previous wars, militiamen had been offered financial incentives to encourage them to pursue their enemy.[38] These payments quickly mounted. After their successful attack on Norridgewalk, Harmon's company netted £425 of Massachusetts money for their twenty-seven scalps and four prisoners, whom they paraded triumphantly through Boston. They earned an additional £100 for 'bringing the Scalp of Sébastien Rale.'[39] Without any question, money was needed to fight.

The war also harmed the fishery, which was one of Massachusetts's few industries. Since the 1660s, fishermen from Boston, Salem, Marblehead, Gloucester, and Ipswich had been fishing off the east coast of mainland Mi'kma'ki. Conflict with the Mi'kmaq between 1722 and 1725 brought further dangers to the fishermen's trade. Neither they nor merchants of New England were amused, and in 1723 and again in 1724 they demanded protection from the 'Indian enemy.' Their 1723 petition to the House of Representatives read:

That whereas its now a very Hazardous time for our Fishing Vessels by reason of the Indian Enemy who have already taken Several, some of wch they Man and Improve as Privateers & with them have taken some others of our Fishermen, there already reports of great numbers of Indians who are marcht down upon the Coast of Cape Sable on purpose to destroy the Fishermen, whereby they are very much & almost wholly discouraged & afraid to proceed on their Fishing Employ, wch if they should not would be a very great Detriment not only to those who are immediately concern'd but even to this Province in General and many of His Majties good Subjects dwelling in Great Britain & other parts of His Majesty's Dominion who Traffick to these Parts. Wherefore pray that Your Honour would please to consider the Matter and all the weighty circumstances thereof and grant us Protection by ordering a Guard Vessel of Thirty or Forty good Hands with Five or Six Guns to be a Convoy to the Fishing Fleet, the remainder of the Summer & the Autumn ensuing.[40]

Both years, the government complied with the merchants' requests, delegating Joseph Marjory as captain of 'the Sloop [*Lark*] appointed as a Guard vessel to protect the Fishery belonging to this Province.'[41] The *Lark*'s presence eased the fishermen's minds and led them to resume their fishing. Many fishermen shifted their operations to Canso, a far safer place than much of the eastern coast. Only after 1724 are there records noting the arrival of fishing vessels at Canso. The number of New England vessels using the port increased between that year and the next one, from 100 to 117.[42] Even after the government deployed the *Lark*, fishermen would have remained uneasy while the war continued.

Besides damaging their fishery and straining their government's finances, the war took an emotional toll on New Englanders.[43] There are no records of the words spoken by those families who had fled from the Kennebec to Boston and Portsmouth, or of the talk between fishermen, or of discussions within the families touched by the war, but that war was surely much discussed. And though not all fishermen would have been able to read, newspaper stories recounting the most recent victims of the war would have circulated through the fishing towns, as neighbours gathered to hear the news from the 'eastward.' One such incident villagers might have discussed appeared in the *New England Courant* on 30 July 1724: 'We have Advice from the Eastward that about 3 weeks since, the Indians had taken 11 Fishing Vessels, 45 Men belonging to the Several Vessels, 22 of whom are killed, and 23 taken Captive. The Indians demand 50 pounds from each Captive. Two vessels with 25 Men each from this Government and two more with 20 men each from New Hampshire, are gone in quest of them.'[44] Between 25 June and 24 September 1722, the three Boston newspapers printed thirteen separate stories describing violent altercations along the east coast of mainland Mi'kma'ki. Though the number of stories declined afterwards – only four appeared in 1723 and five in 1724 – the uncertainties created by the war would have been difficult for fishing families to bear.[45] The story of 30 July 1724 would have offered little comfort to any fisherman contemplating the fishing season, and no comfort at all to those waiting for their husbands or sons to return. True, the war of 1722–5 was less widespread than earlier wars, but there was no certainty that once begun, it would not bring pain and sorrow to fishing families.

Social and economic factors in the Abenaki and Massachusetts communities hastened an end to the war. Saccamakten, one of the hostages taken by the colonists after the Norridgewalk destroyed some settlers' cattle in 1720, mediated an end to the conflict. In early December of 1724 he was given leave by the General Council of Massachusetts 'to go Home & visit his Freinds upon his Parol, To return in Six Weeks.'[46] He travelled eastward across the Penobscot River, and returned to Fort St George on 9 February 1725. He brought with him a Penobscot 'captain,' who advised the fort's commander that his people had held a general meeting 'about fourteen weeks since, [and] all agreed to make a Peace.'[47] Discussions continued over the next four-and-a-half months. In June 1725, two natives arrived at New Castle who said that the 'St. Johns and Cape Sable Indians have agreed to abide by what the Penobscot Indians shall agree, and that the Penobscot Indians have directed him to acquaint your Honour that they are willing to be at Peace ... They are desirous to treat in their own River which hath not been stained with Blood.'[48] The council urged them to come to Boston.[49] In mid-July, two Penobscot delegates, Loron Sagourrab and John Ehennekouit, arrived in Boston. On 31 July 1725, Lieutenant-Governor William Dummer announced a cessation of arms.[50]

There are two accounts of the July conference. One was written by the secretary to the council, Josiah Willard, and records in English a summary of the discussions. The other was written in French and records Loron's response to what he had learned was the council's understanding of the talks.[51] In contrast to Willard's account, the French version was written six months after the July negotiations.

There are significant differences between the two reports. The principal one relates to how the Penobscot delegates responded to Dummer's proposals for ending the conflict. In Willard's account, Dummer emphasized four points, which he understood to form the basis of the ceasefire. First, that the Abenaki were responsible for starting the war;

second, that henceforward they would respect King George's jurisdiction over Abenaki lands and submit to his authority; third, that previous purchases made of Abenaki lands would be honoured; and fourth, that disputes between 'Indians and Englishmen' would be resolved according to British law. Willard's account suggests that the Penobscot acquiesced to Dummer's demands on each of these points. Not so, according to Loron, who offered his own version of Dummer's words and of the responses made to them. Regarding the first point, Loron said he had not accepted that the Abenaki were responsible for initiating the conflict:

> [Dummer] began by asking me, what brought me hither? I did not give him for answer – I am come to ask your pardon; nor, I come to make my submission to you; nor, I come to receive your commands. All the answer I made was that I was come on his invitation to me to hear the propositions for a settlement that he wished to make.[52]

Regarding the second point, Loron recounted that he had not submitted to the authority of King George:

> [Dummer] again said to me – But do you not recognize the King of England as King over all his states? To which I answered – Yes, I recognize him King of all his lands, but I rejoined, do not hence infer that I acknowledge thy King as my King, and King of my lands. Here lies my distinction – my Indian distinction. God hath willed that I have not King, and that I be master of my lands in common.[53]

Nor did Loron admit that the British were 'master' of the lands purchased from the Abenaki. Finally, Loron did not agree that the British alone would resolve disputes between the two: 'I understood only that he should judge his people. And that I would judge mine.'

The two different accounts of the July 1725 meeting suggest how hard it was for delegates to understand the other society's political order, and how this influenced negotiations. Dummer's main objective was to get the Abenaki to recognize King's George's jurisdiction over their lands. This reflected British concerns over France's territorial and commercial ambitions in the region. In contrast, Loron insisted that the king did not have a historical right to Abenaki lands. King George, he said, was king over his own lands but not over Abenaki lands, since these lands had been given to them by the Creator. It was the British claim to their lands that the Abenaki found most puzzling. Then and afterwards, this claim would be a source of disagreement.[54]

The two sides left the July conference with different understandings of their 'agreement.' The 'official' version was recorded in English and was consistent with how Massachusetts officials understood their agreement with the Penobscot. The Penobscots' own interpretation was not part of the 'official' record, which made it a less reliable source of information both in 1726 and afterwards. Indeed, Massachusetts officials would later use the official account of the July conference to demonstrate that the Penobscot had recognized New England's title to lands along the Kennebec. All of this is a good example of how British officials used a written text to enforce agreements that emphasized their own understanding at the expense of native people's understandings. This issue would resurface much later as a problem in Mi'kmaq versus British interpretations of the 1726 treaty.

Loron Sagourrab (also known as Sangaurum) and John Ehennekouit informed the Wabanaki of their discussions with Dummer sometime after leaving Boston in late July 1725. Loron went to Odanak, an Abenaki village east of Montreal, to discuss the proposed peace.[55] Other messengers informed the Maliseet and Mi'kmaq. As Loron was later to tell Dummer, the result of these conferences was that 'all these Tribes have left it to us to act for them in a Treaty of Peace.' This delegation was formalized by an exchange of wampum.[56]

The subsequent treaty, later ratified by each village, was the result of negotiations involving four distinct aboriginal communities: the Abenaki, Passamaquoddy, Maliseet, and Mi'kmaq. These four peoples had jointly prosecuted the war and had social and political ties that had long united them. By negotiating in common, the four communities were maximizing their impact on the negotiations. If each community had negotiated individually, Massachusetts would have found it easier to impose the terms of an agreement.

The joint participation of the Abenaki, Passamaquoddy, Maliseet, and Mi'kmaq gives the 1725 treaty a unique character; so too does the fact that the treaty was negotiated with both Massachusetts and Nova Scotia. Neither the Mi'kmaq nor the Maliseet lived in the area claimed by Massachusetts. However, Boston officials had good reason for wanting to conclude an agreement with both communities. Massachusetts fishermen fished in Nova Scotia waters, and Acadians bought New England wares. By concluding a treaty with the Mi'kmaq, Massachusetts was providing security for local merchants doing business in Nova Scotia. Similarly, Nova Scotia's interests were served by negotiating a common treaty. Like Massachusetts, Nova Scotia would be threatened by any future conflicts with the Abenaki.[57]

On 11 November 1725 negotiations began in Boston. Representing the Wabanaki were four Penobscot delegates, Sangaurum (aka Loron), Arexus, François Xavier, and Maganumbe. Lieutenant-Governor William Dummer was the lead negotiator for Massachusetts, Lieutenant-Governor John Wentworth represented New Hampshire, and Paul Mascarene, a member of the Nova Scotia Council, represented Nova Scotia. Assisting both the Penobscot and the English were three interpreters, Captain Jordan, John Gyles, and Joseph Bean, each of whom had lived for extended periods in Abenaki territory. On 15 December a formal agreement was reached. Copies of the treaties were signed by delegates for each of the British colonies and by the four Penobscot delegates.

Two separate treaties were signed on 15 December: one with Massachusetts and New Hampshire, and another with Nova Scotia. The treaty signed by Massachusetts and New Hampshire was intended to regulate both colonies' relations with the Abenaki communities living between the Saco and St Croix rivers; the treaty with Nova Scotia dealt with that colony's relations with the Mi'kmaq and Maliseet communities of mainland Mi'kma'ki, Unimaki, and the region between the Missiquash and St Croix rivers. In other words, the two treaties together established relations between the region's three main British colonies and the aboriginal communities living in the territories over which these colonies claimed dominion.

Each treaty had two parts: the 'articles of peace and agreement,' and the reciprocal promises. The articles of peace and agreement were signed by the four Penobscot delegates. The reciprocal promises were signed by colonial officials, one for each colony: for Massachusetts, William Dummer; for New Hampshire, John Wentworth; and for Nova Scotia, Captain Paul Mascarene. There were differences between the treaty signed for the Mi'kmaq and Maliseet and the one signed for the Abenaki. While both treaties contained similar 'reciprocal promises,' such was not true of the articles of peace and agreement. These differences will be discussed in the following chapters.

The war of 1722–5 was different from earlier and later conflicts, for two reasons: it did not coincide with a period of conflict between Great Britain and France, and it ended with a treaty between the region's British and aboriginal peoples.

Why did the war start? Quite simply, the war was about land. The Massachusetts government claimed that lands had been bought from the Abenaki between 1639 and 1686, and pressed the Abenaki to allow settlement on these lands. The Abenaki refused, arguing that the land was held in common by all Abenaki and could not have been sold by one person. This argument over private versus communal rights to land was the cause of the war. Though not directly affected by Massachusetts's claims to Abenaki lands, the Mi'kmaq were drawn into the conflict, as much because of their alliance with the Abenaki as because of their own concerns regarding the Massachusetts fishery.

Why did the war end? French neutrality had much to do with the failure of the Abenaki and Mi'kmaq to withstand Massachusetts's military might, and with their desire to end the war once it actually started. But war is rarely so one-sided. The Abenaki were hurt by the destruction of their villages; the New England colonies suffered financially. Neither Massachusetts nor Nova Scotia had the capacity to impose an agreement on either the Abenaki or the Mi'kmaq. Also, when we evaluate the treaties, it is just as important to remember that both colonies were less concerned with defeating their enemy than with incorporating them into Great Britain's political orbit. Their goal in the treaty negotiations was to influence the Wabanaki to become allies of the British king and enemies of the French. The negotiations of 1725 were not one-sided, as both sides had ample reasons for concluding a peace.

The precise terms of the 1726 treaty will be discussed in Chapters 5 and 6. First, however, Chapter 4 will consider the conceptual differences between British and Wabanaki societies, which worked against a complete understanding of their treaty relationship.

Chapter Four

The Languages of Communication

We might conclude from the 1726 treaty that the British and Mi'kmaq understood their agreement in the same way. In this chapter I suggest otherwise. The treaty's text is the most complete and reliable source of information regarding the agreement. However, this document alone is insufficient to evaluate its meanings. Nuances exist. Certain English phrases, such as that the Mi'kmaq would not molest 'settlements already made or lawfully to be made,' and that the Mi'kmaq would make their submission to King George 'in as ample a manner as they have formerly done to the Most Christian King,' breed ambiguity rather than clarity. How were phrases like these explained by King George's representative, John Doucett, and by the Acadian Prudent Robichaux, who translated Doucet's words into Mi'kmaq? Did Robichaux's explanations provide the delegates with an unambiguous understanding of 'lawfully to be made,' and of what the British meant by 'submission'?

To answer that question, we need to evaluate how language affected each party's understanding of the treaties signed at Boston and at Annapolis Royal. In this chapter I use the term 'language' in its broadest context to include any means that people and communities use to communicate with one another. I contend that the different languages used by the British and the Wabanaki in 1726 limited their ability to form a perfectly mutual understanding of each article of the treaty.[1]

Articles of Peace and Agreement: Clause 1, Part 2
... by which Agreement it being requir'd tht the Said Articles Shoul'd be ratified with Full Power & Authority by an Unanimous Consent & desire of the Said

Indian Tribes are Come in Complyance with ye Articles Stipulated by our Dele-
gates as aforesaid and do in Obedience thereunto Solemnly Confirm & ratifie ye
Same & in Testimony thereof with hearts full of Sincerity. Wee have Sign'd &
Seal'd the Following Articles being Conform to what was requir'd by the Said
Majr Paul Mascarene & Promise to be perform'd by our Said Delegates.

The Mi'kmaq and the Nova Scotia officials heard about the treaty in
different ways. The Nova Scotia officials learned of it from letters sent
from Boston by Paul Mascarene, who had represented the colony at the
1725 negotiations. In contrast, the Penobscot sent messengers to tell
their allies of the agreement. These messengers did not carry letters; instead they conveyed the information orally, punctuating their remarks
by referring to belts of wampum, which served as testimonials to their
words.

This reminds us that the British emphasized the written word and the
Penobscot the spoken word. For the British, the written word would
become the principal arbiter for understanding the treaty's meaning.
Not so with the Abenaki and Mi'kmaq, who formed their understanding
during the oral discussions that preceded the treaty's signing.

Mascarene's letter arrived at Annapolis Royal in late March of 1726.
Probably Mascarene was late in relaying information about the treaty because sea travel was hazardous in winter and only rarely did anyone, not
even traders or fishermen, sail north from Massachusetts till early March.
Normally, Mascarene's letter would have been sent to the governor of
Nova Scotia, Richard Phillips. Phillips had been appointed governor in
1719 but was rarely in the colony. He had arrived in 1720, but departed
two years later and would not set foot in the colony again until 1729.
Because of Phillip's absence, Mascarene addressed his letter of early 1726
to the lieutenant-governor, Lawrence Armstrong, who was then the se-
nior military and civil official in British Nova Scotia. But in March of 1726
Armstrong was at Canso, where he would remain till mid-September.
Armstrong being absent, Mascarene's letter was opened by Captain John
Doucett, the lieutenant-governor of the garrison, who read its contents
to the members of the Nova Scotia Council on 21 March 1726.

This council was the king's chief administrative body in British Nova
Scotia. Formed in April 1720 and appointed by the governor, it possessed wide-ranging powers that included the right to overrule the governor's authority and to act as a court of law. Its main responsibility in

1726, however, was to govern the colony's French-speaking inhabitants, the Acadians, who had chosen to remain on their farms after the British conquest of Port Royal in September 1710. In 1726 the Acadians numbered around 5,000.[2] Present at the council's meeting on 21 March were Doucett, the New England merchant John Adams, William Skeen, and the secretary of the council, William Shirreff.

Doucett told the council that Mascarene had sent 'attested Coppys of the Articles Agreed upon by the Indian Deligates in behalf of their Several Tribes of this Province their Consituents.' Since the treaty said that it was to be ratified by the 'Cape Sable Indians and other Indian tribes,' the council decided that the Mi'kmaq and Maliseet should be informed immediately that the treaty had been signed. But this was not so easily done. Though a garrison had been stationed at Annapolis since 1710, the unsettled character of British–Mi'kmaq relations had minimized interactions between the two communities. So the council decided to consult the local Acadian deputies, Abram Bourg and Prudent Robichaux Sr. Robichaux was a good choice, since he was known to have close links with the local Mi'kmaq community – an association attested to by his presence at Mi'kmaq marriages and baptisms.[3] But Robichaux and Bourg were also selected because they had been chosen by local Acadians to represent them in their interactions with the council.[4] Five days later, the two Acadian men conferred with the council's members, and the terms of the treaty 'were read to them and interpreted.' The council 'agreed that Circular Letters be issued out to give Notice to the Indians that the Peace is Concluded at Boston, that they May According to the Articles there Agreed upon their Said Deligates Come or Send their Chiefs to Ratify the Same here Conforme to Agreement, the 4th Day of May Next old Stile on the 15th New Stile.' These letters were given to Robichaux and Bourg; other copies were forwarded to the Acadian deputies at Minas, Cobequid, and Chignecto.[5] Each deputy informed the local Mi'kmaq villagers of the treaty, or as the later correspondence shows, to 'such of them as were present, and that they had used all possible Means to Communicate the Same to those who were absent.'[6]

Mi'kmaq villagers would have also learned of the peace from the Penobscot. Loron said as much when he told William Dummer that after departing from Boston in December 1725, 'we sent Messengers to the other Tribes, and acquainted them of the time the Governour Appointed to meet.'[7] But unlike the 'letters' given by Nova Scotia officials to the Acadian deputies at Minas, Chignecto, and Cobequid, these

Penobscot messengers carried a different written message, made with wampum rather than pen and paper.

According to Sébastien Rale, wampum was often used by the Abenaki to communicate with their allies: 'The custom of these tribes when they write to another tribe is to send a collar or broad belt upon which they make many figures with porcelain beads of different colours. They instruct him who bears the collar by saying to him "This is what the collar says to such and such a tribe to such a person," and they send him away. Our Indians would have difficulty in understanding what we say to them and would not be very attentive if he did not conform to their manner of thought and expression.'[8] Wampum had a similar use in Mi'kmaq society. In the late 1600s, the Recollet Father Chréstien LeClercq wrote that the Mi'kmaq living in the Gaspé region of present-day Quebec 'send ambassadors with collars of wampum to invite these to take up the hatchet against the enemies of the nation.' The Mi'kmaq had used wampum in authorizing the Penobscot to negotiate the Boston treaty. When asked by William Dummer how he was to know that the Mi'kmaq, Maliseet, and Abenaki communities had accepted the Penobscot's role at the Boston treaty, Loron replied: 'The Penobscot Tribe sent belts to those Tribes, & they sent their Belts to the Penobscot Tribe for A Confirmation of their Agreeing to what shall be Concluded, which Belts are lodged with our Chiefs which is equivalent to a Writing or Articles under their Hands.'[9]

Wampum allowed communication among aboriginal peoples separated by geography and language. Algonquian-speaking peoples inhabited a vast territory stretching from Boston in the south to James Bay in the north. Within this region, fifty different dialects of Algonquian were spoken, including Cree, Anishinabe, Abenaki, and Mi'kmaq.[10] Wampum made diplomatic exchanges possible between peoples who spoke similar though distinct dialects.

For facilitating communication over long distances, wampum served the same purpose as an alphabetic script. For recording information, it could not. Wampum was made of small, cylindrical shells roughly half a centimetre long. Pin holes were drilled through the shells, which were then strung together. These strands were then assembled into a belt. The paper used by Europeans generally conformed to a standard size, the product of a manufacturing process that was separated physically from the individual who eventually used the paper for whatever purpose. In contrast, wampum was made by community members and was designed to send a specific message. For this reason, the size of wampum belts varied considerably. One belt made in 1764 that recounted the terms of the Fort Niagara treaty consisted of twenty-two strands, each containing 438 shells 'or a total of a little more than ten thousand beads (10,076).'[11] Most belts were much smaller. According to the Jesuit missionary Jean-François Lafitau, belts were usually 'of eleven rows of a hundred and eight beads each, totalling about 1188 shells in all.'[12] One specimen, thought to have been made by the Mi'kmaq, was smaller still, measuring 235 mm long and 40 mm wide (roughly 9½ by 1½ inches). This belt comprised six rows, with each row holding 87 shells, for 528 shells altogether. Clearly, wampum and paper did not follow the same precepts as to their use. The people who made wampum were also involved in its delivery. In contrast, letters were depersonalized and often devoid of personal interaction between sender and receiver.

Wampum also differed from alphabetic script in that it made use of symbolic figures. In an alphabetic script, the individual symbols per se do not impart information; they are only comprehensible once arranged in a certain pattern. Though there were certainly variations in spelling and grammar, by the eighteenth century great strides had been made in standardizing English. For instance, Samuel Johnson's *Dictionary of the English Language* appeared in 1755, and Robert Lowth's *Short Introduction to English Grammar* in 1762.[13] Furthermore, the symbolic patterns used in written English represent spoken words; this is what makes possible their communication across time and space without recourse to oral speech. This was not true of wampum; its symbols were not exact duplications of spoken words, but rather ideograms used as mnemonic devices to represent concepts. Wampum, unlike alphabetic script, depended on a human intermediary who could interpret the belt's message.[14] For all of the above reasons, a wampum belt was far harder for outsiders to 'read' than an alphabetic script.

Wampum was probably used by the Penobscot to inform the Mi'kmaq of the treaty's signing. Though there is no direct evidence of the message's actual content, some insight into how it was delivered comes from Frank Speck's interviews with Penobscot elders in the early 1900s. These interviews were conducted almost 200 years after the 1726 treaty was signed. In the absence of other direct evidence, they suggest what the protocol was that governed communication between the Penobscot and the Mi'kmaq.

According to Speck, messengers carried two wampum belts. One belt represented the Wabanaki alliance. In the centre of this belt was 'the pipe which symbolized the peace ceremony by which the allies are joined,' and which acted as testimony to the messenger's business. The second belt contained the message. Messengers could relay a variety of messages, though the most important concerned peace and war. Speck wrote that if any member of the alliance was at war, it could ask other tribes for assistance. In such cases, the messenger would hold aloft the war belt, provide details of the impending conflict, and announce the time and place of a council where the issues would be discussed. The counterpart to the war belt was the peace belt, used by the messenger to announce that peace had been proposed and that a council would convene to consider the matter.[15]

There was also a protocol that governed how messages were communicated. When a messenger arrived, the chief and council of the village gathered to greet him. Then a pipe filled with tobacco was passed to each person present; this symbolic re-enactment of the peace that existed among the Wabanaki acted as a pledge of the sincerity of those who were present. Only after the tobacco had been smoked did the messenger rise and deliver his message.

It is difficult to establish precisely when the Penobscot informed the Mi'kmaq about the treaty. There are no written documents that state when the message was delivered or what was said by the messengers. No copy of the belt exists; if it did, it is possible we would know more. But even if such a belt existed today, it would be very hard to translate, since its meaning would be dependent on community memory.

Though nothing is known about the belt sent to the Mi'kmaq, more can be said about its delivery. By 1726 the Penobscot and Mi'kmaq had devised a method of corresponding that circumvented the difficulties posed by geography. In the 1720s there were Mi'kmaq villages in Unimaki, on mainland Mi'kma'ki, and along the east coast of New Brunswick.[16] Because of the large number of villages, messengers probably moved in two separate directions, one group travelling north up the eastern coast of New Brunswick and the other toward Minas, from which point other villages could be contacted.

Sometime in May 1726 the Mi'kmaq received more substantive information regarding the treaty from one of its negotiators, François Xavier, whom we know was present at Annapolis on 4 June 1726.[17] This suggests that he arrived sometime before then to confer with Mi'kmaq leaders. While there is no evidence that Xavier met with the Mi'kmaq, it seems obvious that he did. After all, it would have been strange for him to suddenly arrive at Annapolis Royal without even alerting the Mi'kmaq to his presence.

Xavier's presence prior to the June ratification reminds us how important oral discussions were to the Mi'kmaq's understanding of the treaty. Though they had also received news of the treaty from the Acadians, the Mi'kmaq would have harkened to the words spoken by their Penobscot brethren. The Penobscot and the Mi'kmaq were allies and shared a social and cultural bond. Xavier had also been present at the Boston conference, so his evaluation of the treaty would have been central to how the Mi'kmaq themselves understood its text. In fact, his knowledge would have been especially valued, since unlike the Mi'kmaq, the Penobscot had negotiated previous treaties with the English. After all, before their arrival at Annapolis, the delegates would not have seen a copy of the treaty.

Even after they arrived at Annapolis, the Mi'kmaq delegates' understanding of the treaty would have been informed less by the written text than by the discussions about it. This is apparent from a cursory examination of the treaty. The 1726 treaty was written in English, not Mi'kmaq. Since the Mi'kmaq did not leave Annapolis Royal with a copy of the treaty written in their own language, they would have understood its terms not by reading it but by discussing it.

The Mi'kmaq communities might have placed more importance on the written English text had their delegates been able to be read English or another European language. That none were able to do so is evident in how the delegates signed the treaty. All the delegates either marked an X or drew a totem beside their names – an indication that they were unable to write using an alphabetic script. To be sure, the inability to write does not necessarily mean complete illiteracy. However, there is other evidence to suggest that the Mi'kmaq delegates were not familiar with an alphabetic script. William Pote, captured during the wars of the 1740s, recounted passing through Aukpaque, a Maliseet village on the upper St John River, where he was asked by 'one of ye head of their Tribe to Read a Contract between their Tribe and ye Governour of Annapolis that had been made about 14 years.'[18] William Casteel, captured in 1753, was similarly employed, and was asked by the Shubenacadie Mi'kmaq to read the copy of a recent treaty they had signed with the British.[19] This evidence, combined with the deliberate use of X's, shows that the delegates were unable to read the treaty themselves. This should not be surprising. Why would individual Mi'kmaq have abandoned oral memory, wampum, and other communication forms to learn a skill that was totally useless in 1726?[20]

Though unable to read the treaty, possibly some delegates were able to speak and understand French, and perhaps even English. This would have made it easier for them to understand the text. The Mi'kmaq had interacted with European fishermen, traders, and settlers since the mid-1500s and had made agreements with them. Agreements had been reached, for instance, on the prices paid for furs, on the settlement of Acadian farmers, and on a political alliance with the French king. However, communication was possible without the Mi'kmaq being fluently bilingual. Initially, they would have used signs and gestures. By the early 1600s a unique trade language had developed that combined European and Mi'kmaq words.[21] Certainly, by 1726 many Mi'kmaq men would have heard French and would also have learned to communicate with Acadians. However, occasional encounters such as these should not be equated with fluency.

Scattered evidence suggests that French was imperfectly spoken and understood in most communities. In 1745, while a captive among the Maliseet, William Pote had difficulty speaking with a sakamaw, as he 'was so Imperfect in ye french Tongue, yt I Could not Understand ye true Meaning of his Discours.'[22] Sixteen years later, Gamaeliel Smethurst faced similar problems at Pokemouche on New Brunswick's northeast coast. There, an interpreter was appointed to translate the conversation between Smethurst and the village sakamaw. The translator 'spoke broken French,' making communication difficult.[23] Both examples illustrate that while there was some resemblance between 'French' and the language used in village life to communicate with non-aboriginal peoples, its form at times rendered mutually intelligible conversations difficult.

Both these examples, however, are taken from areas removed from the main Acadian communities of the Fundy coast, where we might expect the Mi'kmaq to be more fluently bilingual. Missionaries had been present in the region since the 1600s, at times even outnumbering their compatriots in Canada. Between 1632 and 1658, 101 priests and lay brothers embarked for 'Acadia.'[24] A seminary was established at Port Royal, ostensibly to instruct Mi'kmaq children, but it closed in 1654.[25] After 1654, missionary activity declined. Between 1660 and the arrival of Antoine Gaulin in 1704, there was not a single missionary assigned to the Mi'kmaq mission. Even after Gaulin arrived, the size of his parish – all of mainland Mi'kma'ki plus Unimaki – and the brevity of the mission season (May to September) meant that he would have spent most of his time performing the most basic duties: baptizing children, solemnizing marriages and deaths, and taking confessions. Only after the arrival of Abbé Vincent in 1724 was Gaulin able to do more. To be sure, some Mi'kmaq would have been exposed to French, and may even have been taught the language by missionaries. However, after 1654 this missionary presence almost vanished, so that by 1726 it is unlikely that any Mi'kmaq would have received instruction in French.

It is possible that knowledge of French among the Mi'kmaq increased after 1735, when three full-time priests were assigned to minister to them in mainland Mi'kma'ki and Unimaki.[26] But discouraging closer linguistic ties were the exponential growth of the Acadian communities, French missionary insistence on keeping the two communities separate, and an intensifying imperial conflict between France and Great Britain. As the eighteenth century passed, these factors tended to widen the cultural, social, and political gulf between Acadians and the Mi'kmaq.[27]

More to the point is that most Mi'kmaq lived far outside both French and British society, and only occasionally interacted with people from either community. For the most part, the Mi'kmaq lived their lives in their own villages, not in European ones. Mi'kmaq was spoken in these villages, not French or English. Indeed, even those few Europeans who ventured into Mi'kmaq communities would have spoken the language of their hosts, not their own.

The exception to all this related to the villages perched along the eastern coast of mainland Mi'kma'ki from Musquodoboit to Cape Sable. Familial and personal ties had evolved in that area between Mi'kmaq and French speakers. Two things fostered a different social and cultural relationship there than in the Acadian communities nestled along the Fundy coast: the limited character of French settlement, and war with New England.[28] Members of the two communities sometimes married each other. Matthew Muse, one of the Mi'kmaq signers of the 1726 treaty, was born of such a mixed marriage. Though Mi'kmaq was the main language spoken in these villages, intermarriage would have led to some knowledge of French among local Mi'kmaq.[29]

But Muse was not skilled enough to translate the treaty, a fact recognized by Doucett, who appointed two Acadians – Prudent Robicheaux Sr and Abram Bourg – to orally translate the treaty into Mi'kmaq.

These oral translations, and the discussions that must have been held about each article, would have done much to influence how the Mi'kmaq delegates understood the treaty. However, we have no way of evaluating the accuracy of the interpreters' words. We might have been able to do so had the minutes of the discussions preceding and following the treaty signing been made and preserved, as was the case with the treaties signed the same year with the Abenaki.[30] It would then have been possible to use the conference minutes in conjunction with the treaty text to evaluate how specific passages were understood by each party. Such documentation, unfortunately, does not exist.

Though we cannot evaluate the interpreters' translations, it seems reasonable to assume that the Mi'kmaq delegates understood the treaty in ways consistent with their own historical experience. They had not been born in England or France, nor had they been educated there. To expect them therefore to evaluate the treaty's words in the exact manner that Doucett and his officers expected them to do, seems unreasonable. Language is historically constructed and so is not easily transferred from one historical experience to another. This was true as much of the Mi'kmaq language in 1726 as it was of the English used by Nova Scotia officials. To contend that every English word contained in the treaty would have been easily translated from English to Mi'kmaq is to suggest that with the treaty, the history of both societies had been merged into the other, so as to make their languages indistinguishable.

But differences there were, differences so profound as to sometimes limit the ability of each side to understand what the other was about. I am not suggesting that there was total incomprehension, only that certain concepts presented more difficulties to translators than others. For good example, consider these English concepts: 'lawful,' 'submission,' and 'subject.' These words were specific to the history of Great Britain. Mi'kmaq history had not evolved in the same manner, so the words used by them to describe the social, cultural, and political aspects of daily life would have been different from those used by the British. How the Mi'kmaq understood 'lawful,' 'submission,' and 'subject' would have been conditioned by their own history and by the history of their interactions with European people. That history will be the focus of the next two chapters.

The 1726 treaty was written in English, and the words used in it embodied the historical experience of Great Britain and its people. We find, for instance, reference to His Majesty King George I, to Massachusetts, and to the Treaty of Utrecht. Yet we also find the names of seventy-seven aboriginal people, most of whom are Mi'kmaq. But here, we do not find their words, but only the marks they have placed beside their names. Though the treaty embodied the cultures of Mi'kmaq and

British alike, it did so unevenly, as it was written in English rather than Mi'kmaq.

That simple but important difference suggests how the Mi'kmaq and British diverged in their understanding of the treaty. For British officials in London, the treaty was an embodiment of its English text. For the Mi'kmaq the treaty was more than this, and included the oral discussions held prior to the treaty's signing. It could not have been otherwise. The Mi'kmaq could not read English. Though some delegates, like Matthew Muse, had a knowledge of spoken French and English, what would have been more important was how the words of the treaty were translated from English into Mi'kmaq by the two Acadian interpreters, Robichaux and Bourg. Though we do not know what words these two men used in their translations, it is reasonable to assume that the delegates understood their words on the basis of Mi'kmaq history, not British.

Chapter Five

The 1726 Treaty and Utrecht

The previous two chapters examined the first clause of the articles of peace and agreement. That clause outlined the historical conjuncture that had led to the treaty's signing and the steps to be taken for its ratification. In the next two chapters I analyse the six clauses of the treaty that created the legal structure intended to govern Mi'kmaq–British relations.

Central to the 1726 treaty was the Treaty of Utrecht, which was signed in April 1713 by France and by Great Britain and brought to a close more than a decade of war. Though most of the battles had been fought – and most of the casualties had been suffered – in Europe rather than North America, the war's end affected Acadians and Mi'kmaq. Buried within the treaty was an agreement by France to surrender sovereignty over Acadia to Great Britain.

Though pleased that Acadia had been added to its burgeoning empire, Great Britain lacked the money to make something of the colony. To be sure, after 1713 a regiment was dispatched to man the fort at Annapolis Royal, a governing council was set up, and some feeble attempts were made to extend British control over the mainland. But without money to grease the wheels of empire, efforts to establish a forceful British presence could not succeed. Acadia was part of Britain's empire, but it was a poor part. The colonial office's decision to rename 'Acadia' Nova Scotia was no more than a symbolic gesture: Nova Scotia remained what it had been before 1713, Acadian and Mi'kmaq.

British efforts to exert control in Acadia were also undermined by the French military presence at Île Royale and by the close political relationship the French enjoyed with the Mi'kmaq on the mainland and elsewhere. That the French provided aid to the Mi'kmaq during the 1722–5 war is an indication of these lingering ties.

The signing of the 1726 treaty ended more than a decade of British ineptitude, and attempted in one bold stroke to shore up Great Britain's claims to the region. Without a peace treaty, New England's attempts to exploit the east fishery would falter, the colony's trade would decline, and the demand for English goods would suffer. Signing a treaty of peace and friendship with a 'local tribe of savages' was a small price to pay for economic stability. But the treaty did more than secure British economic interests; it was also an attempt to undermine France's historical alliance with the Mi'kmaq by establishing guidelines regulating British–Mi'kmaq relations. The long-term goal of the British was to integrate the Mi'kmaq into British civil society. By the terms of Utrecht, Great Britain had occupied 'Acadia with all its ancient boundaries'; the 1726 treaty established the parameters within which that right would be exercised.

The Mi'kmaq and the British understood their new relationship differently. Central to these differences was how each side understood the second clause of the 1726 treaty. British officials interpreted the clause to mean that the Mi'kmaq had agreed to submit to the authority of British law in their interactions with British subjects. The Mi'kmaq understood the clause as creating a relationship between them and the British similar to the one that had existed between them and the French king. The Mi'kmaq alliance with the French had not involved submission to royal authority, but rather a reciprocal obligation of friendship, protection, and trust.

Articles of Peace and Agreement: Clause 2
Whereas His Majesty King George by the Concession of the Most Christian King made att the Treaty of Utrecht is become ye Rightfull Possessor of the Province of Nova Scotia or Acadia According it its ancient Boundaries, wee the Said Chiefs & Representatives of ye Penobscott, Norridgewalk, St. Johns, Cape Sable & of the Other Indian Tribes Belonging to & Inhabiting within this his Majesties Province of Nova Scotia Or Acadia & New England do for our Selves & the said Tribes Wee represent acknowledge his Said Majesty King George's Jurisdiction & Dominion Over The Territories of the said Province of Nova Scotia or Acadia

The second clause of the 1726 treaty focused on one issue – the relationship of the Mi'kmaq to the Treaty of Utrecht, which had been signed in April 1713. On the one hand, that treaty held little significance for the

Mi'kmaq. It had been negotiated thousands of miles away and between two nations with whom most Mi'kmaq would have had little direct contact. But that treaty had important implications for them, as it resulted in France ceding Acadia to Great Britain. However, Utrecht did not end British–French conflict. After 1713 both nations attempted to secure their economic interests in the region, and to validate their political claims to it through its indigenous inhabitants, the Mi'kmaq and Maliseet.

The Treaty of Utrecht formally ended the War of the Spanish Succession. Though Europe had been the main theatre for the war, the conflict had also raged intermittently in North America, pitting New France and its aboriginal allies against the New England colonies. On 2 October 1710 a New England force numbering some 1,500 men and thirty-seven vessels had captured the French fort at Port Royal. Though the fort was manned after this date by New England volunteers, only after Utrecht was signed was Acadia formally ceded to Great Britain.[1]

In negotiating an end to the war, British and French diplomats could not agree on Acadia's physical boundaries. Great Britain argued that Acadia was bounded by the 'River St. Croix on the west, by the Sea on the South and East, and by Canada River on the North,' an area that encompassed all of mainland Nova Scotia, Cape Breton, and New Brunswick, as well as the Gaspé.[2] According to British diplomats, this area coincided with the territory granted in 1621 by Charles I to the Scottish nobleman Sir William Alexander. French officials disagreed. They were unwilling to relinquish Cape Breton, aware that doing so would further reduce their fishermen's access to the rich east coast fishery. Reluctantly, the British agreed to sever Cape Breton from 'Acadia' and to allow France to retain control over the island as well as Île Saint-Jean (Prince Edward Island).[3] But French policymakers remained uneasy with other parts of the British proposal. The French negotiators at Utrecht argued that 'Acadia' meant only the mainland peninsula and did not include lands to the west, and insisted on making the Bay of Fundy the western boundary of British jurisdiction.[4] Because of French intransigence, the negotiations ended without a final agreement on Acadia's boundaries. In the text of Utrecht, Acadia was described in ambiguous terms as encompassing an area 'with all its ancient boundaries.' Both France and Great Britain understood that Acadia's 'ancient' borders would be determined in future negotiations. For various reasons, these discussions were delayed until 1719. Even then the issue was not resolved.[5] When the 1726 treaty was signed at Annapolis Royal, the problem remained of determining 'Acadia's ancient boundaries.'

The negotiations of 1719, however polite, were a foil for the pretensions of both France and Great Britain. After 1713, both nations set out to validate their interpretations of the treaty by physically occupying the disputed areas and by building up their military and political presence in the region. To be sure, these efforts were not immediate, nor did they involve the immigration of thousands of French and British settlers. Even so, the years after 1713 marked a shift in British and French policy toward North America. Both sides strengthened their efforts to establish their respective political claims to the maritime region.[6]

Both nations were well aware that their wealth was directly tied to trade, and that to expand their trade they would have to acquire new territories. The Caribbean islands were a far more lucrative source of trade than Acadia, but the trade in North Atlantic fish was a vital part of that commerce, which linked the maritime region with southern European markets and with the Caribbean islands.

France's immediate goal after 1713 was to establish a presence on Unimaki. This was not going to be easy. No fort awaited the governor of Île Royale, Philippe Pastour de Costabelle. Though a few trading posts had been built on the island before 1714, France had never thought to post a garrison there.[7] When the governor and his men landed on the island in the spring of 1714, they began building a fort to house and defend themselves.

Costabelle chafed at the rustic character of his rooms; his successors fared much better. Within a decade, France had begun the long and costly process of building the fortress of Louisbourg on the northeastern coast of the island. Most of its buildings were completed between 1723 and 1745, at a cost to the French government of some 3.5 million livres.[8] Relative to the forts the French had built at Pentagoet on the St George's River, at Nashwaak on the St John River, and at Port Royal in the 1600s, Louisbourg was immense. In 1705 there had been 192 officers and soldiers stationed at Port Royal.[9] The garrison at Louisbourg was much larger. In 1724 there were 430 military personnel on the island, 370 of them at Louisbourg. By 1734 there were 618, and by 1742, there were 1,191.[10] The fortress served two purposes: it guarded France's commercial interest in the fishery, and it protected Canada from British naval attack.[11]

But Île Royale was more than a military fortress. It was also a home for farmers and fishermen. To be sure, the island presented challenges to settlement that Acadia had not. Île Royale's topography was mountainous, its shoreline rocky, and its climate cool and damp, all of which made it unattractive for farmers. Indeed, though the Treaty of Utrecht had extended to Acadians living in British Nova Scotia the option of relocating to Île Royale, few chose to do so, and of those who did, most returned to their farms in Nova Scotia after experiencing life on the island.[12] But if the island was not graced with the same fertile lands that had attracted settlers to Acadia in the early 1600s, it did offer a staging area for the inshore fishery. For officials in Versailles, this was the island's greatest value. In 1712 the Minister of the Marine wrote that since control over Plaisance and Acadia had been surrendered to Great Britain, 'it seems to me necessary to establish two other fishing posts. I think we can place one on the island of Cape Breton and the other on the coast of Labrador ... It remains only to know where we should make this establishment [on Cape Breton].'[13] Efforts were made to attract fishing families to the island. By 1716, twelve separate fishing communities with a total population of 498 had sprung up along the eastern coast. By 1724, their population was 890, by 1742, it was 4,325.[14] The fishery was the lifeblood of the island's economy. Between 1713 and 1745, perhaps half of all nonmilitary personnel on Île Royale were employed in the fishery.[15]

New French settlements also sprang up on Île Saint-Jean (Prince Edward Island). In contrast to Île Royale, Île Saint-Jean was flat, and its soils were fertile, which made the island attractive for farming families. In 1728 the island's population was 266. By 1735, it was 563; by 1742, it was 2,180.[16] Overall, the French presence in the northeast increased after 1713. Between 1726 and 1739 it more than quintupled from 1,600 to 8,700. This figure does not include those Acadians who chose to remain in British Nova Scotia.

In contrast to French success in populating Île Royale and Île Saint-Jean, British efforts to entice English-speaking Protestants to Nova Scotia failed miserably. Speculators in London and Massachusetts hatched various schemes to capitalize on Great Britain's newest acquisition, but none bore fruit till 1749, when Parliament undertook to fund the building of Halifax.[17] This failure can be attributed partly to the Privy Council's decision that lands within 200 yards of the coast would not be granted to prospective settlers – a move designed to ensure that New England fishermen could dry their fish in coastal areas.[18] Also discouraging new settlers was the presence of the Acadians. In 1703 the Acadians had numbered 1,324; in 1737 they were 6,958.[19] These French-speaking people had immigrated to Mi'kma'ki in the 1630s, and lived mainly along the river systems flowing into the Bay of Fundy.

Fear of the Mi'kmaq also contributed to Great Britain's lack of success. Though land in the older towns and villages of New England was becoming more expensive, Massachusetts and Connecticut had one distinct advantage over Nova Scotia: the aboriginal inhabitants were less threatening than the Mi'kmaq.[20] The most likely people to immigrate from New England were Massachusetts fishermen whose families had been fishing in the area since the mid-1600s. But despite the hardship of leaving their home ports in Massachusetts to fish off the Nova Scotia coast, and the dangers of sailing the North Atlantic, fishing families were unlikely to immigrate without some assurance that the Mi'kmaq would not threaten them. Most fishermen from Salem, Marblehead, and other ports would have been able to recite a long litany of incidents, real or alleged, in which men had been killed or had narrowly escaped death at the hands of the 'savages.'[21] By 1726, little had changed to assuage those fears. If anything, they were greater. Fishermen would have noted the dilapidated character of the British fort at Annapolis,[22] and spread their poor impression of the garrison along the wharves of Marblehead, Salem, Boston, and other New England ports.

Though it failed to attract English-speakers to Nova Scotia, the Board of Trade did try to extablish a stronger presence in the region. In April 1719, Richard Phillips was made governor of Nova Scotia; formal instructions to him were drafted by the Board of Trade, and he was dispatched to shore up the colony's administrative structure.

After arriving at Annapolis in April 1720, Phillips tried to browbeat the recalcitrant Acadians into swearing an oath of allegiance to King George. Among other things, Phillips wanted the Acadians to promise they would take up arms against the French king in war time. He considered this essential to secure the Acadians' neutrality in any future conflict; it might also provide the British garrison with much-needed military assistance. Earlier efforts to extract similar oaths in 1714 and 1717 had failed, with the Acadians arguing that they would incense the Mi'kmaq by making such an oath. The Acadians insisted that they could swear an oath of allegiance only when enough British soldiers were on hand to protect them 'from the Indian nations, who are always ready to make all kinds of wrongs as is clearly evident from the many incidents since the Peace, having killed and pillaged English and french people.'[23]

In the Board of Trade's view, French officials at Île Royale and their Acadian conspirators were sabotaging Great Britain's efforts to lay claim to Acadia 'with all ancient limits.' Indeed, soon after the Treaty of Utrecht was signed, France showed that it was ready to use both the

Acadians and the Mi'kmaq against the British. Witness an incident at Canso, a fishing port on the northeast coast of Mi'kma'ki.[24]

Nowadays, Canso is not an important place. It is not a tourist town, and it has little industry. Its fishery is declining, and it is not on any main highway. Canso is not a place people visit in droves; in fact, most people deliberately avoid the place, since getting there involves a long drive along a bushwhacked road.

Not so in the early 1700s, when Canso commanded the attention of fishermen, merchants, soldiers, and politicians, all of whom measured the port's worth by its proximity to the swarming schools of cod offshore. It was here that Basque fishermen had landed their catch as early as the 1560s, here again where the Compagnie des pêches sedentaire had set up shop in 1682, and here once more where French fishermen were to be found in the years after Utrecht.[25] New Englanders cried foul, claiming that Canso lay in the area surrendered by France. In August 1718 they sent Captain Thomas Smart north to lodge a complaint with Joseph de Saint-Ovide, who a year earlier had replaced Costabelle as governor of Île Royale. Having failed to persuade through argument, Smart returned to Canso, where he seized three French ships and a quantity of fish and goods.[26] Soon after, New Englanders established more control over the area, and Canso became a favourite haunt of their fishermen, in no small part because Nova Scotia established a permanent garrison there after 1720.

Smart's attack on French fishermen at Canso illustrated the simmering boundary disputes between the British and the French territory. For the Board of Trade, the controversy also demonstrated how the French were using the Mi'kmaq quite deliberately to undermine British dominion over Nova Scotia. For the board, the Mi'kmaq were a barbaric and savage people who lacked all civilities of government, and whom the French were using as pawns to sustain their own political and economic aspirations.[27] In September 1722, the board wrote to Lord Carteret, the Secretary of State for the southern department, describing the problems posed by the French presence: 'We find by them [letters lately received] that the French inhabitants remaining in Nova Scotia and the French missionaries who travel up and down that Country are very industrious in instigating the Indian Natives to insult and plunder his Majesty's Subjects there upon all Occasions, so that altho' this Province was solemnly given up to the Crown of Great Britain by the Treaty of Utrecht the Possession by His Majesty has of it is a very precarious One and which in all Probability depends upon the Pleasure of ye French.'[28]

If there had ever been any doubt that the French and the Mi'kmaq were in collusion, Mi'kmaq attacks on British fishermen at Canso put an end to it. In the months that preceded Captain Smart's descent on Canso in 1718, Mi'kmaq had destroyed English houses and stages there. According to one fisherman, John Henshaw, when the attackers were asked 'what reason they had in peaceable times to disturb the English, the Indians replied that Le Sond asked them to do so, as Monsieur Petitpas the French interpreter said, for he had an Order from the Governor.'[29] Two years later, New Englanders fishing at Canso were again visited by Mi'kmaq warriors. A letter written from there recounts the events of the early morning of 8 August 1720: '[A] Company of Indians with some French assisting them ... beset the inhabitants of this Place, and surprized them in their beds, designing to make them prisoners whom they robb'd of all that they had ... it is apparent that there is and was a plain Confederacy between the french and Indians to ruin the people and Fishermen here.'[30] The collusion between French and Mi'kmaq was transparent; according to earlier reports of the incident in the *Boston Newsletter*, the French attackers were wearing 'masquerade' to hide their true identity.[31] But the incidents at Canso were only a handful of the many altercations before 1722 that had demonstrated to the Board of Trade the threat that French–Mi'kmaq friendship constituted to the prosperity of the fishery and to the future settlement of Nova Scotia.[32]

The board's suspicions that the Mi'kmaq were colluding with the French were well founded. French fishermen and traders had been frequenting the shores of Mi'kma'ki since at least the mid-1550s; French-speaking farmers had been living there since the 1630s; and French missionaries had been preaching among the Mi'kmaq since the mid-1630s. While the French political presence before 1710 had never been large, a formal alliance had developed between the king's officials and the Mi'kmaq. This was an alliance born of need, with each side offering friendship as well as support against common enemies. For the Mi'kmaq, this alliance represented a new political conjuncture in their history. To be sure, both before and after 1500 they had made alliances with various aboriginal groups living near them. But these had been with people who lived as they did, without iron and guns, and who inhabited lands adjacent to their own. Their alliance with the French king was different, as it involved a people who lived across the sea and who had come to live among the Mi'kmaq.

After 1710 the French–Mi'kmaq alliance solidified. As tensions between Great Britain and France escalated, Île Royale worked harder to strengthen its friendship with the Mi'kmaq. Beginning in 1719, Governor Saint-Ovide met annually with village sakamaws and elders and distributed to them more presents than they had ever been given, even at the height of the French–English wars of the 1690s. In 1693, for instance, the king had given the Mi'kmaq 2 guns, 500 pounds of powder, 12 shirts, 12 pairs of stockings, 12 laced hats, 12 blankets, 600 pounds of lead balls, and 100 lead bars. By 1732 the annual allotment had increased to 45 grenadier muskets, 15,000 'pierre a fusils,' 35 hundredweight of fine powder, 30 hundredweight each of duck and goose shot, 300 pounds of lead balls, and 80 hoes.[33] Though given as a token of the king's respect, these presents represented much more.[34] French officials were worried that British trade with the Mi'kmaq would facilitate a closer social and political relationship between the two. Officials at Versailles well understood that New England merchants could undersell French traders, and viewed the annual distribution as necessary to 'balance the [prices] offered by the English.'[35] In sum, the presents symbolized French efforts to sabotage a potentially dangerous British–Mi'kmaq alliance.

But if the French were successful in consolidating their relationship with the Mi'kmaq, it was with the help of a British bureaucracy that consistently underestimated the economic value of normalizing relationships with Mi'kmaq villagers. Soon after the French were defeated in October 1710, Mi'kmaq leaders had tried to treat with British officials. In February and March 1711, two delegations had arrived at Annapolis, one from Cape Sable and the other from La Hève, who 'were resolved henceforward to offer no violence to the English, unless they first began with them, and finding we are not disposed to maintain hostilities with them they are come to mediate an Accommodation.'[36] Though the delegates promised that their chiefs would sign 'Articles of Peace,' no further discussions are recorded. Four years later, similar entreaties were made by another Mi'kmaq village on the eastern coast. Pierre Capon, who had been delegated by Thomas Caulfeild, lieutenant-governor of the garrison, to investigate the capture of several fishing ketches near Cape Sable, later reported that two villages were anxious to sign articles of agreement with the British. Later, Capon wrote of his encounter with villagers living near Port Mouton: 'I went ashoar to theire Wigwamms, and told them ye damage ye Indians had done to the English which they Seemd Sorry for, and desired me to meet them in ye Spring on ye Coast, being Sent by theire Chiefs to tell me, that all theire Chiefs and Indians would meet me, and desired Articles then to be drawn relating to trade and other affairs at that Conference, and ye Articles then agreed upon they would Signe and faithfully perform, and pressured me hard to promise to meet them, I answered them if I had ye. Govt orders Soo to doe, I should willingly obey them.'[37] But once again, officials failed to respond to the overtures.

This failure was symptomatic of British policy between 1710 and 1720. Part of the difficulty was that the Board of Trade did not develop policies for Nova Scotia. When Francis Nicholson was appointed governor in 1712, he was not given clear instructions, and at any rate he was present in Nova Scotia only from August to October 1714. After Nicholson departed, the lieutenant-governor of the garrison, Thomas Caulfeild assumed command, but he laboured with little help from the board.[38]

The appointment of Richard Phillips as the new governor of Nova Scotia in 1719 led to only a small improvement in the board's relationships with the Mi'kmaq. While Phillips waited in London for the board's instructions, Captain John Doucett, appointed as the new lieutenant-governor of the garrison, was dispatched to Nova Scotia.[39] But while it began communicating more often with its officers in Nova Scotia, the board continued to dawdle.

Soon after his arrival at Annapolis, Doucett was beset by delegations of Mi'kmaq and Maliseet, who restated their wish to normalize relations. In early February 1718 he described a recent visit by some Mi'kmaq sakamaws: 'I must also Acquaint Your Lordships that Some of the Chiefs of the Indians have been wth me to tell me, that if wee Expected them to continue our Friends they expected Presents Yearly From His Majesty, as they allways receiv'd when this country was in the hands of the French King ... their is no means better than Presents to gain them to our Interest, and keep them from Going to Cape Breton & Canada, where well I am inform'd they have Still Presents if they will goe for them, Now My Lords these Places being so far off, I believe they want not to undertake the Journeys were they taken Notice of by Us.'[40] Soon after, Doucett wrote directly to Phillips in London urging him to inform the board of the importance of sending presents. These presents, said Doucett, would show the king's good faith toward the Mi'kmaq and placate their hostility toward the garrison.[41] But Doucett's repeated requests did not hasten the board's discussions, and the presents were only requisitioned in the summer of 1720. For various reasons, the presents did not arrive in Nova Scotia until one year later and were not distributed until the following year.[42] Soon after, war erupted along the eastern coast of Nova Scotia and the presents had a less positive effect than they might have had.

British policy toward the Mi'kmaq from 1710 to 1726 had been an abysmal failure. Protestant farmers had not arrived, so the colony remained an enclave of the Mi'kmaq and the Acadians, who for the most part remained independent of British civil authority. The social, economic, and political relationships that had developed in the previous century between these two communities did much to limit the British garrison's scope for forming a direct relationship with the Mi'kmaq. So did London's failure to respond to efforts by its officers in Nova Scotia to establish good relations with Mi'kmaq villagers. The conclusion of the 1722–5 war offered the Nova Scotia Council an opportunity to normalize relations with the Mi'kmaq.

For officials in Annapolis Royal and Boston, the treaty was a vehicle for obtaining Mi'kmaq recognition of Great Britain's claims in the region and, it would follow, for integrating the Mi'kmaq into the British Empire. Central to that process was the Treaty of Utrecht. This is evident from the opening words of the second clause of the 1726 treaty: *'Whereas his Majesty King George by the Concession of the Most Christian King made att the Treaty of Utrecht is become ye Rightfull Possessor of the Province of Nova Scotia or Acadia According it its ancient Boundaries ...'* With the ratification of the 1726 treaty, the Mi'kmaq recognized Great Britain's right to regulate the movement of European nationals into 'Acadia according to its ancient limits.' In obtaining Mi'kmaq consent to Article XII of Utrecht, British officials were hoping to undermine French influence with the Mi'kmaq and thereby provide more security to Great Britain's interests in the region. Equally important, the 1726 treaty provided Great Britain with a legal document that it could use to protest the assistance the French gave the Mi'kmaq during times of war. Finally, British policymakers believed that Mi'kmaq confirmation of Utrecht would offer legal support for Great Britain's more expansive definition of Acadia, since the treaty included the 'signatures' of Mi'kmaq and Maliseet villagers living west of the Bay of Fundy. The British could use the signatures of delegates from these communities to demonstrate that they lived in the 'Acadia' that was defined in both Utrecht and the 1726 treaty as bounded by 'its ancient limits.' These signatures challenged France's view that Acadia's ancient boundaries did not extend west of mainland Mi'kma'ki. Thus, it was no accident that the secretary of the Nova Scotia Council, William Sherriff, noted the home villages of the principal headmen present and that these individuals were recognized as chiefs of their communities. In sum, the second clause of the treaty provided British officials with ammunition for their simmering conflict for control over northeastern North America, by providing documentation to prove their own interpretation of the Treaty of Utrecht.[43]

Articles of Peace and Agreement: Clause II, Part II
& make our Submission to his said Majesty in as Ample a Manner as wee have formerly done to the Most Christian King.

Like the previous part of the treaty, this one created a direct relationship between the Mi'kmaq and the British king. The Treaty of Utrecht had made such a relationship necessary. Read literally, these words meant that the Mi'kmaq made their submission to King George of Great Britain in the same way that they formerly had done to the King of France ('the Most Christian King'). It is not clear, however, when this 'submission' to the French king occurred.

This phrase is the most intriguing part of the treaty.[44] Similar ideas are not contained in any treaty signed by Massachusetts with the Abenaki between 1693 and 1717. Nor was such a phrase incorporated into the treaty signed by the Penobscot on behalf of the Abenaki at Boston in December 1725. Rather, the comparable phrase of the Abenaki treaty reads: 'in as full and ample a manner as any of our Predecessors have heretofore done.'[45] The treaty with the Mi'kmaq recognized the unique situation created by the fact that Great Britain had inherited France's century-long relationship with the Mi'kmaq, and incorporated into British law the political and social character of that relationship.

But the meaning of this phrase is not immediately discernible. First of all, how do we define 'submission'? According to the *Oxford English Dictionary*, submission means 'the action of submitting to an authority, a conquering or ruling power; the act of yielding to the claims of another, or surrendering to his will or government.'[46] 'Submission' reflected the hierarchical structure of early modern British society, in which the authority of government was vested in the king's person.[47] Sir Edward Coke, the Chief Justice of England's Court of Common Pleas, wrote in 1608 that individuals born into the kingdom were by the law of nature bound to submit to the will of the king, and so to be faithful and obedient subjects to him. Their obedience, however, was part of a reciprocal relationship. In consenting to obey the sovereign's will,' he is claimed their liege lord, because he should maintain and defend them.' According to Sir Edward, though the king often relied on force to defend his authority, he represented a benevolent force that protected and defended the interests and property of his subjects.[48]

The importance of hierarchy in the king's relationship with his subjects is reflected in the political correspondence of Nova Scotia in the early 1700s. Thomas Caulfeild, the lieutenant-governor of the Annapolis garrison from 1714 to 1717, addressed the Board of Trade as 'My Lords,' and ended his letters to them with the words, 'Your most obedient, most Obliged and humble servant.'[49] Petitions to the king usually began by noting the political relationship between the petitioners and the king. A memorial sent to the king by representatives from the Massachusetts Assembly in August 1701 ended with these words: 'all of which is most humbly Submitted by Your Majesty's Most dutiful, obedient and Loyal Subjects.'[50] In contrast, letters sent by Nova Scotia officials to either Acadians or Mi'kmaq began and ended differently. Armstrong's 1732 letter to Acadian deputies began 'Gentlemen' and ended 'Your most Humble Servant,' while his later correspondence with the Mi'kmaq of Cape Sable started with 'my Friend.'[51] In neither case did Armstrong end his letters by describing himself as their 'obedient servant' – a term that he used most often in corresponding with his London superiors.

The word submission was used to describe the social and political relationship between the king and his subjects. Is this how the term was used in the 1726 treaty? If it was, did the authors of the treaty intend to imply that the Mi'kmaq would henceforth be considered subjects of the Crown? Such an interpretation seems possible, since the Mi'kmaq inhabited an area over which Great Britain claimed dominion. At the same time, the Mi'kmaq were clearly neither British nor French. Surely there were differences between the Mi'kmaq, who were not part of a Christian society, and the Acadian and British inhabitants of Acadia, who were.

Of some assistance here is Sir Edward Coke's summary of a case involving Robert Calvin. This case helped establish the general framework that would govern Great Britain's relationship with North America's aboriginal peoples, and so provides insight into the 1726 treaty.

The case involved two English-born subjects of the king, Robert and Nicholas Smith, who had confiscated the English property of a Scotsman, Robert Calvin. The Smiths' attorney, William Edwards, argued that Calvin did not have a right to own English land since he had been born in Scotland. Since Scotland was not within the Kingdom of England,

Edwards argued, Calvin was not a subject of the Crown but an alien. Because he was an alien, he could not own land. Thus, the Smiths were justified in confiscating Calvin's land, since he had no right to it.

In its decision, the court established the legal status of individuals who by virtue of their birth were not subjects of the Crown, but who later came to live under its jurisdiction. According to the court, 'every man is either alienigena, an alien born, or subditus, a subject born. Every alien is either a friend that is in league, &c. Or an enemy that is in open war, &c.' An alien friend could be a Spaniard, Frenchmen, or German who came to England from another Christian nation that was allied with the English monarch. These alien friends, said the court, could trade with English subjects but could not own land within the monarch's domain 'unless the house be for their necessary habitation.' In contrast to an alien friend was an alien enemy who, because of his hostility to the monarch, could neither trade nor be governed by the same laws as regulated the relationship with alien friends. Alien enemies, the court said, were those people who lived in a Christian kingdom but whose monarchs were at war with England.

Separate and distinct from subjects and aliens were infidels. Infidels were people who did not belong to a Christian kingdom and who therefore were 'in law ... perpetual enemies (for the law presumes not that they will be converted that being a remote possibility) for between them, as with the devils, whose subjects they be, and the Christian, there is perpetual hostility, and can be no peace.'[52] According to the court, infidels were people who were neither subjects nor aliens but inhabitants of a country or kingdom not part of the Christian world. Whether or not the aboriginal peoples of North America were infidels is not clear. The court stated that infidels were perpetual enemies of the Crown, since there was no possibility that they would be converted to the Christian faith. Though aboriginal people might be classified as infidels, the efforts made to convert them to Christianity would suggest otherwise. Indeed, Great Britain was not alone in bringing the Christian faith to North America: the French and Spanish colonial governments pursued similar policies. The missionaries' experience had demonstrated that some communities that were not Christian were not in a state of perpetual hostility.

English policies in North America were inconsistent with the court's 1608 definition of infidels. Since the mid-1600s, British law in the colonies had stressed forming alliances with aboriginal people. It was hoped that these alliances would transform these communities of 'savage folk' from 'alien/enemy to a subject/ally.' This legal transformation always started with some kind of formal ceremony. For example, the ceremony often involved the aboriginal community acknowledging British sovereignty, or agreeing to submit to British law, or expressing its friendship.[53] However peace was made, the hope was always that a period of adjustment would follow in which aboriginal communities would gradually be integrated into a proper understanding of the law, and so learn to behave like members of a civil society.

The 1726 treaty represented a further evolution in this policy. Implicitly, the treaty recognized that the Mi'kmaq would not be integrated into British civil society overnight; a long period of tutelage would be required. The Mi'kmaq simply weren't ready, as they lacked all manner of civilization. British concepts of civilization were closely associated with the Latin term *civitas*, which referred to urban areas where the necessaries of life and culture could be found. Those who lived outside the civitas were 'barbarians,' since they lacked the means to enrich their bodies and their minds.[54] In early modern Europe, these concepts were closely associated with the Christian faith, which had often been employed to 'raise' other cultures out of barbarism into civil society. This view was succinctly articulated in 1718 by the governor of Massachusetts, Samuel Shute, who chastised the Catholic missionary Sébastien Rale's failure to instil in the Abenaki an understanding of the Bible's words: 'I hope I need not tell you, the main design of a Christian mission among the Indians is to bring them from the darkness of their ignorance and paganism to the marvellous light of the gospel; and, under the influence of the divine spirit, to translate them from the power of satan, who has usurped possession of these parts of the world for so many ages, to the kingdom of the Son of God, whose right it is, and to whomever knee shall bow, &c.'[55]

British law would incorporate the Mi'kmaq into civil society by establishing a framework for regulating their interactions with subjects of the Crown. Over time, this framework would be expanded, taming Mi'kmaq excesses and teaching them how to act according to reason rather than emotion. Even though the language of the treaty implied Mi'kmaq submission to King George, the simple fact that a treaty was being negotiated indicated that the British did not intend to impose their will on their new allies. Something more subtle was in the minds of the British negotiators than a literal reading of the word 'submission' would indicate. How this nuance was communicated to the Mi'kmaq delegates is not known.

British and Mi'kmaq delegates may have reached some mutual understanding of the word 'submission,' but it is unlikely that they found
agreement on what the entire clause meant: '& make our Submission to his
said Majesty in as Ample a Manner as wee have formerly done to the Most Christian King.' The British would have assumed that French relations with
the Mi'kmaq were similar to their own relations with neighbouring
aboriginal communities. For instance, Massachusetts had signed a series
of treaties in which the Abenaki had made their submission to the British Crown. The words 'the Submission and Agreement of the Eastern
Indians' were used in the 1693 treaty.[56] But unlike the British, the
French did not sign treaties with the Mi'kmaq.

In contrast to most British settlements in eastern North America, New
France was sparsely populated in the early 1700s. By 1710 there were
perhaps 20,000 people in Canada, Acadia, and Placentia in Newfoundland. In contrast, the British colonies had a population of 339,000. At
least one-third of these people lived in the four New England colonies:
Massachusetts, Connecticut, Rhode Island, and New Hampshire.[57] New
France was compelled by its small population, its continuing reliance on
the fur trade, and (after the early 1690s) its mounting fears of New
England's military strength to establish close political alliances with
neighbouring aboriginal societies. In the early decades of the 1700s
these alliances would be critical to New France's defence. French officials may well have perceived their aboriginal allies as cultural inferiors;
even so, the realities of New France's military situation were such that
they could not treat these people as subjects of the Crown.[58]

There were other differences between the French and British colonies. French settlement in the valley of St Lawrence did not require the
displacement of an indigenous people.[59] On the contrary, by the time
French settlers arrived at Quebec, the Iroquois along the St Lawrence
either had been wiped out by European diseases or had been absorbed
into neighbouring aboriginal societies. And while Algonquin and Montagnais families often visited the French settlements, they were absent
from the St Lawrence Valley for most of the year. All of this meant that
no conflicts over land developed between French settlers and neighbouring aboriginal communities.

British settlement in New England followed a different pattern.
Unlike the French, the first British émigrés in the 1620s and 1630s did
not settle on empty lands.[60] Generally, British expansion in Massachusetts Bay, Plymouth, and (later) the valley of the Connecticut River
required the displacement of aboriginal farming and fishing communi-

ties.[61] Settlement was achieved by either purchasing land from aboriginal communities or by conquest.[62] Massachusetts's relations with the Abenaki were no different. The Abenaki protested that speculators had bought lands without the consent of communities; this did not sway government officials, who upheld these purchases by force. Invariably, each ceasefire ended with the signing of a treaty which confirmed that earlier English purchases of Abenaki lands had been valid.

In the late 1600s and early 1700s, a dynamic evolved in Mi'kmaq relationships with the French similar to the one that had developed in Canada with the aboriginal communities living there. True, aboriginal land use patterns in the two regions were not identical. The Acadians settled on lands that were being used and occupied by the Mi'kmaq. It isn't clear why the Mi'kmaq did nothing while the Acadians settled the land, dyked the marshlands, and expanded their farming activities. Perhaps there were too few émigrés to pose a threat to the Mi'kmaq, or perhaps the lands the Acadians settled were not important fishing or fowling sites. Since there are few records from the early 1600s, there are few answers. Whatever the reasons why co-existence was possible, by the early 1690s Acadian settlement had not resulted in any ongoing hostilities with Mi'kmaq communities. Thus there was no need for either group to resort to military force.

Mainly because land was not a point of conflict in Mi'kmaq–Acadian relations, a peaceful alliance developed between the French king and the Mi'kmaq. This alliance was one of mutual gain: it served France's political interest in eastern North America, as well as the material requirements of the Mi'kmaq.[63] Yet it was not a relationship between equals. The Mi'kmaq perceived their relationship to the French king as that of children to their father. The French king was powerful, but he was also benevolent and kind, and sought to protect his children from harm. Indeed, the French king provided guidance to his children in what had become, by the 1660s, an unstable world.[64] This was not a static relationship; indeed, it required constant nurturing so that the father would be able to assess his children's strength and they in turn would be able to discuss their needs with him.

British officials did not see Mi'kmaq–French relations this way. Indeed, their understanding was quite the opposite. The way they saw it, a hierarchical relationship had been created between an omnipotent king and his obedient subjects.

But if Dummer understood the French–Mi'kmaq alliance this way, the Mi'kmaq who signed the 1726 treaty did not. And however they understood the term *submission*, and however the British took them to understand it, the Mi'kmaq would also have considered it a given that their relationship with King George would be similar to their past relationship with the French king. Undoubtedly, the Mi'kmaq delegates to the treaty-signing did not see themselves as equals to the British king; but neither would they have seen themselves as his obedient and submissive subjects.

All of this points out for us how ambiguous the 1726 treaty really was, and how differently the two parties understood it. The British intended the treaty to regularize relations with a non-Christian, non-European population – in effect, to create a legal relationship between their king and the Mi'kmaq that was different from the one between their king and his natural-born subjects. This legal structure explicitly recognized the Mi'kmaq's special status as inhabitants of a territory over which Great Britain claimed dominion but who lived outside the boundaries of British civil society. A literal reading of the treaty suggests that the Mi'kmaq had made their submission to King George, and had agreed to be governed by British law in their interactions with British subjects. But this literal reading will not serve. By transcribing the existing relationship between the Mi'kmaq and the French king onto the new relationship between the Mi'kmaq and King George, the treaty was incorporating the past customary relations between the French Crown and the Mi'kmaq into British law. These earlier historical relationships thus became the basis on which future relationships would be built. The British thought that these relationships had been premised on the submission of the Mi'kmaq to the will of the French sovereign. This understanding of French–Mi'kmaq relations was at odds with historical realities.

The first clause of the 1726 treaty was an addendum to the Treaty of Utrecht. In 1726, Great Britain acknowledged that proclaiming dominion over a territory in eastern North America required confirmation by the region's aboriginal peoples. To be sure, Great Britain was motivated by an ongoing political dispute with France over 'Acadia's ancient boundaries.' Even so, the 1722–5 war had demonstrated that British efforts to establish their control over Nova Scotia would be sabotaged if an accommodation was not reached with the Mi'kmaq.

Though British officials understood that the Mi'kmaq had 'submitted' themselves to King George in a manner consistent with New England's relations with other aboriginal communities, the Mi'kmaq would not have understood this phrase the same way. Their relationship with the French king had been a reciprocal relationship of friendship and trust. In a word, the Mi'kmaq were not subjects of the French, but neither were they equals to them. They were something in between, and so too would they consider themselves to be in their future relations with the British king.

Chapter Six

Establishing Laws, Establishing Relationships

This chapter analyses the rest of the 1726 treaty – namely, the last five clauses of the articles of peace and agreement and the four clauses of the reciprocal promises (see pp. 63–5). Together, these nine clauses amounted to a framework for regulating relations between the Mi'kmaq and the British.

The second clause of the treaty had formalized a political alliance between King George and the Mi'kmaq. The nature of that relationship was outlined in the remaining clauses. Both parties were concerned mainly about their economic and political interests in the region. The British wanted assurances about the security of their garrison, the integrity of their existing settlements and any future ones, and the right of New England traders and fishermen to tap the region's economic resources without fear of Mi'kmaq interference. Mi'kmaq concerns were less extensive. Mainly, they wanted the British to promise not to interfere with their fishing, hunting, and planting grounds. Two issues were especially nettlesome: How were the lands to be inhabited and used by the Mi'kmaq to be defined? And what would the procedures be for establishing new British settlements? The failure to reach an understanding on these two issues would be a source of irritation for the British and the Mi'kmaq in later years.

Articles of Peace and Agreement
[Clause III] That the Indians shall not molest any of His Majesty's Subjects or their Dependants in their Settlements already made or Lawfully to be made

The Mi'kmaq and the British were grappling with the unique historical situation that the Treaty of Utrecht had created. Great Britain had been awarded the right to occupy Nova Scotia; yet this right stemmed not from any conquest of the Mi'kmaq or from the purchase of their land, but rather from the defeat of France. British officials believed that Nova Scotia's integration into the Empire after 1713 would be best accomplished by settling English-speaking Protestant farmers in the region. This policy was to encounter resistance from the Mi'kmaq and the Acadians. It is doubtful that British officials understood at the time the long-term consequences of the conundrum they faced.

In 1713 the Acadians occupied most of the region's best farmland. While the rest of mainland Mi'kma'ki was not without value, that value was to be measured in timber, fish, and furs, not in fertile lands. These resources constituted Nova Scotia's principal value to British merchants. As long as the Acadians remained docile and did not become entangled in popish plots to reconquer Nova Scotia, policymakers were willing to leave them undisturbed.

For colonial officials in Massachusetts and Nova Scotia, the 1722–5 war had demonstrated the consequences of not establishing guidelines regulating the settlement of land by British subjects. The 1726 treaty did so.

The Mi'kmaq agreed to respect (i.e., not interfere with) the existing settlements of His Majesty's subjects and their dependants. Since the only British subjects living in Nova Scotia in 1726 were members of the Annapolis garrison, of whom only a small number were living outside the garrison's walls, the reference to British subjects was of little immediate consequence to the Mi'kmaq. The reference to settlements occupied by dependants of the British Crown was more problematic. Though 'Dependants' was not defined, it likely referred to the Acadians. Under British law, the Acadians were entitled to a status similar to that of Englishmen who had been born 'natural subjects'; however, they were only eligible for this status if they swore an oath of allegiance to the Crown. Yet British law applied to them whether they swore the oath or not (i.e., whether they were subjects of the Crown or not).

The word 'settlements' was used in reference to the lands occupied and used by the Acadians and the British. How was this word understood by the Mi'kmaq delegates? Did 'settlements' mean, for them, all the lands that the Acadians and British claimed? Did it include all the lands that Louis XIV had granted and where seigneuries had been established? Or did it only refer to the lands the Acadians farmed?

In 1726 the Acadians were living mainly along the rivers that flowed into the Bay of Fundy, an area that stretched from the Annapolis Basin on mainland Mi'kma'ki to the Petitcodiac River in what is now southeastern

New Brunswick. This is a vast area that even today is relatively free of settlement. It was even emptier in 1726. Acadian farmsteads were not built one on top of the other. For instance, Gargas's 1687–8 census shows only 299 acres under cultivation along a twenty-mile stretch of ground running up the Annapolis River from Port Royal at the head of the basin to 'au bout du monde' (Paradise).[1] The quantity of land farmed by Acadians had increased by 1726; even so, they occupied little space.

These Acadian farms would have been clearly visible to the Mi'kmaq, who would have understood 'settlements' to mean lands the Acadians used for their houses and buildings, for growing crops, or for grazing livestock. A similar definition was used by William Dummer in November 1725 when he stated that the Abenaki would have access to all lands except those 'in the Inclosures, or Land that are fenced in.'[2] Fences as well as houses and barns acted as visual markers separating Acadian land from lands used by the Mi'kmaq.[3]

The treaty also indicated that the British would build new settlements. No framework for this was outlined, except that the settlements were 'lawfully to be made.' What did the British mean by 'lawfully to be made'? How did the Mi'kmaq delegates understand this phrase? Did it mean that the British would exercise a unilateral right to make future settlements anywhere in 'Nova Scotia' without Mi'kmaq consent? Or could new farms and forts only be built with Mi'kmaq consent?

At the time, the issue of aboriginal land rights was not unique to Nova Scotia: other colonies in eastern North America faced the same one. The dispute between Connecticut and the Mohegans, which first arose in the late 1600s, highlights some of the political and legal questions that surrounded the British settlement of aboriginal lands. The same questions would arise in Nova Scotia.

The Mohegans lived at the southern end of the Connecticut River. They had sold most of their lands to the colony of Connecticut in the 1630s, though reserving some for their exclusive use. In 1659 these reserved lands were conveyed 'in trust' to John Mason, who in turn transferred the lands to Connecticut with the proviso that the government retain sufficient land for the Mohegans' use. The Mohegans contended that Mason's action violated the spirit of the conveyance; even so, the government began granting these lands in 1687. In 1704 the Mohegans petitioned for redress, arguing that the colony's land grants were illegal.[4] At issue was to what degree the Mohegans, and implicitly other aboriginal people, retained a vested right to the soil. Though the Mohegans had sold some of their lands by treaty to the colony, they had specifically retained other lands for their exclusive use. By granting these lands to non-aboriginal people, the government was implying that it had a legal right to the land, not the Mohegans.

This case exposed the contradictions inherent in the British project of settling eastern North America. Did aboriginal peoples hold title to all their lands both at the time of the first English settlements in Massachusetts and afterwards? Did aboriginal peoples hold title to the lands they used, or only to the lands they occupied and improved? Did they 'occupy' the lands they used for hunting and fishing? Did they have an exclusive right to their hunting and fishing grounds? How was it possible to determine which lands they were using for hunting and fishing? Could these hunting and fishing grounds be defined as encompassing all lands outside European settlements? Or only a portion of those lands? And finally, how was it possible to determine the borders between aboriginal societies? And thereby to distinguish the hunting and fishing grounds of one society from those of another?

A pamphlet published in 1724 by the Reverend John Bulkley, a minister of Colchester, Connecticut, addressed all of these questions and others. Basing his views on the work of the English philosopher John Locke, Bulkley argued that property was an instrument of man's labour. By tilling the land, man invested the soil with his labour and thereby gained the exclusive right to its use. In the same vein, a man who killed a deer, by expending his labour to kill it, obtained the right to use it. But – and this was the crucial point – the land on which the deer lived was commonly shared, since no man's labour had been invested in it. In Bulkley's view, aboriginal communities could hold title to land, but their exclusive right to it was restricted to those areas where they had cultivated the soil; it did not include other lands they might use for hunting, fowling, and fishing. Their right to these other lands was one that they exercised in common with His Majesty's subjects. The right to these lands resided in the Crown. This was so, according to Bulkley, because aboriginal people lived in a state of nature, without laws that regulated, by common consent, transgressions committed against others.[5] Implicitly, Bulkley was supporting Connecticut in its dispute with the Mohegan. Bulkley's views were controversial, not the least because he was a participant in the dispute, during which he acted as an agent for the colony.[6]

Not everyone involved in the Mohegan dispute shared Bulkley's views. One person who did not was Daniel Horsmanden, a justice of New York's Supreme Court of Judicature, who was a member of the review appointed to evaluate the Mohegans' claim. Horsmanden disagreed with that body's findings, and in a minority opinion wrote that the charter granted to Connecticut by Charles II had only given the government the right to dispose of lands purchased from the Indians: 'For I think the Crown looks upon the Natives as the Proprietors of the Soils of these Countries, as is manifested by the universal Practise of purchasing the Lands of them throughout all the Colonys, and the Lands are not absolutely impropriated to his Majesty's Subjects, untill they are so purchased tho' included within the Bounds or Limits of the Royal Grant.'[7] In other words, the act of buying land from aboriginal people was in itself an acknowledgment that those communities held title to the lands they had occupied before the English settled the region.

In Nova Scotia, officials questioned whether the Mi'kmaq had the right to own property, but they were also aware that the Mi'kmaq claimed a right to the land. Witness, for example, these words, spoken by a Wabanaki in July 1713: 'You say, my brother, that the French have given you Plaisance, Port Royal and the surrounding lands, keeping only for themselves the river on which Quebec is situated. He would give you what he wants, but for me, I have my land that I gave to no-one and that I will not give. I want always to remain the master of it. I know the limits and when someone wishes to live there, he will pay. That the English take the wood, fish or hunt game, there is enough there for everyone, I will not stop them.'[8] The Mi'kmaq did not believe that they had an exclusive right to 'hunt, fish, and to cut wood' on their lands, though they did contest the right of the British to do so without their consent. In other words, the Mi'kmaq were claiming sovereignty over the land though they were not seeking to exclude Europeans from ever using it. They also argued that the British did not have a unilateral right to expropriate the land; to use those lands, they would need the Mi'kmaq's consent, which might require compensation. Implicit in the 1713 statement was that any English occupation must involve a joint harvesting of the land's resources by English settlers and the region's aboriginal inhabitants. Co-existence was possible, but only if both societies exercised a joint and consensual guardianship.

The Mi'kmaq expressed their attitude toward the land more clearly in two incidents that took place on mainland Mi'kma'ki in 1720. The first was the attack launched by a combined Mi'kmaq–French force against the British fishing station at Canso in the summer of 1720. An anonymous report of the incident that appeared later in the *Boston Newsletter* recounts that the Mi'kmaq 'told the English they only came for the Merchandise and such things as would suit them on shoar; for the Land was theirs, and they would not suffer any English to live upon it, as for the Vessels and Fish, they would not meddle with either.'[9] As this account suggests, the raiders made a distinction between the 'land' and the 'sea.' The land, they said, belonged to them, though whether they meant the area used by the fishermen or a broader area cannot be determined from the letter writer's account. Other evidence suggests that between 1688 and 1744, Chedabucto Harbour was the site of a Mi'kmaq village. For instance, the Massachusetts merchant Cyprian Southack wrote on his map of 1720 that the Milford Haven River was a place where there was 'trade with Indians if peace.' Similarly, a 1744 map notes that a Mi'kmaq village was situated on the southern shore of what is now Guysborough Harbour.[10] Both these records indicate that for the Mi'kmaq, *land* meant a broad area – it was more than just a village or a river system. In their scheme of things, land included coastal areas where they fished and hunted waterfowl.

Similar sentiments were expressed by Mi'kmaq leaders in response to an incident at Minas in the summer of 1720. In August John Alden, a New England merchant, was trading with Acadians near the Minas Basin. He was accosted by a group of Mi'kmaq. Alden recounted what happened next: 'Eleven Indians with one Peter Nunquadden their Chief came to him and demanded fifty livers for liberty to trade saying this Countrey was theires, and every English Trader should pay Tribute to them to which payment the Deponent agreed being under necessity. A few dayes after the said Chief told the sd Deponant that if any person came there with any Orders from general Phillips that he would make him Prisoner and destroy what he had neither should any Orders of that Government be observed or minded there.'[11] According to an account of the affair that reached Annapolis, Nunquadden and his group, including two children, had confronted Alden while as many as three hundred Acadians were present. The governor of Nova Scotia, Richard Phillips, found the news disturbing, as it suggested that the Acadians either had participated in the robbery or had failed to protect Alden. The council summoned the local Acadian deputies to explain their actions. Before they left, they were to 'assemble the Indians there and demand of them ... their reasons for their thus doing in a time of peace and without the least provocation.'[12]

The council's message was conveyed to the 'Minas Indians,' who sent Phillips a letter of reply on 2 October. This letter, which was not delivered till late February of the following year,[13] was signed by Antoine and Phillip Quaret, both of whom would later sign the 1726 treaty as representatives of the Mi'kmaq village of Minas (Amquaret). The letter began by stating that the Quarets had been shown the letter sent to the Acadians:

> We are therefore assembled to tell you this. We believe that this land that God gave to us, on which we could be counted even before the trees were born, does not appear to us to be disputed by anyone; meanwhile we see that you want to keep us from the places that you inhabit, and the threats you make to us to reduce [us] to your servitude, this you should never hope for. We are masters and dependents of no-one. We want to have our country free. There is the first reason. The second is for the habitants our brothers who tell us that several of them are accused of having been involved in the taking of Aldon. We tell you that this is not true and we have only had advice of the french to do what we believed to be necessary to do in that time. Never think that we will look upon you as a great person; but we put all of us before God; if we would go to England for to live there, what would we be told but to leave, and we by the same reason, do not want the English to live in our lands, that we hold only of God and that we dispute to all men who want to live here without our consent. You ask the reason why we have taken those of your nation, we say to you that it is you who are the cause; that it is you who have caused the seizure of Canso and Aldon, for before you came into our country all were in peace there, but since you have arrived, all is at war by your threats to chase us from possession that our Fathers left to us, of all which we have no understanding; that those of your Nation have never had any authority from us to be free in our country as you would wish.[14]

Before analysing this letter, we must assess its reliability. There are two reasons why. First, it is more than a coincidence that the attack on Alden's sloop took place during a dispute between Great Britain and France over the east coast fishery. There is little doubt that the attack, though not directly instigated by the French, was condoned by the governor of Île Royale and was perhaps precipitated by the inflammatory way in which he described British actions to the Mi'kmaq. Second, the Quarets' letter was probably composed by a Catholic priest: its language and diction suggest a well-educated author. Abbé Gaulin, a missionary then living among the Mi'kmaq, is one possibility, although Felix Pain, the Recollet priest at Minas, is another likely candidate. Whoever the author was, the real question to be posed is this: Did the writer influence the letter's content? Given the close political relationship between the French Crown and the Catholic Church, missionaries like Gaulin and Pain would have viewed the return of Acadia to France as a positive development for their parishioners.[15] For this reason, the letter may reflect French political purposes more than Mi'kmaq notions of sovereignty. Did Pain or Gaulin simply take the council's letter and pen a response? The governor of Nova Scotia, Richard Phillips, certainly thought so, as he noted soon after his arrival at Annapolis that the Mi'kmaq were entirely in the Acadian interest who have 'gott them to play their part and to assert their native Right to this Country, in opposition to that of His Majesty for which end I am told they are assembling.'[16] Indeed, had this not been the ruse employed in 1701, when the Houdenosaunee conveyed lands north of Lake Cataraqui [Lake Ontario] to the British Crown? Whatever the Houdenosaunee intended, had not this action emboldened England's own claims to the region?[17] Or alternatively, did the Quarets' letter reflect the sentiments of a village council that instructed Gaulin or Pain what to write?

Some insight regarding the letter's origins is suggested in the summary of Saint-Ovide's discussions with a group of Mi'kmaq elders and sakamows in late June 1720. This summary, later sent to Versailles by the governor, shows that in 1720 Mi'kmaq villagers were expressing a common concern regarding the scope of British activities in Mi'kma'ki. Indeed, Saint-Ovide's summary of his discussions with the Mi'kmaq suggests that the Quaret brothers' letter was more a reflection of Mi'kmaq concerns than of French interests.

In June 1720 Saint-Ovide met with 'all the Chiefs of the Mi'kmaq nation who had a strong desire to speak to him.' Fearing the displeasure of Governor Phillips, he declined to set foot on the Acadian mainland, and instead arranged a rendezvous along the Fronsac Passage, the narrow strait that divides the mainland from Unimaki. There he met some one hundred men.[18] In his later correspondence the governor did not identify those present. These meetings had yet to become a regular feature of Saint-Ovide's duties, so he was less familiar with the Mi'kmaq than he would be later. Not until 1729 would he be able to identify those he met. In that year he noted the attendance of people from Antigoniche, Mirligueche (on Cape Breton), Piziguit, Chignecto, Baie des Chaleurs, and mainland Mi'kma'ki.[19] It is likely therefore that as in 1729, the 1720 meeting represented a broad cross-section of Mi'kmaq society from mainland Mi'kma'ki and Unimaki.

The discussions in June 1720 focused on British and French policies. The sakamaws began by pointing out the odorous conduct of the British governor toward their 'brothers' the Acadians. Saint-Ovide replied that the British governor had written to him. In this letter, said Saint-Ovide, Phillips had stated that the Acadians would have to pledge an oath of allegiance to King George or vacate the lands that had been ceded to Great Britain by the French king. The Mi'kmaq felt affronted by Saint-Ovide's response, for they interpreted his words as meaning that they too would have to swear an oath to King George or be forced from their lands: 'But learn from us that we were born on this earth upon which you march, before even the trees that you see beginning to grow and to leave the earth, It is ours and nothing can ever force us to abandon it.' Saint-Ovide, realizing his mistake, replied that the earth on which he walked, the Mi'kmaq possessed 'from all time.' He added that by an agreement made between the British and the King of France, the former 'will leave you, your women and children to live always peacefully as you have done until the present time.' The chiefs then voiced their resentment toward those 'who occupy at the present a part of our lands and who destroy all the fish the length of our coasts.' Saint-Ovide continued to counsel caution, reminding them that the King of France had instructed him to tell the Mi'kmaq to live in peace with the British monarch; the chiefs replied adamantly that they would retain their own counsel and do what was 'necessary to save ourselves.'[20]

During the attacks against fishermen at Canso and against Alden at Minas, the Mi'kmaq had expressed concerns about their land. They emphasized that they were the first inhabitants of the soil and had occupied their lands from before time. These lands, whether in the Gaspereau Valley or along the eastern coast, encompassed fishing and hunting grounds that clothed and fed their communities. New England fishermen and traders had occupied or trespassed on these lands. They did so as if they held jurisdiction over both the land and the people who lived on it. The Mi'kmaq rejected this assumed jurisdiction, contending that the right to settle in Mi'kma'ki could not be given by a king in Europe, but could only come from them.

By 1725, British officials in Nova Scotia and Massachusetts had recognized that they would have to make some accommodation with the Mi'kmaq regarding land use. Massachusetts officials, for instance, knew that by failing to address Abenaki concerns over new settlements on the Kennebec and St George rivers, they had precipitated the recent war. The British knew they would have to learn from their mistakes with the Abenaki when addressing land use issues with the Mi'kmaq. Not to do so would be to invite repeated altercations between New England merchants and fishermen and local Mi'kmaq communities.

Mi'kmaq concerns regarding future British settlement were addressed in the 1726 treaty. In the instrument signed by John Doucett on 4 June 1726, the British offered the Mi'kmaq 'all Marks of favour, protection and friendship' in recognition of their expressed intent to 'live peaceably with all His majesties Subjects and their Dependants.' In other words, as long as the Mi'kmaq respected the rights of the king's subjects in Nova Scotia, the British would safeguard the rights of the Mi'kmaq who lived there. In some respects, the relationship between King George and the Mi'kmaq as formulated in the treaty was similar to the one between the king and his natural-born subjects.

But the reciprocal promises made by Doucett did more than offer protection. In the name of King George, Doucett acknowledged the right of the Mi'kmaq to the lands they used. He promised that 'the Indians shall not be molested in their persons, Hunting, Fishing and Planting Grounds nor any other their Lawfull Occasions.' In other words, the British accepted that at the same time as farmers were cultivating land and raising livestock, the Mi'kmaq would live as they had before on other parcels of land outside the British and Acadian settlements.'[21] Though 'other lawfull occasions' was not defined, both parties would have understood this phrase to refer to those other activities customarily practised by Mi'kmaq villagers: cutting firewood, gathering herbs, travelling inland along river systems to hunt during the winter, and so on. The British were agreeing that His Majesty's subjects and their dependents would not interfere with these activities. However, the treaty did not define where Mi'kmaq lands were located. Presumably, their lands would not include areas settled by the British or the Acadians. But this was the only qualification made regarding the extent of Mi'kmaq 'lands.'

Thus, the treaty guaranteed that the Mi'kmaq could continue to exercise customary rights to their 'lands,' and restricted the areas where future British settlement could be made. Settlements 'lawfully to be made' were those which did not infringe on the areas the Mi'kmaq used for planting, fishing, and hunting. In effect, the treaty placed the onus on the British to determine that the lands they wanted to settle were not being used by the Mi'kmaq.

However, the treaty did not provide the Mi'kmaq with an exclusive right to the lands outside the European settlements. The intent of the treaty was to create norms of behaviour that would enable co-existence between the British and the Mi'kmaq in Nova Scotia. To this end, the British were promising not to undermine the ability of the Mi'kmaq to survive. The

British could exercise a common right to use lands outside the British settlements so long as they did not interfere with Mi'kmaq villagers. The Wabanaki speaker in 1713 had suggested this approach when he contended that there was land enough for everyone. A similar sentiment was contained in a 1794 petition addressed to Nova Scotia's governor. In speaking of past treaties, the letter 'writer' noted that when the Mi'kmaq 'made Peace with the English, there was Country enough in Nova Scotia for all the English, French, and Indians then in the Province.'[22]

Though the 1726 treaty did not establish a process to be followed if the land intended for British settlement was found to be in use, representations made later by the Mi'kmaq suggest that they believed that settlement could only proceed with their consent. Such consent might be given after compensation was made, or if the Mi'kmaq continued to have access to fishing and hunting sites. This process had been followed in Massachusetts's settlement of Abenaki lands the century before.[23] Indeed, the experience of the Abenaki would have been central to how Mi'kmaq leaders understood British policies. If anything, the terms negotiated by the Penobscot in 1725 would have reinforced that understanding.

The process followed by the British in their relations with the Abenaki was referred to in the second clause of the treaty ratified at Casco Bay in August 1726: 'That His Majesty's Subjects the English Shall and may peaceably and quietly enter upon Improve and forever enjoy all the singular their Rights of God and former Settlements properties and possessions within the Eastern parts of the province of the Massachusetts Bay Together with all Islands, inletts, Shoars Beaches and Fishery within the Same without any molestation or claims by us or any other Indian and be in no ways molested interrupted or disturbed therein.'[24] 'Former settlements' referred to lands that had been purchased by private merchants in the 1600s. The British had an exclusive right over these lands but not over lands they had not purchased from the Abenaki. The difference between the two types of land had been explained by Massachusetts officials at the negotiations in Boston in November and December of 1725: 'When we come to Settle the Bounds We shall neither build or settle any where but within our own Bounds so settled, without your Consent.' The officials later explained that the Abenaki would be paid for any lands they wished to sell: 'We answer – you will certainly be paid for such Lands as you shall hereafter dispose of to the English.'[25] But what procedures were to be followed in buying land? On this, there was no agreement.

Massachusetts officials were well aware of Abenaki resentment over past purchases. At a 1717 conference, Warneet, a Norridgewalk leader, had voiced his scepticism regarding the legality of some land deeds.'[26] Loron voiced similar concerns during the 1726 treaty ratification at Casco Bay: 'We can't find any Record in our Memory, nor in the Memory of Our Grand Fathers that the Penobscutt Tribe have sold any Land, As to the Deeds mentioned last Winter, made by Medoccewanda and Sheepscut John they were not Penobscutt Indians, one belonging to Mechias Medockewondo, the other towards Boston. If we could find in reality that the Lands were Purchased of the right Owners, we should not have insisted upon it, nor have opened our Mouths.'[27] The Massachusetts government established no policy on how such complaints were to be avoided in the future. Officials did not insist that future purchases be made only with their consent; however, they advised the Abenaki that 'it will be best for you to acquaint the Government there of and they will take care that you be not wronged therein.'[28]

A different situation prevailed in Nova Scotia than in Massachusetts. In Nova Scotia, British claims to the land stemmed from the Treaty of Utrecht. In 1762, Lieutenant-Governor Jonathan Belcher argued that 'the French derived their Title from the Indians, and the French ceded their Title to the English under the Treaty of Utrecht.' However, no supporting documentation exists from 1726 to support this view.[29] But even if this was the Board of Trade's view in 1713 and afterwards, Belcher's supposition that the French had acquired land title from the Mi'kmaq was not as well grounded as he thought.

Acadian settlement before 1713 was at variance with Mi'kmaq land use patterns. Though some Mi'kmaq in the early 1700s planted and harvested corn, for the most part each village's economy revolved around fishing in the rivers, settling in coastal areas, and hunting inland for caribou and moose. This pattern of settlement clashed with European concepts of work and ownership. For the French and for the English after them, life was rooted firmly in the land and did not generally encompass the forests surrounding agricultural communities. The early years of Acadian settlement may have included oral agreements between Acadian farmers and local Mi'kmaq that each would have access to fishing and fowling sites. Similar agreements seem to have prevailed between the Abenaki and New England settlers along the Kennebec River.[30] But the Mi'kmaq enjoyed much readier access than the Abenaki to coastal areas, and this, combined with the small size of the Acadian population, meant that by 1713 Acadian settlement had not adversely affected the Mi'kmaq. In 1713 there were no more than 2,000 Acadians, who lived in five separate communities – a population comparable to that of the Mi'kmaq of mainland Mi'kma'ki. Thus, while the Acadians claimed an exclusive right to the lands they farmed, serious clashes over access to land-based resources would not develop till much later.

Belcher's 1762 letter indicates that the legal issue of title involved establishing that the French actually purchased lands for settlement from the Mi'kmaq. Louis XIV and his predecessors had granted lands to traders and noblemen beginning in the early 1600s, but these conveyances had not involved purchasing lands from the Mi'kmaq.[31] No land deeds exist that attest to the formal purchase of land by Acadians or by early fur traders (similar deeds do exist for large parts of Massachusetts, Rhode Island, Connecticut, and Maine). Nor does any document exist which states that the Mi'kmaq formally ceded their lands to the French king. To be sure, we know of one instance when six Acadians bought land from the Mi'kmaq and thereafter settled on the purchased lands.[32] However, this 'purchase' was made after Utrecht and was likely precipitated by the Board of Trade's instructions that newly granted lands in Nova Scotia be reserved for Protestant subjects of the Crown (which would, of course, render further Acadian expansion difficult).[33]

As much as Lieutenant-Governor Belcher in 1762 believed that Great Britain had acquired title via Utrecht, there is no documentation that the Mi'kmaq had formally ceded any lands to France. Whatever Belcher believed, the Mi'kmaq in theory retained a right to the soil after 1713, since they had not surrendered or sold lands to the French.

Though there are no minutes of Mi'kmaq–British discussions prior to the 1726 ratification, the Mi'kmaq almost certainly believed that any future British settlement in Nova Scotia would proceed only with their consent. That understanding would have been reinforced by their belief that their relationship with the British monarch was to be based on the same customs that had linked them with the French king. Though we do not know what part land rights played in that customary relationship, there is compelling evidence for us to conclude that Acadian settlement happened with the acquiescence of the Mi'kmaq.

Articles of Peace and Agreement
[Clause III, Part II] or in their carrying on their Trade & other affairs within the said Province.
[Clause IV] That if there happens any Robbery or outrage committed by any of our Indians the Tribe or Tribes they belong to shall cause satisfaction to be made to the Parties Injured.

As much as Nova Scotia officials wanted to secure existing settlements, they also wanted New England merchants to be able to tap the region's commercial opportunities. Trade was central to the economic prosperity of the British colonies in North America. New England merchants had been plying their wares in the region since the 1660s, buying furs, skins, fish, seal oil, feathers, sea coal, livestock, peas, and wheat from the Acadians.[34]

The trade between New England and Nova Scotia was important for three reasons. First, the garrison at Annapolis depended on certain items that could only be obtained through Massachusetts. Though the Acadians provided foodstuffs, they could not supply the soldiers with all their needs – namely clothing, guns, ammunition, and other finished goods. Second, though Massachusetts's trade with Nova Scotia was small relative to its trade with other colonies, that market was certain to grow as the Acadian population increased. Third, trade with the Acadians undermined that population's social and cultural ties with Canada and Île Royale; this had political benefits that neither Great Britain nor Massachusetts had any desire to give up.

Friction in Mi'kmaq–British relations threatened to disrupt this trade. New England merchants did not have the capacity to absorb ongoing losses resulting from Mi'kmaq attacks on their shipping. These attacks were far from unheard of. When John Alden's vessel was plundered at Minas in August 1720, he lost 260 New England pounds. And in two separate incidents in 1722, Joseph Bissel and George Lapham lost most of their cargoes.[35]

To stabilize New England's trade with the Acadians, Massachusetts and Nova Scotia officials inserted into the text of the 1726 treaty, articles by which the Mi'kmaq would consent to the commercial activities of merchants like Alden and Bissel. When altercations did occur, British officials would attempt to hold the Mi'kmaq accountable for the merchants' losses. In effect, the Mi'kmaq were acknowledging the right of British merchants to trade in Nova Scotia.

The treaty articles that pertain to trade are far less ambiguous than the preceding ones, and so offer fewer obstacles to a common understanding. At the same time, in geographic terms their wording is vague: they refer to simply 'Nova Scotia.' How would the Mi'kmaq delegates have understood the term 'Nova Scotia'? How was this concept translated from English into Mi'kmaq?

Implicitly, the treaty's signers acknowledged two separate and coexisting political spheres. In the areas inhabited or to be inhabited by

His Majesty's subjects, British law was to apply. Mi'kmaq lands lay outside these settlements, though the exact boundaries were not mapped or described in the treaty. The issue was to what degree His Majesty's subjects could travel through Mi'kmaq areas, either trading or engaging in 'other affairs.' If they could do so, were their actions governed by British law or by Mi'kmaq custom?

By the reciprocal promises made by John Doucett, the British king was extending his protection to the Mi'kmaq and promising that they would not be molested in the areas where they lived. The term 'molest' could be interpreted to encompass harmful actions toward individual Mi'kmaq; however, such a reading would not have accorded with Mi'kmaq spiritual understanding of their lands and the spirits who lived there. In Mi'kmaq cosmology, the distinctions between humans and other living things were not as clear as in Christian thought. The world of the Mi'kmaq was inhabited by animate and inanimate beings. Mi'kmaq people were animate but so too were animals, trees, plants, and sometimes even rocks.[36] Families were associated with a specific landscape, and their identity was tied to this animate world. To trespass through their territory was to disturb the beings who lived there and to undermine families' ability to live in harmony with their world. For the Mi'kmaq, 'to molest' meant more than to interfere with the activities of individuals; it also meant to interfere with the symbiotic relationship between animate and inanimate beings. Thus, when the Mi'kmaq were told that the British would not molest them 'in their persons, Hunting, Fishing and Planting Grounds nor in any other their Lawfull Occasions,' they understood this to mean that in these areas they would exercise some form of control that would enable them to protect their hunting and fishing lands from outside interference. This control would include the right to regulate outsiders' travel through their lands – a right that included regulating the movement of New England traders.

Articles of Peace and Agreement
[Clause V] That the Indians shall not help to convey away any Soldiers belonging to His Majesty's forts, but on the contrary shall bring back any soldier they shall find endeavouring to run away.

After 1710, for various reasons, the British found themselves unable to keep a full complement of soldiers at their garrison at Annapolis Royal. One problem was sickness, and another was desertion; and each of these problems exacerbated the other. As more men fell ill and died, more and more others fled the fort to seek passage back to New England.

After the fort was captured in 1710, the garrison suffered a steady attrition rate. Of the 188 enlisted men posted to Annapolis in October 1710, only seventy-nine remained a year later – 37 per cent of the original total. Eighty-five soldiers died, most of them in February and March. Some companies were nearly obliterated. For example, of the thirty men under captain Samuel Templar's command on 1 October 1710, only nine remained a year later. Though some soldiers were killed or captured in skirmishes with the Mi'kmaq, most were victims of poor living conditions and poor nutrition.[37]

The alien environment may well have contributed to the soldiers' misery. Life outside the fort's walls was no better than life inside. The Acadians were suspicious and uneasy in the Englishmen's presence, a result of the linguistic and cultural gulf that separated them from the garrison's soldiers. The Acadians were French speaking and Catholic, the soldiers were mainly English speaking and Protestant. But despite these cultural differences, the Acadians did not pose a direct personal threat to individual soldiers. Not so with the Mi'kmaq, whose appearance and way of life would have reminded the soldiers of the stories they had heard of these 'barbarous and savage people.' Among these men there were probably descendants of the Marblehead women who had torn the flesh from the bones of two Penobscot prisoners in 1677, or of the Boston mob that in 1705 had protested Samuel Vetch's trade with the Mi'kmaq during a period of declared war.[38] These soldiers were predisposed to view both Acadians and Mi'kmaq with suspicion. In sum, a soldier's life at Annapolis in 1726 was not a comfortable one, either physically or mentally.

Faced with such abominable conditions, soldiers deserted. Of the 105 men who did not die between October 1710 and October 1711, twenty-one deserted – almost one in five. And conditions did not improve after 1711. Complaints were made to the Board of Trade that between June 1712 and June 1715, the men had not been paid. According to the Fort Major, Francis Spelman, the garrison might well have dissolved if the lieutenant-governor, Thomas Caulfeild, had not acquired provisions 'upon his own credit.'[39] Desertion continued, though the number of soldiers who 'ran' is not known. Samuel Vetch, who had been replaced as governor by Francis Nicholson in 1714 and who therefore had many reasons to complain of his successor's policies, reported in September 1715 that the garrison was deserting in great numbers, eighteen men leaving 'at one time in three canoes.'[40] Nicholson reported in August the desertion of five men, who had made their way to French Île Royale, carrying with them two Acadian women and their husbands.[41] Others apparently fled to the east coast, seeking passage home with New England fishermen.[42]

Conditions improved after the Fortieth Regiment of Foot was formed in 1717, its members recruited from the independent companies at Placentia and Annapolis Royal. This regiment would staff the fort's ramparts for the next thirty-two years. Though its strength was fixed at 394 men and officers, its complement was never full.[43] In 1732, for instance, Governor Phillips reported that there were then 324 men and officers.[44] After this regiment was created, the fort's finances began to improve.[45] In large part, this is because Parliament was now providing an annual grant to the regiment's colonel, Richard Phillips, who used it to pay his men, to feed them, and to supply them with other necessaries.[46]

But as the fifth article of the 1726 treaty indicates, officers were still concerned about desertion. To encourage Mi'kmaq assistance, John Doucett promised them that they would be 'handsomely rewarded [for] bringing back any Soldiers endeavouring to run away.' By offering the Mi'kmaq a reward for returning deserters, the British were sending a message to the garrison's soldiers that flight might well result in capture by the Mi'kmaq – a prospect they were unlikely to entertain happily. After all, these men had grown to maturity in Massachusetts, where stories of the frightful tortures inflicted on captives were part of every child's 'education.' Soldiers thinking of flight thought again after the treaty was signed.

There is no reason to think that the Mi'kmaq understood this clause other than literally. In signing it, they were recognizing that the British military exercised sovereignty over its own soldiers regardless of their location, and agreeing that if a soldier sought refuge among the Mi'kmaq, they would return him to the garrison.

Articles of Peace and Agreement
[Clause VI] That in case of any misunderstanding, Quarrel or Injury between the English and the Indians, no private Revenge shall be taken, but Application shall be made for redress according to his Majesty's Laws.

Revenge killings were acceptable practices in many aboriginal communities. These killings were meant to minimize further bloodletting. Generally, a killing involving members of the same community required some compensation: either presents were offered to the aggrieved family, or murder was done for murder.[47] However, it was not absolutely necessary that the murderer be the one who died in return; the only requirement was that revenge be exacted on someone from the same family or clan as the murderer. Compensation always involved the victim's relatives, whether they were offered presents or inflicted death.

When a killing involving two people from different nations, the revenge did not have to be carried out by the aggrieved family or clan. In such cases, revenge was a community responsibility. Similarly, the murderer's nation, not just his family, was collectively responsible for his actions. It follows from this that a killing committed by an Englishman could be avenged by killing another Englishman whether or not the second one had any part in the original slaying. The Mi'kmaq were governed by a similar custom, as indicated by an incident during the summer of 1715.[48]

Some New England fishermen encountered a small group of Mi'kmaq off the coast of Cape Sable and offered to pay them if they went to 'hunt birds.' Two Mi'kmaq took up the Englishmen's offer and were later found dead, their 'bodies floating in the water.' Believing that the fishermen were responsible for the two deaths, local Mi'kmaq villagers seized nine or ten fishing vessels. The captains were kept prisoner, and the crew members released 'all disfigured after cutting their cheeks from the mouth to the ear.'[49] Though none of the fishermen were killed, the fact that the captains were kept hostage suggests that the Mi'kmaq intended to ransom them in compensation for the lives of the two men who had been killed. In this instance, a Mi'kmaq village was exacting revenge on the nation it held responsible for the killings.

The governor of Massachusetts, Samuel Shute, was not amused, and his initial reaction to the hostage taking suggests how Mi'kmaq customary practices regarding intersocietal killings created friction in British–Mi'kmaq relations. According to some Abenaki who were meeting with Shute at the time, the governor flew into a rage, 'and said that all the Indians must be killed,' though he later changed his mind and 'thought that it was more appropriate to send a vessel unto the micmacs to inquire as to the reason for treating the Englishmen so badly.' This was done. The fishing vessels and captains were returned, and further conflict with the Mi'kmaq was avoided.[50] New England officials interpreted the hostage taking as an act of war; the Mi'kmaq believed that their actions had defused a dangerous situation. By avenging the deaths, they had righted a wrong, and prevented further bloodshed.

British law was governed by a different set of customs, which did not condone such unregulated action. From the British perspective, only the New Englanders responsible for killing the two Mi'kmaq were guilty and should have been punished. Among the New Englanders, punishment was governed by the rule of law and by a judicial process that treated every person equally regardless of social class.[51] In disfiguring the fishermen's faces, the Mi'kmaq had undermined this law by appealing to emotion rather than reason. By allowing their emotions to determine their actions, the Mi'kmaq were challenging the social order, creating anarchy instead of order, and making commerce untenable.

By creating a process for resolving disputes, the treaty was attempting to reconcile the different customs each society employed to resolve intersocietal conflicts. The difficulty was that the text did not say *how* disputes were to be resolved; it only said that 'application shall be made for redress according to his Majesty's Laws.' How this was to work is unclear, since there is nothing to indicate that after 1726 the Mi'kmaq ever applied for redress to the lieutenant-governor. The obvious reason why they didn't is that the British and Mi'kmaq did not live side by side. This rendered the clause trivial, at least in the eyes of the Mi'kmaq. Nonetheless, the treaty explicitly stated that the British were responsible for their own subjects' actions. At the same time, it implicitly reshaped Mi'kmaq customs by forcing its leaders to restrain their members from engaging in revenge killings after altercations with subjects of the British king.

Articles of Peace and Agreement
[Clause VII] That if there any English Prisoners amongst any of our aforesaid.
Tribes, we faithfully promise that the said Prisoners shall be released & Carefully
conducted and Delivered up to this Government or that of New England

The last clause of the treaty dealt with an issue that had long bedevilled British political and religious officials: the return of war captives. The British insisted that this clause be included in the treaty for a simple and understandable reason: families wanted their children and parents returned. No doubt, anxiety over the fate of the prisoners was fuelled by the knowledge that they were living among people who, to the New Englanders, lacked all manner of civility and religion.

The fate of the New England prisoners captured between 1722 and 1725 was the subject of a long and bitter discussion between Dummer and the Penobscot. The British were certain that the Penobscot could force their allies to return all prisoners. In fact they could not: the fate of individual captives was determined by the families that had adopted them. However much the Penobscot might have wanted to accede to Dummer's pleadings, they lacked the authority to do so.

To ensure that all captives were returned, the British often had to get the consent of each individual aboriginal community. The Mi'kmaq may not have been holding any captives; even so, a clause holding them responsible for the return of any captives was necessary to the British in political terms. Without it, Massachusetts's political leaders would have been much criticized by their constituents.

The British reciprocated by releasing the Mi'kmaq prisoners they had been holding at Annapolis since June 1722. Twenty-two prisoners had been seized by John Doucett; the number still imprisoned four years later is not known. At the very most, twenty-one prisoners were released, as one man had been executed in 1724 following the killing of an English sergeant during an aborted Mi'kmaq attack on the fort.[52]

The 1726 treaty offered a framework for British–Mi'kmaq relations, and created a measure of economic and political security that neither side had enjoyed before. For the British, the treaty established their claim to sovereignty over Acadia 'according to its ancient limits.' It also secured British interests in other important ways. First, the Mi'kmaq agreed not to interfere with British merchants plying their wares in Acadian communities and to compensate traders for losses incurred from conflicts with local villagers. Second, the treaty secured the political stability of the Annapolis garrison by creating in the minds of its soldiers a belief that desertion would result in their recapture by the Mi'kmaq. Third, the treaty ensured the integrity of existing settlements and suggested that the Mi'kmaq would not interfere with future settlements. Finally, the Mi'kmaq agreed not to unilaterally seek redress to perceived wrongs committed against them by fishermen or traders, but to complain to the governor. The British hoped these measures would minimize potential conflict in the region. For the British, the treaty had accomplished much that was necessary to promote their economic and political interests in the region and to undermine French influence on the Atlantic seaboard.

The treaty also established a direct and personal relationship between King George and the Mi'kmaq. It explicitly made the king responsible for mediating disputes with the Mi'kmaq within the king's dominions in Nova Scotia. 'Indian Affairs,' we might say, was now the responsibility of the king.

The treaty was also important to the Mi'kmaq. First, it brought peace, and provided communities with a security they had not enjoyed for the past thirty years. While the British also desired peace, the Mi'kmaq likely had more need of it, since war had had a far more dramatic impact on them than the British could possibly know. Second, it included British assurances that they would not interfere with the Mi'kmaq family economy. Though the precise areas to be used by families were not described in the treaty, it is plausible to suggest that both parties believed that Mi'kma'ki was sufficiently large that peaceful and comfortable coexistence was possible. After all, there were few British living in Nova Scotia in 1726, and the best agricultural lands were already being farmed by the Acadians. Since the Mi'kmaq were not primarily farmers, it would have seemed fairly certain that they would be able to live undisturbed. But if there was some mutual understanding regarding these parts of the treaty, such understanding was sadly lacking regarding its other clauses. Language, culture, and historical experience separated the British from the Mi'kmaq, and limited their ability to arrive at a mutual understanding of the treaty's other articles.

The treaty did not resolve two important issues. First, the English text of the treaty suggested that the Mi'kmaq had agreed to become subjects of the Crown. If the British thought it meant just that, the Mi'kmaq certainly did not. To begin with, the terms specified that the Mi'kmaq were making their submission to King George in as ample a manner as they had formerly done to the French king. If the British had based this clause on an understanding that the Mi'kmaq had been subjects of the French monarch, they were being blind to historical realities: to the contrary, the French king had been a 'father' to the Mi'kmaq. Also, the cultural differences would have limited the ability of the Mi'kmaq to conceive of themselves as anything more than what they were. The Mi'kmaq were members of a fishing and hunting society, not members of a society in which obedience was owed to one's lord and to one's king. And finally, the very fact that a treaty was negotiated suggests the unique character of the relationship being created between the British and Mi'kmaq. Kings and queens do not usually negotiate treaties with their subjects. Kings rule; they dictate; they impose their will on others just as God imposes his will on humankind. There is a profound contradiction here: the king's intent had been to make the Mi'kmaq subject to his will, yet the treaty was leaving the Mi'kmaq independent of British law. So how could they be subjects? In signing the treaty, the British were tacitly admitting that the Mi'kmaq were *not* subjects – that this mighty, omnipotent British king had not the power to smite the Mi'kmaq into submission.

The second issue left unresolved concerned competing claims to the land. While the treaty stated that both British and Mi'kmaq would use and occupy lands, no boundaries were set. It said that the Mi'kmaq had a right to occupy their lands unmolested by the British. It did not, however, outline the relationship between Mi'kmaq lands and future British settlements. Any new settlements would have to be built 'lawfully.' What were 'lawful' settlements? The treaty did not say, though certainly the onus for showing their legality would be on those who made the new settlements. And though the treaty did not specify the measures for taking the property of another, the historical experience of the French in Acadia and of the British in New England suggests that both sides thought fair purchase would be one possible vehicle to accomplish the transfer.

These ambiguities would not always be evident to the Mi'kmaq and the British over the next twenty years, but they would become so as British and French forces clashed for control of North America in the 1740s and 1750s. The coming struggle between these two titans would be more forceful and more deadly than ever before.

Chapter Seven

British Politics and Treaty Making

The 1726 treaty has been analysed as an oral text written in an alphabetic form. In examining the treaty's oral meanings, two strategies have been employed. First, an emphasis has been placed on how the Mi'kmaq delegates would have interpreted the treaty's articles – an approach complicated by the fact that neither English nor French was widely spoken or understood in Mi'kmaq villages. The problems posed by these cultural hurdles have been addressed by exploring the historical context in which the treaty was created to understand how its English terms would have been understood by the Mi'kmaq. This analysis suggests that British and Mi'kmaq delegates did not share a common understanding of phrases such as 'lawfully to be made' and 'make our submission to his Majesty in as ample a manner as they had formally done to his Most Christian King,' since they understood their historical relationships to these concepts differently. Second, this chapter continues the analysis by examining the British individuals who signed the treaty. I contend that an analysis of the economic and social interests of Nova Scotia officials suggests that they interpreted the treaty in a manner that explicitly recognized that the Mi'kmaq were independent of British law.

In 1726 both Lawrence Armstrong, the lieutenant-governor of British Nova Scotia, and John Doucett, the lieutenant-governor of Annapolis Royal, were representatives of King George in Nova Scotia. As officers of the Crown, they were also responsible for negotiating the ratification of the Boston treaty with the Mi'kmaq. Armstrong was absent from Annapolis in June 1726, but Doucett was not, and as the most senior official in Nova Scotia after Armstrong, it was he who oversaw the ratification of the treaty.

As the senior military and civil officer in Nova Scotia, Armstrong reported to the Board of Trade. This board was a committee of the Privy Council, and corresponded with the governor of each North American colony, providing him with general guidance to adopt in relations with the colony's population. In 1726 the board was exercising little direct control over Nova Scotia's affairs. Its inattention to Nova Scotia is suggested by the irregular character of its correspondence. For instance, a letter from the board to governor Phillips dated the 6 June 1722 shows that the board had last written to Phillips almost eighteen months earlier, on 28 December 1720, even though four letters had been received in the same period from Nova Scotia officials.

The board's inattention to Nova Scotia was symptomatic of its political impotence in the 1720s. This had not always been the case. But by the early 1720s much of the board's power to make patronage appointments and colonial policy had been eclipsed by the king's ministers, notably the Secretaries of State and the Lord Treasurer.[1] Though Phillips, Armstrong, and Doucett regularly sent their correspondence to the minister responsible for colonial affairs, the Secretary of State for the southern Department, the secretary rarely replied. In sum, officials in Nova Scotia were operating in a political vacuum, and without direct advice from either the board or the Secretary of State, except during times of crisis. One such crisis had been in 1720, when French moves on the fishery near Canso had spurred London to pay more attention than it ever had before.[2]

The practical result of such 'salutary neglect' was that Armstrong, Doucett, and the Nova Scotia Council were given little guidance regarding policies to adopt toward the Mi'kmaq. Platitudes there were, such as those contained in the missives sent to Phillips after he was appointed governor in 1719. Phillips was instructed to 'summon the Indian head of the Several Nations or Clans and promise them friendship and protection.' He was also told to encourage intermarriage with the Mi'kmaq, and was to give each man who married an Indian £10 and fifty acres of land, which would be free of quit rent for twenty years.[3] The general tenor of these instructions was that Phillips and his officers were to form a peaceful relationship with the Mi'kmaq. But the board did not give more detailed guidance than that. Significantly, neither the Secretary of State, the Duke of Newcastle, nor the Board of Trade instructed Armstrong and Doucett on how to negotiate a treaty with the Mi'kmaq. A similar situation characterized London's correspondence with the New England colonies. At most, the board offered platitudes similar to those sent to Governor Phillips.[4] The governments of Nova Scotia and Massachusetts were left to negotiate their own terms with their aboriginal populations.

Despite the lack of official direction, both the board and the secretary viewed the 1725 treaty and 1726 ratifications favourably. In response to Doucett's letter of 16 August 1726, in which he had enclosed a copy of the 1726 treaty, the board wrote: 'Their Lordships are glad to find by your said Letter that You have concluded a Peace with the several Indian Tribes lately at War with You, which they hope will be lasting and that you will take care that the said Indians, in their Intercourse with His Majesty's Subjects under Your Command may meet with such kind treatment as to give them no cause of Complaint. This in their Lordships Opinion will be the surest means of continuing a good Correspondence with them.'[5] Both the board and the secretary expressed similar sentiments in reply to Dummer's letter describing the signing of the Boston treaty. The secretary wrote to Dummer that he had 'received your letters of 8th and 18th Jan.; in the former of which were inclosed copys of the conferences held with the Delegates of Indians, and of the Treaty you had thereupon concluded with them. The King is very well satisfied to find, that the endeavours you have used for the interest and security of His subjects in those parts have proved so successful, and that the peace you have made with the several tribes of the Indians seems to be settled upon so good and lasting a foundation.'[6] The board also voiced its approval after receiving printed copies of the July 1726 Penobscot ratification: 'Their Lordships are glad to find ... that the Indians are so well dispos'd to perform their engagements. with the Province, not doubting but care will be taken to continue them in this good disposition.'[7] As this correspondence shows, officials in both Massachusetts and Nova Scotia kept London apprised of the negotiations and treaty signings, sending copies of the treaties and – in the case of Massachusetts – copies of the discussions with the Penobscot ambassadors. Both the board and the secretary had voiced their approval with the treaties made with both the Mi'kmaq and the Abenaki.

Such nonchalance would not have been shown if the treaty had been signed with France or Spain. In such a situation, both King George and his ministers would have been intimately involved in the negotiations, would have been kept informed of the discussions, and would have only signed the treaty after viewing a copy of it. Treaties with aboriginal people were not of the same tenor as those signed with kings of Europe, and so did not require the involvement of the king or his ministers. On the contrary, such tasks were the work of colonial officials, who were left plenty of latitude to negotiate final agreements. The king's ministers might have exhibited a keener interest had it been necessary for the treaties to be consistent with the existing common law. But aboriginal people were not considered to be part of the body politic, so it wasn't necessary that agreements signed by them be considered in the same manner as legislation passed by colonial legislatures. This is implicitly suggested in a letter sent to King George by the board in early September 1721, in which it recommended the signing of treaties with aboriginal nations but did not indicate any need to subject these treaties to the king's review.[8] To a remarkable degree, therefore, the treaties signed by the governments of Massachusetts and Nova Scotia with the Abenaki and with the Mi'kmaq were the work of local colonial officials.

The issues addressed in the treaties varied between colonies. This is because the colonies' governing elites influenced the treaty negotiations in different ways. In the early 1720s, Massachusetts politics was dominated by several prominent families whose wealth and social standing had facilitated their entry into political life. In contrast, life in Nova Scotia was dominated by military officials. That economic interests varied between colonies had profound implications for how the terms of the treaties were implemented.

Political life in Massachusetts was dominated by wealthy men. One of the era's most prominent politicians, for instance, was Elisha Cooke Jr, whose personal estate was valued at about £63,000 sterling in 1737.[9] Cooke was not unique; his public endeavours were imitated by other wealthy merchants, a list which included Andrew Belcher and his son Jonathan, Thomas Hutchinson, Timothy Lindall, Oliver Noyes, Anthony Stoddard, and Adam Winthrop.[10] For these men, public office may have been a noble endeavour, but it also offered an opportunity to advance the financial interests of their families.

The negotiation of the 1726 treaty with the Abenaki is a case in point. Between 1714 and 1721 some prominent Massachusetts families had acquired a financial interest in Abenaki lands, hoping to capitalize on their investment either by reselling the land to prospective settlers or by harvesting the area's rich forests.[11] Two investments had been made. The first of these was known as the Pejopscot Patent, a large area straddling the Androscoggin River. The second tract was known as the Muscongus Patent and included lands between the Penobscot and Muscongus rivers. Both patents had originally been granted in the 1630s by the Council of New England; later, however, the lands were purchased from the Abenaki by the patents' holders.

No effort to settle Muscongus land was made until 1719. That year, the inheritor of the patent, John Leverret – then president of Harvard College – organized a company of ten associates to assist him in exploiting the claim.[12] Each associate invested his own money in the company, agreeing to meet its expenses.[13] Among the associates was Elisha Cooke Jr, a member of the House of Representatives and a leading member of the Popular Party, a group of politicians who in the early 1720s would sharply criticize Governor Samuel Shute for his reluctance to aggressively respond to Abenaki attacks on the Kennebec settlers.[14] By 1720 the company had appointed Thomas Westbrook as its agent, contracting with him to settle twenty-five families on the St George River. Though this settlement was never completed due to the outbreak of war, a fort was built on the east bank of the river.[15]

A different situation characterized the Pejepscot patent. In 1683, Richard Wharton had bought the original patent to lands along the Androscoggin River as well as other lands that had been purchased from the Abenaki. In 1684 he added to his holdings by buying more land from six Abenaki chiefs. However, Wharton was never able to recoup his investment as he died in 1689 without an heir. In 1714 his entire property was bought for £140 by a consortium of merchants: Thomas Hutchinson, Adam Winthrop, Oliver Noyes, John Watts, David Jeffries, Stephen Minot, John Ruck, and John Wentworth.[16] This group's land titles were confirmed by the house and council on 25 May 1715, even though Wharton's claims were known to be controversial since they involved lands purchased from the Abenaki. To encourage settlement, the house also voted £500 to assist the company in building a fort at Pejepscot Falls. No doubt, the house's connivance was assisted by the fact that three of the company's stockholders were sitting members of the House Land Committee.

The house's actions had the desired effects. By 1720 more than one hundred settlers, many of them from Ireland, had built the towns of Brunswick and Topsham.[17] A report prepared in London by the attorney-general, Phillip Yorke, outlined the activities of the proprietors before 1722: 'And in order to prosecute & effectually bring forward the said intended Settlements, they built and finished two strong large block Houses ... & the Petitioners also built a double sawmill to facilitate the Settlements, & bought a Sloop, & hired men to transport People & their effects, besides several other Sloops employed by them in the said Undertaking, and had for above 12 month a Captain & 20 Soldiers whom they paid & subsisted in the said block Houses, & who were provided with great & small Artillery to defend themselves & the Workmen from the Attacks of the french Indians [all] at the sole charge of the Association.'[18] War between Massachusetts and the Abenaki had interrupted each company's efforts to bring new settlers into the region; it had also brought into question whether their land purchases from the Abenaki had been legal. After all, the Norridgewalk had complained that new settlements being made by the proprietors were on lands that had not been sold.

In the treaty conferences at Boston in 1725 and at Casco Bay in 1726, the legality of these purchases was discussed. At the Boston conference, Dummer had insisted that the Penobscot recognize the validity of the purchases made. At the Casco Bay ratification, the issue was discussed again. Loron requested that the New Englanders remove two houses, one from St George's at the mouth of the Penobscot, the other from Richmond on the Kennebec. He proposed that each house be moved west – one to Pemaquid, the other to the English fort at the mouth of the Kennebec. There, the two forts might serve as posts where the Abenaki could trade their furs. Dummer was not amused: 'We Answer, That those Houses on Lands Purchased by His Majesty's Subjects, which we are ready by Commissioners appointed by the Government of the Massachusetts-bay for that Affair, to make evident to you ... by producing fair Deeds under the Hands of the Sachems of those Countrys for the same, as well as divers Treaties wherein you Allow'd and Confrim'd to the English all the Lands formerly Possessed by them, which Commissioners are here present for that Service, Those Lands being for a long time Since Purchased by His Majesty's Subjects, and the Property Vested in them, the Government cannot Disclaim them.'[19] Penobscot concerns were sufficiently assuaged, as Dummer assured them that they would be treated with 'justice' and in the same manner as would any Englishman. But even though the treaty was ratified by the Penobscot, the old problem remained: How was the boundary between New England and the aboriginal lands to be drawn? And where was it to be drawn?

In insisting that the purchases of lands from the Abenaki were valid, Dummer was protecting the financial interests of some of the colony's most prominent families. His political life depended on it. His superior, Governor Shute, had left the colony in December 1722, unable to govern effectively due to the stubborn opposition of men like Cooke and his associates. Dummer could ill afford to alienate men like these. His insistence that the Abenaki accept the legality of the purchases made from them was more than just the fulsome rhetoric of an Englishman teaching the Abenaki to live by the precepts of a written law. He was also ensuring that those families who had a financial interest in developing lands along the Penobscot and the Kennebec would be able to profit from their investments.

The proprietors' private interests and those of the British Empire had become inextricably linked. The government's rhetoric about the deeds' validity reached its fullest expression after 1714, at a time when some families were developing a financial interest in the region. In speaking of the deeds, Dummer clothed his rhetoric in a language which suggested that the Abenaki were to blame for their misfortune, in that they had agreed to sell the land and then failed to honour their agreements. But more than this, Dummer was portraying the Abenaki as the duplicitous puppets of the French monarchy. In the face of such chicanery, New England had no choice but to launch a military campaign against the Abenaki in order to undermine French influence in the region. In sum, the private interests of a few Massachusetts speculators were being portrayed publicly as synonymous with the king's interest in the colonies.

While Dummer and his fellow council members were hastening to protect their financial interest in Abenaki lands, the Board of Trade and the Secretary of State supported them because of their own interest in extending the British Empire. For statesmen like the Duke of Newcastle, there was a direct link between the state's political interests and their own personal fortunes. Though land was still the foundation of these men's wealth, many landowners had diversified their financial interests in the 1700s, seeking better rates of return by investing in the overseas trade and in government stocks and securities. As the scope of Great Britain's trade expanded, and as the government's debt mounted in an effort to protect this trade, more and more families began tying their economic interests to commercial trade and to the income that the government derived from it.[20] The British government's interest was closely identified with the class interests of the wealthier members of British society. Though Newcastle himself may not have dabbled in trade and government securities, his contemporaries certainly did, which suggests that in important ways, government policy was influenced more by wealthy men's desires for personal aggrandizement than by a dispassionate interest in the 'law.'

The fact that neither the king nor his ministers were directly involved in negotiating the 1726 treaties does not mean that their concerns were not taken into account. They were. From their perspective, the treaties

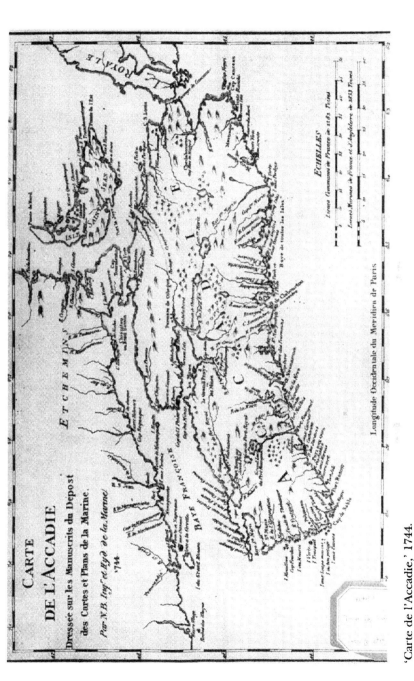

'Carte de l'Accadie,' 1744.

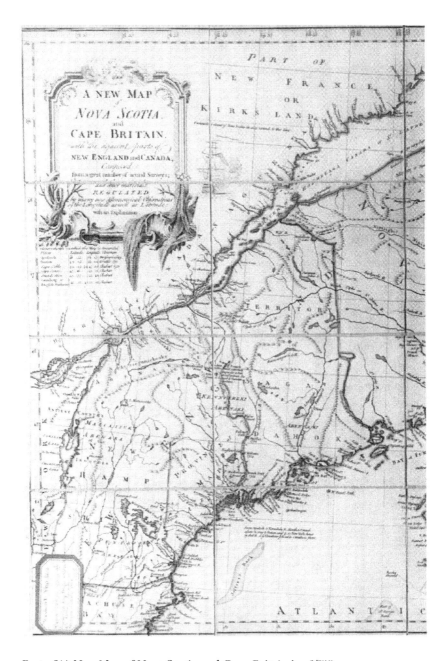

Part of 'A New Map of Nova Scotia and Cape Britain,' c. 1755.

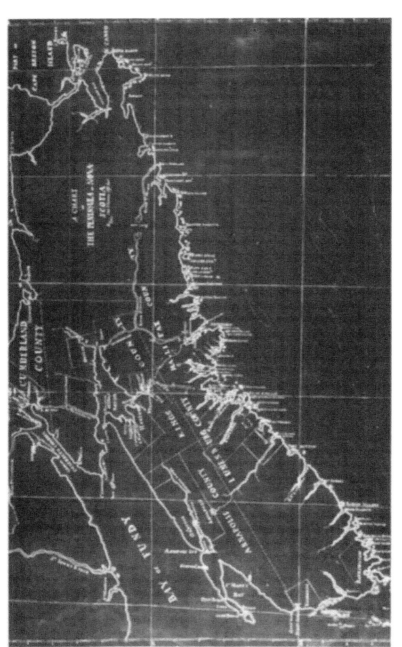

'A Chart of the Peninsula of Nova Scotia,' 1761.

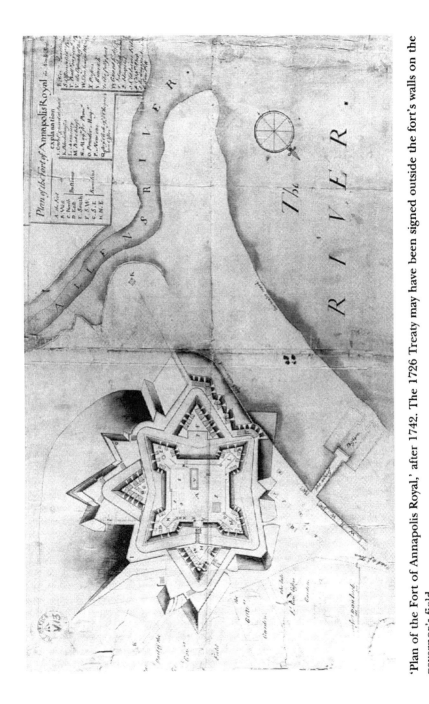

'Plan of the Fort of Annapolis Royal,' after 1742. The 1726 Treaty may have been signed outside the fort's walls on the governor's field.

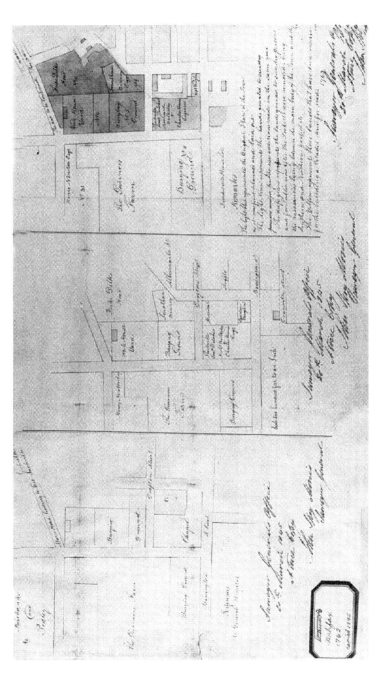

Lands adjoining or near the governor's farm (Halifax). Copy made in 1845 by Charles Spry Morris of a 1762 map. The governor's farm was located near what is today the intersection of Barrington Street and Spring Garden Road. The provincial courthouse now stands there. The treaty of 25 June 1761 was signed at the governor's farm.

Mi'kmaq encampment near Halifax, c. 1791.

Mi'kmaq Chief and European Visitor, c. 1795. Notice the woman in the background putting a lobster into the pot.

Governor's House and St. Mather's Meeting House on Hollis Street also looking up George St., Halifax, c. 1762.

were important mainly because they eroded France's influence on the region. The treaties ratified with the Abenaki and the Mi'kmaq included language that recognized Great Britain's sovereignty in the region. In acknowledging that the British had legally purchased land from them, the Abenaki were in effect recognizing that Massachusetts settlers had the right to live among them. In much the same way, the Mi'kmaq and Maliseet acknowledged King George's dominion over mainland Mi'kma'ki and large areas of present-day New Brunswick. For the Duke of Newcastle, these assurances were critical to protecting Great Britain's trade in the region. In protecting that trade, the treaties were also protecting the ruling elite's financial interest in British trade, and the financial structure of the state which protected that trade. All of this served to erode France's political and therefore economic interest in the region.

The treaty the British signed with the Mi'kmaq in 1726 was consistent with all of this, but the context was very different from that which had led to Massachusetts's treaty with the Abenaki. In 1726 almost the only British in Nova Scotia were soldiers, and there were no more than three hundred of them. There were no English-speaking farmers, and the merchant community was tiny. And since the Acadians were not considered to be subjects of the Crown, there was no elected House of Assembly representing the population's interests. In contrast to Massachusetts, Nova Scotia in 1726 was little more than a garrison post.

The limited nature of British settlement in Nova Scotia affected the content of the 1726 treaty. For members of the Nova Scotia Council, two issues required resolution: the security of the garrison, and the security of trade. Though land was also a concern, no member of the governing council had a personal interest in insisting that the Mi'kmaq not interfere with the establishment of new settlements. As of 1726, no British residents of Nova Scotia had bought land from the Mi'kmaq, nor had they invested their own money in attracting new settlers. Governor Phillips and the Board of Trade had discussed plans for encouraging English-speaking Protestants to settle in the colony. But as of 1726 their efforts had been wildly unsuccessful. In sum, Nova Scotia did not have the population, or an established merchant community, or a level of economic activity, that would have propelled colonial officials to adopt an aggressive attitude toward the Mi'kmaq similar to Dummer's in his negotiations with the Abenaki. Rather, Nova Scotia's interests were limited to ensuring that New England merchants would be able to trade with Acadian communities without fear of the Mi'kmaq.

The lack of an established merchant community with a financial investment in the colony's development had important consequences for how Nova Scotia officials explained the terms of the treaty to the Mi'kmaq. Neither Doucett nor Armstrong would have felt pressure from local elites to insist on an interpretation of the treaty that emphasized British law as the standard for interpreting the treaty's articles. On the contrary, it was possible for Doucett and Armstrong to take a more flexible approach, and to accept an interpretation of the treaty that integrated Mi'kmaq custom into British law.

The reaction of the Nova Scotia Council to the execution of three Mi'kmaq and two French-speaking men by the Massachusetts government in early November 1726 illustrates this dynamic. In justifying the executions of the Mi'kmaq, the Massachusetts government interpreted the 1726 treaty as though the Mi'kmaq had agreed to be subject to English law. This interpretation, however, was disavowed by Armstrong – an indication of just how much Nova Scotia and Massachusetts officials differed in how they interpreted the treaty. This stemmed from differences in the two colonies' economic and political structures. Armstrong was not accountable to men like Cooke and Winthrop, so he enjoyed far more flexibility than his counterparts in Massachusetts, and was able to adopt an understanding of the treaty that was more consistent with the garrison's tenuous relationship with the region's population.

On the afternoon of 25 August 1726, a sloop with five New England fishermen on board sailed into the harbour of Mirligueche (now Lunenburg) on the east coast of mainland Mi'kma'ki. The master of the vessel, Samuel Doty, steered his vessel shoreward to buy rum and other supplies from the local Acadians. Doty saw a Frenchman, Jean-Baptiste Guedry, on shore and signalled him to come aboard. After some discussion, Doty and three of his crewmen went ashore 'to drink some punch' at the house of Guedry's mother. Guedry, however, remained on the fishing vessel with the remaining crew member, Philip Sachimus. Guedry was soon joined by two Mi'kmaq men, James and Philippe Muse (Meuse in the document). Together, the three men seized Sachimus and tied him to the masthead. Four other Mi'kmaq men, accompanied by a woman and two children, paddled out to the vessel. Doty and his men became aware that something was amiss and returned to their boat. On their arrival, they were seized. Guedry informed the five fishermen that three of them would be released to inform Massachusetts authorities that the others would be let go only after prisoners held captive in Boston were freed. These prisoners were relatives of Guedry and the Muse brothers, who themselves were related (Guedry had married one of the Muse brothers' younger sisters). These plans came to nothing, for the next day the fishermen recaptured their boat. Three of the Mi'kmaq men escaped by jumping into the sea; Guedry, his fourteen-year-old son Jean-Baptiste, three Mi'kmaq men (James Meuse, Philippe Muse, and John Missel), and a unidentified woman and her two children remained on board. Doty steered his vessel toward Boston, where he arrived on 3 September.[21]

The five men were tried by the Court of the Vice-Admiralty in early October. The court was responsible mainly for settling colonial disputes relating to marine issues[22] (e.g., disagreements over wages, salvages, and prize vessels won in war) and for enforcing the navigation acts. During the 1720s the Vice-Admiralty Court was also involved in judging those accused of piracy, a crime defined as 'robbery on the High Seas.' It was with this crime that the five men were charged.

The court comprised seventeen men. Each was a prominent member of the Massachusetts political elite. Presiding over the court was the colony's lieutenant-governor, William Dummer. He was assisted by sixteen members of His Majesty's Council, an executive body appointed by the king to assist the governor – and in his absence, the lieutenant-governor – in governing the colony. Among this group were Jonathan Belcher, Elisha Cooke Jr, Edward Hutchinson, and Adam Winthrop, each of whom had a personal financial stake in Abenaki lands.

Though all five men were accused of 'piracy, felony, and robbery,' the Acadians and Mi'kmaq were tried separately. Jean-Baptiste Geudry and his son were tried on 4 October, the three Mi'kmaq men the following day. There were separate trials because the government's prosecution rested on two different sets of legal precepts. The two Acadians were tried as subjects of the Crown according to the terms of the Treaty of Utrecht, whereby the Acadians had, through the consent of their monarch, Louis XIV, become subject to British law. In contrast, the three Mi'kmaq men were to be judged according to the terms of the 1726 treaty. The Massachusetts government was thus acknowledging that before 1726, Great Britain had not held any civil authority over the Mi'kmaq. In effect, the court was accepting the view that up until 1726, interactions between the Mi'kmaq and His Majesty's subjects would have been subject to the customary law that had existed in 1713.[23]

The case against the three Mi'kmaq men was presented by the colony's advocate-general, Robert Auchmuty. According to Auchmuty, at the time the three men seized Doty's vessel their villages had already concluded a peace agreement with the governments of Massachusetts, New Hampshire, and Nova Scotia. By the terms of the treaty signed in Boston on 15 December 1725, the 'Indians' had agreed to end all acts of hostility and to live in 'amity and Friendship with all the English.' The Mi'kmaq had also agreed to 'be ruled and governed by His Majesty's Laws.' These articles, said Auchmuty, had been ratified by the 'chiefs and representatives of the said Indians' at Annapolis Royal on 4 June 1726. Therefore, said Auchmuty, at the time the three men helped seize Doty's vessel, they were subject to 'his Majesty's Laws' – a contractual relationship that representatives from their community had negotiated and signed.

This argument was contested by the advocate for the three men, George Hughes. Hughes argued that the Mi'kmaq men could not be found guilty of piracy, since at the time the offence took place, they thought themselves to be in 'a State of War with us, [and] what they have done, they may well justify, by the Laws of GOD, Nature, Nations, and Arms.' Hughes admitted that a treaty had been ratified at Annapolis Royal in early June, and another one at Casco Bay two months later, but contended that only the later treaty was applicable to the three defendants. He also contended that even though they were subject to the treaty's articles, the government should not expect them to have had a perfect acquaintance with it, 'they living in a far, remote and distant Place of another Government: And being but an inconsiderable Number of People, the Law will not, with Submission, presume a person to be knowing of a thing, unless there appear some Circumstances by which it may be reasonably concluded, he cannot but know it.'[24] In sum, Hughes's defence was making two arguments: first, that the only treaty that applied to the three Mi'kmaq men was the one signed by Massachusetts with the Abenaki at Casco Bay; and second, that the onus was on the Massachusetts government to inform the Mi'kmaq of the terms of the treaty and to ensure that they understood its meaning.

The court dismissed Hughes's argument that the treaty governing Mi'kmaq relations with Massachusetts was the one signed at Casco Bay in early August. In rejecting this argument, the court said that the decision of the Mi'kmaq in early June of 1726 to ratify the treaty meant that they had agreed that their relationship with Massachusetts would be governed by the same terms as had been negotiated between that colony and the Abenaki.

The court found Hughes's argument regarding the defendants' ignorance of the treaty more germane in establishing the three men's innocence or guilt. On this matter, the court's members were interested in the three defendants' testimony regarding what they knew of the 1726 treaty at the time Doty's vessel was seized. In a statement made before the Justice of the Peace for Suffolk County just after he arrived in Boston in early September, James Muse had said that in late July he had been 'at Menis where there were near two hundred Indians with the french Fryar ... the french told the Indians that there was no peace then, and bid the Indians, if they met any English Men to take them. Since which time he hath been at Menis twice from malegash, where he had been at times about thirteen days, and most of the french at Menis, when he was there last, told him there was no peace.'[25] Muse's deposition suggested that he understood that a peace had not been signed. John Missel's testimony was more ambiguous: 'He heard the Indians had been at Port Royal, and heard some of them say that there was Peace with the English and Indians. But he heard some of the Indians say they wondered that if there was Peace, they did not bring the Indian Prisoners from Boston.'[26]

The members of the court weren't satisfied with these responses, since they seemed to suggest that the defendants weren't sure whether the treaty had been ratified by their communities. The prisoners were therefore asked if they had 'seen any of the Indians that were at the Ratification of the Peace at Annapolis.' Each of them replied in the affirmative. James Muse told the court that in early August he had been in company with 'Antoin, one of the Chiefs of the Indians at Menis,' and had also seen the Indian Simon who was Present, as he understood, at the Negotiations of the Peace. Both James and Phillip Muse said that they had also seen 'Captain Walker, alias Piere, one of the Chiefs of the Indians at or near Malegash and Sabuckatook, who was at Annapolis at the treaty.'[27]

Evidence that each prisoner had talked with individuals who had signed the treaty satisfied the court that the defendants should have known about the terms of the peace. The court accepted Robert Auchmuty's opinion that 'the chiefs and Delegates in Duty ought to apprize (as doubtless they did) their respective Tribes, of the said Articles of Pacification and Confirmation and not the Government that stipulated them.'[28] The court believed that it was the responsibility of the Mi'kmaq to inform their people of the treaty's terms. Once the treaty had been signed, it became the legal responsibility of each community to ensure that its members governed their actions according to the treaty's terms. Moreover, as the oral testimony of the Muse brothers showed, there had been ample opportunity between early June and late August for the delegated representatives of the Mi'kmaq to do so. Though there was no evidence regarding what had transpired between the defendants and the individuals who had been at Annapolis, there was evidence that Missel and the Muse brothers had spoken with people who might have told them about the treaty. In effect, the court was ruling that every individual Mi'kmaq was responsible for knowing about British law – specifically, the law prohibiting the seizure of vessels owned by His Majesty's subjects operating within the king's dominions.

On the afternoon of 5 October 1726, the court of the Vice-Admiralty found James Muse, Philip Muse, and John Missel guilty of 'piracy, felony and Robbery' and sentenced them to death. On 2 November, they as well as Jean-Baptiste Guedry and his fourteen-year-old son were hanged at Charleston Ferry in Boston.

The Court's decision was so severe probably because a fishing vessel had been seized. As the government's prosecutor noted in his opening statement, if such actions as those committed by the five men were not 'now timely Corrected by Your Honours experienced Justice, [it] will most certainly terminate in the breaking up of our Fishery, the most valuable Branch of our New-England Trade.'[29] Also a factor in the harshness of the sentence was that piracy was still very much a concern at the time; yet another factor was that the Acadians and the Mi'kmaq had cooperated closely in seizing Doty's vessel. It is likely that all of these factors tugged at the seventeen men of the court and encouraged them to invoke the death penalty. In sum, the court was using the treaty as an instrument for regulating Mi'kmaq interactions with British subjects and for ensuring that the fishery would not be interrupted in the future.

But the court's interpretation of the 1726 treaty was not shared by the Nova Scotia government. Armstrong adopted a more conciliatory policy and did not interpret the treaty as making the Mi'kmaq subject to the laws of Great Britain in their interactions with British subjects. In Armstrong's view, such a policy would have been foolhardy, since he lacked the political and military strength to enforce civil authority over Mi'kmaq villagers living outside the walls of Annapolis Royal. But Armstrong's interpretation was also conditioned by the fact that the executions had been carried out at a critical juncture in his negotiations with the Mi'kmaq.

At the trial of the three Mi'kmaq men, the Court of the Vice-Admiralty had dismissed evidence hinting that the Mi'kmaq may not have been at Annapolis Royal in early June of 1726 to ratify the Boston treaty. Missel's statement that 'some of the Indians wondered ... if there was peace, they did not bring the Indian Prisoners from Boston,' suggests that his community did not consider a final agreement to have been concluded. This perspective was advanced by the defendant's advocate, Hughes, who said that the defendants were told 'by two eminent Cape Sable Indians, Sawcage and Atuoamge, that there was no Peace made, but only talked of.'[30] Though the court dismissed Hughes's arguments, there is evidence that the Mi'kmaq who attended the June 'ratification' did so not to ratify the agreement but rather to hear the terms of the agreement made by the four Penobscot delegates.

Up till now, discussion regarding the 1726 treaty has shown that on 4 June, seventy-seven Mi'kmaq, Maliseet, Passamaquoddy, and Penobscot delegates gathered at Annapolis Royal, and that discussion has also shown that these delegates, by marking the bottom of the treaty, were agreeing to live with the British according to the treaty's terms. This interpretation of what happened at Annapolis Royal on 4 June 1726 would seem to be consistent with each of the extant copies of the treaty.

In all, six copies of the treaty were sent to London by Nova Scotia officials in 1726. Copies were posted on 27 July and 24 November by the lieutenant-governor of Nova Scotia, Lawrence Armstrong, and on 16 August by John Doucett.[31] On each date, one copy was sent to the Board of Trade and another to the Secretary of State, the Duke of Newcastle. Officials in London made additional duplicates; however, the paper copies sent to London were the only ones made from the original.[32] The original was likely made of parchment, and at least three parchment copies would have been made. The Mi'kmaq and Maliseet would each have been given a copy, and another copy would have been retained by John Doucett and kept under lock and key in his chambers at Fort Sainte-Anne.[33] No parchment copy has survived; the paper copies sent to London have since become the principal texts known as the 1726 treaty.

There are both similarities and differences between the six copies of the treaty. There are three main similarities: all are dated at Annapolis Royal on 4 June; all are exact reproductions of the English text of the Boston treaty; and all are signed by delegates representing both parties to the treaty. There is one important difference: the copies sent to London by Armstrong on 27 July and by Doucett on 16 August contain the signatures of sixty-four aboriginal people, whereas the two copies that accompanied Armstrong's dispatch on 24 November have seventy-seven signatures (see pp. 22–3, 155). This dispatch contained the sixty-four names that had been part of the earlier copies plus thirteen additional names. A comparison of all six copies suggests that the copies sent by Armstrong in late November were more accurate reproductions of the original than were those sent in July and August. The most notable difference is that the November copy includes the totems of five individuals; these are absent from the earlier copies, even though these same individuals' names are present on all six copies of the treaties.

All these differences suggest that the treaty was signed in two or more stages. Sixty-four delegates representing the Penobscot, the Maliseet, the Passamaquoddy, and five Mi'kmaq villages signed on 4 June. This would seem so, since Doucett's correspondence regarding that event shows that many Wabanaki men were at Annapolis Royal on that day. Their signatures were on the treaty sent by Armstrong to London on 27 July and by Doucett on 16 August. Each copy was a duplicate of the other and was based on the original parchment copy, which remained with Doucett at Annapolis Royal. In late July, Armstrong was at Canso, so he would not have been at Annapolis in early June; it follows that the copies he dispatched to London were based on the one he had received from Doucett sometime after 4 June. In late September or October, thirteen other delegates representing at least four other Mi'kmaq villages who had not been at the June 'signing' met with Armstrong and signed the treaty. This is suggested in Armstrong's letter to the Duke of Newcastle on 27 July. Armstrong wrote that 'in the middle of September next I shall meet a Considerable body of Indians at Annapolis Royal to Confirme the Peace and all other points that have not yet been Don to make it lasting.'[34] Though no correspondence exists to show that such a meeting did in fact take place, his 24 November dispatch included a treaty text containing the 'signatures' of seventy-seven Wabanaki men, not the sixty-four names that had accompanied Doucett's August letter and his own correspondence of 27 July. The addition of thirteen names hints strongly that sometime after Armstrong's arrival in Annapolis in mid-September, meetings took place with other groups of Mi'kmaq, who signed their marks on the original parchment copy of the treaty made by Doucett in early June.[35]

What is the significance of these later signings? It might be that geography accounted for the autumn adhesions. The five Mi'kmaq villages represented at the June conference – Annapolis, Cape Sable, Minas, 'the Eastern coast,' and Shubenacadie – were all within two days' journey of the British fort. The four villages that later signed – Richibuctou,

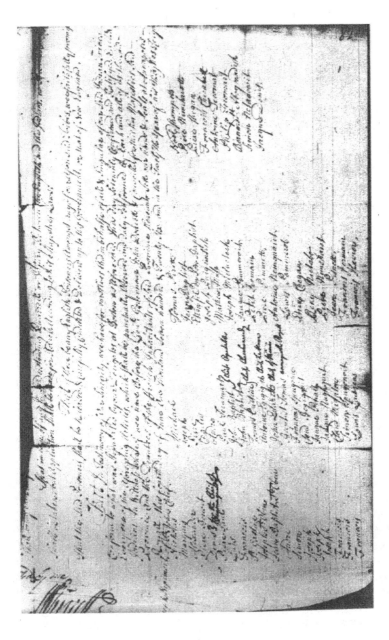

Aboriginal signatures on the 4 June 1726 treaty. This copy accompanied Lt.-Gov. John Doucett's dispatch to the Duke of Newcastle, 16 August 1726.

Shediac, Chignecto, and Unimaki – were not. Geography therefore suggests that those villages located some distance from Annapolis were unable to be present in June, perhaps because they had not been contacted, perhaps for other reasons.[36]

But geography alone does not explain the differences among the six copies of the treaty. In his 27 July letter, Armstrong wrote that he planned to meet 'a considerable body of Indians' to discuss issues that had not been addressed in June. These issues, he wrote, required resolution before a final peace could be concluded. Armstrong's comments suggest an elasticity to the treaty process. This view is reinforced by comments the governor of Île Royale made after meeting with some Mi'kmaq leaders in July 1726. According to Saint-Ovide, some Mi'kmaq and Maliseet had gone to Annapolis more to feast with the British and to receive their presents than to negotiate the terms of a peace. The governor there (Doucett) had explained the articles of the proposed peace, but the elders and sakamows had decided against it.[37]

What we know about the Mi'kmaq polity tells us that intravillage discussions about the 4 June proposals would have taken place afterwards. Though Mi'kmaq villages had been informed of the proposed peace before June, it is likely that the villagers instructed their delegates only to go to Annapolis and learn the treaty's terms. The Mi'kmaq polity was neither hierarchical nor authoritarian; instead, it was governed by a consensual decision-making process that included most adults (a point that was discussed in Chapter 2). To think that the document signed on 4 June 1726 reflected each individual village's acceptance of the terms of the treaty is to ignore both the documentary evidence that suggests otherwise and the consensual character of Mi'kmaq society. Armstrong's statement that he was to meet with some Mi'kmaq during the fall strongly suggests that the treaty required clarification, and that questions about it could only be resolved through consultation with villagers and additional discussions with Nova Scotia officials.

It was during this period of ongoing treaty discussions between Armstrong and the Mi'kmaq that Doty's vessel was seized, and that the five men were tried and executed for piracy. The Massachusetts government's draconian response to the incident did not sit well with Armstrong. Governor Saint-Ovide took pleasure in his counterpart's discomfort, writing to Versailles in June 1727 that 'Mr Armstrong, who has been attempting to continue making peace with the Indians, sent into their villages some presents and told them that he had no part in what had been done by the Council of Boston to their brothers.'[38] The hangings made it more difficult for Armstrong to conclude a final agreement with the Mi'kmaq. Certainly, the trial and execution of the three men did much to lengthen discussions. In late June a great council of the Wabanaki and their Houdenosaunee allies was held on the Penobscot River.[39] That month, John Gyles, a New England trader and diplomat working on behalf of Massachusetts, sent Lieutenant-Governor Dummer a letter containing the information he had received from an Abenaki informer regarding the council:

> He sais yt Gret Disput this spring Concerning Affers, have been between ye Indians of ye several tribes from Cape Saples to ye mountain Indians & ye french, & at their Great Debats & Council was whether their should be a treaty wth ye English or not, the several tribes sd it was Proper to hear what ye English said before any breach made on them, but Arobree ye Jesuitt and Anadahouitt his Decon, & Amareguened & Wewonorawed: Indians Chiefs, usd all Possible mens to force on to Slay the English, before they heard what they had to say & the new Gour sd he was in friendship with ye English & would be well Plesd yt ye English & Indians have a Meeting[40]

Though many issues fed the discussions, the hanging of the two Acadians and three Mi'kmaq figured prominently.[41] After months of talks, the peace was finalized. This was signified in a letter dated July 1728 from the chief Penobscot sakamaw, Wenogonett, in which he noted that Arexus, whom he had sent to Cape Sable, had returned, 'bringing good news to both of us – I have brought the Cape Sable Indians to Real peace which was my intent and grate desier.'[42]

Significantly, in September 1728 a number of Maliseet chiefs and others ratified the 1725 treaty with the Nova Scotia Council. Among those who signed it on behalf of the Maliseet was Charles Maniduphike, who was identified as 'Chief Sachem of the whole Tribe of the St. Johns Indians.'[43] Armstrong wrote to the Board of Trade that the Maliseet signing the treaty had not been present at Annapolis to ratify the Boston treaty. The evidence suggests a far more complex pattern of debate within the Mi'kmaq and Maliseet communities between 1726 and 1728 than Armstrong was willing to admit. For instance, there is little reason to doubt that in identifying himself as 'Chief Sachem of the whole Tribe of the St. John's Indians,' Charles Maniduphike was signifying that his people were ratifying the treaty, thus bringing an end to a process that had lasted two years. Though no documents exist showing that the Mi'kmaq ratified the treaty in a similar way, there is evidence that they did.

Without a text, we can only assume that the treaty in its final form precisely matched the copies sent to the Board of Trade in 1726. In support of this, there is no evidence that at the renewals of the 1726 treaty in 1749 and 1752, Mi'kmaq delegates objected to the terms that were read to them.

The question now is how Armstrong interpreted the treaty's terms after he returned to Annapolis Royal in mid-September. There is no information about the content of these discussions. Even the most basic details are lacking, such as when they occurred, their length, the identity of the participants, and the number of times talks took place. Despite the lack of specific information, we can draw some conclusions from the fact that Armstrong did confer with some Mi'kmaq while a Massachusetts court was trying and executing three Mi'kmaq men for piracy.

A key question during the Massachusetts trial concerned how British law was to apply to the Mi'kmaq villagers who had signed the 1726 treaty. The Massachusetts government's interpretation was obvious from its decision to try the three for piracy. According to the court, British law was to be the basis for regulating relations between the Mi'kmaq and British subjects. Armstrong rejected this interpretation, and softened Mi'kmaq anger by compensating the communities with presents. Armstrong was a pragmatist. He knew that the garrison's military situation was tenuous. Certainly, it could withstand a Mi'kmaq siege, but his men had no stomach for war, and neither did London. But besides that, his actions suggest a more nuanced interpretation of the legal relationship created by the treaty – that he viewed the treaty as a flexible instrument for regulating disputes between both parties. Had there existed in Nova Scotia a large and wealthy merchant community with extensive commercial interests, Armstrong's response to the hangings might have been different. But no such community existed, so Armstrong was able to interpret the treaty in a manner that would assuage the Mi'kmaq and influence them to accept the peace. We cannot say what transpired between Armstrong and the Mi'kmaq between mid-September 1726 and June 1728; we *can* say that those discussions resulted in a peace being concluded.

Why didn't Armstrong send a final copy of the treaty to London? Six copies of the treaty had already been dispatched to London. Armstrong might have been embarrassed to send a seventh with further additions. Doing so might only have underscored his inadequacies in front of the Board of Trade. Like so many officers posted to Nova Scotia, Armstrong longed to be reassigned to a more comfortable station. If there was an omission in his correspondence to the board, it was deliberate, and was intended to maintain his own reputation among those men in London who held so much power over him. Ultimately, his hopes for advancement came to nothing. In 1738 the lieutenant-governor of Nova Scotia, Lawrence Armstrong, committed suicide.

In considering the 1726 treaty, we tend to focus on its English text, since it provides insights into the treaty that other sources cannot. Even so, that text is an oral memory that has been translated into an alphabetic script. It leads us to believe that on 4 June 1726 nine Mi'kmaq villages ratified the Boston treaty. In examining the treaty's multiple texts, we find that this did not happen; rather, the Mi'kmaq and their allies debated the treaty before finalizing the peace sometime during the summer and autumn of 1728.

That Armstrong continued to discuss the terms of the peace accord after 4 June 1726 broadens the time frame within which we must analyse the treaty. We cannot say that the treaty was ratified by the Mi'kmaq in June 1726; it was shaped further by the events of 1726 to 1728, and this fact provides insights into how the treaty's terms were interpreted to the Mi'kmaq. We lack any detailed information about how officials interpreted the treaty's articles, yet the hanging of three Mi'kmaq men in early November 1726, and the lack of a strong mercantile presence in Nova Scotia, suggest that the lieutenant-governor was more willing than the Massachusetts government to adopt a flexible approach toward applying the treaty. His interpretation, as his actions suggest, was premised on an acceptance of the customary methods that the Mi'kmaq had always followed in their relations with other people – methods that influenced their interactions with Europeans after 1600. We can suppose that Armstrong, like his French predecessors at Annapolis Royal before 1710, bowed to necessity and embraced these methods when he interpreted the English text of the 1726 treaty.

PART THREE
Renewing the 1726 Treaty

We can neither disbelieve nor forget what we have heard from our fathers, that when peace was made between Micmacs and the British, and the sword and the tomahawk were buried by mutual consent, by the terms of the treaty then entered into which was ratified by all the solemnities of an oath, it was stipulated that we should be left in the quiet and peaceable possession of far the greater portion of this Peninsula.

Petition of Mi'kmaqs, written by Silas Rand, 25 July 1853

**Treaty of Peace and Friendship concluded by the Governor and Commander in
Chief of Nova Scotia with Paul Laurent Chief of the La Heve tribe of Indians
at Halifax [10 March 1760]**

*I Paul Laurent for myself & the tribe of La Heve Indians of which I am Chief
do acknowledge the Jurisdiction of the Dominion of His Majesty George the Second over the Territories of Nova Scotia or Acadia & we do make Submission to
His Majesty in the most perfect, ample & Solemn manner*

*And I do promise for myself & for my Tribe that I nor they shall not molest any
of His Majesty's Subjects or their dependants in their settlements already made or
to be hereafter made, or in carrying on their Commerce or in any thing whatever
within this the Province of His said Majesty or elsewhere.*

*And if any Insult, robbery, or Outrage shall happen to be committed by any of
my tribe satisfaction & restitution shall be made to the person or persons injured.*

*That neither I nor my tribe shall in any manner entice any of His said Maj-
esty's troops or Soldiers to desert nor in any manner assist in conveying them
away, but on the contrary will do our utmost endeavours to bring them back to the
Company, Regiment, Fort or Garrison to which they shall belong.*

*That if any Quarrel or Misunderstanding shall happen between myself & the
English or between them & any of my tribe, neither I nor they shall take any private satisfaction or Revenge but We will apply for redress according to the Laws
established in His said Majesty's Dominion.*

*That all English prisoners made by myself or my tribe shall be sett at liberty &
that we will use our utmost endeavours to prevail on the other tribes to do the
same if any Prisoners shall happen to be in their hands.*

*And I do further promise for myself and my tribe that we will not either directly
or indirectly assist any of the Enemies of His most Sacred Majesty King George the
Second his heirs or Successors nor hold any manner of Common traffick nor intercourse with them, but on the Contrary will as much as may be in our power discover & make known to His Majesty's Governor any ill design which may be
formed or contrived against his Majesty's Subjects. And I do further engage that
we will not traffick, barter, or Exchange any Commodities in any manner but
with such persons or the Managers of such Truckhouses as shall be appointed or
Establish'd by His Majesty's Governor at Lunenburg or Elsewhere in Nova Scotia
or Acadia.*

*And for the more effectual security of the due performance of this Treaty &
every part thereof I do promise & Engage that a certain number of persons of my
tribe which shall not be less in number than two persons shall on or before September next reside as Hostages at Lunenburg or at such other place or places in this
Province of Nova Scotia or Acadia as shall be appointed for that purpose by His*

Majesty's Governor of said Province, which Hostages shall be exchanged for a like number of my tribe when requested.

And all these forgoing Articles & every one of them made with His Excellency Esq., I do promise for myself and on behalf of my tribe that we will most Humbly keep and Observe in the most Solemn manner.

In Witness whereof I have hereunto put my mark and Seal at Halifax in Nova Scotia this [tenth] day of March one thousand &

Paul X Laurent

The defence lawyers relied exclusively on the 1760 treaty to defend Donald Marshall Jr. The lawyers from both sides focused on two passages in that treaty. The first is found in the first clause of the 1760 treaty, in which each Mi'kmaq chief made his 'submission to His Majesty in the most perfect, ample, & Solemn manner.' The second is found in the seventh clause, in which the Mi'kmaq agreed that they 'will not traffick, barter, or Exchange any Commodities in any manner but with such persons or Manager of such Truckhouses as shall be appointed or Established by His Majesty's Governor.'

Michael Paré, representing the federal government, argued that in signing the treaty the Mi'kmaq had agreed to become subjects of the king and therefore were now subject to federal fisheries laws: 'These treaties represent the formal acknowledgement by the Mi'kmaq people that they are His Majesty's subjects and that they are submitting themselves to His jurisdiction and authority. By doing so, they became subject to the laws of the Province. This included any and all laws then in existence or to be enacted regulating trade and commerce whether Provincial or imperial.' For this reason, Marshall was subject to federal statutes governing the fishery, since the Canadian government was the direct inheritor of the British colony of Nova Scotia. Paré then argued that even if this wasn't the case, by the seventh clause of the treaty the Mi'kmaq had agreed to restrict their trade to government-run truckhouses: 'At most, Mi'kmaq acting in accordance with the terms of these treaties could bring commodities which they had to sell to the approved truckhouse or to such persons as might be appointed by the Crown. At all times, though, these activities were subject to the overriding legislative authority of the State, the jurisdictional authority of which had been accepted by the Mi'kmaq in these treaties. In any event, the treaties do not create any commercial fishing rights.'[1] Both clauses, Mr Paré argued, reflected the Mi'kmaq people's tenuous political situation in 1760. Since the French had been defeated militarily, the Mi'kmaq had few options other than to make peace with the British and to accept any terms proffered to them.

Bruce Wildsmith disagreed. He did not agree that the first clause of the 1760 treaty gave the government the unilateral right to impose regulations on the Mi'kmaq, as Paré was suggesting. Rather, Wildsmith argued, 'nothing was done by the English before, in, or about 1760 and 1761 to bring to the attention of the Maliseet and Mi'kmaq that they were subjecting themselves to unilateral control by Her Majesty. The English did not make a clean breast of what the Crown now says that they were up to.' The 1760–1 treaties, Wildsmith contended, were consensual agreements: 'The pattern that persisted until well after the 1760–61 treaty relationship was established was one in which the Mi'kmaq dealt issue-by-issue with Her Majesty until agreement was reached. Her Majesty did not act unilaterally to impose Her will against the interests of the Mi'kmaq. The relationship was in the final analysis mutual and non-coercive. This is inconsistent with the notion that in the Treaties of 1760–61 the Mi'kmaq would have surrendered themselves up unconditionally to Her Majesty's will and Her Majesty's regulations.'[2] As for the seventh clause of the treaty, Wildsmith argued that the government-run truckhouses also had resulted from an agreement with the British. In return for settling the peace, the British had agreed to set up six truckhouses. However, in about the middle of 1762, the truckhouse operations were discontinued, in part because they were a financial drain on the government, but mainly because the colonial law that had governed their regulation had been overturned by Great Britain's Privy Council. The truckhouses were replaced by a system whereby merchants were to receive a licence from the government to trade with the Mi'kmaq. This system was discontinued in 1783. In Wildsmith's opinion, the British had negotiated in 1760 how trade was to be conducted with the Mi'kmaq. After 1762, the British had unilaterally imposed the terms of the trade. This action, said Wildsmith, was in direct opposition to the framework of the treaty-making process.

Wildsmith did not argue that the Marshall had an unrestricted right to the commercial fishery: 'Mr. Marshall acknowledges for the purposes of this case that he is a citizen of Canada and a subject of Her Majesty, under the sovereignty of Her Majesty and the Constitution of Canada. As such and subject to s. 35 of the Constitution Act, 1982, he may as a matter of law be regulated in his fishing and trading activity through laws that are justified by Her Majesty.'[3]

Wildsmith was referring to *R. v. Sparrow* (1990), in which the Supreme Court of Canada had said that an aboriginal person's constitutional right could be restricted but that such limitation would have to be justified by the government. In effect, this meant that in seeking to stop the Mi'kmaq from fishing, the government would have to make a plausible argument as to why such fishing could not take place. One possible reason, according to the court, was conservation. Public safety was another. Wildsmith followed this line of reasoning in the brief he submitted to Judge Embree: 'Mr. Marshall is not arguing for an unlimited, unrestricted right to fish and sell the fish. The Defence is saying that such justified limits may be imposed to, for example, conserve the species and protect public safety.'[4] However, the court had not provided an exhaustive list of possible justifiable reasons for limiting an aboriginal person's right, nor had it outlined how the government was to proceed in justifying an infringement. For instance, one might argue that the government could inform an aboriginal community of its intent to limit their right to fish and explain to them the reasons for doing so. Such a process, however, would not have to include that the community agree that such an action was justified, only that they be informed of the government's intent. Others might argue, however, that any justification would have to be determined by the courts. This would mean leading expert evidence, for instance, about the negative results to the fishery if an aboriginal community fished a specific species. However, the government in *R. v. Marshall* had chosen not to make a justification argument, explicitly agreeing that, at least in the case of Donald Marshall's actions, eels were not a threatened species.

For this reason, the courts were able to focus entirely on the 1760 treaty in rendering their decisions. The issue before the trial judge, the Nova Scotia Court of Appeals, and the Supreme Court of Canada was how the treaty should be read. Paré stressed the English text of the treaty, reading into its language that the Mi'kmaq had surrendered their rights to the Crown. Wildsmith, on the other hand, focused less on the language of the treaty than on the process of treaty making, which was, in his view, an implicit part of the legal context in which the treaty was written. For Paré, the historical context created by the defeat of French at Louisbourg in 1758 and then at Quebec the following year, suggested that the Mi'kmaq also had been defeated. The 1760–1 treaties were nothing less than treaties of surrender in which the Mi'kmaq accepted what terms they could. Wildsmith, however, interpreted the historical situation differently. For him, what was important was that the British had gone to the trouble of negotiating a treaty with the Mi'kmaq. This seemed to suggest something more was at work than surrender. If this was not true, then why had the British bothered to negotiate a treaty with the Mi'kmaq?

Paré denied that the Mi'kmaq had retained any explicit right to the commercial fishery. If such a right ever did exist, it had ended with the signing of the 1760 treaty. For this reason, Paré argued, the Mi'kmaq could not rely on Canada's 1982 constitution to argue for a share in the commercial fishery. If they were to participate in the fishery, they could only do so through and with the consent of the federal government.

Wildsmith argued back that the Mi'kmaq had such a right, though he did not believe that the right was unencumbered. However, any restriction that was placed on the Mi'kmaq community's right to engage in the commercial fishery would have to be justified by the federal government.

Chapter Eight

The Founding of Halifax:
Re-interpreting the 1726 Treaty

On 12 February 1755, Paul Laurent met with members of the Nova Scotia Council in Halifax. Laurent had been delegated by Mi'kmaq community leaders to speak to the council regarding a proposed peace.[1] Though the Mi'kmaq and the British still considered the 1726 treaty to be the basis of their friendship, by 1755 the nature of their relationship had changed. The British were no longer a negligible presence in Nova Scotia. New settlements had been made at Halifax in 1749, and at Lunenburg in 1753, and new forts had been built: Fort Lawrence in 1750, and Fort Edward in 1751. Though the 1726 treaty had been renewed in 1749 and 1752, not all Mi'kmaq communities had signed, wary of Great Britain's long-term intentions in Mi'kma'ki. Convincingly, the Mi'kmaq pointed to the new settlements and forts that the British had built without their approval. Paul Laurent wanted to renegotiate the 1726 treaty so as to safeguard Mi'kmaq fishing and hunting grounds against the enlarged British presence.

On 12 February, Paul Laurent presented the council with a written text outlining the terms of a proposed peace. This proposal suggested that a tract of land, encompassing much of the northern section of mainland Mi'kma'ki, be set aside for the exclusive use of the Mi'kmaq. The council minutes describe the scope of the area: 'That they should have a tract of Land given them for Fishing, Shooting and Hunting, which Tract should extend from Bay of Verte along the Coast to Canso, from thence along the Eastern Coast up to a Place within three Leagues of the new Eastern Settlement; from thence in a right Line to the Indian Mass-house on the Chibenacadie River, from thence to the Head of Minas Bason, from thence to the western part of Cobequid, and from thence to Beaubassin including the English Fort at Chignecto, which

Fort should be demolished, and that no other Fort should be Erected within the Limits of the said Tract.' After reading the proposals and discussing them with Laurent, the council adjourned, promising to reply the next day.[2]

At ten o'clock on the morning of 13 February, the council delivered Laurent a written reply. In a letter addressed to the 'different Tribes of the Mickmack Indians,' it did not entirely reject Laurent's proposal. Indeed, the council believed that providing lands for the exclusive use of the Mi'kmaq was a reasonable suggestion to safeguard the interests of both British and Mi'kmaq communities. However, the council was unwilling to continue discussions until all Mi'kmaq chiefs were present. In justifying their decision not to negotiate with Laurent, the council members referred to a previous occasion in 1752 when a peace treaty had been negotiated with Jean-Baptiste Cope of Shubenacadie. Though Cope had promised to bring other tribes to ratify a treaty, the treaties were 'immediately and perfidiously broken.' In the council's view, the only solution was to negotiate future agreements jointly with all Mi'kmaq chiefs.[3] Soon after, Laurent left Halifax. Whatever chances there might have been to conclude a peace ended four months later, when the British assaulted the French fortress of Beausejour, opposite Fort Lawrence.

Laurent's proposal that lands be set aside for the exclusive use of the Mi'kmaq was a response to the growing British presence in Mi'kma'ki. In 1726 the British had promised that the Mi'kmaq would not be interfered with in their planting, hunting, and fishing grounds, but they did not specify where such 'lands' were located. Though the treaty referred to British settlements 'lawfully to be made,' it did not explicitly define the process for making settlements 'lawful.' It is plausible that the Mi'kmaq believed that 'lawful' meant they would be consulted on new settlements. In building the towns of Halifax and Lunenburg, however, the British had not consulted them, and this had established new political tensions in British–Mi'kmaq relations. These tensions reflected differences in how the two sides interpreted the 1726 treaty.

This chapter explores the meanings each side attached to the 1726 treaty between 1749 and 1755, and their attempts to reformulate their relationship based on the new political and economic situation in eastern North America. I argue that the oral meanings that were integral to the 1726 treaty were gradually undermined during this period, as British officials adopted a less flexible interpretation of the treaty than had John Doucett and Lawrence Armstrong. The French presence in the region did work to offset the inclinations of the British, and pull them into a more amicable relationship with the Mi'kmaq than would have developed if the French had been absent. The new contingent of British military officials who staffed the governing councils of Nova Scotia did not entirely reject Mi'kmaq interpretations of the 1726 treaty; but at the same time, they interpreted it in a way that privileged their own class background. As a result, the 1726 treaty had become, by 1749, part of a contested battleground in which both Mi'kmaq and British relied on the treaty's words to justify their actions. In the final analysis, however, the fact that the text was written in English rather than Mi'kmaq, and that its memories were preserved in an alphabetic script, favoured an interpretation of the treaty more conducive to British than to Mi'kmaq interests.

The events that led to Paul Laurent's appearance before the Nova Scotia Council had been set in motion five-and-a-half years earlier, on 21 June 1749, when a flotilla of British ships sailed into Chebucto Bay. In the following months, the passengers would build a settlement along the harbourfront and call their new home Halifax. Their arrival marked a significant departure in British policy: Parliament was no longer willing to wait for private speculators to finance the settlement of British Nova Scotia, and had decided to do so itself. To replace the aged Richard Phillips, who had spent only four years in Nova Scotia in his twenty years as governor, it appointed Edward Cornwallis. Parliament's actions were not welcomed by the Mi'kmaq. Their disgruntlement with the founding of Halifax would lead to years of instability in the region, with the British seeking to establish their physical control over the land and the Mi'kmaq attempting to stop them.

When Cornwallis sailed into Chebucto Harbour in June 1749, no English or French were living there. In 1688 there had been a family of three living along the harbour's edge; later censuses recorded no families in the area.[4] Nearby coastal areas were inhabited, however. In 1748 there were seven or eight French-speaking families at Chegekkouck, twenty miles up the coast, and the same number near Mekakanchish.[5] Chebucto Harbour was used by fishermen to catch and dry fish and to hide from North Atlantic storms, and that was the extent of the European presence there.[6]

But while no Europeans had settled at Chebucto Harbour, Mi'kmaq families had been there for centuries. The Frenchman Sieur de Gargas recorded thirty-three Mi'kmaq living in seven 'cabanes' when he visited Chebucto in 1688.[7] However, later French censuses of 1708, 1722, and

1735 do not mention any Mi'kmaq in the region. One reason may be that census makers compiled their information by observing summer villages, and ignored temporary camping sites like Chebucto. But it is also likely that the wars of the early 1700s had subtly altered the Mi'kmaq family economy. In 1708, Abbé Gaulin had recorded 161 Mi'kmaq living at Musquodoboit, just up the coast from Chebucto. In later censuses, in 1722 and 1737, Musquodoboit was not mentioned; rather, the Mi'kmaq living in these areas were identified with Shubenacadie, where a Catholic mission had been established in 1722. The mission's creation, coupled with altercations with New England fishermen, seems to have driven some families inland between 1708 and 1722. Though families continued to live near Chebucto and Musquodoboit in spring and summer, the Mi'kmaq were not using these areas as heavily as before. One Mi'kmaq sakamaw's remarks to the Nova Scotia Council in September 1752 suggest the changed character of Mi'kmaq residency in the eighteenth century. When asked by the council to identity himself, Jean-Baptiste Cope replied that 'he was chief of that part of the Nation that lived in these parts of the province and had about forty men under him.'[8] Thus, while some Mi'kmaq may have been living nearby when British settlers sailed into Chebucto Harbour in June 1749, there is no indication that they used the harbour as anything more than a fair-weather camping site.

The decision by British policymakers to build a settlement at Chebucto reflected Britain's renewed commitment to secure its interests in the region against the French. The need for this had been amply demonstrated during the War of the Austrian Succession, which between 1744 and 1748 had once again pitted Great Britain against France. Just like the war of the early 1700s, this one had spread to North America, with British and French colonists fighting pitched battles. But the war of the 1740s was also different from the earlier ones. While aboriginal communities started out playing a critical role in the conflict, as they always had before, their importance rapidly diminished as naval squadrons and British and French regular soldiers entered the fray in increasing numbers.

This change in combatants was largely a result of the colonies' growth. By 1760 the population of the mainland British colonies would total 1.6 million – an increase of 1.268 million in only fifty years.[9] And while New France's population was tiny by comparison – perhaps 70,000 by 1760 – France had indicated the importance it attached to its North American assets by building Louisbourg.

By the 1740s, when construction was completed, Louisbourg was critical to New France's economic, political, and military health. Economically, it had become a beehive of commercial activity, a focal point for the Atlantic fishery and for the transshipment of goods to and from Canada, France, and the French Antilles.[10] Politically, Louisbourg was important for maintaining contact with both the Acadians and the Mi'kmaq, whose alliance with France was undermining British attempts to extend political control over the region.[11] And militarily, Louisbourg was a forbidding presence, its batteries providing a safe haven for French warships guarding the entrance to the Gulf of St Lawrence, the gateway to any British invasion of Canada.

For all these reasons, a New England naval expedition targeted Louisbourg soon after war was declared in 1744. On 4 April 1745, ninety transports, five men-of-war, and six sloops holding some 4,000 men sailed from Boston. Having landed successfully on 11 May, the New Englanders began a forty-seven-day siege. On 28 June the governor of Île Royale, Louis Du Pont Duchambon, surrendered.[12] The New Englanders occupied Louisbourg for the duration of the war. Île Royale was returned to France in 1748 by the Treaty of Aix-La-Chappelle, which formally ended the War of Austrian Succession. That decision was unpopular in New England; merchants and fishermen alike expressed their resentment toward an Imperial government that with a stroke of a pen had undone the colonies' efforts to reduce French influence in northeastern North America. The founding of Halifax was as much an attempt to soften the colonies' resentment as it was to secure Great Britain's interests.[13]

The ships that sailed into Chebucto Harbour on 21 June 1749 were carrying 2,547 people. Among the immigrants were '161 farmers, 107 workers in the building trades, 19 shoemakers, 11 butchers, 11 tailors, 10 coopers,' as well as[14] ex-military officers and soldiers. These men, women, and children were a motley group with little in common. The world they were now encountering could not have been more different from the one they had just left. Before them was not the urban congestion of London or Bristol, or the rural landscape of Cornwall or Essex, but a country 'quite wild and overgrown.'[15]

In building Halifax the settlers were creating a landscape far different from the one familiar to the Mi'kmaq who had lived there. Finding the land heavily wooded 'so that with some difficulty one may make his way anywhere,'[16] the settlers began cutting down trees. Within six weeks a space had been cleared to accommodate the 2,500 settlers, and the land had been divided into 60 by 40 foot lots. On each lot families set to work building houses. Then in August, work began on five forts around the settlement's perimeter. By the following July, all these forts had palisaded walls. A year after that, the settlement was moving inland, where five-acre lots had been laid out as farms. To protect the farmers on the outskirts, three more blockhouses were built, each twelve or thirteen feet square and surrounded by a double-row of wooden pickets five feet tall. As a further defensive measure, Captain Gorham's Rangers, a group of hardened New Englanders, were recruited to protect the settlement. At the head of the basin they built a small fort, later called Fort Sackville. By the autumn of 1752 the settlers had transformed the landscape into a shape and form more conducive to their culture than the forested lands they had first encountered.[17]

The early settlers of Halifax were changing the landscape by investing it with their labour; they were also establishing a personal claim to it by giving it names. Before the settlers arrived, French and English cartographers had followed the lead of early fishermen and traders and identified the place as Chebucto, from the Mi'kmaq word *k'chibouktouk*, meaning 'great harbour.'[18] After June 1749, British cartographers called this place 'Halifax,' in honour of the George Montagu Dunk, the second Earl of Halifax, who as president of the Board of Trade had spearheaded the drive to establish the new settlement. The basin at the head of harbour, which the Mi'kmaq had called *Asogomapsgiatijg*, the British called 'Bedford Basin,' after the Duke of Bedford, who in 1749 was Secretary of State for the southern Department. And the land across from Halifax, which the Mi'kmaq called *Ponamogoatitjg*, or salmon place, the English called 'Dartmouth,' in honour of the Earl of Dartmouth.[19] Other places would be named in later years. The post farther up the basin would be named Fort Sackville, after the Earl of Sackville; and a new settlement north of Halifax would be named Lawrencetown after Colonel Charles Lawrence, the senior military officer in Nova Scotia, who in 1754 would become lieutenant-governor.[20] In naming the landscape, the settlers were establishing their claim to it and identifying the land with their English past rather than its Mi'kmaq one.

Renaming the landscape was a deliberate exercise by the colonial elite in Halifax. Such a task was not to be left in the hands of the settlers. To rename the land was to create order from disorder, civilization from savagery, Protestantism from superstition, œconomy from indolence. Place names helped *order* Mi'kma'ki under the auspices of men such as the Earl of Halifax, who understood the 'order of things.'

The replacement of Mi'kmaq names with English ones mirrored a conflict over the land between the British and the Mi'kmaq. In building Halifax, the British were serving notice that their rivalry with France would inform all their plans for the region. Though officials continued to acknowledge the importance of the 1726 treaty, the Mi'kmaq alliance with the French during the war of 1744 to 1748 had demonstrated the treaty's weaknesses. The Mi'kmaq had chosen to side with the French and had been involved in several campaigns against the British in Nova Scotia.[21] The lessons were plain. To counteract French influence, the British would have to do more than sign a treaty with the Mi'kmaq: they would need to establish a stronger military presence, and form stronger commercial ties with the Mi'kmaq. As numerous appeals to the Board of Trade had argued, the French alliance with the Mi'kmaq was based on personal relationships created through trade between the two. After June 1749, the British would attempt to forge similar links. The British would try to wean the Mi'kmaq from their friendship with the French by establishing a military and economic presence in Nova Scotia.

But in doing so, the British were undermining the 1726 treaty. British officials like Governor Cornwallis tended to read the 1726 agreement literally. As Cornwallis saw it, the Mi'kmaq had agreed to abide by the 'law.' This law was to be determined by he and his fellow councillors, not through consultation with the Mi'kmaq. Any other approach would be unthinkable. In adopting this view, Cornwallis was blithely ignoring the discussions that had formed an integral part of the 1726 treaty. True, he may have been unaware of what had been said by Doucett and Armstrong. Both were dead and so unable to explain to the new governor how the Mi'kmaq understood the treaty. But even if Cornwallis had been told of such matters, either through hearsay or from Paul Mascarene, he probably would have ignored the advice. After all, Armstrong was a suicide, so what possible credibility could be attached to his words? But more than this, Cornwallis would have been predisposed to treat the Mi'kmaq as a savage and barbaric race that needed to be told what the law was, not to participate in its creation. This was Cornwallis's role in Nova Scotia – to bring law, order, and discipline to an unruly corner of the Empire.

Cornwallis had been instructed by the Board of Trade to keep the peace with the Mi'kmaq and to 'enter into a treaty with them':

And whereas it is highly necessary for Our Service, that you should cultivate and maintain a strict Friendship and good Correspondence with the Indians, Inhabiting within Our said Province of Nova Scotia, that they may be induced by Degrees, not only to be good Neighbours to Our Subjects, but likewise themselves to become good Subjects to Us; You are therefore to use all proper means to attain these Ends; to have Interviews from time to time with the several heads of the said Indian Nations or Clans, and to Endeavour to enter into a treaty with them, promising them Friendship and Protection on Our Part, and bestowing upon them in Our Name such Presents as you shall judge proper.[22]

Soon after his arrival in Halifax, Cornwallis reported that he had met with some of the 'Indian chiefs' who 'say they will send Deputys to enter into treaty, take English Commissions, instead of French and receive His Majesty's Presents.'[23] By mid-August, twelve aboriginal people had arrived in Halifax, brought there by a British ship.[24]

The delegates represented only a fraction of the region's Mi'kmaq and Maliseet populations. Present were François de Salle from the Maliseet village of Aukpaque, Noellobig from the Maliseet village of Meductic, Abbadouallette from the Passamaquoddy, and Jean Pedousaghtigh, a Mi'kmaq delegate from Chignecto. On 14 August, the four met with Cornwallis and members of His Majesty's Council. Among the Englishmen attending were Paul Mascarene, who had attended the Boston negotiations in 1725, and P.T. Hopson and Charles Lawrence, both of whom would later become governors of Nova Scotia.

On 15 August 1749 the delegates renewed the 1726 treaty. This renewal involved more than a verbal agreement: each party also signed the treaty. The text had two parts. In the first, the articles negotiated at Boston were repeated word for word. The second part of the 1749 treaty was a statement in which the four Maliseet and Mi'kmaq delegates confirmed their ability to enter into a treaty renewal.[25]

The decision to formally renew the 1726 treaty demonstrates its significance for both the British and the Maliseet and Mi'kmaq. But their reasons for renewing it were not the same. In the aftermath of the 1744–8 war, British policymakers wanted the Maliseet delegates to formally renew their 'submission' to the Crown. For the Board of Trade this was the key point, since the Governor of New France, the Marquis de la Gallisonière, had renewed France's claim that the territory west of mainland Mi'kma'ki had not been part of 'Acadia' and therefore had not been surrendered in 1713 by the Treaty of Utrecht.[26] British officials thought otherwise, and produced a copy of the 1726 treaty as proof of their claims. In a letter dated the 27 July 1749 and addressed to the Secretary of State, the Duke of Bedford, the Board of Trade noted that in 1726 the St John River Indians had acknowledged His Majesty's claim to

the region west of mainland Mi'kma'ki: 'That they have also acknowledged His Majesty to be the rightful Possessor of the Province of Nova
Scotia, according to its Ancient Boundaries, and have submitted to His
Majesty as such in as Ample a Manner as they had formerly done to the
Most Christian King, as will evidently appear to Your Grace from the
inclosed Copy of their ratification of a treaty made at Boston in New
England in 1725.'[27] Significantly, the only aboriginal delegates who
renewed the treaty in August 1749 came from villages in the disputed
area – indeed, in areas at the centre of a looming conflict between the
British and French. So it is possible that Cornwallis was renewing the
treaty in order to draw those communities in the disputed territory
more closely into the British orbit, and that he was much less concerned
about immediately fostering relations with the Mi'kmaq on mainland
Mi'kma'ki and Unimaki.

But even if this was the British purpose in renewing the treaty, the
response of the aboriginal villages that renewed it shows the importance
each placed on it. The Maliseet and the Chignecto Mi'kmaq, in formally
renewing the 1726 treaty, were establishing their historic relationship to
it. The delegates could have chosen to dismiss the 1726 treaty, pointing
out its meaninglessness or their unhappiness with it. There is no evidence to suggest they did so. We can only conclude that both the Maliseet and the Chignecto Mi'kmaq saw the treaty as central to their
understanding of their relationship with the British.

Cornwallis's purpose in signing the treaty was to ensure that the delegates recognized British claims west of the Missiquash River. This recognition was contained in the 'articles of peace and agreement,' not in the
reciprocal promises. It was these former articles, which included the delegates' 'signatures,' that Cornwallis would send to London, attesting to
the delegates' recognition of British sovereignty. The reciprocal promises made by Mascarene to the Penobscot at the 1725 Boston conference
were not included in the 1749 treaty. One possible conclusion we can
draw from this is that neither side considered them to be part of their
treaty relationship. However, this is unlikely. That the reciprocal promises made by Doucett in 1726 were omitted from the text of the 1749
treaty does not necessarily mean that these articles were no longer considered part of the treaty.

Moreover, the records from the treaty renewal in Halifax suggest that
the Maliseet and Mi'kmaq delegates believed that in signing the treaty,
they were renewing all its articles. The following passage from the Nova
Scotia Council minutes of 14 August underscores this:

Governor: Do you remember the Treaty made with Your Tribes in 1726?

Indians: Yes. Some of us were present when it was made.

Governor: Will you have it read to you?

Indians: We have a Copy of it ourselves & we are come to renew it.

Governor: Have you Instruction from your Tribes to renew the same Treaty?

Indians: Yes.

Governor: Then tis necessary that the Treaty be read:

   Accordingly it was read in French & interpreted from French into their Language by Martin the Indian & Andrew the Interpreter from Minas.

[Governor]: Do you agree to renew every Article of the Treaty now read to you?

Indians: Yes.

Governor: Then I shall order a Parchment to be ready for you to sign tomorrow & Captain How shall carry it to St. John to be ratified.

Indians: Agreed.[28]

As this passage indicates, some of the delegates to the 1749 conference had been present when the 1726 treaty was ratified. Regardless of the actual text read to them, the delegates would have understood that any articles of earlier treaties would also have formed part of the 1749 renewal.

However, few delegates were present to hear Cornwallis's proposals. Maliseet and Passamquoddy delegates were there, but only one Mi'kmaq delegate – from Chignecto – attended, and there is no indication that the treaty was formally ratified by his community. Indeed, a letter from the Jesuit missionary Charles Germain to the Maliseet suggests that the discussions in Halifax in mid-August had not been attended by any of the chiefs, and that 'nothing had been concluded.'[29]

At first glance, the refusal by most Mi'kmaq villages to renew the 1726 treaty seems to have been a backlash against the British establishment of Halifax. This point of view was expressed in an anonymous journal written by an Englishmen who was living in Halifax in the early 1750s. According to the journal's author, the Mi'kmaq had initially believed that the British intended only to build 'a Fishing Town and fortify the little Island to secure it.' Later, the Mi'kmaq realized that something more was intended and began to 'open their eyes.'[30] A period of conflict ensued. However, Mi'kmaq motives were more complex than this; other events interceded to increase their suspicions about British intentions.

Altercations between the British and the Mi'kmaq in August 1749 exacerbated tensions between the two communities. The first incident happened near the Acadian settlement of Beaubassin and involved two British vessels that the Mi'kmaq believed were stopping Acadians from fleeing to Île Saint-Jean. (By early October 1750, six or seven hundred Acadians had moved to the island.[31]) A group of Mi'kmaq were present when the two British ships arrived at Beaubassin. According to an account later transmitted to Versailles, the Mi'kmaq tried to capture the two vessels. A melee followed, and several men on both sides were killed, among them Captain Tom Daniel, who commanded one of the ships, and the 'chiefs of Chebenaakdy (Shubenacadie), Beaubassin, and the sons of the chief of Milligueche.'[32]

The second incident also happened in mid-August. Twenty Englishmen were seized at Canso by a party of Mi'kmaq. Among the prisoners were five Halifax residents who had gone to Canso to cut hay for winter forage. Following complaints made by Cornwallis, the governor of Île Royale secured the release of sixteen of the prisoners.[33] Though there is no documentation suggesting why the attack was made, it is likely that some of the Mi'kmaq involved were seeking to avenge the killing of twenty Mi'kmaq in Newfoundland. This killing had been carried out by a group of men who had been rescued by some Mi'kmaq. The Englishmen had reciprocated by killing the women and children after the men had left their village to hunt and fish.[34]

Both incidents took place far from the two principal British settlements. This suggests that the expanding British military presence in the region resulted in more points of conflict with Mi'kmaq villagers. The building of Halifax meant much more than just the physical occupation of Chebucto Harbour. It also meant the expansion of British economic and military needs. As Halifax grew, so too did the points of potential conflict with Mi'kmaq communities.

Mi'kmaq concerns about increases in British commercial and military activities were expressed in a letter written in their name and delivered to Cornwallis by an English officer in late September 1749:[35]

The place where you are, the place where you live, the place where you are building a fortification, the place where you want now to establish yourself, the place of which you want to make yourself the absolute master, this place belongs to me. Me, the Indian, I come out of this earth like [a blade of] grass. I have been born there the son [and] from father to son. This place is my land, I swear it. It is God who has given me this land to be my homeland forever ... My king and your King together distribute these lands, and it is because of that they are presently at peace, but for me I can make neither alliance or peace with you. Show me where I could, an Indian, withdraw to. As for you, you hunt me down. Show me then where you want me to take refuge. You have taken over almost all of this land, so that the only resource left to me is at Kchibouctouk [Halifax]. Yet you begrudge me even this piece [of land] and you even want to chase me from it. That is what makes me know that you have sworn to not cease to make war on us and to never enter into alliance with us. You are proud of your great numbers. I , who is in very small number, can only count on the God which knows what this is all about ... I am going very soon to go and see you, yes, I shall certainly see you soon.[36]

The letter was as much an expression of French opposition to the founding of Halifax as it was an expression of Mi'kmaq concerns. French opposition is also revealed in the governor of Île Royale's correspondence and in his efforts to enlist Mi'kmaq support in undermining the new British settlement. He recommended to Versailles that it increase its annual allotment of presents for the Mi'kmaq – a recommendation that was later followed.[37] Notwithstanding its strong French 'flavour,' the 1749 letter is useful also for what it tells us about Mi'kmaq reactions to the founding of Halifax. British settlement there sparked fears that further British actions would limit access to fishing and hunting grounds.

Land was the central issue of the dispute. Though the 1726 treaty had not stated how new settlements were to be created, it *had* stated that the Mi'kmaq would not interfere with settlements 'lawfully to be made.' However British officials interpreted that phrase in 1726, its meaning to them by 1749 was unambiguous. In founding Halifax, the Board of Trade was demonstrating its intent to build new settlements in Nova Scotia. These settlements would not require Mi'kmaq approval. It seems that by 1749, British officials were interpreting the phrase 'settlements lawfully to be made' as referring to British law. The only restriction that could be placed on new settlements was that they could not be made in areas used or occupied by the Mi'kmaq for their 'their hunting, fishing, planting grounds,' or other activities. This restriction had been part of the reciprocal promises made by Doucett in 1726. Presumably, the British believed that their settlement at Halifax accorded with the terms of the treaty, since when the settlers arrived at Chebucto Bay in August 1749, there were no visible signs of a Mi'kmaq settlement along the harbour or in the immediate vicinity.

This interpretation of the treaty conflicted with Mi'kmaq understandings of the treaty's provisions. According to the Mi'kmaq, any new settlement should have been negotiated with, at the very least, the Mi'kmaq communities most affected. This interpretation is suggested in the 1749 letter, which refers to the disruption in Mi'kmaq hunting and fishing practices as a result of the building of Halifax. However, these statements are not very explicit; for example, they do not describe the areas used by local families, or how British activity made it harder for the Mi'kmaq to harvest the region's resources.

Having read this letter, the Nova Scotia Council did not inquire into the nature of Mi'kmaq land use. On the contrary, the council members responded angrily, issuing a proclamation offering a reward for Mi'kmaq scalps or prisoners. Pointing to the incidents at Beaubassin and Canso and a more recent attack on a sawmill on Halifax's perimeter, the council argued that an aggressive policy was necessary to defend the colony. Ten guineas were offered for 'every Indian killed or taken Prisoner' – a reward that was increased to 50 guineas in June 1750. As an additional measure, the council voted in early October to raise an independent company of one hundred men to augment Captain Gorham's company.[38] Whatever opportunity might have existed to peacefully resolve the dispute ended with the council's resolutions. As Abbé Jean-Louis Le Loutre, a French missionary then living among the Mi'kmaq, was to later write, the posting of the proclamation prompted 'all the Indians to raise their hatchets' against the British.[39]

Adding fuel to this simmering conflict was Governor Cornwallis's decision to build a fort near the headwaters of the Missiquash River, just west of mainland Mi'kma'ki. This action was in response to the posting of a French garrison on the west bank of the Missiquash in the autumn of 1749. The French detachment was commanded by Captain Louis-Luc La Corne who had been dispatched to the region by Governor LaJonquière to occupy an area that France said had not been surrendered to Great Britain by the Treaty of Utrecht. Commanding the British was Major Charles Lawrence, who landed at Chignecto in April of 1750 with four hundred men. Lawrence withdrew soon after, fearing his men were outnumbered. In mid-September he returned with seventeen ships and two regiments of regulars in tow.[40] Over the next several months both sides constructed fortresses on either side of an expanse of marshland four or five miles wide, the English calling theirs Fort Lawrence, the French calling theirs Fort Beausejour.[41]

The British had succeeded in bolstering their presence in Nova

Scotia, but these efforts had been expensive, and more than Parliament was willing to bear for long. Costs consistently exceeded budgets. In 1751 Parliament had voted an additional £21,000 to make up for the colony's 'exceedings.' The Board of Trade wrote to Cornwallis in early March 1752 that while such costs were necessary to defend the colony, expenditures should be carefully monitored, for 'Parliament will be apt to think no reason sufficient to excuse such an Expense, if be often repeated.' The governor, the board wrote, should pay constant attention to the colony's finances so that future deficits would not force the board to go 'to Parliament with Exceedings': 'We have the highest Opinion of your good intentions for the Publick Service, and mean only to exhort you as it is Our Duty, to prevent the Expense of your Government from always going beyond the Vote of Parliament, by watching over the Manner of conducting necessary Expences, and making the Prescription of Parliament, the Limitation of the whole Expense.'[42]

The board had a remedy: make peace with the Mi'kmaq. Such a measure, they believed, would have several benefits. First, it would allow the disbandment of Gorham's Rangers, who had been employed to protect Halifax. Second, once a 'good Correspondence' with the Mi'kmaq was started, 'a Trade with them, of great Extent and National Utility, might be gradually opened.' This trade would fix them in friendship with His Majesty's subjects and also benefit the 'General Commerce of Great Britain.' Third, peace would increase the colony's agricultural production and so 'reduce the expense of Provisions ... to the Settlers [and] to the Troops.' Fourth, peace would allow the settlers to develop the fishery and other economic pursuits.[43] As the board had written to Cornwallis the year before, the fishery was a resource that the colony could offer 'in exchange for the Manufactures it may receive from hence.' Nova Scotia's agricultural produce and other 'natural products' would also benefit 'His majesty's West Indian Settlements.'[44] For the board, Nova Scotia's value hinged on its capacity to purchase manufactured goods from the Mother Country while supplying it with 'natural products.'

Cornwallis had nimbly anticipated the board's suggestions. The year before, he had sent a peace belt to the Maliseet and dispatched Paul Mascarene to represent Nova Scotia at discussions between Massachusetts and the Penobscot and Maliseet.[45] At the conference at Fort St George in 1751, Mascarene invited the Maliseet and their brethren Mi'kmaq to Chebucto to treat with Cornwallis. Mascarene told them in 'the name of Governor Cornwallis' that in return for laying down their arms they would be given presents annually 'at a meeting of the Tribes at such a time of the year as shall be agreed upon.' Also, truckhouses would be built at convenient places 'where the Indians shall be supplied with provisions and such other Necessaries as they shall want, at the most reasonable Rates.' These proposals were greeted favourably by the Maliseet delegate, who said he would tell all the 'tribes', including the Mi'kmaq, of the governor's words. In the meantime, the Maliseet delegates promised that they would end all acts of hostility against the British, and would urge the Mi'kmaq to do the same.[46]

Cornwallis's overtures did not have the desired effect. Though he reported to the board in mid-February of 1752 that no further hostilities had arisen, he could not report on discussions with the Mi'kmaq or Maliseet.[47] Chafing at the lack of progress, Cornwallis decided to contact the Mi'kmaq directly, employing as his messenger William Piggot, a Halifax merchant. In August 1752 Piggot travelled to Port Toulouse, a fishing port on the southeastern coast of French Île Royale, to seek payment on a debt owed him by Joseph Maurice, a well-known Acadian trader. The timing of Piggot's visit was deliberate, as late July was when Mi'kmaq communities gathered at Port Toulouse to celebrate St Anne's Day.[48] While there, Piggot met with Jean-Baptiste Cope, a sakamaw from Shubenacadie. Piggot offered Cope some presents as a token of the governor's respect, and spoke of renewing the peace between the Mi'kmaq and the British.[49] Cope received the governor's invitation favourably. In mid-September Cope arrived in Halifax, though by this time Cornwallis had resigned and been replaced by Peregrine Hopson, a career military officer.

Cope told the council that he was 'chief of that part of the Nation that lived in these parts of the province.'[50] The territory inhabited by his people was closely associated with the mission built in 1722 at Shubenacadie, forty miles inland from Halifax. Though most families hunted inland in winter, in the late spring they frequented coastal areas between Halifax and Musquodoboit. Since Shubenacadie was near Halifax, Cope's appearance before the council suggests that he had been delegated by many communities to treat with the British, since it was his people who had been most directly affected by the establishment of Halifax.

Cope told the council that he 'had about forty men under him.' This estimate compares favourably with the one made seventeen years earlier by the French missionary Abbé Pierre Maillard. Maillard had counted ninety-five men fifteen years of age or older at Shubenacadie in 1735, but it is likely that half these men came from Mi'kmaq communities near the Acadian settlements at Minas.[51] If we assume that by 'men' Cope meant males older than fifteen, around 126 people lived in his village.[52]

Cope's political position in Mi'kmaq society has been a subject of much controversy. Some Mi'kmaq researchers argue today that he was the Grand Chief of the Mi'kmaq. Some Mi'kmaq contend that Cope had been appointed to represent all Mi'kmaq villages.[53] Non-aboriginal scholars have pointed out that the available English and French documents refer to Cope as 'chief' from Shubenacadie and nothing more.[54] It is probably impossible to resolve this debate. There is no direct evidence that Cope was anything more than 'chief of Shubenacadie'; yet it is equally true that French and British officials could not have known his actual political status, since they were not privy to intercommunity discussions. (In the same vein, most scholars accept that the Five Nations formed the League of the Houdenosaunee before 1600 and were afterwards governed by forty-nine chiefs appointed by the clan mothers. However, this statement is based not on European observations in the 1600s and 1700s but rather on the ethnographic work of later commentators.[55]) While we cannot conclude that Cope was the Grand Chief of the Mi'kmaq, neither can we demonstrate that he was not. What we can say is that at the very least, Cope's influence extended beyond his own village.

At talks with the council on 14 and 16 September 1752, Cope wanted to discuss how to define the territories where the Mi'kmaq and British would live in the future. To Cope, the founding of Halifax and Fort Lawrence had demonstrated the need to refine the 1726 treaty. In his view, 'the Indians should be paid for the Land the English had settled upon in this Country.'[56] At an informal discussion with Captain Edward How at Fort Lawrence in the autumn of 1750, Abbé Le Loutre had suggested that the Mi'kmaq would find it acceptable 'to have a Corner of the Country to themselves, unsurrounded by any Forts of ours ... Shubenacadie would be an acceptable location.'[57] Such an approach would have been consistent with the one the British adopted in Massachusetts, where lands had been purchased from the Abenaki, and then treaties had defined the limits of British settlement. This amounted to an implicit recognition that areas outside this limit were reserved for the Abenaki. However, the proposals made by Cope and Le Loutre introduced a different solution. Cope's was simple: divide mainland Mi'kma'ki into Mi'kmaq and British spheres. The Mi'kmaq would exercise jurisdiction over one area, the British over another. That way, the

British would not need to worry about determining which areas were being used and occupied by the Mi'kmaq. Presumably, the division of lands would facilitate British settlement and minimize potential conflicts.

The council was thinking in very different terms, and did not respond directly to Cope's proposals. Instead, it focused on the general tenor of the instructions sent to Cornwallis in early March of that year and on Mascarene's proposals to the Maliseet the year before. For the council, the main reason to renew the treaty was to facilitate trade between the Mi'kmaq and British merchants. This necessarily meant undermining the close personal ties the Mi'kmaq had long enjoyed with Acadian traders. Thus, the council proposed that a truckhouse be built 'where you may have everything you stand in need of at a reasonable price, and where shall be given unto you to the full Value for the peltries, feathers, or other Things which you shall have to sell.' This truckhouse was to be built at the government's expense and run by officers appointed by them. As a further incentive to Cope and other Mi'kmaq, the council promised that the friendship between them would be confirmed annually, through the provision of presents, which would be offered as long as 'you behave yourselves as good and faithful Children to our great King.' Though the council did not reply directly to Cope's suggestion that compensation be paid for lands the British settled, it promised that the Mi'kmaq would not 'be hindered from Hunting, or Fishing in this Country, as you have used to do.' Moreover, if Cope and his people decided to settle along the Shubenacadie River, neither would anyone 'meddle with the Lands where you are.' However, no attempt was made either then or later to define the lands to be inhabited by the Mi'kmaq, or where they would exercise an exclusive right of occupation.[58]

Cope's responses to the council's suggestions were not recorded. Thus, there is no written evidence that he restated that the Mi'kmaq should be paid for the lands the British had taken. Nor are there any documents indicating that he asked the council which areas the British would recognize as encompassing Mi'kmaq fishing and hunting areas. We only know that he promised to consult with his people and to do his utmost 'to bring here the other Tribes of Mickmacks to make a peace.' He also promised to return in a month.[59]

Cope returned to Halifax in early November to discuss the treaty again.[60] It was not signed until several weeks later, on the twenty-second of that month. There are no records of discussions between Cope and members of the council in the weeks that led up to the signing. And, as with the 1726 treaty, there is little to help us discern the treaty's meanings except the text itself.

The 1752 treaty reflected the changes that had transpired since 1726. It was exactly the same as the earlier treaty except that seven new articles had been added. Each new article addressed an issue not dealt with by the 1726 treaty, and modified the earlier treaty.

In general, the treaty outlined the government's responsibility for managing affairs with the Mi'kmaq. First, the government agreed to provide financial incentives to encourage the Mi'kmaq to keep the peace. If the people of Shubenacadie wished, a truckhouse would be built near them. The government would also immediately allot six months' provisions to every village signing the treaty, and extend on the first of October of each year thereafter a gift of 'blankets, tabacco, some Powder & shot ... so long as they continue in Friendship.'

The British also agreed to intervene on behalf of the Mi'kmaq to protect their interests against the actions of His Majesty's Subjects. The seventh article, for instance, offered a reward to Mi'kmaq who saved the crews (and/or cargoes) of any vessels wrecked along the coast. Possibly, this portion of the treaty was inserted following representations made to the Court of the Vice-Admiralty in late October 1752 by Thomas Gillard, a fisherman. Gillard was upset with the actions of Daniel Malcolm, a fishermen who had been shipwrecked at Ship Harbour, just up the coast from Halifax. Malcolm had been rescued by a group of Mi'kmaq. By chance, Gillard had encountered Malcolm and transported him and his crew to Halifax. Before leaving Ship Harbour, Malcolm had promised to return to the Mi'kmaq encampment and 'carry them flour, Bread in return for the favour he add his Company had Received at their hands.' Gillard complained that Malcolm had not done so and that his renegement had exposed every other fishermen to the wrath of the Mi'kmaq, 'whereby every fishermen who shall be obliged to put into any Harbor along shore or fish near any Harbor Mouth will be in danger of Losing his Life by these Indians as nothing moves their Resentment more than breach of Promise.'[61]

Finally, the treaty promised that disputes between the Mi'kmaq and British subjects would be tried in 'His Majesty's Courts of Civil Judicature.' In some respects, this article was a fleshing out of one of the reciprocal promises made by John Doucett in 1726. In the 1726 treaty the Mi'kmaq had been promised satisfaction according 'his Majesty's Laws.' By 1752 a formal court system had been formed in Nova Scotia. In effect, this phrase of the treaty modified the 1726 treaty by referring to the judicial body responsible for mediating disputes between the Mi'kmaq and His Majesty's subjects.[62]

The 1752 treaty provided for stricter regulation of the colony's dealings with the Mi'kmaq, but it did not resolve the troublesome issue of land. The treaty only repeated those proposals presented to Cope two months earlier, albeit in more compact form: 'It is Agreed that the said tribe of Indians shall not be hindered from, but have free liberty of Hunting & Fishing as usual.' This portion of the 1752 treaty read much the same as the 1726 treaty.

Cope signed the treaty on 22 November, as did three other Mi'kmaq: Andrew Hadley Martin, Gabriel Martin, and François Jeremie. Cope was identified as the 'chief sachem of the Tribe of MickMack Indians inhabiting the Eastern Coast of this Province.' The other three were noted as 'delegates of the said Tribe.' Later commentators have suggested that Cope's co-signers in fact represented various Unimaki villages. For instance Ben Christmas, the leader of Membertou, a Mi'kmaq community on the outskirts of Sydney, testified in court in 1928 that two of the signers of the 1752 treaty came from Cape Breton – Andrew Hadley Martin from Nyanza, and Gabriel Martin from Eskasoni.[63] Though Mi'kmaq were certainly living beside Bras d'Or Lake at the time, there are no documents to validate Christmas's views.[64] Unfortunately, the judge's notes from the trial do not give the source of Christmas's information. There being no evidence to the contrary, it is more likely that both Martins as well as François Jeremie came from mainland Mi'kma'ki. Later records identify an 'Andrew Martin' as 'one of the Cobequid Tribe of Indians,' referring to Mi'kmaq living farther up the Shubenacadie River near what is now Cobequid Bay.[65] François Jeremie and Gabriel Martin are not mentioned in any records; they are names on the treaty, and no more.

Cope had said in September 1752 that he would try to persuade other Mi'kmaq villages to sign the peace. Though other members of his own village had accompanied him to Halifax in November, delegates from other places had not. After he left Halifax in mid-September, he probably talked to other village leaders. These leaders were more reticent about renewing the peace. This was a marked departure from 1726, when at least nine summer villages ratified the agreement. I suggested in Chapter 7 that this process took over two years to complete. Similar heated debates took place in 1752, illustrating the deep political divisions that British expansionism had created. The villages adamantly opposed to the agreement were the ones in Unimaki and on the north shore of the mainland – in other words, the ones most distant from Halifax and the most wedded economically and politically to the French at Île Royale and Île Saint-Jean.[66] These villages could obtain European goods from the French governor or by trading with French merchants. Also opposed to the treaty were the communities west of mainland Mi'kma'ki, at Chignecto and up the eastern coast of what is now New Brunswick. More amenable to the agreement were the villages to the south of the Shubenacadie River, where the British presence was strongest. It is perhaps no accident that, in the spring of 1753, two other Mi'kmaq villages on the mainland, Cape Sable and La Hève, sent delegates to Halifax to ratify the treaty.[67] On April 12, Claude Gisigish from La Hève appeared before the council and signed an agreement declaring that his community would make peace 'on the same conditions with that already concluded with Major Jean-Baptiste Cope as soon as he can bring here an Interpreter and some of his Tribe to ratify the said peace.'[68] As Charles Morris was to write four days later, 'the chiefs of every tribe in the Peninsula [have] sent in messages of friendship, and I believe would have signed articles of peace this spring.'[69]

As Cope was the principal negotiator of the treaty, he likely spent the months following his departures from Halifax in September and November 1752 travelling from village to village to report on the discussions he had held and the treaty he had signed.[70] Discussions continued through the spring of 1753, with both Cope and Claude Gigigish travelling to Chignecto to persuade the people there to ratify the treaty.[71] The Nova Scotia Council also did its part, by posting copies of the treaty throughout the colony.[72] But any chance for a general ratification was undermined by a series of altercations between British fishermen and Mi'kmaq families on the east coast of mainland Mi'kma'ki in the spring of 1753.[73]

Adding even more fuel to Mi'kmaq anger was the council's decision in May 1753 to establish a new settlement at Lunenburg. This new township was to be settled by German Protestants, who had been arriving in British Nova Scotia since 1751. By the spring of 1753 the council was no longer willing to delay establishing the Germans in a new settlement.[74] The council had at one time hoped to place the foreign Protestants near the Acadians. By the spring of 1753, the decision had been reached to settle them instead just down the coast from Halifax, at what had been till then the site of Mirligeuche, a Mi'kmaq village. Some 1500 new settlers were ferried to this site in the late spring of 1753. The council's decision did little to promote friendly relations with the Mi'kmaq. The new settlement was yet another illustration of how hard it was to reconcile British claims to the peninsula with Mi'kmaq claims to favoured fishing and hunting sites. There is no indication that Claude Gigigish, who had discussed the terms of the treaty with the council on 12 April 1753, had been consulted about the new settlement – a surprising omission, given that plans would have already been afoot to move the Germans.

Over the next two years, discussions would centre on a Mi'kmaq proposal that the territory north of the Shubenacadie River be reserved for their exclusive use. Within this area, neither the French nor the British would be allowed to build forts. Nor would Europeans be allowed to settle there. The rest of Nova Scotia would presumably be left for the British and the Acadians. This solution offered many advantages for the Mi'kmaq. First, they would have access to hunting and fishing grounds irrespective of any increases in the Acadian and English populations. This was possibly the most pressing issue: after all, the Mi'kmaq had witnessed their own people diminish as the European presence increased – a process that had begun with the expansion of Acadian settlements and had accelerated with the creation of Halifax and Lunenburg. Second, British settlement would be similarly defined. Third, the creation of separate territories would tend to foster co-existence between the two.

Undoubtedly, French policymakers supported the proposal that an area be reserved for the exclusive use of the Mi'kmaq. They knew that a buffer zone between the Acadian and British populations of Nova Scotia would serve France's interests. A similar strategy had been employed in the 1600s in the St Lawrence Valley, where Abenaki, Huron, and Mohawk missions had acted as a line of defence for French settlements. It is entirely conceivable that Abbé Le Loutre, the trusted friend and confidant of many Mi'kmaq, was instrumental in formulating the proposals that Laurent carried to Halifax in February 1755. Le Loutre had first proposed a partition of lands to Edward How in 1750, and in 1754 and 1755 had written the letters to the Nova Scotia Council that preceded Laurent's meeting with it. But whatever Le Loutre's influence, the proposals were made by Laurent and on behalf of a confederation of Mi'kmaq villages. He would not have proposed such a sweeping revolution in Mi'kmaq life without the support of each village.

Unfortunately, Le Loutre's participation in drafting Laurent's proposals affected how the council responded to them. Le Loutre was well known to the council, and was seen as an incendiary who fanned Acadian and Mi'kmaq hatred of the British. Le Loutre was not a man to be trusted – perhaps the more so since he resided among the Mi'kmaq and therefore lived a life in which gentlemen's decorum mattered nothing. As the council's members would have seen it, Le Loutre was not beholden to the code of conduct they shared with their counterparts in Louisbourg and Quebec; thus, they were predisposed to think ill of him and any proposals he might make. But the council had more reason than this to distrust the proposal presented by Laurent in the handwriting of Le Loutre. Though Le Loutre didn't realize it, the council had been privy to many of the goings on at Fort Beausejour through the traitorous correspondence of Thomas Pichon. Pichon's many long letters to Captain Hussey at Fort Lawrence in 1754 and 1755 made frequent reference to an association between 'Moses' (Le Loutre) and the Mi'kmaq and to proposals to create a separate territory for the Mi'kmaq.[75] Any hope that the Nova Scotia Council might accept Laurent's suggestions died a quick death through association with Le Loutre.

The council's discussions with Laurent in February 1755 reflected the ambiguous nature of treaty making after 1726. On the one hand, the council members interpreted the 1726 treaty in a way that emphasized the centrality of British law in any relations with the Mi'kmaq. The new settlements of Halifax, Lunenburg, and Fort Lawrence were embodiments of the stronger British presence in Nova Scotia, and emboldened British officials to read the 1726 treaty as an expression of British rather than Mi'kmaq culture. This was a marked departure from 1726 and 1728, when Great Britain's tenuous military presence and the circumstances created by the execution of the Muse brothers had influenced Nova Scotia officials to adopt a more culturally relativist view of the treaty's English words.

Nova Scotia's new contingent of officials – Edward Cornwallis being a prime example of the breed – treated the Mi'kmaq differently from the Acadians. Instead of disavowing the 1726 treaty, the British renewed it in 1749 and in 1752, and would have done so again in 1755 had Laurent been accompanied by other village chiefs. The British expected that the Mi'kmaq would continue to live outside civil society and would only be brought into it through constant encouragement. Though the council's members interpreted 'lawfully to be made' to be British law, they recognized that this law did not govern or regulate Mi'kmaq communities. Rather, the treaties were meant to encourage the Mi'kmaq to live peaceably with the British – something to be encouraged by distributing presents and offering rewards to Mi'kmaq who rescued shipwrecked sailors on eastern coast. In sum, the British were unable to impose their law on the Mi'kmaq, or to make them live as if they were king's subjects.

Chapter Nine

The 1760–1761 Treaties

In 1760 and 1761, British officials in Nova Scotia signed separate but similar treaties with nine Mi'kmaq villages. The treaties ended a conflict that had begun soon after British settlers arrived at Chebucto Bay in June 1749. Though another treaty was signed in 1779, it did not substantially modify the earlier treaties.[1] Thus, the 1760–1 treaties constitute the substantive end of the treaty-making period in British–Mi'kmaq relations, a period that had begun in 1726.

With the 1760–1 treaties, the British undermined even further the relationship between the Mi'kmaq and the French. British opportunism was made possible by their victory over the French forces in North America in the Seven Years War (its European name; in the British colonies it was referred to as the French and Indian War). The British committed more ships and men to this war than they had to the earlier one, and invested more money to win it. The Seven Years War, like the previous one, ended badly for France. The principal French fortresses in North America fell quickly to British arms: Louisbourg in July 1758, Québec in September 1759, and Montreal in June 1760. By the summer of 1760 the British were triumphant almost everywhere in North America.

Yet Great Britain's military control of North America was still tenuous. Control of the principal towns of New France meant little if the countryside was not safe for farmers, labourers, artisans, fishermen, and traders to go about their business. British officials faced a similar problem in Nova Scotia. The Mi'kmaq were adept 'forest fighters,' so it was necessary to sign peace treaties with them. Also, the British faced hostile aboriginal populations west of Montreal, and west of the Appalachians, and were afraid that the costs of defending outlying settlements and posts would be crippling. The Board of Trade and Parliament did not want to bankrupt themselves pacifying these territories. It was in this context that the treaties with the Mi'kmaq were signed in 1760 and 1761.

This chapter considers the events between October 1759 and March 1760 that led to the signing of the first of the 1760–1 treaties. This treaty was signed on 10 March 1760 by the villages of La Hève and Shubenacadie of mainland Mi'kma'ki and Richibucto of southeastern New Brunswick (see pp. 163–4). I contend that the 1760 treaty was based on the one of 1726, and that each clause in it corresponded to one clause or another in the earlier treaty. Each article of the later treaty modified a part of the earlier one. In this way, the 1760–1 treaties incorporated the economic and political changes that had taken place in British–Mi'kmaq relations since 1726 – namely, the creation of new British settlements at Halifax and Lunenburg, the expulsion of the Acadians in 1755, and the defeat of French forces in North America soon after.

In the eighteenth century, the process of treaty making was ridden with contradictions, more so when the issues forced the negotiators to grapple with the cultural background of their counterparts. As in 1726, the Mi'kmaq and British had difficulty conceptualizing each other. By 1760, the two sides had been separated even farther by the passage of time. The Mi'kmaq were represented by men who had been present as youths at Annapolis Royal in 1726, or by men who had grown up listening to what their elders told them had been said there. In the same vein, British officials had no personal or familial connections to the people who had negotiated the 1726 treaty. The only relationship these men had to the treaties was through the written English text. This meant that their interpretations of the 1726 treaty were conditioned less by the words spoken by the Mi'kmaq than by their own economic and cultural background.

Between 1755 and 1758 the Mi'kmaq were at war with the British in Nova Scotia. Some Mi'kmaq helped the French defend Beausejour in 1755 and Louisbourg in 1757–8. Mi'kmaq men from Chignecto and the eastern coast of New Brunswick were present at the British siege of Beausejour, though most had left by the time the French surrendered it on 17 June 1755.[2] Considerably more information exists showing that the Mi'kmaq participated in the defence of Louisbourg. For example, an accounting note from 1757 shows that 1,200 livres was paid to 'various Indians for the journey they made by land from Louisbourg to the neighbourhood of Halifax to accompany Mr. Gautier sent to the said place to find out the movements of the English at that place.' Other reports indicate that Mi'kmaq were camped at Louisbourg in 1757. For instance, 61 livres, 10 sous was paid to 'Joseph la Ruine, an inhabitant from the Island of Saint-Jean for the cost of 205 pounds of fresh beef that was supplied for the refreshment of the Indians coming from Miramichi to [Louisbourg].'

Each of these Louisbourg accounts dates from 1757. Together, they indicate that the French expected the British to attack the fortress that summer. According to four Frenchmen captured by the British in 1758, 800 aboriginal people had been camped near the fortress the year before.[3] The prisoners told their captors that an equal number were expected before the year's end; however, it is unlikely that the French military could have supported so many warriors for another summer.[4] However many Mi'kmaq were present at the siege, they weren't enough to hold the fortress, which fell on 26 July 1758. Sometime before then, Mi'kmaq, Maliseet, and Abenaki warriors left Louisbourg and travelled south along Bras d'Or lake to their home villages. The fall of Beausejour and Louisbourg ended France's military and civil presence in the region. After the French departed, Mi'kmaq resistance became more and more untenable.[5]

After the early summer of 1758, the British concentrated on securing the Gulf of St Lawrence, with the goal of mounting a naval expedition against Quebec.[6] William Pitt, the king's principal minister, had hoped to lay siege to Quebec in 1758, but Louisbourg fell too late to make this possible.[7] By late June of the following year, 1759, the first British ships had sailed up the St Lawrence and anchored off of Île d'Orleans, opposite Quebec. Not until 18 September, however, did the capital of New France fall.[8] For the Mi'kmaq and the Acadians, the surrender was a crushing blow.

Among those affected by all this were a group of Mi'kmaq and Acadians who had fled south from Louisbourg in late July of 1758 with Abbé Pierre Maillard, a French missionary who had lived sporadically among the Mi'kmaq since 1735. Settling at Malogomich on the north coast of mainland Mi'kma'ki,[9] this motley gang launched several daring raids against New England ships over the next few months. Between 9 and 25 August 1759 they captured seven vessels. Though they released the crews, they kept the cargoes and six of the vessels.[10] The senior military officer at Louisbourg, Brigadier-General Edward Whitmore, was not amused. In early October he sent Captain Henry Schomberg to root out the troublesome nest of 'pirates.'

On 26 October 1759, Schomberg's small force arrived at Malogomich. According to an account in the *Boston Gazette*, there were 400 Mi'kmaq at Malogomich and a 'larger number of French.'[11] Even if these numbers are inflated, Schomberg's small force was outnumbered. This may have influenced him to adopt a conciliatory policy. Under a flag of truce, Schomberg sent a written message to Maillard in the name of Whitmore, informing him that 'your Capital Quebec has fallen to the arms of the King, my master, your armies are in flight.' Schomberg urged the Mi'kmaq and Acadians to make peace with His Majesty, and offered them favourable terms: 'I am commanded to assure you by His Majesty that you will enjoy all your possessions, your liberty, property with the free exercise of your religion as you can see by the declaration that I have the honour of sending you. If my Reverend father, you doubt the sincerity of my heart, I am ready to exchange hostages and I would be delighted to have the honour of seeing you aboard my frigate.'[12] Discussions between Schomberg and Maillard continued over the next month, and a formal truce was concluded in late November.[13] As part of the agreement, hostages were exchanged. Two or three Englishmen were left at Malogomich; seven Mi'kmaq and thirty Acadians departed with Schomberg to meet with Governor Whitmore, who had remained at Louisbourg.[14]

The identity of the aboriginal delegates who travelled to Louisbourg is unclear. Whitmore wrote that 'among them was Jeannot Peguidalouet, chief of the Indians of this Island.' Later he wrote that 'several chiefs' had come to discuss terms of the proposed peace, though he did not identify them by name or by home village.[15] Schomberg claimed that more chiefs attended. In a letter requesting compensation for the costs of entertaining the seven 'Indians,' Schomberg said that he had brought to Louisbourg 'seven Indian chiefs as Hostages of the Different Tribes of Micmacks Louisbourgh, Saint Johns & others.'[16] While there is no other evidence to show that other Mi'kmaq chiefs were present at the meetings with Whitmore, it is likely that Jeannot was not the only 'chief' who made the trip to Louisbourg.

The only surviving records of the discussions that followed are from Whitmore's own pen. He wrote that the Acadians and Mi'kmaq had surrendered, had sworn oaths of allegiance 'to his Britannick Majesty and had promised to be faithfull good Subjects in all time to Come.' However, Schomberg's earlier discussions with Father Maillard at Malogomich contradict Whitmore's assertions. The Mi'kmaq had not surrendered; rather, they had come to Louisbourg only after

Schomberg had agreed to leave two Englishmen as hostages at Malogo-mich as security for the safe return of the seven 'chiefs.' Whitmore's assertion that the delegates agreed to be 'faithfull and good Subjects' is also suspect: Schomberg's letter to Maillard in October 1759 suggested that the British did not intend to impose unilateral terms on the Mi'kmaq, and that any terms would have to be acceptable to them. These would have to address the security of their possessions, their liberty, and their property, and 'the free exercise of your religion.'

Whatever was said, Whitmore did not treat the Mi'kmaq as 'rebellious subjects.' In Europe, such a term would have been applied to subjects who had joined the French to destroy the king's dominions. At most, Whitmore had requested that the Mi'kmaq swear oaths of allegiance and to live in peace with His Majesty. Indeed, Whitmore's approach was one shared by his counterparts in Halifax, who did not think that the Mi'kmaq had transformed themselves from subjects into rebels by supporting the French cause.

Trade was also discussed, as shown by a casual remark that Jonathan Proctor, a nineteen-year-old New England soldier, made in his diary on 29 November 1759: 'Lt. Shbrey in from Pigto and has Come to a Cap with the french and the Ingens and some of them Com Down with him to Conferme their Peace that they May have Liberty to Trade.'[17] Though further details are lacking, Proctor's observation, which was probably based on gossip circulating in the New England garrison, reminds us that the Mi'kmaq chiefs would have wanted to discuss the resumption of trade. Before 1758 most Mi'kmaq had obtained European goods such as cloth, kettles, powder, shot, and knives through trade – with the Acadians or with French merchants at Louisbourg – or through the annual presents the French king offered to each village.[18] France's defeat was now forcing the Mi'kmaq to develop new trading partners. As Proctor's diary entry shows, trade was discussed at the November meetings, though Whitmore would have tied any exchange of powder and shot to a guarantee of Mi'kmaq neutrality in the ongoing conflict with France.

Whatever was discussed between Whitmore and the seven Mi'kmaq delegates, an agreement was reached sometime in December 1759. No copy of this treaty has been found. Whitmore apparently did not forward a copy of it either to the War Department or to his immediate superior, Jeffrey Amherst, the commander-in-chief of British forces in North America.

Whitmore's purpose in holding talks with the Mi'kmaq was to ensure their neutrality in the ongoing conflict with France. Whatever his intentions, the effect of his actions was to complicate the treaty-making process. It is not known whether the governor of Nova Scotia, Charles Lawrence, was aware of Whitmore's discussions or of the 'manifest' given to Maillard in the name of 'Edward Whitmore, Governor of Cape Breton.' Nor is it known whether Whitmore's discussions centred on the issues that had been part of Schomberg's promises made to the Mi'kmaq on 26 October 1759. Nor is it known how these promises were interpreted. Schomberg's manifest had promised the Mi'kmaq they would 'enjoy all your possessions, your liberty, [and] property.' How did Maillard interpret these words to the Mi'kmaq? Did 'property' mean the lands they inhabited? Or did it mean the lands they used for hunting, fishing, and other activities associated with their family economy? It is possible that Jeannot Peguidalouet interpreted Schomberg's offer in reference to the 1726 treaty, in which similar issues had been addressed.

Considerably more is known about the discussions between the Nova Scotia Council and the Maliseet and Passamaquoddy. These discussions started late in November 1759, while Whitmore was meeting with Jeannot Peguidalouet. In contrast to those meetings, the council's discussions with the Maliseet – and later with the Mi'kmaq – resulted in the signing of a treaty that would later be sent to London. The text of this agreement does exist, and the treaty signed on 10 March with three Mi'kmaq villages would be based on very similar precepts. The importance of the discussions between the council and the Maliseet in February 1760 is that they suggest to us how the Mi'kmaq would understand their treaty relationship. We must take this approach because in general terms, the British did not keep the same detailed records regarding their negotiations with the Mi'kmaq as they did with the Maliseet.

Negotiations began soon after the fall of Quebec. On 12 and 13 November 1759, around thirty-five Maliseet and Passamaquoddy arrived at Fort Frederick at the mouth of the St John River.[19] The fall of Quebec had left the Maliseet and Passamaquoddy with few alternatives but to make peace with the British. As they were later to explain to the Jesuit missionary Father Charles Germain, 'they had done what they had done only inasmuch as they saw themselves as abandoned by the French, from whom they hoped for no further help, Quebec having been taken.'[20] Colonel Arbuthnott, the British commander of Fort Frederick, informed the council that 'some of the Chiefs of the St John Indians ... had taken the Oath of Allegiance to His Majesty and promised to live in Peace and Friendship.' On 30 November the council instructed Arbuthnott to encourage the 'Indians' to come to Halifax 'where they may be sure of having a favourable Reception, and an Opportunity of extending their trade, by the Establishment of Truckhouses amongst them, under such Regulations as shall be agreed upon.'[21] In early February of 1760 the Maliseet and Passamaquoddy delegates arrived in Halifax.[22]

Discussions began on 11 February and continued over the next several days. Representing the British were Governor Lawrence and members of the council. Michel Neptune and Bellamy Glode represented the Maliseet and Passamaquoddy. The talks focused on renewing the earlier treaties and negotiating new terms. The first order of business on 11 February was to establish that discussions would be based on the earlier treaties. After 'the articles of submission and agreement' of 1725 and 1749 were interpreted from English to Maliseet, Lawrence asked the delegates if they were ready to renew the treaty, 'to which they readily and fully expressed their Consent.' Lawrence then discussed three new articles. These articles would make the Maliseet and Passamaquoddy neutral in the ongoing conflict between Great Britain and France, would provide for the building of a truckhouse where the Maliseet might trade with the British, and would require that hostages be lodged with the British as security that the Maliseet would abide by the treaty.

The British were concerned mainly with securing political control over the region. The wars of the 1750s had demonstrated how tenuous their authority was there. Though they had succeeded in capturing the principal towns and fortresses of New France, their political influence was less than the physical presence of their troops would suggest. This was especially true outside the major towns and fortresses. Indeed, during the winter and spring of 1759–60, when Lawrence and the council were negotiating with the Maliseet, the British were far from certain that they now controlled the Gulf of St Lawrence. The British forces in Nova Scotia and Cape Breton were afraid: that Quebec would be retaken, that the British fleet would not arrive before the French one did, that the Mi'kmaq and Maliseet would unite with the Abenaki, Huron, and Houdenosaunee, and that they lacked the means to withstand any assault.[23]

Anxiety about the British forces camped at Quebec in the spring of 1760 is obvious in Proctor's diary. On 14 May 1760, while still stationed at Louisbourg, he wrote: 'This Day is warme and Pleasant and this Day arives hear a vessel from halafex and brings News that the french have Laid Seage to Quebeck and that It Is In Danger of Being tacon.' Fifteen days later, more gossip and rumours ripped through the garrison with the arrival of another vessel from 'Halafex': 'We hear that Quebeck Is Like to Be Tacon a Gain By the French and that the Garison Is Redused from ten thousand men to But three thousand.' But on 17 June the talk among the soldiers was more upbeat: 'This Is a fair Day arives in harbour this Day Sevarel Vessels Som From Boston and Som from Quebeck and I heard that the Englesh have Beet off the french and killd a Good many of them and that the Garison is But Eighteen hundred Stronge.'[24] And finally, two weeks later news arrived that the 'french are holdy Beat off.' Though Proctor was not as well informed of events along the St Lawrence Valley as was Whitmore, his comments suggest how nervous many British were in the late winter and early spring of 1760.

Anxiety for the future was one reason why the New Englanders manning Louisbourg and Fort Frederick talked of rebellion and desertion. By early May 1760, at least 160 soldiers at Fort Frederick had deserted and returned to their homes in New England.[25] Historians now know that the French had to end their siege of Quebec in mid-May after reinforcements failed to arrive from France; but this was not known by Proctor, by his fellow soldiers, by Whitmore, or by Lawrence until more than a month later. They did not know that the British were going to win, and their actions must be considered in that light.

Fear and anxiety over what the morrow would bring informed the agreement that Lawrence reached with the Maliseet in February 1760. For Lawrence, keeping the Maliseet neutral in the ongoing war with France was a tactical purpose of the negotiations. He pointed out to the two Maliseet delegates that at the time the earlier treaties had been signed, Great Britain had not been at war. But the situation in February 1760 was different, and so a provision was inserted into the treaty that guaranteed Maliseet and Passamaquoddy neutrality in the war.[26]

This measure, by itself, was not enough to create a lasting peace. The council now proposed that a truckhouse be built at Fort Frederick where both the Maliseet and the Passamaquoddy could trade their furs with the British. The proposal was similar to a clause in the 1752 treaty that had proposed building a truckhouse at Shubenacadie. The difference was that in 1760 the council was in a position to build this truckhouse, in part because it could defray the expense by imposing new duties on goods entering the colony.

On 13 February the council appointed Benjamin Gerrish to manage the trade with the 'Indians' and to immediately purchase whatever articles he deemed necessary.[27] The council also directed that the Maliseet be consulted on the prices for goods to be sold at the truckhouse. These prices, Richard Bulkley wrote in the council minutes for 14 February, were 'settled very much to their [the Maliseet's] Satisfaction; it being made to appear to them that they would be furnished upon much better Terms than they had ever been hitherto, and much cheaper than any private Trader could possibly furnish them.'[28]

In agreeing to build a truckhouse where the Maliseet could trade for better terms than they might get from private traders, the Nova Scotia Council was adopting a policy that had been pivotal to Massachusetts's relations with the Abenaki. Finding in the early 1690s that private trade was no longer profitable, the government had subsidized it. This ensured that the Abenaki would have continued access to English trade goods; it also discouraged them from trading with French merchants at Quebec, Montreal, and elsewhere. The attendant costs were high, but so were the benefits. On the positive side, trade encouraged personal relationships between individual New England truckhouse masters and neighbouring Abenaki villagers, which helped maintain peaceful relations between the two sides.[29] Also, truck masters were often invaluable sources of information. For example, throughout the 1720s, Massachusetts officials received a steady stream of letters regarding the Abenaki from John Gyles, the truck master at Fort St George.[30] Nova Scotia officials had basically the same reasons to build truckhouses as their counterparts in Massachusetts.[31] On the negative side, the costs of a truckhouse at Fort Frederick were potentially great, as the negotiated settlement included a British promise that the Maliseet would be able to buy goods at far better prices than they could elsewhere.

Because of the tenuous security of Nova Scotia, the council contended that trade should be regulated. It was already clear both in Nova Scotia and in other colonies that British traders sometimes cheated their clients, often by getting them drunk before setting prices.[32] To put an end to this, the council proposed that the trade be subject to government supervision. To be sure, it recognized that private traders might still trade with the Maliseet. But officials hoped that by offering fair prices to the Maliseet and Passamaquoddy, they would be hampering the development of private trade.

The Nova Scotia Council anticipated that the trade would involve the Maliseet – and later the Mi'kmaq – exchanging furs for European goods. This is evident from the price list provided to the council by Benjamin Gerrish on 16 February 1760. Gerrish's list used 'spring beaver' as the basic unit of exchange, which suggests that the most active trading would take place in the early spring, when hunters brought in those pelts for exchange. Spring beaver referred to beaver pelts that had been trapped during the winter. Beaver fur was thickest at this time of year and so more valuable than in other seasons. Though spring beaver was the fur exchanged most often, the British expected that other furs would also be traded. Gerrish's price list included values for otter, sable, martin, fisher, mink, bear, muskrat, and red and black fox, as well as for deer and moose skins.[33]

Though furs were the main item for exchange, other products were also to be traded. For instance, since the mid-1600s Mi'kmaq women had been exchanging leather purses called a 'peschipoty' with European traders.[34] Women also traded fish. The Reverend John Seccombe, an Englishmen living at Chester just south of Halifax, referred to such transactions in his diary in 1761. On 7 August 1761 he wrote: 'Two Indian Squaws brought in a Birch Conoe 5 Salmon & 80 Salmon Trout. One of the Salmon weigh'd 22 pound. One dozen of the Trouts weigh'd 14 pounds.' Later in the month he wrote: 'Two Indian Squaws brought seil skin & ells to sell.' And in late October, while sailing to Halifax, he noted: 'Two Indians came to ye side of ye vessel, wth Ducks & Pinguins on board.'[35] Purchasing food from neighbouring Mi'kmaq was likely a common practice both before and after 1760, with the Mi'kmaq trading fresh meat and fish for cloth, flour, and other items.[36] The agents appointed to run the truckhouses probably welcomed any fresh fish, meat, or berries that the Mi'kmaq brought to trade. Though there is no direct evidence of a trade in food from the truckhouse accounts, such exchanges were common at other British posts. Traders hunted and fished themselves, but they weren't always able to supply their own needs, especially during the spring, when the 'Indian trade' was busiest.[37] In sum, the Maliseet and Mi'kmaq traded a number of items at the truckhouses, though furs and skins predominated.

Though trade was the central issue discussed on 11 February, there was also talk about the British proposal that hostages be lodged as security. This proposal was not received well by the delegates, who, as Bulkeley noted in the council minutes, seemed 'to make some Hesitation.' Apparently their uneasiness was smoothed after Lawrence pointed out that before leaving for Halifax, the delegates had left their families near Fort Frederick, and that they had been 'desrious to have a piece of ground assigned them, near the said Fort for that purpose.' Admitting that this request had been made, the delegates 'expressed their Consent that an Article for the giving Hostages in the manner proposed should be inserted in the Treaty.' These passages suggest some ambiguity regarding how hostages would be lodged. Lawrence had intended for the Maliseet and Passamaquoddy to leave people with the British as a security in case hostilities resumed. The delegates were unwilling to do so. In the face of the delegates' recalcitrance, Lawrence suggested an alternative: the Maliseet and Passamaquoddy would leave some people encamped near the truckhouse at Fort Frederick. Lawrence's remarks, however, can be interpreted in two ways: Were hostages to be kept permanently at the fort? Or were they only to be lodged there when delegations were sent to Halifax? Certainly, the English text of the council minutes is ambiguous, and this ambiguity is more pronounced when the difficulties presented by language and culture are added to the mix.[38]

The treaty signed with the Maliseet and Passamaquoddy on 23 February 1760 reflected the issues discussed with Bellamy Glode and Michel Neptune earlier in the month. The final text provided more specifics as to where trade was to occur and the number of hostages to be kept at Fort Frederick. On the issue of trade, the treaty specified that the Maliseet and Passamaquoddy would only traffic, barter, and exchange their commodities 'with the Managers of such Truckhouses as shall be established for that purpose by His Majesty's Governors of this Province at Fort Frederick or elsewhere within the said Province and at no other place without permission from His Majesty's Government.' The treaty also addressed the question of hostages, specifying that 'not less than three from each of the aforesaid Tribes shall ... constantly reside in Fort Frederick or at such other Place or Places within the Province as shall be appointed for that purpose by His Majesty's Governor.'[39] Though a truckhouse was later built at Fort Frederick, there is no evidence that hostages were kept at the fort. The difference in how each of these articles was implemented after February 1760 shows that while both parties shared a common view of their trading arrangement, there was less common understanding of how the more contentious articles were to be interpreted.

Treaties with the Mi'kmaq were concluded in late February. Representing the Mi'kmaq were Michel Augustine from Richibucto, Paul Laurent from La Hève, and Claude Renée from Shubenacadie. It is probable that these three had been delegated by several villages to negotiate a peace. After all, the war between France and Great Britain had not ended, so each village would have been reluctant to send a delegate to Halifax. It was more than a coincidence that Augustine and Laurent represented villages from mainland Mi'kma'ki and from the coast of New Brunswick. A political separation between the eastern and western halves of Mi'kma'ki had been recognized by the French governor of Île Royale, who between 1719 and 1739 had met most of the mainland communities at Port Toulouse and the western communities at Malpec on Île Saint-Jean. It is likely that Michel Augustine had been delegated by the western villages and Laurent by villages farther to the east – a scenario similar to the process that had led to Laurent's appearance before the council in February 1755. Then, Laurent had set out with Argimeau, a chief from Chignecto, who had fallen ill and had been unable to continue to Halifax. Representation therefore from the Mi'kmaq community in March 1760 likely reflected a common intention among many villages to negotiate a peace with the British.

At a council meeting on 29 February 1760, the terms of the treaty concluded with the Maliseet and Passamaquoddy were read to the three Mi'kmaq delegates, and they 'expressed their satisfaction therewith, and declar'd that all the Tribe of the Micmacks would be glad to make peace upon the same Conditions.'[40] A final text was signed on 10 March. This treaty would later be ratified by six other villages: Pictou and Malagomich, Cape Breton, Chignecto, Shediac, Miramichi, and Pokemouche.[41] Other agreements were made with Cape Sable and Ristigouche, though there is no record as to whether these treaties were similar to to the ones made with other Mi'kmaq villages.[42]

The text of the treaty signed on 10 March and later with other Mi'kmaq villages was both similar to and different from the agreement made with the Passamaquoddy and Maliseet. There were three main similarities. First, the Mi'kmaq agreed not to have any contact with His Majesty's enemies; however, it added a new twist by stating that they would make known to the governor any ill-designs 'against His Majesty's Subjects.' Second, the Mi'kmaq agreed that they would not trade 'in any manner but with such persons or the managers of such Truckhouses as shall be appointed or Established by His Majesty's Governor.' Third, the treaty included a provision that each Mi'kmaq community would provide at least two 'prisoners,' who would live at the nearest English fort 'or at such other place ... as shall be appointed.'

Like the Maliseet treaty, the Mi'kmaq treaty through its 'truckhouse' clause established direct commercial links between the Mi'kmaq and the British. Though there had been sporadic trade between British merchants and the Mi'kmaq before 1760, the treaty formalized their trading relationship. The most important component of this trade clause was that the British would build truckhouses in areas convenient to Mi'kmaq families.

There were also differences between the treaty signed with the Maliseet and Passamaquoddy and the treaties made with the Mi'kmaq. The treaties made with the Mi'kmaq did not refer to the 1726 treaty. The Maliseet treaty included word for word the articles of 'agreement and submission' first signed in 1726 and renewed in 1749; the Mi'kmaq treaty did not. On the basis of this, it has been suggested that the British intended the 1760 treaties to be the beginning of a new relationship with the Mi'kmaq.[43] It would be wrong, however, to think so: the first six clauses of the 1760 treaty addressed the same issues as the first six clauses of the 1726 treaty, and in the same sequence. The differences between the two amounted to modifications, no more.

Consider, as an example, the fourth article of the 1726 treaty. This article had stipulated that 'the Indians shall not help to convey away any Souldiers belonging to his Majesty's forts, but on the contrary shall bring back any souldier they shall find endearvouring to run away.' In the 1760 treaty, this article was only slightly modified: 'That neither I nor my Tribe Shall in any manner entice any of His Said Majesty's troops or Soldiers to desert, nor in any manner assist in conveying them away, but on the contrary will do our utmost endeavours to bring them back to the company, Regiment, fort or garrison to which they shall belong.' Both articles centred on the responsibility of the Mi'kmaq toward soldiers stationed in Nova Scotia. The 1726 treaty had specified that the Mi'kmaq would not help British soldiers desert; the 1760 treaty added that the Mi'kmaq would not encourage soldiers to do so. The 1760 treaty specified that the Mi'kmaq would help the British return the soldiers to their regiment or fort; in contrast, the 1726 treaty only stated that the Mi'kmaq would return them. In this sense, the treaty was addressing changes that had taken place in Nova Scotia since 1726. In 1726 the British military presence had been confined to Annapolis Royal and Canso; by 1760, British forces were located at Annapolis Royal, Lunenburg, Fort Edward, Halifax, Fort Cumberland, and Louisbourg. In sum, the 1760 treaty was not the beginning of a new treaty relationship, but rather the continuation of one that had begun in 1726.

For the most part, the modifications found in the 1760 treaty did not alter the general tenor of the 1726 treaty. The exception to this was the second article, which discussed the creation of new settlements in Nova Scotia. By the second article of the 1726 treaty, the Mi'kmaq had promised 'not to molest His Majesty's Subjects or their Dependants in their Settlements already made or Lawfully to be made' In 1760, this clause was slightly modified: 'And I do promise for myself and my tribe, that I nor they shall molest any of His Majesty's Subjects or their dependant in their settlements as already made, or to be hereafter made or in carrying on their commerce, or in any thing whatever within this the Province of His said Majesty or elsewhere.'[44]

In 1760 the phrase 'to be hereafter made' replaced the 1726 phrase 'or lawfully to be made.' In earlier chapters I showed that the Mi'kmaq would have understood 'lawfully to be made' to mean that the British would consult them before building any new settlements. These consultations might involve the purchase of land or other arrangements. While it is plausible that Armstrong and Doucett either encouraged this interpretation or concurred with it, after 1749 the British understood 'lawfully to be made' differently. From Governor Cornwallis's perspective, 'lawful' meant however the 'law' was interpreted by British officials; it did not incorporate customary rights that had evolved in Massachusetts or Acadia before the New Englanders captured Port Royal. The phrase used in the 1760 treaty was more assertive, which suggests that some agreement had been made regarding how 'lawfully to be made' was to be interpreted.

Underlying this change in the treaty's wording was the British intention to bring more settlers to Nova Scotia.[45] As both Lawrence and the council saw it, the colony's future prosperity depended on attracting farmers to occupy the lands along the Bay of Fundy that had been empty since 1755, when the Acadians were expelled. This expulsion had damaged the colony's long-term economic prospects: only after the land had been put back into production could the colony grow its own food and could a viable internal market be created.[46] Sporadic conflict with the Mi'kmaq after 1755 had made resettlement difficult. In November 1757, Lawrence had reported to the Board of Trade that plans to settle fifty New England families in the Cape Sable area would have to be delayed till the following year, by which time he hoped the region would be more secure.[47] Much to Lawrence's disappointment, 1758 brought more bad news. In the spring and summer of 1758 several Lunenburg settlers were killed by the Mi'kmaq. In December, Lawrence remarked that the killing of an entire family there 'in so bloody and barbarous a fashion' had terrified the populace and driven three-quarters of them from their 'country lots, into the town for protection.' Lawrence despaired; raids like this would retard's the colony's resettlement even further and leave it unable to provide for itself.[48] For Lawrence the capture of Louisbourg and negotiations for peace with the Mi'kmaq and Maliseet had reopened the possibility that settlers could be attracted to the colony. But even after concluding an agreement with the Maliseet in late February 1760, he hesitated to allow immigrants to settle the outlying areas; perhaps he was fearful that troubles with the Mi'kmaq would be broadcast in the Boston newspapers.[49]

British officials acknowledged that they did not have the right to build settlements everywhere Nova Scotia. The 1760–1 treaties reflected an implicit expectation that the Mi'kmaq would continue to trade furs. Five truckhouses were being established under the assumption that Mi'kmaq families would hunt and fish as they had before 1760. These activities were not to be confined to one area, but were to encompass mainland Mi'kma'ki, Unimaki, and eastern New Brunswick. In signing the treaty with the Mi'kmaq, Lawrence and the council were not seeking to regulate where the Mi'kmaq could hunt; in fact, they expected the villagers to continue to use the lands that had historically been identified with family hunting groups.[50] Whether Lawrence understood the implications of the truckhouse clause is unclear, but the effect was to recognize the historical use of hunting territories by individual family groups. In other words, the treaty validated Mi'kmaq villages' own understanding of the customs governing hunting territories and fishing sites.

However, the treaty did not define the areas to be used by each village, nor did it refer to the promise that John Doucett made in the 1726 treaty regarding hunting and fishing rights. In 1726 the British had agreed not to interfere with Mi'kmaq fishing, hunting, and planting grounds, or with any other of the Mi'kmaq community's lawful activities. This article was not discussed in 1760, nor was it specifically renewed. Does this mean therefore that it no longer applied?

There are two reasons for thinking that both the Mi'kmaq and the British understood the promises made by Doucett in 1726 to be still valid. To be sure, the British view of treaty making is not always clear, especially since the Board of Trade at times exercised little direct influence over its colonial officials. At most, officials were counselled to maintain good rapport with the 'Indian tribes,' if only to ensure that the Secretary of State not have to request additional funds from Parliament. However, the board's view of treaty making is at least partly indicated by a legal opinion offered to them by James Marriott, an advocate-general, in February 1765.

The board had requested Marriott's opinion regarding the continuing validity of the Treaty of Neutrality signed between Great Britain and France in 1686. Between 1686 and 1765 the two nations had fought three separate wars, and the board wanted to know whether that treaty's commercial provisions were still in force even though some articles had not been specifically renewed in later treaties. Marriott's opinion was unequivocal: unless specifically abrogated or modified in later agreements, the 1686 treaty still applied.[51] This suggests that even though Great Britain and the Mi'kmaq had been at war between 1744 and 1760, and even though the 1726 treaty was not later specifically renewed, that treaty remained in force until specifically modified or abrogated.

The Mi'kmaq would have adopted a similar perspective, though for different reasons. Mi'kmaq history was remembered and passed down from generation to generation orally. The importance of the spoken word was apparent during the treaty ratification at Annapolis Royal in 1726, where the decision had been pointedly made that sons should be present with their fathers. The Mi'kmaq understanding of the treaty would have included both sides to the agreement, not just the side that British officials chose to renew.

If the reciprocal promises made by Doucett in 1726 had not been abrogated, how did these promises modify the phrase 'to be hereafter made'? Did the Mi'kmaq believe that future settlements would only be established in areas they themselves did not use? Probably. Is this how the British understood this phrase? Probably, with this rider: British officials understood little of the Mi'kmaq economy and even less about the lands where families hunted and fished.

But if there was ambiguity, it was because the treaty negotiators hardly discussed land issues. The question now at hand is why they didn't. From the Mi'kmaq perspective, the actual population of Nova Scotia in 1760 and 1761 was far less than what it had been in 1755. The British had forcibly expelled the Acadians, which left large tracts of land open for new settlers. Indeed, judging from the surveys completed by the colony's surveyor, Charles Morris, any new immigrants would be settling along the rivers flowing into the Bay of Fundy or along the Atlantic coast, and nowhere else. The new settlers who arrived in 1760 and 1761 did just that. By early January 1762, only 3,580 new English-speaking settlers had arrived.[52] It is probable that Mi'kmaq villagers no longer considered these lands central to their own survival. Thus, at least for the present, the British seemed far less threatening than they had been a decade earlier.

At the same time, British officials were reluctant to press the issue of new settlements, mainly because of their own financial interests. Perhaps the colony's gentry were making a deliberate decision not to rile the Mi'kmaq unnecessarily. For proof of this, we need only consider the dealings of four British officials: Jonathan Belcher, Michael Francklin, Isaac Deschamps, and Joshua Mauger. All four were members of the Nova Scotia Council. For these men, Nova Scotia was more than a place to trade in furs; it was also a place to trade in land. After all, wasn't land speculation something that all colonial gentlemen engaged in? Hadn't the French and Indian Wars been precipitated by the eagerness of colonial land companies to buy into the Ohio Valley? And hadn't those lands continued to attract the attention of prominent men like Patrick Henry, Thomas Jefferson, and George Washington?[53] Land speculation in Nova Scotia was the continuation of something that had begun much earlier. In the 1720s, British settlement in Nova Scotia had been only a remote possibility; by the 1760s, times had changed, and the possibilities were enticing. Thus, it is not surprising that men like Belcher, Deschamps, Francklin, and Mauger were granted large tracts of land.[54] Nor should it surprise us that in negotiating treaties with various Mi'kmaq communities in 1761, Lieutenant-Governor Belcher chose not to discuss in depth the issue of land. Better for him to say nothing at all than to say something that might unsettle his own financial affairs, and those of his friends.

Belcher's actions clearly reflected his social status. His grandfather was Andrew Belcher, a wealthy Massachusetts merchant. His father, also named Jonathan, had entered the family firm before becoming governor of Massachusetts (in 1729), and later of New Jersey (in 1747). The Belchers, like many of their class, speculated in land, including Abenaki lands. Jonathan Belcher of Nova Scotia was not his grandfather, nor was he his father; even so, none of his actions suggest that he had broken with his cultural and economic past. As much as the Mi'kmaq remembered their own past, so did Belcher remember his as he mingled with Nova Scotia's political and economic elite. Belcher and Paul Laurent inhabited different worlds, and to suggest otherwise is to believe that culture can be divorced from its historical past.

The 1760–1 treaties were negotiated at a time when the British presence in Nova Scotia seemed more permanent than ever before. The French had been defeated at Louisbourg and Quebec; also, most of the French-speaking Acadians had been forcibly removed, and New England farmers were beginning to settle the lands they had vacated. France's defeat created opportunity.

In negotiating the 1760–1 treaties, the British and Mi'kmaq were attempting to formalize a trading relationship. The benefits of this would be more than financial. Nova Scotia officials knew that by setting up truckhouses, they would be forging personal relationships with the Mi'kmaq, which would in turn help keep the peace and facilitate British settlement.

However, the 1760–1 treaties did not create clear boundaries between Mi'kmaq and British lands. The colonial authorities seemed untroubled by this. If we evaluate their understanding of the treaty by their actions, we must conclude that they believed they could establish settlements where the Acadians once lived. But there was also a more assertive quality to British land-granting policies in these years; there seemed to be less concern about disturbing the Mi'kmaq. After all, Halifax had been built in 1749, Lunenburg in 1753, and Fort Lawrence in 1750 without Mi'kmaq consent. As the British population of Nova Scotia grew during the late 1700s, less attention was paid to how new settlements might interfere with the Mi'kmaq.

The fact that the land issue was dodged during the treaty negotiations was also a reflection of the financial interests of the colony's economic and political elite. Nova Scotia in 1761 was no longer a garrison post. To be sure, the fishery had been attracting New England merchants since the 1660s, and the Acadians had been attracting Massachusetts traders since the 1630s. But the founding of Halifax, coupled with France's defeat, promised opportunities for trade and land speculation for men like Lawrence and Belcher. Nova Scotia offered merchants and political officials a means to enrich themselves in a way they never could in Massachusetts or Great Britain. Here was a land for the taking. In sum, by 1761, economic conditions in Nova Scotia had changed irrevocably.

But there were other likely reasons why land issues were not discussed. Perhaps land was not a point of controversy because of the Acadian expulsion; perhaps it was not because neither the Mi'kmaq nor the British thought that settlements would ever be built except along the region's main river systems. Such an informal agreement would have guaranteed the Mi'kmaq almost exclusive use of the interior. What possible use could these forested areas have for settlers interested in farming and fishing, who would never contemplate living too far from the coast or from a major river? But it is also likely that both British officials and the Mi'kmaq would have understood that villages would continue to fish along the colony's major river systems and in its lakes. Their fishing would not have precluded farming, provided that Mi'kmaq families could continue to travel through farming areas during the spring and autumn fishery. In 1761 this would have seemed a logical assumption for the Mi'kmaq to make. British fishermen were not interested in anadromous fish like salmon, or freshwater fish like trout; they were after the groundfish that swarmed off Nova Scotia's eastern coast.

However, two aspects of the treaties restricted – at least on paper – the unilateral right of the British to build new settlements: the expectation that the Mi'kmaq would continue to fish and to hunt and therefore to trade their wares at the truckhouses, and the promises made by John Doucett in the 1726 treaty that the British would not molest the Mi'kmaq in their 'Hunting, Fishing and Planting Grounds nor in any other their Lawfull Occasions.' That the Mi'kmaq continued to believe that these restrictions were part of their treaty relationship is suggested by their opposition to the creation of settlements after 1760 outside the areas that had been inhabited by the Acadians.[55] Just as in 1749, Mi'kmaq opposition was ignored by Nova Scotia officials, which tells us that the two sides understood this article of the treaty differently. The Mi'kmaq community would keep up a sporadic resistance over the following two centuries. Donald Marshall Jr's insistence that he had a right to fish for eels in Pomquet Harbour in August 1993, free from government interference, was no more than a modern manifestation of the deeply held belief in the Mi'kmaq community that somehow the treaties have been misinterpreted by later generations of Europeans.

PART FOUR
The 1726 Treaty in History and Law

On 27 June 1996, Mr Justice John D. Embree delivered his decision in *R. v. Donald Marshall Jr.* The decision filled forty-six typescript pages, with another nineteen pages of appendices.

Judge Embree first described the historical context in which the treaties had been signed. This included an extensive discussion of the French and English colonization of eastern North America, and of the events preceding the signing of the 1760 treaty. He emphasized that by 1760 the Mi'kmaq had become dependent on European trade goods, including guns and powder, and that they could no longer obtain these items from the French. Moreover, the British defeat of French forces in North America had given Great Britain more confidence 'than ever before in their strength of their position in Nova Scotia.' At the same time, according to Judge Embree, the British still felt uneasy: they 'wanted peace and a safe environment for their current and future settlers. Despite their recent victories, they did not feel completely secure in Nova Scotia.'

Judge Embree then outlined the significance of this analysis for understanding the 1760 treaty: 'It is my opinion that this combination of factors contributed greatly to the atmosphere in which the Treaties of 1760–1 were entered into. The Mi'kmaq had lost their major ally and supplier. Their ability to carry on effective hostilities against the British was substantially reduced. The Mi'kmaq would have perceived the British to be in a superior military position in the Province. At least as importantly, their justification for continuing hostilities against the British largely disappeared when the French departed. The Mi'kmaq also needed a new supplier of European goods and the British had become the primary potential source of those goods.'[1]

What did this mean in evaluating the treaty? On this point, Judge Embree was unequivocal: 'The British wanted their King to be King over all of the land and territory where the Mi'kmaq lived and beyond. The British expected that their King would be the King of everyone who lived in Nova Scotia. By 1760, the Mi'kmaq would have been under no misunderstanding about that.'[2]

Judge Embree added that the Mi'kmaq would have been perfectly capable of understanding British intentions, since they would have been able to converse in European languages: 'I am satisfied that the Mi'kmaq community had members who could communicate in French. So did the British. They could communicate directly with each other.'[3]

Moreover, the long time period during which the treaties were negotiated – from late November 1759 to June 1761 – would have ensured that no misunderstandings could occur: 'There was no misunderstanding or lack of agreement between the British and the Mi'kmaq about the essential ingredients of these treaties as they appear in written form before me.'

These statements helped frame the judge's decision. The question he needed to answer was this: What right, if any, had been conferred on the Mi'kmaq by the trade clause? Did the clause give the Mi'kmaq a right to fish and to sell fish? And was this right therefore protected by Canada's 1982 constitution?

According to Judge Embree, the trade clause gave the Mi'kmaq the right to engage in a commercial fishery. On this issue, he accepted the opinion of the three witnesses who had stated that fish would have been one of the items the Mi'kmaq would have traded at the truckhouse: 'It's my conclusion that the British would have wanted the Mi'kmaq to continue their hunting, fishing and gathering lifestyle. The British did not want the Mi'kmaq to become a long-term burden on the public treasury ... I am satisfied that this trade clause in the 1760–61 Treaties gave the Mi'kmaq the right to bring the products of their hunting, fishing and gathering to a truckhouse to trade.'

However, Judge Embree believed that the right to trade had disappeared with the demise of the truckhouses in 1762 and later the licensing of traders. Here, he adopted a literal interpretation of the trade clause, seeing it as a temporary measure the British resorted to in order to secure Mi'kmaq neutrality and friendship at a time when Great Britain was attempting to establish its suzerainty over the region. Once Mi'kmaq support was no longer needed, colonial officials rescinded trade regulations relating to the Mi'kmaq. After the early 1780s, the Mi'kmaq were treated like every other subject of the Crown.

As a result, Judge Embree found Donald Marshall Jr guilty: 'The Defendant has claimed that the 1760–61 Treaties provide him with a right to fish and sell fish as he was doing here. The Defendant bears the burden of establishing that. He has not met that burden. Rather, I have concluded that these treaties do not convey such a right. The legislative regime under which these charges are brought is applicable to the Defendant ... Based on the admitted facts, the Crown has established the guilt of the Defendant on all three charges beyond a reasonable doubt. I find the Defendant guilty as charged on all three counts.'[4]

Conclusion

On 25 June 1761 various British officials, 'principal inhabitants of Halifax,' and Mi'kmaq leaders assembled at Lieutenant-Governor Jonathan's Belcher's farm to formally ratify a treaty of peace and friendship. Present at the ceremony were many of Nova Scotia's most influential politicians and military officers. Representing the colony were Belcher and four members of his council: Richard Bulkley, John Collier, Joseph Gerrish, and Alexander Grant. Also present were Lord Alexander Colville, commander-in-chief of British naval forces in North America, Major-General John Bastide, the chief engineer in Nova Scotia, and Colonel William Forster, the commander of Nova Scotia's army regiments. These three men were accompanied by a detachment of soldiers. Each man in both groups was clothed in a manner befitting his status and position – Belcher and his fellow councellors in their finest linens, the three military officers in their most formal uniforms, and the soldiers in the red tunics that had become emblematic of the British Army.

There is much less information regarding the Mi'kmaq who were present. At least four 'chiefs' signed the treaty: Jeannot Peguidalouet from Cape Breton, Claude Atouach from Shediac, Joseph Sabecholouet from Miramichi, and Aikon Ashabuc from Pokemouche.[1] All four represented villages some distance from Halifax. Representatives from other villages were also present at the treaty signing,[2] but we don't know who they were or how many.

The Mi'kmaq were dressed much less elaborately than their British counterparts. Many Mi'kmaq wrapped themselves in woollen blankets and furs in the winter, but this was summer. Also present at the treaty signing was Pierre-Antoine Maillard, a French missionary who would interpret for both sides in the discussions. Abbé Maillard had arrived in North America in 1735 to work as a missionary among the Mi'kmaq. Having quickly learned their language, he had often been relied on to mediate relations between the Mi'kmaq and French colonial officials at Louisbourg. After the fall of Montreal in 1760, Maillard was wooed to Halifax by Nova Scotia officials to facilitate the signing of a peace agreement with the Mi'kmaq. Maillard played his part his well in the months and weeks leading up to the June signing, and would continue to do so in the coming months.[3]

The Mi'kmaq and British faced each other near a British flag. On one side stood Belcher, the counsellors, and the military officers, all of whom were probably sitting in chairs. Facing them were the four Mi'kmaq chiefs, who sat cross-legged on blankets or furs.[4] Between them was Abbé Maillard, whose role was critical, as he alone had the ability to convey to each side the meaning of the other's words.[5] As the English summary of the discussions demonstrates, it is possible that Maillard did more than translate – he may also have facilitated the treaty signing by subtlely changing the speakers' meanings.[6]

Belcher rose first to address those assembled.[7] Facing the Mi'kmaq chiefs, he stressed that by signing the treaty the Mi'kmaq were pledging their obedience to the British monarch, George III. In return, their Great Father the King promised to defend them, and to ensure that they would not be cheated by unscrupulous traders. Belcher also promised that the king would protect their religion and would not interfere with Catholic missionaries living among them: 'The Law will be like a great Hedge about your Rights and properties, if any break this Hedge to hurt and injure you, the great weight of the Laws will fall upon them and punish their Disobedience.' However, the Mi'kmaq, said Belcher, must also learn to respect the rights of His Majesty's other subjects: 'I must demand, that you Build a Wall to secure our Rights from being trodden by the Feet of your people.' Belcher then gave presents to each chief. These gifts likely consisted of red woolen tunics, laced shirts, hats, and special medals bearing the likeness of George III. These medals would be passed down from generation to generation as testimony to the words that bound their people to uphold the peace.[8]

Both Belcher and the chiefs then moved to the flag post, where Belcher picked up a hatchet that lay there. This hatchet, he said, will be buried and will never be raised against us but only against our common enemies. Then both he and the chiefs formally buried the hatchet. In doing so, they were agreeing to forget their past disputes. Belcher and the four chiefs then signed the treaty. Belcher signed as a representative of His Majesty George III, writing his full name at the bottom of the parchment. Each chief marked an 'X' beside his name. It is possible that some marked the treaty with an ideograph, but we can't be sure since an original copy of the treaty cannot be found. Finally, the bottom of the treaty was stamped with the seal of King George.

Jeannot Peguidalouet, a chief from Unimaki who had been appointed by the other Mi'kmaq to speak on their behalf, responded to the lieutenant-governor's offer of friendship. He emphasized that the British had demonstrated the goodness of their hearts through their actions, first by being merciful toward the Acadians, and second by their willingness to forgive the 'hostilities that have been committed by us against you and yours.' British generosity and kindness had inspired the Mi'kmaq to come to Halifax to sign the treaty: 'As long as the Sun and Moon shall endure, as long as the Earth on which I shall dwell shall exist in the same State you this day see it, so long will I be your friend and Ally, submitting myself to the Laws of your Government, faithful and obedient to the Crown.'[9]

Here, in the treaty signing at Belcher's farm, we encounter all the ambiguities that had come to characterize British–Mi'kmaq treaty making. And we also find concrete expressions of those ambiguities: pen, parchment, and a summary in English of the speeches by Belcher and Peguidalouet. Remarkably absent from this record is much detail about the Mi'kmaq. There is no mention of their belts of wampum, or of their language; nor is much said about the four chiefs. Indeed, the English summary of the treaty signing is strangely bereft of any information about the Mi'kmaq who were present. When the treaty was reduced to written alphabetic form, the meanings the Mi'kmaq attached to it were subsumed into the political culture of the British Empire.

Accounts of the treaty signing tell us nothing about Maillard's participation; this forces us now to *imagine* what really was said. How did Maillard translate Belcher's words that he had come to offer the Mi'kmaq 'friendship and protection' in the name of George III, 'Supreme Lord and proprietor of North America'? How did he translate that the Mi'kmaq must preserve the chain of friendship 'by fidelity and Obedience' to the king? We only know what English words Maillard used in translating Jeannot's words from Mi'kmaq. While much of Jeannot's speech is consistent with the metaphors he would have used to describe Mi'kmaq perceptions of the treaty-making process, other parts of his speech make it sound as if he and his brethren were a conquered people who wanted little except to be ruled by British law. According to Maillard's translation, the Mi'kmaq were so smitten by the benevolent actions of the British monarch that 'we have no longer a will of our own. His will is ours.'

Had the Mi'kmaq been so impressed with British might that they felt they had no choice but to accept British law? In signing the treaties, were the Mi'kmaq agreeing to become subjects of the British king and to abide by any laws passed by him and his government? Was the treaty Jeannot and his brethren signed on 25 June 1761 nothing less than a surrender, by a people who acknowledged that they had been conquered?

If all this was so, then why were the British bothering to treat with the Mi'kmaq? They hadn't with the Acadians; on the contrary, British soldiers had rounded up the recalcitrants and shipped them out of the colony. If the Mi'kmaq were such a menace to British efforts to colonize Nova Scotia, why wasn't a similar policy adopted toward them? Why didn't the British simply impose their sovereign's will on them? What need was there for this coddling? For this sham of a treaty in which the king offered friendship and protection?

This contradiction between the *act* of treaty making and the *language* of treaty making underlines the paradox of British–Mi'kmaq relations. Treaty making made the Mi'kmaq active participants in creating the laws that would govern their relations with British settlers. Yet the language of the treaties, which included references to the 'submission' of the Mi'kmaq to the British monarch, suggested that the Mi'kmaq community's right to exercise a will independent of the colonial polity was being contrained. This paradox reflects the difficulties that British policymakers faced when incorporating peoples that were neither Christian, nor English, nor agricultural into a political order that was all of these things. The Mi'kmaq were confronting a reverse conceptual problem: how could they incorporate a Christian, English, and agricultural people into Mi'kma'ki?

The world in 1761 was a far more complex place than it had been in 1600, or indeed in 1726. Societies that for the most part had been able to live separate from each other, could do so no longer, and were being forced to create a new political order that would make co-existence possible. In this sense, all of the British–Mi'kmaq treaties reflected a conscious decision by both parties to participate in the creation of a new political order. But at the same time, because the treaties were written in English, they marginalized Mi'kmaq agency; this itself suggests that the treaties were inherently one-sided. The 1760 treaty was written in English, not Mi'kmaq; it is this English copy of the treaty that has survived to the present, not the wampum belt that would have expressed the agreement as the Mi'kmaq understood it. This historical fact reminds us how hard it is in the present day for us to resolve the treaties' contradictions – that it silenced Mi'kmaq voices while simultaneously privileging those voices (by the fact that a treaty existed at all).

The British were prepared to negotiate a treaty with the Mi'kmaq because of the particular circumstances facing them in Nova Scotia after 1713. Great Britain had assumed dominion over Acadia with the Treaty of Utrecht, but it lacked the political and military power to control its newest acquisition. The first tentative efforts by Nova Scotia officials to control the new colony were rebuffed by the Mi'kmaq. The tensions between the two communities eventually developed into a regional conflict pitting the Mi'kmaq, Maliseet, Passamaquoddy, and Abenaki against the three northernmost British colonies, Massachusetts, New Hampshire, and Nova Scotia. Massachusetts wreaked havoc on Abenaki and Mi'kmaq villages but did not have the financial means to wage a war of annihilation against the region's aboriginal inhabitants. To secure Great Britain's interests while undermining the French–Wabanaki alliance, it was easier and cheaper to sign treaties with the Mi'kmaq and the Abenaki.

While negotiating a treaty with the Mi'kmaq in 1726, Nova Scotia officials confronted the customary rules of Mi'kmaq society as well as the customs that had governed French–Mi'kmaq relations. The 1726 treaty was a complex blend of three separate but interrelated legal and historical traditions: Mi'kmaq law, British law, and the customary law of French–Mi'kmaq relations.

Mi'kmaq law was integrated into the 1726 treaty in two important ways. First, in signing the treaty, the British were acknowledging that the Mi'kmaq constituted a political and legal entity that existed independent of the colonial and imperial order. Neither in 1726 nor afterwards did British officials attempt to regulate or interfere in the internal affairs of Mi'kmaq society. On the contrary, British officials acknowledged that Mi'kmaq society was governed by customs over which British colonial society did not exercise authority. Second, the text of the treaty recognized that the Mi'kmaq held proprietary rights over their fishing, hunting, and planting and over other activities associated with their migratory economy. In acknowledging that the Mi'kmaq exercised an exclusive right to their lands, the treaty was in effect placing restrictions on the right of British subjects to use or occupy lands in Nova Scotia.

Mi'kmaq land tenure, organized around the occupation of fishing and hunting territories, had thus become a part of the 1726 treaty.

The 1726 treaty also integrated aspects of the customary law that had governed French–Mi'kmaq relations in Acadia before 1713. For British officials, a key component of the treaty was that the Abenaki and Mi'kmaq were agreeing not to support France during French–British conflicts. The treaty accomplished this purpose by establishing a personal political alliance between the Mi'kmaq and the British monarch, George I. According to the 1726 treaty, this relationship was to be basically identical to the one between the Mi'kmaq and the French king. However, the British did not understand what this earlier relationship had actually meant for the Mi'kmaq, and this would provide a source of confusion.

The treaty also reflected the customary law that had come to govern Massachusetts's dealings with the Abenaki. It suggested that the British would build new settlements in Nova Scotia, but it did not specify a process for determining whether the lands to be settled were already being used by the Mi'kmaq. Nor did the treaty outline how the interests of both the Mi'kmaq and the British would be protected. By the Treaty of Utrecht, Great Britain had assumed dominion over Acadia. Whether or not Great Britain inherited title to Mi'kmaq lands in 1713, in acknowledging that the Mi'kmaq exercised an exclusionary right to use lands for their support, the British were agreeing that any future settlements they established in Nova Scotia would not interfere with the Mi'kmaq economy. To be sure, we lack any minutes of these discussions that might shed light on how both sides understood this issue. Nonetheless, it seems reasonable to suggest that the Mi'kmaq expected that the British would consult with them before building new settlements.

Finally, the 1726 treaty integrated aspects of British law. For instance, the Mi'kmaq agreed that when disputes arose between them and the king's subjects, they would not exact 'private revenge' but would allow these disputes to be resolved in accordance with British law. The Mi'kmaq also acknowledged Great Britain's jurisdiction over Annapolis Royal and other areas occupied by British subjects or by the Acadians; in effect, they were recognizing the legality of British settlements in mainland Mi'kma'ki.

The 1726 treaty was an attempt to resolve the contradictory historical and legal traditions in Nova Scotia; this would allow Great Britain to strengthen its economic and political claims to the region. To be sure, the terms of that agreement were not always understood in the same way by the two sides. These disagreements had as much to do with how each party understood the historical relationships outlined in the treaty, as it did with the cultural differences that limited comprehension. British officials would not have insisted on a literal reading of the treaty's terms, since they themselves exercised little authority over the region in 1726, and indeed, had only a limited interest in exploiting the region's resources.

The contradictions inherent the treaty's terms – both in the oral phrases that had framed its articles, and in the words that had been written on paper – became more evident after Cornwallis's fleet arrived in June 1749. Thereafter, Nova Scotia officials adopted a more literal reading of the treaty, one that emphasized the centrality of British law. This reading of the treaty focused on the English words written at the time the treaty was negotiated and signed. Usually, any oral discussions either in 1726 or afterwards that might clarify or refine the English text were not integrated into British interpretations.

In this way, the British simplified future understandings of the treaty by extracting the written treaty from the oral context in which it had been created, remembered, and later modified. Mi'kmaq perspectives became less important, though at first they were not ignored. In this sense, we can understand British interpretations of the 1726 treaty as part of an ongoing process of reinventing treaties in general to meet the legal requirements of the British Empire. Reinvention of the law was central to the British project of colonizing eastern North America; the written texts of past agreements with aboriginal nations were used to justify British expansionism and the eventual displacement of aboriginal communities. The past was constantly being reinvented. Whatever words the Mi'kmaq had spoken, they would no longer be heeded.

But British officials could not completely ignore the Mi'kmaq after 1749. Nova Scotia officials still faced the threat that the Mi'kmaq and Maliseet would align themselves with the French. This threat, and the financial costs of not developing the colony, prevented the British from pursuing a more aggressive policy toward the Mi'kmaq.

The conquest of New France in 1759 and 1760 afforded the British a rare opportunity to impose the terms of an agreement on the Mi'kmaq and their allies. The French had been vanquished: Louisbourg had fallen in 1758, Quebec in 1759, and Montreal the following June. That the British did not impose terms, but instead continued to employ the 1726 treaty as the basis of their relationship with both the Maliseet and the Mi'kmaq, suggests the importance that both parties placed on that document. However, the two sides' understandings of their relationship had changed since 1726. This was partly due to the ambiguous nature of the treaty-making process – a process that attempted to resolve the fundamental contradictions between a hunting and gathering society in which the spoken word was the principal means of communication and remembrance, and an expansionary trading nation that had reduced its laws to writing and planted them in a legal code intended to defend the economic interests of the country's political and economic elites. Colonial officials like Cornwallis, Lawrence, and Belcher understood this all too well.

For many decades afterwards, various Mi'kmaq communities would appeal to Crown officials, arguing that the British had violated the treaties. Significantly, these petitions did not refer to a specific treaty, nor did they provide the exact wording contained in the treaties' texts. Rather, the petitions spoke of a relationship that had been formed and contended that the king's words had been forgotten or misunderstood by his people in Nova Scotia. The 1794 petition addressed to Lieutenant-Governor John Wentworth spoke of a time when there was land enough for everyone, including the French and British, and explained that gradually all the land had been taken, so that there was no longer any place for the Mi'kmaq to hunt. In 1841 another petition, this one addressed to Queen Victoria, reflected a similar sense of betrayal and sadness: 'Indians poor – poor for ever. No Store – no Chest – no Clothes. All these Woods once ours. Our Fathers possessed them all. Now we cannot cut a Tree to warm our Wigwams in Winter, unless the White Man please. The Micmacs now receive no presents, but one small Blanket for a whole family.'[10] In 1853, another petition was sent to the queen, this time with the assistance of Silas Rand, a Baptist missionary who had begun working among the Mi'kmaq a few years before:

> We can neither disbelieve nor forget what we have heard from our fathers, that when peace was made between the Micmacs and the British, and the sword and the tomahawk were buried by mutual consent, by the terms of the treaty then entered into which was ratified by all the solemnities of an oath, it was stipulated that we should be left in the quiet and peaceable possession of far the greater portion of this Peninsula. May it please Her Majesty. The terms of that treaty have never been violated by the Indians, but the white man has not fulfilled his engagements.[11]

Silas Rand's account of how he had become involved in writing the peti-

Andrew Alex, *put'us*, with Mi'kmaq wampum belts, near Chapel Island, N.S., 1930.

tion is a telling commentary on the difficulties the Mi'kmaq faced in informing the queen of their understanding of their treaty relationship:

> It may not be amiss to furnish your readers with the history of the Indian Petition. It was drawn up by particular request and the substance of it was dictated by an Indian, and in his own tongue. They said: 'We have sometimes got a petition written. We have told some men what we wanted to say. Then he writes, then he reads it, and there are always some words in it of which we know not the meaning. For ought we can tell these words may mean something which altogether undoes the rest. Then we once sent a Petition to the Queen, but never heard from it.'[12]

Like the ones before it, the 1854 petition was not answered. Indeed, one might argue that in deciding to defend Donald Marshall Jr, the Mi'kmaq of Nova Scotia were just continuing something they had been doing for more than two hundred years.

On 17 September 1999, the Supreme Court of Canada issued its decision in *R. v. Donald John Marshall Jr.* Five Justices – Binnie, Cory, Lamer, Iacobucci, and L'Hereux-Dubé – overturned the decisions of the lower courts and dismissed the charges against Marshall. Two Justices, Gonthier and McLachlin, dissented from the majority.

Justice Binnie wrote the decision for the majority. He began by describing Donald Marshall Jr's actions in mid-August 1993 that had led to his prosecution, and then referred to a transaction between two Mi'kmaq women and Nova Scotia minister more than two centuries earlier:

> On an earlier August morning, some 235 years previously, the Reverend John Seccombe of Chester, Nova Scotia, a missionary and sometime dining companion of the Governor, noted with satisfaction in his diary, 'Two Indian squaws brought seal skins and eels to sell.' That transaction was apparently completed without arrest or other incident. The thread of continuity between these events, it seems, is that the Mi'kmaq people have sustained themselves in part by harvesting and trading fish (including eels) since Europeans first visited the coasts of what is now Nova Scotia in the 16th century. The appellant [referring to Donald Marshall Jr] says that they are entitled to continue to do so now by virtue of a treaty right agreed to by the British Crown in 1760. As noted by my colleague, Justice McLachlin, the appellant is guilty as charged unless his activities were protected by an existing Aboriginal or treaty right. No reliance was placed on any Aboriginal right; the appellant chooses to rest his case entirely on the Mi'kmaq treaties of 1760–61.[1]

Justice Binnie first summed up the principal disagreements between the defendant and the government: 'The trial judge ... accepted as applicable the terms of a treaty of Peace and Friendship signed on March 10, 1760 at Halifax. The parties disagree about the existence of alleged oral terms, as well as the implications of the "trade clause" written in that document.' From Justice Binnie's perspective, the problem was that the written text of the 1760 treaty did not sustain the appellant's argument that the defendant had 'the right to trade, but also the right to pursue traditional hunting, fishing, and gathering activities in support of that trade.' The question, according to Justice Binnie, was whether the written text incorporated all agreements made between the Mi'kmaq and the British.[2]

Justice Binnie discussed the trial judge's decision and pointed out the contradictory nature of that judgment. On the one hand, Judge Embree had acknowledged that the 1760 treaty had included the provision that the Mi'kmaq were to bring all their products, including fish, to trade at the truckhouse. However, the written text of the treaty did not make any mention of the items that the Mi'kmaq were to trade but only referred to 'commodities' to be exchanged with the British. But Judge Embree had also concluded that the text contained 'all the promises made and all the terms and conditions mutually agreed to.' In Justice Binnie's opinion, the trial judge either was wrong in concluding that the Mi'kmaq could trade fish at the truckhouse or was wrong that the written text of the treaty contained all the promises made by each party to the agreement.

Justice Binnie wrote that the treaty's text did not contain all the agreements made between the British and the Mi'kmaq, and chastised Judge Embree for saying otherwise: 'The trial judge's view that the treaty obligations are all found within the four corners of the March 10, 1760 document, albeit generously interpreted, *erred in law* by failing to give adequate weight to the concerns and perspective of the Mi'kmaq people, despite the recorded history of the negotiations, and by giving excessive weight to the concerns and perspective of the British, who held the pen' (emphasis added). In other words, when interpreting treaty texts courts were required to assess how both parties understood them. Since there were some records of the discussions that preceded the treaty's signing, the trial judge should have also taken into account these negotiations when rendering his decision. In the minds of five justices of the Supreme Court, Judge Embree had given 'undue weight to the March 10, 1760 document' and not enough weight to other historical documents that informed the written treaty text. In the view of Justice Binnie, courts had a legal obligation to uphold the honour of the Crown, which in this instance meant ensuring that equal weight be given to both British and Mi'kmaq perspectives of their agreement, for the purpose of arriving at their common intent.[3]

Justice Binnie then quoted from some of the documents providing insight into the discussions between the Mi'kmaq and the British prior to the signing of the first treaty on 10 March 1760. This included the discussions between the Maliseet and members of the Nova Scotia Council in February 1760, the 1759 correspondence between Captain Schomberg and a group of Mi'kmaq at Malogomish, and later discussions with Brigadier-General Whitmore.

For Justice Binnie, the key issue was the discussions in mid-February, when members of the Nova Scotia Council and the Maliseet and Passamaquoddy agreed to build a truckhouse at Fort Frederick. Since, this treaty later became the basis of the agreement made with the Mi'kmaq on 10 March 1760, Justice Binnie considered these discussions germane. He quoted directly from the minutes of the Nova Scotia Council on 11 February 1760. During the discussions, Governor Lawrence had asked the Maliseet delegates whether they had anything to propose, 'to which they replied that their Tribes had not directed them to propose anything further than there might be a Truckhouse established for the furnishing them with necessaries, in Exchange for their Peltry, and that it might, at present, be at Fort Frederick.' Subsequent passages from the same date suggest that these proposals were integrated into the written text of the treaty, though by implication rather than by including the language of the discussion in the treaty document.[4]

For Justice Binnie, this short passage was critical, for it suggested how the Maliseet and, by implication, the Mi'kmaq would have understood the trade clause. For both communities, the truckhouses provided an opportunity to trade furs, fish, and other items for 'necessaries.' It follows that the Mi'kmaq treaties conferred on the Mi'kmaq a right to continue to trade the fish they caught to obtain 'necessaries.' For Justice Binnie, however, the term 'necessaries' was the key.

Indeed, the meaning of 'necessaries' had been the subject of intense discussions between Bruce Wildsmith and the seven justices during the oral arguments on 5 November 1998. Before then, neither Wildsmith nor the justices had stressed the word's importance.[5] For Justice Binnie and four of his colleagues, 'necessaries' provided a way out of the historical and legal tangle that the case presented. On the one hand, the Court had few options other than to incorporate the oral discussions between the British and the Maliseet and Mi'kmaq into their understanding of the treaty. On this point, the historical documentation was clear. On the other hand, the justices did not want to make the politically dangerous decision that Marshall had an unlimited commercial right to fish. The word 'necessaries' provided them with a way to preserve the honour of the Crown but also to restrict Mr Marshall's treaty right. Necessaries, according to Justice Binnie, were those items which an individual would need in order to make a moderate livelihood. For the Court, Donald Marshall Jr was doing precisely that when he was arrested for fishing and selling fish without a licence.

The constitutional question was whether or not Marshall's treaty right to fish and to sell fish was accommodated within the fishery regulations under which he had been charged. For Justice Binnie, this right had not been accommodated, since the fisheries minister held absolute authority as to whether the appellant could exercise his right. One might argue, for instance, that having to buy a licence for thousands of dollars placed an unreasonable burden on the Mi'kmaq when they were catching fish to trade for 'necessaries,' and made it impossible for them to make a moderate living. To the Court, the minister's absolute authority limited Marshall's ability to make a moderate living by fishing, and therefore the federal fisheries legislation was an infringement of his treaty right. All charges against Marshall were dismissed.

Wildsmith, the lead counsel in the *Marshall* case, later said that the Court's decision helped clarify how to interpret treaty texts: 'One of the loose ends that had been left by earlier treaty cases is whether there needs to be some kind of ambiguity in the formal document itself before you can look at surrounding negotiations, discussions, and context. They clarified quite directly that there was no problem in the absence of ambiguity to look more broadly to see, for example, if all of the promises had been written into the text.'[6]

Wildsmith's comment that the *Marshall* decision had clarified how treaty texts should be interpreted stemmed from earlier decisions that had left judges and lawyers puzzled about how the Supreme Court viewed the relationship between written treaty texts and the extrinsic evidence that might be used to shed light on a treaty's meaning. This issue had first been raised in 1988 in the Supreme Court decision *R. v. Horse*, when Justice Estey stated that extrinsic evidence should only be used where the meaning of the agreement was unclear. Justice Estey said then that in matters involving 'contractual documents ... extrinsic evidence is not to be used in the absence of ambiguity, nor can it be involved where the result would be to alter the terms of a document by adding to or subtracting from the written agreement.'[7] In *R. v. Sioui*, two years later, Justice Lamer stressed that any interpretation of a treaty must 'choose from among the various possible interpretations of the common intention, the one which best reconciles the Hurons' interest and those of the conqueror,' but he did not explicitly reject Justice Estey's view.[8] Indeed, the lead prosecutor for the federal government in *Marshall*, Michael Paré, had noted in his written submission to Judge Embree in late February 1996 that Justice Estey's comments on the use of extrinsic evidence had been 'cited with approval in *Sioui*.'[9]

In *Marshall*, Justice Binnie stated that the Court had always held that extrinsic evidence should be consulted even 'in the absence of ambiguity.' This was not how the law had been interpreted by practising lawyers in the early 1990s, when Donald Marshall Jr was charged.[10] Indeed, quite the opposite. The point was repeatedly made in discussions between historians and lawyers that in the absence of ambiguity, the meaning of a treaty could not be altered by reference to other historical documents. The only solution to this was to argue that a particular word or phrase was 'ambiguous,' but there was no guarantee that any two justices would agree on whether a word had an ambiguous meaning. Judge Embree had been chastised by Justice Binnie for adopting a narrow interpretation of the 1760 treaty; yet if he had erred at all, it was in taking a conservative approach to the Supreme Court's guidelines for interpreting treaties.

A storm of controversy surged over the Supreme Court's decision in *Marshall.* The controversy was fuelled by the Department of Fisheries and Oceans' lack of preparedness.[11] Taking advantage of this, some Mi'kmaq fishermen began fishing lobster well before the next season's starting date. They were active in two areas: along the eastern coast of New Brunswick, and off the coast of Yarmouth in southwestern Nova Scotia. Their actions sparked an angry and at times violent response from non-Mi'kmaq fishermen. At Burnt Church, a reserve at the mouth of the Miramichi River in northeastern New Brunswick, non-native fishermen destroyed lobster pots that local Mi'kmaq fishermen had set and temporarily shut down a fish plant that had been buying lobster from the Mi'kmaq, wrecking some of the plant's equipment. Violence in the east coast fishery was front page news in both Atlantic Canada and other parts of the country; it was also the subject of national television news broadcasts. An overeager Mi'kmaq community and in injudicious decision by the Supreme Court of Canada were to blame for the violence, or so it seemed.[12]

Fears were raised in Canada's newspapers that the Supreme Court decision might have catastrophic consequences for other resource-based industries in the Maritimes. Kelly Toughill, writing for the *Toronto Star,* cited the opinion of unnamed lawyers who were 'already speculating that the ruling will entitle 20,000 Maritime natives to a hefty portion of New Brunswick's $4 billion timber industry and to Nova Scotia's mines. It also may spawn a new trade in wild game like moose which natives will be able to hunt without a licence at any time of the year.'[13] Later in the month, Robert Fife of the *National Post* wrote that the Court's decision 'is now being used by aboriginals across the nation to justify unregulated rights to cut timber and extract minerals on Crown lands.'[14]

Thomas Flanagan, a political scientist at the University of Calgary, fuelled these sentiments with a column in the *Globe and Mail* in early October. Extrinsic evidence, said Flanagan, could from now on be used to 'produce an interpretation contrary to the plain and simple meaning of the treaty's wording.' He went on to argue that the change in how the Court interpreted treaties should be a cause of concern for the Prairie provinces, as it suggested that aboriginal communities there would continue to possess resource rights. That eventuality, he warned, might well undermine economic development: 'Alberta, Saskatchewan and Manitoba had better get their legal ducks in a row if they expect to continue authorizing companies to run seismic lines, cut timber, and exploit mineral deposits. Otherwise, they could soon find themselves in the resource-development chaos now gripping British Columbia, where Indians are cutting timber on Crown land without license and the province seems unable to enforce the rule of law.'[15]

Some columnists and editors castigated the justices for their 'unreasonable' judgment. Editorial writers for the *Globe and Mail* disagreed with the Court's 'rewriting of history' and suggested that the four justices concurring with Justice Binnie's opinion had 'worked hard to justify the transformation of the Mi'kmaq's obligation to trade only with the British into a broad, explicit and preferential right to hunt, fish and gather game in Nova Scotia 239 years later.' This opinion, the paper declared, demonstrated the Court's 'illegitimate' use of its power: 'The spectre of the Supreme Court functioning illegitimately to create an unintended right based on vague and quasi-historical interpretations is certainly raised by this judgment. It is an example of the court's oversensitivity to the burdens of history, and its desire to assume and ameliorate them, whatever the specific language of a law, treaty, or even the Constitution itself.' *Globe* columnist Jeffrey Simpson was also unimpressed with the Court's decision, though he added that if anything, the reversal of two lower court rulings 'merely underscores how reasonable people can interpret differently historical facts and context.'[16]

Stephen Patterson then entered the fray, complaining that his opinions had been misinterpreted by Justice Binnie. Indeed, the cross-examination of Patterson by Wildsmith on 19 April 1995 had been cited at length by Justice Binnie to demonstrate that the Crown and defence witnesses agreed that the Mi'kmaq had a right to trade fish at the truckhouses established by the 1760–1 treaties.[17] However, Patterson told a reporter for the *National Post* that the Court had not given sufficient weight to his view that the Mi'kmaq also agreed to be subject to the 'laws of the Crown just like everybody else.' The *Post*'s Ottawa bureau chief, Robert Fife, quoted Patterson: 'The contextual evidence shows that the native and governing officials actually discussed this issue of law and the application of law and they were of one mind on the subject. The natives agreed that we are going to live under your laws and the British kept stressing that is what this is about ... All those things were put into words. It is not something you have to make up. You don't have to imply it. It is all there in black and white.'[18] Patterson's comments became the subject of subsequent newspaper columns and political inquiries. The Reform Party's Indian Affairs critic, Mike Scott, requested that the Supreme Court revisit its ruling based on Patterson's allegation that Justice Binnie had misinterpreted the historian's opinion.[19] Patterson's statements were also picked up by *Globe and Mail* columnist Jeffrey Simpson. Simpson seemed to suggest that if the Court had correctly interpreted Patterson's evidence – at least in the way that Patterson told them they should – it might have decided differently.[20]

It was in this context that the West Nova Fishermen's Coalition, an organization representing inshore fishermen in southwestern Nova Scotia, appealed to the Supreme Court to set aside its original decision and rehear the case. The coalition argued that an unregulated Mi'kmaq fishery constituted a threat to the lobster fishery and asked the Court to determine whether the Mi'kmaq community's commercial fishery should be restricted for conservation reasons.[21]

The Court issued a unanimous ruling on 17 November 1999 in the name of six of the seven justices who had heard *Marshall*: Binnie, Gonthier, Iocabacci, Lamer, L'Heureux-Dubé, and McLaughlin. Though Justice Cory had also heard the case, on 1 June 1999 he had retired (though his name appeared on any cases he had heard up until his retirement). When replying to the coalition's appeal, the justices also responded to the criticisms that politicians, media pundits, and fishermen had heaped on their September ruling, and to what they considered the overreaction of some aboriginal people, both in Atlantic Canada and across the country.

The Court restated that a commercial right had been affirmed by the 1760–1 treaties. However, it related only to 'hunting and fishing resources ... together with traditionally gathered things like wild fruit and berries.'[22] The Court squelched media reports and comments by the minister of Northern and Indian Affairs, Robert Nault, that the

17 September decision might be extended to include other natural resources such as timber and minerals.[23]

These rights were the result of treaties signed separately with local communities of Mi'kmaq, and therefore such rights were to be exercised locally. Indeed, the Court referred back to its original decision to expand this interpretation. In the 17 September decision, Justice Binnie had quoted the trial judge's finding that 'all the Mi'kmaq villages in Nova Scotia had entered into separate but similar treaties.' In its 17 November decision, the Court explained that by 'separate but similar treaties,' was meant that 'in the absence of a fresh agreement with the Crown, the exercise of the treaty rights will be limited to the area traditionally used by the local community with which the separate but similar treaty was made.' Moreover, these treaty rights were not individually held; rather, they had been conferred on the community that had signed the treaty. In other words, the commercial rights to fish and hunt and to gather traditional items like berries and fruit were communal.[24]

The Court also said that such rights could be restricted, and that this had been clearly stated in its original decision: 'The Mi'kmaq treaty right to participate in the large unregulated commercial fishery of 1760 has evolved into a treaty right to participate in the large regulated commercial fishery of the 1990s.'

The justices then suggested some ways that the government could regulate the Mi'kmaq fishery. The government could have introduced evidence in the *Marshall* trial that eels were an endangered species and that, therefore, according to the rules set out by the Supreme Court in *Sparrow*, his right to commercially harvest eels should be restricted. However, the Crown had chosen not to make this argument,[25] perhaps because at the time of the offence there was no evidence that eels were endangered. Indeed, this opinion was offered by D. Bruce Clarke for the Native Council of Nova Scotia, whose written statement to the court was quoted in the 17 November 1999 decision: 'Mr. Marshall was fishing for eels. There are no possible conservation issues involving the eel fishery. They are not an endangered species and there is no significant non-native commercial fishery. They are a traditional harvest species, being harvested by Marshall in a traditional method and in relatively small quantities. There is simply no justificatory evidence that the Crown could have led.'[26]

But the Court went beyond this to argue that the Mi'kmaq commercial right did not have to be 'satisfied before non-Natives have access to the same resources for recreation or commercial purposes. The emphasis in 1999, as in 1760, is on assuring the Mi'kmaq equitable access to identified resources for the purpose of earning a moderate living. In this respect, a treaty right differs from an Aboriginal right which in its origin, by definition, was exclusively exercised by Aboriginal people prior to contact with Europeans.'[27] This might justify limiting Mi'kmaq commercial rights: 'The Minister's authority extends to other compelling and substantial public objectives which may include economic and regional fairness, and recognition of the historical reliance upon, and participation in, the fishery by non-Aboriginal groups.'[28] Since such an intervention by the minister would constitute an infringement on a Mi'kmaq community's commercial rights, the Court stated that the Mi'kmaq must be consulted. If no agreement was possible between the government and the community, the matter would have to be resolved by the courts.[29]

The 'public' reaction to the Supreme Court's September ruling, and to its subsequent elaboration of its original decision, reminds us of the difficult political problems that the treaties pose. For the most part, these problems relate not to how history should be interpreted, but rather to how to integrate historical interpretations with the modern rights of an aboriginal population. Some commentators concluded that Justice Binnie and four of his colleagues had made up history to correct a contemporary social and economic problem. But as I have argued in this book, the history of treaty making in Atlantic Canada is far less straightforward, far less transparent, than we as a nation would like to think. To quote one television producer, 'it's complicated' and cannot be reduced to twenty-second sound bites. The words that are found in the treaties are historically constructed. They do not exist outside of history, and to think otherwise is to somehow believe that history itself does not exist and that we only live in the present and never in the past.

Marshall exemplifies the difficult political choices that federal and provincial governments face when considering how the rights of aboriginal people should be exercised in modern times.[30] The trial of Donald Marshall Jr focused exclusively on determining his commercial treaty right to fish. Since 1994, Mi'kmaq communities in Nova Scotia and New Brunswick have defended their members from government prosecution by arguing that they retain aboriginal title to the land in each province. In both *R. v. Bernard* before the New Brunswick Provincial Court and *R. v. Stephen Frederick Marshall*, et al. before the Nova Scotia Provincial Court, the question is whether Mi'kmaq communities in both provinces retain access to unsurrendered Crown lands, and what rights they can exercise on those lands. In both cases, Mi'kmaq loggers were cutting timber on provincial Crown lands without proper authorization. The courts will have to decide whether the Mi'kmaq of Atlantic Canada continue to hold an unextinguished claim to the land. If the courts decide they do, the next problem will be to determine which lands were not surrendered, which rights Mi'kmaq continue to exercise over unsurrendered lands, and what compensation should be made to them.

As in *R. v. Marshall*, Patterson, Reid, and I all testified. In both cases an aboriginal right was advanced by the defence, so a different approach was required than had been adopted in *Marshall*. For this reason, other expert witnesses were also called. In both cases, the defence also relied on the testimony of Stephen Augustine, an employee of the Canadian Museum of Civilization in Ottawa and a member of the Grand Council of Mi'kmaq. A fluent speaker of Mi'kmaq, Augustine testified regarding his oral understanding of his people's history and regarding the difficulties of translating into Mi'kmaq the English words used in the eighteenth-century treaties.

At the trial of Donald Marshall Jr, not one Mi'kmaq had testified. Why the change? Mainly because between the trial of Marshall Jr and the Bernard and S.F. Marshall trials, the Supreme Court of Canada had emphasized the importance of oral history introduced by aboriginal witnesses in determining issues relating to aboriginal rights. How much this testimony will influence trial judges' decisions, we will not know for some years to come.

There is no doubt in my mind that written documentation will continue to constitute the most important body of evidence in cases such as *Bernard* and *S.F. Marshall*. In *R. v. Donald Marshall Jr*, that documentation was absolutely key to the outcome of the case, and became the avenue for Wildsmith to argue for an expansive interpretation of the 1760 treaty. Had this documentation not been available, the case could not have been won. I would expect a similar scenario to unfold in later cases.

Though historians will provide important testimony at trials like this, it is important to recognize that the Supreme Court ruling did not accord with the evidence I gave at trial. To be sure, by accepting Wildsmith's argument it more or less validated the expansive interpretation of the 1760 treaty that I had advanced, as had Reid. But my position was that the British recognized the Mi'kmaq's unrestricted commercial right to fish. After all, the treaty was signed in 1760, not in 1999. It was absolutely clear in the 1760 treaty that the Mi'kmaq would fish, hunt, travel by canoe to anywhere they wished to go, and trade whatever they wished with anyone, except the French. The British did not wish otherwise, so long as the Mi'kmaq did not interfere with British settlers and their 'lawful' activities. And even if the British had wanted to restrict the movement of individual families, they did not have the military means to do so.

But the Supreme Court was never presented with this evidence. Neither Wildsmith nor Zscheile argued that the treaty provided the Mi'kmaq with an unrestricted right to fish and to sell fish. Had they done so, they would have lost the case. The Supreme Court in 1999 was not about to give the Mi'kmaq – or any other aboriginal community in Canada – an unrestricted right to engage in any commercial operation. Wildsmith's and Zscheile's clients – the Union of Nova Scotia Indians and the Confederacy of Mainland Micmacs – were well aware that any successful challenge to fisheries legislation would have to be based on a reasonable interpretation of the treaties. They understood that historical rights cannot be translated unadulterated into political rights.

This is why the word 'necessaries,' which had been used by the Maliseet in their discussions with British officials on 11 February 1760, became so important. None of the expert witnesses who testified in *Marshall* had devoted much time to this word and the possible interpretations that might be attached to it. Rather, as historians we were more concerned with explaining the broader historical events that preceded and antedated the treaty's signing.

But for Wildsmith and the Supreme Court, 'necessaries' was important because it addressed the political realities of the twentieth century. In other words, the justices were reinventing the law, much as British colonial officials had done in the 1700s. The justices gave a meaning to the word 'necessaries' because it coincided with what they considered to be the political and economic realities of the day.

The justices were wrong to believe that 'necessaries' provided them with a politically astute explanation – or at least, some media pundits, politicians, and common citizens disagreed with them. They therefore took the uncommon step of rewriting their decision, reinventing what they had just said instead of waiting to do so in a later court case. As Wildsmith has persuasively argued, they did so in a rather unusual fashion.

The Court's November clarification was unusual in two ways. First, Gonthier and McLaughlin, who had dissented from the majority in September, now joined in interpreting what the majority had said. Second, the Court went beyond the issues addressed in the West Nova Fishermen's Coalition motion. That motion had dealt with conservation issues, so the factums submitted to the court by the plaintiffs, respondents, and intervenors had focused on that issue. In their November ruling, however, the Court chose to address new political issues that had arisen since their September decision, including the rights of local communities whose livelihood was derived from the fishery without first asking lawyers for the federal government or for the Mi'kmaq. Was the Supreme Court acting legally when it chose to address new issues in its November ruling? Or are there no limits on them?

To be sure, the reinvention of the law ultimately resulted in vindication for Donald Marshall Jr. But the price that he and his people will pay for this victory is perhaps too high. The Mi'kmaq may have won in the courts, but they have lost in the court of public opinion. The images that were broadcast nightly over the television and blithely repeated in our national newspapers will not help the Mi'kmaq much in future political and legal battles with federal and provincial governments.

The problem is that the Mi'kmaq are a minority population. They do not exist independent of the Canadian economy, and their prosperity is inextricably bound to the economic and political health of the system from which they are seeking redress. This is different from their situation in the 1700s or even in the 1800s. Regardless of court decisions, Canadian society wields the ultimate power over the Mi'kmaq. Too often their only recourse has been history and the law, which working in tandem have at certain historical moments defended them against the colonial system that took away their land. If the law is to mean anything, it must always be seen to be operating impartially and applying its force equally to all Canadians. While the 17 September 1999 decision of the Supreme Court of Canada demonstrated this, the reinterpretation of the original decision in the wake of 'public' criticism showed that law is far less equitable in its application than the theory suggests. But of course Donald Marshall Jr already knows that, because that has been his, and his people's historical experience. After all, 'Marshall' in *R. v. Marshall* is the same Donald Marshall Jr who was imprisoned between 1971 and 1982 for a crime he never committed. [31]

Glossary of Names

Amherst, Jeffrey (1717–96). Commander-in-chief of British forces in North America, 1757–63.

Armstrong, Lawrence (1664–1739). Lieutenant-governor of Nova Scotia, 1725–39.

Augustine, Michel. Mi'kmaq sakamaw of Richibucto who signed the 10 March 1760 treaty.

Belcher, Jonathan [Snr] (1682–1757). Son of Andrew Belcher, governor of Massachusetts and New Hampshire, 1730–41, and governor of New Jersey, 1747–57.

Belcher, Jonathan (1710–76). Son of Jonathan Belcher, lieutenant-governor of Nova Scotia, 1760–63.

Biard, Pierre (1567–1622). French Jesuit priest who was in Mi'kma'ki from 1611 to 1613. His accounts of his time there are in the first three volumes of the *Jesuit Relations*.

Bourg, Abram. Acadian deputy of Annapolis Royal who translated the English text of the 1726 into Mi'kmaq.

Caulfeild, Thomas (1685–1717). Lieutenant-governor of the British garrison at Annapolis Royal, 1711–17.

Cope, Jean-Baptiste. Mi'kmaq sakamaw of Shubenacadie who signed the 1752 treaty.

Cornwallis, Edward (1713–76). Governor of Nova Scotia, April 1749 to October 1752.

Denys, Nicolas (1598–1688). French fur trader who lived in Mi'kma'ki from about 1635 to 1670. His book, *The Description and Natural History of the Coasts of America*, published in 1672, is considered to be a valuable source.

Doucett, John (??–1726). Lieutenant-governor of the British garrison at Annapolis Royal and captain of the Fortieth Regiment of Foot. Doucett signed the treaty of peace with the Mi'kmaq and Maliseet dated 4 June 1726.

Dummer, William (1677–1761). Lieutenant-governor of Massachusetts from 1716 to 1730. With the departure of Governor Shute for Great Britain in January 1723, Dummer became the acting governor, a position he continued to occupy until the arrival of Governor William Burnet in July 1728.

Gaulin, Antoine (1674–1740). French missionary who lived and worked among the Mi'kmaq from 1704 to 1732.

Halifax, Earl of, or George Montagu Dunk. President of the Board of Trade, 1749–63.

Hopson, Peregrine Thomas. Governor of Nova Scotia, 1752 to 1755.

Laurent, Paul. Mi'kmaq sakamaw of Mirligueche who negotiated with the British in February 1755 and who also signed the 10 March 1760 treaty.

Lawrence, Charles (1709–60). Lieutenant-governor of Nova Scotia, 1754–6, and governor, 1756–60.

LeClercq, Chréstien (1641– ??): French Recollet missionary who lived among the Mi'kmaq of Listiguj from 1676 to 1686. His account of his experiences, *New Relation of Gaspesia*, was published in France in 1691.

Le Loutre, Jean-Louis (1709–72). French priest and missionary who lived and worked among the Mi'kmaq between 1738 and 1755. Captured by the British while on board a French warship bound for France. Le Loutre was not released until August 1763.

Loron (aka Sugauaaram). Penobscot sakamaw who negotiated the terms of the 1725 treaty with Lt.-Gov. Dummer in November and December 1725.

Maillard, Pierre-Antoine (1710–62). French priest and missionary who worked and lived among the Mi'kmaq between 1735 and 1762. Translated the 25 June 1761 treaty.

Mascarene, Paul (1684–1760). British officer and administrator stationed at Annapolis Royal from 1710 to 1751. Mascarene was Nova Scotia's delegate at the negotiation of the 1725 treaty at Boston and at negotiations with the Penobscot and Maliseet in August 1751.

Peguidalouet, Jeannot. Mi'kmaq sakamaw of Unimaki who signed a treaty with Whitmore in December 1759 and with Lt.-Gov. Belcher in June 1761.

Phillips, Richard (1661–1750). Governor of Nova Scotia, 1717–49, but was only in the colony from 1720 to 1722 and 1729 to 1731.

Rale, Sébastien (1657–1724). French Jesuit priest who lived and worked among the Kennebec Abenaki from 1694–1724. Killed by a Massachusetts militia company in August 1724.

Robichaux Sr, Prudent. Acadian resident and deputy of Annapolis Royal who assisted in translating the 1726 treaty from English to Mi'kmaq.

Saint-Ovide, Joseph de (1676–1755). French governor of Île Royale, 1718–39.

Shute, Samuel (1662–1742). British governor of Massachusetts and New Hampshire, 1716–23.

Smith, Titus. Surveyor-general of Nova Scotia who made an extensive written account of his journey across the colony in 1801–02.

Speck, Frank. American anthropologist who taught at the University of Pennsylvania from 1907 and who did extensive interviews with Mi'kmaq residents of Atlantic Canada in the early twentieth century.

Vaudreuil, Philippe de Rigaud de (1643–1725). Governor-general of New France, 1703–25.

Vaudreuil, Pierre de Rigaud de (1698–1778). Governor-general of New France, 1755–63.

Wentworth, John (1671–1730). Lieutenant-governor of New Hampshire, 1717–1730. Following the departure of Governor Shute for England in January 1723, Wentworth became the acting governor of New Hampshire. With the lieutenant-governor of Massachusetts, he signed the December 1725 treaty with four Penboscot delegates.

Whitmore, Edward (1694–1761). British brigadier-general and governor of Cape Breton and Île Saint-Jean after the capture of Louisbourg in July 1758. He signed a peace treaty with a delegation of Mi'kmaq in December 1759.

Wiwurna. Kennebec Abenaki sakamaw who negotiated with Massachusetts officials before 1725.

Wolfe, James (1727–59). Army officer who commanded the British forces that took Québec in September 1759.

Xavier, François. One of four Penobscot Abenaki who negotiated the 1725 Boston treaty.

Glossary of Places

Annapolis Royal. Location of the British fort at the head of the Annapolis Basin in southwestern Nova Scotia. The fort is actually known as Fort Anne and the surrounding area Annapolis Royal.

Canada. French colony located along the St Lawrence River valley.

Fort Beauséjour. French fort built in 1750 on the west side of the Missiquash River. This river today acts as a rough boundary between the provinces of New Brunswick and Nova Scotia.

Fort Edward. British blockhouse overlooking the Avon River in central Nova Scotia. Today the site of the blockhouse is within the boundaries of the town of Windsor. The fort was built in 1751.

Fort Frederick. British fort built in 1758 at the mouth of the Saint John River. Today, the fort lies within the boundaries of the city of Saint John, New Brunswick.

Fort Lawrence. British fort built in 1750 on the east side of the Missiquash River opposite Fort Beauséjour.

Fortress Louisbourg. French fortress built on the northeastern coast of Île Royale. The fort's construction began in 1721 and was completed in 1744. Louisbourg was captured by British forces in July 1758 and was soon after razed. The fortress was reconstructed by the government of Canada during the 1960s and 1970s and is visited by thousands of tourists every summer. It is adjacent to the village of Louisbourg.

Halifax. British town established in June 1749 through a grant of Parliament. Present capital of Nova Scotia.

Île Royale. French colony encompassing the present-day borders of Cape Breton Island. The French occupied Île Royale after the signing of the Treaty of Utrecht in 1713.

Île Saint-Jean. French colony, now called Prince Edward Island. The colony remained under French control until the Treaty of Paris of 1763.

Kennebec River. Major river system flowing into the Gulf of Maine in western Maine. In the 1700s it was home to an Abenaki community.

Lunenberg. A town on the eastern coast of Nova Scotia about an hour's drive south of Halifax. The town was built in 1753 by a large contingent of German Protestants.

Mirligueche. The Mi'kmaq name given to Lunenberg. Before 1753 it was the location of a Mi'kmaq community.

New France. General name given to all areas over which France claimed sovereignty in mainland North America. French sovereignty over these areas ended in 1763 with the signing of the Treaty of Paris.

Norridgewalk. Abenaki village on the Kennebec River that is thought to have been located near the present-day town of Skowhegan, Maine.

Penobscot River. Major river system flowing into the Gulf of Maine in eastern Maine.

Port Royal. French fort located at the head of the Annapolis Basin in Acadia. French forces there surrendered to New England forces in September 1710. The British renamed the fort Fort Anne.

Port Toulouse. French fishing village located on the southeastern coast of Île Royale. It was here that a French garrison was stationed from the early 1720s.

St Croix River. River flowing into Passamaquoddy Bay in eastern New Brunswick. This river generally acts as a boundary between Maine and New Brunswick. In the 1700s it was home to the Passmaquoddy.

Saint John River. Major river sytem flowing the length of the province of New Brunswick and into the Bay of Fundy. In the 1700s it was home to the Maliseet.

Shubenacadie. Also spelled Chebenakady, Chichabenady. The location of a Mi'kmaq community from at least the 1720s, and the location of a Catholic mission from 1722.

Unimaki. Mi'kmaq word describing the territory occupied by Mi'kmaq inhabiting Cape Breton Island. Also includes southern Newfoundland.

Notes

CO 218   Colonial Office Series 218, Nova Scotia, Correspondence of Board
of Trade to Governor of Nova Scotia
WO 34   War Office
UNB University of New Brunswick, Fredericton, New Brunswick

Printed Sources

BRH   *Bulletin des recherches historiques*
CMNF   *Collection de manuscrits contenants Lettres, Mémoires et autres documents*
historiques relatifs à la Nouvelle-France, recueillis aux archives de la Province
de Québec ou copiés à l'étranger (Québec, Imprimerie D'A. Coté, 1883–
1885)
CNLR   *Canadian Native Law Reporter*
CSP   *Calendar of State Papers*, ed. Cecil Headlam (Vaduz: Kraus Reprint,
1964)
DCHNY   *Documents Relative to the Colonial History of the State of New York*, ed. E.B.
O'Callaghan (Albany: Weed Parsons, 1855–58)
DHSM   *Documentary History of the State of Maine*, ed. James P. Baxter (Portland:
Fred L. Tower Co., 1907–16).
JR   *Jesuit Relations and Allied Documents*, ed. Reuben Thwaites (Cleveland:
Burrows, 1896–1901).
NEGHR   *New England Genealogical and Historical Register*
PAC   *Public Archives of Canada Report*
RHAF   *Revue d'histoire de l'Amerique française*
SCR   Supreme Court Reports

Introduction

1 Canada, Province of Nova Scotia, Decision of Judge John D. Embree, *Her
Majesty the Queen versus Donald John Marshall, Jr.*, 27 June 1996, 1–3.
2 Canada, Province of Nova Scotia, *Her Majesty the Queen versus Donald Marshall,
Jr.*, transcripts, 21 November 1994, vol. 1, 1–10.
3 Department of Indian Affairs and Northern Development, *Indian Register
Population by Sex and Residence, 1997* (Ottawa, 1998), 2–3.
4 Bruce H. Wildsmith, Faculty of Law, Dalhousie University, personal commu-
nication, November 1998.
5 *R. v. Sparrow, CNLR* 3 (1990), 160–87; Thomas Isaac, 'Balancing Rights: The
Supreme Court of Canada, *R. v. Sparrow* and the Future of Aboriginal
Rights,' *Canadian Journal of Native Studies* 13, no. 2 (1993), 199–219; Diane
Newell, *The Tangled Webs of History* (Toronto, 1993), 174–9.

6 D. Bruce Clarke, 'Implementation of Aboriginal Fishing Rights,' in *An Introduction to Aboriginal Issues in Atlantic Canada* (Canadian Bar Association, 1994), 4–5; 'Department of Fisheries and Oceans Policy for the Management of Aboriginal Fishing,' 21 February 1993, in Clarke, *An Introduction*; Bruce H. Wildsmith, 'The Mi'kmaq and the Fishery: Beyond Food Requirements,' *Dalhousie Law Journal* 18, no. 1 (1995), 136–40.

7 This was the subject of a protracted argument between the Atlantic Region chiefs and DFO lawyers at an informal meeting in Dartmouth, Nova Scotia, in May 1993, at which I was present.

8 *R. v. Vanderpeet, CNLR* 4 (1993), 221.

9 'Constitution Act, 1982,' in Michael Asch, *Home and Native Land: Aboriginal Rights and the Canadian Constitution* (Toronto, 1984), Appendix A, 111.

10 Dara Culhane, *The Pleasure of the Crown: Anthropology, Law and First Nations* (Burnaby, 1998); Frank Cassidy, ed. *Aboriginal Title in British Columbia: Delgamuukw v. The Queen* (Montreal, 1992).

11 An attempt to analyse this discontent is Ken Coates, *The Marshall Decision and Native Rights* (Montreal, 2000).

12 PANS, RG 1/37 doc. 13 1/2, Charles Morris, 'A Description of the several towns in the Province of Nova Scotia,' in Belcher to the Board of Trade, 11 January 1762. The Mi'kmaq population is a rough estimate gathered from earlier census material, principally the 1708 census, which is found in the Newberry Library in Chicago, the William A. Ayers Collection.

13 Statistics Canada, 'Population and Dwelling Counts, for Census Divisions, 1991 and 1996 Censuses,' *A National Overview: Population and Dwelling Counts* (Ottawa, 1997), 52; Department of Indian Affairs and Northern Development, 'Region 2: Atlantic,' *Indian Register Population by Sex and Residence 1996* (Ottawa, 1997), 2–4.

14 This crisis is analysed in the Task Force on Incomes and Adjustment in the Atlantic Fishery, *Charting a New Course: Towards the Fishery of the Future* (Ottawa, 1993).

15 Rick Williams, 'When Is a Fish Not a Fish?' *New Maritimes* 12, no. 3 (1994), 29–33.

16 Michael Paré, 24 November 1994, in Canada, Province of Nova Scotia, *Her Majesty versus Donald John Marshall Junior*, transcripts, vol. 4, 627.

17 Honourable Judge John D. Embree, *Her Majesty the Queen versus Donald John Marshall Junior*, 27 June 1996; Nova Scotia Court of Appeal, *R. v. Marshall*, 26 March 1997, CNLR 3 (1997), 209–24.

18 *R. v. Marshall*, Stephen Patterson, cross-examination re. qualifications, transcripts, 21 November 1994, vol. 1, 107–12.

19 Stephen E. Patterson, 'Indian–White Relations in Nova Scotia, 1749–61: A Study in Political Interactions,' *Acadiensis*, 23, no. 1 (1993), 23–59; and, '1744–1763: Colonial Wars and Aboriginal Peoples,' in Phillip Buckner and John G. Reid, eds., *The Atlantic Region to Confederation: A History* (Toronto, 1994), 125–55.

20 Normally, the defence would have presented their evidence first, since the onus was on them to prove why Marshall should not be subject to federal legislation. In pretrial negotiations, however, the Crown agreed to present its case first. The difficulties this presented are outlined in Stephen Patterson, 'The Marshall Case: Treaty Rights and the Task of Blending History and Law,' Canadian Bar Association Conference on Aboriginal Law, Winnipeg, April 2000.

21 Reid's main published work on this topic at the time of the trial included *Acadia, Maine, and New Scotland: Marginal Colonies in the Seventeenth Century* (Toronto, 1981); and '1686–1720: Imperial Intrusions,' in *The Atlantic Region to Confederation*, 78–103.

22 William C. Wicken and John G. Reid, 'An Overview of the Eighteenth-Century Treaties Signed between the Mi'kmaq and Wuastukwiuk Peoples and the English Crown, 1725–1928,' Royal Commission on Aboriginal Peoples, 1993.

23 William C. Wicken, 'Encounters with Tall Sails and Tall Tales: Mi'kmaq Society, 1500–1760,' PhD dissertation, McGill University, 1994. At the time the trial began, my published work consisted of three articles,

24 These volumes contained both copies of the originals as well as typescript versions. Five volumes were provided to the defense well before the beginning of the trial. During Patterson's examination-in-chief in April 1995, he introduced an additional volume of materials, containing twelve documents. The Crown prosecutor, Michael Paré, was as much surprised by this addition as was the defence.

25 Judge Embree, '*Her Majesty the Queen Versus Donald Marshall, Jr.*' 1996.

26 The most notable example in Canada is *Delgamuukw v. R.* A number of books and articles explore the problems facing the court and the litigants, for instance, Frank Cassidy, ed., *Aboriginal Title in British Columbia: Delgamuukw v. the Queen* (Montreal, 1992); Dara Culhane, *The Pleasure of the Crown: Anthropology, Law and First Nations* (Vancouver, 1998); the articles by Julie Cruikshank, Robin Fisher, and Robin Riddington in a special issue of *B.C. Studies*, no. 95 (Autumn 1992); and Arthur J. Ray, 'Creating the Image of the Savage in Defence of the Crown: The Ethnohistorian in Court,' *Native Studies Review* 6, no. 2 (1990), 13–29. In the United States, the best known examination of these issues is Jack Campisi, *The Mashpee: Tribe on Trial* (Syracuse, 1991). The

trial was also analysed by James Clifford, *The Predicament of Culture: Twentieth-Century Ethnography, Literature and Art* (Cambridge, 1988), 277–346.

27 Jack Goody, *The Logic of Writing and Organization of Society* (New York, 1987), 124–5, 127–70.

28 Geoffrey Plank, *An Unsettled Conquest: The British Campaign against the Peoples of Acadia* (Philadelphia, 2001), 4.

1: The Mi'kmaq and Land

1 See for instance, the maps prepared by the Nova Scotia Museum for TARR in Shubenacadie. A cartographic summary of more than 200 archaeological sites in Nova Scotia is in Volume 1 of the defence exhibits for *R. v. Stephen Frederick Marshall, et al.*, Nova Scotia Provincial Court, Judge Patrick Curran, July–December 1999. BP stands for 'before the present.' In this case, before the present means before 1950, the date when radiocarbon dating was introduced.

2 See Stephen A. Davis, 'Early Societies: Sequences of Change,' in Phillip A. Buckner and John G. Reid, eds., *The Atlantic Region to Confederation: A History* (Toronto, 1994), 3–21.

3 Kevin James Malachy Leonard, 'Mi'kmaq Culture during the Late Woodland and Early Historic Periods,' PhD dissertation, University of Toronto, 1996, 33–6.

4 Ruth Holmes Whitehead, *Stories from the Six Worlds: Micmac Legends* (Halifax, 1988), 1; Stephen Augustine, Presentation to the Royal Commission on Aboriginal Peoples, 20 May 1992, Big Cove, New Brunswick.

5 Among many examples, Natalie Zemon Davis, *The Return of Martin Guerre* (Princeton 1983); Joy and Richard Buel, *The Way of Duty* (New York, 1985); Laurel Ulrich, *A Midwife's Tale* (New York, 1993).

6 See for instance, W.B. Stephens, 'Literacy in England, Scotland, and Wales, 1500–1900,' *History of Education Quarterly* 30, no. 4 (Winter 1990), 553–4.

7 A description of these divisions is in Frank Speck and Wendell Hadlock, 'A Report on Tribal Boundaries and Hunting Areas of the Malecite Indian of New Brunswick,' *American Anthropologist* 48 (1946), 362–3. Here I have made a clear distinction between the Maliseet and the Passamaquoddy peoples, the latter inhabiting lands contiguous to the St Croix River. As researchers and the historical records suggest, this cultural and political division may not have been as severe as my account indicates. See Edward Winslow, 'A Sketch of the Province of Nova Scotia and Chiefly of such parts as are settled,' W.O. Raymond, ed., *Collections of the New Brunswick Historical Society*, no. 5 (1899), 153; Vincent O. Erickson, 'Maliseet-Passamaquoddy,' in Bruce G. Trigger,

ed., *Handbook of North American Indians*, vol. 15: *The Northeast* (Washington, 1978), 123.

8 E.T. Adney to the editor, *Saint John Telegraph Journal*, 24 March 1939.

9 Refer also to the various historical and ethnographic descriptions of each of these societies in Trigger, ed., *Handbook of North American Indians*, vol. 15: *The Northeast* (Washington, 1978).

10 The following analysis relies on the work of Virginia Miller, 'The Micmac; A Maritime Woodland Group,' in R. Bruce Morrison and C. Roderick Wilson, eds., *Native Peoples: The Canadian Experience* (Toronto, 1986), 326–31; Patricia Nietfeld, 'Determinants of Aboriginal Micmac Political Organization,' PhD dissertation, University of New Mexico, 1981, 306–84.

11 PANS, RG1/7, doc. 7e, p.53, 'A Declaration of ye undermentioned Denis Godet and Bernard Godet Brothers Inhabitants at ye Top of the River of Annapolis Royal,' May 1714; RG 1/7, doc. 7f, p. 56, 'A declaraen and Journall of the Voyage of Peter Arceneau, Inhabitant at Beaubassin from said Place a Trading as farr as Cape Gaspe ye 23rd of May 1714 in a birch Canoe;' AN, AC, C11B 9:12v, Conseil de marine, 11 mars 1727.

12 Chicago, Newberry Library, William Ayers Collection, 1708 Census; Toby Morantz, *An Ethnohistoric Study of Eastern James Bay Cree Social Organization, 1700–1850* (Ottawa, 1983), 89.

13 On hunting groups, see Edward S. Rogers, *The Hunting Group: Hunting Territory Complex among the Mistassini Indians* (Ottawa, 1963), 27–68.

14 Newberry Collection, 1708 Census. In six cases this involved father/son relationships; in the other case it involved a widowed mother and her married son.

15 Denys, *Description and Natural History*, 130 and 349. In May 1604, Champlain reported seeing the stones on Seal Island completely covered with seals. See H.P. Biggar, ed., *The Works of Samuel de Champlain*, vol. 1 (Toronto, 1922), 243; Banfield, *Mammals of Canada*, 368–9; Biard, 'Relation of 1616,' *JR* 3:79.

16 AN, Archives de la Guerre, vol. 3393, M. de La Serelle à Raymond, avril 1753; PRO, CO 217/45, 'A General Return of the Several Townships in the Province of Nova Scotia, the First day of January, 1767'; NAC, MG 23 J6:133; S.W. Prenties, 'Narrative of a Shipwreck on the Island of Cape Breton in a Voyage from Quebec, 1780.'

17 PANS, MG 1 258:20–1 and 24–5, Isaac Deschamps Papers, 'Names of the Indians residing in about the district of Ford Edward with the number of their families, 20 Dec. 1763 and 24 Sept. 1767.'

18 The following analysis relies on David Burley, 'Protohistoric Ecological Effects of the Fur Trade on Micmac Culture,' *Ethnohistory* 28 (1981), 203–14; Virginia Miller, 'The Micmac: A Maritime Woodland Group,' in Morrison and Wilson,

eds., *Native Peoples*, 345; Nietfeld, 'Determinants of Aboriginal Micmac,' 372–7; Eleanor Leacock, 'The Montagnais "Hunting Territory" and the Fur Trade,' *Memoirs of the American Anthropological Association*, no. 78 (1954).

19 For instance, see Denys, *The Description and Natural History*, 173.

20 *Abstracts of English Shipping Records Relating to Massachusetts Ports* (Salem, 1931).

21 Archives départementelles, Charente Maritime–La Rochelle, serie B, vol. 272, Armirauté de Louisbourg, 33v–37r, NAC, MG 6.

22 D.B. Quinn, ed. 'The Voyage of Etienne Bellenger to the Maritimes in 1583,' *Canadian Historical Review* 63 (1962), 341–2; Marc Lescarbot, *History of New France* 3: 265, 268; 'Relation of 1647,' *JR*, 32: 43

23 Denys, *Description and Natural History*, 428–9.

24 Bruce Bourque, 'Evidence for Prehistoric Exchange on the Maritime Peninsula,' in Timothy G. Baugh and Jonathon E. Ericson, eds., *Prehistoric Exchange Systems in North America* (New York, 1994), 23–46; James Bradley, 'Native Exchange and European Trade: Cross-cultural Dynamics in the Sixteenth Century,' *Man in the Northeast* 33 (Spring 1987), 41.

25 Frank G. Speck, *Beothuk and Micmac* (New York, 1922), 83–106; 'The Family Hunting Band as the Basis of Algonkian Social Organization,' *American Anthropologist* 17 (1915), 189–205; and Loren C. Eiseley, 'Significance of Hunting Territory Systems of the Algonkian in Social Theory,' *American Anthropologist* 41 (1939), 269–80. A more extended analysis of Speck's work is Janet E. Chute, 'Frank G. Speck's Contribution to the Understanding of Mikmaq Land Use, Leadership and Land Management,' *Ethnohistory* 46, no. 3 (1999), 482–94.

26 Chrestien Le Clercq, *New Relation of Gaspesia, with the Customs and Religion of the Gaspesian Indians*, ed. William F. Ganong (Toronto, 1910), 237.

27 PANS, RG 1/380:116, Titus Smith, 'General Observations on the Northern Tour,' 1801.

28 Le Clercq, *New Relation*, 237.

29 PANS, RG 1/380:116–17, Smith, 'General Observations, 1801.

30 Robert R. Williams and Graham R. Daborn, 'Spawning of the American Shad in the Annapolis River, Nova Scotia,' and 'Spawning of the Striped Bass in the Annapolis River, Nova Scotia,' *Proceedings of the Nova Scotia Institute of Science*, 34 (1984), 12–13 and 17–21.

31 Ronald J. Nash and Frances L. Stewart, *Melanson: A Large Micmac Village in Kings County, Nova Scotia* (Halifax, 1990), 187–97.

32 'The Journal of Captain William Owen, R.N., during his Residence on Campobello in 1770–71,' in *Collections of the New Brunswick Society*, vol. 1 (Saint John 1894), 202–3.

33 Père Pacifique, 'Le pays des Micmacs – The Micmac Country,' *Bulletin de la société de géographie de Québec* (1930), 126–8.
34 Saint John, New Brunswick Museum, Ganong Scrapbooks, Indian Place Names of New Brunswick, Silas Rand to W.F. Ganong, 8 July 1886.
35 Pacifique, 'Le Pays,' 125, 127.
36 On the importance of place names in aboriginal societies, see Julie Cruikshank, 'Getting the Words Right: Perspectives on Naming and Places in Athapaskan Oral History,' *Arctic Anthropology* 27, no. 1 (1990), 52–65.
37 Richard Basso, '"Stalking with Stories": Names, Places, and Moral Narratives among the Western Apache,' in Stuart Plattner, ed., *Text, Play, and Story: The Construction and Reconstruction of Self and Society* (Washington, 1984), 19–55.
38 Virginia Miller, 'The Micmac: A Maritime Woodland Group,' 349; 'The first relation of Jaques Cartier of S. Malo,' in Edmund Goldsmid, ed., *The Principal Navigation, Voyages, and Discoveries of the English Nation Collected by Richard Hakluyt*, vol. 13, *America*, Part II (Edinburgh, 1889), 91.
39 Since the parents would in some way be related either through the mother or father, they would be parallel cousins and therefore not eligible to be marriage partners.
40 PANS, RG 1/24, Parish registers for St-Jean-Baptiste parish; Newberry Library, Ayers Collection, 1708 Census.

2: The Mi'kmaq Polity

1 PANS, RG 1/430, doc. 145, George Henry Monk to Lt.-Gov. Prevost, 23 April 1808.
2 Abbé Gaulin in 1722 recorded that Claude Couachinauil was chief of La Hève and that Joseph Pidoujacktek was chief of Chignecto. In the treaty, Antoine Egigish is identified as chief of La Heve, and Philip Erqimot as chief of Chignecto.
3 PANS, MG 1/258, Isaac Deschamps Papers, 20–1.
4 NAC, MG 9 B8, 1:19–21, 'Copie des Registres de l'état civil de differents endroits de l'Acadie et de la gaspesie 1680–1757'; PRO CO 217/5:3r, 1726 treaty; PANS, RG 1/188: 255.
5 PRO, CO 5/879:44v, 'At a Conference in His Council Chamber in Boston between His Excellency Jonathan Belcher ... and Arexes and Delegates of the Penobscot Tribe of Indians.'
6 PRO, CO 5/881:21r.
7 PANS, RG 1/186:215, Nova Scotia Council Minutes, 14 September 1752.
8 Virginia Miller, 'Social and Political Complexity on the East Coast: The

Micmac Case,' in Ronald Nash, ed., *The Evolution of Maritime Cultures on the Northeast and the Northwest Coasts of America* (Vancouver, 1983), 43.

9 See Susan C. Prezzano, 'Warfare, Women, and Households: The Development of Iroquois Culture,' in Cheryl Claassen and Rosemary A. Joyce, eds., *Women in Prehistory: North America and Mesoamerica* (Philadelphia, 1997), 98–9.

10 Karen Anderson, *Chain Her by One Foot: The Subjugation of Native Women in Seventeenth-Century New France* (New York, 1991), 127–8.

11 PANS, RG 1/26 'Register of Baptisms, Marriages and Burials at Annapolis Royal 1702–1728,' 242, 244. Though Pierre Pisnet is not explicitly noted as resident at Cape Sable, in the absence of a priest, their son François had been baptized soon after birth by Monsieur [Villat] 'habitant du cap de sable.' This would suggest that they were resident in the Cape Sable region. The Pisnet family also appears in the 1708 census as living at Cape Sable.

12 Jane F. Collier and Michelle Z. Rosaldo, 'Politics and Gender in Simple Societies,' in *Sexual Meanings: The Cultural Construction of Gender and Sexuality* (Cambridge, 1981), 289.

13 D. C. Harvey, ed., *Holland's Description of Cape Breton Island and Other Documents* (Halifax, 1935), 68.

14 AN, AC C11B 10:67v, Saint-Ovide au ministre, 3 novembre 1728; AC, C11B 14:11v, Conseil de la marine, 15 novembre 1732.

15 Upton, *Micmacs and Colonists*, 26–7.

16 Minutes of His Majesty's Council, 4 June 1726, in Archibald MacMechan, ed. *Original Minutes of His Majesty's Council at Annapolis Royal, 1720–1739* (Halifax, 1908), 115.

17 PANS, RG 1/26, 'Baptême de Marie, fille de Mathieu Mieux et de Marie Magdelaine, 18 juin 1726, 'Registres de baptèmes, mariages et sepultures pour la parroisse de Saint jean Baptiste à Annapolis Royal, 1722–1755.'

18 John Robinson, *A Journey through Nova Scotia Containing a Particular Account of the Country and Its Inhabitants* (York, 1774), 37.

19 Henry Grace, *The History of the Life and Sufferings of Henry Grace* (Reading, 1764), 15; Louis Chancels de Lagrange, 'L'isle royale en 1716,' *RHAF* 13 (1759–60), 432; 'The Journal of a Captive, 1745–1748,' in Isabel Calder, ed., *Colonial Captivities, Marches and Journals* (New York, 1935), 16.

20 See Bill Wicken, '26 August 1726: A Case Study in Mi'kmaq-New England Relations in the Early 18th Century,' *Acadiensis* 23, no. 1 (August 1993), 5–22. The quote is from *The Trials of Five Persons for Piracy, Felony and Robbery* (Boston, 1726), 23.

21 Montreal, Séminaire de Saint-Sulpice, série II, vol. 25, 'Copie d'une lettre circulaire écrite par la soeur Chauson ... 27 oct 1701,' NAC, MG 17, A-72 [transcripts].

22 Québec, Archives de l'archdiocese de Québec, Série 312 CN, Nouvelle Ecosse, vol. 1, abbé Thury, 'Les Indiens de l'Acadie,' [c. 1698].

23 Baptiste Tomus [column 3] and Jacques Penall [column 4]. Both might have a French origin.

24 Jacques DeMeulles, 'An Account of the Voyage of Monsieur de Meulles to Acadie,' in William I. Morse, ed. *Acadiensia Nova* 1 (London, 1935), 112.

25 Gamaliel Smethurst, *A Narrative of an Extraordinary Escape (1774); Journal du Voyage de M. Saint-Luc de la Corne* (Québec, 1863).

26 AN, AC, G1/411, Registres de île Saint-Jean, Baptême de Thomas, 29 juin 1722.

27 These were Port Royal, La Hève, Cap Sable, Chebenacadie, Minas, and Piziguit. The more northern villages were located at Unimaki, Antigoniche, and rivière Ste-Marie. At Port La Joye on Île Saint Jean, Mi'kmaq from the eastern coast of New Brunswick – Shediac, Richibucto and Miramichi – as well as from Île Saint Jean, Pictou, Tatamagouche, and Chignecto – met with the governor. AN, AC, C11B 18:3r, Conseil de la Marine, 20 octobre 1735; 20:85v–87v, Bourville au ministre, 16 octobre 1738.

28 Where the dates of the meetings are recorded, the month varies from June to July. AN, AC, C11B 5:340r, Conseil de la Marine, novembre 1721; AC, C11B 7:24r, Saint-Ovide au ministre, 24 novembre 1724.

29 AN, AC C11B 8:34r–34v, Saint-Ovide au ministre, 18 septembre 1726.

30 Saint-Ovide au ministre, 14 novembre 1732, in *CMNF* 3:163. In 1734 there were 250 Mi'kmaq gathered at Port La Joye when Saint-Ovide arrived. AN, AC, C11B 15:3v, Conseil de la Marine, 1 novembre 1734.

31 Saint-Ovide au ministre, 14 novembre 1732, *CMNF* 3:162.

32 AN, AC, C11B 15:142, Saint-Ovide au ministre, 1 novembre 1734.

33 'The Deposition of Walter McFarland,' 27 June 1737, in *Essex Institute Historical Collections* (1942), 175.

34 AN, AC C11B 11:254r–v, Saint-Ovide au ministre, 14 novembre 1732.

35 The geographical limits of these districts are outlined in Philip Bock, 'Micmac,' in Bruce Trigger, ed., *Handbook of North American Indians*, vol. 15 (Washington, 1978), 110.

36 For a biography of Rand, see Dorothy May Lovesey, *To Be a Pilgrim: A Biography of Silias Terius Rand, 1810–1889. Nineteenth Century Protestant Missionary to the Micmac* (Halifax, 1992).

37 Silas T. Rand, *A First Reading Book in the Micmac Language Comprising the Micmac Numerals, and the Names of the Different Kinds of Beasts, Birds, Fishes, Trees, &c. of the Maritime Provinces of Canada* (Halifax, 1875), 81–2.

38 Donald Marshall Sr, Alexander Denny, and Simon Marshall, 'The Covenant

Chain,' in Boyce Richardson, ed., *Drumbeat: Anger and Renewal in Indian Country* (Toronto, 1989), 75–6.

39 James (Sakej) Youngblood Henderson, 'First Nations Legal Inheritances in Canada: the Míkmaq Model,' *Manitoba Law Journal* 23, no. 1 (1996), 12–13; Miller, 'Social and Political Complexity,' 44–5.

40 Janet Chute, 'Ceremony, Social Revitalization and Change: Micmac Leadership and the Annual Festival of St. Anne,' in William Cowan, ed., *Papers of the 23rd Algonquian Conference* (Ottawa, 1992), 45; Nietfeld, 'Determinants of Aboriginal,' 473–5; Ralph Pastore, 'Aboriginal Peoples and European Contact,' in Phillip Buckner and John G. Reid, eds., *The Atlantic Region to Confederation* (Toronto, 1994), 35–7.

41 Patterson, 'Indian-White Relations,' 27.

42 Saint John, N.B., New Brunswick Museum, Ganong Scrapbooks, N.B. Place Names, Samuel Renous to W.B. Ganong, Newcastle 19 August 190[?].

43 David L. Schmidt and Murdeena Marshall, eds., *Mi'kmaq Hieroglyphic Prayers: Readings in North America's First Indigenous Script* (Halifax, 1995), 4.

44 David L. Schmidt, 'The Micmac Hieroglyphs: A Reassessment,' in William Cowan, ed., *Papers of the Twenty-Fourth Algonquian Conference* (Ottawa, 1993), 34; David L. Schmidt and B.A. Balcom 'The Reglements of 1739: A Note on Micmac Law and Literacy,' *Acadiensis* 23, no. 1 (Autumn 1993), 110–27.

45 Ruth Holmes Whitehead, 'A New Micmac Petroglyph Site,' *The Occasional* 13, no. 1 (1992), 10.

46 Julie Cruikshank, 'Getting the Words Right: Perspective on Naming and Places in Athapaskan Oral History,' *Arctic Anthropology* 27, no. 1 (1990), 52–5.

47 AN, AC C11B 8:34, Saint-Ovide au ministre 18 septembre 1726; 10:6v–7r, Conseil de marine, 1727; 10:67v–69r, Saint-Ovide au ministre, 3 novembre 1728.

48 Bruce J. Bourque, 'Evidence for Prehistoric Exchange on the Maritime Peninsula,' in Timothy G. Gaugh and Jonathan E. Ericson, eds., *Prehistoric Exchange Systems in North America* (New York and London, 1994), 34–5; James W. Bradley, 'Native Exchange and European Trade,' *Man in the Northeast* 33 (Spring 1987), 41. See for instance Raymond W. Wood, 'Plains Trade in Prehistoric and Protohistoric Intertribal Relations,' in W. Raymond Wood and Margot Liberty, eds., *Anthropology on the Great Plains* (Lincoln and London, 1980), 98–109.

49 Bruce J. Bourque, 'Ethnicity on the maritime Peninsula, 1600–1759,' *Ethnohistory* 36, no. 3 (1989), 273–4.

50 Bruce Bourque and Ruth Holmes Whitehead, 'Tarrentines and the Introduction of European Trade Goods in the Gulf of Maine,' *Ethnohistory* 32,

no. 4 (1985), 327–41; John Brereton, 'A Briefe and True Relation of the Discoverie of the North Part of Virginia, 1602,' in David B. Quinn and Alison M. Quinn, eds., *The English New England Voyages 1602–1608* (London, 1983), 144–5.

51 Reference to alliances between the Abenakis and Algonquin and Montagnais peoples is in 'Relation of 1652–53,' *JR* 40:195–209. Examples of Houdenosaunee attacks on the Abenaki is in H.P. Biggar, ed., *The Works of Samuel de Champlain*, vol. 5 (Toronto, 1933), 313; 'Relation of 1661–62,' *JR* 47:139–45; and Kenneth M. Morrison, 'The People of the Dawn: The Abnaki and Their Relations with New England and New France, 1600–1727,' PhD dissertation, University of Maine, 1975, 105–6. Mi'kmaq involvement in wars against the Houdenosaunee is in 'Relation of 1642–43,' *JR* 24:147.

52 On the Abenaki and Catholicism, see Kenneth M. Morrison, 'The Mythological Sources of Abenaki Catholicism: A Case Study of the Social History of Power,' *Religion* 11 (1981), 235–63.

53 John Clarence Webster, ed., *Acadia at the End of the Seventeenth Century: Letters, Journals and Memoirs of Joseph Robinau de Villebon* (Saint John, 1934), 99–108.

21 November 1994, Antigonish, Nova Scotia

1 *R. v. Donald John Marshall Jr.*, 21 November 1994, transcripts, vol. 1, 107.

2 Brian Underhill, '$500 m in Native Aid on Way,' *Halifax Chronicle-Herald*, 30 January 2001.

3 *R. v. Donald John Marshall Jr.*, 21 November 1994, transcripts, vol. 1, 36–202 Wildsmith's cross-examination took about two hours.

4 Bruce Wildsmith in *R. v. Donald John Marshall Jr.*, 22 November 1994, transcripts, vol. 2, 213.

5 Judge John D. Embree in *R. v. Donald John Marshall Jr.*, 22 November 1994, transcripts, vol. 2, 220–1.

6 Michael Paré in *R. v. Donald John Marshall Jr.*, 22 November 1994, transcripts, vol. 2, 233.

3: The Genesis of the 1726 Treaty

1 These lands are located within what is now the state of Maine.

2 Proceedings of the Portsmouth Conference, 13 and 14 July 1713, in *DHSM* 23:38–45, esp. 38; PRO, CO 5/931: doc. 10, 'Submission and Agreement of the Eastern Indians,' 13 July 1713. This latter document is in *R. v. Marshall*, Defence Documents, vol. 2: doc 37. It was provided to the court by John G. Reid. A printed copy of the treaty is in *Collections of the Maine Historical Society*, 1st series, 6 (Portland 1859), 250–62.

3 Sir Robert Chambers, *A Course of Lectures on the English Law Delivered at the University of Oxford 1767–1773*, ed. Thomas M. Curley, vol. 1 (Madison, 1986), 286; Yasuhide Kawashima, *Puritan Justice and the Indian* (Middleton, Conn., 1986), 50–3, 69–70; James Warren Springer, 'American Indians and the Law of Real Property in Colonial New England,' *The American Journal of Legal History* 30 (1986), 58.

4 'Treaty of Peace and Friendship between France and Great Britain signed at Utrecht 11 April 1713,' in Clive Parry, ed., *The Consolidated Treaty Series*, vol. 27 (New York, 1960), 35.

5 For an examination of these transactions, see Emerson W. Baker, '"A Scratch with a Bear's Paw": Anglo-Indian Land Deeds in Early Maine,' *Ethnohistory* 36, no. 3 (1989), 235–56.

6 PRO, CO 5/751:64v.

7 PRO, CO 5/931:89r.

8 Villebon au ministre, 27 octobre 1699, in John C. Webster, ed., *Acadia at the End of the 17th Century*, trans. Alice Webster (Saint John, 1934), 121; MSA 29, Report of Commissioners Tailer, Dudley and Stoddard, House of Representatives, 15 July 1720; Bégon to Maurepas, 1725 in *DCHNY* 9:944.

9 *A Conference of His Excellency the Governour, with the Sachems and Chief Men of the Eastern Indians, Georgetown, 9–12 August 1717* (Boston, 1717), 9.

10 AN, AC C11A 45:389v–90r, Conseil de la marine, juin 1723.

11 For instance, PRO, CO 5/868:195r–201r.

12 Willard to Dummer, 30 December 1723, in 'Letters of Col. Thomas Westbrook and others,' *New England Genealogical and Historical Register* 45 (January 1891), 29.

13 Major Joseph Hammond to Samuel Shute, 13 January 1719 in *DHSM* 9:443–5; 'At a Conference with the Chiefs & some others of the kenebeck Indians at Georgetown Novemr ye 25th 1720,' *DHSM* 23:106–7. The archival copy is in PRO, CO 5/869:103v–104r, Willard to Dummer, 30 December 1723; Rale to his nephew, 15 October 1722, *JR* 67: 103–5.

14 AN, AC C11B/5:341r–v, Conseil de la marine, novembre 1721.

15 Norridgewalk was the name given to their principal village. This village was at 'Old Point' on the Kennebec River near the mouth of the Sandy River. This location is just a few miles above the present-day site of Skowhegan. Harald E.L. Prins and Bruce J. Bourque, 'Norridgewock: Village Translocation on the New England-Acadian Frontier,' *Man in the Northeast* 33 (1987), 137–8.

16 'Eastern Indians Letter to the Governour (Governor Samuel Shute),' in *Maine Historical Society Quarterly* 13 (Winter 1974), 179. The manuscript copy of the letter is in PRO, CO 5/869:106r–107r. I thank John Reid for providing me with a manuscript copy of the letter from the PRO.

17 'Journal of the Rev. Joseph Baxter,' *NEGHR* 21 (1867), 58; for similar sentiments, see John Minot to William Dummer, 20 April 1725, 'Letters of Col.
   Thomas Westbrook,' *NEGHR* 46 (October 1892), 361–2.

18 Zach Trescott to Judge Dudley, 1 October 1722, in *DHSM* 10:156–7; Rale to
   his nephew, 15 October 1722, *JR* 67: 115–17

19 *New England Weekly Courant*, 12 February 1722. See also 'Memorial of Father
   Loyard: upon the present condition of the Abnaquis,' *JR* 67:123–5.

20 John Demos, *The Unredeemed Captive: A Family Story from Early America* (New
   York, 1994), 24.

21 For instance, John Minot to Stephen Minot, 4 October 1725, in *DHSM*
   10:344.

22 AN, AC, C11B 5:340–2, Conseil de la marine, novembre 1721.

23 PRO, CO 217/4:116–18, 'Journal of Hibbert Newton,' 16 June 1722; and
   CO 217/4:119, Journal of George Lapham, 26 June 1722; AN, AC C11B:
   6:22r, Conseil de la marine, septembre 1722.

24 *Boston Newsletter*, 25 June 1722.

25 PRO, CO 217/4:118, Doucett to Board of Trade, 29 June 1722.

26 Officially, Nova Scotia only declared war on 1 August 1722. The declaration
   is in the *New England Courant*, 7 January 1723. Some of the events of the war
   are referred to in the *Boston Newsletter*, 20 August, 3 September and 10 September 1722; the *New England Courant*, 20 August, 4 September, 10 September and 24 September 1722; and PANS, RG 1/7 doc. 30, Phillips to Board of
   Trade, 19 September 1722.

27 Figures on the Abenaki, Maliseet, and Passamaquoddy are from David L.
   Ghere, 'Myths and Methods in Abenaki Demography: Abenaki Population
   Recovery, 1725–1750,' *Ethnohistory* 44, no. 3 (1997), 527. Figures for the
   Mi'kmaq have been compiled by computing the 1722 census and adding
   approximate numbers of people from communities in present-day New
   Brunswick. These approximations have been done through reference to the
   1735 census of all Mi'kmaq communities. AN, AC, C11B 6:77r, 'Recensement
   des sauvages dans l'isle Royalle,' 27 décembre 1722; AN, AC G1466, doc. 71,
   'Recensement fait cette presente année,' 1735.

28 The figures for Massachusetts and New Hampshire have been taken from
   Jack P. Greene, *Pursuits of Happiness* (Chapel Hill and London, 1988),
   178–9.

29 Figures from Boston are from Carl Bridenbaugh, *Cities in the Wilderness: The
   First Century of Urban Life in America* (1938; reprint, Oxford, 1966), 303.

30 For instance, the *New England Courant*, 20, 27 August 1722, 9 September
   1723, 30 July 1724; AN, AC C11D 9:65r–v, 'Extrait des nouvelles de l'acadie
   raportée par le père félix missionaire Récollet de l'acadie,' 1724.

31 Fanny Hardy Eckstorm, *Old John Neptune and Other Maine Indian Shamans* (1945; reprint, Orono, 1980), 81.
32 'A Particular Account of Captain Johnson Harmon of His March and Action at Norridgewalk,' *Boston Newsletter,* 27 August 1724. Twenty-six scalps were taken, though Harmon said later that between thirty and forty people were killed. Westbrook to Dummer, 18 August 1724, in *NEHGR* (January 1892), 23.
33 Vaudreuil et Bégon au Conseil de la Marine, 17 octobre 1722, in *DCHNY* 9:911; Vaudreuil au ministre, 28 novembre 1724, in *DCHNY* 9:937–8.
34 *Boston Newsletter,* 11 March 1725; Thomas Westbrook to William Dummer, 23 March 1723, in *NEGHR,* 46 (1891), 31–2.
35 'A Memorial Relating to the Kennebeck Indians,' 8 September 1721, in *Collections of the Maine Historical Society,* 1st series, vol. 3 (Portland, 1853), 352.
36 For the earlier period, see, for instance, 'Meeting of the Selectmen,' 11 March 1700, *Boston Town Records 1660–1701* (Boston, 1881), 241; John Wentworth to Board of Trade, 27 March 1726, in *CSP* (1726–27), 39.
37 *Acts and Resolves Public and Private of the Province of Massachusetts,* vol. 10 (Boston: 1902), 146, 327, 355, 462, 466, 548, 551.
38 For instance, 'An Act to Encourage the Persecution of the Indian Enemy and Rebels,' 8 August 1722, in *Massachusetts Acts and Resolves,* vol. 2 (1715–42), 258–9.
39 MSA 123:298, Treasurer's accounts, 31 May 1724 to 31 May 1725. During this period, the assembly awarded an additional £1,500 to various individuals in payment for scalps and prisoners.
40 MSA 63:406–7, Petition of Nathaniel Norden and forty-four others to William Dummer, 31 May 1723. The 1724 petition is in MSA 63:408–9, John Waldron, Samuel Stacy, et al. to William Dummer and Council, 18 July 1724.
41 Marjory's commission is dated 10 August 1724 and is in 'Documents Relating to Marblehead,' *The Essex Institute Historical Collections* 62 (1926), 116–17; Copies of Marjory's correspondence are in MSA 38A:44–5, 15 August 1723; MSA 63:415–16, 18 December 1724. Other expenses related to protecting the fishery are in PRO, CO 5/784:59r, 66r–v, 68r, Massachusetts Council Minutes for 1722.
42 PRO, CO 217/4:293, 'List of all the Ships and Owners ...' 1724; CO 217/4:287, 'List of all the Ships and Owners ...' 1725.
43 For one example, see Laurel Ulrich, *Good Wives: Image and Reality in the Lives of Women in Northern New England, 1650–1750* (New York, 1982).
44 *New England Courant,* 30 July 1724.
45 The three newspapers were the *Boston Gazette, Boston Newsletter,* and *New England Courant.*
46 Willard to Kennedy, 4 December 1724, in 'Letters of Col. Thomas Westbrook

and others,' *NEGHR* 46 (April 1892), 142. A short first-hand account of the events surrounding the first exchanges leading up to the treaty is in Samuel Penhallow, *The History of the Wars of New-England with the Eastern Indians* (1726; reprint, New York, 1969), 115–19.

47 *Boston Newsletter,* 25 February 1725.

48 John Stoddard and John Wainwright to William Dummer, 28 June 1725, in 'Letters of Col. Thomas Westbrook and others,' in *NEGHR* 47 (April 1893), 161.

49 Dummer to Wentworth, 9 July 1725, in 'Letters of Col. Thomas Westbrook and others,' in *NEGHR* 47 (April 1893), 164.

50 Dummer to Westbrook, 31 July 1725, in 'Letters of Wesbrook,' *NEGHR* 47 (April 1893), 320.

51 It appears that at the conclusion of the discussions in late July 1725, the two Penobscot delegates were given a copy of the proposals made to them by Dummer. Afterwards, the proposals were read by French officials, including Governor de Vaudreuil. However, as Loron's letter deals with discussions that continue until July 1726, his letter could not have been written until after then.

52 Panaouamskeyen, 'Indian Explanation of the Treaty of Casco Bay, 1727,' in Colin Calloway, ed., *Dawnland Encounters: Indians and Europeans in Northern New England* (Hanover and London, 1991), 116. The same account is in *DCHNY* 9: 991–3.

53 Panaouamskeyen, 'Indian Explanation ... 1727,' 117.

54 David L. Ghere, 'Mistranslations and Misinformation: Diplomacy on the Maine Frontier, 1725 to 1755,' *American Indian Culture and Research Journal* 8, no. 4 (1984), 3–26.

55 Longueuil et Bégon au ministre, 31 octobre 1725, in *CMNF* 3: 125.

56 'Conference with the Delegates,' 12 November 1725, Boston, in *DHSM* 23:188.

57 Dummer to Armstrong, 16 August 1725, in 'Letters of Col. Thomas Westbrook and others,' *NEGHR* 47 (July 1893), 322–3.

4: The Languages of Communication

1 The issue of communication is discussed briefly in Andrea Bear Nicholas, 'Maliseet Aboriginal Rights and Mascarene's Treaty, Not Dummer's Treaty,' in William Cowan, ed., *Actes du dix-septième congres des Algonquinistes* (Ottawa, 1986), 225–6.

2 For a short explanation see D.G. Bell, 'Maritime Legal Institutions, 1710–1850,' *Manitoba Law Journal* 23, no. 1 (1996), 104–6.

3 PANS, RG 1/26:243–4, 260, 'Registres des baptêmes, mariages et sepultures de la paroisse de Saint-Jean Baptiste du Port Royal'; Minutes of His Majesty's Council, 22 May 1725, in Archibald MacMechan, ed., *Original Minutes of His Majesty's Council at Annapolis Royal, 1720–1739* (Halifax, 1900), 100.

4 See Naomi E.S. Griffiths, *The Contexts of Acadian History, 1686–1784* (Montreal and Kingston, 1992), 42–4.

5 Minutes of His Majesty's Council, 21 and 26 March 1726, in *Original Minutes of His Majesty's Council*, 110–11.

6 Minutes of His Majesty's Council, 20 April 1726, in *Original Minutes*, 111.

7 PRO, CO 5/870: 75r, 'The Conference with the Eastern Indians, at the Ratification of the Peace, held at Falmouth in Casco-Bay in July and August, 1726.'

8 Rale to his brother, 12 October 1723, in *JR* 67:187

9 'Conference with the Delegates,' 12 November 1725, in *DHSM* 23:188

10 William Commanda Odjigwano, 'Lecture et Interpretation de colliers et cordons de wampum,' in Régent G. Sioui, 'La grande loi du wampum: les chemin des Anishnabek' (Ottawa: Commission Royale sur les Peuples Autochthones, 1994), 4; William Johnson to Arthur Lee, 28 February 1771, in E.B. O'Callaghan, ed., *Documentary History of the State of New York*, vol. 4 (New York, 1851), 436.

11 Quoted in Paul Williams, *The Chain*, LLM thesis, Osgoode Hall Law School, York University, 1982, 92.

12 Jean-François Lafitau, *Customs of the American Indians Compared with the Customs of Primitive Times*, vol. 1, ed. William N. Fenton and Elizabeth L. Moore (Toronto, 1974), 310.

13 Edward Finegan, 'Style and Standardization in England, 1700–1900,' in Tim William Machan and Charles T. Scott, eds., *English in its Social Contexts: Essays in Historical Sociolinguistics* (New York, 1992), 122–5.

14 D.I. Bushnell, Jr, 'The Origin of Wampum,' *Journal of the Anthropological Institute of Great Britain and Ireland* 36 (1906), 173–7.

15 Frank G. Speck, 'The Eastern Algonkian Wabanaki Confederacy,' *American Anthropologist* 17 (1915), 498. Further explanations of the use of wampum among the eastern tribes is made in Speck, 'The Functions of Wampum among the Eastern Algonkian,' *Memoirs of the American Anthropological Association* 6 (1919), 3–74.

16 For a more extensive analysis of village locations, see Wicken, 'Encounters with Tall Sails,' 91–115.

17 PRO, CO 5/870:87v, July 1727, 'The Conference with the Eastern Indians,' John Gyles to William Dummer, 8 April 1727 in *DHSM* 10:376; PRO, CO 5/871:93r, David Dunbar to Board of Trade, 10 Dec. 1729.

18 'Extracts from the Journal of Captain William Pote, Jr., During his Captivity in the French and Indian Wars, 1745–1747,' *Collections of the New Brunswick Historical Society*, vol. 1 (1894), 266–7.

19 Anthony Casteel, 'Journal,' in 'Collection de documents inédits sur le Canada et l'Amérique,' *Canada-français* 3 (Québec, 1890), 117.

20 For a useful social constructivist view of literacy, see Peter Wogan, 'Perceptions of European Literacy in Early Contact Periods,' *Ethnohistory* 41, no. 3 (1994), 407–29.

21 Lois M. Feister, 'Linguistic Communication between the Dutch and Indians,' *Ethnohistory* 20, no. 1 (1973), 25–38; AN, AC C11C 7:6 'Mémoire,' 1710; Peter Bakker, 'Two Basque Loanwords in Micmac,' *International Journal of Linguistics* (1986), 258–61. See also Laurier Turgeon, 'Basque-Amerindian Trade in the Saint Lawrence during the Sixteenth Century: New Documents, New Perspectives,' *Man in the Northeast* 40 (1990), 81–7.

22 'Extracts from the Journal of Captain William Pote,' 266.

23 Gamaliel Smethurst, *A Narrative of an Extraordinary Escape out of the Hands of the Indians*, (London, 1774), 14. Eighty years later, New Brunswick's superintendent of Indian Affairs, Moses Perley, reported that the level of spoken French and English had not appreciably improved. 'Some of the Micmacs here speak a little broken French, but very few of them speak any English.' Moses Perley, 'Report on Indian Settlements,' 12 August 1841 in *Journal of the House of Assembly of New Brunswick 1842* (Fredericton, 1842), ci. During the winter of 1781, men shipwrecked on the northeastern coast of Cape Breton were rescued by a band of Mi'kmaq in the area. Samuel Prenties later wrote that 'one of them could speak a little broken French.' 'Ensign Prenties' Narrative, 1780,' in G.G. Campbell, ed., *Castaway on Cape Breton: Two Great Shipwreck Narratives* (Cape Breton, 1991), 45.

24 Luca Codignola, 'Competing Networks: Roman Catholic Ecclesiastics in French North America, 1610–58,' *Canadian Historical Review* 80, no. 4 (1999), 559, and see the valuable tables listing recorded ecclesiastics in Acadia and Canada from 1610 to 1658 on 570–84. These tables revise the data given in my own 'Encounters with Tall Sails,' 317–20. The 101 missionaries listed by Codignola include 62 Capucins, 19 Recollets, 19 Jesuits, and one secular priest.

25 Ignace de Paris. 'Brêve relation de la mission d'Acadie, 1656,' in *PAC Report 1904*, Appendix H (Ottawa, 1905), 337.

26 Wicken, 'Encounters with Tall Sails,' 309–38.

27 William C. Wicken, 'Re-examining Mi'kmaq–Acadian Relations, 1635–1755,' in Sylvie Dépatie, Catherine Desbarats, et al., eds., *Après vingt ans* (Montreal

and Kingston, 1998), 93–115; Micheline Dumont-Johnson, *Apôtres ou agitateurs* (Quebec 1970), 81–2. This distinction is not made by Geoffrey Plank, who trumpets the old theme of "common marriage." See Plank, *An Unsettled Conquest,* 72.

28 Wicken, 'Encounters with Tall Sails,' 244–55.

29 In a case before the vice-admiralty court in Boston in October 1726, Samuel Doty stated that at Mirligueche on the eastern coast of Nova Scotia he encountered one Jean-Baptiste Geudry [Jedre], who after boarding Doty's vessel called to his son on shoreline in 'a Language unknown' to Doty. I would interpret this to mean that Guedry spoke in Micmac, since Doty would have recognized spoken French. *The Trial of Five Persons for Piracy, Felony and Robbery,* (Boston, 1726), 8.

30 There are many examples. For instance, PRO, CO 5/870:73r–84r, 'The Conference with the Eastern Indians ... held at Falmouth in Casco-Bay in July and August 1726'; PRO, CO 5/870:85r–100r, 'The Conference with the Eastern Indians ... Held at Falmouth in Casco-Bay in July 1727.'

5: The 1726 Treaty and Utrecht

1 On the cession of Acadia, see Brian Slattery, 'The Land Rights of Indigenous Canadian Peoples, as Affected by the Crown's Acquisition of their Territories' (PhD dissertation, Oxford, 1979), 126–31.

2 PRO, CO 195/5:269, Board of Trade to St John.

3 Max Savelle, *The Origins of American Diplomacy: The International History of Angloamerica, 1492–1763* (New York, 1967), 135–48.

4 PRO, CO 218/1:42r, Samuel Vetch to Board of Trade, 19 January 1714.

5 Dale Miquelon, *New France 1701–1744: 'A Supplement to Europe'* (Toronto, 1987), 52. 95–100.

6 In fact, the French Crown's decision to exert a more forceful presence in North America dates to the beginning of the War of Spanish Succession. See W.J. Eccles, *Frontenac: The Courtier Governor* (Toronto, 1959), 336–7.

7 Sieur Malapart, *La Prise d'un Seigneur Escossais et de ses gens qui pillaient les navires pescherus de France ... par Monsieur Daniel de Dieppe, Capitaine* (Rouen, 1630), 10; Bernard Pothier, 'Nicolas Denys: The Chronology and Historiography of an Acadian Hero,' *Acadiensis* 1, no. 1 (1971), 59.

8 Miquelon points out that between 1715 and 1718, the favoured site was Port Dauphin on Baie Sainte-Anne, after which Louisbourg again found favour. Miquelon, *New France,* 111.

9 AN, AC C11D 5:47v, Bonaventure au ministre, 12 décembre 1704; AC, C11D

5:64v, Mémoire du Sieur Brouillan sur les affaires les plus importantes de l'Acadie,' 5 mars 1705.

10 Barbara Schmeisser, 'The Population of Louisbourg, 1713–1758' (Ottawa, 1976), 54; AN, AC, G1 466, doc. 77, 'Recensement générale.' 1742.

11 Miquelon, *New France*, 108–9, 111.

12 Bernard Pothier, 'Acadian Emigration to Île Royale after the Conquest of Acadia,' *Histoire Sociale* 6 (November 1970), 116–31.

13 AN, AC B, 34:363, le ministre à Vaudreuil et Bégon, 26 juin 1712.

14 AN, AC G1466, doc. 54, Recensement de l'isle Royale 1716; G1466, doc. 67, 'Recensement générale de l'isle Royale, 1724; G1466, doc. 77, 'Recensement générale,' 1742.

15 A.J.B. Johnston, 'The Fishermen of Eighteenth-Century Cape Breton: Numbers and Origins,' *Nova Scotia Historical Review* 9, no. 1 (1989), 63.

16 AN, AC G1466, doc. 36a, 'Dénombrement des peuples,' 1728; G1466 doc. 42, 'Recensement de l'île St. Jean,' 1735; G1466, doc. 77, 'Recensesment générale,' 1742.

17 For instance, PRO, CO 218/1:328–9, Petition of Alex Cairnes, James Douglas and Joshua Gee to King George I, 2 August 1717, and for the board's recommendation on the proposed grant, PRO, CO 218/1:199v–201v, Board of Trade to Lords of ye Committee for hearing appeals, 4 June 1719.

18 PRO, CO 218/1:219v–220r, His Majesty's Instructions to Colonel Richard Phillips, 19 June 1719.

19 AN, AC G1466, 'Recensement de l'Acadie de l'année 1703'; G1466, doc. 29, 'Recensement de l'Acadie de l'année 1737.'

20 Kenneth Lockridge, 'Land, Population and the Evolution of New England Society 1630–1790,' *Past and Present* 39 (April 1968), 69.

21 Examples of fishermen alleged to have been killed by the Mi'kmaq are in *Vital Records of Beverly, Massachusetts to the End of the Year 1849*, vol 2: *Marriages and Deaths* (Topsfield, Mass., 1906–7), 416; *Vital Records of Newbury*, vol. 2 (Salem, Mass., 1911), 520; *Vital Records of Gloucestor*, vol. 3 (Salem 1924), 127.

22 PRO, CO 217/3: 31r, Phillips to Board of Trade, 26 May 1720.

23 John Doucett to Secretary of State, 5 November 1717, in *A Calender of Two Letter-Books and One Commission-Book in the Possession of the Government of Nova Scotia, 1713–1741* (Halifax, 1900), 51–3. Geoffrey Plank, in *An Unsettled Conquest* (Philadelphia, 2001), 90–6, chronicles Phillips' efforts.

24 For instance, PRO, CO 218/1:111r, Board of Trade to James. Stanhope, [Secretary of State, Northern Department], 2 June 1715.

25 Marc Lescarbot, *History of New France*, ed. W.L. Grant, vol. 2 (Toronto, 1910), 362–3; AN, AC C11D 1:180r–v, 'Lettres patentes pour la confirmation de l'établissement de la pêche sedentaire de l'Acadie 1682.' On the post-

Utrecht period, PRO, CO 217/2:188r–188v, Cyprian Southack to John Doucett, 9 Jan 1718; PRO, CO 217/2:283, Memorial of James Pitt, et al., to Samuel Shute [Gov. of Massachusetts], 9 June 1718.

26 Donald F. Chard, 'Canso, 1710–1721: Focal Point of New England–Cape Breton Rivalry,' *Collections of the Nova Scotia Historical Society* 39 (1977), 64–6.

27 PRO, CO 218/2:7r, Board of Trade to Lord Carteret. Sec. of State (SD), 25 May 1722.; PRO, 217/2:256r–v, Philippe Riguad de Vaudreuil to John Doucett, 22 September 1718.

28 PRO, CO 218/2:12r–v, Board of Trade to Lord Carteret, 26 September 1722.

29 PRO, CO 217/2:275r, Deposition of John Henshaw, 30 October 1718.

30 Anonymous, Letter from Canso, 29 August 1720, in *Boston Newsletter* 19 September 1720. Other accounts of the incident are in PRO, CO 217/3:128r–145r.

31 *Boston Newsletter,* 22 August 1720

32 PANS, RG 1/15:8, Caufeild to Vaudreuil, 7 May 1714; PRO, CO 217/2: 2(I), 'Extract of a Letter from David Jeffries to Robt Meares, 6 July 1715; CO 217/ 4: no. 18(xii), Deposition of John Alden, 14 September 1720.

33 'Etat des munitions et marchandises ... 1693,' *CMNF* 2:129–30; AN, AC C11B 15:196r, Wicken, 'Encounters with Tall Sails,' Table 7.2, 402.

34 Catherine M. Desbarats, 'The Cost of Early Canada's Native Alliances: Reality and Scarcity's Rhetoric,' *William and Mary Quarterly,* 3rd series, 52, no. 4 (1995), 629.

35 AN, AC C11B 1:343v–344r, Conseil de marine, mars 1716.

36 Anonymous, Letter from Annapolis Royal, *Boston Newsletter,* 19 March 1711.

37 MSA, 38A:15, 'A Journall of a Voyage to Cape Britton on ye Kings Account by Mr. Peter Capon ... 1715.'

38 J. Murray Beck, *Politics of Nova Scotia,* vol. 1, *Nicholson–Fielding 1710–1896* (Tantallon, N.S., 1985), 8.

39 The regiment was formed in 1718 from the independent companies then stationed at Plancentia and Annapolis Royal. Harry Piers, 'The Fortieth Regiment, Raised at Annapolis Royal in 1717; and Five Regiments Subsequently Raised in Nova Scotia,' *Collections of the Nova Scotia Historical Society* 21 (Halifax, 1927), 116–17.

40 PRO, CO 217/2:194r–v, John Doucett to the Board of Trade, 10 February 1718.

41 PRO, CO 217/2:237v, John Doucett to Richard Phillips, [rec'd 24 March 1719]; PRO, CO 218/1:195v, Doucett to Phillips, 29 April 1719.

42 PANS, RG 1/16, Board of Trade to Richard Phillips, 21 July 1720; PANS, RG 1/18, Phillips, 16 August 1721 and Phillips to Board of Trade, 19 September 1722.

43 See for instance, PRO, CO 218/3:71r–72v, Dunk Halifax to the Duke of Bedford, 27 July 1749.

44 My thanks to Robert Sweeny of Memorial University for pointing out the significance of this phrase.

45 'The Submission and Agreement of the Delegates of the Eastern Indians' [Abenaki] in Peter A. Cummings and Neil H. Mickenberg, eds., *Native Rights in Canada*, 2nd ed. (Toronto, 1972), 330. A manuscript copy is in PRO, CO 5/898:175r–176r, 15 December 1725.

46 *Oxford English Language Dictionary*, 3124.

47 For a discussion of the king's relationship with his subjects, see Mark Kishlansky, *A Monarchy Transformed: Britain 1603–1714* (London, 1996), 34–64.

48 Sir Edward Coke, Calvin's Case, *English Reports* 77, 382; Chambers, *Lectures on the English Law*, 268–71.

49 PANS, RG 1/15:43–44, Thomas Caulfeild to Board of Trade, 1 November 1715.

50 CO 5/862, no. 85(ii), Massachusetts Council and Assembly to William III, 9 August 1701.

51 PRO, CO 217/6:227v–29r, Armstrong to Acadian Deputies at Minas, 5 August 1732; PRO, RG 1/14, Lawrence Armstrong to Chief of Cape Sable, 7 May 1736.

52 Calvin's Case, *English Reports* 77, 397

53 Mark D. Walters, 'Mohegan Indians v. Connecticut (1705–1773) and the Legal Status of Aboriginal Customary Laws and Government in British North America,' *Osgoode Hall Law Journal* 33, no. 4 (1995), 793–5.

54 Anthony Pagden, *Lords of All the World: Ideologies of Empire in Spain, Britain and France c. 1500–c. 1800* (New Haven and London, 1995), 19–23.

55 Governor Shute to Sébastien Rale, 21 February 1718, in *Collections of the Massachusetts Historical Society for the Year 1798* (Boston, 1798), 116.

56 PRO, CO 5/751:64r, 'The Submission and Agreement of the Eastern Indians,' 11 August 1693.

57 Jack P. Greene, *Pursuits of Happiness* (Chapel Hill, 1988), Table 8.1, 178–9.

58 Generally, the issue of the French–Algonquian alliance is treated at length in Richard White, *The Middle Ground: Indians, Empires, and Republics in the Great Lakes Region, 1650–1815* (Cambridge, 1991).

59 Cornelius Jaenen, *Friend and Foe: Aspects of French–Amerindian Cultural Contact in the Sixteenth and Seventeenth Centuries* (Toronto, 1976), 160–1.

60 On the New England pandemic of 1616–22, Timothy L. Bratton, 'The Identity of the New England Indian Epidemic of 1616–19,' *Bulletin of the History of Medicine* 62, no. 3 (1988), 351–83; Arthur E. Speiss and Bruce D. Speiss, 'New

England Pandemic of 1616–1622: Cause and Archaeological Implication,' *Man in the Northeast* 34 (1987), 71–83.

61 On the native populations, see Kathleen J. Bragdon, *Native People of Southern New England 1500–1670* (Norman, 1996).

62 The wars of the seventeenth century are documented in Francis Jennings, *The Invasion of America: Indians, Colonialism and the Cant of Conquest* (Chapel Hill 1975); and purchase of lands in Pagden, *Lords of All the World*, 76–86.

63 Olive Patricia Dickason, 'Amerindians between French and English in Nova Scotia, 1713–1763,' *American Indian Culture and Research Journal* 10 (1986), 33.

64 This point is made regarding the Abenaki and Jesuits in Kenneth M. Morrison, 'Towards a History of Intimate Encounters: Algonkian Folklore, Jesuit Missionaries, and Kiwakwe, the Cannibal Giant,' *American Indian Culture and Research Journal* 3, no. 4 (1979), 51–80.

6: Establishing Laws, Establishing Relationships

1 'General Census of the Country of Acadie, 1687–1688 (Gargas), in *Acadiensia Nova (1598–1779)*, vol. 1 (London, 1935), 154, 156–8.

2 'Conference with the Delegates,' 26 November 1725, in *DHSM* 23:202.

3 This is similar to the interpretation of John Foster regarding how the Cree of northern Saskatchewan would have interpreted 'settlement' by Europeans. This view was offered at trial in *R. v. Badger*. See the Supreme Court of Canada's summation of Foster's evidence, Justice P. Cory, *CNLR* 2 (1996), 96–7.

4 Mark D. Walters, 'Mohegan Indians v. Connecticut (1705–1773) and the Legal Status of Aboriginal Customary laws and Government in British North America,' *Osgoode Hall Law Journal* 33, no. 4 (1995), 803–5.

5 Rev. John Bulkley, 'An Inquiry into the Right of the Aboriginal Natives to the Lands in America, and the titles Derived from Them,' 24 December 1724, in *Collections of the Massachusetts Historical Society*, First Series, 4 (Boston, 1795), 159–81.

6 *Collections of the Connecticut Historical Society V: The Talcott Papers* (Hartford, 1896), 53.

7 Daniel Horsmanden's Opinion on the Mohegan Case, 26 October 1743, in *Collections of the Connecticut Historical Society XI: The Law Papers*, vol. 1, October 1741–July 1745 (Hartford, 1907), 156.

8 Rale au Vaudreuil, 9 septembre 1713, *BRH* 37 (1931), 290 [author's translation].

9 Anonymous, 29 August 1720 in *Boston Newsletter*, 19 September 1720.

10 'General Census of the Country of Acadia 1687–88,' 149; NAC, NMC, 107535, Cyprian Southack [1720–34]; NAC, NMC, 000471, 'Plan de la baye de Chedabouctou aujourd'hui Havre de Milfort,' 1744.

11 PRO, CO 217/4: no. 18 (xii), Deposition of John Alden, 14 September 1720. The general context of British-Mi'kmaq relations in 1720 is in L.F.S. Upton, *Micmacs and Colonists: Indian–White Relations in the Maritimes, 1713–1867* (Vancouver, 1979), 38–42.

12 Archibald MacMechan, ed., *Minutes of Her Majesty's Council, 1720–1739* (Halifax, 1900), 13–14.

13 MacMechan, *Minutes of Her Majesty's Council*, 22–23; 'Statement to the People of Minas,' 4 March 1721, in MacMechan, *A Calender of Two Letter-Books*, 72.

14 PRO, CO 217/3:155r–v, Antoine et Pierre Couaret à Phillips, 2 octobre 1720. A printed copy is in *CMNF*, 3:46–7.

15 See William C. Wicken, 'Encounters with Tall Sails and Tall Tales: Mi'kmaq Society, 1500–1760' (PhD dissertation, McGill University, 1994), 357–73.

16 PRO, CO 217/3:35r, Phillips to Board of Trade, 26 May 1720.

17 The context of the transferral is in J.A. Brandao and William A. Starna, 'The Treaties of 1701: A Triumph of Iroquois Diplomacy,' *Ethnohistory* 43, no. 2 (1996), 225.

18 AN, AC C11B 5:125r, 128v–129r, Conseil de la marine, 15 novembre [1720].

19 AN, AC C11B 10:187v–188r, Saint-Ovide au ministre, 1 novembre 1729.

20 NAC, MG 18, E29, Charlevoix Papers, 'Discours des sauvages de l'acadie du gouverneur de l'Île Royale,' 1720.

21 PRO, CO 217/38:100v–101r, 'Articles Signed by Captain John Doucett,' 4 June 1726.

22 PRO, CO 217/65:150r, Petition of the Mickmack Indians to John Wentworth, in Monk to Wentworth, 23 January 1794.

23 PANS, RG 1/186:214, Nova Scotia Council Minutes, 14 September 1752. This issue will be discussed in Chapter 7.

24 Cumming and Mickenberg, eds., *Native Rights*, 301.

25 'Conference with the Delegates' 20 November 1725, in *DHSM* 23:195, 201.

26 *A Conference of His Excellency the Governor, with the Sachems and Chief Men of the Eastern Indians*, August 9–12, 1717 (Boston, 1717), 9.

27 'The Conference with the Eastern Indians, at the Ratification of the Peace, Held at Falmouth in Casco-Bay, in July and August 1726,' in *Collections of the Maine Historical Society*, vol. 3 (Portland, 1853), 389–90.

28 'Conference with the Delegates,' 25 November 1725, in *DHSM* 23:201

29 PRO, CO 217/19:23r, Jonathan Belcher to the Board of Trade, 2 July 1762.

30 Eastern Indians' Letter to Governor Samuel Shute, 27 July 1721, in *Collections of the Massachusetts Historical Society*, vol. 8, second series (Boston, 1819), 180.

31 Printed copies of these seigneurial grants are in Pierre-Georges Roy, ed., *Inventaire des concession en fief et seigneuries fois et homages* (Beauceville, 1928).

32 AN, AC C11B 7:29v, Saint-Ovide au ministre, 24 novembre 1724.

33 PRO, CO 217/8: 77r, Paul Mascarene to the Board of Trade, 16 August 1740.

34 *Abstracts of English Shipping Records Relating to Massachusetts Ports from Original Records in the Public Record Office* (Salem, 1931).

35 PRO, CO 217/2:39r, Francis Nicholson to Board of Trade, 16 August 1715; CO 217/4:116–18, 'A Journall of Hibbert Newton,' 16 June 1722; ; CO 217/4:119, ' Journall of George Lapham,' 26 June 1722.

36 See for instance, Ruth Holmes Whitehead, *Stories from the Six Worlds: Micmac Legends* (Halifax, 1988), 2–18.

37 MSA 91, 92, 94, NAC, MG 18:N8, part 4 [transcripts]; Paul Mascarene to Francis Nicholson, 6 November 1713 in *Report of the Canadian Archives for 1928* (Ottawa, 1929), 47; Plank, *An Unsettled Conquest*, 57–8.

38 James Axtell, 'The Vengeful Women of Marblehead: Robert Roules' Deposition of 1677,' *William and Mary Quarterly* 31 (1974), 650–2; PRO, CO 5/864:82–3, Petition of Samuel Vetch, 1706.

39 PRO, CO 217/2, Francis Spelmen and Andrew Simpson to Board of Trade, 2 September 1715.

40 PRO, CO 217/2:43r, Samuel Vetch to Board of Trade, 2 September 1715.

41 PRO, CO 217/2:39r, Francis Nicholson to Board of Trade, 16 August 1715.

42 Thomas Caulfeild to Colonel Tayler [1716], in *A Calender of Two Letter-Books and One Commission Book in the Possession of the Government of Nova Scotia, 1713–1741* (Halifax, 1900), 42.

43 Harry Piers, 'The Fortieth Regiment,' *Collections of the Nova Scotia Historical Society* 21 (1927), 126.

44 PANS, RG1/18, doc. 49, Richard Phillips to Board of Trade, 24 January 1732.

45 For earlier complaints, see PANS, RG 1/18, Lawrence Armstrong to Board of Trade, 28 February 1716.

46 Colonel H.C.B. Rogers, *The British Army of the Eighteenth Century* (New York, 1977), 45–6.

47 'Relation of 1644–45,' in *JR* 28:49. John Phillip Reid, 'Principles of Vengeance: Fur trappers, Indians, and Retaliation for Homicide in the Transboundary North American West,' in Tina Loo and Lorna McLean, eds., *Historical Perspectives on Law and Society in Canada* (Toronto, 1994), 16; and *A Law of Blood: The Primitive Law of the Cherokee Nation* (New York, 1976), 73–84. See also Hamar Foster, '"The Queen's Law Is Better Than Yours": International Homicide in Early British Columbia,' in Jim Phillips, Tina Loo, and Susan Lewthwaite, eds., *Essays in the History of Canadian Law*, vol. 5, *Crime and Criminal Justice* (Toronto, 1994), 53–60.

48 On the Abenaki, see Kenneth M. Morrison, *The Embattled Northeast: The Elusive Ideal of Alliance in Abenaki–Euroamerican Relations* (Berkeley, 1984), 106.

49 AN, AC C11A 35:12v–13r, MM. Ramezay et Bégon au ministre, 13 septembre 1715.

50 AN, AC C11A 35:13v, MM. Ramezay et Bégon au ministre, 13 septembre 1715; Anonymous, 29 July 1715, *Boston Newsletter,* 1 August 1715.

51 E.P. Thompson, *Whigs and Hunters: The Origins of the Black Act* (London, 1975), 262–3.

52 Nova Scotia Council Minutes, 8 July 1724, in *Original Minutes*, 56–7.

7: British Politics and Treaty Making

1 James Henretta, '*Salutary Neglect': Colonial Administration under the Duke of Newcastle* (Princeton, 1972), 23–34.

2 For instance, PRO, CO 218/1:234v–235v, Board of Trade to the Privy Council, 15 September 1720.

3 PRO, CO 218/1: 440r, Board of Trade to Richard Phillips, 6 April 1719.

4 PRO, CO 5/915:320r, Board of Trade to Governor Shute, 17 March 1721.

5 PRO, CO 218/2:28r, Board of Trade to John Doucett, 16 November 1726.

6 Duke of Newcastle to William Dummer, 7 July 1726, in Cecil Headlam, ed., *Calender of State Papers: Colonial Series America and West Indies 1726–1727* (1936; reprint, Vaduz, 1964), 103.

7 A. Popple to William Dummer, 26 June 1726, in *Calender of State Papers* (1726–7), 309; and for Dummer's letter announcing the peace, Dummer to Board of Trade, 22 August 1726, 137.

8 Board of Trade to King George, 8 September 1721 in *Documents Relative to the Colonial History of the State of New York*, vol. 5, edited by E.B. O'Callaghan (Albany, 1855), 629.

9 William Pencak, *War, Politics and Revolution in Provincial Massachusetts* (Boston, 1981), 70.

10 Clifford K. Shipton, *Sibley's Harvard Graduates*, vol. 4 (1690–1700) (Cambridge, 1933), 209–214, 245–8, 260–4, 349–56, 383–7, 434–49.

11 J.J. Malone, *Pine Trees and Politics: The Naval Stores and Forest Policy in Colonial New England 1691–1775* (Seattle, 1964), 73–5.

12 Roy H. Akagi, *The Town Proprietors of the New England Colonies* (1924; reprint, Gloucester, Mass., 1963), 244–5, 248.

13 On the organization of land companies generally, see Anthony F.C. Wallace, *Jefferson and the Indians: The Tragic Fate of the First Americans* (Cambridge, 1999), 39.

14 Marc Egnal, *A Mighty Empire: The Origins of the American Revolution* (Ithaca and London, 1987), 6, 29–30; Pencak, *War, Politics and Revolution*, 71.

15 Akagi, *The Town Proprietors*, 257–8.

16 Papers detailing these transactions are in *DHSM* 24:199–244. Also see Viola Barnes, 'Richard Wharton, A Seventeenth century New England Colonial,' *Transactions of the Colonial Society of Massachusetts* 26 (1924–26), 260–9; Akagi, *The Town Proprietors*, 244–7.

17 Akagi, *The Town Proprietors*, 259–60; Kenneth Morrison, 'The People of the Dawn: The Abnaki and their Relations with New England and New France, 1600–1727' (PhD dissertation, University of Maine, 1975), 321; Samuel Penhallow, *The History of the Wars of New-England with the Eastern Indians* (1726; reprint, New York, 1969), 83–4.

18 P. Yorke and C. Talbot to Board of Trade, 11 August 1731, in *Collections and Proceedings of the Maine Historical Society*, 2nd series, vol. 6 (Portland, 1895), 409.

19 PRO, CO 5/870:75v, 77r–v, 'The Conference with the eastern Indians at the Ratification of the Peace, held at Falmouth in Casco-Bay, in July and August, 1726.'

20 H.V. Bowen, *Elites, Enterprise and the Making of the British Overseas Empire, 1688–1775* (New York, 1996), 53–60; and on Great Britain's debt, John Brewer, *The Sinews of Power: War, Money and the English State, 1688–1783* Cambridge, 1990), 114–26.

21 *The Trials of Five Persons for Piracy, Felony and Robbery* (Boston 1726); Bill Wicken, '26 August 1726: A Case Study in Mi'kmaq–New England Relations in the early 18th Century,' *Acadiensis* 23, no. 1 (Autumn 1993), 5–6.

22 Charles M. Andrews, *The Colonial Period of American History: England's Commercial and Colonial Policy*, vol. 4 (1938; reprint, New Haven and London, 1964), 230.

23 For a later statement of this legal opinion, see 'Lord Mansfields' Judgement in *Campbell v. Hall*, 1774,' in *Report of the Canadian Archives for 1907* (Ottawa, 1908), 526.

24 *The Trials of Five Persons*, 31.

25 'The Examination of James Mews,' 5 September 1726, in *The Trials of Five Persons*, 26.

26 'The Examination of John Missel,' 5 September 1726, in *The Trials of Five Persons*, 29.

27 Captain Walker is likely Pierre Amquaret, chief of Minas, who signed the 1726 treaty. He is referred to as the chief of Minas in an earlier incident involving Mirligueche. *The Trials of Five Persons*, 30; Letter dated from Piscataqua, 29 July 1715, in *Boston Newsletter*, 1 August 1715.

28 *The Trials of Five Persons*, 33.

29 *The Trials of Five Persons,* 7.

30 *The Trials of Five Persons,* 31.

31 PRO, CO 217/38: 100v–01r, 102r–v; CO 217/38:108r–v; CO 217/4:320r, 321r–v; CO 217/5:3r–5r; CO217/38:109r–v, 116r–v. The multiple copies of the treaty are discussed in Patricia Kennedy, 'Treaty Texts: When Can We Trust the Written Word?' *Social Sciences and Humanities Aboriginal Research Exchange* 3, no. 1 (Summer 1995), 1, 8, 20–2.

32 An example of a later copy is in PRO, CO 217/32:77r–80v. The only extant parchment copy of a Mi'kmaq treaty is the 1749 treaty and is at the Public Archives of Nova Scotia.

33 'Minutes of His Majesty's Council, 4 June 1726,' in MacMechan, ed., *Original Minutes,* 116; PANS, RG 1/186:152, Nova Scotia Council Minutes, 14 August 1749.

34 PRO, CO 217/38:95r, Armstrong to the Duke of Newcastle, 27 July 1726.

35 For instance, PANS, RG 1/14:95–6, 'Lettre Circulaire envoyé aux Sauvages des St. Jean, Pentagouite, Cape Sable, Marligash, Minas ou Chicabnacady & Beaubassin,' 29 juillet 1729.

36 Minutes of His Majesty's Council, 23 June 1726, MacMechan, ed., *Original Minutes,* 120.

37 AN, AC C11B 8:35v, Saint-Ovide à Conseil de la marine, 18 septembre 1726; AC, C11B 9:65v, Saint-Ovide à Conseil de marine, 20 septembre 1727.

38 AN, AC, C11B 10:5v, 'Extrait de la lettre écrite à M. Saint-Ovide, 10 juin 1727.' Further evidence regarding discussions between Armstrong and the Mi'kmaq over the winter of 1726–27 is in AN, AC C11B 9:64r, Conseil de la marine, 20 octobre 1727.'

39 Gyles to Dummer, 28 April 1727, in *DHSM* 10:386.

40 Gyles to Dummer, 22 June 1727, in *DHSM* 10:408.

41 Gyles to Dummer, 14 June 1727, in *DHSM* 10:404

42 Wenungennet to Gyles, 3 July 1728, in *DHSM* 23:231–2.

43 PANS, O/S doc. 511, 'Ratification of Boston Treaty Signed in Presence of thirteen Witnesses at Fort at Annapolis Royal,' 24 September 1728.

February 1996, Halifax, Nova Scotia

1 Michael A. Paré, Brief filed on behalf of Her Majesty the Queen in *R. versus Donald John Marshall, Jr.,* 23 February 1996, 72.

2 Bruce H. Wildsmith and Eric Zscheile, Brief of Defendant in *R. v. Donald John Marshall Jr.,* February 1996, 35, 38–9.

3 Wildsmith and Zscheile, Brief of Defendant, 8.

4 Ibid.

8: The Founding of Halifax: Re-interpreting the 1726 Treaty

1 Lawrence to Monckton, 16 February 1755, in 'Two Letters of Charles Lawrence,' *Cahiers de la Société historique Acadienne* 3 (December 1969), 175.
2 PANS, RG 1/187:185, Nova Scotia Council Minutes, 12 February 1755.
3 PANS, RG 1/187:187–9, Nova Scotia Council Minutes, 13 February 1755.
4 Sieur de Gargas, 'General Census of the Country of Acadie, 1687–1688,' in William Morse, ed., *Acadiensia Nova (1598–1779)*, vol. 1 (London, 1935), 145,147.
5 AN, C11D 10 [np], 'Sur l'Acadie,' 1748. Makkanchisch was possibly what is today called Three Fathom Harbour. See Father Pacifique, 'Le Pays des Micmacs,' *Bulletin de la société de géographie de Québec* 27 (January 1933), 61.
6 For example, Boston, MSA 61:258, 'Deposition d'Abraham Boudrot de Port Royal,' 29 août 1683; Anonymous, 'The Journal of a Captive, 1745–1748,' in Isabel Calder, ed., *Colonial Captivities, Marches and Journeys* (New York, 1935), 10.
7 Gargas, 'General Census ... 1687–1688,' 149, 151.
8 PANS, RG 1/186:214, Nova Scotia Council Minutes, 14 September 1752.
9 Jack P. Greene, *Pursuits of Happiness* (Chapel Hill, 1988), 179.
10 See Christopher Moore, 'The Other Louisbourg: Trade and Merchant Enterprise in Ile Royale 1713–58,' *Histoire Sociale/Social History* (1979), 79–96.
11 Olive P. Dickason, *Louisbourg and the Indians 1713–58* (Ottawa, 1976).
12 Raymond F. Baker, ' A Campaign of Amateurs: The Siege of Louisbourg, 1745,' *Occasional Papers in Archaeology and History* 18 (Ottawa, 1978).
13 George F.G. Stanley, *New France: The Last Phase 1744–1760* (Toronto, 1968), 65.
14 J.M. Bumstead, 'The Cultural Landscape of Early Canada,' in Phillip Morgan, ed., *Strangers within the Realm: Cultural Margins of the First British Empire* (Chapel Hill, 1991), 375.
15 *London Magazine* for 1750, in Beamish Murdoch, *History of Nova Scotia*, vol. 2 (Halifax, 1866), 185.
16 PANS, RG 1/35: doc 1, Cornwallis to Board of Trade, 22 June 1749.
17 *London Magazine* for 1750, in Murdoch, *History of Nova Scotia*, vol. 2 (Halifax, 1866), 185; 'The Evolution of the Halifax Fortress, 1749–1928' (Halifax), 1–3.
18 Pacifique, 'Le pays des Micmacs,' 61; NAC, NMC 107535, Cyprian Southack, 'Western Nova Scotia,' [1720] uses 'Shetboutocer'; 'Carte de l'Accadie' 1744 in Père Charlevoix, *History and General Description of New France*, trans. John Shea (New York, 1902), 248. Charlevoix uses 'Chibouctou.'
19 Pacifique, 'Le Pays des Micmacs,' 64.

20 Thomas Jeffreys, 'A New Map of Nova Scotia and Cape Britain with the adjacent parts of New England and Canada,' 1755.

21 For instance, *Course à l'Acadie: Journal de Campagne de François Du Pont*, Bernard Pothier, ed. (Ottawa, 1982); NAC, Collection Moreau, MG 1 F3/50, 'Journal Concernant ce qui s'est arrivée, chaque jour depuis mon départ de la Baye Verte,' octobre 1748.

22 PRO, CO 218/3:25r–v, Instructions to Edward Cornwallis, 29 April 1749.

23 PRO, CO 217/9:73r, Cornwallis to Board of Trade, 24 July 1749.

24 PRO, CO 217/9:82r, Cornwallis to Board of Trade, 20 August 1749; Charles Germain. 16 août, 1749 in *CMNF* 3:452.

25 Treaty of 1749 in *Canada: Indian Treaties and Surrenders from 1680 to 1890*, vol. 2 (Ottawa, 1891), 200–1.

26 PRO, CO 217/32:39v–40, Paul Mascarene to Mons. de la Gallissonière, 25 April 1749.

27 PRO, CO 217/32:85r, Board to Trade to Duke of Bedford, 27 July 1749.

28 PANS, RG 1/186:158, Nova Scotia Council Minutes, 14 August 1749.

29 Charles Germain, 16 août 1749, in *CMNF* 3:452.

30 Anonymous, 'a Journal,' [1752–57], in *The Northcliffe Collection* (Ottawa 1926), 71–2. For an account that stresses Cornwallis's view, see Plank, *An Unsettled Conquest*, 125–34.

31 AN, AC C11A 95:56v, M. Bigot au ministre, 5 octobre 1750.

32 AN, AC C11B 28:373r–v, Île Royale, 8 septembre 1749; PANS, RG 1/186: 20–21, Nova Scotia Council, 18 September 1749.

33 PRO, CO 217/9:89r, Cornwallis to Board of Trade, 11 September 1749; NAC, MG 5, B1, Archives du ministre des affaires étrangères: Memoires et documents, 1749–53, vol. 9, 'Île Royale,' remis le 3 novembre 1749, par M. Rouillé, 156–8.

34 AN, AC C11B 28:77v, M. Desherbiers au ministre, 9 août 1749.

35 ASQ, Lettres, no. 66, Maillard, 18 octobre 1749.

36 PRO, CO 217/9:117r–118r, Mi'kmaq to Cornwallis, 24 septembre 1749. The letter was dated five days before the feast of St Michel, which is September 29. I have used the translation found in the Government of Canada's documents prepared for *R. v. Marshall.* My thanks to Stephen Patterson of the University of New Brunswick for providing this translation to the court.

'7 AN, AC C11B/28:40r–v, Desherbiers au ministre, 19 octobre 1749; AN, AC C11A 96:51v–52r, Bigot au ministre, 18 octobre 1750.

'ANS, RG 1/186:22, Nova Scotia Council Minutes, 1 October 1749; PRO, ') 217/9:188r, Proclamation against the Micmac Indians published at Hali- in Chebcuto, 2 October 1749; PRO, CO 217/9:108r, Cornwallis to

Board, 17 October 1749; PANS, RG 1/163:41, Commissions and Instructions, 1749–1763, Proclamation of Edward Cornwallis, 21 June 1750.

39 Jean-Louis le Loutre, 'Une Autobiographie de l'abbé le Loutre, *Nova Francia* 6 (1931), 15.

40 PRO, CO 217/10:48r, Cornwallis to Board of Trade, 3 May 1750; Stanley, *New France*, 72–4; C.J. Russ, 'Louis La Corne,' *Dictionary of Canadian Biography* 3 (Toronto, 1974), 331–2.

41 Journal of Charles Lawrence 1750, in John Clarence Webster, ed., *The Building of Fort Lawrence in Chignecto* (Saint John, 1941), 7.

42 PRO, CO 218/4:58r–v, 68r, Board of Trade to Cornwallis, 6 March 1752.

43 PRO, CO 218/4, Board of Trade to Cornwallis, 6 March 1752; CO 217/13:384v, P. Hopson to Board of Trade, 6 December 1752; CO 218/4:221v, Board of Trade to P. Hopson, 28 March 1753.

44 PRO, CO 218/4:15r, Board of Trade to Cornwallis, 22 March 1751.

45 PRO, CO 217/13:20r, Cornwallis to Board of Trade, 4 September 1751.

46 'A Journall of the Proceedings of Jacob Wendell, et al. ... at Fort St. George's the 19th day of August 1751,' in *DHSM* 23:417, 419; PRO CO217/13:27r, Mascarene to Cornwallis, 27 August 1751. Mascarene spells the Maliseet delegate's name as 'Nanjarrett.'

47 PANS, RG 1/35: doc. 67, Cornwallis to Board of Trade, 16 February 1752.

48 AC, C11B 32:163r–v, Prevost au ministre, 10 septembre 1752. Janet Elizabeth Chute, 'Ceremony, Social Revitalization and Change: Micmac Leadership and the Annual Festival of St. Anne,' in William Cowan, ed., *Papers of the 23rd Algonquian Conference* (Ottawa, 1992), 51–2.

49 AN, AC C11B 32:163r–v, Prevost au ministre, 10 septembre 1752. G. Plank contends that Cope had attended the 1726 treaty. Though possible, there is no conclusive evidence that this was the case.

50 PANS, RG 1/186:214, Nova Scotia Council Minutes, 14 September 1752.

51 AN, AC G1466: doc. 71, 'Recensement fait cette presente année du nombre des sauvages Miquemaq portant les armes,' 1735.

52 The assumption is that 31.6 per cent of the population is male and over the age of fifteen. This accords with estimates made of the 1708 nominal census, which gives a complete age breakdown of the entire population. In French census records, fifteen was usually the age for dividing male adults from children. This likely reflected Mi'kmaq attitudes.

53 Donald Marshall Sr, Alexander Denny, Simon Marshall, 'The Covenant Chain,' Boyce Richardson, ed., *Drumbeat: Anger and Renewal in Indian Country* (Toronto, 1989), 82; James [sákéj] Youngblood Henderson, 'Mikmaw Tenure in Atlantic Canada,' *Dalhousie Law Journal* 18, no. 2 (Fall 1995), 252.

54 Stephen E. Patterson, 'Indian-White Relations in Nova Scotia, 1749–61: A Study in Political Interaction,' *Acadiensis* 23, no. 1 (Autumn 1993), 38.

55 For instance, Daniel Richter, *The Ordeal of the Longhouse: The Peoples of the Iroquois League in the Era of European Colonization* (Chapel Hill, 1992), 31; Elizabeth Tooker, 'The League of the Iroquois: Its History, Politics, and Ritual,' in *Handbook of North American Indians*, vol. 15, *The Northeast*, ed. Bruce G. Trigger (Washington, 1978), 145–8.

56 PANS, RG 1/186:214, Nova Scotia Council Minutes, 14 September 1752.

57 Charles Lawrence, 'Journal,' in *The Building*, 9.

58 PANS, RG 1/186:217–18, Nova Scotia Council Minutes, 16 September 1752.

59 PANS, RG 1/186:218, Nova Scotia Council Minutes, 16 September 1752.

60 *Halifax Gazette*, 11 November 1752, 2; PANS, RG 1/186:234, Nova Scotia Council Minutes, 10 October 1752 and RG 1/186:242, Council Minutes, 25 October 1752.

61 PANS, RG 1/492:105, Proceedings of the Court of the Vice-Admiralty, Memorial of Thomas Gillard, Fisherman, 24 October 1752.

62 PANS, RG 1/186:250–4, Nova Scotia Council Minutes, 22 November 1752.

63 Judge George Patterson, Notes from R. V. Syliboy, July 1928, County Court, Port Hood, Nova Scotia, in William C. Wicken, '"Heard it from our Grandfathers," Mi'kmaq Treaty Tradition and the Syliboy Case of 1928,' *University of New Brunswick Law Journal* 44 (1995), 160.

64 For instance, AN, AC G1466: doc. 71, 'Recensement fait des sauvages portant des armes en 1735'; D.C. Harvey, ed., *Holland's Description of Cape Breton Island and Other Documents* (Halifax, 1935), 61–2, 68, 82; PANS, Map Collection, 3.6.4, 1767, Samuel Holland, Plan of the Island of Cape Breton.

65 PANS, RG 1/164:80, 'Pass Given to Andrew Martin,' 26 August 1760.

66 AN, Archives de la Guerre, B1/3393: doc. 25, Raymond à de Rouille, 12 décembre 1752; AN, AC C11A 99:193v, abbé de l'isle Dieu au ministre, 19 juillet 1753; *Boston Gazette*, 1 May 1753.

67 PRO, CO 217/14:38r–v, Hopson to the Board of Trade, 14 April 1753; PANS, RG 1/134, Captain Cotterell to Col. Sutherland, 16 November 1753; CO 217/14:348r–v, Charles Lawrence to Board of Trade, 5 December 1753.

68 PANS, RG 1/186:363, Nova Scotia Council Minutes, 12 April 1753.

69 Quoted in 'Anthony Casteel's Journal,' *Canada-Français* 3 (Québec, 1890), 112.

70 For instance, Cope's travels are suggested in PRO, CO 217/14:3r, Hopson to Board of Trade, 4 January 1753.

71 PANS, RG 1/186:390, Nova Scotia Council Minutes, 16 May 1753.

72 AN, AC C11B 33:159v, Prevost au ministre, 12 mai 1753. See also Patterson, 'Indian–White Relations,' 43–7.

73 PANS, RG 1/186: 365–6, Nova Scotia Council Minutes, 16 April 1753; PRO, CO 217/14:153r–54v, 'The examination before me Charles Morris one of His Majesty's Justices of the County of Halifax of James Grace and John Conner,' 16 April 1753. The Connor/Grace incident was also reported in the *Halifax Gazette*, 28 April 1753, and the *Boston Gazette*, 1 May 1753. On French accounts of the same incident, see AN, Archives de la Guerre, v. 3393, M. De Serelle à Comte de Raymond, avril 1753, NAC, MG 4/B1; AN, AC C11B 33:159v, Prevost au ministre, 12 mai 1753. On the Casteel affair, see PANS, RG 1/186: 391, Nova Scotia Council Minutes, 16 May 1753, 'Anthony Casteel's Journal, while prisoner with the Indians in the months of May and June 1753,' *Canada-Français* 3 (1890), 113–26. PRO, CO 217/14:199r–v, 'Deposition of Anthony Casteel,' 30 July 1753.

74 PRO, CO 217/14:37v, Hopson to Board of Trade, 14 April 1753.

75 Pichon's correspondence has been collected in John Clarence Webster, ed., *Thomas Pichon: 'The Spy of Beausejour,'* trans. by Alice Webster (Halifax, 1937), 37–116.

9: The 1760–1761 Treaties

1 PRO, CO 217/54: 221r–222v, Treaty of 1779, 22 September 1779.

2 'Journal of Louis de Courville,' in John Clarence Webster, ed., *Journals of Beausejour* (Saint John, 1937), 47–8, 50.

3 PRO, CO 5/53, 37r–v, 'Examination of Four French Prisoners, ... 11 March 1758.'

4 AN, AC C11C 14:67r–113v, esp. 73r, 97r–v, 101r, 'Bordereau des payements qui on se fait à la colonie de l'Île Royale pour les dépenses de l'exercise de l'année, 1757 depuis le premier janvier et comprise le quinze décembre de la dite année,' 16 décembre 1757. Other evidence is in AN, AC C11B 37: 209v, 'Etat des vivres, munitions ... de l'Île Royale,' 1757.

5 Stephen E. Patterson, 'Indian–White Relations in Nova Scotia 1749–61: A Study in Political Interaction,' *Acadiensis* 23, no. 1 (1993), 54.

6 For instance, PRO, CO 5/53: 205r–206r, James Murray to James Wolfe, 24 September 1758.

7 George F.G. Stanley, *New France: The Last Phase 1744–1760* (Toronto, 1968), 174–5.

8 Stanley, *New France*, 220–34.

9 Québec, ASQ, Seminaire IV, no. 91, Testament de Mr Maillard, 12 avril 1759.

10 *Boston Gazette*, 10 September 1759.

11 *Boston Gazette*, 10 December 1759.

12 AN, AC C11A 105:50r–v, Henry Schomberg à Maillard, 26 octobre 1759.

13 For instance, see AN, AC C11A 105:50r, Schomberg à Capitaine Le Blanc, 23 novembre 1759.

14 PRO, WO 34/17, Amherst Papers, Whitmore to Amherst, 22 January 1760.

15 PRO, WO 34/17, Whitmore to Amherst, 1 December 1759; WO 34/17:196, Whitmore to Amherst, 14 November 1760.

16 PRO, Treasury 1/458, Henry Schomberg to Lord Commissioners of the Treasury, [nd].

17 Jonathan Proctor, 'Diary Kept at Louisbourg, 1759–1760,' *The Essex Institute Historical Collections* 70 (1934), 32.

18 Louis-Auguste Rossel, 'Journal de ma campagne à l'île Royale (1757),' in *Rapport de l'archiviste de la province de Québec pour 1931–1932* (Québec, 1932), 381.

19 'Diary of Sergeant John Burrell, 1759–60,' *Acadiensis* 5 (1905), 292–3.

20 AN, AC C11A 105:45v, Charles Germain à Monsieur le Marquis de Vaudreuil, 26 février 1760.

21 PANS, RG 1/188:111–12, Nova Scotia Council Minutes, 30 November 1759.

22 *Boston Gazette* 25 February 1760.

23 For instance, see PRO, CO 217/18:81v, Belcher to Board of Trade, 12 December 1760.

24 Proctor, 'Diary Kept at Louisbourg, 1759–60,' 36–7, 40–2.

25 PANS, RG 1/188: 150, Nova Scotia Council Minutes, 1 June 1760.

26 PANS, RG 1/188:119–22, Nova Scotia Council Minutes, 11 February 1760.

27 PANS, RG 1/188:124–6, Nova Scotia Council Minutes, 13 February 1760. Governor Lawrence had appointed Gerrish on 3 February 1760. PANS, RG 1/164:85–6, Commission of B. Gerrish, 3 February 1760.

28 PANS, RG 1/188:127–8, Nova Scotia Council Minutes, 14 February 1760.

29 Yasuhide Kawashima, *Puritan Justice and the Indian* (Middleton, 1986), 85–6.

30 For instance, see the various letters sent to Dummer by Gyles in 1727 in *DHSM* 10: 383–92

31 PRO, CO 217/18:84v, Belcher to Board of Trade, 12 December 1760.

32 PRO, CO 217/19:159v–160r, Gerrish to Belcher, 23 October 1761; PRO, 217/19:31r, 'Message from the Lieutenant Governor [Belcher] to the Members of His Majesty's Council and House of Representatives, 23 March 1762.

33 PANS, RG 1/188: 129–30, Nova Scotia Council Minutes, 16 February 1760.

34 Nicolas Denys, *The Description and Natural History of the Coasts of North America (Acadia)*, ed. William F. Ganong (Toronto, 1908), 447.

35 'The Diary of Rev. John Seccombe,' *Report of the Board of Trustees of the Public Archives of Nova Scotia for the Year 1959* (Halifax, 1960), 20, 24, 33.

36 V.T.H, 'Relation d'un voyage de Paris en Canada,' 14 octobre 1741 in *Rapport*

de l'archiviste de la Province de Québec pour 1947–1948 (Québec, 1948), 25–6; 'Expenses Connected with the Treaty with the Indians, 13 September to 19th Oct. 1778,' in 'Selections from the papers and Correspondence of James White, Esquire A.D. 1762–1783,' *Collections of the New Brunswick Historical Society* 1 (1894), 321.

37 Daniel Francis and Toby Morantz, *Partners in Fur: A History of the Fur Trade in Eastern James Bay 1600–1870* (Montreal, 1983), 85.

38 PANS, RG 1/188:121–2, Nova Scotia Council Minutes, 11 February 1760.

39 PRO, CO 217/18:28v, 29v, 'Treaty of Peace and Friendship Concluded with the Delegates of the St. Johns and Passamaquoddy Tribes of Indians at Halifax, ' 23 February 1760.

40 PANS, RG 1/188:136, Nova Scotia Council Minutes, 29 February 1760. On Claude Renée, see PANS, RG 1/188:131, Nova Scotia Council Minutes, 16 February 1760.

41 La Hève: 10 March 1760. Halifax. BM, Add. Ms. 19071; Richibucto: PRO, CO 217/145, 10 March 1760; Shubenacadie and Musquodoboit: PANS, RG 1/188:137, 10 March 1760; Cape Breton: 25 June 1761. Halifax. PRO, CO 217/18:277r–83v; Shediac: 25 June 1761. Halifax. UNB, Harriet Irving Archives, New Brunswick Indian Documents; Miramichi: PANS, RG 1/165, 25 June 1761; Pokemouche: PRO, CO 217/18: 277r, 25 June 1761; Chig-necto and Missiquash: PANS, RG 1/188: 255, 8 July 1761; Pictou and Malogomich: PANS, RG 1/188: 282, 12 October 1761: La Hève: PANS, RG 1/188: 288, 9 November 1761 and RG 1/430 doc. 20.

42 Cape Sable: PANS, RG 1/165, Charles Lawrence to Francois Shaqwaough, 24 April 1760; PANS, RG 1/188: 149, Nova Scotia Council Minutes, 5 June 1760; Listiguj: CO 5/61, Part II:24r–6r, Robert Elliot to Jeffrey Amherst, 24 January 1761. On Listiguj, also see PRO, WO 34/12 90r–91r, Joseph Claude to Roderick Mackenzie, 7 January 1761; and 12: 95r–v, MacKenzie to Claude, 23 February 1760.

43 Patterson, 'Indian–White Relations,' 55.

44 PANS, RG 1/165: 27–8, Treaty of Peace and Friendship Concluded with Paul Laurent Chief of the La Heve Tribe of Indians,' 10 March 1760.

45 On the council's attempts to bring settlers to Nova Scotia, see John Bartlet Brebner, *The Neutral Yakees of Nova Scotia: A Marginal Colony during the Revolutionary Years* (1937; reprint, Toronto, 1969), 21–7.

46 Brebner, *The Neutral Yankees*, 21–6.

47 PANS, RG 1/36:doc. 30, Lawrence to Board of Trade, 9 November 1757.

48 PANS, RG 1/36: doc. 39, Lawrence to Board of Trade, 26 December 1758; Linda G. Wood, 'The Lunenburg Indian Raids of 1756 and 1758: A New Documentary Source,' *Nova Scotia Historical Review* 13, no. 1 (1993), 107–8.

49 For instance, PRO, CO 5/61:88v, Belcher to Amherst, 19 March 1761. For a fuller explanation, see R.S. Longley, 'The Coming of the New England Planters to the Annapolis Valley,' *Collections of the Nova Scotia Historical Society* 33 (1961), 86–94.
50 PRO, CO 217/20:168v, Committee to Belcher, 5 April 1763.
51 PRO, CO 5/66:17v–18v, 22v, James Marriott to the Board of Trade, 15 February 1765.
52 Figures have been compiled from PRO, CO 217/18:248r–55v, Charles Morris Junior, ' A Description of the Several Towns in the Province of Nova Scotia,' 9 January 1762.
53 See Woody Holton, *Forced Founders: Indians, Debtors, Slaves and the Making of the American Revolution in Virginia* (Chapel Hill, 1999), 3–39; Anthony F.C. Wallace, *Jefferson and the Indians: The Tragic Fate of the First Americans* (Cambridge, 1999), 21–49.
54 PANS, Map Collection, v. 7, 230–1760, Charles Morris, 'A Plan of Lands in the Township of Windsor' [1760]; John Bartlet Brebner, *The Neutral Yankees of Nova Scotia: A Marginal Colony during the Revolutionary Years* (1937; reprint, Toronto, 1969), 28–9.
55 PRO, CO 217/22:211v, Michael Francklin, 'General Heads to Explain,' 26 May 1768.

27 June 1996, Antigonish, Nova Scotia

1 John D. Embree, *Her Majesty the Queen Versus Donald John Marshall, Jr.*, Nova Scotia Provincial Court, 27 June 1996, 32–3.
2 Embree, Her Majesty, 34.
3 Ibid.
4 Embree, Her Majesty, 45.

Conclusion

1 PRO, CO 217/18:26r, Treaty of Peace and Friendship, 25 June 1761; PRO, ADM 1/2590, Captain's Letters, 1764–1771, Samuel Thompson to Philip Stephens, 16 April 1764; Fredericton, UNB, Harriet Irving Archives, Indian Records, Treaty of Peace and Friendship with Shediac, 25 June 1761; PANS, RG 1/165, Treaty of Peace and Friendship with Miramichi, 25 June 1761; Gameliel Smethurst, *A Narrative of an Extraordinary Escape out of the Hands of the Indians* (London, 1764), 14.
2 PANS, RG 1/165, Pass to Augusten et al., 1 July 1761.
3 Quebec, ASQ, Séminaire IV, no. 91, 'Testament de Mr. Maillard,' 12 avril

1759; PANS, RG 1/188:212, Nova Scotia Council Minutes, 10 April 1761; Albert David, 'À Propos du Testament de l'abbé Maillard, *Nova Francia* 2 (1926), 102–3.

4 For a similar seating arrangement for a conference between the governor of New France and Mi'kmaq at Québec in 1749, see Pehr Kalm, *Voyage de Pehr Kalm au Canada en 1749,* Jacques Rousseau and Guy Béthune, transl. and eds. (Montreal, 1977), 295.

5 The complexity of the translator's role in European–Aboriginal discussions is explored in Nancy L. Hagedorn, '"A Friend to Go Between": The Interpreter as Cultural Broker during Anglo-Iroquois Councils, 1740–70,' *Ethnohistory* 35, no. 1 (1988), 60–80.

6 For instance, PANS, RG 1/430: doc. 21, Abbé Sigogne to Sir John Sherbrooke, 9 May 1812.

7 The following summary of the speeches at the treaty-signing ceremony comes from PRO, CO 217/18:279–83v.

8 On medals, see *The Patriot* [Charlottetown, P.E.I.], 18 April 1922, 4.

9 PRO, CO 217/18: 279r–83v, 25 June 1761.

10 PRO, CO 217/179: 407r, Paussanigh Pemmenawweet to Queen Victoria, [received 25 January 1841].

11 PRO, CO 217/213:20, Francis Paul to Queen Victoria, 25 July 1853. A copy of this petition was printed in the *Christian Messenger,* 9 March 1854, 78. My thanks to David Bell of the Faculty of Law at the University of New Brunswick for pointing out this important source.

12 *Christian Messenger,* 16 March 1854, 84. My thanks to David Bell for pointing out this reference.

September to November 1999

1 Justice Binnie, *R. v. Marshall, CNLR* 4 (1999), 167.

2 Ibid., 168, 171.

3 Ibid., 176–7.

4 Ibid., 181. Emphasis as in original.

5 I attended the oral arguments as an observer. The opinion offered here is based on my memory of the discussions between Wildsmith and the seven justices.

6 Quote in Paul Barnsley, 'Fishing Charges Overturned,' *Windspeaker,* October 1999, 11.

7 Justice Estey, *R. v. Horse, CNLR* 2 (1988), 124.

8 Justice Lamer, *R. v. Sioui, SCR* 1 (1990), 1069.

9 Michael A. Paré, Brief (Filed on behalf of Her Majesty the Queen), *R. v. Mar-*

shall, 23 February 1996, 77. And see Justice Lamer, *R. v. Sioui*, SCR 1 (1990), 1049.

10 Justice Binnie, *R. v. Marshall*, 173.

11 Kevin Carmichael, 'DFO Was Unprepared for Marshall Court Ruling,' *Halifax Chronicle Herald*, 7 Dec. 1999, A11.

12 Kelly Toughill, 'Lobster War Boils Over, Three Injured in N.B.,' *Toronto Star*, 4 October 1999, 1; and 'Tensions High in Fish War,' 5 October 1999, 1; Kevin Cox and Daniel LeBlanc, 'Anger Explodes over Fishing Rights,' *Globe and Mail*, 4 October 1999, 1.

13 Kelly Toughill, 'Nova Scotia Fishermen Fear Violence as Feud Brews,' *Toronto Star*, 27 September 1999.

14 Robert Fife, 'High Court Accused of "Distorting" History,' *National Post*, 28 October 1999, 1.

15 Thomas Flanagan, 'The Marshall Ruling Puts Western Canada's Economy in Jeopardy,' *Globe and Mail*, 7 October 1999, A19.

16 'The Burden of Language in the Mi'kmaq Case,' *Globe and Mail*, 6 October 1999; Jeffrey Simpson, 'In the Fishery Verdict, a Win for Chaos,' *Globe and Mail*, 7 October 1999.

17 Justice Binnie, *R. v. Marshall*, 183–5.

18 Robert Fife, 'High Court Accused of "Distorting" History,' *National Post*, 28 October 1999, 1.

19 Robert Fife, 'Ottawa to Buy Commercial Fishing Licenses for Natives,' *National Post*, 29 October 1999.

20 Jeffrey Simpson, 'Mi'kmaq Patty Whack,' *Globe and Mail*, 19 November 1999.

21 'Fishermen Appeal Marshall Ruling,' *Halifax Chronicle Herald*, 19 October 1999.

22 *R. v. Marshall* [#2], *CNLR* 4 (1999), 311–12, 319.

23 Joel Denis Bellavance, 'High Court Fishing Ruling Extends to Logging: Minister,' *National Post*, 16 October 1999.

24 *R. v. Marshall* [#2], *CNLR* 4 (1999), 310–11.

25 Ibid., 304–5.

26 Ibid., 308–9.

27 Ibid., 320.

28 Ibid., 320.

29 Ibid., 322.

30 For this distinction, I have relied on as she was then, Justice McLachlin, *R. v. Van der Peet*, *CNLR* 4 (1996), 259.

31 See Michael Harris, *Justice Denied: The Law Versus Donald Marshall* (Toronto, 1986); Joy Mannette, ed., *Elusive Justice: Beyond the Marshall Inquiry* (Halifax, 1992).

Bibliography

Manuscript Sources

Canada

Archives du Séminaire de Québec, Québec:
Lettre M, no. 35, 37
Lettre N, no. 48, 86, 121
Lettre P, no. 8, 60–64
Lettre R, no. 180

National Archives of Canada, Ottawa, Ontario:
MG 18 E29 Collection Charlevoix Discours des Sauvages Micmaques ... 1749 one
  volume
MG 18 N8 Muster Rolls, New England Expedition against Port Royal, 1710, one
  volume
MG 23 J6 Samuel Prenties Journal 1780–81, one volume

New Brunswick Museum, Saint John, New Brunswick:
W.F. Ganong Scrapbooks

Public Archives of Nova Scotia, Halifax, Nova Scotia:
RG 1 Akin Transcripts
  v. 1–25, 35–57, 166–72, 186–91, 215–17, 286–7, 318–20, 380, 394–8, 491–4
  1603–1800
MG 1
  Isaac Deschamps Papers v. 258 and 258a

In Author's Possession:

Canada. Province of Nova Scotia, Decision of Judge John D. Embree, *Her Majesty the Queen versus Donald John Marshall, Jr.*, 27 June 1996.

Canada. Province of Nova Scotia, *Her Majesty the Queen versus Donald John Marshall, Jr.*, Transcripts, 29 volumes, Nov. 1994 to June 1995.

Paré, Michael A. Brief filed on behalf of Her Majesty the Queen in *R. versus Donald John Marshall, Jr.*, 23 February 1996.

Wildsmith, Bruce H., and Eric Zscheile. Brief of Defendant in *R. v. Donald Marshall Junior*, February 1996.

France

Microfilm copies of manuscripts in France were consulted at the National Archives of Canada, Ottawa.

Archives de la Compagnie de Saint-Sulpice à Paris:
Série II, v. 25, 1701

Archives départementales:
Charente-Maritime
   Amirauté de La Rochelle, Serie B, Cours et jurisdictions, 1634–1646
   Amirauté de Louisbourg, v. 272, 1742–1743
Ille-et-Vilaine (Rennes),
   Registre de Saint-Pierre-du-Nord, Île Saint-Jean, 1725–1758

Archives nationales, Paris: Fonds des colonies:
B – Lettres envoyées aux colonies, v. 3–97, 1671–1753
C11A – Correspondance du Canada, v. 1–99, 122, 1663–1760
C11B – Correspondance de l'Île Royale, v. 1–38, 1714–1758
C11C – Amérique du Nord, v. 1–16, 1705–1771
C11D – Correspondance de l'Acadie, v. 1–10, 1604–1760
F2B – Commerce aux colonies, v.11, 1742–1754
F3 – Collection Moreau de Saint-Méry, v. 5–6, 40, 1678–1755

Archives nationales, Paris: Section ancienne:
Série K. Monuments historiques, carton 1232

Archives nationales, Paris: Section outre-mer:
G1 – Concessions, recensements de l'Acadie et l'île Royale, v. 466

Service historique de l'armée, Paris:
Série A1. – Correspondance générale, opérations militaires, v. 3393, 3499, 1751–
1754, 1758

Great Britain

Microfilmed copies of these records are on deposit at the National Archives of
Canada in Ottawa.

British Museum, London:
Additional Manuscripts #19069–19076, Andrew Brown transcripts

Public Record Office, London:
Colonial Office Papers Series 5 – Massachusetts, v. 751–754, 785–794, 863–869,
1686–
Colonial Office Papers Series 217 – Nova Scotia, Original Correspondence to
the Board of Trade, v. 1–60, 1710–1760
Colonial Office Papers Series 218 – Nova Scotia, Original Correspondence,
Board of Trade to Nova Scotia, v. 1–5, 1710–1760
War Office Papers Series 34 – Amherst Correspondence, v. 11–13, 1756–1763

United States

Massachusetts State Archives, Boston, Massachusetts:
Massachusetts Archive Series, selected volumes, 1686–1776

Massachusetts Historical Society, Boston, Massachusetts:
Belknap Papers
Miscellaneous Unbound Volumes
Parkman Papers

Printed Sources

Abstracts of English Shipping Records Relating to Massachusetts Ports. Salem, 1931.
Acts and Resolves Public and Private of the Province of Massachusetts Bay. Vols. 1–16.
Boston 1869–1909.
Amherst, General. 'Papiers Amherst concernant les Acadiens.' *La Société His-
torique Acadienne* (1970), 256–320.
Anonymous. 'Réglement des Limites (Acadie, 1753), Collection de documents
inédits sur l'Acadie.' *Canada-Français* 3 (Québec, 1889), 60–87.

Baxter, James Phinney, ed. *Documentary History of the State of Maine*. Vol. 1–23. Portland, 1916.

Boston Gazette. 1719–27.

Boston Newsletter. 1704–27.

Buckley, The Rev. John. 'An Inquiry into the Right of the Aboriginal Natives to the Lands in America, and the Titles Derived from Them.' 24 December 1724. In *Collections of the Massachusetts Historical Society*. First Series, vol. 4 (Boston, 1795), 159–81.

Burrell, John. 'Diary of Sergeant John Burrell, 1759–60.' *Acadiensis* 5 (1905), 291–4.

Calvin, Case. In *English Reports* 77 (London, 1907), 377–411.

Campbell, Patrick. *Travels in the Interior Inhabited Parts of North America in the Years 1791 and 1792*. Ed. H.H. Langton. Toronto: The Champlain Society 1937.

Cartier, Jacques. 'The first relation of Jaques Cartier of S. Malo.' In *The Principal Navigation, Voyages, and Discoveries of the English Nation Collected by Richard Hakluyt*, ed. Edmund Goldsmid, 77–97. Vol. 13. *America*, part II. Edinburgh, 1889.

Casteel, Anthony. 'Journal.' In 'Collection de documents inédits sur le Canada et l'Amérique.' *Canada-Français* 3 (Québec, 1890), 111–26.

Chambers, Sir Robert. *A Course of Lectures on the English Law Delivered at the University of Oxford 1767–1773*. Vol. 1. Ed. Thomas M. Curley. Madison: University of Wisconsin Press, 1986.

Chancels de Lagrange, Louis. 'Voyage fait à Îsle Royale ou Cap Breton en Canada, 1716.' *Revue d'histoire de l'Amérique française* 13 (1959), 422–34.

Chronicle-Herald. 1999–2001.

A Conference of His Excellency the Governor, with the Sachems and Chief Men of the Eastern Indians. 9–12 August 1717. Boston, 1717.

'Constitution Act, 1982.' In *Home and Native Land: Aboriginal Rights and the Canadian Constitution*, ed. Michael Asch. Toronto: Methuen 1984. Appendix A, 111.

Courville, Louis de. 'Journal of Louis de Courville.' In *Journals of Beausejour*, ed. John Clarence Webster. Saint John: New Brunswick Museum, 1937.

DeMeulles, Jacques. 'Account of the Voyage of Monsieur Demeulles to Acadie.' In *Acadiensia Nova*, ed. William I. Morse. Vol. 1. London: Bernard Quaritch, 1935, 84–131.

Denys, Nicolas. *The Description and Natural History of the Coasts of North America (Acadia)*. Ed. William F. Ganong. Toronto: The Champlain Society, 1908.

Dièreville, Sieur de. *Relation de voyage du Port Royal de l'Acadie*. Toronto: The Champlain Society, 1933.

Du Pont Duvivier, Joseph. *Course à l'Acadie: Journal de Campagne de François Du Pont Duvivier*. Ed. Bernard Pothier. Ottawa: Editions d'Acadie, 1982.

'Eastern Indians Letter to the Governour July 27, 1721.' *Collections of the Massa-chusetts Historical Society.* 2nd Series, vol. 8. (Boston, 1819), 259–63.

Gargas, M. de. 'Mon séjour de l'Acadie.' In *Acadiensia Nova.*, ed. William Morse. Vol. 1. London: Bernard Quaritch, 1935, 165–99.

– 'General Census of the Country of Acadie, 1687–88.' In *Acadiensia Nova.*, ed. William Morse. Vol. 1. London: Quaritch, 1935, 144–55.

Grace, Henry. *The History of the Life and Sufferings of Henry Grace.* Reading: The Author, 1764.

Gyles, John. *Memoirs of Odd Adventures and Signal Deliverances in the Captivity of John Gyles.* 2nd ed. Cincinnati: Siller and Gates, 1869.

Harvey, D.C., ed. *Holland's Description of Cape Breton Island and other Documents.* Halifax: Public Archives of Nova Scotia, 1935.

Hollingsworth, S. *The Present State of Nova Scotia with a Brief Account of Canada and the British Islands on the Coasts of North America.* Edinburgh, 1786.

Ignace de Paris. 'Brève relation de la mission d'Acadie, 1656.' In *PAC 1904.* Appendix H. Ottawa 1905.

Jeffreys, Thomas. 'A New Map of Nova Scotia and Cape Britain with the Adja-cent Parts of New England and Canada.' 1755.

Journal du Voyage de M. Saint-Luc de la Corne. Québec: A. Coté et. cie., 1863.

'The Journal of a Captive, 1745–1748.' In *Colonial Captivities, Marches and Jour-neys*, ed. Isabel M. Calder, 3–136. New York: MacMillan, 1935.

Kalm, Pehr. *Voyage de Pehr Kalm au Canada en 1749.* Transl. and ed. Jacques Rous-seau and Guy Béthune. Montreal 1977.

La Varenne, M. de. 'A Letter from Louisbourg.' Ed. Kenneth Donovan. *Acadien-sis* 10, no. 1 (1980), 113–30.

Lawrence, Charles. 'The Journals and Letters of Colonel Charles Lawrence.' Halifax: Public Archives of Nova Scotia, Bulletin no. 10, 1955.

LeClercq, Chrestien. *New Relation of Gaspesia.* Ed. William F. Ganong. Toronto: The Champlain Society, 1910.

Le Loutre, Jean-Louis. 'Une autobiographie de l'abbé Le Loutre (1709–1772).' Ed. Albert David. *Nova Francia* 6 (1931), 1–34.

– 'Lettres de M. l'abbé Le Loutre.' *Canada-Français* 1 (Québec, 1888), 19–39.

Lescarbot, Marc. *History of New France.* 3 vols. Transl. W.L. Grant. Toronto: The Champlain Society, 1907–1914.

'Letters of Col. Thomas Westbrook and others.' *New England Genealogical and Historical Register* 45–9 (1890–95).

Malapart, Sieur. *La Prise d'un Seigneur Escossais et de ses gens qui pillaient les navires pescherus de France ... par Monsieur Daniel de Dieppe, Capitaine.* Rouen 1630.

Morrison, Alvin, ed. 'Membertou's Raid on the Chouacoet Almouchiquois: The Micmac Sack of Saco in 1607.' Trans. Thomas Goetz. In *Papers of the Sixth*

Algonquian Conference, ed. William Cowan, 159–79. Ottawa: Carleton University Press, 1975.

Macmechan, Archibald M., ed. *A Calender of Two Letter Books and One Commission Book in the Possession of the Government of Nova Scotia, 1713–1741.* Halifax: Public Archives of Nova Scotia, 1900.

– ed. *Original Minutes of Her Majesty's Council at Annapolis Royal, 1720–1739.* Halifax: Public Archives of Nova Scotia, 1908.

Morse, Colonel Robert. 'A General Description of the Province of Nova Scotia.' *PAC* Report for 1883. Ottawa: Government Printing Office, 1884. xxvii–lv.

New England Courant. 1721–1726.

New England Weekly Journal. 1727–1732.

Owen, Captain William. 'The Journal of Captain William Owen, R.N., during his Residence on Campobello in 1770–71.' *Collections of the New Brunswick Society* 1. Saint John, 1894, 193–208.

Pote, Captain William. *The Journal of Captain William Pote, Junior during His Captivity in the French and Indian War, 1745–47.* New York: Dodd, Mead, 1896.

Proctor, Jonathan. 'Diary Kept at Louisbourg, 1759–1760.' *The Essex Institute Historical Collections* 70 (1934), 38–79.

Rand, Silas T. *A First Reading Book in the Micmac Language Comprising the Micmac Numerals, and the Names of the Different Kinds of Beasts, Birds, Fishes, Trees, &c. of the Maritime Provinces of Canada.* Halifax, 1875.

Robinson, John. *A Journey through Nova Scotia Containing a Particular Account of the Country and Its Inhabitants.* York, 1774.

Rossel, Louis-Auguste. 'Journal de ma campagne à l'Île Royale (1757).' In *Rapport de l'archiviste de la province de Québec pour 1931–1932.* 369–87. Quebec, 1932.

Roules, Robert. 'The Vengeful Women of Marblehead: Robert Roule's Deposition of 1677.' Ed. James Axtell. *William and Mary Quarterly* 31, 3rd series (1974), 650–2.

Saint-Vallier, Jean Baptiste. *Estat présent de l'eglise et de la colonie Française.* Paris: Chez Robert Pepie, 1686.

Smethurst, Gamaliel. *A Narrative of an Extraordinary Escape.* London, 1774.

The Trial of Five Persons for Piracy, Felony and Robbery ... Held at the Court House in Boston, within His Majesty's Province of the Massachusetts-Bay in New England on Tuesday the Fourth Day of October. Boston, 1726.

V.T.H. 'Relation d'un voyage de Paris en Canada,' 14 october 1741. In *Rapport de l'archiviste de la Province de Québec pour 1947–1948,* 21–8. Quebec, 1948.

Vital Records of Gloucestor, Massachusetts to the End of the Year 1849. Vol. 3. Salem, 1924.

'The Voyage of Etienne Bellenger to the Maritimes in 1583: A New Document,' Ed. David Beers Quinn. *Canadian Historical Review* 63 (1962), 328–43.

Webster, John C., ed. *Acadia at the End of the 17th Century.* Saint John: New Brunswick Museum, 1934.

Judicial Decisions

R. v. Badger, 3 April 1996, *CNLR* 2 (1996), 77–113.

R. v. Horse, 28 January 1988, *CNLR* 2 (1988), 112–33.

R. v. Marshall, 17 September 1999, *CNLR,* 4 (1999), 161–96

R. v. Marshall, 17 November 1999, *CNLR* 4 (1999), 301–21

R. v. Sioui, SCR 1 (1990), 1025–74.

R. v. Sparrow, 31 May 1990, *CNLR* 3 (1990), 160–88.

R. v. Van der Peet, 21 August 1996, *CNLR* 4 (1996), 177–286.

Shubenacadie Indian Band v. Canada, CNLR 1 (2001), 282–310.

Secondary Sources

Akagi, Roy H. *The Town Proprietors of the New England Colonies.* 1924. Reprint, Gloucester, Mass.: P. Smith 1963.

Anderson, Karen. *Chain Her by One Foot: The Subjugation of Native Women in Seventeenth-Century New France.* New York: Routledge, 1991.

Baker, Emerson W. '"A Scratch with a Bear's Paw": Anglo-Indian Land Deeds in Early Maine.' *Ethnohistory* 36, no. 3 (1989), 235–56.

Baker, Raymond F. 'A Campaign of Amateurs: The Siege of Louisbourg, 1745.' *Occasional Papers in Archaeology and History* 18 (1978).

Bakker, Peter. 'Basque Pidgin Vocabulary in European-Algonquian Trade Contacts.' *Papers of the 19th Algonquian Conference,* 7–15. Ottawa: Carleton University Press, 1988.

– 'Two Basque Loanwords in Micmac.' *International Journal of American Linguistics* (1986), 258–61.

Banfield, A.W.F. *The Mammals of Canada.* 2nd ed. Toronto: University of Toronto Press, 1981.

Barnes, Viola. 'Richard Wharton, A Seventeenth Century New England Colonial.' *Transactions of the Colonial Society of Massachusetts* 26 (1924–26), 260–9.

Basso, Richard. '"Stalking with Stories": Names, Places, and Moral Narratives among the Western Apache.' In *Text, Play, and Story: The Construction and Reconstruction of Self and Society,* ed. Stuart Plattner, 19–55. Washington: The American Ethnological Society, 1984.

Beck, J. Murray. *Politics of Nova Scotia.* Vol. 1. *Nicholson-Fielding 1710–1896.* Tantallon, N.S., 1985.

Bell, D.G. 'Maritime Legal Institutions, 1710–1850.' *Manitoba Law Journal* 23, no. 1 (1996), 103–31.

Bourque, Bruce. 'Aboriginal Settlement and Subsistence on the Maine Coast.' *Man in the Northeast*, no. 6 (1973), 3–10.

– 'Ethnicity on the Maritime Peninsula, 1600–1759.' *Ethnohistory* 36 (1989), 257–84.

– 'Evidence for Prehistoric Exchange on the Maritime Peninsula.' In *Prehistoric Exchange Systems in North America*, ed. Timothy G. Baugh and Jonathan E. Ericson, 23–46. New York: Plenum Press, 1994.

Bourque, Bruce, and Ruth Holmes Whitehead. 'Tarrentines and the Introduction of European Trade Goods in the Gulf of Maine.' *Ethnohistory* 32, no. 4 (1986), 327–41.

Bowen, H.V. *Elites, Enterprise and the Making of the British Overseas Empire, 1688–1775*. New York: Macmillan, 1996.

Bradley, James. 'Native Exchange and European Trade: Cross-Cultural Dynamics in the Sixteenth Century.' *Man in the Northeast*, no. 33 (Spring 1987), 31–46.

Bratton, Timothy L. 'The Identity of the New England Indian Epidemic of 1616–19.' *Bulletin of the History of Medicine* 62 (1988), 351–83.

Brebner, J.B. *New England's Outpost: Acadia before the Conquest of Canada*. New York: Columbia University Press, 1927.

Brewer, John. *The Sinews of Power: War, Money and the English State, 1688–1783*. Cambridge: Harvard University Press, 1990.

Burley, David. 'Proto-Historic Ecological Effects of the Fur Trade on Micmac Culture.' *Ethnohistory* 28 (1981), 203–14.

Bushnell, D. I., Jr. 'The Origin of Wampum.' *The Journal of the Anthropological Institute of Great Britain and Ireland* 36 (1906), 173–7.

Cassidy, Frank. ed. *Aboriginal Title in British Columbia:* Delgamuukw v. The Queen. Montreal: Oolichan Books, 1992.

Chard, Donald F. 'Canso, 1710–1721: Focal Point of New England – Cape Breton Rivalry.' *Collections of the Nova Scotia Historical Society* 39 (1977), 49–77.

Chute, Janet. 'Ceremony, Social Revitalization and Change: Micmac Leadership and the Annual Festival of St. Anne.' In *Papers of the 23rd Algonquian Conference*, ed. William Cowan, 45–61. Ottawa: Carleton University Press 1992.

Clark, Andrew Hill. *Acadia: The Geography of Early Nova Scotia to 1760*. Madison: University of Wisconsin Press, 1968.

Clarke, D. Bruce. 'Implementation of Aboriginal Fishing Rights.' In *An Introduction to Aboriginal Issues in Atlantic Canada*, 4–5. Halifax: Canadian Bar Association, 1994.

Coates, Ken. *The Marshall Decision and Native Rights*. Montreal: McGill-Queen's University Press, 2000.

Collier, Jane F. and Michelle Z. Rosaldo. 'Politics and Gender in Simple Societies.' In *Sexual Meanings: The Cultural Construction of Gender and Sexuality*, ed.

Sherry B. Ortner and Harriet Whitehead, 275–329. Cambridge: Cambridge University Press, 1981.

Cook, Shelburne. 'The Significance of Disease in the Extinction of the New England Indians.' *Human Biology* 44 (1973), 485–508.

Culhane, Dara. *The Pleasure of the Crown: Anthropology, Law and First Nations.* Burnaby: TalonBooks, 1998.

Daugherty, William. *The Maritime Treaties in Historical Perspective.* Ottawa: Department of Indian Affairs, Historical and Treaties Research Branch, 1983.

Davis, Stephen A. 'Early Societies: Sequences of Change.' In *The Atlantic Region to Confederation: A History*, ed. Phillip A. Buckner and John G. Reid, 3–21. Toronto: University of Toronto Press, 1994.

Dawson, Joan. *A Mapmaker's Eye: Nova Scotia in Early Maps.* Halifax: Nimbus, 1988.

Desbarats, Catherine M. 'The Cost of Early Canada's Native Alliances: Reality and Scarcity's Rhetoric.' *William and Mary Quarterly*, 3rd series, 52, no. 4 (1995), 609–30.

Dickason, Olive P. 'Amerindians Between French and English in Nova Scotia, 1713–1763,' *American Indian Culture and Research Journal* 10 (1986), 31–56.

– *Louisbourg and the Indians: A Study in Imperial Relations, 1713–1760.* Ottawa: Parks Canada History and Archaeology, 1976.

Dumont-Johnson, Micheline. *Apôtres ou Agitateurs: la France missionaire en Acadie.* Trois-Rivières: Boréal Press, 1970.

Eccles, W.J. 'The Social, Economic, and Political Significance of the Military Establishment in New France.' *Canadian Historical Review* 52 (1971), 1–21.

Eckstorm, Fanny Hardy. *Old John Neptune and Other Maine Indian Shamans.* 2nd ed. Orono: University of Maine at Orono Press, 1980.

Egnal, Marc. *A Mighty Empire: The Origins of the American Revolution.* Ithaca and London: Cornell University Press, 1987.

Feister, Lois M. 'Linguistic Communication between the Dutch and Indians.' *Ethnohistory* 20 (1973), 25–38.

Fewkes, Walter. 'A Contribution to Passamaquoddy Folk-Lore.' *Journal of American Folklore* 3 (1890), 257–80.

Flemming, David. *The Canso Islands: An 18th Century Fishing Station.* Ottawa: Parks Canada Manuscript Report #308, 1977.

Foster, Hamar. '"The Queen's Law Is Better Than Yours": International Homicide in Early British Columbia.' In *Essays in the History of Canadian Law* Vol. 5. *Crime and Criminal Justice*, ed. Jim Phillips, Tina Loo, and Susan Lewthwaite, 41–111. Toronto: The Osgoode Society, 1994.

Francis, Daniel, and Toby Morantz. *Partners in Fur: A History of the Fur Trade in Eastern James Bay 1600–1870.* Montreal: McGill-Queens University Press, 1983.

Ghere, David Lynn. 'Abenaki Factionalism, Emigration and Social Continuity: Indian Society in Northern New England, 1725 to 1765.' PhD dissertation, University of Maine, 1988.

– '"Mistranslations and Misinformation": Diplomacy on the Maine Frontier, 1725 to 1755.' *American Indian Culture and Research Journal* 8, no. 4 (1984), 3–26.

Gonzalez, Ellice B. 'An Ethnohistorical Analysis of Micmac Male and Female Economic Roles.' *Ethnohistory* 29 (1982), 117–29.

Goody, Jack. *The Logic of Writing and Organization of Society*. New York: Cambridge University Press, 1987.

Griffiths, N.E.S. *The Contexts of Acadian History, 1686–1784*. Montreal: McGill-Queen's University Press, 1992.

Hagedorn, Nancy L. '"A Friend to Go Between": The Interpreter as Cultural Broker during Anglo-Iroquois Councils, 1740–70.' *Ethnohistory* 35, no. 1 (1988), 60–80.

Henderson, James [Sákéj] Youngblood. 'First Nations Legal Inheritances in Canada: The Mí'kmaq Model.' *Manitoba Law Journal* 23, no. 1 (1996), 1–31.

Henretta, James. '*Salutary Neglect:' Colonial Administration under the Duke of Newcastle*. Princeton: Princeton University Press, 1972.

Holton, Woody. *Forced Founders: Indians, Debtors, Slaves and the Making of the American Revolution in Virginia*. Chapel Hill: University of North Carolina Press, 1999.

Isaac, Thomas. 'Balancing Rights: The Supreme Court of Canada, *R. v. Sparrow* and the Future of Aboriginal Rights.' *Canadian Journal of Native Studies* 13, no. 2 (1993), 199–219.

Jaenen, Cornelius. *Friend and Foe: Aspects of French-Amerindian Cultural Contact in the Sixteenth and Seventeenth Centuries*. Toronto: McClelland & Stewart, 1976.

– 'The Role of Presents in French-Amerindian Trade.' In *Explorations in Canadian Economic History: Essays in Honour of Irene M. Spry*, ed. Duncan Cameron, 23–50. Ottawa: University of Ottawa Press, 1985.

Johnston, A.J.B. 'The Fishermen of Eighteenth-Century Cape Breton: Numbers and Origins.' *Nova Scotia Historical Review* 9, no. 1 (1989), 62–72.

Kawashima, Yasuhide. *Puritan Justice and the Indian*. Middleton: Weslayan University Press, 1986.

Leonard, Kevin James Malachy. 'Mi'kmaq Culture during the Late Woodland And Early Historic Periods.' PhD dissertation. University of Toronto, 1996.

Malone, J.J. *Pine Trees and Politics: The Naval Stores and Forest Policy in Colonial New England 1691–1775*. Seattle: University of Washington Press, 1964.

Marshall, Donald Sr, Alexander Denny, and Simon Marshall. 'The Covenant Chain.' In *Drumbeat: Anger and Renewal in Indian Country*, ed. Boyce Richardson, 71–104. Toronto: Summerhill Press and the Assembly of First Nations, 1989.

Miller, Virginia. 'Aboriginal Micmac Population: A Review of the Evidence.' *Ethnohistory* 23 (1976), 117–29.

- 'The Micmac: A Maritime Woodland Group.' In *Native Peoples: The Canadian Experience*, ed. R. Bruce Morrison and C. Roderick Wilson, 324–51. Toronto: McClelland & Stewart, 1986.

- 'Social and Political Complexity on the East Coast: The Micmac Case.' In *The Evolution of Maritime Cultures on the Northeast and the Northwest Coasts of America*, ed. Ronald Nash, 41–53. Vancouver: Department of Archaeology, Simon Fraser University, 1983.

Miquelon, Dale. *New France 1701–1744: 'A Supplement to Europe.'* Toronto: McClelland & Stewart, 1987.

Moore, Christopher. 'The Other Louisbourg: Trade and Merchant Enterprise in Ile Royale 1713–1758.' *Histoire Sociale/Social History* 12 (1979), 79–96.

Morantz, Toby. *An Ethnohistoric Study of Eastern James Bay Cree Social Organization, 1700–1850.* Ottawa: National Museum of Canada, 1983.

Morrison, Kenneth. *The Embattled Northeast: The Elusive Ideal of Alliance in Abenaki-Euro-American Relations.* Berkeley: University of California Press, 1984.

- The People of the Dawn: The Abnaki and Their Relations with New England and New France, 1600–1727.' PhD dissertation, University of Maine, 1975.

- 'Towards a History of Intimate Encounters: Algonkian Folklore, Jesuit Missionaries, and Kiwakwe, the Cannibal Giant.' *American Indian Culture and Research Journal* 3, no. 4 (1979), 51–80.

Nash, Ronald J. *Mi'kmaq: Economics and Evolution.* Halifax: Nova Scotia Museum, 1986.

Newell, Diane. *The Tangled Webs of History.* Toronto: University of Toronto Press, 1993.

Nicholas, Andrea Bear. 'Maliseet Aboriginal Rights and Mascarene's Treaty, Not Dummer's Treaty.' In *Acts of the 17th Algonquian Conference*, ed. William Cowan, 215–29. Ottawa: Carleton University Press, 1986.

Nietfeld, Patricia. 'Determinants of Aboriginal Micmac Political Structure.' PhD dissertation, University of New Mexico, 1981.

Pacifque, Pere. 'Le pays des Micmacs – The Micmac Country.' *Bulletin de la société de géographie de Québec* (1930).

Pagden, Anthony. *Lords of All the World: Ideologies of Empire in Spain, Britain and France c. 1500 – c. 1800.* New Haven and London: Yale University Press, 1995.

Pastore, Ralph. 'Aboriginal Peoples and European Contact.' In *The Atlantic Region to Confederation*, ed. Phillip Buckner and John G. Reid, 22–39. Toronto: University of Toronto Press, 1994.

Patterson, Stephen E. 'Indian–White Relations in Nova Scotia, 1749–61: A Study in Political Interaction,' *Acadiensis* 23, no. 1 (Autumn 1993), 23–59.

Pencak, William. *War, Politics and Revolution in Provincial Massachusetts.* Boston: Northeastern University Press, 1981.

Piers, Harry. 'The Fortieth Regiment, Raised at Annapolis Royal in 1717; and Five Regiments Subsequently Raised in Nova Scotia.' *Collections of the Nova Scotia Historical Society* 21 (Halifax, 1927).

Plank, Geoffrey. *An Unsettled Conquest: The British Campaign against the Peoples of Acadia.* Philadelphia: University of Pennsylvania Press, 2001.

Pothier, Bernard. 'Acadian Emigration to Ile Royale After the Conquest of Acadia.' *Histoire Sociale/Social History* 6 (1970), 116–31.

Reid, John G. *Acadia, Maine and New Scotland: Marginal Colonies in the Seventeenth Century.* Toronto: University of Toronto Press, 1981.

Reid, John Phillip. *A Law of Blood: The Primitive Law of the Cherokee Nation.* New York: New York University Press, 1970.

– 'Principles of Vengeance: Fur trappers, Indians, and Retaliation for Homicide in the Transboundary North American West.' In *Historical Perspectives on Law and Society in Canada,* ed. Tina Loo and Lorna McLean, 14–34. (Toronto: Copp Clark Longman, 1994).

Rogers, Edward S. *The Hunting Group: Hunting Territory Complex among the Mistassini Indians.* Anthropological Series 63, National Museum of Canada Bulletin 195. Ottawa: 1963.

Rogers, Colonel H.C.B. *The British Army of the Eighteenth Century.* New York: Allen and Unwin, 1977.

Schmeisser, Barbara. 'The Population of Louisbourg, 1713–1758.' Ottawa: 1976.

Schmidt, David L., 'The Micmac Hieroglyphs: A Reassessment.' In *Papers of the Twenty-Fourth Algonquian Conference,* ed. William Cowan. Ottawa: University of Carleton Press, 1993.

Schmidt, David L., and B.A. Balcom. 'The Reglements of 1739: A Note on Micmac Law and Literacy.' *Acadiensis* 23, no. 1 (Autumn 1993), 110–27.

Schmidt, David L., and Murdeena Marshall, eds. *Mi'kmaq Hieroglyphic Prayers: Readings in North America's First Indigenous Script.* Halifax: Nimbus, 1995.

Shipton, Clifford K. *Sibley's Harvard Graduates.* Vol. 4, 1690–1700. Cambridge, 1933.

Speck, Frank. 'The Eastern Algonkian Wabanaki Confederacy.' *American Anthropologist* 17 (1915), 492–508.

– 'The Family Hunting Band as the Basis of Algonkian Social Organization,' *American Anthropologist* 17 (1915), 189–205.

Speck, Frank, and Loren C. Eiseley. 'Significance of Hunting Territory Systems of the Algonkian in Social Theory.' *American Anthropologist* 41 (1939), 269–80.

Speck, Frank, and Wendall Hadlock. 'A Report on Tribal Boundaries and Hunting Areas of the Malecite Indian of New Brunswick.' *American Anthropologist* 48 (1946), 355–74.

Speiss, Arthur E., and Bruce D. Speiss. 'New England Pandemic of 1616–1622: Cause and Archaeological Implication.' *Man in the Northeast* 34 (1987), 71–83.

Springer, James Warren. 'American Indians and the Law of Real Property in Colonial New England.' *The American Journal of Legal History* 30 (1986), 25–58.

Stanley, George F.G. *New France: The Last Phase, 1744–1760.* Toronto: McClelland & Stewart, 1968.

Stephens, W.B. 'Literacy in England, Scotland, and Wales, 1500–1900.' *History of Education Quarterly* 30, no. 4 (Winter 1990), 553–4.

Turgeon, Laurier. 'Basque-Amerindian Trade in the Saint Lawrence during the Sixteenth Century: New Documents, New Perspectives.' *Man in the Northeast* 40 (1990), 81–7.

Upton, L.F.S. *Micmacs and Colonists: Indian–White Relations in the Maritimes, 1713–1867.* Vancouver: University of British Columbia Press, 1979.

Wallace, Anthony F.C. *Jefferson and the Indians: The Tragic Fate of the First Americans.* Cambridge: Harvard University Press, 1999.

Walters, Mark D. '*Mohegan Indians v. Connecticut* (1705–73) and the Legal Status of Aboriginal Customary Laws and Government in British North America.' *Osgoode Hall Law Journal* 33, no. 4 (1995), 786–827.

Whitehead, Ruth Holmes. 'A New Micmac Petroglyph Site,' *The Occasional* 13, no. 1 (1992), 10.

– *Stories from the Six Worlds: Micmac Legends.* Halifax: Nimbus, 1988.

Wicken, William C. 'Encounters with Tall Sails and Tall Tales: Mi'kmaq Society, 1500–1760.' PhD dissertation, McGill University, 1994.

– 'Re-examining Mi'kmaq-Acadian Relations, 1635–1755.' In *Après vingt ans*, ed. Sylvie Dépatie, Catherine Desbarats et al., 93–111. Montreal and Kingston: McGill-Queen's University Press, 1998.

– '26 August 1726: A Case Study in Mi'kmaq–New England Relations.' *Acadiensis* 23, no. 1 (Autumn 1993), 5–22.

Wildsmith, Bruce H. 'The Mi'kmaq and the Fishery: Beyond Food Requirements.' *Dalhousie Law Journal* 18, no. 1 (1995), 116–40.

Williams, Rick. 'When Is a Fish Not a Fish?' *New Maritimes* 12, no. 3 (1994), 29–33.

Williams, Robert, and Graham R. Daborn. 'Spawning of the American Shad in the Annapolis River, Nova Scotia,' and 'Spawning of the Striped Bass in the Annapolis River, Nova Scotia.' *Proceedings of the Nova Scotia Institute of Science* 34 (1984), 12–13 and 17–21.

Illustration Credits

Index

CHOICES

CHOICES

by

NANCY TODER

alyson
books
LOS ANGELES • NEW YORK

Printed in the United States of America.
Printed on acid-free paper.

This trade paperback is published by Alyson Publications Inc.,
P.O. Box 4371, Los Angeles, California 90078-4371.
Distributed in the United Kingdom by Turnaround Publisher Services Ltd.,
Unit 3 Olympia Trading Estate, Coburg Road, Wood Green,
London N22 6TZ, England.

First published by Persephone Press: 1980
First Alyson edition: May 1984
Tenth-anniversary edition: December 1991

01 00 99 98 97   10 9 8 7 6 5 4

ISBN 1-55583-061-7
(Previously published with ISBN 0-932870-61-9.)

This book is dedicated to all the brave women who have defied so much in their love for women, and to those women who, for whatever reasons, were unable to make that commitment or live by it; in our common pain and rage, let us affirm that our daughters will have more choices.

And in my own individual journey, this book is for Alice Bloch, whose strength and support helped me rediscover my courage, and who has so lovingly shared in my personal struggles and growth.

Special thanks to Andrea Nachtigall, Jan Oxenberg, Marcy Alancraig, Florence Toder, Emanuel Toder, and Connie Katzenstein, whose belief in this project helped keep me going; and to Pat McGloin, Deborah Snow, and Gloria Z. Greenfield, who have built, in Persephone, a press I can wholeheartedly support.

INTRODUCTION

It was my hope when I wrote *Choices* twelve years ago, a time when there were so few stories of lesbian lives, that I would help a little in our communal search for definition and courage. Many of us in the women's community were struggling with creating our own culture and some of us were exploring the philosophy and politics of separatism. In my frustration of wanting to read a novel that would portray lesbian relationships honestly and positively, I decided to write my own. I wanted to make lesbian experience the center of the world in my novel, a world where women were valued and the bonds between women were taken seriously.

Today, we have a wider selection of lesbian and women-identified novels and nonfiction available to us. The public voices of lesbians have become more diverse as many of us recognize a variety of cultural heritages, identifications, and commitments. Large segments of the lesbian community are forging links with a variety of liberation movements and are attempting to envision a global perspective cognizant of worldwide economic, social, and ecological realities.

There is much about such changes which is positive; the diversity of voices has provided a way for more of us to relate to the women's community and has strengthened and enriched our politics. But unfortunately our energy and economic resources are limited. Some lesbian organizations and centers have dissolved recently, leaving many women without a safe refuge, as well as putting us at risk of assimilation into the mainstream where we may lose our vitality and independent vision.

On a individual level, many of us have also experienced disillusionment, as the simple comforting idealizations of women and lesbian relationships which gave us such a righteous sense of purpose in the '70s no longer seem to apply to our more complex view of ourselves and the world we live in. In the face of these uncertainties, we look for something to hold onto. At such moments I think we must reach to our core, the place from which our love and commitment to women springs. For it is in returning to those personal and intimate bonds that we may find a sustaining vision to guide our lives and our work.

Choices is the story of several women's struggles to articulate their love for women. I have been very fortunate that this book has been so well received and that many women have let me know that they were able to use this story to more fully understand and create their own lives. And in listening to their stories, I have found more freedom to live and create my own.

Nancy Toder
Topanga, California

Part I

1

The noise of the planes was comforting to Sandy. The louder the engines, the less likely her mother would try to make conversation with her. Sandy watched a plane taxi into the hangar. She loved airports: they meant escape and freedom.

Her mother hated airports for a corresponding reason: they meant desertion and loneliness. Esther was a little shorter than Sandy, but like Sandy, she appeared taller than she was. Her clothes were inexpensive but in good taste: a black skirt, white blouse, and dark red cardigan, an old pocketbook of Sandy's from junior high — Sandy often told her to throw it out — and a casual pair of stacked heels. Her hair was messy, as always. There was nothing to be done about that, so to compensate, Esther had put on some lipstick that morning.

Sandy's father hated airports, too, but for an entirely different reason: they made him feel small and useless. Small, because the deafening noises and huge crafts came from a word of powerful men, a world Sid had never felt a part of. Useless, because he didn't know how to say goodbye to the daughter who was so estranged from him, and even more, because he didn't know how he would deal with his wife's sadness when they got home. After Sandy's departures, Esther would be so very quiet — staring off into nowhere, crying on and off for no apparent reason. In his life Sid had known what it was like to feel helpless, and knowing that had made him softer than most men. But he had never gotten used to it, and it always frustrated him. Sid was Sandy's height (although Sandy looked taller since she had started teasing her hair), medium built, slightly balding, once good-looking. The years of hard work had taken their toll; he was a very nervous man, and the lines of continual worry showed on his face.

Esther looked at her daughter and sighed inwardly. The black leather jacket, the short black skirt, the blacktoned stockings and black pointed shoes. Sandy looked as though she was on her way to a funeral. No, it wasn't that; her daughter looked like a

1

hoodlum. The teased hair, the makeup, and the constant gum chewing (in which Sandy never closed her mouth, no matter how many times Esther carefully pointed it out) were the final touches to this carefully groomed image. Esther imagined how a stranger would see her daughter. Another tough New York adolescent. Seventeen going on thirty-five. How would they ever know that underneath the war costume was an exceptionally brilliant and sensitive young woman? A young woman who would some day do something great. Some day.

Sandy wished her mother would quit staring at her. Esther had that wistful expression that always made Sandy particularly creeped out. The three of them had been waiting by the gate for about fifteen minutes. Other college kids and their parents stood around in various stages of silence and awkwardness. Sandy wished her parents would go.

"You guys don't have to hang around or nothing."

"Oh, we don't mind. Do we, Sid?" Esther didn't bother to look at her husband for his answer. "It's the last look I'm going to have for a long time."

Sandy was exasperated. Why was her mother always making such a big deal out of everything? "Shit, Mom. I'll be home for Thanksgiving. It's not like this is the first time I've been away from home." Sandy was sorry as soon as she said that last line. Her mother's face whitened and her father got even more tense. Why couldn't she keep her mouth shut? It just seemed as though things popped out without her having any say in it. Sandy felt a twinge of guilt. Hadn't she hurt them enough?

Esther chose to ignore that reference to Sandy's disappearance last year, when she had run away from home for six months. Six awful, panic-filled months during which Esther and Sid had gone over every interaction with Sandy, every child-rearing memory, every possible explanation for their daughter's dropping out of high school and running away. Thank God that was all in the past.

"No, but this is the first time my baby is going off to college. And the first time you're flying. And Sandy, you know I don't like it when you use language like that. Your friends may think it's smart, but it's not becoming for a young lady."

Sandy chomped on her gum. She had heard this lecture a million times. Her lines were just as inevitable as Esther's. "It's not the first time, Mom — I flew once to Washington. And I know in your day young ladies didn't say SHIT or FUCK or SCREW or . . ."

Esther interrupted. "Sandy. Your language."

Sandy was in her smart-ass routine now. "Just making a point, Mom. Times have changed."

"Well, I certainly don't like the changes you young people are going through." Esther threw that in for good measure, but she knew she was defeated. There was nothing she could do. Sandy would talk the way she wanted, and God only knew, dress the way she wanted, and now there wouldn't be anyone to tell her otherwise. No one to bug her, as Sandy would say. Esther remembered what an unusual child Sandy had been — so bright, and enthusiastic and honest, so idealistic and sweet. How could such a miracle of a child turn into such an angry, bitter teenager? The psychiatrist had said it was simply a phase Sandy was going through, just normal teenage conflicts and problems, except they were a thousand times magnified. Esther had never thought about it before, but she wondered if he really meant a thousand times. No, surely he must have been exaggerating.

Sid paced back and forth, looking around tensely. He had walked to the other side of the waiting room so they could have a chance to talk. To be alone. It was funny how that still hurt him — being left out. He took a quick glance at the two of them standing there. They were ordinary-looking people. Yet they were so important to him. It wasn't fair. But then nothing in life was fair. He approached them.

"We should go, Esther. We'll get a ticket. I told you we shouldn't park there — the spot is reserved for airline personnel."

"Sid, it's only a few minutes. There's nothing to worry about." Esther's voice was mildly annoyed. She was tired of his worrying all the time.

Sandy saw her chance. "Dad's right, Mom. It's crazy to risk getting a ticket. Besides, there's nothing you can do here. Let's say goodbye now."

Esther looked from her daughter to her husband, who nodded toward the exit. There was nothing she could do; Sandy and Sid rarely formed an alliance, but when they did, it was a strong one.

Sid walked over to Sandy. "Take care of yourself, Sandy." He embraced her awkwardly and quickly walked away.

"I will, Dad," she replied to his back.

Esther had tears in her eyes. "Will you write?"

Sandy hated it when her mother cried. The sick feeling in her stomach started to grow. "I ain't gonna promise, Mom. You know how I am. But we'll talk on the phone some. Okay?" Sandy was afraid she was going to throw up.

Esther wiped the tears from her eyes in a way not to call attention to them. She hated crying, especially in front of Sandy. "Just remember that your father and I love you." Esther prayed that Sandy would hear that, that she would be okay. What else could she say to make it all right?

Sandy only partially heard it. She was mostly just embarrassed by that kind of intimacy, period, let alone in an airport. What if someone had overheard? Sandy looked around quickly, but no one seemed to be paying attention. They would think she was some kind of baby or something. The only thing to do was to end this quickly.

"Yeah, I know, Ma."

Much to Sandy's relief, her mother was done talking. She hugged Sandy and then walked off quickly to join her husband. Sandy sighed with relief. Then she turned to look at the other people in the waiting room. Other mothers and fathers were fussing over their kids. "How disgusting," Sandy thought. "They all look like babies."

Walking over to the window, she stared out again. She smiled to herself when a plane skidded in its landing. The discomfort from before had quickly dissipated; she had forgotten about her parents and all those weird feelings she had around them as soon as they walked out of her sight. No one would bug her now.

2

Looking out the window was one of Sandy's favorite activities. It was a way she could be invisible, yet continue to see all that was going on around her. This was ideal, because she didn't like to talk. Actually, she didn't know how to talk, but her pride made her describe herself as "a person who didn't go in for much talk." That way, she could pretend to prefer things as they were.

High school had been very difficult for Sandy. She hated the teachers, hated the kids, and most of all, hated her school. It had been her mother's idea that Sandy take the city exam for placement at the one special school for extra-bright students. (Actually, there were three special schools in New York City, but only one of them admitted girls.) Sandy had gone along with it for laughs; she never thought she'd pass the exam. But she did pass — and then it was three long years with those kissing-ass brownies. Sandy was constantly getting into trouble for telling off nosy teachers, smoking in the bathroom, playing hooky, and other typical teenage behavior. But at Bronx Science no one else acted that way, and certainly not a girl.

The hardest time was lunch period in the cafeteria. Sandy sat with a bunch of girls from her homeroom. They would talk about school, boys, clothes, and other subjects that Sandy considered trivial. Sandy never joined in on those conversations; she answered "yes" or "no" when one of the girls asked questions in an effort to make Sandy feel a part of things. But Sandy never did, and that hour was grueling — for as much as she told herself that she was more mature than the other girls and she didn't really want to be included in their stupid chatter, there was still a part of her that wanted to fit in.

4

"Excuse me, is this taken?" A weird-looking girl pointed to the seat next to Sandy. She had a big smile and nervous, exuberant energy as she swung her tennis racket with one hand and held a big bag of packages with the other. She was wearing matching sweater and knee socks with a plain skirt and sneakers.

Sandy shook her head and looked back out the window.

"You mind if I sit here?"

Sandy turned to look at her a bit more closely. She decided the girl was definitely crazy and wished she would go away, but what could she say? The seat wasn't taken. She shook her head, once again turning to look out the window.

"Oh, great." The girl seemed oblivious to Sandy's unfriendliness. Full of enthusiasm, she placed her racket above the seat. Sandy wondered if she was losing her touch. She was sure she had flashed one of her mean, don't-bother-me looks. While Sandy was worrying whether her toughness was slipping, the girl interrupted her for a third time.

"Do you play?"

Sandy turned to look at her again. "Huh?"

"Tennis?"

Sandy found herself answering the question despite herself. "Not exactly, I got a racket, but we don't have none of those courts where I live. But I used to play against the project garage. Squash."

"Oh." The girl didn't seem at all taken aback by what Sandy had said. There was something really strange about this kid. "My name is Bernice Bernstein. My friends call me Bunny."

"Sandy Stein." Sandy was kind of liking Bunny. There was something sweet about her.

"Pleased to meet you. Oh, I'm so excited, I can hardly stand it. This is the first time I'm flying. Have you flown before?"

Sandy slipped into her cool, sophisticated older woman act, despite the fact that they were the same age. "Sure. Many times." To her amazement, Sandy felt herself grow protective towards Bunny.

"Oh, I'm glad I sat next to you. You seem so calm and like you know just what to expect. This is also the first time I'm going to be away from home. Well, not exactly — I went to summer camp, of course. But that doesn't count. This is different. I'm going to college. In Buffalo. There's a state university there." Bunny paused here for a breath.

"I know," Sandy replied, amused by Bunny's quick chatter. Talking to Bunny was easy. Her excitement was almost contagious. Almost. Sandy reminded herself that she was cool.

"Oh. You wouldn't by any chance go to the university? . . ."

"Yeah."

"Oh, how wonderful. Are you going there now?" Sandy

nodded. "Oh, I was lucky to sit next to you. Maybe we can go together."

"Sure, if we can find some other students, we can split a cab. What dorm are you in?"

"Goodyear. How about you?"

"We're batting a thousand." Sandy wondered if all the girls would be like Bunny. She tried to imagine a dorm full of sweet babbling kids. She couldn't grasp it.

"Oh, we're in the same dorm. How exciting. My first friend." Bunny smiled at Sandy affectionately.

Sandy had never met anyone like Bunny before. She was really weird. "Where are you from, anyhow?"

"Woodmere." Sandy didn't recognize the name. "One of the five towns." Sandy was still blank. "It's on Long Island."

"Oh, the Island." That explained why Bunny was acting so strangely. Everyone knew that people on the Island were different. They were all rich. She probably even owned her own house.

"Where are you from, Sandy?" Bunny's look was curious.

"The Bronx," Sandy said with an edge of defensiveness and pride.

Sandy looked out the window as the stewardess' voice came on the intercom. As the engine started and the plane began to move, Bunny became agitated. Sandy was too engrossed in the changing view outside to pay much attention. She was back in San Francisco, walking the streets in the middle of the night. The light drizzle justified her pulling up the collar of her trenchcoat as she walked. Sandy liked to look at herself in the mirror with her trenchcoat collar pulled up around her ears. It made her feel tough. She'd dangle a cigarette from her lips like Bogart. Or Bacall. The smoke from her butt would stream up her face, but Sandy had carefully learned how to place it so that none of it got into her eyes, making them tear. That had taken hours in front of the bathroom mirror; if someone yelled for her to get out of the john, she flushed the cigarette down the toilet. But those days of hiding were over. Sandy was her own person now. All grown up.

"Would you mind if I held your hand?"

Bunny's voice shook Sandy out of her daydream.

"Huh?"

"I said would you mind if I held your hand? I know that may seem kind of silly. But I'm frightened and holding your hand would help."

"Well . . . sure." Sandy hesitated for a moment but then came to the conclusion that there was nothing for her to be ashamed of. She wasn't the one who was scared. She tried to reassure Bunny. "Hell, there's nothing scary about flying. You won't feel a thing."

Bunny smiled gratefully and grabbed Sandy's hand as the plane lifted and started to gather speed. Sandy's attention re-

6

turned to the window. She became oblivious to Bunny and her hand. All she saw was the city drifting away.

3

The dormitory room felt like a prison. A walk-in closet on the right gave more of a feeling of space than did the rest of the room. A single bed and a bureau were on the immediate right against a gray cinderblock wall, and a metal-frame double-decker bed and another bureau filled the other side wall. The third wall, which faced the door, was also cinderblock, but had windows looking out across the campus. Against this wall, two desks had been squeezed in.

Sandy paced and smoked furiously. She was still embarrassed about having thrown up on the plane. Bunny hadn't seemed to think anything of it, but Sandy felt she had lost face. She tried to be oblivious to the other two girls in the room, but with each sweep of the floor they were in her peripheral vision. Sandy had never been to sleep-away camp. Nothing in her life had prepared her for living in such intimate quarters with two total strangers. She felt miserable. Why had she ever let her mother talk her into giving college a chance? She could tell already that she wasn't going to like it.

Jenny had set her hair on big curlers and was filing her nails. All week she had been looking forward to this evening. Her first day away from home. College. She was embarking on a mysterious adventure full of exciting events. Jenny was hungry for experience. She wanted to try everything at least once. Maybe even twice. She had bided her time carefully. Her parents had been strict with her: curfews were rigidly enforced, both male and female friends inspected for their desirability, and good grades insisted upon. For the most part, Jenny obeyed their rules as long as she lived in their home. The few times she secretly broke their rules, she felt much guilt; but now she was on her own, and their rules no longer applied. She had waited a long time for this day, and now it was here. But this first day had already turned into a big disappointment. Jenny surveyed her new roommates. Mary was sitting on top of the double-decker, writing a letter. She had volunteered to take that bed. Sandy and Jenny had flipped a coin to see who would get the single. Luckily, Jenny had won. Mary was dressed in a long pink robe. She had straight blond hair and pointy speckled glasses. Jenny thought she was attractive in a small-town farm-girl kind of way. Mary seemed okay, not exactly her first choice for a roommate, but next to Sandy she appeared a gem.

Jenny watched Sandy pace back and forth. Jenny was

seriously afraid that Sandy was a lunatic. They had only been together for a few hours, and Sandy was already starting to get on her nerves. She reminded Jenny of a caged lion, resentful of captivity, and constantly vigilant lest it miss an opportunity to escape. Jenny had always been fascinated by the big cats she saw at the zoo. Their restlessness and sudden capacity for savagery excited her. But Sandy was not a big cat and this wasn't the zoo. Jenny started to bite a cracked nail, then caught herself, and started to refile.

"Do you always pace like that?" Jenny was unable to control herself any longer.

Sandy stopped for a moment and looked at her. "Yeah." She continued pacing, trying harder than ever to ignore them. Boy, did she have luck. Mary seemed straight off the farm. At least she was quiet. She had a reserved, no-nonsense attitude that Sandy liked. She could be tolerated. But Jenny. She *looked* like a baby doll in her pink sheer baby-doll pajamas. The product of an assembly line gone berserk — the long dark hair wrapped around fat ugly curlers, fixed in place by a pink hair net. And that nose. Who had ever seen a baby doll with a long thin Jewish nose? She looked ridiculous. Sandy imagined that she wouldn't be bad-looking if she put on a T-shirt like Sandy's and let her hair down. She had beautiful hair; it was thick and straight and shiny. Everything that Sandy's wasn't. And an interesting face. Not pretty like Bunny's, but attractive in an unusual way. Sandy shook her head and quickened her pace. There was something about Jenny that made her uncomfortable.

"I still can't believe they put three of us in a room this size," Jenny said. The silence had been getting to her, and even complaining seemed better than no conversation at all.

"And I asked for a single," Sandy snapped. "I don't know why they bothered asking us what we prefer on that application."

"And I asked for a nonsmoker," Mary said mildly, as Jenny lit a cigarette.

"Well, we can speak to the head RA tomorrow. Maybe there's been some mistake." There had to be a way out of this, Jenny thought to herself. No one could expect three such diverse people to live in a room barely big enough for two.

"That's a waste of time." Sandy's voice came booming back to Jenny, shaking her out of her thoughts. "They couldn't care less." Jenny felt uncomfortable but intrigued by Sandy's blunt and caustic style. She was so different from anyone Jenny had ever known.

Jenny turned to Mary, who was a safer bet for moderate conversation. "You just got here. Who are you writing to already?"

Mary continued writing without looking up. "My boyfriend," she replied.

8

"Oh. Have you been going together long?" Jenny was suddenly interested in Mary. She always liked to listen to other girls talk about their boyfriends. She had done a lot of dating in high school, but the boys who asked her out, though nice enough, were rarely the most popular ones, and Jenny had secretly harbored crushes on the captain of the basketball team and one of the star players on the tennis team. She watched them flirt with the cheerleaders and the more popular girls, and tried to figure out a way to get close to these boys, but was unable to come up with any good ideas. She had seen other girls make fools of themselves, running after the boys, and she never wanted to put herself in that position. So she dated the boys who asked her out, went steady with a few, but never got very emotionally involved with any of them.

Now, Jenny listened and marveled at how matter-of-factly Mary talked about her fiance. About their plans to marry when he graduated and she could transfer to a nursing program near him. Jenny tried to imagine what it would be like to know what your future would be. She had no idea what she wanted to major in, let alone which man she would spend the rest of her life with. It seemed very far away.

When Jenny imagined the man she would marry (and there was never any question in her mind that she would marry some day) she pictured him as tall, dark, and handsome. A Jewish boy who looked Italian. Her parents had never let her go out with Christian boys, because they were afraid she might marry one. Jenny had explained that she was only fourteen and had no desire to marry anyone yet, but they insisted that if she dated *goyim* she might get used to them. And if she got used to them she might marry one. There was no way to argue logically with her parents, so Jenny often told boys she would have liked to date that she was busy, until they stopped calling.

Jenny was philosophical about the rules her parents made. She often knew that their rules didn't make any sense, but it didn't seem worth it to fight. When she tried to argue about a particular point, like the time she contested her curfew, which was an hour earlier than most of her friends', her mother got hysterical, her father turned livid, and the household was upset for days. And her curfew didn't change.

Her parents often told her that it was important for her husband to be a good provider. That didn't seem very important to Jenny, who just assumed she would always live comfortably. Besides, she was going to have a career and expected that she would bring in good money some day, too. The man she would marry would be exciting. They would travel all over the world, eat at exotic restaurants, and experience strange cultures. When she was with him, Jenny would never have to fear anything. He would protect her from other men. Jenny knew that a single woman couldn't travel freely, especially in many parts of the world. But if she was married, nobody would bother her. They would know that she was spoken for. It had always seemed like a shitty reality to Jenny, but she accepted it as the way things were. There was no point getting upset about the rules; one bent them when possible and followed them when necessary.

Sandy continued to pace, blocking Jenny and Mary's view of each other during their conversation. She tried not to hear them talking, but the words insisted on finding their way through her resistant membranes. Boys, boys, boys. She had only been in the room a few hours and already they had found the number-one topic of interest. The universal language of all teenage girls. Except for Sandy. She was some kind of freak, she guessed. She had never had a crush on Elvis Presley when all the other girls were going wild about him. They had always seemed kind of foolish. But Ann Southern or Gale Storm — now those were people who made Sandy's tough heart soften.

Jenny finished her nails and yawned loudly. "I'm about ready to go to bed," she said. Mary closed her writing pad and slipped down under her covers.

"I'm not tired yet, but you can turn the lights off," Sandy said. She felt relieved that they were going to sleep. Now she would have a chance to think without feeling their presence as a constant intrusion. Sandy continued pacing back and forth along the narrow lane between the beds. Her cigarette glowed in the dark, an orange spot that pinpointed her movements.

Jenny lay in bed, telling herself to turn over and forget about that swirling orange light. She faced the cinderblock wall, but she could still feel Sandy and the cigarette moving back and forth. Back and forth. Jenny reminded herself that this was their first night together and that she should try to be good-humored about the situation. But she wasn't feeling cheery.

"Hey, I'm having trouble sleeping, with you pacing up and down like that. It makes me nervous. Aren't you about ready for bed?"

Sandy's orange dot had stopped momentarily. Her voice was surprisingly quiet as it came out of the darkness. "Huh uh. I'll do it in the bathroom."

Jenny heard Sandy get her cigarettes and ashtray and take them with her into the bathroom, closing the door behind her. A thin stream of light came through the bathroom door. Something in Sandy's voice had upset Jenny. The usual harshness was absent. Instead, Jenny detected a note of vulnerability. Well, it had been a hard day. Jenny drifted off to sleep.

Sandy stood in front of the mirror, her expression forlorn. She had never felt so alone. And in such alien territory. Sandy knew that she was facing a new situation. And that something had to give. But she was damned if she knew what. There was a sickly sour taste in her mouth that refused to go away, even when she swallowed. She felt her fear start to turn into panic, and calmed herself by grabbing tightly onto the cool white porcelain sink, until all she could feel was the tension in her fingers. She reminded herself that she had lived through rougher times and that she would also survive this. Slowly, she loosened her grip and began to breathe again.

4

Much to their surprise, Sandy and Jenny became friends. It started with the discovery that they both liked to play cards. Because the school imposed an early weeknight curfew, there was little to do in the evenings (unless you were a creep and studied), so the two girls initiated a pinochle game in the dormitory lounge. What originated as a casual venture soon turned into a nightly endeavor. Sandy and Jenny became partners and began to take on all comers. Starting the game immediately after dinner, they sat around the bridge table for hours, while empty Coke bottles and potato stick, Twinkie, and ice cream wrappers piled up on the sofa and chairs. No matter how late it got, Sandy and Jenny always wanted to continue the game. After all, they were unbeatable as a team. When the other girls sleepily begged off to bed, they would hang around the lounge a bit longer, touting their victories and unwinding together from the tension and excitement of the game.

But it wasn't just shared victory that brought the two unlikely girls together. There were also those horrendous mornings when the alarm clock went off at 7:30, after they had played cards till 4:00. Sandy would automatically roll out of bed, a moving zombie. Mary was usually up and gone. Jenny always slept through the alarm, so Sandy shook her roughly by the shoulder on the way to the bathroom. If Jenny didn't respond to this first measure, Sandy came back into the room and contemplated which steps to take from there. Sometimes she set the alarm to Jenny's clock radio, so that a loud blast of rock and roll burst from the radio, jerking Jenny immediately out of bed. Other times, she would drip cold water on Jenny's face or toes after gently lifting the covers. And as the familiarity between them grew, Sandy became brave enough to break the barrier of touch and to experiment with the always-reliable tickle-torture. These early morning antics usually resulted in shouts and laughter. Even though they weren't big on studying, Sandy and Jenny depended on each other to at least get up for class.

Groggy and half-asleep, they straggled down to the cafeteria. Oatmeal, the texture of dripping cement, was ladled into beige porcelain bowls. The eggs, scrambled from a powder mix, were runny with water. The toast, which came in two varieties — burnt or soggy — provided a difficult choice at that time of the morning. The orange juice was the color of piss, the coffee indescribably putrid. Sharing harsh realities is bound to create strong bonds between the people who suffer through such inhumane conditions. And in fact, Sandy and Jenny participated in secret rituals to express their muted resistance. They would sit at the table, staring at their plates, then looking at each other. Jenny would begin by tasting the juice and grimacing. Sandy would remove her juice from her tray and then pick at the watery eggs, finally working up the courage to taste them, then immediately spitting them out with disgust. Jenny would take the eggs off her tray and reach for her toast, which was hard and brittle and broke into little pieces. They tasted the coffee together, simultaneously making a face. Nodding and standing up in unison, they put the food back on their trays, and carried them directly to the huge plastic-lined garbage cans, where, averting their eyes, they would scrape their aborted breakfasts off the plates. When they were done, they would turn and face each other and shake hands in a silent pact.

The final welding of their friendship occurred during morning and afternoon jaunts to empty movie houses, where they sprawled low in their seats, their feet hanging over the vacant chairs in front of them. Their bodies leaned against each other as they chomped on the buttered popcorn, absorbed in watching the screen. Hands touching as they both reached for popcorn out of the same greasy container, they shared the intimacy of noisily sucking their fingers clean.

They ate together, went to classes together, played together, studied together, and dated together. They became best friends.

5

Sandy tried to put on her mascara properly this time. Usually she caked it on too thick, so that by the end of the evening her face was smeared and smudged. Once on a double date in high school, the other girl had figured out the problem. They were driving, she in the front seat with Tom, the other girl with her date in the back, when suddenly the girl shrieked, "That's it, look!" Sandy looked all around but didn't see anything particularly interesting. "Not out there, dummy, your hand." Sandy examined her hand, and it was the culprit. She could see black streaks running lengthwise on her fingers. But Sandy couldn't imagine not scratching your eyes if they itched. It was like pissing. If you had to go you went. It was a good thing they didn't make you wear cosmetics on your crotch.

Jenny walked into the bathroom, dressed in slip and bra. Her underwear wasn't black, so Sandy guessed that she didn't know her date well.

"Who are you going out with tonight?"

"Bob Klein." Jenny was putting on her eyeliner now. Sandy noticed how graceful the arc of her elbow was — it was slender yet steady. The line Jenny made was very straight. "He's pledging Sami." She finished her left eye, then tilted her head to the right and peered into the mirror to confirm that she had done a good job. "I met him in Calculus . . . how about you?"

Sandy had gone back to staring into the mirror over the bathroom sink, and now she put on a few last strokes for good luck. Jenny hovered over the other bathroom sink, doing her right eye. It always seemed strange to Sandy that when girls talked in bathrooms they rarely looked at each other. Instead they stared into the mirror, fixing their blouse so it was neatly tucked in, or "doing' their face. But it seemed to be part of an important custom, so Sandy continued to face the mirror as she talked, even though there was nothing left for her to do.

"It's a blind date. Bunny talked me into it. He's supposed to be a doll." Sandy's voice was skeptical. Actually, she had never had a blind date before, but everyone had always said they were terrible. "I think he's pledging Sig. What time is yours picking you up?"

"Eight."

"Same here." There was more enthusiasm in Sandy's voice as she said this than when she was talking about her date. Sandy wouldn't have minded staying home that night if it wasn't bad for her reputation. She would have liked to go down to the TV room in her jeans and T-shirt and just relax with whoever was there But she hadn't had a date last Friday night, and some of the girls had acted as though it was really important that she have a date this weekend. Sandy didn't want it getting around that she was unpopular or anything like that, but she didn't see any reason to start panicking just because she hadn't had a date in a couple of weeks. In high school she often didn't date for a few months. Then she'd meet someone, usually at a frat party at NYU or Columbia or CCNY. She had liked the boys at CCNY the best; they didn't push so hard to make it all the time; they seemed to respect girls more. They usually didn't have much money, so instead of going to fancy places, they would sit in coffeeshops after the movies and talk for hours. Sandy liked that. It was a way she could let them know right away that she had a brain. That way they always treated her with a lot of respect and didn't push her or call her a cock-teaser in the car. Sandy had heard that this happened to other girls when they said no. The shame of it made her flesh crawl whenever she thought about it.

Jenny was fully dressed now and inspecting herself in the

mirror. She frowned slightly as she looked at her profile. Sandy had to admit that Jenny did have an awfully big nose. But Sandy thought it gave her face some character. Jenny didn't buy the character argument. In high school she had thought about having a nose job but decided against it. All the other girls had gotten one, but Jenny held out. Sandy liked that about Jenny. In her own way she was a bit of a noncomformist. Like Sandy.

Sandy no longer felt quite as isolated as she had those first few weeks. She had made some friends, and everyone on the floor seemed to respect her. They treated her like she was older and wiser, and Sandy liked that a lot. She had been around more than the other girls, and it showed. It was one way that growing up in the Bronx had been an advantage. Nobody could say she wasn't streetwise. And Sandy often felt superior to the silliness and girlishness of the other freshmen and even sophomores on her floor. Wasn't she the only one who had been politically active in high school? The other girls would just listen attentively when Sandy talked about the demonstrations she had been to, the things she had seen. And one time she talked about religion with several of the other girls. She and one Catholic got into a whole discussion about afterlife and the existence of God. Sandy was the first atheist the Catholic girl had ever spoken with, and she saw in the eyes of the other girls that her arguments were far superior. So, Sandy enjoyed some of the notoriety she had earned in her first few months at the dorm.

But sometimes she still felt alienated from everyone else. It mostly had to do with money. The other girls had huge allowances and spent their money frivolously. Sandy had to watch it real close, so when they ordered in a pizza, she would often say she wasn't in the mood. And then too, she didn't have any of the appliances the other girls had. And her pride made it difficult to borrow anything if she couldn't offer something in return. Sandy was amazed by the possessions most of the other girls had and how they were taken for granted — hair dryers, typewriters, stereos — the list was endless. Sandy and her mother had gone shopping before she left, to buy a good light. So she wouldn't hurt her eyes when she studied late at night. They had gotten an expensive one, the latest thing on the market, a combination of fluorescent and regular lighting at the same time. It was made with springs, so it stretched and turned in whatever direction you wanted it to. The lamp, her transistor radio, and an alarm clock, which her mother had gotten with green Safeway stamps, were the only possessions Sandy had. She looked at the other girls' things and felt uncomfortable. Her pride would never have let her admit it, but she was slightly ashamed of her things, or her lack of things. She told herself that the other girls were shallow and spoiled, and in many ways they were. Sandy felt proud that she was a working-class child, that she had earned a scholarship to pay her tuition, that her parents had sacrificed so she could go out of town to college. Very few of the students came from Brooklyn or the Bronx, and Sandy realized how unusual it was for someone like her to be at a state university. So, on the one hand, Sandy felt special and different and liked her uniqueness. But every now and then, like when the girls talked about what their fathers did, Sandy found herself getting defensive and embarrassed. And then she felt even more ashamed of herself, for not being proud to say her father was a factory worker. Most of the girls had professional parents — doctors, lawyers, businessmen, a few civil servants — and when they heard what Sandy's father did, there was an awkward silence and then someone would say, "Oh, how interesting." But it couldn't have been too interesting, because no one would ask her anything about it and the conversation would quickly continue elsewhere.

Jenny picked up her purse and turned to Sandy. "Are you ready?" Sandy nodded. "Great. We can go down together. That way I can see this gorgeous date." They walked out of the room, down the long corridor to the elevator. They were really comfortable together now. The earlier defensiveness and caution had dropped. Sandy had always had a best girlfriend, ever since she was eight and the boys had started to get a little weird with her, and now she felt that closeness with Jenny. It was a good feeling.

A group of girls were standing around the main desk in the lobby of the dormitory, waiting for their dates. Sandy and Jenny joined the girls and watched the guys come in.

"He's supposed to be tall, with blond hair. I told him I'd be wearing a purple blouse." Sandy was chomping on a piece of gum, her mouth wide open. Jenny had told her that it looked lousy, but after Sandy replied that she sounded just like her mother, Jenny laid off.

A very tall, very skinny guy walked in. He was wearing a leopard-skin leotard, which left half of his hairy chest exposed. His walk was gangly and awkward. Sandy and Jenny exchanged a look of horror. They started to giggle as Sandy poked Jenny in the ribs. "Let's hope that's not my date," Sandy said under her breath. She wasn't really worried, as Bunny had told her he was cute. He looked around at the girls and started walking towards Sandy. She blanched.

"Oh, no. He's coming this way."

"Hi, I'm Butch. Are you Sandy?"

Sandy gulped. This couldn't be happening to her. When she got her hands on Bunny. . . . "Yeah." At the moment she was desperately wishing she weren't Sandy.

"Well. Here I am."

Sandy looked him over, not quite believing what she saw. Jenny tried to stifle her laughter, but didn't succeed entirely.

"Uh . . . what's with the Tarzan outfit?" An edge of sarcasm crept into Sandy's voice, although she was trying to be polite.

Butch seemed proud of himself as he looked down at his costume. Sandy began to wonder if he was mentally defective.

"Oh. Didn't I tell you? It's a Hawaiian party."

"No, you didn't mention that." ("Because if you had, you creep, I would have never accepted the date," she thought.) The annoyance in her tone was obvious. But Butch seemed to misinterpret her irritation as worry over not having a costume.

"Don't worry about it. I figured you might not have anything right to wear, so I brought a grass skirt. It's on the back of my motorcycle. You can put it on when we get there."

Sandy was too flabbergasted to maintain her irony. "Motorcycle," she squeaked out.

"Yeah. Come on, let's go." Butch was pleased with himself. He attributed the thinness of her voice to her natural feminine fear of riding on his motorcycle. He thought to himself that on the way he would do some dips and S's so she would really see what a good driver he was.

"Have fun." Jenny's voice was cheerful; she was rubbing it in and Sandy knew it. Sandy flashed her a dirty look as Butch grabbed her arm and dragged her off. She would get back at Jenny later. And that Bunny was going to get it.

6

It had been a long evening. The only things that had helped her get through it were the acts of revenge she planned. She would enlist the help of a friend and throw Bunny into a cold shower. She would put a snake in her bed. (It was only a small inconvenience that there were no snakes in the area.) She would make her go out with Butch — but that was almost too dreadful to wish on anyone. Sandy watched him throw a glass of beer on several of his frat brothers. Perhaps all men were mentally defective and Butch was just a little less attractive than most. It was a chilling thought. Sandy reminded herself that she had dated some older men in their 20's and 30's who had seem civilized. She had enjoyed listening to them talk about the different places they had been, usually in the service. Sandy was now anti-military, but maybe the Army did make boys into men. Anyway, the men she knew who had served overseas seemed different, gentler. As if they had seen things that made them more mature, more serious. That youthful boyish exuberance which always had an underside of violence was gone, as if they had shed a skin that chafed and irritated, causing them to behave as erratically as they often did. But Sandy speculated that soldiers stationed far away from the familiar also got disgustingly drunk and immature, throwing beer at each other. So maybe it had nothing to do with the military. It was more their coming home and the "then what" that did it. Or perhaps just the process of aging. She really did prefer older men. They didn't act like children or treat you like one. They also had other things on their minds besides sex, which made dating college men so boring.

When she lived in San Francisco for six months, she dated several ex-sailors. They talked about the poverty they had seen in Singapore, Hong Kong, Tokyo, and Seoul. Their eyes seemed far away as they described people living in the streets, dirty children running barefoot, the horrors of disease and starvation. Sandy knew they had been profoundly touched by these experiences, humanized. She liked those men. For she had shared their nightmares, despite the fact that she had never seen these things. She had seen a different kind of poverty in New York, not quite as extreme, but also devastating in its impact. She remembered being downtown one day, when she was about eleven, and seeing an old woman dressed in a housecoat full of holes, talking to herself as she rummaged through the garbage cans. Sandy had started to cry, then stopped herself. If she cried for every poor and desperate and miserable person she saw on the streets, she'd never stop crying. Soon after, she stopped crying entirely, and she had not cried since.

Men who had been in the Far East also seemed different with women. Sandy knew that many of those men had been with prostitutes and that the experiences in those brothels had shaken them. It had made them realize that it wasn't just getting laid that they needed. They had come back to the States looking for something to kill the loneliness, to create meaning in their lives. They wanted women they could talk to, who would hold them and nurture them through the horrors they had seen. Sandy felt that compassion for them. But even more, she felt a great compassion for the young women whose poverty had forced them into prostitution. She couldn't imagine anything more horrible. Yet she had toyed with the idea when she was in San Francisco. She wanted to know what life was about. She felt sure that those other girls knew more than she, and that in their agony they saw truths that Sandy could only barely imagine. It seemed that pain was the way to enlightenment. It made you tough. It made you grow up. And if you lived out your worst fears, then there would be nothing to be afraid of.

She had imagined that in ten years she would look back on those days, after having been a prostitute and seen the seamy side of life, and she would have raised herself from the gutter and created a meaningful life for herself. A life of freedom and independence from petty social constraints. A life devoid of the hypocrisy she saw everywhere. Some people would be shocked by her. Others judgmental. But Sandy would put them in their

17

place, with their phony moralities that condemned others who were less fortunate. It was not fair that women were scorned for trying to survive.

So, a week after Sandy turned sixteen, she picked up an ex-sailor in a bar in San Francisco. There was no excuse for her still being a virgin. Wasn't she a liberated woman? A woman who believed in free love? But when it came down to it, it never occurred to her to take money. She had chosen the experience freely. She had said, "Why don't we go back to your place." Now she would know what the other women knew. She was a woman.

A loud shriek brought her back to the frat party. Two of the older brothers had pinned Butch down and, pulling his leotard out at the chest, had poured a pitcher of beer down the front. Sandy turned away, disgusted. She hoped he wouldn't make a scene in the car. Then she remembered that they had come by motorcycle. She smiled. At least there was one positive note to the evening.

It was cold as they drove up to the dorm, Butch still dressed in his leotard, Sandy wearing the grass skirt for extra warmth. That was another difference Sandy had noticed. Men didn't seem to get cold. They walked around without their shirts on days Sandy wore a sweater. Her teeth were chattering. Butch seemed perfectly comfortable. She really didn't like him.

In front of the dorm was the usual jam-up of cars, as everyone was coming back from their dates a few minutes before curfew. All the girls complained about curfew, but there were times when it served a valuable function, Sandy thought to herself. Now if only she could make it through the "fishbowl" without incident. She walked quickly to the dorm, and Butch followed.

The fishbowl was a small area between the outside and inside doors of the nine-story female-occupied dorm. It was usually empty, just an entranceway to the building. But on Friday and Saturday at 2 AM it was filled with couples saying goodnight to each other. A hundred people would be squeezed into a fifteen foot by ten foot area. Some of the couples were making out passionately. More often the girls were trying to fight off their dates.

Sandy spotted Jenny in the far corner with her date. He was attempting to kiss her and she was politely trying to keep him at arm's distance. In that crowd it was quite a feat. Their eyes caught and Jenny flashed Sandy a look that indicated she couldn't wait to get rid of her date. Sandy, who was shaking her head sympathetically, was jerked back to her own situation by Butch lunging at her and pinning her against the glass door. Sandy turned her head in the nick of time to avoid his kiss. It landed on her ear.

18

"That was a great evening." Butch pressed his body against hers.

"Yeah. Yeah, it was lots of fun." Sandy pushed him away and started to force her way through the crowd. Years of fighting to get on the subway during rush hour had prepared her for this new combat zone. "Listen, I have to go now." She was almost at the inner door. Butch was clinging to her right shoulder.

"Well, when can I see you again?"

Sandy went for a space in the crowd. Butch didn't make it, instead jarring into a heavy-set boy who turned to him and said, "Watch it, buddy." As Butch apologized, Sandy managed to get through the door into the safety of the interior lobby. She ran to the elevator, where several girls, including Jenny, were standing. They looked at each other and sighed in relief. Then they started to giggle.

"Did you see him? All night people were coming up to him and calling him Tarzan. So then he'd bang his chest with his hands and do the call of the apes." Sandy demonstrated this for Jenny as they stepped into the elevator. Jenny laughed hysterically, rolling around the sides of the elevator, bent at the middle. The other girls laughed too, but kept a distance from Sandy, who seemed a little weird. But Sandy didn't notice. All she cared about was Jenny.

"How was yours?" she asked when Jenny had gained some control.

"Yours may have looked like Tarzan but mine acted like him." They stepped out of the elevator and walked down the corridor. "He was all over me the entire evening. On the way home in the car we were in the back seat. At one point, I pushed him so hard he fell off the seat."

Jenny demonstrated as they both burst into gales of laughter and entered the room, flopping on Jenny's bed.

"It's good to be home."

"You know it."

7

Most of their important talks took place on the top bunk. Mary rarely spent any time in the room; she had made friends in the pre-nursing program and only came back to sleep. Sandy and Jenny's favorite time was early afternoon, when the other girls were in class and the dorm was quiet.

"It's funny how things have turned out." Jenny was chewing a piece of gum as she talked. She had picked up the bad habit from Sandy. "When I first met you I thought, 'Oh, no. Is she weird.' Especially the first night." She laughed. "You pacing back and forth in the dark. I figured if anything, Mary and I might end up being friends." She puckered her lips, then, looking at the tip of her nose, she blew a bubble. It got larger and larger until it popped neatly. She opened her mouth and sucked it back in. She looked at Sandy, who was staring out the window.

The more Jenny got to know Sandy, the more she realized just how different Sandy was from the girls Jenny had known in school and at camp. Jenny always had several girlfriends, but she never got too close to any of them. She never had a best girlfriend and didn't particularly want one. It didn't make any sense to get dependent on another girl, as people would come and go in your life and it wasn't healthy to get too close. Besides, she had never felt she could trust the other girls. It wasn't just that they might steal your boyfriend, as *Seventeen* said; it was more a general and vague feeling that made Jenny keep her distance. Her other girlfriends seemed to feel the same way. Although they did things together — shopped, went to frat parties, studied or double-dated — their relationships with each other were always pretty casual. Occasionally Jenny would be disappointed by one of her friends; they would promise to call and wouldn't, or promise to go somewhere with her and then cancel at the last minute. Although Jenny was badly hurt at the time, she would recover quickly. The friendships were just not that important.

But her friendship with Sandy was different. Sandy was so intense. She felt very strongly about many things that Jenny had rarely given a thought to. Jenny admired that about Sandy. Most of the girls Jenny had known were silly and superficial; she could talk to them for hours about the clothes at Saks vs. the clothes at Bonwit, or about the latest article on different makeup for different complexions in *Mademoiselle*, but she often felt bored. With Sandy, Jenny never felt bored. Sandy's perception of the things around her was often astute, and they would talk for hours about books and movies and philosophy. Jenny had always gotten good grades in school, and thought of herself as smart, but not until she and Sandy talked did she realize just how smart. Sandy encouraged Jenny to share her perceptions, and nodded her head in enthusiastic agreement. Jenny discovered that for years she had been noticing things about people and society, without even realizing.

"I guess I did act kind of strange at first," Sandy said. "I was really freaked out." She reached for a cigarette and shook her head. "That first night I thought both of you were creepy. Mary, the sweet, small-town hick who doesn't know anything about life . . . and going with the boy next door. Jesus, how corny. And you, a rich, spoiled Jewish princess, with your stereo and your

20

hair dryer, and probably as much depth as saran wrap. Inside, I was cursing the computer that matched us. But it's really turned out okay." Sandy wanted to look at Jenny but couldn't. Lately it was getting hard to meet her eyes.

"Yeah. It took me a while, but I finally got you to talk. At first you answered all my questions with one-syllable replies. The other girls started calling you 'the mystery woman.' It's been a challenge getting you to talk about yourself."

Sandy suddenly became very serious. Could Jenny know? Know the fear that had kept Sandy silent for years? She had sworn to herself, after seeing the ways people lied, after hearing the silly and inane conversations of her peers, that she would never talk unless she had something to say. She had started to watch her words carefully, making sure that they expressed exactly what she intended and that her intention was meaningful. The closer she watched, the fewer words she had to say. The fewer words she had to say, the more she could scrutinize the words she did say. It became a growing cycle until Sandy simply stopped talking.

"How did you know that under that silence there'd be anything worth talking to?" Sandy felt like she was at the edge of a deep crevice, with Jenny standing behind her. Sandy couldn't see Jenny and was helpless; if Jenny wanted, she could just give a small push.

"I just knew." Jenny's voice was also serious now. She didn't quite understand what was going on with Sandy, but she sensed that whatever it was, it was important. There was a long silence.

"You know ... I've never talked to anyone else like this ...," Sandy stumbled over her words, ". . . about myself and stuff. I don't think I've ever said this to anyone before, but . . . sometimes . . . I feel kind of scared."

Sandy was looking away as she said this. Jenny was also avoiding eye contact. There is a painful awkwardness in certain moments of closeness. Perhaps one of them has gone too far. Crossed an imperceptible line which will nonetheless electrocute you or trap you in an invisible barbed-wire fence. At such moments the natural growth of a friendship is at stake. It is courage that is required.

Jenny broke the tension by putting out her hand and placing it on Sandy's. It was not a familiar or comfortable gesture for her, but it seemed right. For Sandy, it was the embodiment of her worst fear and most coveted desire. She froze for a moment, torn between the old reflex of avoiding touch and the new feeling of wanting contact. Hesitantly, she tightened her own grasp on Jenny's hand.

Not looking at each other, they sat in silence.

8

Jenny was sitting Indian style, her textbook propped on her knees, in the chair they had stolen from the lounge. Sandy tried to imitate Jenny's position but was unable to. Her legs just wouldn't bend that way. She had always had trouble in gym class. Since she was an excellent athlete, the teachers had assumed she was being a smart-ass when she couldn't do the exercises that required flexibility. Sandy would remain silent as they accused her of not trying. Her code of ethics did not permit defending herself in such situations. It didn't matter that the accusations were unfair. Nor that a few of the teachers, reacting to Sandy's indifference and bristling arrogance, had tried to humiliate her. What mattered was that you never showed you cared. Or that anything anyone could do would hurt you. Her teachers, English and Social Studies in particular, had attempted to reach her. She was obviously very bright but refused to participate in any of the classroom activities. Actually, that wasn't true, although that was the way they saw it. Sandy would answer a question if she was directly asked, but she never volunteered an answer. This irritated them considerably. The fact that her answers showed an unusual understanding of the material further frustrated her teachers. They tried talking to her after class, when that failed referring her to the guidance counselor. But hard as they tried, no one was able to break through the walls she had created around her. All these attempts felt like an invasion of privacy to Sandy. Why didn't they just leave her alone? She had a right to her silence.

Sandy felt a wetness trickle out of her vagina. She reached into her underpants with her index finger, ignoring Jenny's presence. She would never have done anything like that before, but in the four months they had been living together, she and Jenny had become more comfortable with each other than Sandy could ever have imagined. There wasn't anything they couldn't talk about or share. Well, almost. She pulled out her finger and looked at the dark brown substance which had managed to get under her nail. She'd have to scrub her hands — it was always hard to get the blood out from under the nail.

"Shit, I just got my period." Sandy threw down her text and stood up. "And I think I'm out of napkins, too." She would have to go door to door and try to borrow some.

"You can use some of my Tampax if you want." Jenny looked up from her book.

"Oh, I can't use that stuff."

"Why not?" Jenny seemed surprised.

Sandy was embarrassed. She liked to think of herself as a grownup, certainly older and more experienced than most of the girls on the floor even if she was one of the youngest. Jenny didn't seem quite as babyish as the others.

"I can't get them in," Sandy admitted sheepishly.

Before Sandy had a chance to resist, Jenny had handed her a Tampax and pushed her into the bathroom, and was giving her instructions from the other side of the door.

"Did you do it?"

"Nah, nothing's happening." Sandy grunted as she struggled to push it in. The sweat was beading on her forehead and under her arms. Maybe there was something wrong with her.

"Okay, try standing up. Put one foot on the toilet seat and balance yourself with the other."

That sounded like a very awkward position to Sandy. "Which foot should I put on the seat?"

"It doesn't matter, dummy. Whichever feels better." Jenny sounded exasperated. Sandy tried each foot.

"They both feel lousy." Sandy wished she had never said anything. Her vagina was feeling very sore.

"Well, pick one, and then separate your lips and put it in."

Sandy tried that, but she couldn't bend over far enough to see what was going on. Damn her inflexibility.

"I can't find it."

"You can't find what?"

"My hole. I can't find my hole."

"I don't believe this. You mean you don't know where your hole is?" Jenny was incredulous. "But you've had intercourse."

"So what?" Sandy replied defensively. "I was up here, not down there at the time." Sandy felt like two cents. Didn't everyone have as much trouble finding their hole?

Jenny chuckled to herself. Sandy made such a big deal about being so sophisticated and she didn't even know where her hole was. In some ways Sandy was really a baby. Intellectually she was precocious but emotionally — she still had a lot to learn. Jenny couldn't remember a time when she didn't know about her hole. At ten she was already masturbating regularly, sometimes inserting her finger into her vagina. She'd been wearing Tampax since she was fourteen, when one of the JCs at camp showed her how to put it in. It was no big deal. Even the first time she had intercourse, it was she who showed Frank how to get it in. He said he had done it before, but he certainly had a lot of trouble. She finally put her hand over his and showed him what to do. She was fifteen that summer, the youngest student in the special summer school class for prospective college kids. Frank was a college sophomore, making up classes he had failed in the winter quarter. He wasn't very bright but he was unusually good-looking, and seemed to know his way around girls. He was on the make that first night, but after Jenny firmly said no, he really slowed down and acted like a gentleman. Jenny liked that. She was tired of guys who pushed so hard that they made the whole evening uncomfortable. She and Frank went out every night for three weeks and he still didn't try anything. One night she got a little high and decided that was going to be the night. On the way back to the dorm she asked him if he had any condoms. He seemed shocked at first, then quickly recovered his cool. They went back to the frat house and did it in the room of one of his friends. Some couple was using his room.

Jenny heard Sandy grunt with pain. "This is silly. Open the door and I'll put it in for you," Jenny said in a reasonable voice.

"What?" Sandy shrieked. "Are you crazy? Get out of here." Sandy had never heard such an outrageous suggestion.

"It's no big deal, Sandy. Stop being childish."

There were many names that Sandy had been called and could be called without flinching. But "childish" wasn't one of them.

"How do I know you know what you're doing?"

Jenny opened the door and squeezed into the small cubicle that she and Sandy and the RA shared. She had a fresh Tampax in her hand and seemed very calm, much to Sandy's amazement. She motioned for Sandy to put her foot up on the seat.

"Just take it easy, will you?" Sandy remembered how much it had hurt the first time.

"Will you relax?" Jenny had the air of a doctor performing a professional task. You had to respect her for her cool.

Jenny spread Sandy's lips apart with one hand and with the other pushed the Tampax up, angling it in the direction of Sandy's back rather than straight up as Sandy had done. Sandy felt a small rush of pain and then Jenny stood up.

"Hey, where'd it go?" Sandy couldn't see it anywhere. "It's gone."

"Where do you think it went, dummy?" Jenny was smiling at her in a superior way but Sandy didn't care.

"We did it. We did it," Sandy exclaimed excitedly, jumping up and down as she hugged Jenny in gratitude.

Now Jenny was embarrassed. "Will you stop hugging me? It's no big deal."

Jenny turned to look at Sandy, who was pulling up her underpants, a proud expression on her face. "So how does it feel?"

Sandy very slowly hobbled out of the cubicle. Knees bowed, she gazed down at her crotch as she moved. She looked disheveled and sweaty, like she had been through a war. Gingerly, she took each step.

"Not bad. Not bad."

9

Sandy had never had very good study habits. In elementary school she had done her work on time but that was before she went through her adolescent rebellion, a rejection of all authorities including those at school. Getting good grades with the least amount of studying was an art Sandy had mastered.

Jenny, on the other hand, had always been a responsible student. She didn't love learning any more than Sandy (both of them would prefer a good pinochle hand any time), but the prospect of poor grades was much scarier for Jenny. How would she explain to her parents? So she studied moderately throughout the semester, keeping up with the reading. When Jenny wasn't available to play, Sandy would find one of the other girls and they would horse around in the lounge, or go down to the TV room. That was one of the things Sandy loved about the dormitory — there was always someone to mess around with. The only time she regretted her style of studying was during finals week.

Sandy was frantic now as she raced back and forth across the lounge, holding her book open with tightly clenched hands and muttering to herself to help memorize the material. She was oblivious to the papers and notebooks which littered the floor; she had already read them, and looking at the clock on the wall which read six, Sandy knew she wouldn't have time to go over them again. She kicked a bunch of notes out of her way so she could pace in a wider circle. There were only eight more hours until the exam, and she needed at least fifteen minutes to wash up; it wasn't the dirtiness she was concerned about — she had been wearing the same sweatshirt and jeans since finals week had started five days ago — but the cold water would help her stay awake through the test. Then it would take her another fifteen minutes to walk briskly to the exam, which was on the other end of the campus. That only gave her seven and a half hours more to study. Sandy started to panic and was unable to concentrate. She read over a line three times and still didn't understand it. Her panic grew as she looked out the window and saw that the sun was starting to rise. No one else was up, except for Jenny, who was underlining her book for the second time. Sandy couldn't believe Jenny's study habits; the book was underlined in two different colors of ink, which meant that she had read the material three times, as Jenny never underlined her first time through. Three times. Sandy quickened her pace and returned to the difficult sentence. She breathed a sigh of relief as she understood it this time.

Jenny could hardly keep her eyes open. Why had she let

Sandy talk her into pulling an all-nighter? She would never be able to take the exam in this condition. She closed her book. It was six now. She could get four hours' sleep and still have three hours left to review. Sandy's pacing rarely bothered her anymore; she had gotten used to it. But now Sandy's repetitious motion was having a hypnotic effect on Jenny. She stood up and stretched, shaking her head to clear it. Sandy looked upset; her mouth was frozen tight and her brow was wrinkled.

"How's it going?" Jenny asked.

"Terrible. I'm going to fail."

"You're not going to fail."

"Yes I am. Do you realize this is the first time I'm reading most of the material?"

"Yeah, but you did that for the midterm and you aced it. In fact, you bastard, you did better than I did — and I really studied for it."

Sandy did not feel reassured. She continued pacing frenetically, mumbling louder under her breath in response to this interruption.

"Do you realize it's been 24 hours since I slept?"

Sandy ignored Jenny's last remark. She was totally absorbed in her studying. The rhythm of her pacing was interrupted only by her about-face when she approached the two walls at either end of the lounge. Sandy and her book seemed like one object hurtling across the room, propelled by an inexhaustible force.

"You're amazing. You haven't slept for close to two days. And look at you. Still going strong. Well, I've had it." Jenny started to walk out of the lounge. "Wake me up in four hours."

Sandy nodded without looking up. Every second counted. She was afraid she would fail the exam, and that would be a humiliation. She had never failed anything in her life. It was a matter of pride. When she got sleepy she told herself that she would sleep after the exam. When she got bored she told herself not to be self-indulgent. She had a task to do and she would do it. If there was one thing she hated it was weakness.

They were laughing as they came back into the room, dripping wet. It had started to rain while they were taking the exam. Jenny dumped her books on the floor.

"That's it. The end of finals. Boy, am I beat." She unzipped her raincoat. Sandy was looking out the window.

"Let's go for a walk."

"Are you crazy? It's pouring out there.'

"So what? It'll be fun."

"Go away."

"Come on. What's the matter, you chickenshit? Does the princess melt in the rain?"

Those were fighting words to Jenny. Besides, it would be fun to run amok in the rain. "Okay. We'll see who runs for shelter first."

They linked their pinkies. "Gentlemen's bet."

The campus was deserted except for a few people hurrying to and from exams, with umbrellas and books protecting their heads. They stared at the two girls dressed in jeans, sweaters, and green rubber raincoats, leisurely strolling on the grass. As they walked by a huge puddle, Sandy pushed Jenny in. Then she took off, followed closely by Jenny.

"I'm going to drown you in the next puddle, you creep," Jenny shrieked.

Sandy ran through a row of pine trees, pulling back the branches and letting them go quickly so they would spritz Jenny as she followed in close pursuit. At the next large puddle, they eyed each other and broke into laughter at the sight of soaked hair plastered to their faces, jeans wet from the knee down, and sopping loafers which squished with every step.

Sandy walked casually into the middle of the puddle, the water around her calves. Then, very slowly, very dignified, she sat down. Her eyes said to Jenny, "I dare you." Jenny walked around the puddle flirtatiously, and then flopped down next to Sandy. Laughing hilariously, they rolled against each other.

They were still laughing and banging into each other as they burst through the door.

"First in the shower," Sandy called as they peeled off their clothes.

Jenny jumped up and headed for the bathroom. "Oh, no. I'm going first."

Sandy grabbed her by the arm and pushed her aside. "Oh no, you're not. I called it first." Sandy headed for the bathroom.

Jenny grabbed her by her half-opened blouse and tried to stop her from getting past the entryway. Cackling, they banged against the walls in vigorous wrestling. "Hey, watch my boobs!" Sandy shrieked as Jenny elbowed her. Continuing to struggle, they fell onto Jenny's bed. Sandy was bigger and stronger and finally was able to pin Jenny down by half-sitting and half-lying on top of her.

"Got you," Sandy said as she fortified her position. She smiled at Jenny, who was looking at her questioningly. Sandy's heart had been pounding from the wrestling but had slowed down for a moment. Now it started to pound again. She felt Jenny's breast against her thighs, her own calves resting on Jenny's hips. They both quickly averted their eyes.

Sandy got up and Jenny darted for the door to the bathroom. They started wrestling again and laughing, pushing each other against the walls, but now they were a little more self-conscious and controlled. What they had felt was not only unspeakable but also unthinkable. Sandy told herself that Jenny couldn't possibly feel the same way. But Jenny knew better.

10

It was a typical afternoon. They had made it to classes that morning, even though the game last night had lasted until after 4, and now they returned to the room after lunch and collapsed on top of the double-decker bed. Jenny was propped up with pillows against the backboard as she looked at Sandy, who was leaning against a pillow on the concrete wall. Sandy seemed so much more relaxed these days. Her face was beautiful now as the afternoon light enhanced the softness of her features. You would never know that Sandy was Jewish — her nose was perfectly straight, refined in the way it blended in with the rest of her face. Sandy's eyes were closed and Jenny took the opportunity to examine her closely. There was a roundness to her bottom lip which had always intrigued Jenny, whose own lips were thin in comparison. The fullness of that lower lip.

Jenny's eyes followed the line of Sandy's lips down the bottom side of her face, along her throat, and to the opening of her blouse, which puffed out like a sail in full wind, pulling Jenny's attention to the roundness of her partially exposed breast. Jenny looked away to swallow. There was an unfamiliar lightness in her head.

Her feelings for Sandy had passed the boundary of friendship. In the beginning it had been easy to deny, to see their friendship as just being closer than any other she had had. But three weeks ago in a dream she and Sandy were lying next to each other in a field of tall grass. Sandy was tickling Jenny behind the ear with a long green blade, and they had started to wrestle, as they often did. But then they stopped, exhausted, and Sandy leaned over and kissed her on the lips. Jenny was not surprised. She returned Sandy's kiss as if it were the most natural thing in the world.

When she awakened, Jenny was amazed by the dream. She asked herself what it meant, and then quickly told herself that dreams meant nothing and that this had been a sillier dream than usual. But during the following weeks Jenny had noticed herself staring at Sandy, watching her as she studied or slept, averting her eyes when Sandy got undressed. There was no longer any doubt. She had sexual feelings for Sandy.

Jenny remembered in grade school, someone calling one of the girls a lezzie. It had been clear that that was a terrible thing and the girl had denied it and cried. At the time Jenny had not understood, so she had asked her older brother George what it meant to be a lezzie. He had said a lezzie was a queer, someone who was perverted.

Later Jenny learned that "lezzie" meant lesbian. Lesbians were sick and disgusting women who had sex with each other. But she and Sandy weren't lesbians. How could they be? Lesbians were ugly women who couldn't get a man. But that wasn't true of her and Sandy; they both dated and were reasonably attractive. She had heard that lesbians hated men because they were unable to get one and because they wanted to be one. That didn't make total sense to Jenny, but she knew that neither she nor Sandy hated men. They both liked men. So there was nothing abnormal about them. It wasn't like she wanted to have sex with other girls. She had never felt this way before, and she didn't feel it now with anyone except Sandy. Jenny was sure it was the same for Sandy too. Which meant that they just cared for each other in a special way.

Jenny had never heard of two "normal" girls feeling this way. That meant that what was happening between her and Sandy was very rare. Maybe it had never happened before. She sensed that other people wouldn't understand. They would think that she and Sandy were sick because they wouldn't know it could happen between two nice girls. That would mean that they would have to be very discreet.

Jenny abruptly stopped her thinking here. She must be crazy. Was she actually considering telling Sandy? Let alone doing something about it? This was ridiculous. Of course she wasn't going to say anything.

But a couple of days ago Jenny had decided that she was going to tell Sandy. She had to know if Sandy felt the same way. And besides, there was no one else to talk to about it, and Jenny felt a strong need to tell someone. Sandy wouldn't make fun of her. She was pretty sure of that. Today would be the day to say something. She had tried yesterday but every time she got up the courage, Sandy cracked a joke or started a serious conversation. It just hadn't been the right time. But Sandy was quiet now, preoccupied with trying to make smoke rings.

"Sandy."

"Uh huh." Sandy's cheeks were billowed as she gently pushed out small tight smoke rings which loosened and became more amorphous as they floated up to the ceiling.

"I don't know exactly how to say this. I don't want you to misunderstand it, but sometimes . . . sometimes when we're lying next to each other, or fooling around — you know, like wrestling — I have these feelings. . . ." Jenny paused, hoping Sandy would say something. But Sandy was quiet. "I'm not sure what they are but . . . at times like that I feel like holding you." This last sentence was blurted out. Jenny felt relieved to have gotten it out.

Sandy sat there motionless. She even stopped breathing. She was afraid to look at Jenny and was embarrassed by that, so she didn't see that Jenny was also not looking at her. She had been aware of those feelings in herself for a long time, but it had never occurred to her to say anything about it. The risk was too great. You couldn't say anything unless you knew for sure that the other girl felt the same way. And since there was no way to know for sure, you never said anything. But Jenny had broken the taboo of silence. That had never happened to Sandy before, and she didn't know what to do.

"Me too," she whispered.

"What?" Jenny asked. Her heart was pounding so loud that she wasn't sure she had heard right.

"I understand. I have the same feelings." Sandy couldn't believe she had said that. She felt out of her body, as if she was hanging by a strap from the ceiling, watching this scenario take place on the bed below. It had never occurred to Sandy even to hope that Jenny might feel the same way. But if Jenny felt that way, and Sandy felt that way, then . . . Sandy couldn't finish the thought.

"Well, I don't think we should do anything necessarily." Jenny's voice betrayed her anxiety. "I just wanted to let you know."

Sandy took a quick look at Jenny, saw her averted eyes, her long thin fingers twisting the bedspread cover, her lips compressed as if she wanted to suck back in the words that had just slipped out.

"Yeah, I agree. It's good we talked, but there's no reason we have to do anything." Sandy tried to sound mature and confident, even though she was feeling neither. There was no hurry for them to decide whether or not . . . Sandy still couldn't complete that thought. She reminded herself that she needed to breathe and took a shallow sniff of the air around her. But her heart wouldn't stop pounding.

11

They didn't talk about it for two weeks, although neither of them thought about much else. Each wondered whether it showed on her face, or in her inhibited movements. Each at times wished she had the courage, then thought better of it. Sandy had had these feelings before, although never so intensely. She had learned to keep them under control. For Jenny the feelings were new; they took her off-guard. She tried to dismiss them, but they kept coming back, and each time they grew stronger.

The two girls came into the room laughing. It was Sunday, so they were wearing skirts, blouses, and loafers. This was one of the dorm rules: for Sunday dinner, all girls had to wear skirts and stockings, or not be admitted to the dining room. Sandy thought it was a stupid rule. It never occurred to her to think of the origin of the rule, to realize that Sunday was the Christian day of prayer. If she had known that, she would have been doubly pissed. Despite the fact that she argued philosophically about the existence of God, or the profound corruption of religion, it never sank in that other people really believed that hocus pocus, let alone that it affected their lives. She was unaware that some interpretation of God's law mandated that she wear stockings on Sundays. She thought the enemy was Miss Ogleby.

Miss Ogleby was tall, thin, and prunish. She stood somberly at the entrance to the cafeteria and inspected each girl as she walked in. Sandy despised Miss Ogleby. She offended her sense of the important. Today they had had a confrontation.

"Young lady, you're not wearing stockings and you know the rules about dress for Sunday dinners," the old bag had chided.

"But Miss Ogleby, how do you *know* I'm not wearing stockings?" Her philosophy class had paid off after all. "Unless you're 100% positive, and have some other evidence to corroborate your visual sense, I'm afraid you really don't have the right to refuse me entrance to the cafeteria." Sandy tried to sound as snotty as Miss Ogleby.

Miss Ogleby was pissed. Sandy could tell because her breathing had gotten funny. A long line of girls had gathered and were staring at the duo.

"And how do you expect me to get this evidence?" She fell right into Sandy's trap.

"Well, there's one sure-fire way, Miss Ogleby. God gave you a pair of hands."

Ogleby had turned bright red. Several of the girls had snickered. She was losing face. So in the pressure of the moment, she had done it. She had jabbed at Sandy's bare legs, then all huffy, said, "Don't you ever pull another stunt like this on me, young lady, or I'll see to it you'll never eat in this cafeteria again."

Sandy and Jenny had turned around, barely stifling the laughter that erupted when they were out of Miss Ogleby's sight. They were still laughing as they entered their room. Sandy slipped out of her skirt, putting on a pair of jeans that had been lying on the floor. Jenny stared appreciatively at her while lighting a cigarette. Sandy, unaware of Jenny's look, flopped on the bed, still laughing to herself. Never to be allowed to eat in the cafeteria again. As if that would be punishment.

"Get me a cigarette, Jen."

Jenny walked over to her purse, pulled out a second cigarette, and lit it from the first. She sat on the edge of the bed and gave Sandy one of the cigarettes.

"Thanks."

They both smoked in quiet. Sandy sat up, repropping her pillows.

"God, I love being lazy." Sandy became aware that Jenny was preoccupied. She seemed unusually quiet.

"Is something the matter?"

Jenny had been staring at the linoleum floor. An endless parade of grey diamonds. She had been waiting for Sandy to bring it up, but it was clear she wasn't going to. If anything was going to happen it would be up to Jenny. She had never wanted anything the way she wanted Sandy. Her entire body ached from the effort of trying to keep her feelings under control. She didn't want to fight it any longer. She looked up at Sandy.

"I want to kiss you."

Their eyes met and held. They paused, holding their breath in the stillness. Then very slowly, they both leaned forward, their faces meeting halfway. The tension was expressed in the stiffness of their jaws, the tiny quiverings of the bottom lip, which was getting two messages from the brain at once. Yes. No. Let it go. Control. Very gently their lips touched and explored each other. The room dissolved. Everything but their faces was out of focus. Only their lips touched. Their bodies were rigidly braced. Exhausted, they placed their heads together — forehead against forehead, nose to nose. Their heads were too heavy to hold up. Slowly their faces slipped to the side so they were cheek to cheek, their chins resting on each other's shoulder. It had taken them a long time to get to this place. Now they rested.

That first kiss was unlike any experience Sandy had ever known. She felt desire surge through her body, pulsating with an entirely new rhythm that was at the same time hauntingly familiar. As their lips started to explore each other again, refreshed from the pause, her desire grew. The rhythmic pounding in her wrists and ears and chest and vagina overpowered her; the pounding would grow louder, deafening, rampaging out of control, then gradually start to subside, almost becoming inaudible. Then it would suddenly start to grow louder again, until its thundering threatened to burst her skin, as a rubberband bursts when it is stretched to the point where the force pulling it apart matches the natural tension that binds it together.

Jenny was the first to explore further. Her lips moved from Sandy's cheek, down toward her neck, lingering, then slowly, every so slowly, continuing down Sandy's throat, moving her face lower, her nose nuzzling the space between Sandy's breasts, her hair gliding across Sandy's face and throat, slipping into her blouse and gently caressing her there.

Sandy felt selfish in her pleasure. She lifted Jenny's head and kissed her more strongly now, taking Jenny by surprise, and

32

felt her yield as Sandy repeated the beginning rites of passage — from cheek, to neck, to throat, down to chest. Her mouth hungrily searched for what she did not yet know. Moved by a force so powerful that she was weakened by its simple presence, she lay her head against Jenny's chest. Jenny's hands caressed the back of her head and played with her hair, swirling its ends through her fingers, now gentle, now forceful.

Sandy felt like she could lie there forever. Nothing should feel this good. She sat up. They pulled apart and looked at each other. Their eyes held, and Sandy felt the longing surge up again. Sandy watched the same passion grow in Jenny's eyes. It fed her, aroused her, which in turn further excited Jenny. Sandy marveled at how she could feel this way without even a touch between them. It was as if the air between them was full of desire, and with each shallow breath the desire was transmitted, caressing her body with a light tingling that had started in her hands and had spread up her arms, to her shoulders, and simultaneously up her neck to her scalp and down the front of her torso, collecting especially in the throbbing in her groin which was bound tightly by her jeans.

Jenny reached over and unbuttoned the top button on Sandy's blouse. Sandy felt afraid she would pass out. Instead, she breathed deeply and undid Jenny's top button. Simultaneously, they undid the rest of the buttons, letting their blouses part. Together, they reached over to each other, Jenny first helping Sandy out of her blouse, then Sandy helping Jenny out of hers.

With a brazen smile, Jenny reached around Sandy to undo the clasps of her bra. Jenny's long dark hair fell across Sandy's shoulder and chest as her breasts lightly brushed against Sandy's. While Jenny was leaning over, Sandy reached around and unclasped her bra, watching it billow and expose more of Jenny's cleavage as it loosened. Together they gave that slight push, letting the bras slip unheeded into their laps. They stared at each other. Surely it was a miracle, Sandy thought. She had never looked closely at another girl's breasts. Oh, there had been quick glances in the locker room at school, and a few times a friend had undressed in front of her, but Sandy had always averted her eyes, afraid they might express something other than the boredom she felt expected to feel. Now she hesitatingly allowed her eyes to explore every curve, taking in the way the swelling of Jenny's breast tapered ever so gracefully into her nipple, which was darker than Sandy's, and the way one nipple stuck out and the other hid.

Jenny's initial shyness had disappeared. She saw how scared and timid Sandy was. This surprised her, as Sandy was usually so certain in her motions. Now she seemed like a very young girl, younger than Jenny. Jenny felt herself soften, grow protective

33

towards Sandy. She had known that she would have to take the initiative. She reached out and rested her hands on Sandy's breasts, then circling them slowly, marveled at their fullness. Sandy's breasts jutted directly out as if to say, "Here I am, free and full." Jenny's breasts drooped a little; she had often worried that she might end up like those old women she had seen in the dressing room at the pool. Their breasts sagged down to their belly buttons, their nipples were withered and pocked by age. Jenny hoped that Sandy found her breasts beautiful. She looked at her, but Sandy was staring down, her face flushed and vibrant. Sandy reached up and placed her hand on Jenny's cheek. Then she lay down, gently pulling Jenny on top. They began to kiss, their excitement growing as their legs entwined; they rolled around the bed, turning and turning with each new touch, each new kiss. They stopped for a moment, and Jenny lay her head in the crook of Sandy's shoulder.

"If we're going to make it to the library, we'd better get dressed," Jenny said teasingly.

"Fuck the library." Sandy leaned over and gave Jenny a long kiss. "This is wonderful." Their lovemaking became more fervent. The bed shook and the springs groaned with resistance. Jenny hoped that the bed wouldn't break. How would they explain it? A pillow fight, she thought. That would do it. She lost herself again in Sandy's mouth, her tongue following every fold of her cheek.

Their inner clocks were suspended for a rare moment. Time didn't go by quickly and it didn't stop. It simply was. After a while, they lay quietly in each other's arms.

"Jenny?" Sandy's voice was quizzical.

"Yeah?"

"Do you know what to do?"

"Huh uh." She looked at Sandy. "I was hoping you did."

Sandy was embarrassed and sheepish as she shook her head. They looked at each other and burst into laughter.

"I don't believe this. Here we are, supposedly women of the world," Sandy's voice was sarcastic, "and neither one of us has the slightest idea how to. . . . " Both girls burst into giggles. "Well, what happens now?"

Jenny sat up on one elbow and looked down at Sandy, who was on her back. "Don't worry about it. We'll think of something."

12

They did think of something. They thought of things they had never heard of. Things that seemed to come from some intuition that guided them when they felt stuck or confused. It was as if their bodies were discovering a new sense that they had never known existed. They made love endlessly, interrupted only by classes, pinochle games, and the rare times Mary was in the room. Their lovemaking became natural and uninhibited, blossoming in the familiarity that grew with time. Each came to know the other's body as one knows a favorite place: the landscape is stared at, etched in one's memory; attention is paid to every detail, so that the slightest change triggers an instant exclamation of surprise. And in those surprises is great pleasure as more and more is known, as the senses discover new ways of perceiving the same thing. Sight and smell and touch and sounds and taste and motions merge, until what is known is as complex and varied as the counterpoint in a piece of music, or the shades in an impressionistic painting.

And as they discovered each other, they also discovered themselves. They had been taught not to be selfish, so it was only now, under the desire to give pleasure to each other, that they explored their own pleasures for the other and unwittingly for themselves. And the discovery was monumental; many of Sandy's philosophical concerns and cynical preoccupations paled by contrast with these new feelings. She had never expected to love. Certainly not like this, anyhow. All those songs of romantic love weren't just crap to feed children. Was it possible that others felt this passion, this total dedication to and involvement with their loved ones? Sandy didn't think so. She had heard a lot of people talk, but their words seemed vacant, trite, and silly, unconnected to real desire. Sandy remembered what it had been like for her with men: uninteresting and uninvolving. They had seemed to get into it more, but the sex had a rushed and frantic quality, as if they were hurrying to get to some unknown place. It wasn't exactly that they all had been clumsy, but just that it had been so regimented, predictable and uninspiring. Sandy hadn't realized it at the time, but none of them had really known how to touch her body, how to take pleasure from giving her pleasure. It was so different with Jenny. Sandy was as excited from touching her as she was from being touched. The sight of her, often in places where touching was forbidden, like the cafeteria or the library, made Sandy rush with heat. When they were close, sometimes just standing near, not even touching, a wave of desire would sweep over Sandy, making her legs weaken, her knees ready to buckle. And when they embraced, Sandy's knees would give, jerking a little before they lost all solidity, so that she would usually be able to warn Jenny and they could sit down. It was during this period that Sandy softened. She often smiled now and laughed without a bitter ring. She stopped teasing and spraying her hair, letting it hang loose and feeling the sensuousness of it on her neck and shoulders. She became sweet, almost childlike. Yet she also seemed more womanly. It was a peaceful time.

13

At all hours of the day and night they talked. Each was hungry to know everything the other felt, thought, dreamed, and had experienced. They shared from their past in a way that neither had ever done before. Sharing what they understood and exploring what they could only begin to grasp. Each accepting and encouraging the other to test her honesty to the limit, to set no bounds on the trust between them.

"How do you think your parents would react if they knew . . . about us?" Sandy asked one day as they sat on Jenny's bed.

"Why even ask?" Jenny shook her head. "They couldn't handle it. It would destroy them. Besides, I would never tell them. Never. They've been through enough."

"You mean the war?"

Jenny nodded. Lately she had been thinking a lot about them. She would remember the stories her mother had told her when she was a little girl. Her mother would sit Jenny down next to her and tell stories about what life had been like before the Nazis came. And what it had been like after. It amazed Jenny that after all these years she still got upset when she thought about how her mother had lived during the war. Always running and hiding from the Germans. Knowing that her whole family had perished in the camps. Jenny felt tears start to form in her eyes, but she resolutely pushed them down. Her mother had never cried when she told Jenny the stories. Neither would she.

And then of course there was her father. He hadn't had it quite as bad. He had fought in the Polish army. When the Nazis took over, he got out of the country with forged papers. No close escapes like her mother. After the war, service groups were set up to help people find out whether their relatives were still alive. But he had never been able to find out anything. He figured his family had probably died in Warsaw. He didn't talk much about the past. When they came to America, he explained to Jenny that they were beginning a new life. They would work hard and mind their own business. He raised her and her two brothers to be good American citizens. Jenny knew that he had once been more sophisticated than that, but that fear had forced him to simplify things. His roots were in Europe, but Europe had betrayed him. Jenny sighed.

"My two brothers and I are all the family they have left. Great expectations, I'm afraid . . . I couldn't disappoint them."

Sandy was thoughtful. She remembered what Jenny had told her about her parents. It was hard to understand what it must have been like. The fear. The uncertainty. Her own parents had been born on the Lower East Side. They hadn't talked much about the war. Their thing had been McCarthy. Sandy remembered the time she had come home one afternoon from a civil rights meeting in the Village. Her father had gone crazy — screaming and hitting her when she walked through the door. He thought she was getting involved with the Communist Party. Later that night, her mom talked to her, tears in her eyes. She told Sandy never to become politically involved, because then they would put her name on a list and it would always be there. Always, her mother stressed. She told Sandy never to forget that she was Jewish. That people would look for an excuse to give her a hard time, especially when things got rough.

"How about your parents?"

Sandy looked up. "I was just thinking about what my parents told me about being Jewish. During the Depression, the only way my mother could get a job was to pretend that she was Christian. She got some priest to back her up. And later, during the war, she said that pro-Nazi rallies used to parade down New York City streets. Can you believe that? It wasn't safe for Jews to be out in many parts of town. They hid in their homes."

Sandy got up, walked over to the desk and got a fresh cigarette. "My mother said that the anti-Semitism stuff continued even after we entered the war," Sandy said angrily. "I guess the feeling was as long as the Nazis were killing Jews, they couldn't be all bad."

Sandy lit the new cigarette from the old and put the old butt out by grinding it into a coffee cup until it was demolished. It was just too much to deal with. She knew how badly shaken her parents had been after what they had seen. Her parents were good liberal union people. It hadn't made any sense for her father to flip out the way he had. . . . Now Sandy knew that he had just been scared for her. Sandy couldn't even imagine how surviving in Europe during the war must have affected Jenny's parents. She sighed, walked back to the bed, and flopped down.

So how would her parents handle it if they knew? They had always worried about her. It seemed as though she had gotten into one kind of trouble after another. Like the time she had gotten suspended from school for passing out "Communist" literature — all it had been was a few lousy civil rights flyers telling about a demonstration downtown. What an asshole the dean was. A big pompous cigar-smoking guy who really hated Sandy. Hated her because he couldn't intimidate her. So he had called her mother in. Sandy had been so proud. Her mother had come to school to defend her. Of course, she had given her hell when they got home, but she had stood by her when it really counted.

"You know, I don't think they'd be freaked out if they knew."

Jenny looked up, still distracted by her own thoughts. "If who knew?"

"My parents. About us." Jenny looked skeptical. "No, I mean it. They wouldn't like it or nothing, and they'd worry about me and stuff, but I think they'd accept it."

Jenny waved her hand to dismiss Sandy. "You're crazy."

Sandy shook her head. She didn't know for sure, but she thought they would accept it. Shit, they had always stood behind her before. This might be harder for them, but they would get through it.

14

It was almost summer, and Sandy found herself tuning out in class, hearing the teacher's voice in the distance as a light hum. It had been particularly hard to pay attention to this morning's psychology lecture. Jenny had dutifully taken notes so Sandy could get them from her.

They threw down their books and purses as they came into the room. "Boring. I thought psychology had something to do with people. If I hear one more story about the eating or shitting habits of Albert the Rat, or the hearing problems of Freddie the Frog, I . . . am . . . going . . . to . . . scream . . . or maybe I'll just go crazy." Sandy was waving her arms as she walked around the room. "I can see the headlines now. Coed driven mad by psychology class."

Sandy started walking around the room, doing her monster act which included weird faces and grunts, hitting her hand against her head, and other acts that Jenny found lovable. Jenny had sat down on the bottom bunk and was laughing at Sandy's antics. Jenny motioned for Sandy to come over. Sandy got into her gorilla routine, grunted a little and lumbered over to the bed. Jenny pulled her down on top of her.

"I thought we were going to take a nap."

Jenny began playing with Sandy's hair, nibbling on her ear. "We will," she whispered seductively. They started to make out. By now their lovemaking was totally natural. They undid each other's pants. Jenny pulled them down and started to kiss Sandy on her stomach, and then her hips. She stopped suddenly. "Did you lock the door when we came in?" she asked.

"I don't remember."

"Go lock it. We don't want Mary walking in on us."

Sandy jumped out of bed. Her pants were down around her knees, so she hopped awkwardly to the door, locked it, and hopped back to the bed, falling semi-exhausted on top of Jenny.

"Take them off," Jenny said between giggles. They both removed their pants and their blouses, leaving their underpants on as they lay down again on their sides. Sandy reached over and took Jenny's breast in her mouth, as her hand slid over Jenny's thighs, buttocks, and lower back. With one hand pushing Sandy's face closer to her breast and with the other fondling Sandy's nipples, Jenny wrapped her legs around Sandy's thigh. Teasing each other, they gently caressed the inside of each other's thighs, squeezing the hips and gently licking a nipple until the desire grew and they were gyrating their hips in synchrony. Jenny slipped her hand under Sandy's underpants, pulling on her pubic hair with a few gentle tugs, then stroked her vulva. Sandy lifted her hips, forcing Jenny's hand down onto her lips which were lubricated and swollen, and hurting for the need of direct stimulation. Jenny's hand squeezed her vulva tightly, relieving the pain, as her fingers slipped into Sandy's vagina, then out again, rubbing their way up to her clitoris where they lingered for a while, playfully stroking, then rotating in a slow circular motion. One of Sandy's hands had been squeezing Jenny's buttocks, and now she moved that hand to Jenny's anus as she gently caressed the opening and with the other hand started to manipulate Jenny's clitoris with a similar patting motion in which direct touch was interrupted by very brief intervals of no touch. By this time each knew what kind of stimulation the other liked. Their breathing became more labored. Jenny started to moan softly. With a free hand she placed a pillow over her head so no one would hear her sounds. The rhythm of their lovemaking grew faster, the tempo no longer controlled cerebrally but by an instinctual sense that took over at a certain point. Sandy's face was buried in Jenny's breast, muffling her panting, which had been increasing with the shorter, faster revolutions of their bodies. Jenny reached a climax first, her hips thrusting forcefully against Sandy's thigh and hand. Sandy felt as satisfied as if she had come with Jenny. It was one of the mysteries of making love with each other — they became so involved that it was hard to tell whose thigh or hand or breast was whose. In the tangle of their bodies, their excitement grew together, and the release of one felt like a release for the other. Jenny removed the pillow from her face and slid down on the bed to be at eye level with Sandy. They kissed gently. Sandy rubbed her back with a very light ticklish touch, which released the last tension in Jenny's body.

"How was that for you?" Jenny asked.

"Great," Sandy murmured through her smile.

"You want to come?" Jenny said as she pulled on a few of Sandy's pubic hairs.

"It's not important." Sandy was feeling very content.

Jenny's hand moved in between Sandy's lips, spreading them apart as she ran her fingers up and down the channel that ran from clitoris to vaginal opening. "Still think it's not important?" she said with a mischievous smile.

Sandy laughed from way down deep. "You certainly

have a way of convincing." Sandy barely got a chance to finish that sentence as Jenny kissed her hard, her mouth open, her tongue filling Sandy's mouth, as it pushed farther and farther in. Jenny's fingers played with Sandy's clitoris, then slipped into her hole, moving round and round as Sandy rotated her hips. With her thumb, Jenny started to caress Sandy's clitoris, at first lightly, then harder as Sandy's excitement grew. Jenny could always tell right before Sandy would have an orgasm. She would be panting in a steady rhythm, and then suddenly take in a deep breath and hold it, until it exploded in a scream as her body released its tension. Now Sandy had taken that gulp of air, and Jenny shooshed to warn her not to be too loud. Sandy held her sounds in, climaxing in relative quiet. Afterwards, she allowed herself to breathe deeply, filling her lungs with the wonderfully scented air that cushioned their lovemaking. Sandy rolled over on her back, laughed and slid her hand under her head. Jenny, who was on her side, lay down next to her, her head resting on Sandy's arm. Jenny lifted her head to look at Sandy.

"It's your turn to get the cigarettes."

"No, I got them last time."

"Well, you're so much better at getting cigarettes than I am," Jenny said sweetly.

Sandy shook her head. She knew she shouldn't reinforce Jenny for a bunch of crap like that, but she sure did look beautiful. And it really wasn't such a big deal. Sandy got up and went to Jenny's purse, which was sitting on one of the chairs by the desks. She pulled out two cigarettes and lit one. Turning around to light the second one off the first, she suddenly froze.

"Oh, my God," Sandy whispered.

"What's wrong?" Jenny sat up.

Sandy motioned to Jenny to be quiet. She was very agitated as she gestured for Jenny to come over. Sandy pointed to the top of the double-decker bed. Mary was "sleeping" there, huddled in the corner against the wall, directly above where they had just made love. Her body was very still — unnaturally still.

Sandy thought she was going to die. Smiling hysterically, her face expressed a mixture of embarrassment and fear. Jenny looked horrified. Her eyes were bulging and she seemed about to cry. Sandy told herself that maybe Mary really was sleeping. She didn't usually take afternoon naps, so maybe she had been very tired. Exceptionally tired. Dead on her feet. Sandy wished *she* were dead on her feet.

15

They never talked about that incident. That was a first. It had been two weeks and Jenny still couldn't believe it had happened. How could she and Sandy not have seen Mary? Sure, she was never in the room in the afternoons, but how could they have been so careless? Jenny wondered if she should say something to Mary. But what was there to say? She only prayed that Mary wouldn't tell anyone. Dear God, please keep her mouth shut. Sandy had been nervous for a couple of days, but then when she saw there wasn't going to be any immediate catastrophe, she had reverted back to her usual outrageous self. Jenny didn't say anything, but she felt angry with Sandy. How could she act so carefree? It was as if she had already forgotten what had happened. As if she didn't realize that this could ruin their lives. If Mary went to the RA, it would get to the dean. If it got to the dean, their parents would probably be notified. Jenny went to the closet and got a heavy cardigan. Even though it was summer, she had been cold lately. During the night, she had had some awful dreams, dreams of being chased by unknown figures. She would wake up in a cold sweat, afraid to go back to bed. Looking over, she would see Sandy sleeping peacefully, one arm dangling over the bed, and the other cupping her face. Jenny couldn't count on Sandy to handle things. She walked around in a cloud, oblivious to what was going on around her. Several times Jenny had run into one of the other girls on campus, and they had asked where her "other half" was. As if they never expected to see Jenny without Sandy. People were talking about them. It was one thing to be best friends, but she and Sandy spent almost all of their time together. It had to stop. It was dangerous.

Jenny looked up as the door opened and Mary walked in. She had spent even less than the usual amount of time in the room lately, often not even coming back to sleep. Every time she saw her, Jenny cringed. She felt helpless and ashamed. Mary acted as though nothing had happened, but Jenny knew that she must know. No one could have slept through that. My God, the bed had been shaking. And the sounds. Jenny forced herself to stop thinking about it while Mary was in the room. She felt she was going to vomit.

Mary nodded hello and then put her books on her bed. Now she turned to Jenny. They hadn't said more than a few words to each other since. . . .

"I've decided to share a room with Elaine. A double opened up in Clement and we've already signed for it. I'm sorry I didn't let the two of you know earlier, but it kind of happened all of a sudden." Jenny looked up at Mary. She seemed as uncomfortable as Jenny. That made Jenny feel a little better.

"Oh, that's great," she said. "I know you and Elaine have been wanting to live together for a while. It'll be good for your studying . . . you both being in pre-nursing and all."

"Yeah, that's what we thought. Anything to help our grades some." It was a lame joke, but they laughed anyhow.

"Well, I have to be going. I thought I'd have an early dinner and get a fresh start at the library." Mary turned to get her purse and then turned back to Jenny. "Will you tell Sandy if I don't see her before you do?"

"Sure. I'll tell her. No problem."

"Great. See you later."

"Yeah." Jenny didn't watch Mary as she walked out. She didn't look up until she heard the door click. That had been awful. But she had learned what she needed to know. Mary wouldn't tell anyone. At least not intentionally to hurt them. But there was no way to know with time what she might say to whom. She wasn't a malicious person, but you never knew. Jenny felt one weight lift and another replace it. They were in the clear for now. But this must never happen again.

16

Sandy was ecstatically happy. She had never known that she could feel the way she did. It was as if she had been dead all her life and now every cell in her body screamed with the joy of being alive. Life was beautiful. Who would have believed it?

She was sprawled out on the bed, enjoying her cigarette with long sensuous puffs. Everything was better when you were in love. She smiled as she remembered the conversation they had had a week ago. It was the first time she had told Jenny she loved her. She had never said that to anyone before. Sandy had always been amazed at how lightly people used those words. Love. What did it mean if you said it to everyone? Then it wasn't special. That's why Sandy had never said it before. When she said it, she wanted it to mean something. Jenny had told her that she loved Sandy, too. It had brought tears to Sandy's eyes. To love and be loved. Sandy was sure there was nothing better than that. Certainly nothing as good had ever happened in Sandy's life before.

Jenny was unusually quiet. She had a lot on her mind. She had decided to tell Sandy today. She had been putting it off for several days. Last week Sandy had told her she loved her. That had scared her. The way Sandy had said it, it sounded like she thought they were married. Like boyfriend and girlfriend. Jenny had to set things straight. For both of them.

"What's the matter?" Sandy asked, noticing Jenny seemed preoccupied.

"Nothing. I was just thinking about the reading I have to do for the History exam. It's only a week away and you haven't done any of the reading yet." Jenny looked at Sandy and then quickly looked away.

"Ah, who cares? Besides, we've got plenty of time." Sandy refused to get uptight about the exam. About anything. She yawned and stretched languidly in bed. Life was good.

Jenny sat up, bringing her knees to her chest and wrapping her arms around them. It was her serious talking pose. "You remember that guy I mentioned in Economics — Steve? We're going out on Friday. Probably catch a movie." Jenny's voice was casual, but her body contradicted her.

"What?" Sandy turned around to look at Jenny.

"We're going to a movie at the Student Union — 'La Strada,' I think." Jenny was still avoiding looking at Sandy. Sandy sat up in bed. She felt a vague apprehension in her belly.

"You interested in this guy?" Sandy's voice cracked a little. She told herself to calm down; she must be misunderstanding what Jenny meant. But her apprehension was growing.

"I don't know. He seems like a nice guy."

Jenny's voice was evasive; she didn't sound like she was very interested, but then why would she be going out with him? Something didn't fit here. It wasn't making any sense.

"I mean, is it a date?"

"Well, of course . . . you didn't think we were going to stop dating guys, did you?" Jenny looked at Sandy as if she was crazy. From Sandy's expression, it was clear that was exactly what she had thought. "Don't be silly. We have to date." Jenny was feeling annoyed now. Sandy had no right to look so hurt.

"Why?" Sandy felt tears welling up. She pushed them back and stood up.

"Because. Because we have to. Girls date boys. That's what we're supposed to do. It's expected of us." Jenny was flustered. She had assumed all this was obvious. What could Sandy be thinking? Sandy was acting so childish. Jenny began to feel scared. Maybe they shouldn't have done it. It was too complicated. And Sandy was making it worse.

"I don't want to date guys. It's you I'm in love with."

Jenny could see that she was really upset. She felt herself harden against the pleading look in Sandy's eyes.

"But what will people think?" Surely Sandy must realize that people would talk if they didn't date. It would be obvious.

"I don't know." Sandy misunderstood Jenny's fear. "We'll just tell them we're in love."

Jenny's voice was shrill. "Sandy, no. Never. You must promise me you will never tell anyone. If you do I'll never talk to you again. Promise me."

Sandy felt sick to her stomach. There was a desperation and vehemence in Jenny that didn't make any sense. Jenny was acting as if Sandy was the enemy. What had she done? She couldn't remember doing anything wrong. She loved Jenny. She felt panic at the thought of losing the first love she had ever known.

"Well, okay. I don't have to tell anyone if it's that important to you." Sandy was pacing frenetically around the room now. She was tearful. "But I don't understand why we have to date.

The idea of some immature creep clawing at me, reduced to a panting jelly if he touches me under my bra." Sandy felt disgusted at the thought. How could she let a man touch her now? Not after what she and Jenny had shared. It would be a sacrilege. What the hell was she talking about? She didn't believe in religion.

She reverted to a different argument. "And besides, the guys up here are so boring. They're so young and shallow. All into playing some big-shot fraternity jock." Sandy's voice was filled with contempt. "A bunch of rich spoiled kids from the Island." After all, Jenny had picked her and she was different. Because she was different. How could Jenny go back to them? She tried again.

"You try to start an intelligent conversation about the Civil Rights Movement or the Peace Movement and they look at you with that dumb stare: 'What's that?'" Sandy imitated a big dumb jock with a deep voice. "Babies and idiots. I don't want to date."

Jenny sat silently throughout Sandy's diatribe. She had a stubborn look on her face.

"We have to date. I'm going to. No one must know. Not even suspect." Why was Sandy trying to ruin their lives? Where did she think they were, in some sort of fairy tale? This was the real world. You obeyed the rules or you didn't survive. And Jenny was going to survive.

Sandy tried once more. She felt a growing helplessness, but her mind told her that Jenny must not have understood what Sandy had been saying. She couldn't have understood, because otherwise she would see that what Sandy was saying made sense. Very slowly she began to speak, accentuating each word.

"Jenny, I'm in love with you. I've never felt this happy, or strong, or proud. I feel like I can take on the whole world." Sandy paused here and looked at the girl she loved. A girl she would do anything for. A girl she would die for. This was the love of her life. There would never be anything like this again. Sandy felt sure of that. She pleaded.

"What can they do to us? They can't hurt us, not if our love is strong, not if we stick together. I don't need anyone else but you." Sandy was getting angry. That anything should get in the way of their love. With the greatest conviction she said, "I don't give a fuck about what *they* think."

"I do," Jenny said quietly.

Their eyes met and held. It was said.

17

Nothing was ever quite the same after that. In a very secret place, carefully hidden, Sandy lived with a pain like the pilot light on a stove: it was always there, sometimes small and unobtrusive, but with the turn of a switch it could ignite into a searing flame. As they lay in the bottom bunk, kissing and fondling each other's breasts, Sandy hoped that it wouldn't hurt as much tonight as it had last weekend.

Jenny had started dating. Sandy tried to act nonchalant when Jenny put on her makeup, got into a particularly sexy sweater and skirt, and then breezily said good-bye when her date rang from downstairs. Sandy had begun to hate the phone. And the different men's voices that asked for Jenny. She tried not to think about what they looked like, or where they took Jenny on their dates, or what happened on the way home in their cars. But she was plagued with images of Jenny and different men, sitting in the car, Jenny smiling at them, a man's hands reaching out, touching her hair, her face, the hand moving down her body, a rough hand, an unloving hand, someone else's hand, and the rage would begin to erupt so she'd ball her hands into a fist, her nails pressing into the skin until the pain would shoot through her entire arm, the indentations in her palm lasting for minutes, then hours. Only physical pain could distract her from this inner ache which seemed to have a mind of its own, a will that was stronger than Sandy's, that laughed at her meager attempts to stop the thoughts, to bring the feelings back under control.

Last weekend, they had also been lying in the bed, making out before Jenny's date. The making out turned into lovemaking. Sandy even forgot that Jenny had a date. Then the phone rang. Jenny jumped out of bed and disappeared into the bathroom, on the way asking Sandy to get the phone. Obediently, Sandy answered it and heard the male voice, telling of his arrival downstairs. When she got off the phone, she felt like crying. Her vagina was throbbing, and a shooting pain had spread from the opening up into the deeper end. Confused and frightened, she sat down on the bed, clasping her knees tightly to her chest. Oblivious, Jenny came back into the room to grab her purse, and then she was gone. Sandy didn't know how long she had sat there, her legs tightly clenched, her hand holding her vagina over the jeans, futilely trying to comfort herself. She had wanted to say something to Jenny, started to, then changed her mind. What was there to say? Jenny knew she didn't want her to date. And she was doing it anyhow. Sandy had no power; Jenny was throwing her tidbits, and she was gratefully grabbing them.

Now Jenny started to unzip Sandy's pants. Sandy wanted to tell her to stop. Jenny's date would be here any minute and she didn't want a repeat of last Friday. And besides, she was hurt and angry, and her mind was jumping from one thing to another. This was no time for them to make love. Jenny's hand slipped farther into her pants, and Sandy knew she wouldn't say anything. How could she stop this? This was so wonderful, so right. Fuck her pride, fuck her anger, her body cried out in the strength of its desire. Sandy felt her excitement grow quickly, felt the forcefulness in the thrusting of her hips as she met Jenny's hand halfway, more than halfway. The room began to spin as her breath became quick and shallow; she gasped as every muscle and cell strained and stretched to reach that mysterious place where all of her joined together, funneled and focused down a path which became a spot which exploded into thousands of pieces, parts of herself that scattered wildly. She was almost there. Almost at that place where there was no going back.

The phone rang.

Instead of exploding, the spot just hung there for a moment, and then simply disappeared. Suspended in ether, Sandy felt the invisible coils which held her snap, and she fell a very short distance, landing on the bed bruised and aching. Mutely, she watched as Jenny got up and headed for the bathroom.

"Would you get that, Sandy?" Jenny called over her shoulder. "And tell Sam I'm running a few minutes late." This last fiat was muffled by the sound of the faucet.

The phone continued to ring. Sandy lay there on the bed, her body motionless, her eyes fixed on the steel springs which stretched when Mary used to lie there but were now tightly bound. She felt something tear inside her. She no longer cared what Jenny would think or say. A fierce anger laced with a reckless giddiness grew paradoxically in the stillness of her frame.

Jenny came out of the bathroom, wiping her hands on a towel. "Will you please get that, Sandy?"

"No."

Jenny started back into the bathroom, then turned around, shocked, when Sandy's response registered.

"What?"

"I said no." The phone rang once more and stopped. "I will not answer the phone. I will not tell Sam you are running a few minutes late. In fact, when he calls again, I will tell him to go fuck himself." Sandy felt herself start to breathe again. She swung her legs off the bed, her back stiff as her feet landed on the floor, her hands clenching the rounded edge of her bed.

"I want to know why you're going out with him."

"Look, Sandy, I don't have time for this crap now." Jenny walked back into the bathroom. Sandy followed her.

"Well, you're damn well gonna make time." Sandy stretched her arms and braced them in the door frame, feeling her control slip, her anger spiral in a heated swell. "You don't give a damn about him. Yesterday you told me you weren't even sure you liked him. So why the fuck are you spending the evening with him instead of me? You're supposed to love me. Or have you forgotten?"

Jenny unscrewed her mascara brush and, leaning over the sink, began to darken her already dark lashes with swift expert strokes. Sandy knew Jenny was deliberately taking her time with an answer, in order to frustrate her.

Jenny finished one eye and turned to Sandy. "We've been through this before. I don't want to go through it again." She started on the other eye.

Sandy suddenly wanted to grab the brush and poke out one of Jenny's eyes. The thought frightened her. Then made her feel guilty. She said she loved Jenny. And she did. How could she feel such hatred?

"I know we've been through it before. But I still don't understand it. It doesn't make any sense to me. Explain it again." Sandy could hear the pleading in her voice. She was trying hard to be reasonable. To give Jenny a chance to explain the necessity for this violation of their love.

"Damn it, will you leave me alone?" Jenny was yelling now. "Just get out of here!"

Sandy didn't move. She was too hurt to move. Any motion might cause the tears that filled her eyes to spill over. That would be the final humiliation. Sandy stared down at the floor.

"You hear me, get out of here."

The phone rang. Sandy felt the hurt abate and transform into an intense fury which turned her around, and almost yanked the door off its hinges as she slammed it open and strode down the corridor.

She found herself walking across the golf course that was adjacent to the campus. The sound of the wet grass crunching under her sneakers reminded her of the long walk she had taken her first night at the dorm. It had been a warm night, the stars shining brilliantly after an unexpected shower that morning. She had been feeling terrible. Lonely. Isolated. Scared. Just as she was feeling now.

Damn that Jenny. She was a bitch. A fucking cocksucking bitch. Sandy couldn't imagine how she had gotten involved with her anyhow. Her anger warmed her, made her feel more powerful as she kicked the grass with a vengeance. She didn't need Jenny. She didn't need anyone. Those words, words she had often repeated to herself, had a hollow sound now. Sandy tried to muster her false bravado. Putting her hands in the pockets of her jeans, she told herself that she didn't give a fuck; she had been through rough things before and this was nothing compared to the shit she had seen. A vague uneasiness stirred in her chest. There was something wrong with what she was thinking. Something untrue. Half-formed thoughts and images collided in the confused pandemonium of her mind. Her father red-faced, puffing, eyes bulging, his arm swung back in an arc ready to connect with her terrified face. I need her. Her mother shocked, slapping her again, this time Sandy returning the slap defiantly, then inwardly torn and screaming for forgiveness as her mother's eyes filled with tears. Jenny's face in front of her, laughing that cynical yet self-conscious giggle which was filled with contradictions. Yet so familiar. This is the person I love. The girl I love. It seemed strange, but not really, to say "girl." Sandy had always thought it would be "boy" or "man." This is the boy I love. This is the man I am going to marry. But that was silly. Sandy had known for a long time that she was never going to get married. By the time she was thirteen, Sandy had decided that she was going to be some man's mistress. Preferably a married man.

There seemed to be two kinds of women in the world: wives and mistresses. And Sandy was sure she didn't want to be any man's wife. Everything she had read in books and seen in movies made it clear that men took advantage of their wives — treating them like maids, ignoring them when they got home, holding them responsible for the way the kids turned out. You had to be crazy to want that kind of life, Sandy had often thought to herself. She'd listen to the other girls talk about the men they would marry, watch their eyes cloud over with romance, and realize that she'd rather be the "other woman" any day. Shit. You had your own pad and a lot of freedom. He'd come over one or two nights a week, which seemed enough, and when he did come over it would be because he wanted to, not because he had to. Sandy didn't like the idea of feeling trapped, so she certainly didn't want any of her men to feel that way. Sandy was realistic; she knew there'd be more than one man. She'd have several, no, many affairs with different kinds of men. That way she would really see it all.

In the movies the mistresses were always lonely and miserable. Sandy didn't understand that. They never seemed to have any friends. Sandy would have friends. People she'd really like. They'd run around downtown in the Village and have lots of fun. Besides, Sandy would have a career. She wanted to do something with her life. She had watched her father come home every night stiff and sore from the same stinking job. There was no way that was going to happen to her. Her mother had often told her, "Sandy, get an education. Look at your father. He had no choice. You make sure you have one."

Choices. In all her wildest imaginings she had never envisioned falling in love with a woman. But was that really true? She'd always had close girlfriends. And she usually enjoyed being with the girlfriends more than going out on dates. And when she was a kid she'd had crushes on some of the older teenage girls. And at times she wanted to be comforted by those girls, held close and . . . Sandy stopped suddenly. There was something in her head that wanted to get through but she couldn't quite get a handle on it. It was very frustrating. Then she remembered Jenny.

Jenny. All of this other shit was academic now. She had met Jenny. And fallen in love. And now not only didn't she want to be a man's wife, but she had no desire to be a mistress either. All she wanted was Jenny. To spend the rest of her life with her. It was really very simple. When people fell in love they spent their lives together. And there was no doubt in Sandy's mind that their love would last. It was a lifetime love. A special love. And what difference did it make that they were two girls? People were people, weren't they? Hadn't she marched in civil rights demonstrations where the placards called for equality and justice for all people? And laughed about the sign of a friend that said, "So you're a liberal — but would you let your sister marry one?" Something made Sandy uncomfortable again. There was a piece missing in her thinking, but she couldn't put her finger on it. Whatever it was, it frightened her. An image of Jenny, standing close to her, looking her in the eye as she said, "I do." An amorphous dread seized Sandy. The woman she loved was out there, right now, with a man she didn't even like. It all seemed so crazy. So wrong. Yet she was helpless to change it. She had tried to make Jenny see. But she had failed.

Sandy felt very close to a new and unknown despair. She quickened her pace, pitching herself into the darkness which grew blacker as the campus lights receded behind her. Simultaneously, an inner darkness, at first just a spot, began to enlarge, advancing steadily, filling her brain with jeering shadows that threatened to suffocate her, stopping the air from her lungs, her mind panicking as she broke her stride, gasping for breath. Falling on her knees, head bent, her fingers clawed the grass until they reached soil. Twisting her thumbs and forefingers into the moist earth, Sandy felt a respite from the fear that had suddenly gripped her, coming out of the darkness so swiftly that she hadn't had a chance to cement her defenses.

She knelt there for a long time, concentrating on the coolness of the soil on her fingers. The anxiety began to abate. Sandy stood up slowly and began to walk again.

It was quiet when she got back to the dorm. Too late for the girls who had stayed home to be up, and too early for the ones with dates to be back. Automatically, she waited for the large steel elevator which silently carried her to her floor. There were no sounds as she walked down the corridor, whose gray and white linoleum floor sparkled eerily in the fluorescent lighting. The room was dark as she entered it. Sandy left the lights off and sat down at her desk. The huge concrete street lamps which edged the campus driveway shone brilliantly in the moonless night. Concentric circles of light around the base of the lampposts were bordered by more mysterious areas where objects were not totally discernible. The campus was deserted; Sandy sat in the darkness waiting for something, anything to break the surrealistic silence that surrounded her.

Slowly, the cars began to trickle in. Feeling strongly compelled and uncomfortably voyeuristic, Sandy sat in the darkness and watched the couples get out of the cars. A boy and then a girl. Once in a while a girl and then a boy. But always a boy and a girl. The pattern was never disrupted. Sometimes two boys and two girls would pile out of the car, but they were always in couples. Walking back to the dorms, the boys would invariably put their arms around their dates. This gesture seemed a statement of possession rather than one of affection. How come these men, many of whom hardly knew the girls they were out with and couldn't give a shit about them, had the right to put their arms around their dates' shoulders, while Sandy, who loved and respected and cared for her girl, couldn't do the same? In the last few months Sandy had often felt an urge to touch Jenny when they were in public, but something had inhibited her natural impulse. They had never talked about it, but she knew that Jenny wouldn't like it. She had thought of saying something but had been afraid to bring it up. Jenny had been so moody lately, ecstatically happy at times, then strangely withdrawn. And Sandy hadn't wanted to do anything that would displease Jenny, anything that might interfere with this sudden and great happiness that she had discovered. Maybe she was being silly to make such a big deal out of Jenny's dating. After all, it was Sandy that Jenny loved. What difference did it make if she went out with some different *schmucks* every now and then if she felt she had to? It was the feeling that she had to which disturbed Sandy greatly. The anxiety began to spill again, and she resolutely pushed it away. She loved Jenny. Loving meant not being selfish. If Jenny wanted to date, if it was that important to her, even for reasons that didn't make any sense to Sandy, then if she really loved her she should be able to accept that. And to control her childish tantrums that threatened to destroy their beautiful love. She would not let this men thing get the best of her. They just simply weren't worth getting excited about. Even Jenny, with her crazy ideas about boys, must know that somewhere.

The cars were beginning to pile in now, the sounds of approaching engines and men's voices and an occasional female laugh drifting up the eight flights to her window. Sandy turned on the light by her desk. Quickly she grabbed the closest textbook, her Chemistry book, and opened it randomly. She looked at the equations and figures on the page and smiled to herself. What a bunch of crap, she thought. What does this nonsense have to do with anything?

Sandy had asked this dangerous question about most of her classes. Even the Psychology courses she had taken seemed irrelevant to life, to the things that concerned her. The two exceptions were her Philosophy class and her Contemporary Lit seminar. She was taking Epistemology, and she loved the debates about what was real, what we know and what we just think we know. Philosophy was fun. And it was serious. It raised questions about the meaning of life, of reality, of morality. These were questions she had pretty much kept to herself. Now she had discovered that not only did these concerns have names — Epistemology, Metaphysics, Ethics — but that other people shared her interest.

Lit class was also exciting. Instead of reading the usual garbage — Dickens, Hawthorne, Thoreau — all those old-time creeps who had lived in a totally different and thus useless world, she was reading Camus, Sartre, Marx, and Albee. In high school, she had thought everyone who had ever lived was an idiot. Except for Freud, and Hesse, and Huxley, whom she had discovered on her own. Now she was finding that there had been other good thinkers, guys who were concerned about the more serious issues of life, who had something else on their minds besides who had won the Pennant and where they would get their next fuck.

As the girls returned from their dates, laughs, screams, and heavy footsteps echoed down the hall. Sandy picked up her textbook and pretended to read it. She didn't want Jenny to come in and think she had just been sitting there, waiting up for her. That would make Jenny angry. And she wanted them to reconcile tonight.

There was a knock at the door. Surprised, Sandy got up and opened it. A girl she had never seen before was standing in the corridor.

"Are you Sandy?"

Sandy nodded.

"You live with a girl by the name of Jenny?"

"Yeah." Sandy felt herself begin to panic. Oh God, she thought, let her not have been in an accident.

"Well, we have her over by the elevator. We wanted to make sure this was the right room."

"What's wrong with her?" They started walking down the corridor to the elevator. "Is she okay?"

"Oh yeah," the other girl said nonchalantly. "She just really tied one on. I rode home with her in the same car. She was in the back seat stretched over four of us. Threw up all over her date."

Jenny was leaning against a wall. A second girl was standing next to her, holding her up.

"I found her roommate."

The girl turned around, letting go of Jenny for a moment. Jenny slid to the floor, her head bobbing like an apple in a pan of water. Sandy rushed over and heaved her up with the girl's help.

"Will you give me a hand with her to the room?"

"Sure."

They half-carried, half-dragged Jenny to the room by throwing her limp arms around her shoulders. Sandy felt a protective fury grow inside her. If Jenny's date had done something to get her so drunk, Sandy would knock the shit out of him. She kicked open the door.

"Hey, thanks a lot." Sandy grabbed Jenny tightly around the waist.

"Are you sure you can . . ."

"Yeah, I can manage from here," Sandy interrupted. "Thanks again." With great difficulty, Sandy hoisted Jenny up and dragged her into the room. They slammed against the walls some, as Sandy lost her balance from kicking the door shut. Jenny was no help at all.

"I'm going to be sick again," Jenny mumbled in the voice of a zombie.

"Oh, no. Okay, Jenny. Just hold on. Here we go." Sandy dragged her into the bathroom, propping her up against the wall with one hip as she lifted up the toilet seat. Just as Sandy let her down, Jenny started retching. Sandy held her head for support with one hand and her hair out of her face with the other. Just as her mother had done for her when she was a child. It had always comforted Sandy when her mother did that. She had never understood how her mother wasn't disgusted by her vomit, how she had been able to be there without gagging. But now, as she held Jenny's head, she felt no repulsion. She hadn't had a chance to think about it; it had just been the most natural thing for her to do. She loved Jenny just as much when she was vomiting as when she was well. There was nothing she wouldn't, nothing she couldn't do for Jenny.

Sandy helped Jenny up after she seemed to have finished. They started back into the room.

"I have to piss," Jenny muttered in that unknown voice.

Sandy stopped pulling her in one direction and, catching her balance, pulled her back the way they had come.

"Okay, Jenny. Just let me get your pants down first." Leaning her against the wall, Sandy unzipped Jenny's pants, pulling them down with one hand as she tried to lower the seat with the other. But Jenny fell on the toilet before Sandy could get the seat down.

"Wait a second, Jen. The seat."

Jenny sat there staring dully ahead, her eyes half closed.

"Okay, Jen. Never mind. Just stay there and piss. I'm going to fix your bed. Call me when you're ready to get up."

Sandy raced into the bedroom and pulled back the covers on Jenny's bed. She heard a loud bang and Jenny was standing in the doorway, her pants around her knees, dangerously swaying back and forth. Sandy barely had time to grab her before she keeled over. Holding her from behind, Sandy pulled her to the bed just as Jenny crashed onto the mattress, her feet still hanging over the side. Picking up Jenny's feet and lifting them onto the bed, Sandy maneuvered her into a less awkward position. Jenny was out cold. Sandy undressed her, leaving only her underpants on. As she pulled the covers around her shoulders, she smoothed the sweaty tangled strands of hair out of Jenny's face. For the first time it occurred to her that Jenny had probably gotten drunk because she had been upset by their fight. Jenny didn't like these battles any more than she did. Sandy looked at her strangely ashen face and knew that Jenny did care about her. About them.

"Oh, Jenny. Why does it have to be like this?" Sandy asked in a soft sad voice.

Jenny continued to breathe heavily, lost in a stupored sleep, oblivious to Sandy and to the question which neither of them understood, nor would understand for many years.

18

Jenny was humming softly as she read her Political Science textbook. All morning the refrain from "Teen Angel," an oldy but goody, had been circulating through her mind. She tried to concentrate on the words in front of her but it was difficult. Her mind was on Bruce.

It had happened so quickly. One minute she had been playing the field and then Zap — she was going with Bruce. They had hit it off right away, talking excitedly about music (he seemed to know so much, and Jenny hoped to learn a lot from him) and art and literature. He was an English major, a senior, and far more mature than any of the boys she had dated that year. Or ever, for that matter. His energy was contagious; one minute he'd have her laughing hysterically at some wise crack, and then in the next he would have grabbed her hand and literally dragged her off to see something. To see anything. He was excited by everything around him, from the small pine growing crooked in front of the Student Union, to the Ionic designs on the History Building. And on top of that, he was a nice guy. He seemed to care genuinely about people and about her in particular. She felt very lucky to have met and now to be going out with such a great guy. Well, she really didn't know him well enough to call him great — but he certainly was good. And better than most.

Jenny looked down at the page before her and realized she had read it without even registering what it was about. So there were two houses in the German Federal Council: the *Bundesrat* and the *Bundestag.* She repeated that sentence over to herself without looking at the text, which was draped across her knees. Sandy would be back soon. Her Bio class would just be ending now. Jenny nervously pulled her upper lip into her mouth by tugging at it with her lower teeth. She had seen Bruce almost every night this week, and Sandy had stomped around the room, silently sullen, when they were together in the afternoons. Jenny knew Sandy was upset because she was spending so much time with Bruce rather than with her. That wasn't fair of Sandy. She should be happy that Jenny had finally met someone she could get serious about. Hadn't Sandy all this time said that the guys Jenny dated were *schmucks*? That she would understand if Jenny went out with someone decent, but dating guys who were idiots was crazy? Well, now she had met someone worthwhile. And Sandy was acting worse than ever. Jenny was getting tired of coming home and greeting the accusing hostility in Sandy's eyes. Sandy was being a pain in the ass. If only Sandy would start dating. If she put out half an effort, she wouldn't have any trouble meeting guys. But Sandy insisted that she wasn't interested; all the guys were immature and creepy and she didn't see any point wasting her time. Well, now that Jenny was going to be gone more, maybe that would change.

Jenny felt a pang of guilt. She knew that Sandy was hurting; she was sullen and hostile because she missed Jenny and was jealous of her new boyfriend. But there was nothing Jenny could do about it. She had to go on living. Her first responsibility was to herself. And she wanted a boyfriend. Someone she could spend close weekends with, someone she could go to movies with at the Student Union, their arms linked and greeting their mutual friends; someone she could take home to meet her parents.

Whoa, Jenny, she thought to herself. Don't rush things. You hardly know him and you're already imagining him coming home for dinner. She could envision Bruce asking her if he had to wear a white shirt and tie, and her saying, "No, don't bother; my parents are informal." Her parents would like him. He was a gentleman, and very intelligent, and could be ever so charming when he wanted to. Bruce had talked about renting a motel room this weekend. Just for the fun of it. Jenny had never done it in a motel. It seemed very glamorous and mature and a touch illicit. She would wait in the car as he paid for the room. The woman behind the counter would peer out through the shades to see if anyone else was in the car. Jenny would brazenly look back at her and the woman would quickly yet disapprovingly turn her eyes away. Jenny felt a wild excitement stir inside her. She and Bruce would do many outrageous things together. And they wouldn't care what other people would think.

Jenny was startled when Sandy pushed open the door and came into the room, dropping her notebooks loudly on the floor. She felt mildly irritated that Sandy had come in now just as she was starting to get some serious studying done. She nodded at Sandy over her shoulder and returned to the book. Sandy sneaked up behind Jenny and kissed her lightly on the neck.

"Cut it out," Jenny said, annoyed.

"What's the matter?" Sandy sounded hurt. She was always

hurt lately. Jenny was sick of Sandy's walking around like a sad-eyed cocker spaniel whose master had kicked it.

"I'm trying to study." Jenny was amazed at how angry her voice was. At how angry she was beginning to feel.

Sandy took a step back and looked at her closely. She seemed to hesitate, then decided to pursue what was on her mind.

"You've been acting strange for a couple of days. Is something else going on?" Sandy stood there, looking as if she expected a guillotine to fall any minute. Something in Jenny snapped.

"I don't want us to do that anymore." The words tumbled out, propelled by a momentum that Jenny hadn't been aware of. It was all clear now. She knew what she had to do. She couldn't risk complicating things with Bruce. And she never wanted to get drunk again the way she had on that night with Sam. That had been the most horrible night of her life. Totally out of control. Helpless to stop herself from acting like a fool. And completely vulnerable and defenseless, so that anyone could have done anything they wanted to her. Jenny shuddered to remember that night. And the self-loathing she had felt the next morning. With the acute crystalline vision that one has only at important choice points, Jenny saw Sandy freeze, and the horror she had felt a moment before started to cross Sandy's face.

"Do what anymore?" There was a long silence.

"We're friends. Good friends. That's all." Jenny looked at Sandy squarely. There was no running away from this. It had to be dealt with here and now.

"Jenny, what are you talking about? We're a lot more than that." But Sandy's voice didn't sound convincing. An edge of panic had crept in.

"Not anymore," Jenny said simply. Sandy stared at her in amazement. "I just can't deal with it anymore. It's too complicated, and you start making demands on me for time. It's no good, Sandy. We're going to have to stop." From a distance, Jenny heard her firmness, felt the careful articulation as she uttered these words she hadn't even known were there.

"I can't believe you're saying this. You don't mean it." Sandy really did seem flabbergasted. She was close to tears. For a moment Jenny felt a crack in her armor, then resolutely, like a warrior sure of his blessing from God, she pushed forward.

"I do mean it. Bruce and I are going to be spending a lot of time together."

"And there'll be no time for me." Sandy seemed to have gotten a second wind. Her inflection was angry.

"I didn't say that." Jenny felt herself take a step back. Suddenly she felt on the defensive.

"You didn't have to. He's more important to you than I am." Sandy pressed on her momentary advantage.

"That's not true, Sandy." Jenny wanted to say, "Yes, yes,

he's more important," but instead found herself denying it. She couldn't seem to get those words out. Why? Why couldn't she say them? Jenny felt backed up against the desk with nowhere to move.

"Then what the hell are you saying?" Sandy's eyes were piercing her, her heart was pounding so fast and hard that her chest hurt. At the same time she felt like she wasn't getting any air. She felt faint. Somewhere a more resilient part of her took over. This was one battle she could not afford to lose. There simply wasn't any choice.

"I can't handle two relationships at the same time." Jenny watched Sandy get confused. She obviously hadn't been expecting that. Sandy hesitated for a moment, then resumed her attack, but this time it didn't have the same sureness.

"That's great. You can't handle it, so I get the shaft."

"I'm not shafting you, Sandy. We're still roommates and friends. Best friends." Sandy threw up her hands and made a face. Now Jenny felt angry and hurt.

"So that doesn't mean anything to you, our being best friends. Well, thanks a lot." To her surprise Jenny heard herself yelling. "I thought you cared more about me than that." The anger on Sandy's face was replaced by a bewildered expression.

"I don't know what's going on here." Sandy's eyes were pleading. "Of course I care about you. I love you. And our friendship is very important to me. What does that have to do with anything?"

"It has to do with everything." Jenny felt sure again that she was in the right. It was Sandy who was being unreasonable. "Our friendship is not enough for you."

"You're damn right it's not enough for me," Sandy shot back at Jenny vehemently. "You expect me to be pleased and say, 'Thank you, Jenny,'" Sandy mimicked the intonations of a sweet Pollyana, "'thank you for the few crumbs you throw at me.' Well, fuck that and fuck you." Sandy stomped to the door, then turned around. Her face was twisted in a tormented expression.

"You think because he reads Proust and listens to Wagner that he's different from the rest of them. Well, he'll end up using you just the way the others have. You want him, you got him." The last words were spat out with a venom that shocked Jenny. Sandy opened the door, then turned around for one last sting. "Lots of luck," she said bitterly, slamming the door as she walked out.

Jenny stood very still. In the silence, the only sound was of her irregular breathing. She stood there stunned, as if Sandy had slapped her in the face. Emotionally drained, she tried to remember what they had said to each other. But all she could see was Sandy's contorted face, her features distorted into a grotesque parody of pain. Jenny shivered, although if anything, it was uncomfortably warm in their room. Their room. The look on Sandy's face said that she, Jenny, had become her mortal enemy. How would they continue to live together? Tears began to slide down her cheek and drip from her chin as she stood motionless, trying to imagine what it would be like not to live with Sandy. A wave of fear swept over her, through her, chilling in its acuteness and suddenness. She might lose Sandy. It seemed inconceivable but it could happen. She would have to face that possibility. Jenny struggled to regain her composure, to suppress the broken sob that was lodged at the base of her throat. Suddenly, a second thought exploded into her consciousness, bringing with it a flood of panic. What if it didn't work out with Bruce? Then she would have no one. She would have thrown Sandy away for nothing. She would be alone. Empty. A desperate urge to run after Sandy filled her, but she arrested it quickly. There was no going back now. She would try to make it work with Bruce. And prove Sandy wrong.

19

During the next months, Sandy wandered through an unfamiliar wasteland. The landscape around her hadn't changed, but Sandy was oblivious to everything except the gripping despair which held her with the strength of a steel-toothed vise. There was no escape from the anguish that demanded her total and undivided loyalty. But it wasn't only that grief had seen fit to conquer her body and deplete her spirit. What was unendurable was that she felt mutilated, as though her insides had been ripped apart. She could see no sign of injury when she looked down at her gut, but something doubled her over, forcing her down to her knees on the bathroom floor, convulsed with dry heaves and spasms of pain. Within a few weeks the pain had become constant. She went to the Student Health Center, where a doctor prescribed valium for her "nerves." At one time her pride would have refused to cater to such a visible sign of weakness. But now she gratefully swallowed the pills and prayed for the anesthetized intervals. The absence of pain seemed the most she could hope for in life. Like her pain, her tears came in waves, bursting out at the most inappropriate times, then mysteriously dissipating into a foggy blur, in which her anguish would temporarily subside into a relieved numbness. She stopped eating and lost twenty pounds. Looking in the mirror, she reminded herself of a concentration camp victim, each rib clearly defined in parallel with the barbed wire fence. But like the prisoners, who had no reason to survive, she lived. Against her will. Her body refused to die.

It had occurred to Sandy to take her own life. But that

required a decisiveness she did not feel. And what was there left to kill? She felt she had lost not only Jenny, but also herself. There had been times before when Sandy had philosophically struggled with the meaninglessness of life, but in the past, at least she had always had some things to cling to. Like her toughness. She had been proud of the fact that she never cried or showed any weakness. But now even that was lost. Her love for Jenny had turned her into a weak blubbering slob, who had no pride or self-respect. For if Jenny wanted her back, Sandy knew she would be there. And somewhere in her mind was a hope that Jenny would discover her mistake and come back to where she belonged.

Sandy would never remember much about that time. As the months passed, the acuteness of the pain subsided, replaced by an amorphous ache. She cut back on taking the little yellow tablets, reserving them for real emergencies. Now that curfews had been abolished, Jenny was rarely in the room. Their class schedules were different, and Jenny often stayed out late "studying" at Bruce's. Once in a while, Jenny would stop by the dormitory on a Saturday afternoon and spend a few hours washing and setting her hair, filing her nails, and making other preparations for her date that night. Sandy made a habit of spending those afternoons in the room, hoping Jenny would come back and they could have a little time together. Sometimes she thought it was better this way. Cold turkey. But she still looked forward to seeing Jenny, even for only a few moments.

Her life seemed to be full of contradictions. Always tired, Sandy was unable to sleep. Thoughts scattered and incapable of real concentration, she found herself studying more than she ever had. She was constantly cold, even on hot days. The weekly phone conversations with her mother were the hardest. Sandy wanted to be able to let her mother know something, but what was there to say? When her mother asked her how she was doing, Sandy would say fine, aware that her monotone betrayed her words. Screaming for help inside, she would respond with an angry "Don't bug me" when her mother asked again if she was sure everything was okay. They would get off the phone quickly then, her mother worried and hurt, Sandy guilty and confused. There was no one to talk to. No one could understand what had happened. She grieved alone.

It was in September that her old friend Evelyn first came up for a weekend. She was visiting her boyfriend Kevin, a graduate student in Philosophy. Sandy and Evelyn met for coffee on campus and talked old times. In high school they had had long discussions about philosophy, politics, Freud. Now, after a long separation, they renewed their friendship. When Evelyn left that Sunday, Sandy felt better than she had in months. Talking with Evelyn about the people they had known, the stoned escapades in the Village, Sandy remembered her old self. She had been an independent SOB in those days, downright feisty, and scared of no one and nothing. If she had been that way once, she could do it again. This thing with Jenny had thrown her, beaten her down like nothing else in her life, but she'd be damned if she wasn't going to start fighting back.

Sandy eagerly looked forward to the weekends when Evelyn came up from the city. Kevin had to study a lot, so Sandy and Evelyn would take long strolls on campus or explore some of the surrounding neighborhoods. Sandy was surprised to see that she could still laugh.

One day while they were walking along a quiet suburban street, Sandy told Evelyn about Jenny. Sandy had expected that it would be very difficult to get it out. She had thought for weeks about breaking her vow to Jenny and decided that she really needed to tell someone, and it wouldn't really be wrong to tell Evelyn, who didn't know Jenny and didn't even live in the same town. Besides, she asked herself, what did she owe to Jenny? But somehow, despite the fact that Jenny was acting as though she didn't exist, Sandy still felt bound to her oath. So before she told Evelyn, she made her swear that she would never tell another living soul. Evelyn smiled as she took the childish oath, crossing herself and repeating the ritual words. Surprisingly, Sandy found it easy to talk about falling in love with Jenny, the good months they had had, and then the changes. When Sandy was finished, she saw that Evelyn was crying. Sandy felt her own eyes start to fill, then spill over as Evelyn threw her arms around Sandy, rocking her back and forth as they stood there on the sidewalk. Embarrassed, Sandy stood still with her hands by her sides. She couldn't quite believe she was crying in public. But she was. And the remarkable thing was that a part of her didn't even care.

20

As Sandy watched the three of them play out the hand, she acknowledged to herself that Evelyn had been absolutely right about Mike. He was different from the other men she had known. He was bright, sensitive, and warm. It had taken Evelyn two months to convince her that meeting Mike, who was Kevin's roommate, would be a good idea. Good for her, Evelyn had said. Sandy had insisted that she had no desire to go out with anyone. The whole idea of dating seemed preposterous. First the obligatory movie, then a boring conversation about who was majoring in what, and other inane personal statistics. And how could she possibly participate in the wrestling match at the Fishbowl? She couldn't tolerate such humiliations now. It was too ridiculous to think about such things, let alone seriously contemplate them. But Evelyn had persisted. She didn't have to go out on a date with him. Evelyn would cook a meal, and the four of them would simply have dinner together. If they liked each other, fine. If they didn't hit it off, that would be the end of it. Sandy had continued to resist, but less vehemently. Maybe it wouldn't be such a bad idea. After all, it wasn't a date. She was under no obligation to like him, or even to spend any time alone with him. And it was time for her to pick up the pieces of her life. She couldn't go on mooning after Jenny forever. Besides. She was lonely.

She had known that very first night she met him. She immediately liked the contradictions in his face: rugged features with baby-soft skin. When he laughed, the natural sound filled the room, putting Sandy at ease. She liked the way he held his pipe, thoughtful but unpretentious. And she liked the way he talked: deliberate when he knew what he was saying, meditative and open when he wasn't sure of his thoughts.

He obviously liked her, too. He seemed interested in what she had to say and impressed by her intelligence. But not intimidated. During dinner, he encouraged her to take the frontal attack in an argument about the validity of logical positivism. They both agreed that there were serious limitations to this model, and Kevin played devil's advocate, smugly sitting behind his philosopher's mask. After dinner they went to Mike's bedroom to talk some more. The room was sparse and clean — a double bed, a desk and chair, a big recliner. The one splash of color was the rug made from carpet samples sewn together, which added immediate hospitality to the room.

Sandy smiled as she remembered that first night. Their conversation was still clear in her mind. He had been sitting on the bed, she on the chair.

"I've really enjoyed being with you — dinner, talking," he said. "You're very sharp."

"You're not so bad yourself."

Mike blushed. His vulnerability decided it for her.

"I don't believe in beating around the bush," she said. "I'd like to have an affair with you."

Mike looked shocked. His mouth hung open for a brief moment, until he regained his composure.

"You don't have to answer right away," she added generously.

"Uh, it's just . . ." Mike shook his head and laughed. "I don't know what to say. No girl has ever said anything like that to me . . . been so direct about it."

"I understand. My style is kind of abrupt at times. Think about it and let me know what you decide." Looking at her watch, Sandy knew this was the time for her exit. She was feeling

60

quite pleased with herself, but she really wasn't ready for anything to happen that night. "I should be getting back to the dorm. Will you give me a ride?"

Mike jumped off the bed and hastily put on his shoes. "Oh, I'm sorry. Sure."

Sandy had left the room first, but out of the corner of her eye she caught him looking at her appreciatively. She liked the way he looked at her. There was no doubt he was attracted to her, but underlying his desire she felt his respect.

It was hard to believe that had happened only three months ago. She felt like she had known Mike for years. They were amazingly comfortable with each other, right from the beginning. Even about sex. She had been scared that first night they spent together, but felt foolish since she had passed herself off as so sophisticated. Mike had sensed her fear and been very gentle with her. Later, he was amazed when she told him that she had only done it a couple of times before. He laughed and told her she was full of surprises. She joked that there were many more. Turning over, Sandy quietly cried herself to sleep. She still didn't know why she had done that.

"Hey, you're not even paying any attention while I lose this hand for us," Mike interrupted her thoughts, with a wide smile on his face.

"Shit, what kind of partner are you?" Sandy shook her head as she looked at the cards stacked in front of Kevin and Evelyn. Bridge was a lot like pinochle, except more complicated. She still didn't know how to keep score. Mike had showed her a couple of times but she couldn't seem to keep it straight in her mind. Everyone said that bridge was a better game because it was more difficult and thus more challenging, and Sandy supposed that was true. But she liked pinochle better. It was simpler.

21

Mike put down his copy of Kuhn's *The Structure of Scientific Revolutions* and lay back against the spongy cushions of his gray and blue flowered armchair. It was such a pleasure to have Sandy around. For the first time she had agreed to spend the entire weekend with him. Over the last few months she would spend the night, but insist on going back to the dorm for at least a few hours, even if they had a date for that next evening. It was baffling to Mike, but he hadn't pressed it. He sensed that she needed room, and he gave it to her without asking any questions.

Sandy was a mystery. Not in the usual *femme fatale* way that Mike had learned years before was a distraction from the underlying emptiness — delicate and tantalizing cream puffs that revealed huge cavities of air when one enthusiastically dived in for the first bite. Sandy didn't play any of the games Mike had thought necessary to dating. She opened her own car door, lit her own cigarette, said what was on her mind, and laughed rather than giggled. How many nights had Mike listened to inane female titters and tried to squelch his irritability before it soared to a height where it could no longer be controlled? It was as if there was a certain sign post, and once he had passed it, he was suddenly transformed into a different character. A Dr. Jekyll-Mr. Hyde syndrome, he supposed. His cruelty at times surprised him. It wasn't that he really hated these girls; it was more that their stupidity annoyed him, grating on him until he felt his usual good nature disappear, to be replaced by a sarcastic, contemptuous alter ego. He would watch himself as he exhaled a venomous dart, noticing from a distance the reaction of the stunned victim, and feeling a confused mixture of excitement and guilt. He enjoyed his manifest superiority, his ability to control the situation so totally, attacking and disarming his prey at leisure. Suddenly Mike remembered as a child, catching salamanders and chopping off their feet with a sharp rock, and watching them struggle frantically to crawl away with their now useless appendages. A surge of guilt and disgust swept through him. Senseless cruelty. How could he have done those things? But it didn't matter any more. Or not as much. He didn't have any of those feelings with Sandy. Not that he had felt that way about all the girls he had dated. He had dated some girls he liked, who had a brain and with whom he could talk. But no matter how much he had liked them, or enjoyed their company, he had always felt himself withdrawn, watching a play that had been scripted long before he came on the scene.

Yet all of his closest friends since high school had been girls. But that was different. The girls you dated and the girls who became close friends. It was very confusing. Why hadn't the girls he had dated turned into good friends? Was he attracted to the wrong type of girl? Or was there something about the dating scene that ruined any relationship before it had a chance to grow? Mike heard the bathroom door open and Sandy run barefoot across the cold wooden floors. She must have forgotten her socks and shoes when she went in for her shower. It was funny how he felt about Sandy. From that very first evening, he always felt an excitement when he was around her. An unusual slow burning excitement which seemed to grow gradually, warming more and more of his insides. He had never felt so relaxed with a girl before. He didn't have to prove how smart or urbane he was, nor did he have to be your all-American guy. Sandy was as bored with he-men as he was with the "helpless female." There was no need to play the boy-girl games, and that was a great relief. Mike hadn't realized how tired he was of having to make all the decisions: where to go eat, what movie to see, what to do this weekend. It was emancipating to be able to loosen up some, knowing that if he asked Sandy what she wanted to do, she would tell him, instead of saying, "I don't care, what would *you* like to do?" In fact, everything about Sandy was decisive, even the way she related to sex. He still couldn't quite believe the pass she had made at him. Actually, it couldn't really be considered a pass. A pass implied something subtle, some ritualized way of letting the other person know you found them desirable. But there had been nothing subtle about what Sandy had done; she had quite matter of factly propositioned him. What a redemption from the usual cat-and-mouse chase, which left both participants wearied and wasted, making the actual coming together anti-climactic at best. Mike had never understood why getting a girl to bed had to be such a big deal. If he wanted to and she wanted to, one would think things could proceed smoothly. The problem seemed to be that he almost always wanted to and she almost always didn't. Men and women fit perfectly together physically, but they sure didn't seem to match well in other ways. In fact, when it came to sex, men and women seemed to be at war with each other. But there were no brilliant maneuvers and no consummate victories. Instead, the skirmishes took on a demeaning character, in which both parties were reduced to dishonorable manipulations; he would attack the fort with charm, logic, and persevering insistence, and she would buttress her defenses with evasions, disclaimers, and unfulfilled promises. If nothing else, clearly an inordinate waste of time.

But still, infinitely better than being around men. Mike had never felt a part of the world of men. The backslapping always seemed phony and forced. In high school he had tried to be "one of the guys" — but the experience had left him feeling hypocritical when he went along with the ridiculous rituals (the incessant dirty jokes, show-and-tell in the bathrooms, and the obligatory cursing) and isolated when he managed to beg off. Not only wasn't he one of them, but he felt a deep mistrust that cautioned him to keep his distance. One by one they were okay, but when they got together in a pack something important changed; their group identity seemed different from the sum of their parts. Mike couldn't quite put his finger on it, but something about that pack mentality frightened him. Somehow he feared that the group might turn on him — but that didn't make any sense either. What could a bunch of guys do to one guy?

Of course, it was possible, Mike reminded himself, that he was rationalizing this whole business. Maybe it was just a question of his feeling inadequate. Unable to make it as a "man's man." After all, he hadn't been a very good athlete. Not the last one chosen for the basketball teams that formed on the playground after school — but by no means one of the first selections either. But shit, he played a damn good game for someone his height. Those words still gave him a chill at times. Sometimes, before asking a girl out for a date, he would remind himself that Alexander the Great was a small man, and he would feel himself lifting his head up higher, stretching his neck muscles until he felt like a deplumed ostrich. But he didn't have to do that too often. After all, he was five feet six inches, and most girls were his height or smaller.

It was different when he was with a group of men. Often he was the smallest. Walking down the street, he would be aware that his eyes were at the level of their shoulders, that to look at them directly he would have to tilt his face backward, looking up to catch their eyes. In the subways, packed and jostled by the crowd, Mike would secretly envy the men over six feet. What was it like to stand tall above the peons beneath you? Not to be intimidated by any guy who might bump into you, not to have to rush an apology lest you get your head kicked in? Bullies picked on small men, and Mike had had to learn to think and talk quickly to avoid potentially dangerous confrontations. He had hated his fear, felt ashamed of his weakness. The one comfort had been knowing that he was superior to these mute, dim-witted jocks who wore big letters on their sweaters. He had often privately mused that they had to wear those oversized symbols because they couldn't possibly remember what they were captain of unless they had some sign right in front of them. Of course, this was predicated on the very doubtful assumption that they were capable of symbolic cogitation — but then again, even simians were capable of making simple discriminations based on differential visual cues.

Mike smiled as he followed this last line of distinguished reasoning. He didn't need to be as threatened as he had been in high school. Things had gotten better in college, and now, as a graduate student, it was he who had the status and the choices. It was they who had been in for the Big Shock when they hit college. Being big and athletic didn't help you pass the classes. And in the city college where Mike had gone, there was no emphasis on sports at all — no athletic scholarships and no special privileges extended or excuses made for the host of jocks who had come in that first year. And been gone by their second. They had ended up with lousy-paying physical labor jobs, getting some girl pregnant and having to get married, then living in an overcrowded apartment with lots of bills and Thursday night out with the boys to tell the same stupid dirty jokes and the same lies about making it with every hot number in town. And here he was, a graduate student in one of the finest schools in the country, living modestly but comfortably, enjoying all the stimulation and excitement any man could want. And going out with some of the finest young women in the country. *La creme de la creme*: the combination of brains and beauty that prevented the fatal boredom that often descended after the first fuck.

Mike relit his pipe, short sucks until the embers flamed. It hadn't occurred to him before, but that was what was so different with Sandy. He wasn't bored. Christ, they had known each other for several months now, spent all these weekends together, and he was still enjoying her company. But it was more than that. It felt like a process of discovery. Every day he was learning something new about Sandy: the way she felt about things, the way she got shy when someone complimented her on an astute comment she had made. And he found himself taking great pleasure in unearthing her secrets. He wanted to know her, to understand what made her tick. But it really wasn't as analytical as it sounded, it wasn't that he wanted to pick her apart and see the pieces. No, it was something more subtle than that, something vaguer and less defined. And in the process he was discovering parts of himself that he had never experienced before. A tenderness without shame. An inner calm that was simultaneously exciting.

"Where's your hair dryer?" Startled by her sudden entry, Mike spilled the ashtray in his lap. "Jesus, are you a clod."

"Thanks for the vote of confidence. It's in the second drawer in the bathroom bureau." Mike watched her as she bent her head down, whisking the towel in short certain strokes as her long brown hair fell out and down in tangled strands. She was oblivious to him as she continued to dry the hair at the back of her neck, tilting her head to one side. Not at all concerned that she was in a ridiculous position or that her hair was a mess. Mike felt a wave of excitement surge through him. He imagined making love to her, right there in the living room, oblivious to Kevin and Evelyn, who might come in any time. She turned and walked out, unaware of his passion for her. It didn't make any sense. She hadn't even looked particularly pretty. And yet he had never felt such intense desire.

22

The door was closed. But the water was running. Sandy knocked just in case. "Come in."

Mike was standing by the basin, half of his face covered with shaving cream, a bridge of white foam snuggled between his upper lip and nose. A tiny blood-stained patch of toilet paper stuck on the smooth side of his face was a testimonial to the sharpness of his razor. Staring at the four-inch blade, and imagining it carving immense chunks out of her legs, Sandy tugged at the extended tails of his pinstripe shirt, now converted into a nightgown, and sat down on the toilet with her customary energetic plunk, which almost landed her in the bowl.

"Shit." Standing up, she pulled down the seat with a loud crash, and sitting again, this time more gently, she proceeded to piss. Mike was intently watching his hands in the mirror, his head cocked to one side, one hand stretching his skin, the other holding the blade poised just above his check.

"How can you use that thing? It looks like you're going to cut yourself to shreds!"

"Sandy, I'm trying to concentrate."

"Well, why do you use something like that? It should be registered with the FBI as a lethal weapon. Besides, you just shaved this morning."

Mike, who had just bravely started the unsweep towards his ear, nicked himself at this last oration. "Shit. Sandy, would you please shut up. You're making me nervous."

"Okay, okay. I won't say another word." Sandy tore a wad of paper off the wall and wiped herself. She flushed the toilet, still sitting on it. With a detached curiosity, she watched his arm graze across his face, mowing narrow rows in the soapy lather. Her hand unconsciously caressed her cheek as she tried to imagine what it would be like to take a razor to her face. Was it like shaving one's legs or underarms? It seemed so much closer, more intimate somehow. Arms and legs were more distant, not so close to oneself. But then, maybe men didn't see it that way. For them, shaving their faces might just be the same kind of inconvenience that shaving her legs was for her. At least women didn't have to shave daily. What a total pain that would be.

"What's the matter?" Mike gave her a shy grin as he washed the last of the shaving cream off his razor. Snatching a towel off the old-fashioned ceramic rack, he tenderly patted his face.

"Nothing. Just looking."

"You are weird," he teased as he leaned over to kiss her.

Sandy stood up and walked to the door. "Uh huh. So what does that make you, buster?" She could hear him chuckling as she walked down the corridor to the bedroom, across the room and to the small rectangular window, which looked out on several of the other duplexes that lined the street. The trees were still bare, their gnarled trunks and weatherbeaten branches stretched to the sky in forlorn protest, waiting for warmer and more soothing days. Soon spring would arrive and the abandoned trees would once again bask in the sun. They would forget their grievances and joyously create those first fragile buds, and then in early summer they would flourish and burst into full bloom.

Spring always creeped her out. It made her feel edgy, off-center. Somehow, no matter where she was, she felt as if she was supposed to be someplace else, but she had no idea where that someplace else was. It was a confusing, vague feeling, and Sandy hated that more than the feeling itself. She was used to being able to analyze things; but this feeling defied labeling, let alone analysis, making Sandy very annoyed with herself for being so foolishly enigmatic. All she had ever been able to figure out was that it was some kind of obscure longing. There had only been one spring when she hadn't felt it. That first spring with Jenny. Angrily, Sandy walked to the nighttable and, jerking out a cigarette, lit it furiously. How many times had she told herself that she was not to think about Jenny on the weekends. That was the time she spent with Mike, and she didn't want Jenny making her upset and ruining things with Mike. Mike was the best man she had ever met. They had a good thing. She felt more comfortable with him that she had ever expected to feel with a guy. She was very lucky to have met him. Sandy's anger dissolved, and she plopped down heavily on Mike's stuffed chair. She often teased him about how dignified he looked when he smoked his pipe while reading a particularly classy book. One by Hume, or Bertrand Russell. He would act like she was full of shit, but he loved it. He loved her attention and a part of him liked the idea of being a distinguished philosopher. Sandy couldn't imagine him looking distinguished. Not with his boyish face. Maybe in forty years when his hair had turned gray — no, white — and he had grown a small beard. Sandy laughed at the idea of Mike in a beard. He would look ridiculous. Besides, he was a really good-looking guy; he didn't need all that stuff on his face. And he sure wasn't going to have it as long as they were together. She hated the scratchiness of beards. It was like kissing a porcupine. And they always had those disgusting food particles lodged in their beard where everyone could see it except them. Thank God Mike didn't want a hairy face. It was enough that men had so much hair over the rest of them, without overdoing it when they had the choice.

Jenny had a mustache. Sandy hadn't even noticed it, but it made Jenny uptight. Once every three or four months she would dye it with hydrogen peroxide. She looked so funny with that bubbling froth over her lip. Sandy used to love to tease her about how good she looked with that crap under her nose, and how she should wear it out sometime and start a new fashion. Jenny squealed with mock rage and punched her playfully in the arm. Sandy always wanted to wrestle, but Jenny would scream, "Stay away from me! You're gonna mess up my face." They usually ended up doing something sedate like playing two-handed pinochle until it was time for her to take the crap off her face. Sandy never noticed that the dark lip hairs looked any different after a treatment, but she didn't have the heart to tell Jenny.

Jenny would always smile a lot after the application, as if she actually thought she looked more beautiful. As far as Sandy was concerned, Jenny always looked beautiful. Well, not really. There were days when Jenny looked tired, her complexion sallow rather than dark, the nervous lines around her mouth making her skin look one size too big for her. Objectively Sandy knew that on those days Jenny wasn't a particularly beautiful girl. But at the same time, she was always beautiful to Sandy. Somehow those two truths didn't seem to contradict each other.

Jenny.

Sandy felt that old familiar aching. It would start in one spot directly beneath her belly button, and then radiate until her entire abdominal cavity was filled with a diffuse discomfort. At least it no longer incapacitated her.

Now that Sandy was also going out, Jenny was more friendly. On Saturday afternoons when she stopped by the dorm, Jenny would chatter about what she and Bruce had done that week, how her classes were going, and other newsy topics. Obligingly, Sandy told her what she had been up to, but she rarely talked about Mike. It seemed disloyal to her to mention his name. But Jenny clearly felt the opposite: she wanted to know all about Mike, what he was like and what they did together. Sandy continued to frustrate her, replying to Jenny's questions in staccato phrases. It was a graceless *rapprochement*, but Sandy sullenly accepted it. She would have fought it longer if she had known any other weapons to use. But all of her earlier maneuvers had left Jenny curiously untouched. Neither tears, nor threats, nor tirades had had any effect on the impervious mask Jenny wore for such occasions. Sandy marveled at Jenny's heartlessness. Could this be the warm and tender girl that she had fallen in love with? How could intense passion be transformed into such a self-contained detachment? It didn't make any sense. Unless Jenny had never really loved her. Sandy relentlessly searched her memory for evidence. But how could she deny the hours they had spent lying next to each other, their eyes searching for any hint of deceit or discontent? And time after time, her anxious probing had eased as Jenny's eyes incontestably conveyed her love for Sandy. After all, it was Jenny who had vigorously pursued her, pushing for closeness, passing every test and obstacle Sandy had put in her way to discourage the fraudulent. Could it have been just a game for Jenny? A challenge? Sandy refused to believe that Jenny could be so diabolical. Nor did she believe that she could have made such an asinine mistake. She was no dummy. She had to trust that what they had shared was real. To deny that was to disown her most basic instincts and to welcome a flood of emptiness and despair that made her present condition seem jovial by comparison.

Staring out the window as she and Mike drove back to

the dorm, Sandy wondered if Jenny would be there that afternoon. She almost hoped she wouldn't. She needed to do some thinking about her and Mike. Did she love him? The question seemed academic; it sprang from her intellect and seemed related to a more general concern about life. Lately she had begun to ask herself that question again: "Is life meaningful?" Unlike her younger days, she was no longer able to answer with a categorical "no." Meeting Jenny had changed that. But losing her had thrown Sandy back into a quandary that no longer seemed as clear as it once had. How could a quandary be clear? Sandy chided herself on her sloppy use of concepts. She had read somewhere that one's brain cells started to deteriorate after the age of fifteen. And here she was, almost twenty. Maybe she was starting to get senile. What once would have been a chilling thought didn't seem so repugnant now. Sandy's mother had often told her she was too serious, she should stop thinking so much. If her brain started to drop dead maybe she'd be a happier person.

23

Jenny watched the bubbles as they slowly began to rise to the surface of her coffee cup. The electric coil looked like a one-eyed deformed monster that had expired on the bottom of the beige and brown landscaped mug. It was time to get up and find the instant coffee, but Jenny felt too tired to begin what was sure to be a protracted search through overflowing ashtrays and mounds of unattended texts. Instead she continued to watch the bubbles splash against the walls of the cup. It wasn't until a wave sloshed over the side and onto the desk that Jenny got up and carelessly started shoving some of the mess aside. Under a pile of sweaters and old nylons, the Yuban jar lay on its side. Jenny shook her head as she lifted the stockings and dropped them to the floor. She had told Sandy for weeks that she should throw out those stockings. But Sandy said they were still good for hanging around the dorm. At least she had enough sense not to wear them out on dates.

Dates. Tonight was the first Saturday she would spend in the dorm in months. Jenny pulled out the plug, removed the coil, and poured some coffee from the jar into the mug, stirring it with a long bobby pin. Maybe she'd use tonight to do some of the studying she had been putting off. Looking around the room for her books, Jenny felt the tears start to drip down her cheek. She jumped out of her chair, strode angrily across the room, jerked a tissue from its box, and hastily wiped the wetness from her face. She was not going to cry. It wasn't like it was all over between them. Bruce had just asked for some time to himself. And here she was getting herself all worked up over nothing.

Walking to the window, Jenny looked out at the gray overcast sky. The campus appeared drab; the dull beige buildings were scattered haphazardly in the bleak landscape. Jenny sighed deeply. There was no point lying to herself. She had known for a while that things were no longer as good as they had been. She just hadn't wanted to recognize that Bruce was getting bored with her. At first he was irritable, snapping at her for no apparent reason. Then he became quiet and moody, withdrawing into himself and ignoring her presence for long periods of time. In the beginning Jenny teasingly asked him what was wrong, calling him Old Grump Boats. But he didn't find that funny and told her to stop acting like a juvenile. She was very hurt but didn't know what to say. Thinking he might be uptight about not having heard from any graduate schools yet, Jenny just let it drop. But his crankiness didn't go away; instead his sullen brooding continued and worsened.

Jenny then tried to be extra considerate, buying him a new lighter when his broke, cooking him a special meal. And he would respond to her thoughtfulness by brightening up, and they would have a good evening, laughing and teasing and ending up in bed. But after they'd made love he would get moody again, and Jenny could sense a new distance between them. And it didn't seem to be the sex; he would always say it was good afterwards. But something was obviously bothering him, and Jenny had no idea what it was. And no idea how to find out when her tentative questions were received with hostility. So she decided to deal with it by just hoping it would pass. And then this morning over breakfast, Bruce said they had better have a talk. He did all the talking. She didn't know what to say, so she didn't say much of anything. Then they drove back to the dorm in silence.

Jenny told herself that there really wasn't anything she could do but wait. Maybe spending time alone would show Bruce how much he really cared for her, and he would call her up tomorrow and say he missed her. She would play it cool at first, not get excited right away. After all, this whole thing had been his idea and he hadn't taken her feelings into account at all, so why should she let him off the hook? No, she would make him insecure for a while, tell him she had other plans for that night. That would put him on the defensive. What the hell was she doing? Jenny felt a wave of self-disgust. She sounded like a game-playing sorority girl. She and Bruce had something better than that; they didn't have to play games. Or was that the problem? Maybe she should have played harder to get. She had slept with Bruce right away, that first night, and he had said that he really respected her for not playing the usual coy role. But had he really? Maybe he had lost some respect for her. Jenny felt a surge of anxiety sweep across her entire body. The anxiety was quickly followed by guilt, which insidiously wormed its way into her gut. Her parents would just die if they knew that their baby girl had slept with six different men. Six. That was a huge number. Jenny wondered if that made her a whore. She felt herself start to get sick. She tried to force herself to burp the way Sandy did, but she had never learned how to do that satisfactorily. Instead she would strain at the throat, making a face similar to the one Sandy made, and nothing would come out. Sandy often teased her about not having gotten the knack of it after all this time.

She forced herself to take a few deep breaths and sit down at her desk. The afternoon was passing and she still hadn't cracked a book. She was looking out the window when the door opened behind her.

"Oh, hi, Jenny. I didn't expect to see you here this late on a Saturday."

"Hi." Jenny watched as Sandy put down an overnight bag and some dirty clothes she was carrying. Sandy unpacked some dirty underwear and threw it in the laundry bag she kept near her bed.

"How's Mike?" Jenny said, feeling the need especially tonight for conversation. Sandy looked like she was in a hurry, as she raced to the bureau to get some fresh underwear. But maybe she'd stay a little while and talk.

"Oh, fine. Last night we went to another philosophy party. I met some other philo grad students and most of the faculty." Sandy pursed her lips and sucked in her cheeks to imitate an English accent. "A very intellectual group, if you know what I mean." No matter how hard she tried, she always sounded Bronx. "And tonight we're going out to a nice restaurant and movie. We pooled our resources and decided we could afford a splurge. How about you?" She changed her clothes as she talked, going to the closet and getting out a nice sweater and a pair of pants.

"Oh, I don't have any plans for tonight," Jenny answered, turning back to looking out the window. She had wanted to sound casual but her voice was unmistakably strained. She felt Sandy stop what she was doing and look at her.

"Is something wrong?"

Jenny didn't want to let Sandy know how upset she was. It was a question of pride. Besides, hadn't Sandy pronounced that she and Bruce would never last? Turning around, she had trouble meeting Sandy's eyes.

"Well . . . Bruce has been feeling that we've been seeing too much of each other lately. He wants to cool it for a while." Jenny stood up and walked around the room so she wouldn't have to look at Sandy. She couldn't stand the expression of concern and sympathy on Sandy's face. It made her feel like she was choking. "And I suppose it is a good idea. It'll give us a chance to re-examine the relationship, a breathing space to see . . ." Jenny felt her voice rise and hang in the silence. She was repeating to Sandy exactly what Bruce had said to her that morning. It was ludicrous.

"Oh, Jenny." The sincere upset in Sandy's voice did it. Jenny felt the streams of tears running down her face and was unable to stop them. She didn't want to stop them this time. Jenny turned to face Sandy.

"Why is he doing this, Sandy? Why? Things were going so well." Jenny started to sob. And then Sandy was there, holding her, rocking her back and forth, her lips pressed against Jenny's hair. Jenny buried her face between Sandy's neck and shoulder and wept shamelessly. After a while the tears stopped. Taking a Kleenex from Sandy, Jenny blew her nose resoundingly. She realized she hadn't blown her nose like that in months. Early in their relationship Bruce had cracked a joke about some guy in the theater who had blown his nose loudly, and since then Jenny had been careful to be more tasteful when she was around him. Screw him, she thought, and let out a tumultuous blast. Sandy laughed appreciatively.

"You'd better go, Sandy . . . Mike is waiting." Jenny wiped her nose with the tissue. Sandy looked at her watch.

"Yeah. You want to wear that or get into something else? You're coming with us," Sandy said matter-of-factly.

"Sandy . . ." Jenny started to object but was cut short.

"Dinner and a movie will do you good. You didn't think I was going to leave you here in this pigsty, did you?" Sandy looked around the room with obvious repugnance. "Come on, I don't got all day. Get dressed."

"Sandy, you have a date with Mike. He's not expecting . . ."

"You don't know him. He's an incredible guy. No bullshit. No game-playing. And he really knows how to care." Sandy looked embarrassed. "Come on, will you get dressed or do I have to do the honors?"

Jenny felt her spirits climb as she laughed with relief. "Okay, okay, I'm getting dressed." She walked over to the closet and took down her brown cashmere sweater and beige wool pants. It was one of her favorite outfits. Sandy said she looked classy in it, like one of those women who shop at Saks. Maybe it would be a fun evening. She had been wanting to meet Mike for months, but Sandy always said they had other plans when Jenny tried to arrange a double date for the four of them. The smile left her lips as she thought about Bruce. Pulling the sweater over her head, she resolved to have a good time. Two could play this little game of his. And she'd be damned before she'd let him make a fool out of her. She pulled down the sweater and stepped out of the closet smiling. Sandy was standing over by the window, staring out thoughtfully.

"How long am I going to have to wait for you?" Jenny teased.

Sandy turned around slowly. "Huh? Oh, are you ready? Good, let's go then." Sandy picked up her purse and started to walk past Jenny, then stopped and smiled. "Hey, you look great."

"Well, you didn't think I was going to let Mike think you roomed with a *schlub*, did you?"

"Why not?" Sandy replied. "I ain't exactly high fashion myself."

"But you're *not* a *schlub*, Sandy."

"Whatever you say, *schmuck*. Can we go eat now?"

Jenny shoved Sandy out the door. "Who are you calling *schmuck*?" Sandy went to push her back but Jenny had already dashed down the hall. "You fucker!" Sandy yelled as she chased after her.

Giggling, they shoved each other into the elevator.

24

Sandy knew exactly how long it had been since the three of them went out to dinner. Sixteen days, each one adding a smidgen of courage to her slowly garnered stockpile. Every morning she awakened early, her usually fuzzy brain lucid, wondering if today would be the day.

She had been absolutely right about Mike. He had acted very gallant that evening, making Jenny feel a welcome addition rather than a third wheel. He even suggested on the way to the restaurant that Sandy and Jenny share the passenger seat in his Citroen so that all three of them could ride in front. Jenny perched on Sandy's lap, easily making conversation with Mike, as Sandy quietly took it all in. It felt strange to be sitting next to Mike, with Jenny on her lap. But people often wanted their good friends to meet, so why should it feel so different with Mike and Jenny? Of course, Mike didn't know about her and Jenny. She might have considered telling him, if it weren't for her promise to Jenny. Actually, Sandy knew that wasn't the total truth. She would be scared to say anything to him. As fine as he was, how could he understand what the two of them felt for each other? After all, he was still a man.

During that evening, it became unmistakably evident that Jenny was the one she was in love with. Sandy wondered how she could ever have felt uncertain of that. Sitting around the red and white checkered tablecloth, the bread crumbs crunching under her elbows, her fingers tugging at the loosened strands from the near-empty Chianti bottle, Sandy accepted the feelings that now became clear. There was no way to even make a comparison between what she felt for Jenny and what she felt for Mike. They were two totally different experiences. Worlds apart. And nothing could shake the plain truth of that.

When Jenny left the table to go to the bathroom, Sandy explained to Mike that Jenny had just broken up with her boyfriend. He was very understanding, even when she said she wanted to go back to the dorm that night, in case Jenny needed to talk. She felt a little deceptive about that explanation, but justified it on the grounds that it was true. It just wasn't the whole truth. But how could she have explained to Mike that her desire for Jenny had been rekindled that night. That throughout dinner, she had looked at Jenny, the scented red candles throwing a warm shadowy light across her face, and fantasized their return to the dormitory where they would fervently make love. No, there were many reasons why she couldn't tell Mike that. She just hoped that she wasn't becoming a sell-out and hypocrite like her parents' generation. Sandy had always believed that there was no excuse for ever telling anything but the whole truth. But in the last few years she had had to compromise that principle. Sometimes it was hard to know what was the most ethical thing to do. But this was not a night for philosophizing. Sandy hadn't felt so happy and alive in many months. They spent the rest of the evening giggling over the second bottle of Chianti they bought instead of going to the theater.

When Sandy and Jenny got back to the dorm, they flopped down on Jenny's bed just as they used to in the old days. Fixing a cup of coffee, they decided to play two-handed pinochle. They played until the sky began to get light, the thick fluffy clouds illuminated from behind as if by a spotlight. Washing up before going to bed, Jenny turned to Sandy and told her how lucky she was to have a great guy like Mike. Sandy tried to change the subject, but Jenny persisted in her praise of Mike, stressing that he was really crazy about Sandy. Sandy felt awful.

Since that first night back at the dorm, Sandy had thought of little else besides Jenny. Yearning raced through her, electrifying her waking moments. In her dreams she imagined them walking slowly across a room. Controlling their excitement, they would stare into each other's eyes as they relished the growing fury of their feeling. Standing next to each other, but not touching, their nipples erect, they would bend their faces closer until their lips gently met. Melting, they would sink to their knees and lose themselves in each other's arms.

Sandy didn't look at Jenny as she took the joint from her fingers. She was afraid what she had been fantasizing about would show in her eyes, and she wanted to make sure that when she approached Jenny it would be the right time.

"I can't wait until we move into the new house," Sandy said excitedly. "After three years, we're finally getting out of the dorm."

"Halleleujah," Jenny replied as she took a long draw off the dying butt and sank back against the pillow. She seemed more relaxed than Sandy had seen her in weeks. Sandy decided she couldn't wait any longer.

"It's good to be spending time together again. I've missed you."

Jenny looked up and smiled at her. "I missed you, too." Jenny relit the joint and passed it to Sandy. As their fingers touched, they both lingered. Was Jenny trying to tell her it was okay? Or was she just very stoned and having trouble coordinating the transfer? Sandy resolutely plunged on.

"I want you back, Jenny. I haven't thought of anything else in weeks." Her heart was pounding furiously.

Jenny sat up and pulled back simultaneously. "That's not possible, Sandy."

"Why not?"

"We've been through this so many times. Can't you let it go?" Jenny sounded annoyed. But Sandy had risked too much to let it go so easily.

"No, I can't. And now there's no reason to keep us apart." Jenny's look was one of surprise. She acted as if she didn't know what Sandy was talking about. "You and Bruce aren't seeing each other any more. So there's no conflict," Sandy insisted.

"That has nothing to do with it."

"What do you mean, that has nothing to do with it?" Sandy heard her voice become guarded. She sat motionless as Jenny lit a real cigarette.

"We can't be lovers because . . . we just can't. Whether we have boyfriends or not isn't the point." Jenny was impatiently looking at the ceiling, then around the room. Everywhere but at Sandy.

Now the pounding was in her head. Sandy vaguely recognized the feeling, the suspended stage before an explosion. She silently told herself to calm down. She knew that once she erupted, she would never get the answers to her questions. "You told me the reason we couldn't be lovers was because you couldn't handle two relationships at a time. Are you saying now that wasn't the real reason?" Her voice was low.

"Look, Sandy, I don't remember exactly."

"Bullshit, you don't remember," Sandy interrupted angrily. "It was that unimportant, huh? Did you or did you not tell me that was why we couldn't be lovers?"

"Sandy, stop yelling," Jenny shouted back.

"I will stop yelling," Sandy hollered, "when you answer my question. It's very simple. Yes or no."

Jenny stood up now and walked to the other side of the room. Sandy got up and walked towards her. The two women were squared off.

"I don't remember," Jenny answered. "And besides, I don't have to answer to you. Who the hell are you?" Jenny brushed by Sandy, walking in the direction of the bathroom. Sandy followed her. Her last shreds of control were rapidly disintegrating.

"Damn you. Yes or no. Answer me, fucker. You lied to me."

"I didn't lie to you," Jenny screeched. Sandy saw she was frightened but pressed on, her words having a will of their own.

"Yes, you did, you lied, you used him as an excuse. You didn't even have the common decency to tell me the truth — you phony, you coward." Sandy spewed out the words with hate. Her intent now was to hurt Jenny in any way she could.

Jenny was crying. "Stop it. Stop it," she pleaded. "Leave me alone. I can't stand any more of this. I'm leaving. Are you happy now? I'm leaving. I hate you. I hate you," she shrieked. Rushing to the closet, she tore down a valise off the top shelf and began throwing pants and sweaters into it.

Sandy walked over to the closet and deliberately planted herself by its entrance. "Put that down and answer my question. You can leave if you want — but first you're going to tell me the truth."

Jenny ignored Sandy and continued to pack. Enraged, Sandy yanked the valise away from her, dumping the clothes and valise into the room in a jumble. "I said put it down," Sandy barked between clenched teeth. Sobbing, Jenny started to leave the closet. With a harsh shove, Sandy hurled her against the wardrobe back wall. "You're not going anywhere till you tell me why you lied."

"I may not have told you the whole truth but . . . all you care about is One Thing." Seeing the look on Sandy's face, Jenny stopped, aware she had said something terrible. Sandy felt herself freeze, her face contorting in rage.

"You fucker. You dirty-minded fucker." Without thinking, Sandy pulled back her arm and slapped Jenny hard across the face. Jenny's mouth hung open as she looked surprised and hurt. Sandy was horrified by what she had done. She looked at her hands as if they belonged to someone else. As if they had committed the worst crime imaginable.

"I'm sorry," Sandy whispered. She turned around and walked out of the closet and into the bedroom. She sat on her bed, hands extended in front of her, staring at the floor. Jenny approached her slowly.

"Sandy," she said gently.

Sandy motioned her away. "You can go," she whispered. "I won't try to stop you." All the fight was out of her now. She felt defeated.

"That was a terrible thing I said. It's not true, Sandy." Jenny was upset now. She was worried about Sandy, and she wanted to take back the hateful words.

Sandy was preoccupied with herself. With what she had done. "It doesn't matter what you said. I had no right to hit you. No one has a right to hit you. I'm not fit to love."

Jenny crouched down, placing her hands on Sandy's knees. "That's not true. I provoked you. I said the thing I knew would hurt the most."

Sandy looked up at her. "Why? Why would you say something like that?"

Jenny started to cry again. "I'm sorry, Sandy. I get so scared."

Bewildered, Sandy started to ask Jenny to explain what she meant, but Jenny, sensing the question, cut her off. "Don't ask me to explain it," Jenny said as she took Sandy's face in her hands. "But you must know that doesn't mean I don't love you."

Tears started to spill out of Sandy's eyes. They were both crying now. "I do . . . Oh, Sandy. I do love you."

Sandy pulled Jenny up to the bed so they were sitting side by side. Rocking, their arms fiercely wrapped about each other, they both sobbed out of control.

25

As she walked slowly across the campus, her hands stuffed in her pockets, Sandy reassured herself that what she was about to do was the right thing. The only fair thing to do. She hadn't seen Mike in two weeks and she owed him an explanation. She couldn't make any more excuses about being busy or taking care of Jenny. His initial patience had changed to puzzled concern and then to hurt silence. She had to tell him. Even though it meant breaking her promise to Jenny. She owed him at least that much.

But how was she going to tell Mike that she couldn't be lovers with him anymore without hurting his feelings? He deserved better than he was getting from her, and Sandy felt sick with guilt. She knew what it was like to really want someone and not be able to have them. She hoped Mike didn't feel about her the way she felt about Jenny. She couldn't bear the idea of causing him that much pain. Thinking more about it, she felt her panic recede. Mike wasn't in love with her the way she was with Jenny. How could he be? He really didn't know her the way Jenny knew her or she knew Jenny. It seemed like it was a different thing between men and women. Both parties were more careful about keeping their distance. There just seemed to be some natural boundaries that kept you from feeling too intensely. But then again, maybe it was just her. Or her and Mike. The other girls in the dorm would talk about their fraternity boyfriends as the "love of their life." Yet their feelings always seemed very superficial to Sandy, as they chatted about the ring they wanted, or how they were holding out to keep him interested. None of that made very much sense to her, and she was glad of it. She'd rather be an old maid than worry about how many carrots were in her diamonds.

But Mike wasn't some stupid fraternity guy. He had feelings. And he'd been good to her. And now she was going to tell him that . . . that . . . What was she going to tell him? In the last few weeks she had tried to figure out what her and Jenny being together meant. But it was all so confusing. Jenny insisted that they were two normal girls who had just happened to fall in love with each other. That it was a one in a million thing that happened occasionally. It didn't mean that they "liked" girls and didn't like guys. They weren't queer or anything. Sandy never argued with Jenny when she talked like that, but recently she had begun to wonder whether that was the way it really was. She had begun to suspect that she and Jenny were different. Maybe it had been a freak accident for Jenny. But Sandy wasn't so sure it was the same for her. She vaguely sensed that something more complex was going on. But she couldn't seem to grasp the significance of it. It. She wasn't even sure what she was thinking about. Her love for Jenny? What could be confusing about that? Above all else, that was certain. As usual, she was making a big deal out of nothing. Making it more confusing than it had to be.

Opening the big glass door to the Student Union, Sandy walked across the corridor and started down the concrete slab steps. Hands in pants pockets, she shuffled down the stairs with an irregular hop as she had seen countless guys do in the subway. She had always taken pride in the fact that she never used the bannisters for support.

Jenny endlessly bawled her out for the way she descended stairs. "Can't you walk down the stairs like a normal person?" she would say while shaking her head in disapproval. "Come on, slow poke," Sandy would retort, "you're just jealous because you're such a clod." "Clod," Jenny would squeal as she raced down the stairs after Sandy. Sandy would agilely keep ahead, sticking out her tongue and yelling "Na na na na na" to sustain

Jenny's interest. Right before Jenny would quit, Sandy would feign fatigue and let Jenny triumphantly catch up with her. Jenny would grab her by the collar and drag her through the union like a mother finally disciplining a spoiled kid. They usually ended up in the Rathskeller, where they'd order a cheeseburger and fries and a big grape drink. Sandy would drink half of her grape drink as they stood in line for the burgers; then she refilled it before they reached the cashier. Jenny always rolled her eyes as Sandy refilled her cup.

Sandy smiled at the thought of the good times they had had and the good times they were going to have again. Then she remembered why she was there, and her smile vanished instantly. What the hell was the matter with her? There was nothing funny about today's venture into the Rathskeller.

Standing quietly for a moment in front of the wood-carved doors, Sandy took a deep breath, then resolutely pushed the doors open. She hesitated as she searched the near-empty chamber. It was an off-time, too late for lunch and too early for dinner. Mike was seated at a table at the far end of the room. She appreciatively noticed that there was no one sitting near him. He waved as she started to walk over.

"Hi."

"Hi. I think I'll get a cup of coffee too. Do you want a refill?"

"No, thanks."

Sandy walked quickly over to the counter and filled the porcelain cup she had removed still steaming from the green rubber tray. Mike seemed pensive. He was waiting for her to explain.

Mike was pushed back in his chair, the front two legs off the ground, when she returned to their table. Sitting down, she decided to lay it out quickly.

"I don't know exactly how to say this," she began. "It has to do with me and Jenny." Sandy could see a couple several tables down tongue-kissing. She was sitting on his lap, her skirt pulled up around her thighs, his hand a huge mass weighing down on her stockinged limb. The girl looked like a miniature toy swallowed in the arms of a gorilla. It was a normal scene for the Rathskeller, but today it creeped Sandy out. "Jenny and I," Sandy continued and then stopped. "Jenny and I are more than friends."

Sandy waited for his explosion. But it never came. Instead Mike still sat there quietly, waiting for her to go on.

"You don't seem surprised."

"I guess I'm not."

Sandy looked at him closely, and he really didn't seem surprised. It had never occurred to her that others might know about her and Jenny. But then Mike was pretty sophisticated. Maybe he had known that these things happen sometimes. He seemed to be taking it pretty well. Sandy decided to plunge ahead.

"Well, we've been lovers on and off since freshman year. For the last year or so it's been off. That was Jenny's idea, I've never wanted it that way. Anyhow, a couple of days ago, she and I, well, we got back together again. And it feels right. I really like you, Mike. Shit, I love you. But it's Jenny I want to be with. And I can't do both. It wouldn't be fair to you, Mike." Sandy had been looking down at the table. Now she sneaked a look at Mike and saw that his eyes were also averted. He stared at his spoon as he swirled it around in his coffee. He was upset and trying hard to control it. Sandy felt a stab of guilt and forced herself to sit quietly now. Mike sighed several times.

"I don't know what to say," he began. "I've felt like we had a good thing. I'd sensed that there were ways you were still holding back, but I thought it was just a question of time." Putting the spoon down, Mike nervously rubbed his hand several times against his cheek.

"We do have a good thing, Mike." Sandy felt like she was going to cry. "Your friendship is very important to me. You're very important to me. And I'm closer to you than I've ever been to any man." She didn't want him to think that their relationship had meant nothing to her. How could she explain it? "But it's different from the way it is with Jenny," she continued, struggling to find the right words. "I feel like you're more a good friend. Jenny is the one I'm in love with. I'd like to keep our friendship. But I realize that you may not want that. From here on, you call the shots, Mike. I'm willing to play it any way you want."

Mike shook his head, still looking into his coffee. "I don't know . . . I need to think about it."

He looked so dejected. Sandy started to reach out her hand to touch his, then stopped herself. She didn't want him to misinterpret that. Besides, he probably wouldn't want her hand now and would think it hypocritical of her to offer that phony gesture of concern. He was no *schlub*. He had his own pride. Sandy didn't know what to do next. She had said what she had come to say.

Mike looked up at her. Suddenly, a huge chasm had opened up between them. "Well, thanks for telling me how it is. I think I'd like to be alone now," he said in a subdued voice.

"Okay, Mike. Whatever you say." She stood up, hesitating, trying to think of something to make it feel less painful. But there was nothing left for her to say. She turned and walked across the Rathskeller, feeling his eyes bore into her back, and her eyes brim with tears.

26

For Sandy and Jenny, 1968-69, their senior year, was the most exciting part of college. The entire campus sprang alive with people marching and chanting. Every lounge was filled for teach-ins and strategy sessions with long-haired, jeans-clad young men, and women in green bush jackets two sizes too large. They were a sight for sore eyes, as far as Sandy was concerned. Somehow the school had transformed from a sorority-fraternity playground to a sophisticated, politically concerned student body. Sandy couldn't figure out how it had all happened so quickly, and she really didn't care. For the first time since coming to college, she felt a part of something bigger than herself, something important that involved other people she could identify with. It was a bloody miracle.

Jenny also seemed to come alive during this period. On the picket lines and in the sit-ins, her eyes radiated excitement. Face flushed, she chanted the political slogans with fervor. For the first time in her life she cut classes, ignored homework assignments, and broke rules for which there were serious punishments.

Amid the late-night emergency meetings, the endless passing out of leaflets, the frequent confrontations with the administration and sometimes the riot police, Sandy and Jenny rediscovered their love. And it was different this time. The things they had been through, separately and together, had changed them, and this change was reflected in the new quiet and calm of their love-friendship. Jenny was more comfortable with their relationship, more accepting of their bond as lovers. Sandy, now that she felt more certain of Jenny's affection for her, made up her mind that she would not give Jenny a rough time if she decided to date again. And it was as if Jenny sensed this, for she showed little interest in dating, occasionally going out with an old friend or seeing a new guy two or three times. Sandy had no idea why men no longer seemed important to Jenny, but she accepted it with the same unquestioning elation she felt toward the radical transformation of consciousness among her peers. There had been so much unhappiness between her and Jenny, and Sandy wanted this year, their last together, to be a happy one.

It was very difficult for Sandy to acknowledge that after their senior year they would graduate and part. "Go their separate ways," as Jenny often said. Both of them were applying to graduate school in Psychology. Some of their choices overlapped, and Sandy hoped they could go to the same program. But Jenny vehemently opposed that. She made it clear to Sandy that their love affair would end with graduation. That was non-negotiable, as Sandy discovered the times she tried to bring the subject up. Jenny simply refused to discuss it.

Sandy didn't know that this flat rejection of a future for them was what permitted Jenny to feel comfortable with their love in the present. As long as Jenny knew that the end was in sight, she and Sandy were safe, and they could make the most of the limited time they had together. With less than a year left in Buffalo, Jenny knew there was no point starting a serious relationship with a man. That would have to wait for graduate school. And in a way she felt relieved. It meant she and Sandy could really have this year to themselves. And as long as Sandy didn't get weird or try to change the agreement they had reached, Jenny could relax.

They moved into a big, two-story dilapidated wooden house. For three years they had wanted to live off-campus, but girls were allowed to move out of the dorms only in their senior year; the guys were allowed to move out their sophomore year. The college explained this rule with a bunch of gobbledy-gook that translated into the assumption that the girlish goods had gotten to college without being damaged, and it was the school's duty to maintain the first-rate quality of the merchandise during that four-year period of storage known as "liberal education." Sandy and Jenny had often joked about the naiveté of their parents and the administration. Who did they know who was still a virgin? No one except Bunny. She still had this thing of not sleeping with a boy till she was in love, and although she had done a fair amount of dating, she hadn't met Mr. Right.

Bunny moved out of the dorm with them, and they found a fourth roommate, a townie none of them had known before. Pat was a sophomore who had lived at home her first year and was desperate to find another place to live. She had been a friend of one of the girls on their floor in the dorm, and they decided to risk living with her. She didn't quite fit in with the three of them, but she wasn't around much, and her bedroom was on the bottom floor. Pat was stoned or tripping most of the time, and she talked, with a faraway wide-eyed expression, about the stars, and Buddha, and chants and reincarnation, and spirits and telepathy and a whole bunch of other stuff that didn't make much sense. Floating in and out of the house, Pat never seemed to touch ground. She was on a different wave length, and the three of them decided to try to make her feel comfortable when she was around. After all, she was a really nice girl even if she was a little strange. And she couldn't help it that she had been born in Buffalo. That was bound to make anyone impressionable and uncritical. Just as she couldn't help being born Christian. She had been taught to believe in angels floating around in heaven, and holy spirits, and some guy being the Son of God, and women getting pregnant without screwing, and other weird things. Who knew what kind of permanent damage believing that stuff did to your mind? Instead of believing in an afterlife replete with haloed angels, Pat now speculated about her previous lives and what she would be born as next. Sandy and Jenny sometimes joked about the things Pat said, until Bunny chastised them for their intolerance. Bunny would rightfully remind them that everyone had a right to their own personal beliefs, and who were they to feel so superior? But they did feel condescending: Jenny because she thought it was all so stupid, and Sandy because she thought it was a waste of time. After all, there were important things to worry about, like fighting social injustice and creating a better world. Who had time to worry about where a nonexistent "soul" went when what was real was that your body would rot six feet under?

One had to live in the now. And they had never had so much fun living in the now, for there was no one to tell them what to do, and in that freedom the girls went playfully berserk. They slept during the day and stayed up all night, smoking and laughing and going on excursions to the local hot dog stand at three in the morning. Skipping and singing through dark and deserted snow-filled streets, they felt immune from the chilling wind and the disapproving old man behind the Dog House counter.

At times the playfulness was tinged with frantic overtones. In an earlier time, Sandy and Jenny would have condemned Pat's childishness as she mixed the ketchup and mustard with the salt and pepper in a multi-colored heap on the formica table. But now they laughed, even getting into the act a little with their own contributions of green relish and chopped onions, which added revolting lumps to the pasty mess.

They both sensed that this was the last year of their newly discovered childhoods, the last year of freedom from the responsibilities that were waiting for them. Now that they were living off-campus, they each had a room of their own. Sandy tried to talk Jenny into sleeping with her sometimes, as she now had a double bed, but Jenny staunchly refused, reminding Sandy that no one was to know and this would be a sure giveaway. But then they had never slept next to each other — the single beds in the dorm precluded that possibility — so Sandy told herself that being in separate rooms really wasn't so different. Yet she missed being able to look at Jenny at night, and sometimes, when she had trouble sleeping, Sandy would get out of bed and walk across the cold floor to the entrance of Jenny's bedroom, where she would stare at the familiar sleeping face and the dark tangled hair wildy strewn across the white pillow. Reassured, with teeth chattering, Sandy would race back to her bed, her socks slipping on the smooth wooden floor. And then she would sleep.

But if sleeping in separate rooms was a drawback to having their own home, there were many advantages. For one thing, they now had a kitchen. They had quit the cafeteria two years before and had been forced to live on the food they were able to cook on a hot plate. Now, with a refrigerator and stove, they could cook anything they wanted, and they started making regular family dinners and took turns shopping, cooking, and cleaning.

And more important, they now had privacy. On the many days when Bunny and Pat were out of the house, Sandy and Jenny would lie in bed, giggling and fooling around and making love without worrying that someone might hear. They could make noise. When they made love they didn't have to stuff a pillow over their faces. Sandy could look at Jenny the whole time. It was wonderful.

In spite of herself, Sandy kept thinking about the future. What was she going to do with her life? Should she go on to graduate school? If not, what would she do instead? It was the latter question that had gotten her to fill out the exhausting application forms. Everyone told her she should go to graduate school; she had excellent grades, high GREs, and good recs from her professors, as well as a senior thesis based on original research. All hot shit stuff, according to her thesis advisor. All she had to do was swear that she loved research and never wanted to do therapy, and he assured her that she could get into any Psych program in the country.

Going to school for another five years sounded like a drag. More teachers, more exams, more cramming, more bullshit classes; when would this student routine ever end? But then again, getting a job seemed even worse. What could she do? She had worked as a waitress when she lived in San Francisco years before, and done office work in New York. That had been okay for the summer, but she sure didn't want to do that shit for the rest of her life. Maybe becoming a psychologist wasn't such a bad idea; you got to be useful and help people when they were in pain. And she'd earn enough money that she could always support herself and live the way she wanted. If you had a good skill, you didn't have to take shit from anyone. Her father had told her that, and it was one of the few things she thought he was totally right about.

It was the prospect of doing therapy that attracted her to psychology, but the system was such that you had to prove you could do boring stuff like statistics before they'd even let you take a Personality or Abnormal Psychology class. Her thesis advisor had explained that too many people wanted to major in Psychology, and this was how they weeded out the less serious students. Sandy resented the fact that after she had gotten through all the requirements, there wasn't much time to take the interesting classes. That definitely seemed like false advertising. Now they were telling her that she had to go to grad school before she'd learn the things she really wanted to know. Like what made people tick? That had always fascinated her, even when she was a kid. She would watch the adults around her as they talked, seeing who kissed ass to who, and who said one thing but really meant another, and log that down in the informal chronicle of life experiences she kept in her head.

Learning more about why people acted the way they did and what made them get fucked up seemed interesting. And supposedly in graduate school they stopped treating you like stupid babies. That sounded good to Sandy, who was tired of people assuming she was an idiot until she proved otherwise, which always took some special effort and made her nervous in the beginning of her classes until the teachers got to know her.

She still didn't know where she would be going to school, and so even though things were great with Jenny, and she didn't have to read any of the books for her classes any more because she would be accepted to grad school before those transcripts were out, Sandy felt a slowly growing nervousness. Everything in her life was up in the air. She would leave Buffalo, which was just beginning to feel like home, and move to a strange city where she wouldn't know anyone. And she'd be enrolled in a graduate program she didn't know she'd like, to prepare her for a career she wasn't really sure she wanted. And then of course, she and Jenny would be separated.

That was the killer. She could handle anything if she knew she and Jenny would be together. That was all she really wanted in life. The only thing that felt necessary. Jenny's grades weren't as good as hers, so she wasn't likely to get into the better schools, but Sandy would go to Oshkosh U if she could be with Jenny. But Jenny had said no.

Sandy tried to put their impending separation out of her mind. But as June grew closer, she had trouble sleeping and lost interest in the family meals. She had never believed that the day would actually come when she and Jenny would say goodbye to each other. Now, it was slowly becoming real.

27

Closing her eyes, Jenny concentrated on the warm sunlight that basted her face, arms, and legs. A lazy peacefulness radiated inward from her limbs to her midsection. The occasional stirrings of a soft June breeze cooled her bared flesh. Half-smiling, she amused herself with the kaleidoscopic light show that flashed across her eyelids. If she opened her eyes too much, the darting lights vanished; if she shut her eyes too tightly, all she could see was one orange dot that inexplicably migrated from one end of her eyelid to the other, disappeared, then magically reappeared in the original location, repeating the same process over and over. The repetitiveness of that journey irritated Jenny. Her irritation reminded her that she was supposed to do something this morning, but she couldn't remember what. Sitting up on the dilapidated, once rose-colored sofa that had braved the winter rain and snow, she brought her knees to her chin and stared out across the quiet street of old two-story houses. Several houses down, she could see an old woman, also sitting on a porch, rocking on a cushioned chair as she read a magazine. It was definitely a lazy day. Who would believe that by next week she would be a college graduate? Her parents' pride and joy. Her parents. Shit. Her mother had asked her to confirm the reservation at the motel, and she still hadn't called. She had told her mother that the reservation would be fine — they had made it four months ago — but her mother said please to double-check it, just to make her father happy. When it came to traveling, he was a nervous wreck, always making sure that everything was in perfect order. Having them around for three days was going to be a strain. Sandy had told her parents that she didn't want to go to graduation, expecting that they wouldn't think it was a big deal. She was surprised when her mother told her that they had been looking forward to the trip to Buffalo for years. After all, they had never seen the city or the campus, and this was a good excuse to do that. Sandy said there was nothing to see, but then gave in without a fight when her mother insisted. Listening to Sandy on the phone, Jenny had marveled at her naiveté. How could she not know that parents made a big deal out of their kids' graduations? Jenny felt exactly the same way as Sandy, but it had never occurred to her to try to get her parents not to come.

Jenny became aware that she was biting her index nail, started to stop herself, then let herself continue, figuring she could grow them back over the summer. She'd have plenty of time to be virtuous later. Graduation, then a few weeks to get her things in order, and then she'd be at home for six weeks before her parents drove her out to Ohio. Ohio. It had such a strange sound. Like a mountaineer yodeling. That would be her home for the next four or five years. She had been lucky to get into their Ph.D. program and to get financial assistance too. Everyone told her it was a good program, though not as good as Sandy's. Poor Sandy. She was still heartbroken that she hadn't gotten into Berkeley, her first choice. But she had gotten her second, UCLA, and Jenny didn't see that Sandy really had anything to complain about. Jenny would have loved to go out to

California for school, but her advisors had told her not to even bother applying. Her grades just weren't spectacular enough. So, she was going to another cold place, while Sandy would be in warm and sunny California, and it was Sandy who was complaining. Sandy didn't even know when she had it good. She had been moping around lately, getting quieter and more withdrawn. Jenny hated to see Sandy down in the dumps like that, so she teased her about growing up to be a morose old lady, and Sandy would start to smile despite herself. Jenny sighed deeply. She was worried about Sandy. Sandy was such a big baby, so delicate and fragile at times. How was she going to get along without Jenny to whip her into shape? Jenny was surprised by the tears that suddenly welled up in her eyes. She wasn't *that* concerned about Sandy. Sandy knew how to take care of herself, and she could be damned tough and difficult if she wanted to be. No one knew that better than Jenny. So what was she crying about like some silly schoolgirl? It wasn't like they would never see each other again. They'd both be back in New York for the holidays, and they'd get together then. Probably not Thanksgiving — Sandy couldn't afford to fly back from California just for a weekend — so they'd see each other during Christmas break. And the stories they'd have to tell. Who knew? Maybe by then they'd both have met some fabulous guy, and they could compare notes. After all, they were best friends. And best friends often got separated when they moved to other towns or one of them got married, but they still stayed in touch.

Jenny saw Sandy as soon as she turned the corner. She was wearing cut-off shorts and a sleeveless blouse, and her long, thin legs strode gracefully along the concrete sidewalk. She reminded Jenny of a high-strung race horse.

"Hi. What did you get?" Jenny smiled as Sandy took the stairs two at a time.

"Some groceries for tonight." Sandy nodded to the brown bag balanced on one hip; with her free hand she pulled her long wild hair out of her eyes. "It's my turn to cook. I'll join you in a minute."

Jenny heard Sandy tromp into the kitchen and crash the groceries onto the gray formica table they had found in the street when they first moved in. Sandy came back and plopped herself down on the couch next to Jenny, moodily lighting a cigarette and flicking the match onto the sidewalk below.

"What are you thinking about?" Jenny asked.

"Oh — I was just thinking I owe Mike a letter. It's been almost a month since I got his," she replied guiltily.

"He said he was liking it up there?"

"Yeah, pretty much. The university is okay and he likes teaching. His major complaint is that there aren't any intelligent women." Sandy shook her head. "They're all just off the farm."

"I thought Calgary was a big city."

"I thought so too. But Mike says it's more like a frontier town. The guys wear ten-gallon hats and spurs on their boots."

"You gotta be kidding!" Jenny was horrified. God, she hoped Ohio wasn't like that.

"No, and in the city, too. Besides, Mike is used to New York women, and I can't imagine the girls up there would be very sophisticated." Sandy turned to look at Jenny with big eyes. "Jesus, it never occurred to me — you think there are any Jews there?"

"In Calgary?" Jenny feigned surprise. "Sure. At least the one who runs the kosher pizzeria."

Jenny and Sandy burst into giggles simultaneously. Sandy poked Jenny in the ribs with her elbow. "Get outa here."

"No," Jenny replied as she started to tickle Sandy. Laughing and wrestling, they fell back against the couch. They were smiling as they sat up, their shoulders grazing each other's lightly.

"Jen," Sandy's voice was serious. "I know I'm not supposed to bring it up again but . . ."

"Sandy, you promised." Jenny felt herself getting stiff and cold.

"It's just graduation is next week and then you're going to be leaving in less than a month."

Jenny's eyes narrowed as she focused on the house across the street. There was no room to be kind. "We agreed not to talk about it, Sandy. There's nothing more to be said. I made it clear from the beginning that after graduation . . ." Jenny left it unfinished, then decided it needed to be stated clearly. She had never been guilty of misleading Sandy on this issue. ". . . that we would go our separate ways." Jenny now turned to look at Sandy, who was sitting unusually still as she stared at her feet.

"I know." Sandy's voice was almost inaudible. "It's just it never seemed real before. It always seemed so far away."

Sandy turned her face away to look down the street. Jenny sensed that Sandy was crying and wanted to hide her tears. Jenny felt her own tears rise and fought to keep them from spilling over.

"I'm sorry I'm being such a baby. I don't know what's wrong with me." Sandy looked at Jenny apologetically, her feelings now under control.

"Things have felt so good the last few months. Please don't ruin it, Sandy." Jenny was still looking away, but she knew her voice had softened. It was the most she could do.

Sandy stood up. "I'm going inside to get some lemonade. You want anything?"

"Huh uh." Jenny made believe she was absorbed in the street, as Sandy walked into the house. Biting her lip, she tried to keep back the tears that refused to stay inside. They spilled over and splashed silently onto her clenched hands.

28

The sun was shining through the thin red curtains, casting psychedelic shadows on the walls and filling the room with a cheery pink glow. Sandy had always loved waking up in this bright aura, but today it seemed a mockery. She turned over onto her back and gazed at the sloped ceiling over her bed. It was by far the nicest room in the house. She had won the flip of the coin and gotten her first choice: the sloping ceiling, the big windows facing two directions, and outside one window, a slanted alcove, which she used as a second-story porch. She had been so happy when she picked this room. A tune kept repeating in her head. What were the words? "Happy days are here again, the skies are . . ." Sandy threw back the covers impatiently and walked down the corridor to the bathroom. There was water all over the floor, and half-drenched towels surrounded the tub. Someone had obviously tried to take a shower with the homemade attachment. "Shit," she mumbled as she turned the faucets on, knowing it would be minutes before the water would begin to get warm. Taking a deep breath, she threw some icy water onto her face, then looked into the old mirror above the sink. The water ran down her cheeks, caught on her chin, and then dropped to her breasts. The face in the mirror was gaunt and wore a grim expression.

With a brusque swing of her arm, she wiped the water off her chest, and began to wash up. She kept her mind empty as she brushed her teeth with the last of the paste from the flattened tube. On the way back to her room, she stopped for a moment at the top of the stairs and listened to the noise coming from the kitchen. Someone was fixing coffee. Concentrating on the sounds in the kitchen, Sandy forcibly blanked her mind again. Behind the blank space were the tears and the pain, which she could not afford to feel. Reminding herself that there would be time later, plenty of time, she walked back into her room and put on her favorite pair of blue jeans, which were lying near the bed on the floor. She walked over to the wooden straight chair next to her desk, picked out a black danskin from the pile of clothes, and pulled it over her head.

Jenny was sitting at the kitchen table, smoking a cigarette and drinking a cup of coffeee.

"Good morning," Sandy said as she walked over to the stove.

"Good morning. You're up early."

Sandy poured herself a cup of coffee. "What time is the cab coming?"

"7:15." Jenny put out her cigarette, then lit another one.

"Are you sure you don't want me to borrow Bunny's car?" Sandy sat down at the table next to Jenny. "I could drive you to the airport."

Jenny shook her head. "No, it's a hassle borrowing the car, and there's no need for that." Jenny got up and fixed herself another cup of coffee from the hot water on the stove. Sandy felt strangely relieved. At least this way it wouldn't be drawn out. The cab would come and Jenny would go. It would be a simple and clean amputation. Jenny sat down and nervously played with her spoon. Lighting a cigarette, Sandy watched her from what seemed a great distance. It was as if she were looking at Jenny through a telescopic lens; the closeness of their bodies had the unreality of watching the characters in a movie.

"So when are you leaving for Ohio?" Was that her voice that had cracked? She had felt almost casual.

"School doesn't start for another two months." Jenny seemed relieved by her question. "I'll probably spend a few weeks in the city, and then my parents will drive me out there." Sandy wasn't paying attention to Jenny's words; instead she found herself watching Jenny's lips opening and closing. This was the last day, and Jenny still had no trouble chattering on. She really didn't care. "Once we've found me an apartment, then I'll buy some secondhand furniture and get settled in. How about you? When are you leaving for California?"

"First week in September," Sandy said abruptly. Were they really having this inane conversation? Was this the way it was going to end? As if they were two acquaintances? "Well, I guess we won't see each other for a while . . . probably not till Christmas," she ventured. Please say something, Jenny.

"Well, the time will go by fast. We'll both be busy."

"Yeah, sure." Sandy felt like she had just been slapped. The anesthetic was beginning to wear off. Jenny was acting as if nothing were happening, as if their saying goodbye were not of any consequence. Sandy felt crazy.

"Well, I'm going upstairs to get my bags." Jenny stood up and left the kitchen. Sandy heard her clomp up the stairs, the sound of each footstep ringing individually. She got up and paced around the kitchen table, fighting back her tears.

"Just be cool, kid," she whispered to herself. "It'll all be over before you know it. Then you can fall apart. But not until after she's gone." Sandy lit a new cigarette, unaware of the one still smoking in the ashtray. She heard Jenny stumble down the stairs and carry her suitcases into the living room. Sandy climbed up the few stairs to the lower landing, and then down the stairs on the other side to the living room. Jenny was looking out the window for the cab. She would be leaving any minute now. Knowing that she was defeated, Sandy tried once again, for the last time.

"Are you sure it has to be this way, Jenny?"

Jenny's expression was pained. "We'll see each other in a few months."

"Yeah." The hurt engulfed Sandy, blinding her for a moment. Far away she heard a cab honk.

"Well, there's my taxi." Walking quickly to Sandy, Jenny gave her a fast hug and a peck on the cheek. "Bye, Sandy. I'll call you." She picked up her bags and walked out.

"Goodbye, Jenny," Sandy said quietly as she stood in the doorway and watched Jenny get into the cab and the driver put her bags in the trunk. And then he got back into the car and they drove off.

Sandy stood motionless for what seemed a long time. Then she closed the door and leaned back against it.

"Well, kid . . . you're on your own again." A huge wave of grief crashed in on her. She crumpled to the floor, sobbing. "Jenny," she screamed. "How could you leave me?"

Part II

29

"I had this dream. . . . But I'm not sure I want to talk about it." Marilyn halted and looked around the room, waiting for someone to try to convince her. Then she could argue the point. But the women sat quietly. Patiently.

"Okay." She took a deep breath. "I was walking down a long corridor, holding hands with Joe — he's a man I work with — and we came into a room filled with people. I realized they were all women. Then I saw some masculine-looking women, and I realized all the women in the room were lesbians. I got very red in the face and embarrassed, so I grabbed Joe's arm and we cleared out of there. I was afraid he'd know I was one of them."

Marilyn's hands tugged nervously on the red and blue tassels of her cloth belt. She was wearing the same dark blue polyester pants she had worn the first night she came to group. Uneasily looking at the other women during her turn at rounds, Marilyn had said then that she didn't know whether she belonged. Her problem was that she had recently been left by her lover of eight years. But they never had any contact with other women, and after all, she wasn't really sure she was a lesbian. And besides, she had nervously tacked on, she was the only one in the group wearing polyester pants.

Sandy smiled to herself as she remembered that initial burst of anxiety. How fitting it was that Marilyn's semi-conscious fears should have been summed up in her observation that she was dressed differently. Those first few weeks in group, she kept everyone at arm's length. The doubts about her lesbianism dropped out almost immediately, and then she loosened up and began to respond to the other women. Her quick sarcastic humor often triggered a needed release, and by now she had become fully a group member. Last week she even wore a pair of blue jeans and a sweatshirt, for the first time relaxing her fabric armor. And now she was wearing the polyester again, to accompany a dream of lesbian panic.

Well, they had all been through that process. Sandy reminded herself that some of the women in the group were just beginning the long and painful trek. She surveyed the room quickly to see if any of the other women looked anxious. No, the curious open faces told her it was still too early. Tonight would be interesting.

"Tell us more about the corridor."

"Well, it was long and narrow. Like the corridors in a hospital or an institution. Maybe a mental institution." Marilyn's words trailed off and she seemed unsure.

"What about the masculine-looking women? How did it feel to find yourself in a room with them?"

"I felt very angry at them for being so obvious and identifiable," Marilyn blurted out. A nervous chuckle escaped as she shook her head. "I'm surprised to see that I'm still so uptight."

"We don't work through deeply ingrained prejudices overnight. Tell us more about how you felt." Sandy leaned back into her chair.

"Well, I didn't want to identify with them. But people see us all as lesbians and so I get identified that way. I felt real threatened. They are objects of ridicule. And that means that I'm more likely to be ridiculed. And it's not fair. I don't believe in acting like a man, it's wrong, but people think we all want to be men."

Marilyn seemed uncomfortable with what she had just said. Hurriedly, as if to forestall an attack, she added, "You know, I've changed some. I walk into a bar now, and I see them, and I feel separate at first, like I wouldn't want to be seen with them, but it's funny. Once I start to talk with them, it all disappears."

Sylvia broke in. "I feel fucked up about it, but it scares me. I stay away from women who look like lesbians. I just haven't been ready to deal with being open about it. Today, I was talking to Peter — he's the gay guy at work — about a T-shirt I've been designing. I wanted to use the double women's sign, but then I thought, who would wear a T-shirt like that? Peter said I was chicken, so I asked him if he would wear a T-shirt with two interlocking men's signs, and that shut him up. I've been trying to find some design that would use the women's symbol subtly."

"You mean invisibly," Marsha quipped.

"No, just something that a lesbian who wasn't 'out' could wear, that would make her feel proud without anyone having to know. Except for other lesbians, of course." Sylvia threw up her hands in frustration. "I guess what I'm saying is that I wanted to design a T-shirt that a woman like me could wear."

Jane was perched on the edge of the brown tweed sofa. She rarely talked in group and was still self-conscious about being considerably less educated that the other women. She had come close to quitting at the end of her first month; hesitant and stumbling, she said that she had nothing to offer and she didn't belong in this group.

One by one, the other women told Jane about their own insecurities and doubts. Marilyn, a college professor, said she often felt dumb and inarticulate too. Sylvia shared her initial fear that she would never be able to open up like the women who had been in the group longer; as a photographer, she thought in visual images, and she was intimidated by the more verbal women.

Jane was flabbergasted. It had never occurred to her that educated women might be insecure about such things. Then several of the women told her that they really wanted to get to know her; and Marsha, a radical lesbian feminist, said she counted on Jane's presence, and just having another woman in the room who looked like a dyke was reassuring.

Since then, Jane had seemed somewhat more comfortable, but she still usually needed some encouragement before she would speak up. Sandy looked in her direction and said gently, "You look like you've got something on the tip of your tongue."

Jane smiled in appreciation. "Yeah, I guess I do. You know, I've gotten a lot of shit for being masculine. My hair is short. I dress in jeans. But I feel like a woman. Sometimes I feel feminine, sometimes I don't. But people have ridiculed me a lot. At work or on the street, some wise guy will say, 'Is it a girl or is it a boy?'"

She cracked her knuckles and looked down at the floor. "But I'm just being myself and I don't want to be any other way." Her voice became stronger, more certain. "I don't wear a dress. That's not my way of proving I'm a woman. And I've known a lot of different women. Some tough. Some dykes, some femmes. I like seeing the butch women, though. I feel like they're saying, 'I'm proud.'"

"You know, I used to have very long hair." Laraine gestured in the air as if to comb a flip. "It was camouflage. When I first became involved with a woman, I cut it to shoulder length. Now it's even shorter. But you know, I'd like to wear it shorter still, but I've been afraid. That people would know."

Sandy nodded in agreement. "I passed for years with long hair, not wanting to be seen as masculine. Which would mean I wasn't a 'real woman.' Words that strike terror in the hearts of all females. We've been taught to stick with 'appropriate sex roles.' It's no accident that when a woman steps out of line she gets called a cold bitch, a castrator, and finally, if nothing else works, a dyke. But you know, after they've called me a dyke and that doesn't shut me up, there's nothing left they can call me. I'm free."

She searched the room to see how her comments were being

received. She didn't usually go on like this, especially in such a political vein, but it seemed important for the women to see to what extent their fears and anxieties had been culturally programmed by a society intent on keeping them immobilized, if it was unable to eradicate them entirely.

"I feel like we owe a great deal to the identifiable lesbians of the past," Sandy continued. "They stood out there in small numbers in a terribly hostile society and said, 'This is who I am.' There were millions of women-loving women who hid and passed, but a few women had the courage to risk being targets so that they could have more freedom. In a way, they gave us all more freedom. I may not agree with the mimicking of men that often occurred. They were limited by the choices they knew: masculine or feminine, butch or femme. But within those limited concepts, they were very brave in their refusal to compromise."

"You know, that's true. Society does set that up," Sylvia said excitedly. "Being tall, and having short hair from the back, I sometimes get mistaken for a guy. That really upsets me. So even though I think tailored clothes look best on me, I'm careful about what I wear. Just as I'm careful about whom I'm seen with. I want to thank you, Jane. I may be embarrassed occasionally, but when I think about what you had to put up with . . . you gave me a good kick in the ass. I really needed to hear that from you." There were tears in Sylvia's eyes as she regarded Jane, who was sheepishly clenching and unclenching her hands.

"But wait a second," Marilyn interrupted, looking skeptically at Sandy. "Do you mean to tell me that you'd wear a T-shirt saying 'I'm a homosexual'?"

"No, but I would wear a T-shirt with two women's signs interlocked."

"I don't agree," Marilyn challenged. "It seems wrong to me to broadcast. Why do you need to do that? It's personal. You don't see women in T-shirts saying 'I sleep with men.'"

"No, but you do see them wearing T-shirts with such goodies as 'I'm a virgin' or 'I'm easy, baby.'"

"That's disgusting," Marsha said, sticking out her tongue and making a nauseated face.

"Or what about 'No nukes,'" Sandy persisted.

"That's not personal."

"Sure it is. It says something about what you believe, what is important to you."

"Well, I guess that's true, but it's not personal like sex. That's private. You don't tell people personal things indiscriminately." Marilyn looked upset. More upset than was merited by a theoretical discussion. Sandy decided to pursue it.

"Why not?" she said.

"You just don't."

"I wonder if this is a cultural issue. Growing up in New England . . ."

Marilyn shook her head. "It has more to do with my mother. She told everyone everything. And they weren't interested, but she didn't care," she spat out, her hand clenched in a fist.

"You must have felt humiliated," Sandy said softly.

Marilyn looked at Sandy, an ironical smile twisting her lips higher on the left side. "Yeah, well, I guess I learned to be a good listener. And now I have trouble talking."

Sandy nodded, reflectively tapping her index finger against her upper lip. She always found that gesture pretentious in others, but it did seem to help clarify her thoughts.

"Sometimes people create moral principles to support their personal styles. I'm not saying that you should talk without caring, just to hear your own voice, or that you should be indiscriminate, but I do think that it's important to be able to disclose freely." Sandy waited a moment to see how that intervention would be received. Marilyn was a stubborn woman and usually fought each new insight.

Marilyn shook her head back and forth as if she were having a conversation with herself. "Okay, but just tell me one thing. Would you walk into a store and say, 'I'm Jewish and a lesbian'?" She looked proud of herself.

"Well," Sandy drawled, "I might not use exactly those words but I might say, 'Hi, I'm Jewish and a lesbian, and I'm buying a Chanukah present for my lover. What would you recommend?'"

The group exploded in laughter. Marilyn, amused and defeated, shook her head. "I'll have to try that some time." She became reflective. "You know, I thought that dream was a step back. That's why I didn't want to tell it."

"Not at all." Sandy leaned forward in her chair, her thumb and index finger joined to complete the point. "We don't have dreams like that until we've already reached a certain point and are ready to deal with them. Often the dream content will seem most negative or regressive right before we're ready to make a big change. I can remember when I was first dealing with my fear of being gay and being discovered. In the dream I was pregnant," Sandy stretched her arms out in front of her, "with my belly out to here. That way everyone would think I was normal. No one would know my terrible secret. And my dreams progressed from there until I became more comfortable, and didn't feel like I had to hide."

"You know, I really envy and respect you for being 'out.' I'm not sure I can do it. At first I thought the dream meant I was attracted to men, but I'm not. He was some kind of security."

"You were different from the other lesbians. No one would suspect."

Sylvia let out a long whistle. "I had a dream this week about sex with a man. It was nice. But then I was embarrassed to tell you about it. I was afraid you'd think I was regressing. But now I see that the dream came out of my work in group last week, when I said there was no way I wanted to be with a man again."

"The dream is telling you that you could still have sex with a man," Sandy said. "Is sex the only reason you are with a woman now?"

Sylvia shook her head vigorously.

"Of course not," Sandy agreed. "The dream is only a problem if you interpret it as meaning you're not really a lesbian. That's why we talk about sexual *preference* — actually, a better label would be affectional-sexual preference, because it's not just an issue of sexuality. But it's not like there are two separate slots — gay or straight — and we fit completely into one or the other, with no overlap. If a straight woman had an occasional dream about a woman, she probably wouldn't question her identity. But gay people are always vulnerable."

"Wow," Laraine exclaimed. "Gay people are walking on tip-toes all the time. I bet all that energy worrying about small things really breaks up relationships . . . You know, the other night I was really freaked out about getting a notice from the gay chapter of the ACLU. I tore it up. The idea of being on a list, and who knows where it goes — maybe even Washington." Laraine sighed. "I worried about that for two days."

"I saw a program on '60 Minutes,'" Marilyn interrupted. "They have access to our checks, and that tells all. My first thought was, how do I explain all these checks to Sandy Stein, the well-known lesbian psychologist." The group laughed. "But I decided there was nothing to do. If they want to know, they will."

"It sounds like you've come around some," Marsha commented.

"Maybe. But if you wear a T-shirt with interlocking women's signs, it's like saying 'Fuck you.' That's not right."

"No," Sandy cut in. "I think it depends on the woman. One woman wears that T-shirt and is saying 'Fuck you.' And another woman wears the same shirt and is saying 'I love women.'"

"That's me," Marilyn exclaimed. "I'd like to wear a T-shirt saying 'Fuck you.'" She laughed at herself. "Maybe that will be the sign of my cure. When I can wear a T-shirt that says 'Fuck you.'"

Sandy turned on the car radio, then quickly turned it off again. She wasn't quite ready to be distracted by the music she usually listened to during the long drive home. Today's group had been unusually energetic and integrative. The women knew that she was about to go to a convention where she would give

100

a lecture on "coming out" issues, and then Marilyn dutifully brought in an exemplary dream.

Sandy chuckled as she imagined Marilyn's horrified reaction to the idea that this dream might have been a going-away gift, a fresh example to spice up the lecture Sandy had already prepared. Which reminded her, she needed to go over her notes on the plane. She wasn't satisfied that her transitions were smooth enough.

Feeling her anxiety level skyrocket, Sandy switched on the radio, leaned back, and forced herself to observe the foliage that sheltered the houses along Overland Drive. The street looked like many others in this section of Los Angeles: stucco houses with tiled roofs, all in a neat line, with lawns that Japanese gardeners cropped closely in the fashion of a Marine haircut. This green order was pleasant, even comforting, but something in Sandy rebelled against the uniform trimness of the landscape.

Driving a little faster, she spotted a patch of long grass and overgrown foliage, and she cheered inwardly for the brave owners who managed their own property and refused to capitulate to neighborhood custom. No doubt the other neighbors complained about the aberrant plot, calling it a blemish on the neighborhood, a depreciator of property values. Imagining an elderly couple with physical impairments who couldn't afford to hire a gardener, Sandy grew indignant over the insensitivity of the neighbors' reaction. A familiar tirade started in her mind, about the obscenity of societal attitudes toward old people.

Sandy paused to analyze her thought process. It was much more comfortable for her to be angry than anxious. And at the moment, thinking about injustices to the elderly was less threatening than thinking about her upcoming presentation.

This would be her first lecture at the annual National Psychological Association conference. She had attended the convention once, and it was a peculiar experience. Drifting in and out of the seminars situated in plush but sterile conference rooms, Sandy felt very much alienated from her colleagues.

What a strange word "colleagues" was. It implied that she was supposed to feel a bond with the thousands of people who invaded San Francisco like a storm of locusts. The streets swarmed with psychologists, immediately identifiable by the program in hand. Embarrassed by the way they engulfed the city, changing its personality and identity, Sandy withdrew into herself and became an alien among aliens.

Now she imagined calling up the panel chairperson and telling him she was deathly sick. She would put on a pathetic bull frog voice, which would make her sound already six feet under. Then she would crawl under the covers, get comfy, and sleep all day.

There was no doubt about it. She still hated giving presentations. According to behavioral principles, she should have gotten over this by now. But she hadn't. Oh, it had become easier over the years. Instead of starting to dread a planned talk three months in advance, she now began to worry only a few days before. And instead of suffering from stomach pains, accompanied by a riveting nausea, she now felt the tension in her calves and thighs.

Of course, this wasn't going to be just any old academic presentation. The topic was "Gay Adolescents: The Struggle for Identity." A professor had once told her always to start a presentation with a joke, but it was difficult to find humor in such topics as suicide, drug addiction, alcoholism, and the other problems that can result from that little-understood but well-loved attitude known as homophobia.

Sandy exhaled a deep sigh as she stretched her back, pushing her hands against the wheel of the car. Patting the dashboard, she whispered sweet nothings into the air vents. Baby was her first car. And a first car was as special as a first love. Sandy snorted at her own inanity. Maybe Shelly was right to insist that they turn this business trip into a vacation. Sandy hadn't taken any time off work in over a year, and lately she had been tired, even a little depressed.

She wasn't sure what the problem was. The last few weeks, until this afternoon's group, she had felt dissatisfied with her work, and that seemed crazy, because she loved what she did. There was a special kind of gratification in therapy work. Every moment was pregnant with potential, and almost every session brought some change. And yet recently it hadn't seemed enough.

Guilt. She wasn't doing enough. That was what she felt. She was one of a handful of lesbian clinical psychologists who were publicly "out," and all she was doing was private practice. Not only hadn't she taken a respectable academic position, as was expected by the professors who had groomed her at one of the top schools in the country, but she hadn't even gotten an administrative job in a mental health center or government agency. Instead, she had ended up doing direct service work. Sandy remembered the embarrassed expression of her faculty advisor when she told him what she was doing now that she had finished her dissertation. And just setting foot on that campus triggered the shakes, accompanied by acute stomach distress. Graduate school, with its pretensions of scientific rigor and uninvolved objectivity, had almost killed her spirit. Certainly she had learned there her first hard lessons in humility and compromise. How else could a woman like her get through a sexist, homophobic, authoritarian factory that passed itself off as a learning institution? No, she reminded herself, that wasn't totally fair. She had learned some important skills in graduate school. But she had paid a heavy price.

That was why she had decided to go into private practice. There was no way she could publicly come out as a political lesbian and stay in the university or any public institution. Other women had tried, and for the most part, they were thrown out or mysteriously denied tenure.

Poor Shelly. She still had another year before she would come up for tenure. Sandy didn't quite understand how Shelly survived at the University, half in and half out. Somehow she managed to walk that very thin line: not hiding who and what she was, yet not making her lesbianism public in a way that would threaten her colleagues or the administration. Maybe it was easier in a field where standards of normality were not constantly discussed or applied to individuals; Sandy's field adhered to the belief that clinicians should be well-adjusted themselves. Nothing wrong with that, except homosexuals were always talked about as patients, not doctors.

Even in grad school, Sandy had never actually lied about her sexual preference. Rather, she remained silent when certain predictable conversations came up. It was a very uncomfortable truce for Sandy, and over the years she felt personally compromised. She knew that if she stayed in that system, it would kill her. So, she did the only thing that would preserve her sense of integrity: working for herself, doing therapy. And therapy was what she most loved, anyhow; it just didn't fit her image of herself as a political activist. Psychotherapy was nice, but it only reached a very small group of women, and mostly privileged women at that. She had set up a sliding scale so that she could work with some less affluent women, but that didn't eradicate her guilt. She had skills that very few public lesbians had. It was her responsibility to use those skills to counter the oppression her sisters struggled with daily. But that meant going really public, talking at college symposia, doing TV and radio spots, and finally educating her own profession, which had done such serious damage to lesbians. That was why she had accepted Jim's invitation to speak at the NPA convention. It didn't matter that she hated public speaking, nor did it matter that she was scared to death. It was a responsibility she could not evade.

Sandy opened the door to the cozy wooden house she and Shelly had bought several years before. Two cats ran in and wove around her legs.

"Hi, Sappho. Hi, Emma. What a sweet way to welcome me home." Sandy put down her briefcase and squatted to rub the cats. That was always the first order of business when she came home. Emma began to purr loudly. She was a small tiger-striped cat with a lot of spunk. A fighter. She loved to be petted, but she was also fiercely independent. Sappho, on the other hand, was sweet and affectionate, almost clingy. She was a black cat, rounder and softer than Emma. She liked to sit in Shelly's lap for hours while Shelly read. Sandy stood up. "Come on. Let's see what we have for a late lunch."

She walked across the living room to the kitchen. The living room was wood-paneled, with an old-fashioned fireplace. The room was decorated in warm, natural colors, and furnished with traditional rocking chairs and bunches of bright pillows. The walls were covered with macrame, weavings, and paintings of women and of abstract female imagery. There was a view of brush-covered mountains through a large picture window. The mountains were dark green now; the rain had been good this winter.

Sandy often felt that the view seemed phony, like a picture postcard. Nothing could really be that beautiful. Living in California for ten years had softened her, loosening the tension that had been in her body during most of her adolescence and early adulthood. But the remnants of having grown up in New York were still there. Didn't vegetables just come from cans? And electricity from a switch? And one got water by turning a tap. It was still hard to grasp the notion that things came from somewhere.

In the kitchen Sandy opened a can of cat food and spooned it into two bowls. She took off her jacket and watched the cats eat. Sappho ate her food steadily, totally involved in the process. Emma was more distracted. She would eat a little, then look around to see if anything was happening. She had a little of that New York paranoia in her. Very Jewish. Sappho on the other hand seemed *goyish*. She was secure and complacent in the world. Enjoying her life without question, happy to be alive. Sandy had known some Protestants like that. Usually they came from money. They seemed so damned comfortable all the time. Sandy felt torn between envy and the reassurance that it was all phony. Like the picture postcard.

Returning to the living room, she started to organize some of the toiletries that were lying next to two partially packed suitcases in the middle of the room. Then she walked down the stairs and through the redwood bathroom to the bedroom, a large room with windows facing the mountains. In the middle of the back wall, an old wooden bed dominated the space. It was intricately carved, with alternate pieces of mahogany and an unidentifiable hardwood stained a slightly different color. Everyone always commented on how beautiful the bed was. Even the relatives.

Sandy picked up some clothes that were lying on the bed and went back upstairs. Emma was sitting in one of the suitcases.

"Would you mind, Emma? I'm trying to pack."

Emma looked at Sandy, stretched languidly, and started to lick herself. Obedience was not one of her virtues. Sandy tried to be philosophical about it. Teasing, she said, "Who's in charge around here, anyhow?" Emma looked at Sandy with bored eyes, then curled up to take a nap. The answer to the question was obvious to both.

30

Shelly Cohen was delivering her last lecture of the quarter. The classroom was huge, and Shelly had to use a microphone pinned to her shirt to reach the last of the students sitting way up in the back of the auditorium. It hadn't been easy learning to lecture to 300 students at once, but practice had made it tolerable and occasionally even enjoyable. Commanding so many people's attention was at the same time embarrassing and intriguing. Shelly turned to look at the clock and resumed her lecture.

"Okay, that's a summary of the major anthropological theories of the past two centuries. Now, the thing to keep in mind is that all these theories are trying to answer the same three questions: Why do cultures differ? How do they differ? And what is the relationship between the individual and his or her society? . . . I think this is a good place to stop for a moment. Are there any questions? . . . Yes?"

A young man sitting in the back had raised his hand and now stood up, slowly and with something of a swagger. The appropriate adjective was "cocky."

"How much of the final is going to cover material we had to learn for the mid-term?"

Shelly nodded her head as if to give serious attention to his question. "Let me make sure I understand." Now her voice began to show the irony she felt. "I'm trying to summarize the essential questions and issues raised in the last 10 weeks, and you just want to know whether you have to read the first 200 pages of the textbook again . . . or perhaps for the first time?"

The students laughed. Her sarcasm was appreciated. But the young man seemed unabashed. Shelly found the *chutspa* of some of her students astonishing. She remembered what she had been like in college. A serious student who always did her assignments and more. Respectful of teachers, but even more so, worshipful of knowledge. Grades? You just always got A's. Grades made your parents brag and laugh, and serve a glass of wine with dinner.

"Right," the young man answered her question. Shelly was resigned. Except for a handful of students, scholarship was dead in the university. God help us. But then God was dead too.

"Okay, I am now entertaining questions about the final. As for your question, yes, you will have to read the first 200 pages, plus the paperback reference books."

There was a loud groan from the class. But that was okay with Shelly. She had gotten used to it, gotten over making apologies, trying to appease the students. She might be anachronistic, but she would continue to demand some modicum of scholarship from her students.

"Are there any other questions?" Shelly surveyed the classroom, her eyes sweeping along the invisible line that separated the enthusiastic students in the front of the room from the bored ones at the rear, close to the exits they bounded for as soon as the bell rang. She vacillated between feeling angry with those vacant faces and feeling upset and guilty that the system was failing them. That she was failing them.

She looked again at the clock: five more minutes to the end of class. There was no point in dragging out this torture any longer. Over the years she had learned to write off the last two or three class sessions. The students who intended to go to graduate school were far too anxious to learn anything new, and the players were already transported to the blissful state of vacation. She was for all practical purposes talking to herself. Maybe she should take that into consideration and squeeze the important material into the first nine weeks of the quarter.

"Let's stop here, then, and I'll take any further questions after class. Thank you."

To her surprise, the class began to applaud. Even some of the students in the back had modified their usual prison-break exit to participate in this gesture of respect. Was it possible she had reached some of the students her colleagues termed the "Mediocre Mass"? It was so easy and tempting to ignore them, to focus instead on the few bright and motivated students who came to your office hours and engaged you in interesting dialogue. But lately it had really started to bother her that so many of the students drifting through her classes seemed so alienated, so utterly untouched by the learning experience. Their faces already mirrored the dulled, deadened expressions of their parents.

It was frightening to watch this generation growing up without curiosity or interest in the world around them. Zapped out on drugs or compulsive sex, these young people seemed to have lost sight of the substance as well as the subtleties of their experience. Over the last five years, she had charted a steady decline in writing ability and critical thinking in the papers she graded. Some of the students literally could not write a complete and comprehensible sentence. Many more could neither spell nor be grammatical in their sentence structure, and only a handful of students showed clarity of thought and style.

Some of her colleagues blamed TV for transmitting the mediocre images of the culture to these docile, passive tube kids. It was true that the previous generation had learned about the world by reading, a much more active process; but Shelly didn't really think that television was an adequate explanation for what she saw around her. It was as if these children, born in the late fifties, adolescents in the 70's, had given up hope. They seemed to have no dreams as they wandered through the classrooms in a dreamlike state.

The apathy of these students seemed a sign of ignorant and repressive times. And indeed, the backlash was here. Maybe that was the truly upsetting thing about the students who sat in the back. They were the same students who would sit quietly if the administration ever decided to fire her because she was a lesbian. Some of the votes in favor of the Briggs amendment would come from her own students.

It was horrifying to personalize it like that. The other night when she was staffing the "No on 6" office, she talked with a young algebra teacher. He had finally worked up the courage to ask his parents how they were going to vote on 6 in the fall. His mother said vehemently that she would vote in favor of the proposition; of course you couldn't let those perverts near children. His father was more casual about it: "I haven't made up my mind yet. The whole thing seems like a big deal over nothing."

Nothing. The stupidity of people who could say those things to their own son and never know it was he who might lose his job, who might be scarred by the vicious lies they helped perpetuate. The young man had tears in his eyes as he told Shelly that he had been too ashamed and frightened to "come out" to his parents as he had planned. Instead, he had gone home angry and sickened by his own cowardice.

Shelly felt for him, but she could think of nothing to say to give him comfort. She had wanted to reach out and touch his hand, but then she hesitated and the moment passed. Now, she felt angry with herself for letting him down. She would hug that boy the next time she saw him.

Shelly loved the drive home from the university. She would turn the radio to her favorite classical music station and lose herself in fantasy until she got to the ocean. Then she would once again become aware of the world around her. There were no mountains quite like the California coastline; the graceful sloping of the hills often reminded her of women's bodies.

The car ahead braked suddenly, and she barely had time to stop herself from plowing into it. Two boys with surfboards darted across the highway. Once they were safely on the other side, they laughed and jostled each other. Shelly was always amazed by the way males related to one another, expressing physical affection with a punch or a push, laughing loudly together. These boys were still young, probably only thirteen or so, and there was an awkwardness and hesitancy in their bantering, as if they hadn't quite learned the rules yet and were afraid of making a mistake.

Shelly's thoughts wandered to the things she had to take care of before Friday. The list was overwhelming: pick up the clothes at the cleaner, get to the bank, show the house-sitter where everything was, pack her clothes for the trip (it wasn't the packing that was the problem, it was deciding what to pack), finish business at school — which reminded her that she had forgotten to give the TA instructions for the final, and damn, there was that meeting tomorrow where she would have to convince Mathews to hire another woman for the department. That would certainly turn into a battle, and she didn't feel she had the energy right now.

It had been a difficult quarter. Preparing a new class in physical anthropology, which was not her specialty, had been tedious. And then there was the extra worry and work caused by Prop 6. At least next term she would be teaching through the Women's Studies program. For the first time, an anthropology teacher would be affiliated with the Bastard Child. It had taken a while, but things were slowly coming together. Those first few years, before Amanda was hired, Shelly had been the only woman at the weekly faculty meetings. The jokes and whispers. Her face a mask of politeness, the seething inside. Shelly shook herself from her memories. There was something else she was forgetting. What was it?

She stopped for a light and looked at herself in the rear-view mirror. Same old face: Jewish nose, glasses, pale complexion. She was looking forward to getting some sun in Hawaii. The streak of gray hair at her left temple was definitely more pronounced. Shelly had always liked her hair, its thick texture, its rich, black color. She had mixed feelings about the streak; but Sandy thought she looked more beautiful, more mature. Shelly had to agree it did lend an air of dignity to her face. But it was also a sign of aging, like the slight discoloration under her eyes, the few more lines around her mouth, and the drying out of her skin. As a child Shelly had never expected to live past 30. Now she was 34 and often surprised that she had moved into adulthood.

The drive up the canyon road was invigorating. The wild lilac bushes were in bloom, and their slightly sweet scent added a richness to the cool breeze. Her anxiety about getting ready for the trip dissolved when Shelly saw Sandy's car, a battered beige VW. Sandy drove very fast and often made Shelly nervous. But seeing her car in the driveway was one of the nicest things about coming home. A certain empty spot in her stomach got magically filled. Shelly was humming as she walked down the steps to the entryway. Sliding open the glass door, she saw the suitcases in the middle of the room.

"Honey, I'm home."

Sandy came bouncing up the stairs. "Hi." They put their

arms around each other and kissed lingeringly. "How was your day?" Sandy asked.

"It's finals week . . . How about yours?"

"The usual insanity," Sandy replied. Walking over to the pile of clothes and toiletries by one opened suitcase, Sandy kneeled and picked up a few items. Emma was still sitting on top of the pile.

"I'm just putting away the last of the things, if her majesty will kindly remove her butt."

Shelly walked over, picked up Emma, and began talking to her.

"And what kind of a day have you had, Emma?"

Sandy answered for her. "A busy one. There's a dead gopher under the bed."

Shelly turned to look at Sandy. "That sounds like the present tense . . . or did you clean it up?" Her voice was skeptical.

"Hell, no. I left it for you." Sandy made a disgusted face. "You know how that stuff creeps me out."

"My poor fragile woman." Shelly walked over to Sandy, putting Emma down. She punched at Sandy playfully. Sandy ducked and laughingly grabbed Shelly's waist from her position on her knees. She pulled Shelly down. "Come here. I'm going to miss you."

"Sure. Who's going to kill whatever bugs you find in the tub?"

Sandy played with Shelly's hair. She lifted the short strands at the nape of her neck and watched them fall back into place. "No. I'm serious. Three days. That's a long time."

"I would think not long enough, if you really want to get a taste of what it's like to be a single woman again," Shelly said sarcastically.

"Damn it, Shelly, I thought we had gotten that straightened out." Sandy shook her head in frustration. "You know I'm all talk. It's you I love and you I want to be with. And I'm such a swinger that I can't even imagine not seeing you for three days."

Shelly's voice softened. "There'll be plenty to do at the conference. Lots of people you haven't seen for a long time."

"I know. But I still wish you were done at school."

Shelly nibbled on Sandy's ear lobe. Her voice was somewhat muffled. "Me too. But I'll join you on Friday and then we'll have eight days together for that romantic vacation you've been promising for the last year."

"Says who. I noticed that stack of books you got ready for the trip." She nodded to a pile on the counter. "How are we going to be romantic with all those books to read?"

This was an issue of contention between them. Shelly was a reader. Sandy, needing escape when she came home, often put on the TV. Since they liked to be physically close at night, this presented a problem. Shelly thought they watched too much TV. Sandy felt jealous of Shelly's books.

"I love the books. And I love you. There's no conflict."

They both smiled at Shelly's intelligent use of diplomacy and enjoyed a long gentle kiss. Shelly was just starting to get into it when Sandy jumped up, remembering she was supposed to be efficient. Shelly was startled, the way she often was with Sandy, who bolted from one mood to another without any apparent strain.

Shelly watched Sandy continue to pack, her brow furrowed as she concentrated on making sure she had included everything on her list. Sandy's energy never ceased to amaze Shelly. One hundred percent involvement with whatever she did. Sandy never permitted herself to be distracted by the many things that were constantly disrupting Shelly's attention: the cats wanting petting, a series of interesting images or thoughts, the dishes to be washed, a forgotten memory, a book that caught her eye. Which reminded Shelly, she had forgotten to buy film for the trip. She got up to put that on the list she was keeping so she wouldn't forget anything. Except that she hardly paid any attention to the list. List-making was a habit she had picked up from Sandy, but like a plant transported to foreign soil, it never quite blossomed as it had in the old country. Shelly laughed to herself at the thought of Sandy being a representative of the old country; she had never met anyone less interested in ritual or custom. Sandy didn't care much about the past. Did something work now? If not, well, back to the real business of living.

This whole question of attraction was still a mystery to Shelly. Sometimes she thought she and Sandy had so little in common, they were almost extreme opposites. At other times she was sure Sandy was the only person in the world who saw things from exactly the same perspective as she.

Shelly reminded herself that there were things she should be doing and this was no time to wonder why and how they had chosen each other. Sighing, she picked herself up and began to pack her books in her battered green tote bag.

31

Rush-hour traffic had not started yet, and they zipped by the endless gasoline stations, supermarkets, and fast-food places that lined Lincoln Boulevard on the way to the airport. When Sandy first came to Los Angeles, she was overwhelmed by the ugliness of that part of Santa Monica, with its flat buildings thrusting their signs toward the boulevard, clamoring for attention in a very aggressive way. She had heard that L.A. was plastic, but now she understood just what that meant.

For the first year Sandy rode the buses, occasionally hitching when she had to get somewhere promptly. She had loved riding back and forth to the university. It was the only time she was able to lose herself totally, to be completely unself-conscious. The streets and people would flash by as if in a kaleidoscope, a constant blur of complex motions. When the bus stopped at a red light, Sandy would stare at the people with unabashed curiosity. If she had ever done that on the subway, she would have gotten her ass kicked in. But on the bus she was invincible.

Off the bus, she was alone, hurt, and scared. The pain of losing Jenny had become less intense, but she still spent many days wandering by the beach, or sitting in front of the TV. "Star Trek" was her favorite program then. She religiously made sure to get home by 6, and she watched all the repeats, as well as the few episodes she had missed the first time around. The competent and fearless captain, the analytic and emotionless Spock: no wonder she had been drawn to these characters. They were such simple and pure symbols, so comforting to her confused mind. Then, in her third year of graduate school, she met Shelly.

They met in a gay center and talked for hours. Sandy was immediately impressed by Shelly's intelligence and thoughtfulness. There was something very special about the warmth of her voice, the softness and roundness of her body, the generosity of her eyes. By the end of that evening, Sandy knew that she was in love with Shelly.

During their first two years together, the intense intimacy that they shared shattered every conceivable barrier between them. They spent every free moment, and some that weren't free, in passionate lovemaking or in long flowing talks that unraveled the mysteries of their lives. Sandy discovered that there was nothing she could not say to Shelly, that there were no parts of herself that she had to hide for the sake of this remarkable love. Old nightmares, some from past relationships, others of unknown origin, haunted Sandy, reminding her that such happiness could never last. She lived in a state of joy, but also in terror that someone or something would steal this most precious experience from her life.

From the very beginning their lovemaking was extraordinary. After the initial hesitation and shyness, they discovered that their bodies were like two finely tuned instruments of full and resonant tone, always in perfect harmony. In the beauty of their lovemaking, Sandy discovered an enigmatic sadness in herself. She sobbed uncontrollably, as Shelly held her and rocked her until she simply had no energy left for weeping. They analyzed everything and came up with many brilliant explanations for Sandy's pain. And yet the circumstances of her life did not seem to explain

111

entirely this intense sorrow; it was as if her own individual pain had tapped into a larger, almost impersonal source.

Somewhere in their second year together, the tumultuousness of Sandy's emotions began to abate. She finished her dissertation, and the pressures of graduate school drew to a close. For the first time in her adult life, Sandy felt no anxiety or distress.

The next couple of years were among the best she'd ever known. It was a peaceful time, a time of healing. Sandy increased the hours of her private practice, but made sure she never worked more than four days a week. Shelly's job at the university, although demanding, still permitted flexible hours, and they spent a great deal of time together. During this period, Sandy developed an inner confidence that changed the way she related to the world. She became much softer in her interactions with people; and she even gained some weight, one sign of the rounding off of her sharp edges. She refined her therapy skills and became in her own eyes a damned good clinician. Both she and Shelly were increasingly active in feminist and lesbian political groups. Now that Sandy was finished with graduate school, she felt free to come out publicly in any way she wanted. It was a utopian time.

Sandy didn't know exactly when the restlessness began, but she had been aware of it, on and off, for a few years. And with the restlessness came a desire to have an affair. Like most people, Sandy had always assumed that when someone in a couple wanted to have an affair, it meant that there was probably something wrong with the relationship. But she was still deeply in love with Shelly, and she couldn't imagine a better relationship. She had never felt so contented and safe as she did now.

Sandy couldn't help wondering if there wasn't a perverse streak in her after all. For years she had been searching for a stable and loving relationship, and now that she had attained that goal, she found herself growing nostalgic for the wild, loose, carefree days of college, when relationships were anything but stable.

More ridiculous still, Sandy couldn't even think of anyone she wanted to have an affair with. It was an abstract desire that seemed to have nothing to do with an actual woman.

She brought up the whole issue to Shelly, who was threatened and upset, and they spent several months talking about it. Shelly didn't like the idea, and Sandy agreed it probably wouldn't work.

But still, the fantasy kept returning. Sandy didn't know how not to tell Shelly about these feelings when she had them, and Shelly began to get annoyed. She was tired of hearing Sandy complain, and at some point she said, "Just go ahead and do it already!" Shelly's permission immediately killed the desire, and Sandy concluded that she had probably just been testing the limits. But after about six months the fantasies came back again, and Sandy felt closer to action. All she needed was a promise that Shelly wouldn't get too upset and that their relationship wouldn't be ruined. Shelly said, rightfully, "That's a crock of shit. You're going to have to take responsibility for your own choices."

But taking responsibility was exactly what Sandy didn't want to do. Between her work, which demanded that she always respond maturely and sensitively to her clients, and her public political activities, which demanded that she conduct herself as a model lesbian, Sandy was growing tired of responsibility. She wanted to be free, uncomplicated, and even irresponsible if she damn well pleased. That was part of the allure of an affair. The problem was that all of the women Sandy knew who had experimented with non-monogamy now had more headaches than ever. Consequently, Sandy set about making careful calculations to minimize the risks involved.

She tried to figure out who the perfect woman would be, so that the situation would not become too sticky. The woman obviously couldn't be a friend or even an acquaintance, because Shelly would not want to socialize with her. A single woman wasn't a good bet, as she might fall in love with Sandy or want more than Sandy could offer. But if the woman was in a committed relationship and looking for an affair, it probably meant that she and her lover were having troubles. And Sandy didn't want any part of that; she dealt with troubles all day at the office. So, it had to be a woman who was in a happily committed couple, and whose lover would not be jealous. (Sandy didn't want to feel guilty about causing another sister any pain.) But why would a woman let her lover have an affair if they were happily committed, unless she wanted an affair? Sandy noted that Shelly was an exception to this rule, but then Shelly was an exception to most rules, and it was highly improbable that Sandy would run into a woman who had a lover like hers. So, Sandy was looking for an unknown woman who was in a happily committed couple, in which both women had decided it would be interesting and growth-producing to have outside affairs.

Unfortunately, in the last seven years Sandy had been attracted to only three women, and none of them fit her rapidly narrowing eligible category. And even if she could find such a woman, she still had to deal with the unfair imbalance, that she would be having an affair and Shelly wouldn't. This made her feel tremendously guilty, so for a while she tried to convince Shelly to have an affair too. But Shelly insisted she didn't want to sleep with anyone else, and furthermore, she quite accurately pointed out that Sandy would not like it. In fact, when it came to Shelly, Sandy was irrationally jealous.

At this point, Sandy began to wonder whether she was ready for an affair at all. Her fantasies up to then had focused on getting to know some woman over a period of time, becoming attracted, and finally sharing a passionate kiss by the ocean at sunset. But now Sandy tried to imagine what it would be like actually to make love with another woman. She would visualize them getting into bed and kissing. Then the other woman would start to unbutton Sandy's blouse, and Sandy would burst into tears. Unable to stop crying, Sandy would get out of bed, put on her shoes, and apologize profusely to the bewildered woman: it was nothing personal, she just felt too guilty to go through with it. Then she would drive home, tell Shelly what she had done, and spend the rest of the night sobbing in Shelly's arms.

This fantasy was discouraging to Sandy. She liked to think of herself as a liberated woman, and she didn't really believe in sexual fidelity. In fact, in earlier years she had often had multiple relationships, and she had never thought of herself as a particularly jealous or guilt-ridden person. But Shelly was the first committed lesbian she had gotten involved with, and the first woman who was willing to make as deep a commitment as Sandy wanted. And that had changed everything around. The only other time Sandy had felt insanely jealous and loyal had been in her first love affair, with Jennifer Chase. But she had had to bury those feelings quickly, or be driven insane under the circumstances.

Now Sandy began to see that she was not really interested in a casual affair, although she knew that would be the easiest and most practical. She had no desire for casual sex. What she wanted was to fall in love again. It seemed that she was going through a mid-life crisis of sorts. It wasn't that she feared getting old; if anything, she found older women more appealing. But she had missed the romance and intense passion that had been present in the first few years of her relationship with Shelly, and throughout her relationship with Jenny.

She found herself wondering, for the first time in years, what had happened to Jenny. The last time she had seen her was at Jenny's wedding, shortly after they both started graduate school. Sandy wondered whether Jenny had panicked and grabbed the first nice guy who came along. In any case, the wedding was an awful experience for Sandy, and she never heard from Jenny again.

Sandy still missed the idealism and youthful exuberance of her affair with Jenny. She knew she was probably romanticizing the past, but she remembered it as a time of unparalleled innocence and excitement.

Once she realized that she was just trying to recapture the past, she gave up all notions of having an affair. But at times, she still felt an urge to be somewhere new by herself. After all, in the past four years, she and Shelly hadn't been separated for even one night. So Sandy casually suggested that it might be a nice change of pace if she went to the conference alone. But unbeknownst to Sandy, Shelly had been reading books about Hawaii and looking forward to a romantic vacation for the two of them after Sandy's presentation. Shelly was terribly hurt that Sandy didn't seem to want to vacation with her. The fact the the conference was also around the time of their anniversary added insult to injury.

It had taken some convincing to get Shelly to believe that Sandy loved the idea of a romantic holiday; then they agreed that the trip would be their anniversary present for each other. That was that, until today. Sandy looked over at Shelly to see if she seemed uptight or angry. Shelly was staring out the window with her far-away look. That was normal enough. Sandy made a mental note to buy something special for Shelly in Honolulu.

The airport was a madhouse, as usual. Shelly imagined what an aerial photograph of the place would look like. Actually, a silent movie would capture the scene more closely: little figures jumping in and out of odd moving vehicles. If one was far enough away, the figures and cars would blend together and probably appear like ants scurrying to important business that was always happening somewhere else.

Shelly often imagined what different Earth customs and situations would look like to foreign beings — not just foreign, but aliens from another world, a civilization that did not share the common human assumptions. No doubt they would see Earthlings as bizarre. For if Shelly found it all bizarre at times and she shared the assumptions, one could only speculate at how silly this frenetic motion would seem to a real outsider. But then, who was to say that they would be any less frenetic? That was the optimist's dream: a more mature and sophisticated civilization was out there somewhere that would positively influence the savages on Earth. Besides — how did she know they would find Earth silly? Maybe they wouldn't even have a sense of humor.

She was suddenly self-conscious. She took a quick glance to see whether Sandy was staring at her. Sandy could never understand how Shelly didn't see that bargain sign in the store-front window, or notice the gorgeous sportscar four lanes over. She would say, "Were you spaced out again?" Shelly would nod, as she didn't want to waste her breath trying to explain to Sandy that she hadn't been "spaced out." (God, how she hated that phrase; it was a perfect example of the way the language was being destroyed by inaccurate and inane expressions.) Sandy couldn't understand not being conscious of one's environment at all times. Maybe that was because she had grown up in the city, vigilant against potential attackers who could come out of nowhere for no apparent reason. For Shelly, the outside world also seemed a danger, but her way of coping had been to ignore it. Why worry about something that you couldn't control and that might not happen anyway? Besides, if you didn't look, you wouldn't see many of the things that might bother you, and so not looking was one of the best protections. They often argued this point, with Sandy trying to convince Shelly that the best protection came from knowing reality and trying to deal with it as effectively as possible.

This line of thought was abruptly interrupted, as Sandy maneuvered the car into a small space that had opened up in front of the baggage check-in. She looked proud of herself as she gave a guy in a big American car the bird for honking her when she crossed his lane to get the space. Sandy never seemed intimidated by the larger cars she shared the roads with. If anything, she felt she had more of a right on the roads, as the big cars hogged so much space all the time. They were like men: their mere presence made you feel your space was shrinking as they moved around, freely ignoring the smaller things in their environment.

Shelly stepped out of the car, grabbing one of Sandy's suitcases. The two women stood on the curb and looked at each other.

Shelly broke the silence. "Call me when you arrive."

Sandy nodded and walked over to her. They embraced, arms tightly wound around each other, faces buried in each other's neck. Sandy loved the smell of Shelly's neck; it reminded her of leather, her favorite smell. Other people would look at a shoe closely before trying it on; Sandy would sniff at it first to make sure it had a good leather smell. If it didn't smell good, she wouldn't buy it. Now she nuzzled in Shelly's neck, knowing she wouldn't have access to that smell for several days.

Passers-by took quick startled glances as the two women embraced in the front of the terminal. Several people did double takes when they realized that both lovers were women. But the two women were oblivious to this attention. It hadn't always been that way. There was a time when Sandy was afraid even to link arms in the street. Shelly had told Sandy that the women in Europe did it all the time and it didn't mean anything. But Sandy had retorted that this wasn't Europe and it did mean something and others would be able to see it too. Over the years, both women had grown comfortable with being lovers in public. At least most of the time.

They separated slowly. The noise of the airport traffic was persistent.

"Models of independence, aren't we?" Shelly smiled.

Sandy laughed fully. "I love you."

Shelly reached over and kissed Sandy delicately on the lips. Then she turned around, walked to the car, and got in. Sandy didn't want to watch her drive away, so she quickly picked up her bags and entered the terminal.

116

32

The airplane ride was typical. The usual businessmen compulsively made passes at the stewardesses; a couple of tourists drank a lot and got rowdy on the plane; the enraged father of a screaming infant kept telling the mother to control her child; a young hippie couple went back to the bathroom several times, giggling, getting stoned; a pilot, with the required deep masculine voice, told jokes nobody laughed at.

Actually, the woman who sat next to Sandy was very nice. She lived on the main island and had been visiting her married daughter in Los Angeles. They talked about smog and traffic, and the woman recommended some remote places for Sandy to explore on Maui.

It was the leaving of the airplane that upset Sandy and put her in this bad mood. As she exited from the plane, standing on top of the stairs, she watched a drunk middle-aged man kissing and pawing one of the young Hawaiian women who greeted the passengers as they stepped off the plane. The woman had placed a lei around his neck and was now trying to disengage herself politely; his wife stood by awkwardly, taking quick looks at her husband, then looking away.

Sandy felt disgusted and angry as she walked down the steps. Standing in line at the Tropical Rent-A-Car booth, she told herself not to be silly. There was no point in getting upset. But she couldn't seem to control it. No matter where women went, they were always put in that double-bind situation. If you got angry or acted insulted, you might get hit or at least yelled at. If you were sweetly polite, you felt like a coward, a hypocrite.

A woman she knew had been at a singles bar just a few weeks ago. A man had asked her to dance, and when she politely refused, he hauled off and slugged her. Even when you were polite, you weren't necessarily safe. The threat was always there.

The area surrounding the hotel was chaotic; cars and taxis were jammed everywhere. A huge blue and white banner waved from a canopy over the entrance. It read, "Welcome National Psychological Association." Sandy wondered whether the people who lived here paid any attention to the conventions. Did they see differences among the psychologists, dentists, teachers, and post office employees who gathered here? Sandy put her car into first gear and illegally used a lane to bypass the waiting cars, pulling into the parking lot under the hotel. She felt a twinge of guilt but told herself it was a small injustice.

After parking the car, she pushed her way through the crowd

of psychologists to the main desk. The drinking had already started. As Sandy moved forward, a woman bumped into her and spilled her drink on Sandy's jacket. She apologized profusely. Sandy furiously opened her mouth to tell her off and then thought better of it. She knew it wasn't just the drink. The image of that guy pawing the woman had stayed with her. That's where her anger belonged.

Now, as she picked up her key and took the elevator to her room, Sandy mumbled to herself. Her lips moved ever so slightly as she cursed herself for coming to this damned convention. She hated conventions. Especially the national ones. Everyone was so pompously academic. It was as if they didn't know how to speak English when they gave their presentations, each one trying to outdo the other to see who could be more incoherent. An understood maxim was that: The less understandable your presentation the more intelligent you must be. And then there was the politicking. The big boys would get together for their annual business meetings and discuss the state of their profession. A few women had been let into these higher echelons, primarily to soothe egos if tempers flared.

Sandy walked to the bathroom to check for towels (to get her money's worth), then looked in the empty closets and around the room to make sure no one was there. She didn't really expect anyone to be there, but it was an old habit, and it certainly didn't hurt to be safe. She collapsed on the bed and reached for the phone. She'd only been gone for a few hours. She couldn't miss Shelly already. That would be disgustingly dependent. Sandy thought about it for a moment and decided she was disgustingly dependent. Shelly not only was good company, but she helped Sandy face the insanity around her. They did that for each other. If Shelly had been there, she would have put her arm on Sandy's shoulder, they would have exchanged a look of disgust, and Sandy would have felt some validation for her feelings. But to the rest of the world she was a crazy woman, upset by everyday things that average people would never think about. A drunk man being a little too affectionate. What was the harm? How could you explain to them that it was one more instance of the mentality that raped and brutalized women, that abused children, that created "dirty jokes" as a euphemism for woman-hating, that forced women to live in a state of perpetual fear, and that, worst of all perhaps, made women feel guilty and soiled, as if somehow they were responsible for the lewdness and humiliation that were continually directed against them. Sandy liked that last thought. It had a melodramatic ring to it. Maybe she should use something like that in her presentation. She picked up the phone and hoped Shelly was home.

33

Although the cocktail lounge was very crowded, Sandy noticed the small group as soon as she entered. They were standing off to one side of the bar, a little self-consciously, as if they sensed they didn't fit in with the rest of the room. Barbara, Jan, and a woman Sandy didn't recognize wore the customary three-piece tailored suit. Julie and Pat were dressed more casually, like Sandy, in a blouse and pants. Margo was a knockout in a red and white caftan, and Catherine looked very much the part of an English professor in a bright multi-colored dress from South America with long shell beads and feathered earrings. "A handsome motley bunch of women," Sandy thought. Walking over to the bar, she ordered a whiskey sour. She didn't like hard liquor very much, but she had acquired a taste for whiskey sours at all the bar mitzvahs she attended as a teenager.

Julie, a tall redhead in her mid-thirties, was the first to notice Sandy standing at the bar. She broke into a big smile, walked over, and gave Sandy a hug. Their arms still around each other, they walked back to the group. Sandy noticed several people stare, then look away when she stared back. Gawkers. She reminded herself that this was another reason she hated coming to conventions: most of her colleagues were jerks.

Sandy hugged Barbara, a good friend who was a New Yorker and Jewish, and then kissed Jan on top of her dark curly hair. Jan was Italian and from Philadelphia. She had grown up in a poor neighborhood, and her strong working-class consciousness endeared her to Sandy, even though Jan was an "old dyke" and was constantly saying offensive things. Her latest *mischugas* was to try to get her friends to call her "Rocky," after the "Italian Stallion." Of course, none of the women would do it.

Margo reached over and kissed Sandy on the cheek. She was a strikingly beautiful woman, tall and stately, of West Indian origin. In the last few years, her hair had started to gray, making her Afro an astounding blend of dark and light. Sandy bent to kiss Catherine, who turned her cheek and puckered her lips. Catherine was a weird bird, a combination of romantic spirit and self-proclaimed lay analyst. Sandy had never quite figured out how to relate to her, but she assumed there must be something worthwhile hidden under the pretentious gushing; after all, Catherine was Margo's lover, and Sandy respected Margo a great deal. Pat gave Sandy a warm hello and introduced her to Dolores, the woman she hadn't recognized, who was from Northern California. Sandy didn't know Pat very well, but there was something about her that she liked and trusted. Maybe it was Pat's down-to-earth honesty or her hearty enthusiasm that often made Sandy smile.

"You just arrive?" Julie asked as she put her arm around Sandy and squeezed her close. She and Sandy had gone to graduate school together. They had both more-or-less fallen in love with the same guy. Naturally, he had turned out to be gay. When they finally compared notes and discovered he had been reciting the same malarkey to both of them, they forgot about the guy and became best friends. Over the years, as Sandy became more certain of her lesbian identity and Julie had a series of affairs with men Sandy found creepy, their friendship slackened. Then, about a year ago, Julie had an affair with a woman. Sandy still didn't know quite what that meant. But despite the distance between them, there was always a warm camaraderie when they saw each other.

"Guess what we were just discussing," Barbara said with a wry smile.

"The Briggs Amendment," Sandy replied, holding the fingertips of her right hand to her head, as mediums often did.

"Hey, how did you know that?" Jan exclaimed in surprise.

"One of the first criteria for acceptance into a clinical psychology program is clairvoyance. Didn't anyone ever tell you, Jan?" Margo's sarcasm was droll.

"Is that why you became an experimental psychologist?" Sandy retorted. "When you discovered you weren't clairvoyant, you took second best."

Margo laughed. She was the only academician in the group, and she and Sandy had a longstanding dispute over the relative contributions of their fields. Margo thought clinical psychologists were flaky, and she called Sandy the "High Priestess" to imply that Sandy was practicing religion, not science. Sandy, on the other hand, thought most experimental psychologists were rigid and uptight types who reduced human experience to a quantitative denominator that their concrete and non-introspective view of the world could accommodate. In each woman's mind, however, the other was an exception to the rule, and this enabled them to tease each other.

"No, I'm serious, Sandy," Jan persisted impatiently. "How did you know what we were talking about?"

"I overheard something about orange juice when I was standing at the bar," Sandy said. "It wasn't a difficult deduction, given the times."

"My favorite drink used to be a screwdriver," Catherine complained, "but you know they use Florida orange juice at all the bars. What a sacrifice we make for our politics."

"Did you ever try drinking the California orange juice?"

Barbara made a face. "I gave some to Marian the other day, and she said, 'Gee, that's funny-tasting grapefruit juice.'" The women laughed.

"The sacrifices are just beginning, if that damned bill passes," Dolores said angrily. "I know women who are starting to arm themselves."

"What?" Catherine's voice sounded shocked. "What for?"

"Because we will fight before we'll let them put us in detention camps." Dolores was dead serious.

Catherine looked around the group for support. The other women were quiet. "It could never happen here. I don't want to sound corny, but this is America. There are some elements of justice."

"Tell that to all the women who are in jail serving five-year sentences for bouncing checks to supermarkets to feed their children." Jan was angry now.

"That really isn't quite the same point," Margo said in defense of Catherine. "Whether it's compassionate or not, a crime was committed."

"Tell that to the Japanese-Americans who were imprisoned in our great state of California 35 years ago," Pat added quietly.

"But that was during a war," Catherine said.

"You don't think we're in a war now . . ." Dolores began.

Barbara interrupted her: "Margo, in most states homosexuality is still a crime." The group was silent.

Sandy broke the silence. "Shelly and I have talked about it. I think we've basically come to the decision that we'll leave the country if things get too bad. Go to Canada, I guess."

"You're really taking this seriously?" Margo was now shocked.

"Prohibiting homosexual teachers from working was one of the first repressive steps the Nazis took," Julie said. "Who's to say it couldn't happen here?"

"Women are freaked out," Sandy continued. "I see it in my practice. Women come in and they're scared. Even the non-political ones. But it's the Jewish lesbians who are really panicked. They talk about concentration camps for gays. It's very real for them." Sandy shook her head. "Them. It's very real for us."

"That fucking Gospel-preaching asshole. She's really affected our lives," Jan said bitterly.

"Well, I don't think Anita realized how much this campaign was going to affect her life either," Pat said. "She can't get her hair done anywhere now." The women snorted with laughter. The tension was broken.

"I guess we should thank her in a way," Barbara said. "Nothing has ever mobilized the gay community more than her Campaign to Save the Children."

"Did you see the slogan the Parents and Friends of Gays have come out with?" Sandy said. "Save our children — from Anita

Bryant and the others like her who want to deprive our children of their civil rights."

"Oh, that's dynamite." Jan laughed appreciatively. "Well, we're going to give those pious bastards a run for their money."

"I really don't understand what the fuss is about. We're hardly a new phenomenon," Catherine said. "We've been around at least as long as recorded history."

"But we've never come out in large numbers before and demanded that society deal with us," Pat argued. "It was okay when we were a few flamboyant individuals adding a little color to the monotony of heterosexual life."

"That's exactly right, Pat." Dolores put her hand on Pat's shoulder. "The threat is political."

"Let's not forget the psychodynamic factors," Barbara interrupted. Sandy smiled in anticipation. Barbara had gone to graduate school during the early 60's, and her orientation and training were traditionally analytic. She had modified her theory some to include a feminist perspective, but she was still basically Freudian in her approach and would thus focus on the intrapsychic factors in homophobia.

"All people have gay feelings," Barbara continued. "Highly homophobic straights probably have more gay feelings than other heterosexuals, and thus have to defend against those feelings more strongly by overcompensating in their disgust and anger towards gays. The primary mechanism is fear, fear of the emergence of their own repressed feelings."

"You have a point, but I think it's a lot simpler than that," Pat said with a smile. Pat's usual role in such heady discussions was to simplify things humorously. She had no patience with excessive intellectualization. It wasn't that she lacked intelligence — the subtlety of her anecdotes often knocked Sandy on her ass — but she didn't have the propensity to verbal abstractions that characterized the academically trained members of the group. She was an ex-alcoholic who ran a peer counseling program for women. Sandy had never seen her work, but she was sure Pat was fantastic.

Now Pat offered her tongue-in-cheek analysis. "You see, gayness is contagious. It's like a social disease." Barbara was shaking her head and laughing. She also got a kick out of Pat's outrageousness. "So you better watch which toilet seat you sit on, 'cause you never know who was there before you." Pat pulled on her ear lobe for serious effect. "Us queers, are the American . . ." she hesitated for a moment, "what do you call those guys in India — the untouchables?"

"Pariahs," Catherine volunteered.

"Any relationship to Elliot Ness?" Jan joked.

"Jan, that was awful."

"Who asked you, Dolores? Well, I might as well throw in

122

my two cents," Jan said. Sandy waited for what was bound to be a socialist analysis of the problem. Despite her adolescent style, Jan was very astute about people and power. She divided the world between the haves and the have nots. Without labeling herself along any political dimension, she would often gravitate to a near-Marxist perspective.

"They're afraid that more people will choose to be gay if it becomes acceptable," Jan went on.

"Which doesn't fit into the propaganda that their life style is more satisfying or that God is on their side," Julie intercut. "If they really believed heterosexuality was so much more appealing, then why are they worried that exposure to even one gay role model is going to undermine the conditioning of the entire American fabric?"

"That tells you how strong the fabric is," Dolores added sarcastically.

"Well, my point is," Jan interrupted excitedly, "that the straights are afraid their life style will become a minority and they will no longer be holding the reins."

"That's not very likely," Margo contended.

"Then why are they so uptight?" Jan argued back. "I think it is because they are afraid if we get power, we will do to them exactly what they have done to us all these years."

"From a sociological perspective, that certainly does seem to be the fear of the majority group," Julie commented. "Giving blacks and women the vote in this country ran up against the same opposition, although it was often disguised in less blatant terms. What's happening now in South Africa is another example, although the ruling class in that situation was always the minority. Look at the fears in the white community: that the women will be raped, the men murdered, and all of the survivors shuttled off to a white ghetto and forced to live in subhuman conditions. Those are exactly the realities that blacks live with now under white rule!"

"We don't have to go to South Africa to see that principle in action," Dolores remarked. "Just look at Southern California and the Chicanos. We're the fastest growing minority in this state and we will be the majority by 1985. You don't think that's got the *gringos* scared? All of a sudden the politicians are showing up in the *barrio*. They think we're stupid Mexicans, we'll forget the years of humiliation. But we remember who our friends are." Dolores delivered this last prediction with considerable resentment. There was an awkward silence. She had hit too close to home.

"Hey, you've been awful quiet, Sandy, what do you think?" Jan asked, trying to change the subject.

"Sandy's been playing therapist so long she's forgotten how to talk," Barbara quipped with a smile. In the group, they were the only two committed to the anachronism known as individual therapy. They were both socially quiet women and often teased each other about the primary hazard of being a psychotherapist: chronic muteness.

"Thanks, friend." Sandy acknowledged Barbara with a formal bow. "Well, the only point of view still unexpressed is the feminist analysis that sees nontraditional sex roles as the primary threat to patriarchy." Sandy cleared her throat. "What I'd like to know is why this analysis has been forgotten by such a staunch group of feminists." She surveyed the group with mock disapproval.

"It's not that we forgot about it," Julie said quickly. "It's just that we were saving it for last so it would have its proper place."

"The grand finale," Barbara supplied.

"Exactly," Julie said, looking pleased with herself. "And besides," she made a grandiose wave of her arm in the direction of Sandy, "we were saving it for you."

"Touché." Catherine lifted her glass.

"What do you think, I'm crazy?" Sandy noticed her voice take on more of a New York inflection, as it did when she was excited or embarrassed. Right now she was acutely uncomfortable, from all the attention. "Who would say anything after an introduction like that? I know when to keep my mouth shut."

"Oh, come on, Sandy," Catherine urged, "entertain us in the great spirit and tradition of Sappho, Colette, Vivien . . ."

"I'm entertaining you bums tomorrow," Sandy said in her most definitive voice. "That's plenty for one week."

"Oh, I forgot all about that," Barbara cut in quickly. Sandy knew she was changing the focus and flashed her a grateful smile. "You all prepared?"

"I'll give it the once-over tomorrow morning. It's stuff I know, I'm just worried about whether I'll be eloquent." Sandy nodded in the direction of Catherine.

"You don't have to be eloquent, Sandy." Pat put her arm around Sandy's shoulders. "Just tell it like it is."

Marian, Barbara's lover, now joined the group. "Hi, all you gorgeous gals," she said as she hugged Sandy and Margo and walked over to Barbara's side.

"I haven't been called a gorgeous gal for some time," Pat said, amused but feigning ruefulness. Pat was in her early sixties, with thin graying hair and a lined face. She grew up in the South, the daughter of a trucker who got her hired to drive a rig when there were no women truckers at all. She'd been a lesbian all her life and could tell stories about the days back when. Sandy knew that when Pat was in her twenties, she had driven supply trucks up in the Yukon. She had lived with a prostitute who was killed by a john. After that Pat bummed across the country, becoming jack of all trades and getting involved with a lot of

124

different kinds of women. Fifteen years ago she sobered up with AA, and for the last five years she had worked as an alcohol counselor.

"Oh, nonsense," Marian said, putting her hand on Pat's cheek and kissing her lightly. "I should only have a tenth of the number of friends you've had." The emphasis on the word "friends" made it clear she was talking about lovers.

"What's the status of 'gals,' anyhow?" Dolores asked Sandy. "Is it PI?" Sandy shrugged.

"What's PI?" Margo asked.

"Politically incorrect," Julie offered.

"Hey, where's Shelly?" Marian looked around the group as if she would discover Shelly hiding somewhere.

"She's not coming till Friday," Sandy said.

"Aha." Jan hit Sandy with her elbow. "What do you say we go out on the town and look for some action?"

The women groaned. Sandy was annoyed. She knew that Jan had recently separated from Mary, her lover of six years, and that Jan was very much upset and compensated for this by presenting herself as a superstud, but there was no need for comments like that.

"Come off it, Jan. Stop being obnoxious." Sandy tried to control her irritation.

Margo turned to Sandy. "To hear this woman talk, the exploits of Don Juan pale in comparison."

Dolores was looking skeptically at all five feet of Jan. "The last of the great lovers, huh?"

"Only by self-report," Sandy threw in.

"Hey, this is my reputation you guys are making fun of."

"Times have changed, Jan," Pat said with a twinkle in her eye. "I've cleaned up my act since the Women's Movement and if an old-time dyke like me can change, so can you."

Sandy saw that Jan was pouting. Jan had taken a lot of teasing lately and didn't quite seem to understand why. Sandy wondered whether she would have the same problem if she had been born ten years earlier. No, it wasn't simply a question of age. As Pat had pointed out, she had changed, and Sandy knew other women in their forties and fifties who had never been into role-playing. No, it wasn't age. It was a certain kind of rigidity.

"I think that would make an excellent toast, ladies," Julie said, raising her glass and putting an arm around Jan. "To the Women's Movement."

Jan raised her glass grudgingly along with the other women. "To the Women's Movement," they replied in unison.

Sandy took a long sip from her drink and felt the tension drain from her body. Her friends would make the next few days bearable. If the presentations got too stultifying, they would go out for dinner and talk. And what she would say to them would be understood and shared. Sandy felt relaxed for the first time since she got off the plane.

34

Sandy waited at the message desk. Her line, for the R's, S's, and T's, was the longest one in the hotel corridor. She looked at her watch. It was almost 5:00, and the presentation on child abuse was starting at 5:15. Sighing deeply, she fidgeted impatiently in place. The woman in front of her turned around.

"You'd think they'd have a separate line for the S's." The woman was in her late fifties, her dyed, reddish-blond hair neatly coiffed in a beehive. The kind of woman who had given Sandy a hard time in graduate school — always looking at her sandals or jeans in disapproval but never making an honest or direct comment. But now there was a note of camaraderie in this woman's voice. Sandy was obviously an equal now, another professional.

"They never do. That would take intelligence," Sandy replied angrily. Her anger was partly in response to the wait and partly in response to this woman, who reminded her of past supervisors, the supervisors who had insisted that Sandy was going through a stage, an extension of her adolescent rebellion, when she rejected their assumption that the therapist should be an authority figure, distant and professional. "I'm going to come back later. This is ridiculous," she said in an irritated voice.

She pushed her way through the other lines and headed back to the main lobby. Now why had she done that? She had spent minutes there, made an initial investment of her time. Was she trying to impress the woman that she, Sandy, would not waste her time in such a way?

Sandy now remembered exactly which supervisor the woman reminded her of: the intake supervisor at the Veteran's Hospital. The one who had told her that she was an excellent clinician, committed to her work, doing very well for a third-year student, but that she had to give her a B (in graduate school, one step from failing). And when Sandy asked why, the woman explained in a motherly tone that Sandy simply wasn't professional enough. Yet. When Sandy was done with school, however, she was sure that would change. What a bunch of crap. Sandy smiled to herself. There was no way she wanted to identify with such a pompous and archaic point of view, and a part of her was still stubborn enough to resist the mild association of standing in the same line. That childish part of herself had gotten her into a lot of trouble. But it also helped keep her honest.

As Sandy crossed the main lobby, she noticed a woman standing in the corner, reading a convention program. Sandy stopped and stared at her. It had been a long time; the hair was shorter, shoulder-length and fashionably styled, but it looked like Jenny. She felt her heart stop. She approached the woman hesitantly, hoping it wasn't Jenny. Hoping it was.

"Jenny? Jenny Chase?"

The woman looked up. There was no longer any doubt.

"Yes, that was my maiden name. Do I know you from somewhere?"

Sandy felt the smile tense on her face. "You might say that, Jennifer." She accentuated the name, the way she used to do when she was angry.

Jenny swallowed. She had always expected they would run into each other some day, but she hadn't been prepared for today. She hoped Sandy hadn't seen her swallow. Sandy looked so sure of herself.

"Sandy Stein? I don't believe it. Running into each other like this. God, how long has it been?" Somehow the words came out. They sounded natural enough. But she felt light-headed, and her voice was far away.

"Since the wedding. 1970, I believe."

"Eight years . . . and you look so different. Your hair is short, you never had it short . . . you just look so different. Put on some weight, I see. I didn't even recognize you." Jenny couldn't stop noticing how short Sandy's hair was. She had always liked Sandy's hair when it was long. This way it was — masculinizing.

Sandy stared openly at Jenny. Jenny was uncomfortable with that look. It spoke of past intimacies. She automatically reached for her cigarette case in the purse she had slung over her right shoulder.

"You here for the convention?" Jenny said, hoping to stop that look. But Sandy was still staring at her.

"Yeah, and then a short vacation on one of the islands."

Jenny fiddled with her case and lighter. She crumpled an empty pack and started to open a new one. That gave her some time to think. Barry was going to meet her in a moment. Sandy was older now. She would certainly have to be civilized.

"Are you here alone . . . or?" Jenny looked up questioningly.

There was a hint of a smile in Sandy's eyes, as if she had been able to follow Jenny's thoughts. Jenny had always hated that about Sandy. Her knowing looks, her quiet air of superiority.

"At the moment. My lover is going to join me in a couple of days. How about you?" Sandy looked at Jenny's wedding ring. "You here with your husband?" Sandy hoped she had said that casually. She had been worried she would choke on the word "husband." Friends had often criticized her inability or refusal to hide her feelings when necessary and make small talk. Who said she couldn't pretend and have a "normal" conversation?

"Yes, I'm here with Barry." So, Sandy had a lover. No ring,

127

so she had probably never gotten married. Maybe they should all have cocktails together. It could be interesting. Jenny finally pulled out a cigarette. She offered one to Sandy.

"No thanks, I don't smoke anymore."

"You're kidding. You used to smoke two packs a day. I never met anyone who enjoyed smoking more than you did." Jenny paused for a moment. "You don't have a child, do you?"

"No, why?"

Jenny sighed in relief. Why would Sandy's having a child upset her? This was no time to stew about it. "Because I remember how we used to say that cigarettes were killing us . . . and you said you loved smoking so much that you'd only quit if you had a child, if someone else's life really depended on you."

Sandy was quiet for a moment. There was a familiar quality to the way she got reflective. Jenny observed that Sandy was still attractive despite the haircut.

"Huh. It's funny. I stopped smoking just after Shelly and I got together. I guess for the first time I felt I had a strong stake in living." Sandy was surprised by the intimacy of her response. She thought to herself that she must be crazy to be vulnerable with this woman after all that had happened. And then it occurred to Sandy that what she had said might hurt Jenny, by implying that their relationship hadn't been very important. Was she still trying to hurt Jenny? To pay her back for those awful months? Awful years. Jenny did seem somewhat taken aback by that last remark. Bull's eye.

"Oh." Jenny recovered herself. "Well, is Shelly the guy you're going with now?" Sandy laughed. What the hell was so funny?

"Yes, Shelly is the person I'm living with, but she's not a guy. The Shelly is short for Michelle."

Jenny tightened. She could feel her jaw freezing and her shoulders going stiff. Her mind had that hazy blankness which came on whenever she was taken by surprise, and it made her feel uptight. So Sandy was with a woman. She should say something. Something cool. "Oh." Now why did she say that? Sandy would know she was uptight. She tried to think of something else to say, but nothing appropriate came to mind. The weather was always good in Hawaii.

There was an awkward silence. Sandy didn't know what to say either. Surely Jenny must have realized that Sandy was a lesbian? How could she not have known that? But she seemed genuinely surprised. This was crazy. They were acting like strangers.

Sandy noticed a man approaching them from across the lobby. It was Barry. He had lost some of his hair and had gained a small pot-belly. He was wearing a short-sleeved banlon shirt and a pair of bermudas, baggy around his thighs. He even had some of that white crap on his nose, the stuff that prevented peeling. Well, at least he looked a little more mature and self-confident than she remembered from the wedding. That initial shock of seeing him — a *schlubby* Jewish kid. This was the man Jenny was going to marry? Sandy noticed how awkwardly he made his way through the crowd. He must have been a poor athlete as a boy. Probably took a lot of ribbing from the other boys who were able to assume their expected roles more easily. Barry looked at Sandy as he walked up.

"Hi." He was friendly.

"Hi."

Jenny turned to Barry and put her hand on his arm. The unmistakable gesture of wife to husband.

"Honey, you remember Sandy Stein? My roommate in college."

Barry nodded. "Sure. I recognized her when I first saw her." He turned back to Sandy. "It's the way you stand." He was looking at her openly. More openly than Jenny had.

"Yes. I recognized you from your walk too." Sandy returned his stare. There was that mutual recognition of the other's importance. Sandy felt a tinge of respect for him. He really was a nice guy. Probably as decent as men got. At least Jenny hadn't ended up with one of those macho guys she used to date. Sandy turned to look at Jenny. She seemed confused by the way Sandy and Barry were interacting.

"Well, I should be going." Sandy had been polite, but there was no reason to overdo it. "I'm meeting some friends at a symposium. Maybe we could have a drink some time." It was clear the invitation was for Jenny alone.

"That sounds great. We have a lot to catch up on."

35

Sandy found herself pacing the narrow hotel room. There was no doubt about it. She was freaked out. It had taken a while to hit her. Initially, she had mused over the coincidence. Then she decided to skip the lectures; she wasn't really in the mood. She went back to her room, lay down on the bed, and, staring up at the gold-flecked stucco ceiling, ran through the conversation in her mind. Jenny seemed like a stranger. Sandy felt nothing in particular, mostly the separation and distance between them. Except she wanted a cigarette. That was the first tip-off something was wrong: only on rare occasions did she ever feel the urge to smoke anymore.

She decided to call Shelly. Shelly would really get a kick out of this situation. But no one was at home. Sandy got annoyed, then anxious. She felt off-center, like the first time she had worn a pair of Roots and her center of gravity had changed. It was then that she remembered Jenny's face — and realized that she was upset.

Jenny's face was as familiar to Sandy as her own. The shape of her nose, the color of her eyes, even the texture of her skin. Sandy knew every line and crease and mole and freckle on that face. It was as if the eight years of not seeing each other had never happened. As if she and Jenny were still connected by a bond that could never be severed. How could Sandy feel this connection in one moment and feel that Jenny was a stranger in the next? Sandy didn't know which experience scared her more. They both scared her.

She suddenly wondered whether Jenny was happy with Barry. Barry still seemed totally devoted to Jenny. At the wedding, Sandy had sensed that Jenny was already running the relationship. Barry was obviously more in love with her than she was with him. And unless Jenny had undergone a total personality change, an imbalance of power in her direction would at least result in her taking him for granted, and might result in her not valuing him at all. Not exactly the ingredients for a satisfying marriage. It wasn't that Sandy doubted that Jenny loved Barry; it was more a question of what *kind* of love she felt for him.

Sandy went to the window and looked out at the people on the crowded street below. From the eighth floor, they seemed very tiny and insignificant. If the ground opened up and swallowed them, she would feel pity but no real empathy. She wasn't connected to them. But if before they died, she went down there and talked with them, heard something about their lives, their concerns, their dreams, then she would feel sorrow when they died. Even a five-minute conversation might do it, might make the connection strong enough so she would experience their deaths as a loss. What was the bond that made us real for each other?

And what happened that those to whom we were closest were often the ones for whom we had the least empathy? She didn't wish bad things on strangers, but over the years she had often hoped that Jenny would get hers — that someone would do to her what she had done to Sandy. But that had never happened, because Jenny had picked a man who would never dump her. So, vengeance had come in an unexpected way to Jenny, a way that would have never occurred to Sandy ten years before. Jenny had settled for safety and its inevitable companions: boredom and mediocrity.

Sandy would have wished her a painful love affair in the unconscious equality of "an eye for an eye, a tooth for a tooth." But this current destiny that Jenny had chosen, or fallen into, lacked the passion of punishment, and for that very reason it made Sandy uncomfortable. A part of her might gloat that Jenny had gotten a fate worse than any Sandy had wished for her, and yet another part of Sandy was upset by Jenny's choice. How could Jenny go from what they had shared to this? It wasn't that Barry was a bad man. Sandy was sure he made an excellent husband. But it was impossible to imagine that life with Barry was exciting. Jenny must be restless.

Then again, who was Sandy to talk? In the last year or two she had also felt somewhat restless in her work, in her relationship with Shelly. Perhaps restlessness was a twentieth-century condition, a barometer of the existential crisis of the times. Not that it hadn't existed in earlier periods, but then each generation narcissistically assumed that its historical dilemmas were unprecedented.

Sandy realized that she was missing an important point in her current line of thinking, and rubbing her hand back and forth over the top of her head, she tried to relax and stimulate her scalp so that clarity would magically emerge. It was an old studying trick she had learned in college, and she still occasionally used it when her mind refused to release an idea.

Both she and Jenny were restless in their relationships, but Sandy was sure that there was a significant difference between the two of them. She knew she was less restless than Jenny, but it wasn't really a question of quantity. The difference was in the process by which they had arrived at this point. Sandy was coping with the inescapable realities of long-term relationships: with time, some of the romance and passion was bound to dissipate. No, not exactly dissipate, change. Jenny, on the other hand, had no real passion or romance with Barry in the first place. Sandy imagined that Jenny's restlessness had been there from the very beginning. But did it really matter how each of the women had gotten here, if now they were in the same place? And was it the same? Sandy sensed that the intensely ardent beginning of her love affair with Shelly had given their relationship a wholeness, even though some of the ardor had diffused into other regions. When she thought of her and Shelly together, she had an image of roundness, an egg-like form which was slowly transforming its shape in a continual process of change. Perhaps that was a key difference between her and Jenny. It wasn't that her restlessness was any more existentially meaningful than Jenny's, but rather that Jenny seemed stagnant, as if she had hit a road block and simply retraced her steps a few miles and set up camp.

Sandy went back to the bed and tried calling Shelly again. Still no answer. How would Shelly react to hearing that Jenny was at the conference? She'd probably be irritated and a bit threatened, and she'd deal with it by making a few snide comments. Shelly hated Jenny for hurting Sandy the way she had. She always said she couldn't understand how Jenny had given up such a prize as Sandy. Wait still she saw Barry. Shelly would think anyone who was stupid enough to give up Sandy for him didn't deserve Sandy in the first place. But then Shelly couldn't see how any woman would choose a man over a woman.

That was it. The missing question from her consciousness. The $64,000 question for tonight: Was Jennifer Chase Berkowitz heterosexual? Or was she really a lesbian who had run from women in fear?

Sandy laughed at herself. Such melodrama. "Tune in tomorrow for the next thrilling episode of 'As the World Turns Gay.'" She picked up her wallet and quickly left the hotel room. Maybe a walk along the ocean would do her good.

It was dark when she got outside. Sandy appreciated the darkness; she felt like being anonymous. She walked across the sand to the shoreline. Taking off her shoes, she continued along the water's edge. The water slowed her brisk pace. Conflicting feelings alternated insider her. Like an electric current. AC-DC. Someone in a Hollywood bar once said that about some woman. She was shocked that Sandy didn't know what the expression meant. The woman had great difficulty explaining it. "You know, AC-DC," she kept repeating. Finally she said, "Swings both ways." "Oh, you mean bisexual," Sandy said. "Yeah," the woman said, "AC-DC."

A shiver ran through Sandy's body. The evening breeze had suddenly turned cold. She stopped walking, took a deep breath, and looked out over the ocean. The deep breath didn't help her chill, and the constant lapping of the waves tonight had an irritating effect, rather than calming her as it usually did. She turned around and headed back to the hotel.

In the small bathroom sink, Sandy washed off the sand that clung to her feet, hiding between her toes. There was no reason for her to be upset. She was overreacting, as Shelly often said she did. Jenny was from her past, and the distant past at that. There was no way Jenny could hurt Sandy now, even if she wanted to, and she didn't have any reason to want to. After all, everything had gone her way. There were still some questions Sandy had never asked, or had never gotten satisfactory answers to, and this might be an ideal time to get those answers.

She wanted to know, was Jenny bisexual, or what? For the most part, Sandy thought bisexuality was a crock of shit. It wasn't that people weren't capable of relating sexually or emotionally to both sexes; most lesbians she knew had related to men at one time, and some heterosexual women had had significant relationships with women. It was the denial of a preference that was the crock. When it came right down to it, almost everyone preferred one type of relationship to the other. And in Sandy's experience, the great majority of women who called themselves bisexuals were in fact lesbians who were frightened of the oppression and contempt they might have to face if they accepted the label "lesbian." Those women said they didn't like labels. What they really meant was that they didn't like what happened to you if you took the wrong label. After all, there weren't many straights living in fear of being labeled heterosexual. Sandy was sure that Jenny thought of herself as a heterosexual. She didn't live in fear. But what was she really? Sandy stopped a moment before asking herself the next question. What did she want Jenny to be?

Sandy didn't like that question at all.

36

So Sandy was with a woman. Jenny knocked some of her ashes into the ashtray on the night table and leaned back against the cloth-covered headboard. She had been repeating that thought for hours. She would feel her entire body tighten, her teeth would start to grit, and then, shaking her head defiantly, she would free herself of that unpleasant thought. For a while. As long as she kept busy, she was okay. But as soon as she had a moment of quiet, she would find those words slipping back into her consciousness.

A three-quarter moon was casting a pale light across the green floral bedspread. The light was interrupted by the window shutter, which created a pattern of dark and light bars crossing the bed and her body diagonally. Jenny ran her index finger along one of the dark bars across her thigh. The smoothness of that skin surprised her. It was so soft, yet firm at the same time. She started to run her fingers up the slope of her thigh, stopping suddenly when Barry sighed in his sleep and turned over on his side, facing away from her. He was still sleeping soundly; Jenny had watched him on and off through the night. He looked so much younger in sleep, the fullness of his face reminding her of a child's baby fat, innocent and inexperienced. Sandy had put on some weight too. Her body wasn't quite as lean and firm as it had been in college. Her hips and breasts were fuller than Jenny had remembered, making her seem more womanly in figure, at the same time that her haircut and clothes made her appear more masculine.

Jenny put out her cigarette with a vehement twist, which pushed the ashtray against the lamp, making a loud bang. She held her breath and waited to see if that would wake Barry up. Usually when she was unable to sleep, she would find some way to awaken Barry and then would insist that he stay up to keep her company. But tonight she wanted to be alone, to listen to the quiet, to empty her mind of all thoughts and just sit and stare.

So Sandy was with a woman. So Shelly was a she. The image of Sandy's condescending smile flashed through her mind. That image made her want to punch Sandy in the face. Whenever she saw that smile, a deep rage flowed through her body. It felt irrational and wild, and that made Jenny very uncomfortable. There was no reason for her to get so upset. She didn't give a fuck who Sandy related to. If Sandy wanted to live that way, that was her business. She had just never outgrown it, the way Jenny had.

Jenny wondered what kind of woman Shelly was. Was she pretty or plain? More masculine than Sandy or more feminine? What did she do for a living? How was she in bed? Jenny observed herself as she went through this thought process: her fingers twirling her wedding band in a compulsive motion; her big toe wrapped around its buddy in a deathlike embrace; the train of thought ending with a predictable emphasis on sexuality. Freud certainly had a point.

Perhaps that was all there had ever been between her and Sandy. Adolescent passion. No one ever wrote books about that subject matter. It was commonly assumed that women didn't get excited about their sexuality until they were in their thirties and men had already passed their prime. That certainly wasn't true of her; she'd always been aware of her sexuality, and during that time when she and Sandy were roommates, the strength of it had often overwhelmed her. Jenny wondered if she was unusual in that way. She had never heard another woman talk about her early sexual experiences as passionate. Most women laughed when they described the awkward scenes in the backs of cars, the big letdown when he finally put it in, and then in a few moments it was all over. No, she couldn't think of any women who had had adolescent passion. Except for Sandy. Sandy and her.

She found herself standing by the shuttered window, with a cigarette in her hand that she couldn't remember lighting. This was ridiculous. She had rarely thought about Sandy over the years, a clear sign that Sandy hadn't been very important to her. She was just tired and grumpy. She rarely had trouble falling asleep, and tonight's insomnia was upsetting her more than she had realized. She looked at Barry, sound asleep.

Smiling to herself, she walked back to the bed, put out her cigarette, and sat down with a harsh bounce, pulling the covers over her. Barry's leg jerked a little, but it was clear she would have to take more drastic measures to wake him up. He would enjoy the novelty of a middle-of-the-night escapade, and she would be able to sleep afterwards.

She rearranged her pillow and leaned back against the headboard with a loud thump. Barry didn't move. Jenny took in a deep breath and exhaled loudly. Out of the corner of her eye, she saw that Barry hadn't stirred in the slightest. She felt an edge of irritation. He wasn't usually this insensitive to her moods. But she really wasn't being fair. If she wanted him to wake up, she should take the responsibility and just awaken him. Maybe he really needed his sleep. He had seemed very tired when he went to bed. And he was sleeping so peacefully. But she wasn't sleeping at all. And if she didn't get any sleep, she would be a real bitch tomorrow and ruin the day for both of them. That settled it. She leaned over his pillow and kissed him on the ear, and then on the top of his head.

"Barry . . . Barry." She fondled his hair.

"Huh."

"Are you awake?"

Barry turned onto his back and rubbed his eyes. "Uh . . . I guess so."

"Good. I'm horny."

Barry looked at her with confusion. Turning to the night table, he reached over and grabbed the travel alarm clock.

"Honey, do you know what time it is? We have to get up at . . ."

Rolling on top of him, Jenny moved her hips in a circular motion, grinding her pelvis against his. Barry put down the alarm clock, laughing. She could feel him start to harden. She was very much turned on tonight, and she didn't want to waste any time with preliminaries. Pulling her panties down around her ankles, she pulled out his erect cock and pushed it up into her vagina. Her fingers touched her crotch, and to her surprise, she found that she was already lubricated. She pushed down on him harder and harder each time, wanting to feel herself filled with his cock, enjoying the slight pain of the powerful thrusts. Barry stimulated her clitoris with a free hand, and she came immediately. They stopped fucking, and Barry looked at her in surprise. They both laughed. Barry's penis was still hard inside her. Pulling herself off him and lying by his side, she started to give him a hand job. Barry's hand stopped hers.

"Why don't you just come closer and let me hold you?"

Jenny slipped into his arms, resting her head against his chest. Suddenly she felt very tired. She drifted off to sleep.

Now Barry found himself unable to sleep. His left arm was going numb, yet he didn't want to move it for fear of waking Jenny up. Seeing Sandy had upset her more than she realized. That was the way Jenny dealt with things. She wouldn't let herself get upset immediately, and, telling herself she was fine, she would put off a reaction for days, sometimes weeks. Then, when she was ready, she would choose the time and place to deal with whatever was disturbing her. Barry had learned to let her have the time she needed. He would have preferred to talk about things more quickly, but he had learned over the years that there wasn't any point in rushing her.

Gently, he moved his arm out from under her head, letting the tapering of his arm cushion the drop to the bed. Jenny sighed in her sleep, then turned over, clasping her arms to her chest, her legs bent at the knee. Barry got out of bed and quietly walked to the bathroom, shutting the door and then turning on the light. There was something very satisfying about watching urine spurt out in a long clean arc, ending at the exact center of the bowl. As a boy he had often experimented with different distances, and he had gotten pretty good at it, able to control his muscles so that he could direct his piss all along the circumference of the toilet, making sure it never got on the seat, even when he was hitting a fraction of an inch away.

Barry had never been a very good athlete. In fact, he had been terrible; if it hadn't been for Wormface Wolowitz, his childhood would have been even more difficult than it was. Thanks to Wormface, he was never the last one to be picked for ring-o-levio or basketball, and that helped him to maintain a shred of dignity in the excruciating torture known as recess.

People often talked about wanting to return to the innocent joys and irresponsibilities of childhood. They acted surprised when Barry said he was mighty pleased to be an adult, to have survived the "joy and innocence" of childhood. Barry wondered if most people did have a fun-filled childhood or if they just for some strange reason denied the cruelties and injustices that children suffered at the hands of adults and other children. But he had never forgotten the taunting, the small humiliations, which he had tried to ignore but which hurt him so badly that at the age of eight he had developed terrible stomach pains. A pre-ulcerous condition at eight. Oh yes, the joys of childhood.

He remembered Sandy walking away from them, across the hotel lobby, moving easily through the crowd. There was a sureness and grace in the way she moved that identified her as an athlete. Barry had often envied the nonchalant self-confidence of other men: the way they sat in a chair with their long legs spread easily and loosely in front of them, or the way they leaned against a wall, the body just naturally assuming the correct pose to accentuate the tailored Arrow shirt they wore. Sandy was like those men. It wasn't that she was man-like. There was a definite woman-liness in her manner and her figure. But there was a similarity in the way she seemed at ease in her body, the knowledge that her torso would do what she wanted, could be counted on in emergencies, the reflexes ready, so that her muscles could now be relaxed and fluid, in full assurance that they could be mobilized at a moment's notice.

How different he and Sandy were from each other. Yet

Jenny picked them both as lovers. Jenny had dated some "men's men" in college, so maybe her tastes had changed with age. Besides, maybe what Jenny needed in a man was different from what she had liked in a woman. Sandy may have been athletic, but that was her only resemblance to the men Jenny had dated. There was a seriousness and an honesty to Sandy that he had seen the first time he met her at the wedding. He had liked her right away; there was something intriguing about her bluntness, her refusal to play the expected social games. Barry had hoped they might become friends, but Sandy clearly didn't want that. And neither did Jenny.

At the foot of the bed Barry stopped and gazed at the woman lying there, his wife. She was on her back now, one hand flung out across his side of the bed, her dark hair strewn across the light pillowcase in a wild array of textures. Women's hair was so different from men's. It seemed to have a sense of body, a fullness that was absent from the scrawny strands of most men's hair when they wore it long. In the early 70's Barry had tried to wear his hair moderately long, but it had stubbornly refused to look stylish, instead parting foppishly at the nape into three distinct clumps. Jenny told him to either get a haircut or start wearing a jester outfit to match his new image. He cut his hair the next day.

She was beautiful. Even with her mouth slightly agape and her body unnaturally twisted, she was still alluring to him. Even after all these years. Other men talked about being sexually bored with their wives, wanting to get some action on the outside, some "fresh pussy." It was as if a pussy got rank or tired with continued use, and they wanted to catch a fresh fish. Barry had never understood that. Of course he was occasionally attracted to other women; he was as human as the rest of them. But the idea of sex with a stranger wasn't appealing. There would be so many problems. Like not knowing what she wanted, and then what would you talk about afterwards? It didn't seem quite appropriate to make small talk after you had just fucked, but if you didn't know her, how could you do otherwise? It didn't seem worth the awkwardness or the hassle. Besides, he'd always been a pretty private person, and what was more private than sex? No, he would joke some with the other guys, and make his share of comments about some attractive lady at the office, but he wasn't really interested. It was Jenny he wanted.

Walking to his side of the bed, Barry gently pulled back the covers, lifting Jenny's arm just enough so he could slip into bed. Sighing, but not awakened, she turned over onto her side facing away from him. He sidled closer and rested his head in the hollow of her neck. With her hair nestling his cheek, he drifted off to sleep.

37

Jenny sat in the next-to-last row of the large conference room. She had been tempted to take a chair in the first row, but then decided that would be too conspicuous. From her position on the inner aisle, she could survey the entire room without being obvious herself. The room was packed, and noise wafted around her like strands of smoke. She had felt self-conscious as she entered the hall, fearful that people would be looking at each new arrival and wondering "was she or wasn't she." Jenny smiled wryly to herself. Not even the hairdressers knew for sure.

This was the first time she had come to such a symposium. Her specialty was family therapy, and attending the symposia and lectures in her own area usually kept her plenty busy. In the last five years she had noticed an increasing number of programs on the Gay Problem. Jenny regarded this change with minor interest and felt pleased that those people were getting themselves organized and insisting on their civil and psychological rights. A Gay Psychologists Caucus had been established a few years before; for some reason Jenny had always thought of them as men. And in the front left side of the audience, she noticed a group of men sitting together, talking and laughing intimately. But there was also a group of women, sitting in the front too but on the right side. They all seemed to know each other well; some had an arm hooked around the back of the next woman's chair, and they leaned close together as they talked, their faces barely inches away from each other. In the middle and back sections of the audience sat random groupings of people, men and women mixed in various proportions; these people were quiet, restless, and very conscious of the borders of their body space. There was little physical contact among this group, although some of the people seemed to know one another. Jenny's eyes kept returning to the group of women sitting together in the front. Every now and then, their laughter would reach her in the back of the room. The women seemed very self-contained, as if they were a world unto themselves.

Facing the audience, two men sat behind a long speakers' table; the two seats at their left were empty. Jenny saw Sandy and another woman enter the room together and greet the two men with hugs and kisses. Sandy and her friend sat down and surveyed the room, and Sandy waved to a couple of the women sitting in the block in front.

Jenny took advantage of her inconspicuous position to stare unabashedly at Sandy. She had matured into a handsome woman.

One had to use the word handsome; she wasn't pretty or beautiful. But there was something strong yet delicate in her facial features, and a certain nobility of carriage. She was wearing a highly tailored tan suit with a brown-and-rust satin shirt, which brought out the auburn highlights in her short layered hair. She had on gold hoop earrings, and a simple gold chain necklace that sparkled even in the fluorescent lighting. The gold chain was mesmerizing; Jenny found it difficult to break away from staring at that chain and the triangle of skin on which it rested.

One of the men got up to speak first. He worked in the Probation Department with juvenile boys. He was a tall, stately-looking man, his hair graying at the temples. Not effeminate in the least. You'd never know he was gay, except that the description under the panel heading made it clear that all of the psychologists who would be talking were gay themselves. Jenny looked around the attentive crowd. She wondered how many had come to learn, to listen to the gay point of view, and how many had come to gawk at the queers. She felt herself grow angry, wanting to protect those four people who had the courage to put themselves out there and risk the contempt and ridicule of their colleagues. Sandy was listening carefully, and occasionally she wrote something down on a pad as her gay brother talked. Jenny shook her head. Gay brothers and sisters. She had heard some minister of a gay church speak once when she was in graduate school, and he had used that phrase. She hadn't even realized it had impressed her one way or the other.

The man in front of her was whispering to the woman next to him. They chuckled together, and without thinking Jenny leaned forward.

"If you can't keep respectfully quiet, then why don't you leave now, so others won't be disturbed?"

Jenny saw the shocked expressions on their faces and realized that her voice had been harsh. She had just assumed they were making fun of the speaker. What was the matter with her, anyhow? She didn't know what they were laughing at; it could have been anything. She was being paranoid. Or was she? There was no way of knowing. If one was gay, one would never really know where other people were coming from. They might be polite to your face but derisive behind your back. There would be no one you could really trust. Except maybe other gays.

She wondered how many of the people in the room were gay. It was impossible to tell. There were some effeminate-looking men in the audience, but they could just be sensitive heterosexuals. And as for the women, Jenny recognized some of the more masculine-looking ones around her and knew that some of them were married. It seemed as if there was no sure way to tell. So then how did gay people recognize each other?

Jenny heard some applause and then a woman's voice in

the background. She was remembering a few years ago, when she and Barry and another couple had gone to a gay bar downtown. A men's bar. After their eyes adjusted to the dark, they saw male faces and bodies stretching from one end of the bar to the dance floor at the other end. There was a strange, overpowering odor that nearly suffocated her in its insistent intensity. Later she realized it was the smell of sweat from hundreds of perspiring male bodies. Jenny remembered in the locker room in high school, how the girls used to hold their noses as they undressed after gym class, giggling and making faces at the odor accompanying the beads of sweat that trickled between their breasts until they were captured by miserly belly buttons that hoarded the moisture. But the smell in the bar was totally different, more sour than the scent Jenny remembered; it felt alien.

She and Barry maneuvered their way to a small space along one side of the dance floor. The men ignored them as if they were invisible. Jenny had never been in a situation where there were so many men — and none of them looked her over. It was a very strange sensation, realizing that they had no sexual interest in her at all. It didn't matter whether she had set her hair that day, or taken time with her makeup. There was nothing she could do, short of something bizarre, that would catch their attention.

The boys had been pretty uptight. When she and Rita got up to go to the bathroom, Jim insisted that they go separately so one of them would be at the table at all times. That seemed very silly to Jenny, as none of the men were paying the slightest attention to Barry or Jim. But she and Rita humored them, and there was only one stall in the women's room anyhow.

Jenny and Rita had really enjoyed themselves that evening. They couldn't stop commenting on how unusually attractive the men were. There was something in their movements that hinted at an unusual sensuality. And the way they danced exploded the hint into a blatant exhibition of uninhibited eroticism. The dancing made Barry and Jim very uncomfortable; after one or two tries, they refused to get back on the floor. Jenny couldn't blame them. Compared to the other men, they seemed like mechanical mannequins, operated by a covert puppeteer who jerked the strings attached to their limbs to produce awkward, jarring movements, totally antagonistic to the rhythm of the music. Even Jenny felt clumsy in comparison with some of the more graceful dancers.

The sound of Sandy's voice brought Jenny back from her reverie. Sandy was speaking from behind the podium, to the left of the long table. "My expertise in this area is not only from my work with lesbian clients. My own struggle to achieve a positive lesbian identity has also taught me a lot about some of the unique problems that lesbians face, generally in the world and specifically in the therapeutic situation."

Jenny marveled at the confidence of Sandy's voice. Sandy had always been able to argue her points convincingly, but the youthful insecurity which had manifested itself in an overdramatic accentuation of all her ideas was gone. Instead, her voice now had a softspoken quality. Her manner was open, sharing, yet one felt strongly that this was not a woman to be trifled with.

"One of the most acute problems the adolescent gay person faces is the extreme feeling of isolation from those around her or him. To this day, despite the Gay Revolution and the Women's Movement, many gay youngsters mistakenly feel that they are the only ones. They are very much aware of the social and familial pressures to be heterosexual, and they often live in great fear that someone will discover their innermost thoughts and feelings."

The only ones. The only ones. Those words kept repeating themselves, as when the needle of a phonograph becomes stuck on an imperfection in the record. They had thought they were the only ones. Jenny had hoped they were the only ones. She had known there were lesbians, but she had wished for a different, rare experience untouched by any of the labels that would degrade what she and Sandy had shared. It never made sense to her that people insisted on having labels. Labels were a trap, a way to rob you of your individuality. No one was upset if they heard two women loved each other (unless they were really archaic), yet many people were turned off by the label "lesbian." What was the point of using a word that upset so many people? Yet Sandy kept on repeating that word, and Jenny had heard other gay spokespeople talk about how important it was to stand up and be counted as gays.

It was obviously an artifical distinction. Kinsey had not developed his seven-point scale for nothing. Jenny tried to remember from her graduate school classes which end of the continuum was for gays. Was it a zero that meant you were a total homosexual or was it a six? She couldn't remember, and she told herself it wasn't important. The important thing is, Kinsey had found that most people weren't a zero or a six. Most people had homosexual as well as heterosexual thoughts, fantasies, and behaviors. Some people were more on one end of the continuum than the other, but very few people were pure heterosexual or pure homosexual.

Now where had the word "pure" come from? She was sure Kinsey would never have used a concept like that. That's right, it was from the film she had seen the other night, "Doctor Strangelove," with that crazy general talking about returning the world to the purity of the white race. As if there were a pure race, or as if "white" were a meaningful concept. Jenny tried to focus on Sandy's talk again. She chided herself for spacing out like this. She had come to hear Sandy speak, and here she was thinking about some ridiculous film.

"Additionally, as gay teenagers most often have internalized the prevalent stereotypes, myths, and general garbage about homosexuals, they face the additional stress of recognizing that what they feel is considered sinful by some, sick by others, and illegal by most. You add the pressures that come from feeling that one is immoral, depraved, and criminal to the ordinary pressures and crises that adolescents must deal with — and you have one hell of an explosive situation."

Sandy paused here to let that last point sink in. So many people didn't understand the agony the young gay individual went through. The confusion and overwhelming fear. That something was very wrong and it might never be right again. Never. For those who believed in a Day of Judgment and an afterlife, the "never" took on eternal proportions. People lived in constant fear of exile to Hell. With no hope of salvation anywhere, the isolation and fear grew, pushing the weaker ones past their own personal boundaries of sanity. No wonder many analysts had "discovered" great pathology associated with homosexuality. One had to be a superwoman to cope with the combination of external and internal pressures.

As Sandy surveyed the crowd, she saw Jenny sitting in the back of the hall. She had never seen Jenny at any of these workshops, and it was likely this was her first time. "What could she be thinking?" Sandy mused. "Has she put our experience in this context? Or does she still think that what we did wasn't lesbian?"

Jenny wondered if Sandy hated men. Was that another myth, or did most lesbians hate men? She hadn't hated them in college. In fact, Sandy had gotten along with men better than many of the other girls. Sandy was the kind of girl the boys respected. She was no dumb chick, and she had a certain ease and camaraderie with the guys. Jenny had envied Sandy's ability just to be herself, not at all worried about what people would think of her. She'd had quite a reputation as a character, someone who was different in a positive way.

The two men on the panel were sitting together, and then the two women. Just as the group of men were separate from the group of women in the front rows. So the men were with the men and the women with the women. Yet Sandy and the other woman had hugged the two male panelists when they entered; obviously, men's bodies didn't repulse them. But then again, maybe it didn't count, as these were gay men.

The sound of applause jerked Jenny from her thoughts. She joined in, watching Sandy return to her seat. One of the men announced that the panel would now take questions and comments.

"Yes, this is for anyone on the panel." A tall man in his early fifties stood up, placing one hand in the pants pocket to his three-piece suit, and clearing his throat until the room was absolutely quiet. "I was under the impression that today's symposium was going to be a scholarly presentation from a psychological perspective. Instead I found myself listening to political rhetoric in the guise of scientific objectivity."

There was a low groan from some of the people sitting in the front. Undaunted, the man pressed on, seemingly pleased with his role as devil's advocate. "Frankly, I am from the old school that sees psychology as a scientific endeavor pursuing the complexities of truth. That position doesn't seem to be held in high regard these days. Instead, we find a handful of small interest groups pressuring the profession to make political decisions, such as holding this convention only in states that have ratified the ERA, or the recent maneuvers which resulted in homosexuality being removed as a disorder from the APA Diagnostic Manual. I'm not saying that homosexuality per se should be labeled as pathological necessarily, but the point is that political pressure, not scientific data, was used to make these decisions. I think there is too much activism in the profession at the expense of solid, responsible, and scientific research. If we are to survive as a serious profession, we can't be subject to the political whims of today."

There was silence as the panel members looked at each other to see who wanted to respond to this challenge. Sandy was nodding her head thoughtfully. "You're absolutely right. Instead, we should be subject to the political whims of ten years ago." The audience broke into laughter.

"I don't think that's a very serious answer." The man sat down.

"No, I suppose it isn't." Sandy stood up and walked back to the podium. "Let me give you a serious answer. I think that one of the most dangerous illusions our profession has perpetuated is that psychology as a science is objective, apolitical, logical, reasonable, and appropriate. This attitude is not only naive about the way values and perspectives influence scientific research and conclusions, but it is also a pernicious myth used to justify the status quo and whatever inequities come with the cultural package. A couple of examples may clarify my point. Ten years ago, homosexuals were labeled as sick and deviant. These conclusions were drawn from clinicians' impressions of the patients they saw in psychiatric settings. In order to draw conclusions about heterosexuals, on the other hand, our colleagues studied non-patient populations. This small discrepancy in accurate sampling was the work of some of the 'best' scientists of the time. You call the 'scientific truths' of that recent time rational? Apolitical?

"Scientific objectivity can also be seen in action in the area of female sexuality. Fifteen years ago, the scientific community had no idea of the importance of the clitoris to women's sexual responsivity. The idea of the vaginal orgasm as different, more mature, and superior to clitoral orgasm, although totally unscientific, was endorsed by the scientific community. And of course this idea reflected the bias of the times, as well as the fact that theories about female sexuality were created by men, with virtually no input from women. Now we can safely say that our knowledge of women and female sexuality is more accurate, as we have finally gotten round to asking the real experts on female sexuality: women. You want to know about gays and lesbians? Then ask us."

Sandy surveyed the room as a couple of men and women called out in support. "Let's take another question. Yes, the woman in the black suit."

"If an adolescent comes into my office and says, 'I'm frightened, I think I might be gay,' how do I know whether he is or isn't?" The woman shook her head. "I don't want to coerce anyone into being straight, but how do I handle a situation like that?"

Jenny listened half-heartedly as the other woman on the panel made suggestions. Her heart was still pounding from the interaction that had taken place earlier between Sandy and that man. What a pompous asshole. She had been furious when he first started talking; she just wanted him to sit down and shut up. But as he continued talking, she had felt an anxiety inside her start to grow, until by the time he had finished making his comments, she was in a virtual state of panic. Then she laughed appreciatively when Sandy came back with her retort, and gradually, while Sandy went into a fuller statement, Jenny felt the anxiety begin to abate. But she was still unnerved and she didn't know why. It had something to do with the way that man had stood, the way he had looked at Sandy. He had been polite enough, but his body language had communicated measured contempt.

There was another round of applause, and then the people around Jenny started to disperse. She was relieved by the milling around; the tall bodies standing in front of her blocked her vision of Sandy as effectively as if she were a small child in an adult crowd. That gave Jenny some time to think. Did she want to go up and say something to Sandy? Sandy would probably be with her friends. Maybe it would be better to call her room later and ask her out for a drink, as she had suggested. Or Jenny could leave a note at the message desk. The crowd thinned a little, and Jenny could see Sandy talking to a group of her friends in a tight circle. "I'm being cowardly," Jenny thought. "What am I frightened of?"

She stood up resolutely. She did not like to pamper herself when it came to small insecurities. The worst that could happen would be that she might feel uncomfortable. And besides, she was curious. Who were these women who had sat together and were now with Sandy? She didn't even know whether they were lesbians. It would be an interesting experience. Jenny felt herself relax. She had handled many different situations, and she could handle this one too.

Sandy was pleased with herself. Not only was the presentation over, but it had also gone well. Her initial relief was already beginning to transform into excitement. That was one of the strangest things she had discovered about giving talks: her excitement would come afterwards. Anxiety and performance pressures always made it impossible for her to enjoy the talk while she was giving it. Her goal was, if not to look forward to presentations, at least to be relaxed before and during — but that still seemed a long way off.

She walked around the front of the table and joined the group of women who were standing there. Julie, then Margo, gave her a big hug. Jan put an arm around her, beaming like a proud parent whose precocious child had just won the spelling bee.

"Dynamite presentation, Sandy," Julie said.

"Every time you said the word 'lesbian,' the woman sitting next to me winced," Margo added. The women laughed.

"You should have seen this one guy. Nervous fellow. By the end of your talk he had developed a tic." Jan mimicked a tic in one eye.

"Well, we all deserve a celebration," Dolores said as she snapped her fingers and twisted her frame sensuously. "The name of the club is the Gay Nineties."

"Sounds like our kind of place," Jan said, punching Sandy in the arm. Sandy put up her arms to spar, and from the corner of her eye she saw Jenny approaching. She lowered her fists.

"Hi."

"Hi," Sandy replied. "We were just talking about the presentation. Everybody, this is Jenny. Jenny, this is Margo, Julie, Dolores, and Jan."

"That was a very impressive presentation. You've really gotten articulate over the years."

"Thank you."

Jan was looking back and forth as they talked. "The two of you sound like old friends."

Sandy chose to ignore the undercurrent in Jan's voice. "Yeah, we go back to college," she said abruptly.

Dolores cut in. "Listen, I have to go and we still need to make plans for tonight. What do you say we meet in the lobby at nine?"

"Things should be hopping by then." Jan hopped from one foot to the other, then turned to Jenny. "We're all going out dancing tonight. You want to join us?"

Sandy felt her irritation at Jan turn into rage. What the fuck was the matter with her? It was just like Jan to assume that because they had known each other in college, Jenny must be gay. And even if she was, Jan didn't know anything about their relationship. What right did she have to make the invitation without checking with Sandy first?

"Oh . . ." Jenny hesitated a moment. "That sounds like fun."

"We're going to the Gay Nineties. It's a women's bar," Sandy blurted out, aware of how uptight she sounded but unable to control herself.

"Well, of course it's a women's bar," Julie said impatiently. "Who's going to the rape workshop?"

"Me," Dolores said, heading for the door. Julie and Margo followed.

"You coming, Sandy?" Jan asked.

"No, I think I'll pass on that. I need to unwind from this. Go ahead. I'll see you later."

"Okay." Jan turned to Jenny. "It was nice meeting you. Hope you join us tonight." Jan walked to the door, then jokingly called back over her shoulder, "D.F. tonight, girls."

The conference room was now empty. Sandy found herself unable to look at Jenny. Jenny hadn't committed herself either way, but Sandy felt very uncomfortable about the prospect that Jenny might indeed show up at the bar. Damn that Jan and her goddamned assumptions. Sandy looked at Jenny and saw that she was staring at Sandy with a quizzical expression.

"What's D.F.?"

"Dyke finery . . . You really going to come?"

"Sure," Jenny replied breezily, starting to walk toward the door. "Why not?" Sandy followed Jenny out in silence.

In the main lobby, Jenny turned to Sandy and smiled broadly. "Well, I think I'll go up to the room. Lie down for a bit. See you later." She winked at Sandy before making her way across the lobby to the elevator.

Sandy watched her mutely as she crossed the lobby, her small compact frame swinging slightly as she walked. It was the walk of a straight woman, her hips subtly swaying in an intentionally provocative way. Sandy found herself staring at Jenny's ass as it receded in the distance. It was a nice ass.

38

It wasn't until Jenny got up to the room, that she realized she had no idea what dyke finery meant. Did lesbians wear some special sort of clothing to go out at night? She had heard there were leather bars, and also bars where men dressed up to look like cowboys, but it was hard to imagine a room full of women dressed in black leather jackets or looking like Roy Rogers. Jenny laughed to herself as she imagined Sandy dressed up in a fringed leather jacket and pants. But then again, maybe the look in a lesbian bar was more like Dale Evans and she'd be wearing a fringed leather skirt instead. Whatever the fashions, Jenny knew Sandy would never show up looking like a cowboy or cowgirl.

Jenny visualized what the women had been wearing at the conference. They had all looked normal, no one was in any weird get-up. Walking to the closet, Jenny took down the orange flowered dress she had gotten on sale at Bloomingdale's when she went into the city to shop last year. It was long and flowing, made out of a soft shimmery synthetic that clung to her frame. The cleavage was subtly exposed in such a way that one's eyes were inevitably drawn to the faint outline of breast revealed.

Reaching into the bureau, Jenny selected a new pair of hose, started to tear the plastic, and stopped. None of the women had been wearing stockings. And now that she thought about it, all the women had been wearing pants, and none of the tops had the frills and lace that were so common in today's fashions.

Jenny put the dress back into the closet. She didn't want to look too feminine. She wondered if all lesbians wore tailored clothing. And perhaps found that look most attractive. Or perhaps if none of them were lovers, maybe their lovers wore the more feminine clothing?

She tried to remember what had turned Sandy on in college. Had Sandy been more turned on when Jenny put on a dress and stockings? No, she didn't remember Sandy caring one way or the other how Jenny dressed. Clothes had never seemed very important to Sandy; she had liked hers roomy and comfortable, and she virtually lived in her favorite pair of jeans.

It was very confusing. Jenny felt like she was walking into a strange and foreign culture where she knew none of the customs and rules. Slightly anxious, she went through the clothes on the rack until she came to the kelly green pant suit with its colorfully flowered blouse that scooped at the neck. That was safe.

Later, as she dressed, she tried to imagine what the club would look like. Would it be a small, dark, dingy place, the stereotype of a gay bar, or would it be just like any of the bars she went to back home? Tying a matching silk scarf around her neck, Jenny gazed dissatisfied at her reflection in the mirror. Her face was beginning to show her age, in the pockets beneath her eyes. Reflexively Jenny smoothed the skin above her cheek, as if she could iron out the wrinkles. Frowning, she grabbed her purse and left.

A sea of women filled the huge room, which was lit by dozens of old-fashioned chandeliers. There were women sitting at tables in small groups, women standing by the bar three deep trying to order drinks from women bartenders, women dancing together on the spacious wood floor. The walls were covered with red velvet, and darker, almost burnt red sashes and curtains added a three-dimensional texture along the perimeter. Balustrades and wooden railings separated some of the tables on the second floor, which had an excellent view of the tables and the dance floor on the main level. The room was magnificent.

Jenny was amazed by the diversity of the women. Young and old, Asian and white, stylish and not so stylish. Most of the women were dressed in pants, as Jenny had suspected, but some were wearing long dresses and skirts similar to the type she had discarded. Many of the women were dressed flamboyantly in the latest disco silks and cut-out tops, while other women wore conversative polyester suits with stacked heels.

On the way over, the eight of them had crowded into Sandy's rented car. That was fun, reminiscent of college days. Jenny was squashed with Julie, Jan, Margo, and Catherine in the back seat, and they joked about how this setting seemed perfect for a marathon encounter group. There was one wisecrack after another. Now, here she was, in an alien setting, trying to act like one of the girls.

She felt uncomfortable as they walked through the club to a table in the back. What was she doing here? She didn't belong. She had hoped to talk with Sandy, but Sandy seemed to be avoiding her. She had said hello to Jenny when they met in the hotel lobby, but then proceeded to ignore her during the entire car ride. Jenny hoped Sandy wouldn't be unfriendly all evening. After all, they were old friends.

Sandy, Jan, Pat, and Dolores were already seated, and both chairs next to Sandy were taken. Shit. Sandy had to know this situation would be somewhat awkward for Jenny — being in a group of strangers like this — and yet she wasn't making any effort to put her at ease. Feeling annoyed and insecure, Jenny sat down next to Julie. Margo and Catherine took the remaining chairs, on Jenny's other side.

"Where are you from, anyhow, Jenny?" Julie asked as she lit a cigarette.

"Well, I'm originally from New York, but I'm living in Ohio now." Jenny pulled out a cigarette and lit it. At least some lesbians smoked.

"It's been an interesting experience living in the Midwest," Jenny continued, taking her mind off her irritation with Sandy. "I had expected that the people would all be hillbillies, but there's a surprising degree of sophistication."

"You call Ohio the Midwest?" Julie smiled. "Sister, I'm from the plains of Iowa. Where I come from, Ohio is considered a suburb of the east coast."

Jenny smiled back. She liked Julie's friendliness and warmth, and she was grateful to Julie for trying to make her feel more comfortable.

"Ohio," Catherine said quizzically. "I've never been there, I'm afraid. Do you live in a big city or a small town?"

"It's a nice-sized town for southern Ohio, but a small town by New York or Los Angeles standards."

"I've lived exclusively in big cities," Catherine said. "That must make it a lot more difficult."

"It's no so bad." Jenny wasn't sure what Catherine meant. "We don't have the same cultural activities that you get in Los Angeles, but the people are very nice." Jenny felt on the defensive. Catherine was a snob, no doubt, thinking that big cities were the only places an aristocrat like herself could live. There was a pretentiousness in the way she spoke that annoyed Jenny.

"Well, I'm delighted to hear that Middle America is becoming more tolerant," Catherine said with a surprised look.

Jenny felt as though her face had been slapped. She hadn't understood that Catherine was talking about the plight of gays in small towns. But what was even more stunning was that Catherine had assumed she was one of them. It had never occurred to Jenny that they would think she was a lesbian. She remembered her initial discomfort when she walked into Sandy's presentation, wondering if anyone thought she was gay. But then she had assumed that one of the straights would make the mistake. She had never figured that a gay would or could make an error like that. She had heard that they could always tell when they met another one like them. She had obviously heard wrong.

She looked around the table and wondered which, if any, of the other women also thought she was gay. Did they all assume that any acquaintance of Sandy must be a lesbian, or was Catherine particularly insensitive? There was so much about this situation that she didn't understand. Did lesbians only socialize with other lesbians? Surely they must know some straights.

Now where did she get that word? It was an awful word. Jenny used the word "straight" to describe rigid, uptight, and conservative people, people who weren't hip. Gays used the same word to label anyone who wasn't gay. How could they assume that just because you were heterosexual, you must be uptight? It wasn't fair of them to make such generalizations.

Then again, maybe the word "straight" had come from heterosexuals; it also meant that one was honest, as in "straight-talking," or not crooked, as in "going straight." What was the opposite of straight, anyhow? Crooked, deviant, perverted, criminal. It was just as unfair for heterosexuals to think that all gays were deviant. But they were different, not deviant perhaps, but definitely different, as she was now learning. And if she found them and their world different, then they must feel separate from her world.

But how could there be major differences if they couldn't even tell that she wasn't one of them? Obviously she could pass. Jenny felt pleased with herself; she was a sophisticated woman who could travel in many different circles. If a bunch of lesbians couldn't even tell whether she was the Real McCoy, then she must . . . she must be what?

An anxious feeling appeared suddenly, then started to spread. Was she giving off cues that told them she was gay? That was crazy. She was just acting naturally. And how could they not know she was married? After all, she was wearing a wedding band.

Jenny sneaked a look at Julie's fingers. She had an Indian turquoise silver band on the middle finger of her left hand; it was obviously not a wedding ring. Reaching for another cigarette, Jenny noticed that Margo had a gold band on her ring finger. It was more detailed than a typical wedding band, done in antique gold, but Jenny had no way to know if it was simply decorative or if it meant something. She tried to see whether Catherine was wearing a similar band, but Catherine's hand was under the table. Perhaps lesbians who were in relationships also wore gold bands; then they might assume she was married to a woman somewhere.

This was crazy. Hadn't she mentioned anything about Barry? No, she couldn't remember saying anything about him. He just hadn't come up in conversation.

But just because she had not mentioned her husband, that was no reason for anyone to assume she was gay. Unless Sandy had said something to them about . . . Jenny had trouble finishing that thought. It was too horrible to imagine. Jenny looked at Sandy, who was talking to Pat. It wasn't possible that Sandy would have told them all about her relationship with Jenny in college. Sandy was naive at times, and occasionally had trouble being discreet, but there would be no reason for her to go into their past. It was none of their business. But then maybe Sandy didn't feel that way.

Maybe? It was *obvious* Sandy didn't feel that way. After

150

all, she had publicly come out in her presentation, and Jenny had to assume that she was open about herself in other circumstances too. Sandy was acting as though she had nothing to lose. Her point of view, or personal preference, as they called it, was open to public scrutiny. So why shouldn't she have felt free to tell anyone she damn well pleased?

Because she promised me, that's why, Jenny thought, feeling much relieved. Of course, Sandy would never tell. She would not violate the oath she had taken in college, even if it was now ten years old.

Trustworthiness was one of the qualities that had attracted Jenny to Sandy in the first place. Jenny had sensed that if she could win Sandy's friendship, it would be for life. Whatever shortcomings Sandy might have, when it came to loyalty she was true-blue. Jenny felt an old familiar affection for Sandy; she was in many ways an exceptional person.

Jenny found herself sneaking glances at Sandy. There were many attractive women in the bar, but somehow Sandy stood out. When they all walked in, Jenny had noticed several women following Sandy with their eyes. The way she moved, the way she carried herself commanded attention. In college, the girls in the dorm had always treated Sandy like something special. But even here, Sandy still seemed special. The expression "a man's man" flashed across Jenny's mind. That was it. Sandy was a woman's woman.

Jenny watched the women dancing and noted their sensuousness. She had wondered how two women would dance together, and she always imagined that they would bump breasts awkwardly, but these women didn't seem to have any trouble. In fact, many of the women dancing together were the same size, and when they held each other tightly, they were able to rest their faces against each other, their bodies blending tightly together. Jenny realized with surprise that the dance floor looked different because of this. In heterosexual bars, there was usually considerable difference in the heights of the dancers, the women resting their heads on the men's shoulders or chests. Some of these couples were different in size and looked like that, but the great majority of couples were more equally matched. Jenny wondered what it would feel like to dance with someone your own size. She was a relatively short woman, and all of the men she had dated were much larger. It seemed strange.

Jenny watched with an amused smile as Sandy and Jan got up for a fast number. To her surprise, Jan was pretty graceful. But it was Sandy who captured the attention. Her movements were elegant, with her arms swirling and her torso bending and snapping to the percussion beats. Jenny found herself staring at Sandy's hips, watching them alternate between slow rotations and swift incisive cuts, which seemed to bisect the space around her body. Slowly lifting her eyes, Jenny followed the buttons of Sandy's blouse upwards to the place where the last button held the tautly stretched blouse. The full outline of Sandy's breasts was visible, and Jenny noticed with fascination how they swung and bounced with each shake. Sandy no longer wore a bra. And in spite of the fact that her breasts were fuller than they had ever been.

Sandy looked in her direction, and Jenny quickly averted her eyes, but not quickly enough to prevent Sandy from noticing that she had been staring at her. Jenny felt mildly uncomfortable, as if she had been caught doing something she wasn't supposed to do. Sandy probably now knew that Jenny still found her attractive, and Jenny felt one-down for having let that piece of information slip.

She wondered whether Sandy found her attractive, too. Sandy certainly wasn't encouraging any conversation or eye contact. And Jenny had noticed that Sandy touched the other women freely but seemed to keep some distance from her. Was she no longer interested, or just good at hiding it? Jenny surveyed the table and decided she was as good-looking as any of the women seated around her. But as she scrutinized the rest of the room, she saw that many other women in the club were more attractive than she. Pinching the small roll of fat underneath her breast, Jenny resolved to take off the five pounds she had put on during the holidays. She had pretty much kept her figure since college, and the five pounds didn't really show in her clothes, but they would show in a bathing suit.

Sandy and Jan switched into a lindy and began to whirl each other around the floor. Perhaps Sandy was still very much attracted to Jenny, and was overcompensating for it by paying little attention. That was just like Sandy, to play it cool. After all, she had once found Jenny attractive, so why shouldn't she still?

Jenny took a comb out of her purse and arranged her hair, staring into the small mirror of her compact. She moistened her lipstick with her tongue, returned the compact and comb to her bag, and placed an arm behind one of the other chairs, so she could gaze more freely at the crowd. Sipping her drink and smiling at Pat and Dolores, who were at the other end of the table, Jenny felt a new sense of confidence. The song ended and the couples dispersed to the tables.

"Would you like to dance to the next number?" Dolores called above the din.

"Sure," Jenny replied with a full smile. She and Dolores headed for the dance floor. When they passed Sandy and Jan, who were returning to the table, Jenny gave Sandy a wink. She noted with pleasure that Sandy looked uncomfortable. If Sandy thought Jenny was just going to sit there and wait for Sandy to ask her to dance, she was in for a surprise.

39

Sandy watched Jenny out of the corner of her eye. She was now in a deep conversation with Julie and seemed totally enthralled. What the hell was she doing here, anyhow? Sandy felt a strong urge to grab Jenny by the arm and drag her out of the bar. She had no right to be here. This was a lesbian bar, and Jenny didn't belong. She had made her choice of husband, normalcy, a safe life. She had copped out on her lesbianism, and she didn't deserve to sit and drink with all these other women, women who didn't have her heterosexual privilege, women who survived and loved on the edge of a very flat world.

Sandy often felt angry with the heterosexuals who came to gay bars, women clinging to their men, waving the banner of their heterosexuality so no one would assume that they were lesbians. At first they seemed fearful that some wild lesbian would beat up their husbands and drag them off by the hair. But as the night progressed, the paranoia, tinged with more than a little excitement, would abate, and a sad pout would take its place. The women would leave, disappointed, and go home and tell their friends there was nothing interesting about the gay bars — just a lot of women dancing together. What they never had the honesty to admit to themselves was that they had been ignored. They, the *real* women, had been rejected by lesbians. It was inconceivable.

And then there were the straight men. They usually came in pairs. They were there to look, to gawk at their own private three-dimensional porno show. They would sit at a table and drink as they watched the girls dance. The more adventurous or drunk ones would try to start conversations, hoping they would hit upon some kinky lesbian and get laid. Many lesbians treated the men politely, and some women went out of their way to prove they weren't "man-haters." Sandy would get nauseated as she watched these interactions, the women trying to show that they liked men okay, and the men capitalizing on the women's naiveté and good faith as they quickly moved into dirty jokes and tried to get in a few freebie touches. The men's judgment was usually impeccable. They seemed to know which women they could do their number on and which women to avoid. They read women's insecurities as adeptly as a computer scanning an entry card. All Sandy could do was fume inside, then tune it out, focus on the women, and blot out the intruders from her peripheral vision.

Now Jenny was the intruder. Sandy watched as Jenny picked up a cigarette and Jan, who had moved down to that end of the table, offered to light it. That Jan made her sick. It was just like her to treat a new woman in the crowd as if the woman was Scarlett O'Hara and she was Rhett Butler. A very miniature Rhett Butler. Sandy chastised herself; it was not right to put Jan down extra for being short.

What really got Sandy pissed was that Jenny seemed to be having such a damned good time. Sandy would have felt more comfortable if Jenny seemed uptight, if she recognized how little she fit in. But on the contrary, she seemed to radiate an excitement in this situation. In fact, she was acting downright seductive. It wasn't just that her blouse exposed a good portion of her breasts. Sandy had caught that number when they got into the car, and it made her blood boil. But now Sandy was also noticing how Jenny held her cigarette, the way she took a little extra time to inhale, her lips pursing just enough when she exhaled to draw attention.

This was ridiculuous. Here Sandy was in her own territory with her own friends, and she was the one who was having a miserable time. She was acting jealous, as if she gave a shit what Jenny did with herself. How could she feel jealous over a woman she hardly knew anymore, a woman she hadn't seen in ten years? It defied the laws of common sense and reason.

Sandy forced herself to pay attention to the women moving on the dance floor. She had always loved to watch the different ways women moved. Shelly said you could tell what a woman would be like in bed by watching her dance, but Sandy didn't think that was always true. A woman could look sexy on the dance floor but freeze up when it came to making love; just as someone else might be shy about being sexy in front of so many women but could be wonderfully uninhibited in privacy with her lover. Nonetheless, Sandy immensely enjoyed observing the different dancers and speculating on what kind of women they were, and occasionally, when the movements of a particular woman intrigued her, wondering what it would be like to make love with such a woman.

Her thoughts annoyingly returned to Jenny. Why had Jenny come here? To have an "experience," like the other straight women? Or to see what she had missed by marrying Barry? Sandy wondered whether Jenny even thought of herself as having anything in common with these other women. She had never thought of herself as a lesbian, so she might use the label to keep herself distant, to forget that she too had once been in love with a woman. A woman. "It wasn't just any woman," Sandy reminded herself. "She was once in love with me. Or so I thought."

Sandy took a gulp of her drink, aware that she was holding her glass and swirling its contents thoughtfully, lending an air of sophistication and reflectiveness to her appearance. It was all a question of appearances. Jenny appeared comfortable, when Sandy damn well knew she must be shitting in her pants. And Sandy sat here playing it cool, being polite but not acting too interested, so that Jenny would never suspect that she hadn't been able to think of anything else since she first laid eyes on her yesterday.

"How about a go-around, ole buddy?" Jan yelled from across the table.

Sandy laughed, relieved for her unpleasant thoughts to be interrupted. Maybe what she needed was to dance and get rid of all this tension and uncertainty. Nodding to Jan, she got up, and they made their way around the crowded tables to the dance floor. Sandy wondered whether she was supposed to ask Jenny to dance. What was the etiquette for a lesbian after not having seen her first lover, who was now straight, for ten years? If she asked her to dance, should it be slow or fast? Emily Post didn't seem to have thought about this situation.

The band was taking a break, and the jukebox started with a Supremes hit, "My World Is Empty Without You, Babe." Sandy closed her eyes and, repeating the verses in her mind, tried to concentrate on the music and her body. She often got compliments on her dancing; she rarely allowed herself to flirt, so women were often surprised when they saw her blatant sexual energy released on the dance floor. Now she wondered if Jenny was watching her dance and what conclusions she would draw from the way Sandy moved. She found herself making some unusually seductive gestures with her hands, then stopped herself abruptly. What the hell was she trying to do?

Sandy looked towards the table and caught Jenny staring at her. Jenny quickly turned away, and Sandy mentally noted the answer to one of the questions she hadn't wanted to ask herself. Yes, Jenny was still attracted to her. It was there unmistakably in her eyes, in the way she guiltily jerked away. Sandy felt her discomfort grow. What did she want?

It was difficult for Sandy to admit to herself that she was still attracted to Jennifer. She decided to call Jenny "Jennifer" in her thoughts, to remind herself of the very real distance between them. What was she doing, being attracted to a straight woman? That was from an earlier phase she thought she had outgrown long ago. There was nothing more regressive than a committed lesbian finding herself fascinated by a heterosexual woman. Sandy had listened to that heartbreak story a thousand times in the office. It was a stage that many lesbians went through, particularly in their transition to a lesbian identity, when they didn't know or were afraid of other lesbians. But she was no half-assed kid with traditional notions of feminine beauty. There was no excuse for her.

Another part of Sandy argued back: "That isn't exactly fair. Jenny was once very important to me. It's only natural that I would be curious about her, be interested in what she's been up to all these years, want to spend some time with her, and wonder what it would be like to go to bed with her." A devilish voice quickly squeezed in these last words.

Sandy was appalled by the cavalier quality of this thought. The whole thing was ridiculous. She didn't even know Jenny now, so how could she possibly want to have an affair with her? Then again, maybe she had no desire for an affair with Jenny; perhaps the fantasy was just to do it once. For old times' sake. That was a line out of a grade-B movie. And she had mistakenly thought she was liberated from most of that shit. What was going on with her? It wasn't like her to be so juvenile and single-minded. Sandy found herself thinking in clichés: playing with fire, the temptation of the devil (now where did a weird phrase like that come from to enter the pure mind of a nice Jewish girl?), forbidden love. What could be forbidden about making it with Jenny? It seemed almost incestuous. This woman was someone she had known when she was so much younger. A childhood sweetheart, one might say. If they were to make love again, there would be a confusion between their two different selves, a merging of the past and present, which had no right to be connected. What on earth was she thinking? Sandy looked down at her glass to make sure she was drinking ordinary booze. If the coherency of her thoughts was any sign, she was getting plastered. She'd have to ask Shelly to drive them home.

Jesus Christ. Shelly. She really was out of it. And after only two drinks. Maybe it was because she hadn't eaten all day. Sandy wondered what Shelly was doing tonight. She hadn't even tried to call her today, and Shelly would be waiting, expecting to hear how the presentation had gone. Shelly would have a fit if she found out that Sandy had been drinking without eating anything. Sandy wished Shelly were here, with her. It was strange sleeping alone all night, not having Shelly to cuddle against, her heat warming the sheets for both of them.

But if Shelly had been here, Sandy wouldn't now be wondering whether Jenny was still turned on to her. Sandy felt a pang of guilt. It was one thing to be attracted to another woman, but *Jennifer* of all people. Shelly would have a conniption when she heard about this.

And where was Sandy's pride? This woman had treated her like shit for four years. Sandy felt herself grow angry, then cut it short. She preferred to be a sweet drunk instead of an angry drunk any time. But the anger was an important sign of some unfinished business she had with Jennifer Chase. Berkowitz. It was hard to incorporate the idea that Jennifer had a new name, as if the old one had had babies. Or wasn't good enough. Hadn't Jennifer ever heard about feminism? Didn't she know that many women were now hyphenating their own last names with their husbands'? Not that it really made any difference at all, as far as Sandy was concerned, until the men also hyphenated their names, but Jenny wouldn't be hip to that more sophisticated objection. Sandy turned to look at Jenny, who was talking with Margo. Where had she been for the last ten years? The various liberation movements seemed to have passed her by, or just left her unaffected.

The song ended, and Sandy and Jan headed back to the table. As they made their way through the crowd, Sandy saw Dolores and Jenny approach them, obviously on their way to the dance floor. Sandy started to frown, then wiped the expression off her face. She smiled at Dolores and nodded perfunctorily at Jenny, turning her body to the side so their breasts would not brush. For a moment their eyes caught, and Jenny smiled impishly and winked.

So Jenny was going to play flirt with her. Well, that was a game two could play. Sandy decided to call Jenny's bluff and see who would chicken out first. She turned her chair to face the crowd of dancers as a Tina Turner song came on the jukebox. She stared brashly at Jenny as she and Dolores began to dance. Jenny looked back at the table, saw Sandy gazing at her, smiled uncertainly, and then turned back to Dolores. The uncertain smile said that Sandy had won one for the home team: Jenny had probably hoped to catch Sandy copping a look, but didn't know what to make of the blatant attention. Jenny was on Sandy's turf now, and there was no way Jenny could bamboozle her.

Sandy felt herself toughen in a way she used to do a lot as a kid, and now only did occasionally, when she was threatened by something that didn't feel clean or simple. Putting self-doubts out of her mind, Sandy rated Jenny as about an eight for her dancing; she was good but not exceptional. Jenny knew her steps and knew how to manipulate her body, but she lost one point for lacking originality, and another point for a certain tightness that was evident to Sandy's discerning eyes. Guiltily, Sandy recognized she was objectifying Jenny, turning her into a number, critically evaluating her as if she were a term paper. And vaguely, she realized she was doing that as a defense against an even vaguer fear that seemed to persist despite her self-admonishments that everything was okay.

Jan came over and sat next to Sandy. She motioned to a group of women sitting at a table near them. "Did you notice that good-looking blonde?"

Sandy turned around to look in the direction Jan pointed,

reluctantly taking her eyes off Jenny. "No. She looks nice." Jan nodded in appreciation. "Go ahead," Sandy laughed. "Ask her to dance."

"Looks like you got something cooking yourself," Jan chuckled.

"What are you talking about, Jan?" Sandy realized she sounded defensive. Jan's comment had caught her offguard.

"That old college chum of yours," Jan said. "You haven't taken your eyes off her all evening. And you a married woman."

"Married," Sandy replied angrily, now feeling very annoyed. "What the fuck are you talking about, Jan? Will you just go ask your blonde to dance?"

"Okay, okay," Jan said, backing off. "I was just kidding." Jan got up and pulled her velvet vest down, fixing the collar of her shirt. "Wish me luck," she said as she started off.

Sandy watched her for a moment, then turned to look at Jenny on the dance floor. There was no point getting upset about what Jan had said. Jan was an asshole. Sandy's eyes followed Jenny as she came back to the table at the end of the song.

"You look like you're enjoying yourself," Sandy said.

"I'm having a wonderful time." Jenny stopped briefly by Sandy's chair. "All I need to make my evening complete is a dance with you."

Sandy laughed. "Okay, Jennifer, you got it."

Sandy watched the band return to the stage, and start to tune up for the next set. There were six women: two guitarists, a drummer, a pianist, a flutist, and a violinist. They had been playing a Latin-American piece before their break, and they had sounded pretty good. Sandy was looking forward to hearing them play some more.

The lead guitarist picked up her mike and waited for the crowd to quiet some. "During the break we had a request for a polka." Some women whistled. "So here goes, ladies."

To Sandy's amazement, the band broke into a foot-stomping rhythm. Women hooted with glee and raced to the floor. Pat virtually dragged Dolores, screaming for help as the women at the table guffawed. Sandy found herself clapping and humming along with the music. She watched with a smile as Jan and the blonde got up and started to cavort wildly around the floor, bumping into other couples who would stop while they continued on their merry way. Sandy laughed at the ridiculousness of the scene: in what looked like a fancy turn-of-the-century brothel, on a remote island called Oahu, six female rock musicians in glittery psychedelic clothing were playing a polka for an enthusiastic crowd of cheering dykes. This was turning out to be one hell of an evening.

When the music stopped, the women *en masse* got to their

feet, cheering and screaming, "Encore." The band leader shook her head and raised her hand to quiet the crowd.

"Well, we've had some strange requests tonight," she said good-humoredly. "First there was the Charleston." Sporadic cheering and clapping. "Then there was the hora." A group of women on the other side of the bar yelled and clapped their approval, as Sandy regretted not having gotten to the bar earlier. "And now we've done the polka. Before we get back to some contemporary sounds, do I have one last unusual request?"

"A waltz," an older woman yelled from the back. Some of the women clapped. Others booed. The band leader turned to the other musicians. "Ladies, we have a request for a waltz. What do you say?" The band nodded agreement as they tuned up. The woman playing the electric violin undid her pickup, setting up a microphone in front of her. Sandy stood up.

"Well, you said you'd like to dance with me." She looked at Jenny with a half-formed smile. "This is it, kid."

"Are you kidding? A waltz?"

Sandy very gallantly offered Jenny her elbow. Jenny laughed and got up, slipping her arm through Sandy's as they walked onto the nearly empty dance floor. The band struck up "The Blue Danube."

"Would you like to lead or should I?"

Jenny shook her head. "This was your idea, Sandy, go ahead. I don't even know if I remember how to do a waltz."

Looking at their feet and laughing, Sandy and Jenny began to dance. Sandy liked the feel of Jenny's hand in hers, liked the way Jenny's waist filled the cup of her other hand. This was the closest she had been to Jenny in years, and after she was sure she had the steps down pat, she took the opportunity to look at Jenny secretly. Jenny had undoubtedly aged some, but there was a freshness about her that reminded Sandy of the girl she had once known. She felt affection swell inside her; how could she have thought this woman was a stranger? Jenny looked at Sandy, and Sandy smiled at her openly. Jenny returned the smile, and they continued to look at each other as they danced, the pace of the music picking up slightly. Sandy realized she had no desire to play games with this woman; this was a woman she had once loved, and what they had shared was too valuable to desecrate with superficial bullshit.

As they relaxed together, their dancing became more graceful and flowing. She had suggested the waltz as a joke, but suddenly it became more serious; there was nothing silly about their dancing. When the music stopped, they held each other for an extra moment, the seriousness turning into a shy smile.

"Thank you, madam," Sandy said as she bowed formally.

"Thank you." Jenny returned the bow. They walked back

to the table, somewhat self-consciously.

"You know, that was the first time we ever danced together," Sandy said, not wanting to let the moment go.

Jenny looked surprised. "Was it?" she said casually. Jenny continued to the end of the table, where Dolores and Catherine were singing a Bing Crosby croon tune. Sandy couldn't figure how a young radical woman like Dolores would even know such a song, let alone sing it in public, but then tonight had brought out the beast in all of them. Sandy plopped down next to Julie, who was looking at her thoughtfully.

"How you doing, kid?" Sandy put an arm around the back of Julie's chair.

"I'm doing fine," Julie answered quietly. "How about you?"

"Me, just great." Sandy scrounged through the glasses on the table, looking for her scotch on the rocks. She stopped a passing waitress and ordered another drink. Then she turned back to Julie, who was still looking at her. Sandy felt herself become a little uncomfortable.

"What's on your mind, Julie?"

"You really want to know?"

"Yeah, of course I want to know."

"Okay." Julie put out her cigarette. "Is she somebody important to you?"

Sandy sat there for a moment. Then she smiled ruefully. "Is it that evident?" Julie was quiet. Sandy sighed deeply. "That's Jenny. My roommate in college."

"*The* Jenny." Julie whistled through her teeth. "I'm amazed you're still in one piece."

"You think it's a big deal?" Sandy asked, unsure.

"Unless I've gotten my stories confused, you were very much in love with her, no?" Sandy nodded. "How long has it been . . ."

"Since the wedding." There was a long silence. "And he's here, too." Julie nodded in understanding. Sandy was grateful not to have to explain who he was. She didn't want to have to say the word "husband." She hated that word. It wasn't only that the word had a feeling of property ownership about it, but it also implied that everything that happened to Jenny before her marriage was unimportant. Sandy had been an affair; he was the real thing, her husband.

"If you want to talk, later tonight, or some other time, I'm available." Julie put a hand on Sandy's arm. Sandy smiled and laid her hand on top of Julie's, squeezing it tightly for a moment. It felt good to hear Julie confirm that it was a heavy thing for her to have run into Jenny again; she hadn't quite been sure she wasn't making a big deal over nothing. So, she had a right to be upset.

Sandy's drink came, and she let herself stare into the rusty

160

brown liquid. It had been years since she last ordered a scotch on the rocks — she didn't actually like the medicinal taste of the stuff — but tonight she felt like playing at grown-up drinking. She had first started drinking scotch when she was a teenager; she had probably gotten the idea from watching old movies, where the male hero always ordered a stiff drink. Nothing sissyish passed through his lips nor through Sandy's. She was a tough hombre who would only order a real drink. Over the years, Sandy had decided there was no point in ordering a drink she really didn't like, and to her amusement, she found that the drinks she liked were the sissy drinks: whiskey sours, banana daiquiris, all the cocktails that didn't taste like liquor. But tonight Sandy felt the old urge for a scotch. Was she trying to impress Jenny with her sophistication? Or was it more that she was trying to recapture the atmosphere of the time when she had first met Jenny, almost fifteen years ago? God, what a child she was then, so innocent and worldly at the same time. On the dance floor tonight she had felt for a moment that old tender shyness from when she and Jenny had first fallen in love. It was amazing that Jenny could still elicit that very special innocence.

Sandy suddenly felt very tired. She had a lot to think about, and her mind didn't seem equal to the task. She was confused; the past and the present kept sliding into each other, and she didn't know how to keep them apart.

Sandy surveyed the table: all the women were present and accounted for. Everyone seemed a bit drunk — even Pat, who had been drinking seltzer all evening — and Sandy smiled as she watched Pat and Dolores play a game of patty cakes, while Margo and Catherine sang the limerick.

"Hey, I'm getting tired," Sandy yelled across the table, looking at her watch for extra effect. "You women ready to head back?"

"Sandy's watch says she's tired," Margo looked at her wrist to make fun of Sandy. "My watch says I'm still having a good time." The women laughed.

"Aw, come on, Sandy. Don't be a killjoy." Jan lifted her head off the arm it had been resting on.

"Yeah, you old stick in the mud," Pat teased.

"Say what you like, I have to drive us home," Sandy said in her most rational voice.

"Don't worry about it," Dolores mumbled. "I'll drive us home."

"Uh huh," Sandy answered skeptically.

"Actually, I'm about ready to go," Jenny said.

Sandy felt excited. It had never occurred to her that she and Jenny might have some time alone. She hoped none of the other women were ready to leave.

"Well, I don't want to go yet," Julie said. "Why don't the

161

two of you cut out? We'll grab a taxi home."

Sandy looked gratefully at Julie. She was a good friend. "Is that okay?" Sandy asked the group. Julie smiled, Margo nodded, Jan shook her head no, Catherine waved goodbye, and Pat and Dolores giggled as they wrote messages to each other on their napkins. Sandy looked at Jenny, who nodded, and standing together they said goodnight.

"The fresh air feels good," Sandy said as they headed for the parking lot.

"Yeah, it's a beautiful night." Jenny wrapped her arms tightly around herself. Sandy felt an urge to put her arm around Jenny to warm her, but she put her hands in her pants pockets instead.

It wasn't until Sandy sat behind the wheel that she realized how drunk she was: she couldn't find the ignition. She cursed as Jenny laughed. Finally, she found it. "I know that wasn't very encouraging," she said, starting the car, "but I promise to get you home safely."

Jenny leaned back in the seat. "I have the utmost confidence in you, Sandy. I know you won't do anything to hurt me." Sandy found it difficult to swallow. She was having a hard enough time getting them out of the parking lot as it was; this was no time to pay attention to Jenny's seductiveness. She rolled down the window and forced herself to keep her eyes on the road, but she couldn't help noticing with her peripheral vision that Jenny was looking at her and liking what she saw. Sandy imagined pulling off the road and forcefully taking Jenny into her arms. Her lips would press hard against Jenny's, her tongue pushing into Jenny's mouth, as her hands ran along Jenny's sides, squeezing her thighs, until Jenny's excitement was close to bursting.

"So, did you have a good time tonight?" Sandy asked casually.

Jenny lit a cigarette. "You mind?" She pulled the ashtray out. Sandy shook her head. "Actually, I had a wonderful time. Your friends are very nice."

"You sound surprised."

"Not really." Jenny took a few drags and knocked her ashes into the tray. Some particles landed on Sandy's thigh. Jenny brushed them off quickly. "Frankly, I didn't know what to expect."

"A bunch of wild and ferocious beasts is the common stereotype." Sandy tried to keep her voice light. She was disappointed that Jenny didn't seem more shocked by what she had seen.

"I never expected that, Sandy. I don't know where you think I've been since the last time we saw each other." Jenny sounded irritated. Sandy cursed herself for being such an asshole. She was feeling good with Jenny, so why was she going out of her way to alienate her? "I didn't mean that as it sounded,"

Sandy said, feeling chickenshit to be taking it back. "Actually, sometimes I think it might do me some good to be a little more brutish and a little less controlled." She smiled, and Jenny smiled back.

"I don't know, Sandy. You still seem pretty outrageous to me." They laughed.

"You remember that time I was stoned and you dared me to get up on the table in the Rathskeller and sing 'Love Is a Many Splendored Thing'?" Sandy chuckled.

"Do I! I wanted to crawl under the table. I can't remember when I was so embarrassed." Both women laughed. "I don't know if I ever told you this, Sandy," Jenny paused for effect, "but you have the absolutely worst singing voice I have ever heard."

Sandy looked at Jenny with mock hurt. "What kind of thing is that to say to an old friend?"

"Well, at least I got back at you," Jenny said proudly. Sandy was puzzled. "Don't you remember? You were in the shower, singing 'Old McDonald Had a Farm.'" Sandy shook her head. "I invited all the girls on the floor into the bathroom, and when you pulled back the curtain, there we were."

Sandy blushed. "Christ, I forgot about that. That was awful, Jenny."

"So was your rendition of 'Love Is a Many Splendored Thing.'"

Sandy pulled the car into the garage under the hotel. It was brightly lit, and the two of them squinted until they reached the main lobby. Now that she had gotten them home safely, Sandy allowed herself to be drunk. She staggered a little on the way to the elevator.

"Wow, you know what I'm in the mood for," Sandy said excitedly. Jenny shook her head. "Golf." Getting her torso into a drive position, and wobbling a little before she was balanced, Sandy made a mock swing and fell into the wall. Jenny giggled.

"There's supposed to be a really beautiful course on the north side of the island," Sandy said.

"Well, let's play."

"You're kidding."

"No, I'd love to." Jenny sounded sincere. "I never get to play anymore. Barry's not interested in golf, and I don't have any girlfriends I can go with."

"But we don't have our clubs," Sandy said, trying to solve what felt like a very difficult problem.

"We can rent them."

"Good idea. Okay." Sandy turned around and started to walk. "Let's go." Jenny grabbed her arm and pulled her back.

"Not now, Sandy. Tomorrow."

"But what about the conference?" Sandy said guiltily.

"Would you rather play golf or sit indoors listening to boring presentations all afternoon?"

Sandy thought about it for a moment. The elevator came and they walked in. It was not a difficult decision. "I'd rather play golf."

When the elevator door opened to her floor, Sandy stepped out, turning to face Jenny, who was still in the elevator. "Well, this is where I get off. Goodnight, Jenny." The elevator door closed, then opened again.

"Wait a minute," Jenny said, holding the door open. "All night you've been hugging women. Don't I even get a goodnight kiss?"

Sandy put on a Mae West imitation. "Are you flirting with me, Jenny, or just glad to see me after ten years?"

"Probably a combination of both."

Sandy hesitated for a moment, suddenly sober, then leaned over and kissed Jenny deliberately on the cheek. Then she turned and walked down the corridor without looking back.

Sandy sat in the green flowered chair for what felt like a long time. She found herself remembering strange things: the first time she made out with a boy, an English teacher from junior high, the rubber duckie she had bathed with as a child. Seeing Jenny had upset some balance in her psyche, as if her mind were layered like the earth and an underground disturbance had cut through the strata, folding them like the striations in a marble cake.

She wanted company, but it was two o'clock in the morning, and her friends were probably asleep. Julie had invited her to drop by, but Sandy wasn't sure it was fair to impose on her, especially since they hadn't been very close in the last couple of years. She could call Barbara, but then Marian would want to know what was going on and would be insulted if Sandy said she wanted to talk to Barbara alone.

But then maybe Julie was still awake; they might have all just gotten back from the bar. Sandy took the staircase down to the floor below. It was eerie walking through the brightly lit corridors, which remained unaffected by day or night. Outside Julie's room she hesitated and put her ear to the door. A humming from the fluorescent lights in the hallway made it difficult to determine whether she was hearing running water or the buzz of machinery. She didn't want to take the risk of waking Julie, so she turned around to leave. Then she had the brilliant idea that she might be able to see a light from under the door. Walking back quickly, she got down on her hands and knees and put one eye to the crack. It was very dusty down there, and Sandy sneezed before she had a chance to stop herself.

The door jerked open.

"Jesus Christ, Sandy! What the hell are you doing?"

Sandy looked up and saw Julie standing over her in a nightshirt, with a vase in one hand, raised above her head.

"Would you believe I was just in the neighborhood?" Sandy smiled weakly.

"Get off the floor and come in here."

Sandy stood up dizzily and stumbled into the dark room. Julie turned on the table lamp by the bed.

"I didn't want to wake you up," Sandy said apologetically.

"So you decided to frighten me half to death instead."

"Maybe I'd better go, Julie. I'm sorry . . ."

"Would you shut up and sit down?" Julie slid back under the covers and propped the pillows behind her head. "After all this, if you think I'm going to let you out the door without finding out what's going on in that half-crocked skull of yours, then you know nothing about Midwestern grit."

"I thought grit was something you ate," Sandy said, still abashed.

Julie laughed. "You really are provincial, aren't you? Come sit down." Her voice softened.

Sandy sat on the edge of the bed, feeling sheepish; she knew she was acting like a child, but she felt safe with Julie. They went back many years, and Sandy trusted that Julie wouldn't judge her harshly for being a little confused.

"I'm feeling kind of fucked up. I don't know what's going on or what I'm getting myself into. I made plans to play golf with her tomorrow. I haven't even told Shelly about any of this. How am I going to explain it to her?" Sandy's voice was frantic; she felt like she had just stepped onto a rollercoaster and she was getting nauseated around the bends.

"Whoa, slow down, Sandy." Julie threw back the covers and moved behind Sandy, placing her hands on Sandy's shoulders and slowly beginning to knead them. "I don't know when I've seen you so tense," she said as she massaged the back of Sandy's neck. Tears started to run down Sandy's cheeks and splash on her hands, which lay limply in her lap. Her anxiety dissolved immediately; it was this complex sadness she had been avoiding.

Sandy felt Julie's arms around her shoulders, and the tenderness of that gesture made her weeping more intense. For a while there was nothing in her consciousness except the sounds of her sobs and the wetness on her face and chin.

"You got any tissues here?" Sandy asked when her crying abated.

"Yeah, I got some tissues here," Julie said in an affectionate imitation of Sandy's New York accent. She walked to the bathroom and brought back the box. Sandy blew her nose loudly.

Some women would have brought back a handful of tissues, but Julie had brought the whole box; Sandy felt grateful for Julie's generosity.

"Nothing like a good cry to clog the sinuses." Sandy turned for the first time to look at Julie, who sat next to her on the bed. "What happened to us, Julie? We used to be so close and then we just let it slip away."

"Changes." Julie shrugged. "We started moving in different directions."

"You're being kind. It was my fault."

"Oh, come on, Sandy."

"No, it was. I couldn't handle the men you were dating. It upset me to see you go with one jerk after another."

"Looking back on them, I'm not thrilled with any of them either." Both women laughed. Then Julie sighed. "It really hurt me that you didn't want to hear about my men friends. I was pissed at you, Sandy. I felt like you were putting a crazy limit on our friendship. But I understood, and a part of me agreed with you — none of those men were worth very much."

Sandy gathered up her courage to say what she had never been able to say before. "When I told you that I couldn't stand putting any more of my energy into your self-destructive relationships with men, I wasn't being totally honest with you or myself. I wanted you to be a lesbian, Julie." Sandy shook her head. "You were one of my closest friends. Shelly and I had just gotten together, I wanted to share it all with you: becoming a lesbian, finding my anger. . . . I'm sorry."

"It wasn't all your fault, Sandy. You know I love Shelly, but it was hard to be around you two. You were so much in love and so damned good for each other, it wasn't easy to watch that and then go home to my man or pick up some creep in a bar." Julie looked at Sandy intently. "It was a long time ago, Sandy. I'm willing to let it go if you are."

"I think you're getting the raw end of this deal." Sandy stood up. "Why don't you yell at me or something? Tell me how unfair I am, what a *schmuck* I've been."

Julie had a little smile on her face. "If you wanted me to be a lesbian so much, why didn't you do something about it?"

"What do you mean?"

"For an intelligent woman you certainly have some blind spots, Sandy." Julie continued to look at Sandy, and Sandy felt herself start to blush.

"Shit, Julie, we were friends."

"Oh, you only make love to enemies." Julie was sarcastic. "How charitable of you."

Sandy regarded Julie closely. "We didn't sleep together because we decided not to." Julie looked surprised. "Don't you remember? We were talking, and I don't remember how it came up, but one of us said something about being attracted to the other, and the other said she felt the same way, and we agreed not to do anything about it. We didn't want to fuck up our friendship."

"It does sound vaguely familiar."

"You were going with William at the time."

"Oh my God. William." Julie reached over to the bureau and picked up a cigarette. "What a terrible relationship that was."

"I thought you were in love with him."

"I was." Julie got an ashtray from the bathroom. Standing in the doorway, she looked at Sandy with an ironical smile. "He always thought you were real sexy. If it hadn't been for our friendship, I'm sure he would have tried to get into your pants, as the expression goes."

"What do you mean, would have," Sandy said resentfully. Julie walked over to the bed and stood in front of Sandy. "What did you mean by that comment?"

Sandy looked up at Julie in surprise. "The night of the party on 20th Street. When he was drunk." Sandy saw by Julie's expression that Julie had no idea what she was talking about. She cursed herself silently; she thought she had told Julie about that night, but obviously she hadn't. "Hey, it's no big deal, Julie. Let's forget it, huh?"

"I want to know what happened, Sandy." Julie's voice was insistent.

"It was nothing. You and he had gone to sleep in the living room. I was in my bedroom. Anyhow, he came into my room, and . . ." Sandy knew she wasn't looking at Julie and that made it worse, but she couldn't bring her eyes up to face her. ". . . and he got into the bed and started to . . ." Sandy exhaled the breath she had been holding.

"He started to what?" Julie stood stiffly in front of her.

"He came on to me," Sandy said quickly, hoping to end this awful conversation.

Julie's face was hard. "What happened?"

"Shit, Julie. We tangled for a while, and then I finally got him out of the room. Nothing happened."

"He tried to rape you." Julie's face was furious. She walked across the room and clenched the drapes tightly in her hands.

"Julie, he was drunk. He didn't know what he was . . ."

"What are you saying?" Julie screamed. "Are you listening to yourself? He was drunk . . ." Julie jeered, "Is this the Sandy Stein I know, a radical feminist who won't let any man make a sexist comment within hearing distance? Is this the same woman, making excuses for him because he was drunk?" Julie grabbed Sandy's shoulders. "Look at me, Stein, damn it, look at me. Why didn't you tell me?"

Sandy stood up and walked to the other side of the room. Hands in pockets, she turned to Julie. "I don't know why I didn't tell you. I should have. I guess I was trying to protect you. I didn't want to hurt you."

"You're acting so casual about this. Like it didn't upset you in the least." Julie clenched her fist. "That bastard." She turned back to Sandy. "Don't you think I'd want to know that about a man I was living with? How could you not tell me?"

"How could I tell you?" Sandy retorted. "What would you do? Leave him? If you did, you'd hate me for it. And if you didn't, I'd hate you for continuing to see a man who could do something like that. Either way it would have ruined our relationship." Sandy shrugged. "I guess I didn't want to risk it."

"Do you really have that little trust in me, Sandy?" Julie's voice was quiet.

Sandy looked at Julie directly. "I never met a straight woman who would break up with her man because of a friend, or because of anything as remote as a principle." She sighed. "Maybe I should have trusted you, or at least tested you, Julie. I don't know. But at the time, I just didn't know what to do. I felt so . . ." Sandy struggled to get the word out. ". . . humiliated," she whispered.

"Oh, Sandy," Julie cried out, "I'm so ashamed." She turned away from Sandy and stood rigidly by the wall. "To think that the next night I let that fucker into my bed . . ." Julie shuddered.

Sandy walked over and put a hand on her shoulder. "It wasn't your fault, Julie. There's nothing for you to be ashamed of." Julie shook her head. "Listen to me," Sandy said as she turned Julie's face toward her own. "You're not responsible for him. I'm sorry I didn't tell you. I should have. But it was too soon after Jenny; she was my lover and she put men first, so how could I know to trust you to take our friendship seriously?" Sandy put a hand on Julie's cheek, smoothing her tangled hair. She felt her eyes fill with tears as she looked into Julie's open face.

"You should have told me, Sandy." Julie put her arms around Sandy, and Sandy hugged her back. "We should have handled that together."

"You mean you would have gone with me to beat him up?" Sandy teased.

"Why are you still joking about it, Sandy?" Julie sounded pissed.

"Damn it, Julie, if I don't joke about it . . ." Sandy walked to the window and banged one fist into the other hand, making a cracking noise. "I wanted to kill him," she snarled, "but he wasn't just any prick. He was your man. And you were my best friend . . . I think I was just as furious about what he was doing to you as about what he tried to do to me." Striding across the room, Sandy kicked the straw wastebasket into the air, and it crashed against the opposite wall. The women looked at each other and laughed.

"Maybe we should try starting this conversation over." Julie pointed to the bed, and Sandy plopped down. "So you've got a golf date for tomorrow."

"Shit. I forgot all about that. Jenny. I don't know where to begin." Sandy sat up, swinging her feet to the floor. "For one thing, I'm really pissed at her. When I think of the way she treated me and the shit I put up with, it makes my blood boil. If I had been male she never would have treated me that way. Shit, we probably would have gotten married." Sandy smiled. "But then again, if I had been male, we would never have loved the way we did."

Sandy turned to Julie with a quizzical expression. "That's the part I don't understand. If she loved me the way I remember, how could she leave me? And end up with some man?" She shook her head. "The intensity of what we shared . . . how could she be straight? It's one thing for a woman who's never known what it's like to be with a woman. I can understand how they date men, get married, go through the whole routine. And many of the lesbians I've worked with go that route until they discover their lesbianism. But to have known the difference from the start, and still to get married."

Sandy looked at Julie, who was sitting on the cushioned arm of the chair. For the first time she saw why she had been hesitant to talk to Julie about this, and why she had been drawn down here in the middle of the night. Sandy had always thought of Julie as being one of the "real" heterosexuals; Julie seemed to really enjoy men sexually, and to find some vitality in her struggle with men. And then Sandy heard through the grapevine about a year before that Julie was having an affair with a woman.

"I guess what I'm trying to figure out," Sandy continued, "is whether Jenny is a lesbian." There was no doubt in Sandy's mind that Jenny's most intense sexual and emotional experiences had been with Sandy, and probably would be with other women. But Jenny, who Sandy suspected was really a lesbian, was with a man, and Julie, who Sandy had been sure was straight, was now experimenting with women, and Sandy was beginning to wonder what the hell it was all about anyhow.

40

They were on the next-to-last hole, and Jenny had been joking nervously about her game for some time. At first Sandy tried to reassure her that she wasn't playing badly, considering how long it had been, but Jenny persisted in her self-rebukes.

Something was bothering her, and it probably had to do with their being together, but Sandy had no idea what it was. The whole situation was disconcerting, particularly because Sandy had expected that their playing golf together would restimulate some of their old closeness; instead it seemed to be having the opposite effect. And that was exactly what Sandy didn't want.

Jenny swung and hit the ball too high. "Shit." She picked up the tee with a vengeance. "I really am rusty."

"Since I'm hanging around you, maybe I ought to get a tetanus shot?" Sandy teased. Jenny groaned, but Sandy could tell she liked the pun. They walked on.

All morning, to keep from nodding out during a presentation of meaningless findings on "Women's Decision-Making Processes," Sandy had tried to figure out what was going on between her and Jenny. A few things began to fall into place. Like her preoccupation with going to bed with Jenny. When Sandy imagined them making love, at first the fantasy was lovely and erotic, but then it turned cold and mechanical. Afterwards, all Sandy felt was an acute emptiness. She couldn't imagine anything more horrible than feeling detached while making love to a woman; she had carefully protected herself from that experience, and the idea that she and Jenny could create such a nightmare was sobering, even chilling.

The fantasy exercise told Sandy she was off the track; and then she realized that all she really wanted from Jenny was for the two of them to make contact. To touch. Like most Americans, she had immediately translated that need into a sexual one. Then too, the urge to go to bed with Jenny was something of an ego trip: a chance to prove to Jenny what a mistake she had made by leaving Sandy, a chance to show her what she was missing. Sandy's magical lovemaking would instantly convert Jenny into the ranks of women-loving women. Now, while Jenny hit her ball again, Sandy laughed at that moment of megalomaniacal insanity; but she was also embarrassed by the baseness of some of her motivations, and this was more difficult to accept.

Why she needed intimacy with Jenny was a different story. That felt ego-motivated too, but it also felt important. It was more hazy in her mind, but she knew she had to prove something to herself before she could let Jennifer out of her life this time.

When they reached Sandy's ball, she squatted and looked closely for the direction of her next shot. She took her stance and swung, concentrating on the projected path for the ball. The club and ball made a good, solid contact, and Sandy smiled as she watched the ball arc in the air and land squarely at the end of the fairway.

Jenny was looking at Sandy closely. Sandy couldn't tell whether she was examining her or her swing.

"You always had good form," Jenny said enviously.

"Do you remember Miss Johnson?" Sandy tried once more to deflect Jenny's competitiveness.

"Who could forget her?" Jenny stuck out her chest and boomed, "Good morning, girls." Sandy and Jenny laughed.

"I'll never forget the day she walked up to me and said, 'Let's see your form, Stein.'" Sandy forced a tenor voice by tucking her chin down into her neck.

"That's right," Jenny interrupted. "She always used to call you Stein. The rest of us got called by our first names."

"Yeah. Remember? I made a beautiful swing . . ." Sandy stopped walking and positioned herself, empty-handed, ". . . and she said, 'You swing like a man, Stein. Keep practicing, you might be a golfer some day.'"

The two women started walking again. Sandy gazed thoughtfully over the lush green course, which was dotted with grandiose coconut palms and banana trees. "At the time I thought that was the greatest compliment one woman could give to another. Aaagh!" She stopped in her tracks and made a terrible face. "Isn't that incredible?"

Jenny smiled and continued walking, giving no verbal response to Sandy's question. Sandy felt as though a door had opened and then slammed shut again. Was it possible that Jenny hadn't understood what she meant? No, it wasn't possible. Jenny was obviously not involved in the Women's Movement, but she must have been affected by it anyway. So why hadn't she responded? A more upsetting thought occurred to Sandy. Maybe Jenny didn't give a damn.

At the next tee, Sandy asked, "How come you don't have any female friends to play with?"

"I don't know." Jenny shrugged it off. "Most of my close friends are men. I guess I'm more comfortable with men."

Sandy felt an urge to grab Jenny by the shoulders and shake her. How could Jenny say such an ignorant thing? Didn't she know that not liking women meant not liking herself? And where was her loyalty to her sisters? Sandy chose her club, positioned herself momentarily, then hit a powerful, long drive, her anger moving down her arms, smashing the ball into space.

"Whew." Jenny put a hand to her eyes to gauge the distance. "That's two hundred yards at least." Sandy picked up the tee and wordlessly, briskly walked in the direction of the ball. Feeling Jenny hesitate behind her, then slowly start to follow, Sandy tried to calm herself with the thought that Jenny hadn't really meant what she said. She was just defensive; she was uncomfortable with Sandy, so she generalized the discomfort to all women. Sandy began to feel more composed, although a part of her suspected that she was deceiving herself in order to restore peace. For it was only in the spirit of harmony that she would get the answers she required.

They finished the last hole in relative quiet, each woman pretending to concentrate on the game. On the way back to the clubhouse, Jenny tried to make light conversation: "Have you stayed in touch with anyone from Buffalo?"

"Nah Once I moved out west, that ended most of my friendships from college. How about you?" Sandy chastized herself inwardly for going along with Jenny's game, rather than steering the conversation to more important subjects.

"You remember Doris?"

"Sure "

"Well, the last I heard, he was doing his residency, and she was finishing her Master's in Special Ed. They finally got married, and they're very happy."

"How wonderful for them."

As they entered the clubhouse, Sandy regarded Jenny sideways, to see whether she was being so obnoxious on purpose. But Jenny looked as though she had made the most perfectly normal comment. And on the surface, it sounded pretty ordinary, but surely that little bit about the joys of marriage was intended for Sandy's benefit. Or was Jenny really that unconscious? Or, in all fairness, was Sandy being oversensitive?

The clubhouse was filled with local members and tourists, who were boozing it up after their nine holes. Sandy identified the tourists by their brightly colored shirts and polyester pants. Walking to a table by the window, she felt the eyes of different men upon her and Jenny. The irritation of being looked over far outweighed the pleasure of having gotten a window table, and this made Sandy realize she was in a snotty mood. She must have caught it from Jenny, who was now looking quite cheerful.

Just a few seconds after they ordered, the waiter brought their drinks to the table: a dry martini for Jenny and a whiskey sour for Sandy. This was obviously a classy place. Sandy wiped the sweat off her face with the cloth napkin, then dipped it into her glass of water and pressed the cool cloth to her cheeks. Looking up, she saw Jenny shaking her head and smiling.

"You haven't changed much, Stein," Jenny said as she sipped her martini.

Sandy decided to let that remark pass. "So what kind of work are you doing?" She fished out the plastic-looking cherry and dropped it into the ashtray.

"I'm working in a community mental health center," Jenny replied. "My specialty is family therapy, and recently I've become interested in child advocacy."

"Child advocacy." Sandy was impressed. "I don't know much about that."

"Well, it was a natural development from my work with families," Jenny explained. "I'd watch those crazy parents bring in a poor little kid whom they blamed for all the problems at home." Jenny's voice was angry now. "The average American family sees their children as property. That gives them the right to treat kids in any way they deem reasonable. So under the banner of individual freedom, sanctity of the family, and rights to privacy, parents abuse their children physically, sexually, and psychologically." Jenny paused to take a sip of her drink. Sandy was surprised by Jenny's passion and conviction; she'd turned into something of a fighter. "Am I boring you?"

"Not at all. Go on." Jenny looked skeptical. "Really, Jenny."

"Well, child advocacy takes the position that children should have certain inalienable rights, just like adults. As mental health professionals we have an obligation to establish children's rights in relation to incarceration, educational practices, and diagnostic labeling, as well as guaranteeing certain basic minimal conditions within the family, such as the right not to be abused." Sandy shook her head and laughed. "What?"

"Women, children, and queers," Sandy said.

"What are you talking about?"

"The last frontiers of American inequality. Not that poor people or people of color get a fair shake, but theoretically they're supposed to, and when they don't it's a weakness of the system." Sandy picked up her spoon and banged it lightly against her glass. She was beginning to enjoy herself again. "But with women, children, and gays, it's another story. It's incredible that there should be any question about whether parents have the right to abuse their child. Just as it's unbelievable that the country should vote on whether women are entitled to equal rights. Or that lesbians and gays should need special protective legislation to ensure their right not to be discriminated against, and that the struggle for this most basic of Constitutional rights is losing." Sandy looked at Jenny with an amused smile. "It's funny, but in some ways we're working toward similar goals."

Jenny, looking uncomfortable, paused for a moment. "Why do you say you have no involvement with children's rights?" she said quietly. "You just gave a presentation on gay adolescents."

Sandy laughed. "That's true. I guess I don't think of adolescents as children. Of course, legally they are, and that's what gets us into so much trouble when we try to help them form a positive lesbian or gay identity, which the parent may strenuously object to. It's interesting . . . one of the things you didn't mention was the sexual rights of children. Is anybody working on that?"

Jenny whistled. "You just put your finger on the question that every child activist is scared to touch with a ten-foot pole. The field is safe when it talks about the right of a child not to be abused sexually by an adult, but as to the rights of that child to his own sexuality," Jenny shook her head, "that's messing around with the strongest cultural taboos. It's a downright explosive issue."

173

"But in the case of adolescents it has to be dealt with," Sandy insisted. "In fact, American youth are having sex earlier and earlier. Good or bad, it's reality."

"Good or bad," Jenny said with a smile. "I get the feeling that you don't approve of adolescent sexuality."

"The idea of a twelve-year-old girl having intercourse is not very comfortable to me. I could justify my discomfort by pointing to the problem of teenage pregnancies, but it's not just that. I don't know, maybe I'm a bit conservative in this area. I don't worry about the boys, but the girls . . ." Sandy looked out the window. "I don't think I have a double standard. It's just that the girls get hurt, given the fact that society has a double standard. And I think the girls are looking for something else when they go to bed with a teenage boy than what the typical boy is looking for. That's the problem with the whole sexual revolution. It's a revolution created and designed to serve men, not women."

"I see." Jenny smiled into her drink. "Unless I'm mistaken, doctor, didn't you have adolescent sexual experiences that weren't destructive?"

Sandy blushed. "That's different. I was sixteen the first time I went to bed with a man . . ." she paused, then looked straight at Jenny, ". . . and seventeen when I had my first experience with a woman. Sixteen or seventeen is different from twelve or thirteen. I guess that' at I meant about feeling like adolescents aren't children. Tv e seems like a child to me, sixteen doesn't." Sandy pretend o look out the window again, but focused instead on Jenny's reflection in the glass. "And sex between teenage girls is different. Nobody is used or taken advantage of. At the risk of sounding heterophobic, it's more pure."

Sandy knew Jenny was looking at her closely, but she was afraid to meet Jenny's eyes. She swallowed so hard that she was sure everyone in the room could hear. She knew they were on the verge of making contact, breaking through the double entendres, and although she had thought she really wanted that, she now felt frightened. What were they playing with?

"It sounds as though your adolescent experience was quite remarkable." Jenny's voice was quiet and sure. The fear simply disappeared as Sandy met her gaze.

"It was."

For the first time since meeting, they really looked at each other. Sandy felt her excitement grow until she was close to tears. Now Jenny looked down, picking up an unused spoon and moving it around the surface of the table. Sandy could see that Jenny was frightened, torn between maintaining the intimacy and running from it. Sandy didn't want to lose this moment, and she tried desperately to think of some way to reassure Jenny.

"How'd you gals like some company?" a voice boomed in her left ear.

Sandy turned and saw two men, both in their early 40s, standing by the table. They had drinks in their hands, and the more aggressive one stood inches from her shoulder, with a big smile on his face.

"As you can see, we're in the middle of a conversation, so . . ." Sandy tried to keep her irritation under control. The man near her pulled out an empty chair, and the other guy came closer.

"Conversation happens to be one of my strong points," the first man said as he started to sit down.

"What the hell do you think you're doing?" Sandy spit out her words, stopping him in midair. "How dare you come busting in like that! What gives you the right?"

The man stood up, scowling. "Looks like we found ourselves a castrating bitch, Ralph," he said. He's trying to save face with his friend by taking the offensive, Sandy thought; she was further incensed by his unwillingness to apologize.

"I don't see much around here worth castrating," she said icily.

"Why, you . . ." the first man began, but his friend grabbed him by the arm.

"Come on, Dave, it's not worth it."

"Cunt!" Dave snarled, and then they left.

Closing her eyes, Sandy tried to force the adrenalin out of her system by taking several deep breaths and slowly letting them out. When she opened her eyes again, she saw Jenny staring at her.

"Why did you pick a fight?" Jenny sounded irritated.

"Why did I pick a fight? You gotta be kidding . . ." Sandy stopped to scrutinize Jenny. "You didn't resent their intruding on us like that?"

"They were just trying to be friendly."

"Friendly!" Sandy exploded. "Do you think they would have done that if we were two men in a conversation, or a man and a woman? No way. Our privacy would have been respected." Jenny's face showed no comprehension. "But two women by themselves," Sandy emphasized the last two words, "well, he said it: 'Would you like some companionship?' Meaning that two women don't provide companionship for each other." Jenny was still staring at Sandy as if she were a lunatic. "Doesn't that offend you?" Sandy demanded.

"Well, when you put it that way, yes. But that's not the way I look at it." Jenny reached for a cigarette and lit it. Sandy fumed quietly, trying to calm herself down. Did Jenny believe what she was saying, or was she just trying to aggravate Sandy? And why would she want to do that?

"What just happened is the way it is," Jenny commented thoughtfully. "You must get angry a lot."

Sandy sighed, some of the tension relieved. Jenny wasn't playing with her; she really didn't understand Sandy's anger. Sandy regarded her with a new compassion. There was so much Jenny didn't understand. And it was bound to catch up with her some day. Sooner or later, every woman had to deal with being a woman in a man's world.

"Actually, I've calmed down quite a bit in the last few years. You're looking at a woman who's successfully resolved much of her anger. You should have seen me five years ago." Sandy chuckled. "Every time a man made a noise at me, or an 'innocent remark' . . ." Sandy shook her head, ". . . I walked around in a constant rage."

"I don't know that I envy you, Sandy," Jenny said in an unfamiliar voice. Sandy didn't know what Jenny was getting at, so she just continued.

"I've felt the same way myself, at times. Once you see," Sandy looked around the dining room, "you're never quite the same again." She felt a familiar sadness, a muffled aching that originated from a place deep inside her. "But I guess I never learned how not to see." She suddenly felt foolish and wanted to change the subject. "So, where were we?"

"Well, we were talking about what happened to different people from Buffalo," Jenny said, moving the conversation to a safe place. "Do you know about Bunny?"

"No. What about her?" Sandy was unable to disguise fully the irritation in her voice. At another time she would have been very curious about Bunny. But now she wanted to return to the intimacy she and Jenny were sharing when those creeps interrupted them, and Jenny's sudden enthusiasm for gossip meant they would have to start from scratch again.

"I recently ran into someone who knows her," Jenny continued, seemingly oblivious to Sandy's lack of interest. "It was just by accident that we were able to figure out it was the same person." Jenny seemed very much involved in telling this story. The incident with the men had not simply set them back a half-hour; it had set them back ten years. "She married a philosophy student in graduate school, and now nobody knows her by her maiden name. It was terribly lucky that we were able to figure out we knew the same Bunny." Jenny paused for breath and continued. "Now, what is her married name? Krakerhauser, Kraushauser, something like that. Anyhow, he got a job teaching at some college on the Island, and she's teaching high school."

"I thought she got an advanced degree in political science." Sandy's voice was quarrelsome.

"I think she might have," Jenny said, "but you know, there are no jobs at the college level now."

"Oh sure. There's no need for political scientists, but there's still a great demand for philosophers."

"So, you haven't seen anyone at all from Buffalo?" Jenny seemed nervous; Sandy's sarcasm was finally getting through to her.

"Actually, I did run into one woman from school," Sandy said defiantly. "Andrea Goldman."

"Oh, sure," Jenny said with a big smile. "How is she?"

"Okay. It's not likely her name will change, though. She's a lesbian." Sandy saw Jenny's discomfort and pressed her advantage. "Unless she changes it to Goldwoman."

There was a long, awkward pause.

"So how are your parents?" Jenny finally asked.

"They're doing great. They're happily married and living in Dade County. They hawk orange juice on the corner to supplement their Social Security. . . . Look, Jenny, is this what you want to do? Pass the time with superficial gossip?"

"Asking about your parents isn't superficial," Jenny protested. "I really liked them. Is there something on your mind?"

"Damn right there is. I'm filled with questions. Questions I never got answers to." Sandy stared at Jenny, who looked out the window in exasperation.

"I don't see any reason to make this any more difficult on either of us," Jenny said, barely controlling her annoyance.

"Difficult!" Sandy yelled. She no longer cared whether she was being strategic. "Christ, woman. Do you know who I am?" Jenny glanced around the room in embarrassment. Sandy lowered her voice slightly. "I'm the woman who lived with you for four years. I held you when you were scared, I put you to bed when you were too drunk to do it yourself. I loved you and I fought with you, and I grew up with you. Now I listen to you talk, and I'd never know we were once lovers."

Sandy realized her voice had changed from anger to pleading. She wanted urgently for Jenny to acknowledge who she was, and what they had been to each other. Jenny's face was ugly, her lips tightly pursed as they prevented her anger from spilling out. Sandy wanted to pry them open and force the feeling out. If only she could get Jenny angry, then maybe she could get her to admit she cared.

"That was a long time ago, Sandy." Jenny's voice showed a determination to stay in control. "There's no point in dredging up the past. What do you want from me?"

"Dredging?" Sandy roared. "You make it sound like our past is something disgusting, like a dead body in a mire. . . . What do I want from you? I want to know what happened. I want to know why you didn't stay with me. I want to understand how you married and how you've stayed married all these years. I want to know if I'm crazy or if you really did love me the way I remember you loving me."

Sandy felt as though a huge weight had been heaved out of her body with these words. What was happening to her was becoming more clear. She wondered how she could have thought not getting angry was the answer; for it was usually in anger that she discovered what was really on her mind.

"What is the point of this?" Jenny hollered back for the first time. Sandy noticed with pleasure that Jenny seemed really pissed. "You want to know if I loved you? Yes, I loved you." Her tone was venemous. "You want to know if I'm as satisfied with Barry as I was with you? Well, I can't answer that question. I refuse to compare my feelings for you with my feelings for Barry. It's different. I've made choices in my life. And I've chosen to live with a man. I like men." She looked at Sandy challengingly. "I'm comfortable around men. I don't know what you want from me."

Suddenly, Sandy felt guilty. What *did* she want from Jenny? Here she had put both of them through this, and she still wasn't feeling satisfied. She was relieved to hear that Jenny had loved her, but something still didn't feel quite right.

"I owe you an apology, Jenny," Sandy said, looking at her spoon. She forced herself to raise her eyes to meet Jenny's. "I don't know what's the matter with me." She found herself nervously tapping a spoon against her glass. She always hated it when men did that as an outlet for their anxieties. She put the spoon down. "Look, I'm sorry for pushing you into a corner. I had no right to do that. I didn't mean to put you uptight."

Sandy felt sheepish. When she looked up again, Jenny had a small smile.

"The apology is accepted. You know, you still have a terrible temper. How does Michelle put up with it?"

"It was hard in the beginning, but she learned how to fight back." Sandy was grateful to Jenny for normalizing the conversation. "Besides, we don't have as many blow-ups as we used to. How about you and Barry?"

"We go through our rough times. But nothing major. . . . So how *are* your parents?" The women laughed.

"They're fine," Sandy answered. "They really did just retire and are starting to enjoy life for the first time in years." Sandy hesitated, then added, "And they've ended up being real supportive of me." Jenny looked uncomfortable. "Maybe it's because they adore Shelly. She gets along with them even more smoothly than I do." Sandy remembered Jenny's prediction years before and she didn't want Jenny to think she was saying "I told you so."

"Well, my parents are absolutely crazy about Barry," Jenny said defensively. She looked at her watch. "Speaking of Barry, I told him I'd meet him at 4."

"Oh. Okay." Sandy picked up the check. Jenny started to object, but Sandy cut her off. "Jenny, please. This one is on me."

"Okay." Jenny smiled. "Will I see you again?"

"You still want to?" Sandy said in surprise.

"Yeah, if you promise to be on good behavior," Jenny teased. "How about dinner tomorrow night? Barry's got some kind of business meeting anyhow."

Sandy felt a warmth spread through her body. It must finally be the drink, she thought. "Okay. Let's make it early, though, say 5:00. I'm supposed to pick Shelly up at the airport at 8."

Jenny nodded in agreement as they stood up and walked to the cashier. Sandy marveled at how casually they had begun to mention their respective mates. But then why shouldn't it be easy? After all, they were two mature adults.

41

Jenny pushed the revolving glass doors and whirled quickly into the hotel. Her first few steps were wobbly; the sensation was a familiar one, taking her back into her childhood in New York, where most of the department stores had that kind of entryway. As a little girl she had liked to jump into the small compartment and push the door with all her might, staying on the merrygoround the whole way around until she landed exactly in the same place she had started from. But she had rarely gotten to do that; her mother would stop her and explain it was very dangerous, it wasn't nice behavior for a little girl, and she was being a nuisance to the other people.

Walking across the lobby, Jenny realized that she had to piss something fierce. The whole time she and Sandy were talking, neither one of them had gone to the bathroom. No wonder she felt like she was going to explode. She passed a ballroom in which the tables were set, but no one was there yet. She walked in and looked around. There was a hallway off to the left. Feeling very much like an explorer, she strode around the edge of the room until she reached the corridor. As she had suspected, there was a men's room sign immediately to her left, which meant that the ladies' room should be nearby. She found it and entered. The bathroom had pink flocked wallpaper, with brightly lit crystal chandeliers hanging in front of the enormous makeup mirror. Five pink, round chairs with low iron backs were lined up along the marble counter.

Pushing the door open to the inner chamber where the stalls were, Jenny was struck by the absolute silence. She sat down and began to sort out her feelings from her meeting with Sandy. She smiled wryly to herself; it felt more like a meeting than a casual get-together. That Sandy had really interrogated her. Jenny was annoyed. She hadn't asked Sandy any personal questions, so what right did Sandy have to put her on the spot? Sandy made such a big deal about honesty and fairness, but she certainly hadn't been evenhanded with Jenny.

And it was none of Sandy's damned business why Jenny didn't have many female friends. *Any* female friends, a small voice corrected. Well, there was nothing unusual about that, Jenny answered the voice. Many women preferred the company of men. Men were easier to be around; they were often good storytellers, and they had interesting perspectives on what was happening in the world. Besides, they were usually more direct about their desires than women were. If they were attracted to you, it would come up early in the relationship and get resolved one way or another. Jenny understood men; their desires were simple and straightforward, and even when they weren't totally above-board with her, she never had any problem figuring out what was going on with them.

But females were another thing entirely. When Jenny was around them in social settings, she often felt mildly uncomfortable; she never quite knew what they were going to do. That was it, Jenny decided: they were unpredictable. They would say something, and you would know that there was more, but you wouldn't really know what it was. Women seemed to be more convoluted; maybe it was because they were more emotional than men, and so the extra complexity of their feelings got jumbled with their intellects. If that was true, Jenny speculated, then women were more tied to primary process, as Freud had implied in his theories about the more infantile nature of women, or as exhibited in their inferior morality.

But Freud was wrong; certainly she didn't feel less moral or less intellectually capable than any of the men she met, and in graduate school she had known many women who were exceptionally competent, often more so than their male peers. No, it was just in the area of emotion that she had trouble relating to other women, Jenny concluded. Maybe she was more similar emotionally to men?

Jenny usually thought of men as more in control of their feelings, less prone to irrational decisionmaking. Not that men didn't have to deal with unconscious primitive urgings too; of course they did. But they seemed more able to oversee their emotions, to make sure their feelings remained subservient to the whole person. Or to the restraints of the social system they operated in. In the business world, emotions were seen as handicaps, and society at large was still quite intolerant of emotional men, who were often seen as less masculine. Perhaps a fear of homosexuality was hidden in men's unwillingness to lose control of their feelings.

The thought of homosexuality brought Jenny back to Sandy. Sandy was one of a kind. It was impossible to figure out where she belonged on the masculine-feminine scale. Jenny would have thought she was more male-like, but then Sandy didn't seem to like men, so she probably wouldn't agree. Certainly Sandy seemed to have control over her life and over situations with other people. Sandy was no wilting lady. But then, the way Sandy had just acted in their argument at the clubhouse was not typically male either; most men wouldn't have laid out their feelings the way Sandy had. It was very strange: Sandy seemed able to expose her emotions without losing power. Sandy had been highly emotional during their talk; she had raised her voice in public, and even had tears in her eyes at several points. But all of that feeling seemed to come from strength, not weakness or hysteria.

At some point Jenny became aware that she was thinking about everyone and everything but herself. It was perfectly fine to try to make sense out of this situation, but why avoid her own feelings so carefully? Why did they frighten her so much?

Jenny ran over the conversation she and Sandy had just had. She sensed that this conversation contained clues, and if she could only find them, she would understand everything. The question was where to begin looking.

Jenny got up and left the stall, stopping at the large mirror to study her own face. It was not a beautiful face: her nose was too Jewish, her skin too dark, her lips too thin. But she had nice eyes, beautiful hair (everyone always said that was her best feature), and a pleasant if not very interesting expression. Jenny now suspected that this familiar face belonged to a woman she really didn't know. What mysteries lay behind, covered up by that commonplace veneer? Was she an ordinary woman inside and out? Certainly the life she had chosen for herself was very conventional: a good marriage, a good home, a good job. Very humdrum and uninspired by current standards. Sure, she was a professional woman, and that was worth points in some circles. And she had decided she didn't want any children; this attitude was considered odd by many, particularly her parents, who still asked, "When?" and she still answered, "Later." But certainly there was nothing exceptional about this woman who stared back at her without compassion. When it came right down to it, Jenny wasn't sure she even liked this sad person hiding behind mascara and a nervous smile.

But she did like Sandy. As weird as she was, and as demanding as she was, Sandy was a *mentsch*. Jenny smiled to herself. That was a word she hadn't heard in years; living in a small town in Ohio had not done wonders for the little Yiddish she had absorbed from her parents. It was funny that her parents had never asked about Sandy. They had never questioned why Sandy, her constant companion in college, had suddenly disappeared from her life. For the first time Jenny wondered whether her parents had suspected about her and Sandy. No, it just wasn't in their frame of reference.

But it was in hers, at least sort of. She found it hard to keep in mind that she and Sandy had actually been lovers. Was that simply because it had happened so long ago, or were there other reasons why she felt dissociated from that aspect of her past? Until now, she had rarely thought about Sandy. There had been a lot of publicity about the Gay Movement in the last few years, but Jenny had always thought of that in terms of men. She had read Kinsey in graduate school and learned that a large number of people had adolescent homosexual experiences, but she never really connected that information with herself. There was no reason to blow such an experience out of proportion, but she seemed to have done the exact opposite, minimizing it out of existence. Why?

That question made her very uncomfortable. Grabbing her purse, she headed for the lobby elevator. Barry would be upstairs by now, and he would want to know what they had talked about. Jenny felt very irritated. The gall of Sandy asking her how she had married Barry and why she was still with him! The answer was obvious: she was with him because she loved him. What did Sandy think, anyhow? That she had married Barry on the rebound from their friendship? Sandy had quite an ego. She was so damned sure of herself, so contented with her life style. Who did she think she was? She acted like she was better than anyone else, and especially, better than Jenny. The nerve of Sandy, to imply that Jenny's life with Barry was anything less than ideal.

What did Sandy know about Jenny's life, anyhow? She didn't know her at all anymore, and here she was, criticizing Jenny for not living the same way she did. Well, if Sandy found it necessary to be that defensive, then she couldn't be very happy in her own life. That thought consoled Jenny. Maybe Sandy was just pretending to be happy and secure, and underneath that phony veneer she was as fucked up and frightened as the rest of us.

Jenny caught herself. What did she mean, the rest of us? She didn't think of herself as confused or fucked up. She had a good life. Sure, she got bored sometimes, a bit restless, wondering if she was missing out on things, but that was a normal part of living. A normal part of being married.

Jenny tried to remember whether she had told Sandy off for implying that Jenny couldn't possibly be as happy with Barry as she had been with Sandy. Let's see, she had said something about not being able to compare her feelings for the two of them. Now, why had she said that? She could damn well compare them, and she was far more satisfied with Barry than she had ever been with Sandy. The love she had with Barry was mature; she and Sandy had been just a couple of kids experimenting.

The elevator came and Jenny got in. The woman next to her was wearing very sweet perfume, and Jenny thought she was going to be sick. This whole business with Sandy was very aggravating. She should not let herself get upset about it. She was sure Sandy wasn't upset. That damned Sandy never seemed out of control. She played her life like she played her golf: well, with style, and always on top. Jenny felt like a *klutz* next to her on the course; it was a mistake to play with Sandy without warming up first.

The more Jenny thought about it, the more displeased she was with how she had handled their talk. She couldn't quite believe some of the things she had said; like all that crap about how good marriage was for people. She sounded just like her mother. And then avoiding the question of whether she was more satisfied with Barry or Sandy. She couldn't figure out why she hadn't laid that one out. Maybe she was trying not to hurt Sandy's feelings. No, more probably, she didn't want a confrontation. Well, that was chickenshit of her, and she wouldn't do it the next time they got together. No way was she going to let Sandy run the show again. You couldn't be polite with a person like Sandy; she was the kind who took a foot when you gave an inch.

Jenny walked down the corridor to the door of their hotel room. It was painted an awful shade of yellow, bright and shiny like some kitchens. Putting the key in the lock, she swung open the door.

Barry was sitting on the bed, propped against the wall with pillows as he read the newspaper.

"Hi, hon," he said with a smile. "How'd it go?"

Jenny waved her hand in a gesture of dismissal. "It was ridiculous. How was your afternoon?"

"Fine." Barry threw the paper onto the floor and sat up straighter on the bed. "I met with Tim and his partner Steve Williams. We went over the contracts and it looks good. I think I'll be able to close this without much hassle." Barry pulled out two cigarettes, lit them, and held one out for Jenny. "So what happened with you and Sandy?"

Jenny took the cigarette and sat down on the bed. "I don't want to talk about it. She's a bummer."

"Come on, Jenny, get it out of your system. You seem annoyed."

"Furious is the word." Jenny looked at Barry, who appeared amused. "Okay, okay." She stood up and paced to the center of the room. "We played eighteen holes. That went along fine. She was kind of moody, but otherwise it was okay. I played lousy." Jenny stretched her back by arching it. "Then we went to the clubhouse for a drink. We were having a perfectly pleasant conversation and then all of a sudden she got nasty — inserting little snide remarks." Jenny walked into the bathroom and picked up an ashtray, which she carried back into the bedroom. "I don't know why I'm surprised. It's just like her."

Barry looked puzzled. "What do you mean, she got nasty?"

"Just what I said," she snapped. "She was lecturing at me the whole time. Every other word out of her mouth was 'lesbian.' So she's a lesbian. So big fucking deal." Jenny was puffing furiously on her cigarette. "She brandishes her sexuality like a badge of courage. And all the rest of us plain ordinary heterosexuals are inferior by comparison."

"It sounds pretty unpleasant."

"She was picking on me the whole afternoon," Jenny said, ignoring Barry's remark. "I didn't do this and I didn't do that." She threw herself angrily into the armchair.

"Well, it was a bad experience, but you don't ever have to see her again," Barry said.

"Not so," Jenny sighed. "We're having dinner tomorrow night."

Barry felt his body stiffen. If Jenny had such a bad time with Sandy, why did she make plans to see her again right away?

"We're supposed to have dinner with Tim Collins tomorrow night." Barry endeavored to keep his voice calm.

Jenny shrugged. "I didn't think it was important that I join you."

"Well it is," Barry blurted. He took a deep breath. "Besides, I told him you were coming and he said he'd bring his wife. . . . What do you want me to tell him? That you have a date with your ex-lesbian lover?"

"Knock it off, Barry," Jenny said, looking very uptight. "We may have been lovers but we were never lesbians."

"Okay," Barry conceded, "but how come you want to see her again if she irritated you so much?"

"I don't know." Jenny looked away. "I guess I've always had a masochistic streak," she said, smiling coyly.

"What's going on with you, Jenny?"

"What are you talking about?" Jenny looked startled.

"I know you," Barry said more gently, "and I know something is eating at you."

"Stop playing shrink with me, will you?"

"I'll stop playing shrink when you start dealing with this, Jenny." Barry's voice was firm. It was obvious to him that Jenny wasn't just bullshitting him; she was also bullshitting herself. From experience, Barry knew that was dangerous. "Sandy was your first love. And that was a very powerful love. It makes sense that you would be upset." Jenny stared at him in amazement. "You didn't have to tell me these things for me to know . . . nor for me to know that with us it's been different . . . a quieter love, growing slowly with time." As he spoke, he could see Jenny's rigid posture soften. Good, he thought, she is listening.

"I know I'm not the most exciting man in the world, nor the best looking," Barry went on, "and I know you weren't madly in love with me when we got married." He was quite serious now. "And since then you've been attracted to other men, and some day it might be a woman again. But that's okay. I understand."

Jenny was sitting absolutely still. Her eyes bore into him, and he forced himself to return her gaze. "You know it's different for me," he said. "Don't get me wrong, I'm no martyr, it's just that I have no desire to be with any other woman." Barry felt tears well up in his eyes; resolutely he forced them down. It was important that Jenny hear him out and not get distracted by guilt.

"You're my first woman and my first love. I feel very lucky that you chose me to be your husband." He smiled. "I may not be an exceptionally smart man either, but I do understand you." Barry looked down. There was nothing more for him to say. It was up to Jenny now.

Jenny walked over to the bed and sat next to him, placing her hand on his cheek. Slowly he raised his eyes.

"You're a very exceptional man, Barry. You give so much . . ." Jenny looked at him with love. She seemed open to him in a way she hadn't been in a long time. She kissed him lightly, grazing his lips back and forth until they both started to smile. "But you are making a big deal out of this Sandy thing," Jenny admonished in a playful tone.

"Good. Then you won't mind canceling with her?" Barry said innocently.

She hesitated for just a moment. "No. Of course not." She lay down next to him, placing her head on his chest. He held her tightly, and now that she couldn't see, he let the tears fill his eyes and well at the bottom lid.

They lay there for a long time. Gradually, Barry's composure returned. It was hard to know how serious this Sandy business was. It wasn't a question of Jenny's consciously deceiving him;

it was more an issue of her sometimes not knowing how important something or someone was to her.

Once before Jenny had acted very casual about a "friendship" with one of the guys at school. Barry had suspected they were having an affair, but he assumed it was unimportant like the others. It bugged him, but he waited patiently for it to pass and for Jenny to come back to him, as she always did. But instead, she told him one night that she wanted to separate; she was in love with this man. The next few months were awful. They had ups and downs, fights and reconciliations, all depending on how things were going between Jenny and her lover. Barry had to face the possibility that he might lose Jenny; it frightened him the way nothing else ever had. Then Jenny started seeing the other man less, and finally they broke up. It took months before Barry felt safe again in his own home.

That series of events taught him a very important lesson about Jenny: she would always act casual about her attractions, regardless of her true feelings. There had been no warning signs for him, so he had foolishly imagined there were none for Jenny, either. But she had simply kept her knowledge underground, until one day it popped up.

Many times Barry had considered forbidding these affairs. But something always stopped him short; he sensed that laying down rules would only propel Jenny to test and then break them. She seemed to need an inordinate amount of space. Barry didn't know why, but he accepted this reality and made his moves from there.

The issue now, Barry reminded himself, was to assess how much of a threat Sandy presented. Sandy was a good-looking woman. Not the kind of woman he found attractive, by any means, but he could see how someone else might find her appealing. Like Jenny, for example. Jenny had once been very much attracted to Sandy. Could she feel that way again?

Barry remembered how upset Jenny had become when he called Sandy her lesbian lover. Jenny certainly didn't think of herself as ever having been a lesbian. But then she didn't seem to think of Sandy as a lesbian either, and Sandy was definitely a lesbian now. Had Sandy always been a lesbian? Or had something happened to her since Jenny knew her? And if so, what was it that made her change?

Barry didn't understand this sort of thing at all. He had never felt attracted to someone of the same sex, and he couldn't quite imagine what it was like to have such a tendency. He had read in some magazine recently about the gay sensibility in art; but that didn't seem to have much relevance to Jenny. She and he pretty much agreed on what they liked. And although he didn't know Sandy at all, he didn't imagine she had any unusual esthetic tastes. In fact, she didn't seem the type to be greatly interested in art in the first place. So what made someone gay?

Barry shifted his weight, and Jenny stirred. "Did you fall asleep, hon?" he asked.

Jenny looked at him groggily. "I guess I dozed. What time is it?"

"About six."

"Oh." Jenny stretched across him. "I think I'm going to take a shower. I feel like I could sleep through the night." Pushing herself off the bed, she walked to the bathroom. There were a few noises, and then he heard the water go on.

Barry tried to remember whether he had ever met any homosexuals. There was that one time he and Jenny and another couple had gone to a gay bar, but they hadn't talked to anyone. No, Sandy was the only homosexual he knew. And Jenny was the only person he knew who had had a homosexual experience. It wasn't much to go on.

He wondered how someone knew that they were homosexual. He had once thought homosexuals didn't like people of the opposite sex; but he knew from Jenny that Sandy had dated in college, and he had read somewhere that gays were quite capable of having sex with an opposite-sex partner. Recently he had heard a new expression being bandied around, what was it, something about being partial to one or the other, "sexual preference," that was it, and this seemed to imply that some people were capable of both but preferred one over the other. Barry imagined that those people were bisexuals. So there must be two types of bisexuals then: those who liked same-sex partners better and those who liked opposite-sex partners better. A frightening thought exploded in his mind. Could someone be a lesbian and not know it?

He reached for a cigarette, found the pack empty, and crumpled it forcefully, throwing it in the direction of the wastebasket across the room. Then he opened the night-table drawer for a new pack. It had never occurred to him before that someone might not be sure what they were; he had always been so certain about himself that he just assumed everyone else was pretty much the same, one way or the other. But if someone was bisexual, how did they decide which way to go? If the person was screwing around, there would be no problem; they could do both at the same time. But if they fell in love with somebody and made a commitment, that would be entirely different. Maybe that was it. A bisexual ended up with whoever they fell in love with. If it was someone of the same sex, then they were gay, and if it was someone of the opposite sex, then they were normal.

That seemed to make a lot of sense. What was interesting, though, was that none of Jenny's affairs since they were married had been with women. So, maybe Jenny was really more heterosexual, with only a slight tendency towards homosexuality.

Perhaps if she had never met Sandy and fallen in love, she would never have had a homosexual experience. Maybe the affair with Sandy was a fluke; for some unknown reason, Jenny was powerfully attracted to Sandy, even though she was really heterosexual. If so, all he had to worry about was keeping Jenny away from her. With Sandy out of the picture, things would settle down to what they had always been.

Barry felt very proud of himself. Not only had he handled this situation remarkably well, but he also was being pretty smart about what was going on. If his analysis was right, there was no cause for alarm.

Jenny came back into the room and went to the closet to pick out some fresh clothes. Barry watched her with pleasure as she dressed.

"You know, I was thinking, hon," Jenny said as she undid her toweled hair, letting it fall onto her cheeks, "it might be nice if I stopped by Sandy's room and told her I can't make it tomorrow night." She picked up a brush and ran it through her hair several times. Then she walked over to Barry and sat next to him on the bed.

"If I don't see her tomorrow night, then I probably won't see her again, and I'd rather say goodbye in person than over the phone." Jenny's expression was casual and her voice matter-of-fact. Barry could detect no guile. "Is that okay with you, hon?" she asked.

Barry smiled. "Sure, babe. Go ahead, and then we'll go out for dinner afterwards." He leaned over and picked up the paper. "Besides, this way I get to read Ann Landers," he said jokingly. "You know how I like to stay in touch with what your colleagues are doing." Jenny punched him lightly in the shoulder.

Jenny walked to the door and turned around to regard Barry, who pretended to be engrossed in the paper. "I'll be back in a few minutes," she said. Barry raised his head briefly, smiled, then lowered it again. He didn't want Jenny to think he was worried about her. After all, what could happen in a brief goodbye?

Jenny left the room. When the door closed, Barry put down the paper. He was in an exceptionally good mood. They would go out and celebrate tonight, have a good bottle of wine with dinner. This incident was coming to a close.

42

For some reason she was upset. Jenny walked slowly down the long hall. Here she had just had a wonderfully intimate time with Barry, and they were closer to each other than they had been in months, and nonetheless she was filled with a vague sadness.

It didn't make any sense. Unless Barry was right; perhaps seeing Sandy again was heavier than she wanted to admit.

Jenny realized she didn't even know what room Sandy was in. She'd have to check with the desk downstairs. Stepping into the elevator, she felt on the verge of tears. Just in case the man and woman in the elevator with her were noticing the sudden buildup of liquid in her eyes, she pulled out a tissue and blew her nose. This way they'll think I have a cold, Jenny thought.

There was a long line at the desk, and Jenny took her place at the end. It just didn't make any sense that she should be so volatile. She felt as if she were losing her best friend. Which was ridiculous. But then again, in many ways Sandy *was* her best friend, at least her best girlfriend. She had never been as close to another woman as she once was to Sandy. And in some mysterious way, they were still close.

Jenny suddenly panicked at the thought that she might never see Sandy again. In a few minutes they would say goodbye, and then they would leave each other's lives as completely as they had years before. Fighting back the sense of desolation, Jenny told herself that she was overreacting. She would miss Sandy, of course, but she would get over it. She had the first time and she would now.

The woman in front of her was complaining to the clerk: she had asked for twin beds and gotten a double by mistake. There was no way she and her husband could possibly share the same bed; he was a very restless sleeper, and she wouldn't get a moment of sleep. Jenny found herself smiling sympathetically at the man behind the counter.

"You wouldn't believe some of the people we get here," he said, shaking his head, as she approached the desk. She got Sandy's room number and headed back to the elevator. The woman was now repeating her complaint to some man who stood there awkwardly, obviously a stranger who happened to be in the wrong place at the wrong time. Jenny tried not to laugh.

She thought about Sandy again. If only they could have put aside the anger and really talked to each other, woman to woman. Jenny had a lot of questions she would have liked to ask Sandy; she would have liked to find out what Sandy's life was like, what it was like to be a lesbian. Jenny smiled wryly. If she had asked Sandy those questions, Sandy probably would have accused her of making small talk again. With some shock, Jenny realized it wasn't that way at all. The answers to those questions were very important to her.

On the way up in the elevator, she decided to invite Sandy to come visit any time she was in the area. Jenny smiled ruefully. The likelihood of Sandy coming to her neck of the woods was less than zero; but maybe she would get an invitation from Sandy, and it wasn't at all improbable that she might find herself in

Los Angeles some day. She just couldn't bear the idea of never seeing Sandy again. Who would she fight with? She and Barry had occasional arguments, but they were nothing like her battles with Sandy. Jenny was rusty with those kinds of altercations, as today's skirmish indicated, but Sandy had clearly stayed in shape. It looked as if she'd have to practice her yelling as well as her golf before she'd be ready to see Sandy in L.A. Jenny realized with surprise that she was serious about visiting Sandy in California. She'd have to do quite a job of finagling to get Barry to take that trip, but it wouldn't be impossible.

She knocked on the door. Sandy opened it and looked startled.

"Hello."

"Hi," Sandy stammered. "Uh . . . come in."

Jenny entered and looked around. Sandy seemed uncomfortable to have her in the room. It suddenly occurred to Jenny that they were in a hotel room. Alone. Except for the big queen-size bed.

"I can't believe it," Jenny said, turning around. "Your room is decorated exactly like mine." She realized, as soon as she had said it, that she had used the singular "mine" instead of the plural "ours." What was she doing? "These hotels remind me of dormitories," she blurted out, much to her horror.

"Well, not quite." Sandy seemed amused and completely in control once again. There was another awkward silence.

"Listen. The reason I came up is that I'm not going to be able to have dinner with you tomorrow night." Jenny saw the look of disappointment flash across Sandy's face before she had a chance to disguise it. So she wasn't Superwoman after all. "I'm sorry about having to cancel," she continued. "It turns out that Barry's plans included me."

"Oh." Sandy put her hands in her pockets. She suddenly looked very young to Jenny. "Then I guess we won't see each other again. Shelly and I are leaving for Hana Saturday afternoon."

"Hana! You aren't going to that place that was advertised in the *Psych Gazette*, are you?"

"Yeah." Sandy sounded surprised. "Paradise Cove." She began to mimic a travel brochure: "Secluded cabins, nestled in luxuriant foliage . . ." Jenny joined in, and they finished the sentence together: ". . . by our own private beach." Both women laughed.

"Barry and I saw the same ad. We reserved a cabin starting next Wednesday. I wonder who the other eighteen couples are," Jenny said, tickled by the possibilities.

Sandy was shaking her head back and forth like someone watching a tennis match. "I don't believe this," she repeated several times.

"Well, this is great," Jenny said. "We can have our dinner on Maui."

"Sure," Sandy said with enthusiasm. "Let's do that."

Jenny reached over to Sandy and gave her a quick hug. Sandy seemed startled again. "Great," Jenny said, walking to the door. "See you then."

She whistled as she skipped to the elevator. She was feeling very silly, almost schoolgirlish. Calming herself down, she walked sedately into the elevator. She could relax now; she and Sandy would still have some time together.

43

Hands in pockets, Sandy stared out the huge windows of the passenger lounge. She was glad Shelly's flight hadn't arrived yet; she wasn't at all ready to see her. That made Sandy feel guilty. But not half as guilty as she felt about not having told Shelly that she had run into Jenny. It wasn't like her to keep secrets from Shelly; usually she blurted out everything, even her plans for Shelly's surprise birthday parties.

Sandy rationalized to herself that she hadn't wanted Shelly to hear about it on the phone. She wanted to be able to see Shelly's face and deal with both of their reactions, and there was no way she could do that long distance. But Sandy knew that wasn't the whole story; for the first time in their relationship, she was feeling secretive. She didn't want to share her emotions toward Jenny with Shelly. How she felt about Jenny had nothing to do with Shelly, and Sandy knew herself well enough to know that once she told Shelly, her own feelings would be influenced by Shelly's. She would begin to respond to Shelly's fears, insecurities, and demands; and then she would never know what she really felt herself.

It made sense, but it wasn't very comfortable for Sandy. She didn't like to think of herself as a selfish or devious person, and in the last few days she had been both. And tonight would be her Judgment Day. No wonder she wasn't looking forward to Shelly's arrival.

She hoped Shelly would be understanding. She usually was, about most things. But Shelly did have a few blind spots, and Jenny was one of them. Shelly always made snide remarks any time Jenny's name came up. At first, Sandy attributed this to jealousy; she never hid from Shelly how important Jenny had been to her, and she could understand why Shelly would feel threatened. But even after their fifth year together, the final proof that her union with Shelly was far more substantial than the four-year affair with Jenny, Shelly still persisted in making disparaging comments about Jenny whenever Sandy mentioned her.

Of course, Sandy reminded herself, she was at least partially responsible for Shelly's attitude. When had she ever said good things about Jenny? No wonder Shelly thought of her as an ogre; like most people who had been abandoned, Sandy tended to present her ex-lover's shortcomings rather than her virtues. She had learned that lesson early on in her therapy work. In one of her first cases, she listened for weeks to her client's description of a brutish, uncaring husband. Sandy came to hate him passionately and couldn't understand why her client stayed with him. Then the husband came to therapy, and Sandy was shocked: the savage husband turned out to be a mild man who was obviously very much in love with his wife. It was a hard lesson to learn, particularly for Sandy, who craved simple situations where she could easily tell the right and wrong of it, and choose her side. Perhaps she had been as guilty of distortion as her client.

Which didn't help her a damn bit now, Sandy told herself harshly. She had created this situation and now she was going to have to deal with it. She didn't know what was the matter with her; she wasn't usually this cowardly about taking her medicine. But then again, she wasn't usually this much in the wrong.

It was with a sigh of relief that Sandy realized just how guilty she felt. She had never lied to Shelly before. Not that this was technically a lie; it was a misleading omission. By most people's standards she had probably not done anything horrible, but by her own code of ethics she had engaged in a severe violation of principle. In her book, lying by omission was just as bad as outright lying — well, perhaps not *quite* as reprehensible, but almost, and she certainly didn't deserve any gold stars for the way she had handled this. Sandy grinned self-mockingly. It had been years since she last thought about the gold stars her teachers handed out in grade school. But that was exactly the feeling: she had been a bad little girl and was undeserving of any rewards.

It was funny how doing something wrong so quickly reduced you to feeling like a child. Perhaps she should meet Shelly with a diaper tied around her waist and a pacifier in hand. No, Shelly would not find that amusing. She was coming to the islands to vacation with her adult female lover. The least Sandy could do was to face this thing squarely — "and take it like a man," a sardonic voice whispered. She must be really wigging out if she was getting into a John Wayne mood! It was one thing to feel childish and strictly another to slip into male bravado. "That's what you get for hanging around straight women," her sassy voice quipped. "Oh, shut up," Sandy retorted.

She took several deep breaths and tried to relax. If she

didn't calm herself, Shelly would know something was wrong from the moment she stepped off the plane. Usually Sandy appreciated Shelly's sensitivity, which made it easier for her to talk about herself. But she didn't think it was fair to lay a bummer on Shelly as soon as she arrived. That meant she had to get her head together in the next three minutes if the plane was on schedule, which it was sure to be now that she needed some extra time.

Shelly would be excited when she got off the plane. And she would expect Sandy to be jubilant too. Jubilation was not what she was feeling, and she knew there was no point even attempting to feign such an exacting emotion. Shelly would say that she had missed her. She would surely notice when Sandy changed the subject, rather than responding in kind. Desperately, Sandy tried to reconnect herself to the woman she loved and the life they shared in a distant place called Los Angeles. She thought about their home. She could visualize their living room, but all the objects appeared static and two-dimensional; some important perspective was missing.

Everyone always said that when you loved two people at the same time, the two distinct and separate feelings had nothing to do with one another. But if that was true, then why in hell was she suddenly cut off from her feelings for Shelly? All the humanistic psychologists talked about the unending supply of love that people have available, just waiting to be tapped; hadn't those guys ever heard about the natural phenomenon called drought? With some shock, Sandy realized that she wasn't feeling anything for Jenny either. Her insides were parched.

She stood motionless and watched the plane taxi up to the terminal.

44

The sky began to change. At first it had been clear, an endless pale blue which stretched across the horizon. Shelly had picked up her copy of *The First Sex* and begun to read it for the second time. Elizabeth Gould Davis was a good example of a creative thinker without adequate scholarship to back up her work; this text would demonstrate both the limitations and the advantages of abandoning traditional modes of scientific inquiry. Now, Shelly rested the book on her lap and gave her attention to the flock of pudgy cottonballs that enveloped the plane.

It wasn't until she got away that Shelly ever realized how bored she was with the almost constantly sunny weather of L.A. She missed the tempestuous thunderstorms of the East, the rumbling belly of gray-black sky, ripped by streaks of lightning. In fact, she sometimes thought that growing up in the moderate climate of Southern California left an indelible imprint on the native children: they were beautiful, healthy, and incontestably dull. Even the Jews didn't seem Jewish.

Sighing, Shelly leaned back and stretched her feet out in front of her. She was really looking forward to this vacation. It would be wonderful to have some quiet time alone with Sandy. For a few months now she had been feeling unusually romantic; one night she even came home with a dozen yellow roses, and she and Sandy had a special dinner with wine, for no reason at all. But then Shelly got busy reading student papers and working on the "No on 6" campaign, and Sandy began to worry about her presentation for the convention. In a way, Shelly was glad she had missed Sandy's panel; at least now when she arrived Sandy would be free of that pressure, and they could start their vacation in Hawaii without any anxieties.

Sandy probably wouldn't have eaten dinner yet, so maybe they would go out and start celebrating immediately. Shelly smiled to herself. She was beginning a vacation with the woman she loved, on an idyllic island in the Pacific. What more could a woman want?

She did want to spend some time looking for petroglyphs, and that was bound to present a slight problem, as Sandy had no interest in "looking for some stupid rocks." They would have to negotiate a deal: Shelly would go snorkling with Sandy, something she was frightened to do, if Sandy would accompany her on a field trip. Sandy would complain some, but she would be reasonable; half of her fun came from making believe she didn't want to do things that Shelly could tell she was actually curious about, by the incessant questions she would ask. But Sandy would deny it to the end. Shelly could just imagine Sandy's response to the first petroglyph she saw. "Feh," she would say, making a face, "this isn't a very good drawing. For this you *schlepped* me five miles into the hills?"

Sandy's lack of respect for tradition and her impatience with the sublime were among the things that Shelly loved best about her. All day at work Shelly was exposed to the pretentiousness of her academic colleagues. Sandy was her daily breath of fresh air. Of course, sometimes Sandy was infuriating, like an invigorating breeze that suddenly transformed into an annoying draft. This happened when Sandy refused to see the value of something dear to Shelly; opera was the best case in point. Not only was Sandy unwilling to go to an opera even once, but she made disrespectful comments the few times Shelly went with friends. Over the years Shelly found herself going to the opera — which had once been a real passion for her — less and less, and this was one of several grudges Shelly harbored.

194

She didn't know how, but one day she would get her stubborn lover into an opera house.

Shelly allowed herself to be carried along by the stream of passengers leaving the plane. Sometimes the noise and proximity of a crowd made her feel disconnected; but tonight she was in harmony with the people pushing and jostling their way through the narrow passageway. With a growing sense of excitement, Shelly searched the crowd for Sandy. Hurriedly scanning the reunited families, she spotted Sandy leaning against a pillar. She waved frenetically, and Sandy finally saw her and smiled. Shelly moved quickly across the room and threw her arms around Sandy, who hesitated for a moment before returning the hug. Surprised, Shelly stepped back and looked at Sandy closely.

"You okay?"

"Of course I'm okay. How could I not be okay in Hawaii? ... How was your flight?"

"Fine." Shelly pulled back slightly in response to Sandy's evasion. Sandy seemed a bit withdrawn, almost distracted.

"Let's get out of here, honey," Sandy said warmly, putting her arm around Shelly's shoulders. Shelly immediately relaxed. After all, it had been three days since they last saw each other; maybe it was just taking Sandy a little while to get comfortable again.

"I sat next to a woman who lived on the islands all her life," Shelly said. "She told me about a beautiful waterfall near Hana." Shelly looked at Sandy, who was now watching the people passing them on the escalator in the opposite direction. "Are you listening to me, Sandy?" Shelly squeezed Sandy's wrist.

"Sure, I'm listening," Sandy replied a bit guiltily, jerking her head back. "You met a woman on the plane . . ."

"Yes, and she told me about a secret waterfall. I thought you loved waterfalls and were looking forward to doing some exploring." Shelly heard some peevishness creep into her voice, and she felt irritated with herself.

"It's so good to see you, babe." Shelly kissed Sandy on the tip of her ear.

Sandy smiled awkwardly. "That waterfall sounds really great, hon. It's just like you to do research, even on the plane."

Shelly sneaked a look at Sandy as they stepped off the escalator. It wasn't only that Sandy was being so undemonstrative; there was a listlessness even in the way she moved, and her face had the lackluster quality of unattended copper.

"So how are you?" Shelly tried to keep the concern she was feeling from entering her voice. Sandy watched each piece of luggage intensely as it slid down the metal chute and crashed into the low containing wall by their legs. There was no longer any doubt that Sandy was acting strangely; the question now was why.

"Okay," Sandy said noncommittally. "Actually, not bad," she added after a pause.

"Didn't anyone ever tell you New Yorkers that the English language has more than four descriptive adjectives?" Shelly teased. She imitated a Bronx accent: "Okay, not bad, could be worse, decent."

Sandy laughed. "It *is* good to see you," she said, really looking at Shelly for the first time. She quickly kissed Shelly on the lips. Then she spotted Shelly's luggage and rushed around to grab it before it was lost to the next revolution of the turntable. Shelly smiled. This was the Sandy she knew.

Shelly debated whether she should press Sandy for an explanation. The airport wasn't the place; it would be better to wait until they were in the car and had some privacy. They walked to the parking lot in silence, Sandy seemingly absorbed in watching the cars and people around them.

Shelly began to get annoyed. It was obvious that if she didn't initiate conversation, there wouldn't be any. Why was Sandy so damn grumpy all the time? There was always something bothering her. She never gave herself any time off; as soon as one crisis was resolved, she was already worrying about the next. And she expected Shelly to be right there with her, compliant to her moods. Well, she was sick and tired of Sandy's demands and Sandy's moods. It was time for Sandy to accommodate to *her* needs for a change. And right now her need was to enjoy their vacation. The last thing she wanted was to turn this trip into some kind of heavy encounter. You'd think Sandy got enough of that at the office.

Suddenly Shelly felt guilty. Sandy didn't usually get upset over nothing. Maybe there was something wrong. Shelly tried to figure out what that might be. Perhaps Sandy had really missed her and was angry with herself for being so dependent. No, that wasn't likely. Sandy was pretty comfortable being a "dependent slob," as she often joked.

Then maybe something really terrible had happened. It wasn't the presentation; Sandy had told her it had gone fine, and she wouldn't lie about that. Perhaps one of their friends was sick. God knew everyone was having hysterectomies lately. Shelly hoped it was nothing more serious than that. Or maybe some couple was breaking up. It would have to be close friends of theirs, or Sandy wouldn't be upset about it. Maybe it was Barbara and Marian. They seemed to be going through a rough period lately, and they certainly had a strange enough relationship, with Barbara's outside affairs that were never talked about. Perhaps one of those casual affairs had turned serious.

Sandy did have a tendency to protect Shelly from bad news; she would carefully pick a time when she thought Shelly could handle it. What she never seemed to realize was that the bad news was written all over her face, and Shelly's fantasies during Sandy's silence were usually far worse than the reality Sandy was trying to protect her from. Shelly decided she should bring it up now, so they could get whatever it was out in the open. Just as she was about to speak, Sandy swerved the car out of the fast lane into the right lane, cursing at the old jalopy to her left.

"That's the fast lane, you creep!" Sandy yelled out the window at the old driver and his wife, who were staring straight ahead like rigidified mummies. Sandy's angry outburst and the tightness with which she clenched the stick warned Shelly this was not a good time for questions. She controlled a strong urge to make conversation. Better to let Sandy blow some steam off now, and then Shelly could ask her questions at the hotel, if Sandy didn't get to it first.

As she unpacked her suitcase, Shelly watched Sandy pace back and forth across the room, the way she used to when they were first together. "Sounds like the conference has been pretty boring," Shelly said cautiously.

"That's the understatement of the year." Sandy's tone was indifferent, rather than irritated. All of her reactions seemed slightly off-kilter. "How are the girls?" she blurted out suddenly.

"Fine." Shelly laid the last of her things in a drawer. "They missed you. Sappho kept jumping on the bed and sniffing your side, and Emma tried to climb into the car every time I left."

Sandy nodded, then walked over to the bed and lay down, her hand tucked under her head. She moved around restlessly on the bed, finally turning on her side and distractedly flipping the pages of the convention program. For the first time it occurred to Shelly that Sandy might need her help in getting out whatever was bothering her. She walked over to the bed. "Are you sure everything is okay, hon?"

Sandy looked up. "Huh. Why?"

"Well, you seem a bit preoccupied. I felt it last night, too, when we talked on the phone. It was as if there was something you wanted to tell me, then decided not to."

Sandy sat up. "Don't you ever get tired of being astute?" she said with a weak smile. "Come sit by me." She patted the bed next to her. Shelly sat down. She tried to be patient as Sandy struggled to find the right words.

"I don't know why this is so hard for me to talk about," Sandy began, then paused. "I . . . I ran into Jenny a couple of days ago. Jenny Chase." The addition was unnecessary; Shelly knew instantly whom Sandy meant.

"Well, it was bound to happen one of these years," Shelly said, switching to an automatic pilot system, which led her involuntarily to the right thing to say. Inside her body, from which she now felt quite removed, she heard an alien voice screaming.

"Yeah, I guess so," Sandy continued, visibly relieved by

Shelly's moderate response, "but I wasn't really prepared for how it would feel."

That makes two of us, Shelly thought. Sandy looked very far away, and between them was a thick cushion of invisible padding, which muffled the sounds emanating from Sandy. This was a familiar state, Shelly reminded herself; she often reacted this way when she was taken by surprise. There was nothing to be frightened about. She forced herself to focus and turn Sandy's sounds into words.

"It's just felt so strange," Sandy went on, "and each time it's felt different." The words "each time" rang in Shelly's head with the persistence of an approaching fire engine. Some of the fogginess in her head cleared, and she felt a hot flash of anger.

"Diversity is the spice of life," Shelly said, only vaguely aware of mocking Sandy. "I'm glad you're having such a good time."

"Oh, for Christ's sake, Shelly!" Sandy's voice was angry. "Would you please have the decency to be upfront about this? If you're pissed, just say so, but don't give me any of that sarcastic bullshit."

Sandy's anger thrust Shelly further into confusion. What the hell was going on? If Shelly was the one who was supposed to be angry, then how come Sandy was doing the yelling? Shelly wished she had never come to Hawaii. She imagined herself getting back on the plane and returning to her quiet, safe house.

"Goddamn it, Shelly, will you answer me instead of sitting there like a zombie?" Sandy hollered. Jolted, Shelly realized she was going to have to deal with this; fantasies of returning to L.A. would not help. She pushed away the remaining clouds, leaving only a thin film between her and Sandy.

"I'm sorry," Shelly said. "I know I'm not being very supportive. I wasn't prepared for this either. Go on and tell me what it's been like." Sandy looked hesitant. "No, really, Sandy, I want to know." And she did want to know; she needed more information. That was the task for now. There would be plenty of time later to throw a fit.

Her neck went rigid and arched at the base. Maybe she was overreacting. After all, Sandy had only been gone for three days. What could happen in 72 hours? Shelly was immediately sorry she had translated the time into hours; the considerably larger number of 72 made it sound as though a lot more could happen. She forced herself to stay calm and pay attention to what Sandy was saying.

"Sometimes I look at her and she seems like a stranger. But then the other times . . . I look at her face and it's as familiar to me as my own."

Or mine, Shelly thought reflexively. Irritated with herself

for making such a comparison, she nodded encouragingly at Sandy.

"I just can't seem to make sense out of my feelings for her," Sandy went on. "All I know is that they're intense. And then I'm not sure if they're really about her or about something else." Sandy threw her hands up.

Shelly could see how upset Sandy was, but she was reluctant to sympathize with her. What about *my* needs, she thought. She felt torn between consoling Sandy and resenting the entire situation.

"I feel like I've been transported back in time. But there are two me's, the one I am today and the one I was ten years ago with Jenny." Sandy's eyes were now full of tears. Shelly softened considerably. "I just feel so damned confused. I can't get those two me's to agree on anything, and every time they have a fight about what I'm feeling or what I'm doing, they each start to tear at me." Sandy looked at Shelly with trust. It was hard to stay angry with her when she was so vulnerable. Shelly's love for Sandy swelled inside her, and she gently placed her hand on Sandy's cheek. Sandy's tears started to spill over.

"Shelly, is this okay with you?" Sandy was crying a little harder, and some liquid was hanging from her nose in a thin strand. Shelly nodded. "I mean, you are sure . . . you're not threatened by all this?" It was a silly question, but Sandy needed some reassurance.

"Of course I'm threatened by it," Shelly answered, trying not to express her impatience. "I felt my stomach knot as soon as you mentioned her name. I've hated that woman and been jealous of her for years. And having to hear about your feelings toward her on the first night of our vacation is not exactly what I had in mind." Shelly realized with pride that she had kept her sarcasm to a minimum. "But it's happened and I want to be supportive. . . . Is this the first time you've let yourself cry?"

"Pretty much," Sandy said in a small voice. "I don't want this to mess up our vacation either." Shelly's irritation disappeared; Sandy was in pain, and she needed her now.

"Come here," Shelly said softly, opening her arms wide. Sandy scuttled down and snuggled against her, laying her head on Shelly's breast. When Shelly caressed her hair, Sandy released a big sigh and burrowed in a bit further.

With Sandy lying peacefully in her arms, Shelly became more agitated. Sandy had gotten the guilt and anger out of her system, and now she was fine; but Shelly was just beginning to feel the weight that had been dumped on her. This is exactly like Sandy — going to such a length to avoid a peaceful vacation, Shelly thought. Even if it wasn't intentional, Sandy had to be responsible for it in some way. There was no such thing as co-incidence; things happened to people when they wanted them to happen. After all, Shelly had gone to many professional meetings, and she never ran into any of her ex-lovers. So Sandy must have done something to cause this encounter. And now she, Shelly, would have to live with the consequences.

It simply wasn't fair. First she had to listen to Sandy's endless monologues about her desire for an affair. And no sooner was Sandy off that kick than she "accidentally" ran into Jenny and was preoccupied with her. This was really the last straw.

Sandy shifted her position, moving her head lower onto Shelly's lap. Shelly suppressed an impulse to pull out a clump of Sandy's hair in one big yank. Sandy was very vain about her hair; she fretted all day when it didn't look right. She deserved a bald spot that would take months to grow back.

Shelly frowned. This line of thinking was not making her feel any better. If anything, she was slightly ashamed of her reactions. She had every right to be pissed, but Sandy's seeing an ex-lover a couple of times was not quite legitimate grounds for dismemberment. And although Shelly had a stockpile of resentments from the past, her fury did seem a bit extreme. But this isn't just any ex-lover, she reminded herself. And that was true. She had harbored a passionate hatred for Jenny ever since Sandy first talked about her. She hated Jenny for the spineless cowardice that made her leave Sandy for the safety of marriage. She couldn't stand Jenny's sycophantic need for security, her fear of facing the unknown or taking an unpopular position, her passive compliance with the powers that be. And on top of all that, she was important to Sandy. It was hard to imagine how Sandy could have fallen in love with such a woman, but she had.

That someone like Jenny had witnessed Sandy's transformation from adolescent to woman, was very difficult for Shelly to swallow. She wished that she had known Sandy during that time, that she had been the one to share in Sandy's discovery of love and sexuality. But all of that beauty had been wasted on a woman who didn't have the good sense to appreciate it. A woman who treated Sandy terribly and hurt her very deeply.

And despite all this, Sandy still had an idealized image of Jenny in her mind. She seemed to feel that she owed Jenny a big debt, for having taught her how to love. Most importantly, for having taught her how to love women. Shelly was sure that Sandy had actually learned how to love women from her mother, who adored Sandy and had taught her that women were to be respected.

In Shelly's view, Sandy was meant to love women, and if it hadn't been Jenny, it would have been someone else. But Sandy was convinced that having known Jenny was crucial to her development of lesbian feelings, and there was no arguing with her on this point. In some very basic way, Sandy was still loyal to

Jenny, and she always defended Jenny against Shelly's criticisms.

The only comforting thought was that if Shelly and Sandy ever broke up, Sandy would not let anyone say negative things about her, either. At least Sandy was consistent. That thought made Shelly feel warmly toward Sandy again.

"You're a very loyal woman, Sandy," Shelly said, breaking the silence.

"Huh." Sandy rolled off her lap and sat up. "What do you mean?"

"Nothing. . . . Well, at least we'll be getting off this island, and that will be the end of it." Shelly noticed with alarm that Sandy looked uncomfortable.

"Uh . . . not exactly." Sandy hesitated, to check Shelly's response. "They've got reservations, she and her husband, at Paradise Cove."

"What?" Shelly's fist slammed down on the bedspread. "How could that happen?"

"They saw the same ad in the Gazette," Sandy answered apprehensively. "But they won't be coming till Wednesday."

"Shit . . . of all the people." Shelly scowled. A diabolical force in the universe was out to get her.

"You got to admit it's pretty funny," Sandy said without conviction.

"How come I'm not laughing, then?" Shelly stood up and walked to the bathroom.

"Where are you going?" Sandy sounded panic-stricken.

"For an intelligent woman, you certainly lack imagination at times." Shelly slammed the door behind her. She heard Sandy say "shit," and then it was quiet. Looking around the tiny room, Shelly decided to seat herself on the edge of the tub. She rested her hands on the smooth, cool porcelain surface and stretched out one leg in front of her.

She was reminded of her childhood, when the bathroom was the only place where she could get any privacy. She had often retreated there to escape from the squabbling of the other kids. It had gotten much worse after her father died, when she was ten. Her mother had to go back to work, and Shelly, the oldest, took the responsibility for looking after her brothers and sisters. At the time it never occurred to her to resent it; she just assumed the burden without question.

It wasn't until years later that Shelly saw how that experience had affected her. Putting other people's needs before your own was definitely habit-forming, and she had to fight that tendency in herself constantly. Sandy would never consciously take advantage of her as some others had, especially the men, but Sandy's healthy egocentrism was often overwhelming to Shelly. Sandy was so easily able to identify what she felt and what she wanted; for Shelly it sometimes took days to figure out how she felt about something. Over the years, Sandy had helped Shelly learn to recognize her full emotions more quickly. But with that improvement had also come some drawbacks, from Sandy's point of view: Shelly was now much more hot-tempered and much less patient.

There had been a time when Shelly would never have left the room as she did just now, and Sandy hadn't quite yet accommodated to the changes. It felt good to be able to pick yourself up and leave a situation; Shelly enjoyed the power of knowing that Sandy was fretting in the other room. At least she was no longer the only one concerned about the other's reactions.

Shelly knew she wasn't being totally fair. Sandy had always been sensitive to her moods, and Sandy had helped her out of her shell, just as Jenny had helped Sandy out of hers. Perhaps that was what was so threatening about Jenny: Shelly wondered which of them had done more for Sandy. Now she was the one asking stupid questions. Jenny might have given Sandy her first taste of love, but it was Shelly who had shown her that love could be solid and healthy.

Shelly watched her fingers tap a rhythm on the tub ledge. Why was she making so many comparisons between herself and Jenny? She must be frightened, although that certainly didn't seem like the logical response. She and Sandy had a good relationship; there was no way Jenny's ghost could ruin it. Sandy was probably blowing this encounter way out of proportion, and it was foolish of Shelly to do the same when she should know better. Of course Jenny had been an exceptionally important person in Sandy's life, and running into her was bound to be a bit traumatic; but that was old history, and even if Sandy didn't know it yet, there was no reason for Shelly to lose her firm footing.

A calm settled over Shelly. This situation had taken her by surprise, but things were beginning to fall back into perspective. There was no need to cancel their reservations on Maui; they wold have their holiday as planned, and Jenny be damned. It would take Sandy a little while to assimilate all that had happened, but she processed things quickly. They were both resilient women, and there was no reason for this to set them back substantially.

In fact it might prove interesting to meet Miss Jennifer Chase, or Mrs. Berkowitz, as she called herself now. Shelly had been curious about Jenny for a long time, but it had never occurred to her that she might actually have the opportunity to behold her in the flesh. It might be a kick for the three of them to get together; she would enjoy witnessing Jenny's reaction to seeing her and Sandy together, living the life Jenny hadn't had the courage for. Besides, it would give Shelly a chance to see what kind of woman Jenny really was.

The only complication might be Sandy's residual feelings for Jenny. After all, Jenny had abandoned Sandy, and that always left a person hanging in the air, wondering what she would now select if she had all the options. Shelly knew that on some level Sandy must be asking that question, and this explained her confusion between past and present.

Shelly stood up and stretched, her hands reaching for the ceiling, then dropped quickly to touch her toes several times. She was pleased to see her body was still flexible, even though she had stopped her morning excercises when things got hectic at school. Perhaps she would do some stretches early in the morning on the beach. She felt greatly relieved. Sandy often said that intellectual understanding of a problem wasn't sufficient, but she certainly was in better spirits.

She opened the bathroom door and stepped into the room. Sandy had turned the armchair to face the window, and was staring out pensively.

"Hi, babe," Sandy said as she stood to face Shelly.

"Hi," Shelly said, equally wistful in tone. Both women smiled.

Sandy walked over to her and put both hands behind Shelly's ears, cupping her head. "I'm really sorry about all this, Shelly. I want to make it up to you."

"Good," Shelly teased. "You can start by making all of the phone calls while we're in Hawaii."

"All?" Sandy shrieked. "I could get more leniency from the Parole Board."

"So go live with the Parole Board."

"You drive a very difficult bargain."

"I live with a very difficult woman."

Sandy laughed. "Okay. I'll take care of the calls to make any arrangements while we're on vacation. Now that is a task we both hate, but out of my generosity . . ."

"Guilt," Shelly interrupted.

Sandy nodded. "But out of my guilt I will assume this abominable chore. Case dismissed?"

Shelly rubbed her chin with her thumb and index finger. "The court will take a close look at the defendant's behavior in the next few days, before coming to a final decision."

"Got you, kid," Sandy said, pushing Shelly in the direction of the bed. "You want a good vacation, huh? Well, what's a vacation without a few laughs?" Sandy fell on the bed, and pulled Shelly on top of her. "And what's laughs without a few tickles?" she yelped, grabbing Shelly's waist and tickling her.

The women wrestled on the bed, laughing and squealing. Then Sandy collapsed on top of Shelly. She raised her head and kissed Shelly gently. "I'm glad you're here, babe," she said. They kissed again, longer this time. Shelly moved her hand down

Sandy's back, to her buttocks, which she squeezed sensually.

"I don't think I can handle it tonight," Sandy said softly, moving Shelly's hand up to her waist. "Okay?" Shelly nodded, even though she felt a little hurt. "But I will let you know when I can."

"Good," Shelly said as she flipped Sandy over onto her back and lay down on top of her. Sandy enfolded Shelly in her arms, and Shelly rested her face between the crook of Sandy's arm and her breast. Sandy reached for the light by the bed, turned it off, and they snuggled in the darkness.

45

A school of angel fish, their skins glowing brilliantly, passed within a few feet. Shelly held her breath, afraid to disturb them, but they seemed oblivious to her presence. Ahead she could see Sandy's flippers gently oscillating as she glided along effortlessly. Sandy seemed to belong in this world of stillness and shocking colors. She moved gracefully by instinct, like the other creatures in this underwater universe.

It was very difficult for Shelly to lose her self-consciousness. Even here, among such sensuous beauty, she couldn't help wondering whether she was disturbing this natural wonderland, throwing off the ecological balance somehow. Even so, she was glad she had agreed to come snorkeling with Sandy. The diversity of the coral was astounding, much more spectacular than what they had seen off Catalina. Snapping her ankles suddenly, she skimmed along the surface until she reached the rocks at the other side of the cove.

There was such a sense of freedom in the water. Motion was almost effortless, and the slightest action translated immediately into a change of position. Gravity was something we took for granted, until for some reason it was called to our attention.

She felt a sudden tug at her flipper, and then Sandy was there, her hair flapping in the water, as she gave Shelly a seductive wink from behind her mask. Then she was off again, her body straightening, speeding along the ocean floor. Shelly went after her without thinking. Only after she was deep underwater did she remember that she had trouble clearing her snorkel once it filled with water. Well, it was too late to worry about that now.

They hit the air about the same time. A tall stream of water shot out of Sandy's snorkel. Shelly pulled hers out of her mouth and inhaled deeply. Then she swam over to Sandy, who was laughing playfully and paddling in place.

Shelly said, "Okay, smart aleck, you want to get sexy with me?"

The masked figure nodded with great enthusiasm. Shelly took a deep breath and dived under. Grabbing Sandy's legs, she squeezed her face into her thighs, her hands pinching Sandy's butt under her suit. The sudden motion forced Sandy beneath the surface. She grasped Shelly's trunk as they whirled round and round in the water, their bodies pressed together in an amphibious embrace.

When they came up for air, Sandy pointed to the shore. They swam leisurely side by side until they reached the beach. Shelly removed her flippers as soon as she could stand; she watched Sandy clump through the waves in penguin fashion.

"You're an awfully cute *klutz*," Shelly called as she ran past Sandy, who still had on her webbed feet.

"*Klutz!*" Sandy yelled indignantly. Throwing off her flippers, she tore after Shelly. They raced along the hot sand and collapsed gasping on the blanket. Shelly turned over onto her back, her arms and legs spread as she tried to catch her breath. Sandy lay next to her, panting in counterpoint.

Shelly rolled over and nestled into Sandy's neck, her tongue licking beads of water that clung to the skin like transparent fruit. She had always loved that part of Sandy's body; it was as soft as Sandy was during their lovemaking. Arching her neck in pleasure, Sandy exposed more of her tender flesh to Shelly's inquisitive mouth, as if she knew what Shelly was thinking.

"You taste so good," Shelly murmured as her tongue traced a path along one of the delicate bones which strained against the skin as Sandy trustingly rolled her head backward.

Staring up at the clear sky, Sandy allowed Shelly to nibble on her as she dug the back of her head into the warm, soft cushion of sand. She curled her back in pleasure, and relished the knowing touch which sent a tingle down her spine, along her thighs, down to her feet. Serene and aroused at the same time, Sandy bent her head to one side and nuzzled into Shelly's underarm. Drops of freshly-scented water sprinkled onto her face. With catlike strokes, Sandy groomed the small mat of hair until each individual strand stretched joyously from its root. Feeling Shelly's body tense with excitement, Sandy very slowly brushed her lips down Shelly's side to the swell of her breast.

She slipped the strap of Shelly's bathing suit off one shoulder and pulled it down to the elbow, where Shelly assisted her in getting it off. The suit cut diagonally across Shelly's chest, covering one breast and exposing the other in a style reminiscent of men's swimwear at the turn of the century. Perhaps that's the kind of garment the Amazons wore, Sandy thought.

Shelly leaned back with an amused expression. "Are you sure you can handle this?" she said with mock concern.

Stunned, Sandy opened her mouth wide, her eyes returning to Shelly's face. "Huh?" she said, then remembered the night

Shelly arrived. "Oh, Christ, Shelly," she groaned. "Are you going to give me a hard time about that?"

"Hard time?" Shelly acted surprised. "I just didn't want you to do anything that might . . ." Shelly never got to finish her sentence. Sandy sprang at her, and they both toppled over, laughing. Sandy's lips found Shelly's, and their tongues began to encircle each other in the artful dance of advance, contact, retreat.

Pressing Sandy's arms to her sides, Shelly stretched the straps of Sandy's suit and pulled them down along her body until the top dangled around her waist. Lovingly, Shelly smiled at the new territory suddenly exposed. She cupped each breast in a hand and gently licked the nipples, a few strokes for one, then a few for the other, so that neither would feel left out.

Sandy grasped the back of Shelly's head with her hands, her fingers massaging Shelly's neck in rhythm with the motion of Shelly's lips on Sandy's nipples. Aroused by the heat that started in her breasts and spread to her genitals, Sandy wrapped her legs around Shelly's waist and squeezed her thighs tightly. She smiled ecstatically and Shelly sucked her nipples with a lover's expertise, and their bodies pulsated to a gradually increasing tempo. Wanting to intensify Shelly's excitement, Sandy made a trail with her tongue around the edge of Shelly's ear. Shelly was exceptionally sensitive there, and Sandy used this touch only on special occasions. She darted her tongue in and out of Shelly's ear, just giving a hint of pleasure to come. Shelly was now biting Sandy's erect nipples, which throbbed with excitement. Sensing Sandy's agitation, Shelly pulled Sandy downward on top of her and slipped one of her thighs between Sandy's legs, so that Sandy would have the pressure she needed to keep from aching.

Sandy answered by pressing her cunt against Shelly's and thrusting her tongue farther into the recesses of Shelly's ear. Shelly was sucking furiously now at Sandy's breast, one hand gripping Sandy's hip and the other down her bathing suit, squeezing Sandy's buttocks between her insistent fingers.

Sandy rolled them both onto their sides and slipped the strap of Shelly's suit off the other shoulder. Her lips moved down Shelly's neck to the soft cup of flesh between her collarbone and shoulder. Shelly leaned on one hip and elbow, allowing Sandy to pull the suit down to her waist and then off completely as she raised her hips off the ground, stretching her torso from elbow to feet. She lay back licentiously as Sandy threw the suit to one side and ran her eyes eagerly over Shelly's body. It had been a long time since Sandy had felt this level of arousal, and she wanted to prolong this delectable state. Shelly's hips were thin and angular, rising in sharp contrast to the flatness of her stomach. The curve of her hip indented dramatically to form the narrow waistline, which Sandy could almost grasp around with her hands. But to Sandy's continual surprise and delight,

206

Shelly's breasts were large and full, spilling out from her thin frame in willful abandon. They refused to be constrained by the body, and they flapped wildly with any sudden motion. Heavy and soulful, they were a place of safety as well as desire.

Watching Sandy take her in, Shelly laughed deeply and lifted her hips slightly in invitation. Sandy ran one finger lightly from the base of Shelly's neck, down to her chest, along the channel between her breasts, and down across her stomach, grazing the navel as the finger continued to the fuzzy covering of hair. When she arrived at the furrow between Shelly's thighs, she gently caressed the whispy strands of hair. Shelly moaned softly, lifting her cunt to try to capture Sandy's finger between the lips. But Sandy kept the finger tantalizingly on the surface, now moving it along the edge until she reached the area above the opening, where she stroked the hairs in a circular motion.

Sandy loved to watch Shelly become aroused, and her own body always responded to what she saw. There was no doubt that women's bodies were beautiful, but somehow Shelly appealed to Sandy in a way no other woman did. It certainly wasn't because Shelly had the most exquisite body in the world; Sandy had always been objective enough about her lover's attributes, although she did feel that Shelly's face was spectacular, the long nose and cheekbones giving her appearance a dignity and character that made cover girls seem silly in comparison. No, it had more to do with the way Shelly's personality radiated through her body, reminding Sandy constantly that this was the woman she loved. The woman with whom she would share her life.

Now Sandy allowed all five fingers to tickle Shelly's pubic hairs. "Tease." Shelly sat up so they were side by side, their legs extended in opposite directions to form a long, straight line. Supporting her weight on both hands, Shelly lowered her face onto Sandy's belly. Her mouth glided softly across the smooth expanse of flesh which hinged at the hip. Sandy leaned over on one elbow, her mouth caressing Shelly's breast until she landed at the nipple, where she sucked the fleshy bulb between pursed lips.

Shelly moved her face downward to nestle it in the downy pile. She breathed in deeply the pungent aroma of earth and body salts, as her tongue scouted its way through the dense growth. Suddenly she came upon a sparser place, and she ran her tongue along this thin patch.

Sandy's tongue now followed the imaginary line she had drawn a moment before with her finger; from cleavage to abdomen she licked a path until she reached Shelly's navel, where she inserted her tongue, simultaneously separating with her hands Shelly's buttocks and running a finger around the anus. Both women were squirming with pleasure and anticipation now. Shelly broke the tension by unfolding Sandy's vulva with her mouth, her tongue plunging into the wet canal as Sandy thrust her hips forward to meet Shelly's probing.

Parting Shelly's swollen lips with her fingers, Sandy ran her thumb from vaginal opening to clitoris and back again. Shelly's vagina was moist with juices that intoxicated Sandy and beckoned her to enter. Mouth slightly parted, and heart pounding furiously, Sandy burrowed her face into Shelly's cunt, her tongue slithering along the channel, mixing the luscious fluids from Shelly's vagina with her own saliva until the wetness was everywhere. Sandy gently licked the clitoris, her lips massaging the vulva as Shelly tightened her thighs around Sandy's face. As Shelly's excitement swelled, Sandy inserted two fingers into her vagina and swirled them slowly against the lubricated walls.

Now both women were lapping at each other's vaginas, their bodies rolling back and forth, oblivious to the sand that gradually coated them. Mouth to vagina, vagina to mouth, they gyrated their hips and heads to a rhythm that oscillated between one woman and the other like an electric current. Their passion raced back and forth, increasing with every body rotation.

Shelly felt herself approach an edge. Her legs stiffened, and then she crossed over, her entire body shaking in spasms, as Sandy's mouth followed her, refusing to let go, insistently passing on its message. When the contractions stopped, Shelly parted her thighs slightly, and Sandy moved her mouth to Shelly's upper leg, which she kissed tenderly.

Both women sighed contentedly. Resting their heads on each other's thighs, they lay quietly, savoring their closeness. The sun baked their bodies with a different kind of heat from the one that had fueled them moments before.

Sandy ran her fingers lightly over Shelly's ass and lower back. Feeling her desire return, Shelly kissed Sandy's inner thigh, her lips moving from cunt to knee and back again. Then she began to massage Sandy's buttocks, her fingers kneading the pliant muscles. Her mouth teased Sandy, brushed her cunt but refused to make a firm commitment. Soon Sandy was wiggling, thrusting her pelvis this way and that, hoping to capture that elusive mouth.

Aching intensely, Sandy dove into Shelly's cunt and began to lick furiously. Shelly's body trembled with surprise. Then Shelly suddenly plunged three fingers into Sandy's vagina and thrust strenuously in and out, round and round. Throbbing with delight, Sandy pushed against Shelly's hand.

Shelly began to kiss Sandy's vulva, her mouth slipping in the wetness that poured from Sandy's vagina. Her tongue slowly parted the vulva and gently rotated the clitoris until Sandy became frantic with excitement. Her pelvis bore down on Shelly's face, insisting that Shelly seize her more forcefully. And just at the point where Sandy felt she couldn't take any more tenderness, Shelly started to lick her more vigorously, until Sandy felt on the verge of explosion. Then Shelly began to suck softly on the concealed bud, coaxing it to come out again, to meet her mouth fully, so that Sandy felt more mild ripples merge into the tide that was carrying her outward from her body at the same time that her sensations were only of her body and Shelly's. And the sucking became intense, then fervent, and Sandy was on the crest of a huge wave, as the lower part of her body was being pulled one way and the upper another, and at the peak where she felt her body would snap, the wave broke and she crashed downwards, her body erupting in several charged outbursts that released a flood of feeling.

Sandy was sobbing, deep painful sobs that wracked her body as intensely as the spasms that had occurred a moment before. Immense tears splashed on Shelly's thigh, mingling with all the other fluids. Suddenly frightened, Sandy turned her body so that she was now lying face-to-face with Shelly. Shelly did not seem startled by her crying. She wrapped her arms around Sandy, and her hands secured Sandy's face on her breast. Sheltered by the certainty of Shelly's love and the comfort of snuggling in her arms, Sandy allowed herself to release the mysterious sadness. She wept for a long time.

When there were no more tears, Sandy ran her hand along Shelly's spine, grounding herself by this trusted reality. A familiar sign post.

"Do you want to talk about it?" Shelly smoothed Sandy's matted hair off her checks. Sandy appreciated that Shelly was giving her a choice: she was asking, not demanding an answer.

"I'm not sure I understand where all that pain came from." Sandy leaned over and kissed the sleek indentation of Shelly's waist. "It must have something to do with running into Jenny, I guess." She rolled onto her back to look at Shelly, who propped herself up on one elbow, holding Sandy's head with the other hand. "What do you think?" Sandy often counted on Shelly to make sense of things when she was confused.

"I think some of it has to do with Jenny. And some of it has to do with us," Shelly said matter-of-factly.

"Us?" Sandy was shocked. "Why would I be crying about us?"

"You've been estranged from me for the last week. That's never happened before." Sandy began to cry again. "It frightened you more than you let on, babe," Shelly said calmly.

"I didn't know, Shelly," Sandy whispered.

"I know."

Sandy felt as though her tears were washing away the last barriers between her and Shelly. Of course she loved Shelly. How could she have ever doubted that? Who else knew her inside and out and loved her none the less? Tilting her head backward, Sandy looked up at the sky and watched a flock of sea gulls passing overhead. They seemed at one with their world in a way that was hard for Sandy to imagine. Shelly was more like the gulls; she had a natural wisdom and grace which seemed to carry her through even the most difficult of situations. Her common sense was one of the qualities that had cemented Sandy's love years before. Cemented. Leave it to the Bronx kid to find an urban image.

"We should be heading back. You've got goose bumps." Shelly rubbed Sandy's arms vigorously. Sandy nodded. She felt very young and nonverbal. Standing up, they brushed the sand off themselves. A strong wind had suddenly sprung up, dusting all their possessions with sand. They dressed, gathered their things quickly, and headed for the jeep.

"Why don't you drive, honey?" Sandy said as she hopped into the passenger seat.

"And to what do I owe this honor?" Shelly got behind the wheel and started the engine. Sandy almost always preferred to drive; she claimed that she got carsick when she wasn't steering.

"I'm not old enough," Sandy said in her most adorable baby's voice.

Shelly grinned affectionately at the guileless child who sat next to her, playing patty cakes with an imaginary playmate. Sandy didn't regress often, but when she did, she went all the way.

"Well, make sure itsy bitsy Sandy doesn't fall out of her seat," Shelly warned. She wished she had paid more attention earlier when Sandy had veered off the main road toward the ocean, guided only by a faint trail and the Stein sense of direction. Now Shelly drove up the hill, trying to look composed as her stomach lodged in her throat. Sandy was happily singing childhood ditties to herself, bouncing joyously in the seat every time they went over a bulge in the earth.

With considerable relief, Shelly drove the jeep onto the main road and headed for the motel. Once they were on the highway, she began to enjoy the ride. There was a wondrously open feeling in the jeep as the wind rushed by, catching and holding her hair. She looked over at Sandy, who was slouched down in her seat, feet propped on the dashboard. It was good for Sandy to give up some control; she had been tightly wound for some time. Sandy noticed Shelly look her way and smiled at her. She was an adult once more, but she seemed softer and more vulnerable now. Shelly smiled back. Very few people ever got to see this side of Sandy; Shelly felt very fortunate.

It was late afternoon when they got back to the cottage. They stripped and jumped into the shower, and the hot spray immediately dispersed the chill of the ocean breeze and the ride home. Sandy wrapped her arms around Shelly's waist, hugging her tightly and pretending to wash her back.

"When was the last time I told you how beautiful you are?" Sandy scratched some sand off Shelly's calf with her foot.

"Oh, about yesterday," Shelly said, wrinkling her face.

"Has it been that long? Tut tut." Sandy shook her head disparagingly. Then her face broke into a grin. "How can I love you so intensely after all these years?" Sandy turned off the shower as she asked this familiar rhetorical question.

"All these years? You ain't seen nothing, kid. We're not going to reach our prime for another twenty."

Shelly stepped out of the shower, grabbing a towel for herself and throwing one at Sandy. Sandy had the crazy idea that romantic love couldn't last past a certain arbitrary point. The more years they spent together, the farther ahead she pushed the deadline. That type of thinking had really irritated Shelly when they were first together, but she had decided not to fight about it, because Sandy's emotions never followed her preconceptions anyway. Sandy might play at being the hardened cynic, but in reality she was more romantic than just about anybody Shelly had ever met.

46

She woke up with the melody from a Mozart sonata still resounding in her head. The dream had taken place in her grandmother's house: the wrought iron gate on which she used to swing, until her mother told her, "Little girls don't do things like that"; the big dark front door with its brass knocker, which she got to pound after pleading with her father to pick her up; and inside, the tall oak coat rack and oval mirror of the entryway.

After hugging Grandma, she would run down the hardwood floors, her patent-leather shoes clicking behind her until she reached her favorite room, with its heavy wooden sliding doors indented for a giant's hands. Placing both of her hands in one hollow, she would push the door open to congratulatory shouts from Grandma: "*Shaynele, Shaynele,* she is as strong as she is beautiful." Then Shelly wandered through the room, running her hands along the two velvet wing-backed chairs which sat in front of the stone fireplace; or she rushed into the kitchen, where there was always the smell of *kreplach* soup, or *borscht* in the summer.

But her favorite memory was of sitting beside Grandma on the piano bench, the huge piano shaking with joy as Grandma's skilled hands brought forth sounds that made her tremble. After Grandma finished playing, they would sit quietly, and Grandma would sigh, and then place her hand on Shelly's thigh, her expression suddenly sad and remote. Shelly threw her arms around Grandma's neck, trying to bring her back; and then Grandma would smile a sad smile and take Shelly by the hand. They walked to the corner where Grandma kept the family pictures, and Grandma would say, "This was my mother, Sarah. She was a very beautiful woman. She married my father, who was one of the few Jewish lawyers at that time, when she was only seventeen. And this was my older sister, Hannah. I told her to come to America but she wouldn't listen, she was too set in her ways." And Grandma would take her through all the pictures, telling stories about each, making little *Shaynele* repeat after her, until the faces and names were inscribed in her mind.

Sandy's hand was resting on Shelly's thigh, her fingers cupped around the curve of the leg. Shelly gently moved back the covers, picked up Sandy's hand, and placed it on the bed, then got up very quietly. She pulled back the curtain and inhaled the moist morning air. Dew was still clinging to the hala trees outside the window, but the sun was already bright and hot.

Shelly examined her face as she brushed her teeth. Her skin was tanned, and she looked rested. The last few days had been good days: plenty of rest, food, and lovemaking. Just what they had needed when they left L.A. Quickly Shelly tried to push L.A. out of her mind; they only had a few days left, and she was determined not to ruin them by worrying about the responsibilities waiting for her at home.

Should she get back into bed, or go for a walk? It would be beautiful at the pool, and probably uncrowded. She decided to go there with a book. She had noticed a few chaises longues the other day, and nothing seemed better than to lie down, gaze at the mango and guava trees and coconut palms which surrounded the area, and listen for the distinctive calls of the *amakihi*, an endemic bird, and the Japanese white-eye, which had been introduced in the early 1900's. Shelly was pleased with herself; at least she remembered something from the book on Hawaiian flora and fauna that she had checked out of the university library. She really should have read more, but with finals and politicking, she just hadn't gotten around to it.

She put on her bathing suit, left Sandy a note, and started down the shaded path to the pool. A spirit of exhilaration swept over her, and she began to run, her thongs flapping wildly against her feet. She slowed down as she reached the pool area. A man was lying in one of the two lounges at the other end of the pool. Shit, she thought. Why did anyone have to be here, and a man at that?

She walked to the pool, slipped one foot out of its thong, and tested the water. It was cool but not cold; maybe she would take a dip before returning to the room. But first she wanted to lie in the sun for a while, allowing her skin to warm so that the pool would be invigorating when she went in. The only problem was that man; he was sitting beside the only other available chair. She really didn't want to sit that close to him; after all, he might be a talker, and she was in no mood for idle conversation, let alone with a strange man. Sandy would say, "Grab the chair and move it to the opposite end of the pool," but that seemed rude. Yet the chair was awfully close to him, and she knew his presence would annoy her. This is ridiculous, she thought. I'm wasting this perfectly wonderful morning on a decision about whether to move a stupid chair. Resolutely, Shelly marched towards the chair and the man.

"Excuse me . . . is anyone using this chair?"

The man opened his eyes. "Well, my wife is going to be out in a few minutes . . ." Shelly started to turn away, ". . . but you're here first, so go ahead and take it." Shelly hesitated, but the man insisted. "No, go ahead."

Shelly pulled the chair a little away from the man, but not as far as she would have liked to. How could she drag the chair away from him as if he had the plague, when he had been so nice about it? There was no way to win with men.

"You been here long?" The man sat up and put some suntan lotion on his legs. He was probably in his mid-thirties, an average-looking Jewish man. Nothing extraordinary except his voice, which had a softness and warmth that made Shelly less irritated.

"A few days," she said noncommittally.

The man nodded. "This is my first trip to the Islands. They're more beautiful than I ever imagined. A welcome change from the Midwest."

"I know what you mean," Shelly replied, starting to get involved in the conversation in spite of herself. "I'm from the Midwest originally myself."

"Yeah? Where are you from?"

Shelly heard the approaching footsteps before she saw the woman. When the man waved, she turned around, and the woman was only a few feet away. Shelly's heart began to race.

"Did you take the suntan lotion?" The woman walked up to her husband's chair and smiled in Shelly's direction. "I couldn't find it anywhere."

The man nodded and pointed to the bottle. Suddenly the sun was scalding her, and Shelly felt faint. She wanted to stand up and get out of here, but her body refused to move.

"Honey, this is . . ." The man scratched his head. "I never got your name, did I? I'm Barry and this is my wife, Jenny."

"Yes, I know." Shelly forced herself to turn to Jenny and look at her directly. "I recognized you from your picture. . . . I'm Michelle." The words sounded heavy, almost ominous to her ears.

"Sandy's lover?" Barry cried. "Oh, wow. This is really funny."

"The twists and turns of fate." Shelly stood up. She was disgusted with herself; the last comment sounded like a line from a soap opera. Damn these people for making a fool out of her. "Well," she started awkwardly, then simply left it hanging in the air. All she wanted to do was run, run away from this humiliating scene with its horrendous characters.

"There's no need for you to get up." Jenny was being so damned nice. "I can get a chair . . ."

"No, please," Shelly interrupted her. "Don't bother, I have to be getting back to the cabin anyway. I promised Sandy I'd wake her up."

"So she still likes to sleep in," Jenny said. There was an awkward silence.

Shelly fumed inside: Was Jenny just crass and insensitive, or had she meant that as a barb to Shelly, a reminder that she too knew Sandy intimately? Shelly started to walk away, but was stopped by an excited exclamation from Jenny.

"Listen. I just had an idea. Why don't the four of us get together some time?"

"Well, why don't you phone later and we'll see," Shelly said over her shoulder.

"Fine. Bye," Jenny called in a friendly tone.

Shelly felt like a buffoon as she fled. Why hadn't she told Jenny just what she could do with her "idea"? This was one situation where rudeness was called for. And no matter how crude she got, she couldn't possibly be as boorish as that Jenny.

Why now? She and Sandy were just starting to enjoy themselves. Seeing Jenny again was bound to upset Sandy, and she would likely react by withdrawing from Shelly, and then they would be right back where they started when she first arrived in Honolulu. Damn them for intruding on us, she thought. What gives them the right?

The longer Shelly stewed about it, the madder she got. She was blind to the tropical foliage along the path; all she could see was images of Sandy and Jenny in the dormitory: eating, sleeping, making love. And beneath those images were burning questions, questions that seared her viscerally, leaving her insides raw. How could Sandy have loved this woman? A woman who didn't even deserve her respect, let alone her love. And why had Shelly's proud and strong-willed lover allowed this twerp to humiliate and demoralize her? It made Shelly's blood boil. At least if Jenny had left Sandy for another woman, Shelly could understand. But to have manipulated Sandy so mercilessly because of men, and out of cowardice? That was unforgivable.

But it wasn't only Jenny she was furious at. She was also irate with Sandy. Given that Sandy had fallen in love with this woman, for whatever inexplicable reasons, how could she still care about her after all these years and after everything she knew? It didn't make any sense. Sandy had to be either stupid or masochistic.

This thought terrified Shelly. Perhaps there was a masochistic side to Sandy that she had never seen. A side that had been lying dormant, just waiting to be triggered by the appropriate signal. Perhaps Shelly had made a tactical mistake by treating Sandy as well as she did. If she had been more cool and distant and given Sandy a rougher time, then maybe Sandy would have appreciated her more, instead of taking her for granted as Shelly often felt she did. What Shelly and Sandy had was healthier than what Sandy and Jenny had; but which was stronger? Was it this fear that made Shelly react so violently now?

No, Shelly decided, it was really very simple. No one liked running into her lover's ex-lover under any circumstances, and especially on vacation. There was nothing excessive in her reaction; she just didn't want to deal with this nonsense, and there was no reason why she should have to. It was Sandy's fault for getting them into this mess in the first place; if she hadn't gone out with Jenny on the main island, none of this would have come up. Sandy had had the choice to ignore Jenny or to get herself embroiled again. And she had chosen the latter course without any consideration of Shelly's feelings.

Shelly stomped into the cottage, slamming the door behind her. Sandy stirred and slowly opened her eyes as she stretched her arms over her head.

"Hi, honey." Sandy's tone was mellow, further fueling Shelly's rage.

"Don't you honey me!" Shelly threw down her towel. Sandy sat up, looking dazed.

"Guess who I ran into down at the pool," Shelly said. "Mr. and Mrs. Straight America." She threw one hand behind her head and batted her lashes. "'Darling, did you take the suntan lotion? I couldn't find it anywhere.' How did you ever have an affair with that woman, anyhow? She's downright pathetic."

Sandy sat quietly for a moment, then got up and walked to the bathroom.

"Where the hell are you going?" Shelly snapped.

"To throw some cold water on my face," Sandy said as she disappeared into the bathroom. Shelly heard the water run. "I have a feeling we're going to have a scene, and at the moment I'm not at my fighting best."

Shelly followed Sandy into the bathroom and stood behind her bent-over frame. She stifled an impulse to kick Sandy in the ass; Sandy's head would smash into the porcelain and probably break open, and then Shelly would have to take her to the hospital. There was no way Sandy was going to get out of this so easily.

"She actually had the *chutspa* to suggest that the four of

us get together. Who is she kidding? She's acting like we're all long-lost buddies." Shelly waited for Sandy to defend Jenny or get angry; but Sandy just wiped her face with the towel. Her silence enraged Shelly. "Well, I don't want to spend any time with them." Now Sandy would have to respond.

"I didn't imagine you would," Sandy said matter-of-factly. "If she calls, I'll take care of it."

Sandy walked out of the bathroom and back into the small bedroom, which at the moment was feeling claustrophobic. So far she had been able to avoid a fight, but if Shelly pushed much harder, she was going to blow it.

"I bet you will." Shelly's tone was bitter.

"What the hell is that supposed to mean?"

"You've been running hot and cold ever since I arrived. It doesn't take a genius to figure out what's been on your mind." Sandy recoiled from Shelly's sarcasm. This was a side of Shelly she had rarely seen: a Shelly who could be venomous with her darts, and who was out to draw blood.

"I'd say that's hitting below the belt, Shelly," Sandy said, trying to shame her.

"Well, that seems to be where the center of your conscious-ness is lately." Shelly was revving up; Sandy felt a wave of anxiety. "So at least I'm on target."

"Look, Shelly, you don't want to see Jenny, that's fine. Nobody asked you to. But just back off, huh? You're really pushing your luck."

"Pushing!" Shelly screamed. "This is nothing. I'm just getting started."

"Will you please lower your voice?"

"I will not lower my voice!" Shelly was still yelling, for no obvious reason. "I have not finished what I intend to say, and you will sit there and shut up for a change."

Sandy found Shelly's shouting very embarrassing. Many of the other cabins probably housed her colleagues, and this wasn't going to help her professional reputation. And somewhere out there were Jenny and Barry; it was humiliating to imagine that they might overhear any of this. Sandy sat down. If she coop-erated, maybe Shelly would be calmer

"For the last two years you have pestered me, like a whiny child, about your desire to have an affair. I have been patient through this, irritable at times but goddamned patient, waiting for you to decide, listening to your nonsensical bullshit about the how, why, where, and when of it, as though you were con-templating some historically significant action. Well, let me set you straight. Whether you end up diddling some woman or not, this conflict is not earth-shattering; in fact, it is not even inter-esting. But in your imaginary philandering, you have reduced both of us to this banality, and I refuse to participate any more. I don't want to hear about it ever again. Is that clear? Ever again." Shelly repeated as if she were talking to an idiot.

"Now, as to this Jenny business," she went on. "I don't like that woman. I don't know what you saw in her, and I don't know why you are still attracted to her. But I refuse to have her in my life. You may say I'm being unreasonable. Okay, I'm being unreasonable. But I do not want her in my life. Which means I do not want her in *your* life. Unless you no longer want our lives to overlap, in which case I will pack my bags and catch the next plane out of here."

Shelly's voice lost some of its anger. Sandy sensed that Shelly was as frightened of what she was saying as Sandy was. In all the years they had been together, Shelly had never threatened to leave. Sandy was stunned.

"You have a choice to make, Sandy. It's me or her. You can't have both. I told you once you could have an affair, but that didn't apply to her. I didn't write an exclusion clause into our agreement, because it never occurred to me that she might be back in the picture. I don't want you to see her. I've never forbidden you to do anything, but I am now forbidding you to see her."

Sandy tried to put the pieces together, but she couldn't quite make sense out of what was happening. One minute she had been sleeping contentedly, and the next minute Shelly was threatening to leave her. It was crazy, like the action in a surrealistic experimental film, where everything is symbolic and none of the characters seem real.

"I do think you're overreacting, Shelly, but that's not the point. I've never seen you this vehement before. If seeing Jenny means any kind of serious threat to us, then I won't see her again. It's important to me to see her, but nowhere near important enough to risk what we have."

"So it's settled?"

"It's settled. When she calls, I'll tell her I've decided not to see her again. In fact, there's no reason we even have to stay on this island. I doubt we could get reservations on any of the other islands now, but I'm sure we could get a flight home early. Why don't I call the airlines and see if we can get a flight tomorrow?"

"You'd be willing to leave now?" Shelly's voice was small.

"Well, of course."

"Then there's no reason for us to go." Shelly walked closer to Sandy. "I don't want to end our vacation early. We've looked forward to it for such a long time."

"Honey, it hasn't been much of a vacation. Maybe we should just go home and try to get calmed down and reconnected. I think we've both had about all we can handle."

"No, I want to stay." Shelly shook her head stubbornly. "And I want you to see her again."

"What? Goddamn it, Shelly, what kind of shit is this?" Sandy was bewildered.

"Now, don't get angry with me," Shelly pleaded. "I want you to meet with her again. You want to, don't you?"

Sandy threw up her hands. "I don't know. What's the difference?"

"You need to talk to her and finish it. And that's important for both of us."

"Shelly, two minutes ago you were threatening to leave me if I ever saw her again. Now you're telling me you're not going to be happy unless I see her one more time. What the hell am I supposed to believe?"

"Two minutes ago I wasn't sure that you loved me enough to let go of her."

"So that's what it was." Sandy sighed in relief. "You had me really scared, kid. I thought there was something seriously wrong."

"I'd say this was pretty serious."

"No, I don't mean it that way. It's just that when you talked about leaving me, I felt like my whole world was turning topsy-turvy, and I didn't know what to do to make it all right again." Sandy walked over to Shelly and stood in front of her, hesitating to touch her. "I'm really sorry I caused you so much pain." Sandy saw Shelly's eyes fill up, and her own eyes became misty.

Shelly suddenly began to laugh, with tears running down her cheeks. "Look at us. We're both a little *meshugeh*, no?" She rested her hands on Sandy's shoulders. "Maybe that's why we get along so well together."

"I don't think our record for this week is terribly impressive," Sandy said dryly.

Shelly stepped over to the dresser for a kleenex and wiped her eyes hastily. "You're absolutely wrong, Dr. Stein," she said in a parody of Sandy's professional manner. "Our performance this week has been remarkable, considering the stresses we've been under. I would think a crisis intervention specialist like you would be aware of that."

"Aren't I lucky to have such a hotsy-totsy lover?" Sandy exaggerated her Bronx accent. "Are you sure you didn't go to finishing school? I can't believe you learned to talk that way on the streets."

"You're impossible," Shelly said, shaking her head in amusement.

"Well, then, that must make me the impossible dream."

47

"Are you sure there's nothing wrong?" Barry twisted the tennis racket nervously in his hands.

"Yes. That's the third time you've asked me this morning. Will you stop bugging me already?" Jenny's voice was peevish. As soon as she finished speaking, she returned to staring out the window.

"Well, okay. I guess I'll go down to the courts then."

Jenny nodded. Barry stood around awkwardly, wondering whether he should make one last attempt at communication.

"So what are you hanging around for now? Would you please go play?" Jenny looked at him for a moment and then smiled. "I'm okay. Now go and have a good game."

Barry returned Jenny's smile, quickly walked over, and kissed her on the forehead. Then he left the room and started on the path up to the tennis courts. Glancing at his watch, he saw he still had a half-hour before he was supposed to meet John. He turned around and headed in the direction of the ocean.

He felt somewhat relieved by the warmth in Jenny's voice when she told him to have a good game. She had been acting so irritable the last few days, so critical of everything he did, that he was beginning to wonder whether she even liked him anymore. She would be excited one minute and depressed the next. In the afternoon she would talk enthusiastically about the nice dinner they would have that night, and then when they got to the restaurant, she stared silently at the other patrons.

He didn't mind her moodiness, nor did he begrudge her the two new suits she had bought on Oahu, even though she had two perfectly fine suits already packed. What really disturbed him was her constant picking on him to tuck in his shirt because he looked like a slob, or not to order dessert because he needed to lose a few pounds. Those flippant comments stung him deeply, and he was still too hurt to talk about it with her. He just didn't understand how she could say those things. She knew how insecure he was about his body image and how many years it had taken him to feel okay about the way he looked. In the first few years of their marriage, Jenny had been very supportive, often reassuring him that he was built just fine, and if she had wanted a jock she would have hung out at the Phys Ed department instead of the business school.

Those first two years had been good. He and Jenny really enjoyed each other's company then; they talked for hours about what had happened each day. Because most of the other grad students weren't married, their house became a center for singles who needed a home-cooked meal or wanted to talk about their problems. After the bachelors went home, he and Jenny would talk some more about them, and then they would lie together, sometimes making love, secure in the knowledge that they had a good life, protected from the instability everywhere around them.

But at the end of their second year together, Jenny started having affairs, and things slowly changed. They just didn't seem as close to each other anymore. It was as if a transparent plastic wall had been constructed between them, and they could touch each other, but there was always something else there when they made contact. Maybe he should never have agreed to an open marriage; he had certainly never taken advantage of it. It just didn't seem fair to forbid Jenny to do something she really wanted to do. He liked neither the idea nor the reality, but he comforted himself with the knowledge that she loved him, and casual sex shouldn't be a threat to a mature relationship like theirs. And it was tolerable, especially because Jenny knew how to be discreet. Until Roger.

Barry clenched his racket tightly as he watched the waves break against the shore, the small mounds of foam forming, then disappearing. It was hard to imagine what life would be like without Jenny. The word Empty reverberated in his mind. When she was seeing Roger, there had been many sleepless nights, as he lay in bed and stared at the unoccupied space beside him. Sometimes he awakened in a cold sweat, feeling like his body had been pounded all over with a flatiron.

He shook his head forcefully, as if to dispel the painful images from his mind. He tried not to think about those days, and recently there had been no cause for alarm. Jenny had even seemed to lose interest in the casual affairs she once desired. He had felt safe again, and he decided it had just taken Jenny a few years to get used to married life, and now they could enter the peaceful portion of their lives, a time to relax together and enjoy themselves.

Now they had enough money to do the traveling they had always wanted to do; but when they took a trip to Nassau and then a longer one to Brazil, Jenny seemed more restless than excited. She would set a demanding itinerary, constantly *schlepping* them to museums, public buildings, and markets, and then at the end of the day collapse exhaustedly in bed. They ended up having less time together on vacation than at home. That was why this trip to Hawaii seemed perfect: they would mix business with pleasure, for the tax break, and finally have a tranquil holiday on Maui after having gotten some of the frenzy out of their system in Honolulu.

But instead of getting closer, they now seemed farther

apart than ever. Damn that Sandy for coming into their lives just when things were beginning to go smoothly. Barry squatted on his heels and clasped his hands in front of him. He wasn't being totally honest with himself. The problems between him and Jenny hadn't just started this week; he had been avoiding some distressing thoughts for a long time, and now he was going to have to take a good look at what he had suspected but refused to accept. There was something missing from their relationship. He didn't know exactly what, but he knew it was important.

It seemed as if they had stopped having fun together. He could remember what it had been like when they were first married: both of them so full of love, each of them wanting to share everything with the other. One day he had found a baby bird and brought it home. Jenny said he was crazy, the bird would die without its mother, and there was no way they could take care of the bird in an apartment, with their crazy schedules. But they kept it warm, fed it flies, and even chopped up some worms for it. It lived, and left them a few weeks later.

What had happened to them? It was as if each day sucked a little more of their life away, leaving them without the joy that had once been abundant. They had so much, compared to most people, and yet Jenny was bored and he was dissatisfied. Or was he? Maybe he was just thinking that because he knew Jenny was dissatisfied. Damn it, what do people expect out of life, anyhow? You try to lead a good life, take care of your family, and be relatively happy. It wasn't glamorous, but it was real. But Jenny had the romantic notion that life should be exciting. And now she was probably imagining that she could find that excitement with Sandy. Well, he was getting fed up with her fantasies. He wanted something that you could count on, that gave your life meaning. He wanted a family.

Ever since he was a child, he had looked forward to having many children. He had been an only child, and he promised himself that his kids would have brothers and sisters, the large ebullient family he had always wanted. He got good grades so that he could go to graduate school, so that some day he would be able to support his family comfortably and give his children the things that his parents had been unable to provide. It seemed like a very achievable dream, very ordinary and mundane.

But Jenny didn't want children. The subject first came up almost a year after they were married. He was talking about when would be a good time to start a family, taking into account their financial situation and the importance of timing properly Jenny's break from her work. Jenny looked at him with surprise and said, "I don't know if I want children."

He hadn't taken it very seriously at that point — after all, they were still in grad school, they had no money, and both of them would be getting careers started, so it was natural for her to feel that way. But even after they had both finished school and worked for a few years, Jenny still showed no interest in having children. It wasn't that she ever categorically said no; she just didn't feel it was the right time. At some point, it became clear to him that it would never be the right time. They had a couple of big fights, and one time Jenny screamed, "If you want children so much, then go get knocked up and *you* have them!" Their laughter broke the tension for a while. They agreed to table the issue, and except for a few comments here and there, nothing had really been resolved.

A lot of experts thought that when a woman didn't have children, she became neurotic and frustrated. That might explain Jenny's restlessness. He was sure Jenny wouldn't buy that; he could just hear her saying it was a bunch of sexist garbage. And maybe it was. With the population problem, there certainly was no reason why every woman had to have children. But children would have been good for their marriage. Children's laughter brought joy into the home. Barry didn't know where he had heard that. It certainly didn't describe his own childhood. His birth seemed to have split his parents into warring camps, each wanting him as an ally. But even if children didn't improve your life, somehow it seemed wrong to live just for yourself. It was so . . . self-indulgent.

For some reason, Jenny didn't agree. She insisted that their lives were important, and she wouldn't even consider having children unless she felt it was something she really wanted to do, rather than something that was expected of her. And then she worked with all those crazy families, so Barry could see where she had gotten that attitude. Certainly many people had kids who never should. But why shouldn't he and Jenny have children, just because so many others had blown it?

If Jenny didn't want to have a lot of kids, they could have just two. A boy and a girl. Barry laughed as he imagined the four of them going for a picnic on Sundays. The American dream. He really was a square in some ways, but the idea of a family felt important to him.

He wanted to see his children enjoy some of the things he had enjoyed as a kid. Like ordering hot dogs at the stadium. Barry caught himself. There was no baseball team near where they lived, and the latest *Consumer Reports* on what went into franks was enough to ruin anyone's appetite forever. He certainly couldn't feed such shit to his kids. But avocado and granola sandwiches didn't sound like much fun either. Something had definitely gotten lost in the last twenty years.

What did children do for fun these days, anyhow? Drugs and sex, a sarcastic voice answered. That's just what he would need. What if his daughter became a junkie, and then a prostitute to support her habit? He couldn't handle that. It was hard to comprehend what it would be like to be a parent, to create some thing, someone, out of your own body, and to watch this small helpless beautiful thing, this little person who looked like you and sounded like your wife — no, better reverse that, Jenny had the good looks in the family — that this little child whom you loved with all your being, could become corrupted, and maybe even destroyed. His heart went out to those poor parents he had seen on TV, who were looking for their teenage runaways or whose kids had gone to the Moonies or some other lunatic fringe.

Children had a way of not turning out the way you wanted them to. His mother had never adjusted to the fact that he hadn't become a doctor, and his father was terribly hurt that Barry and Jenny hadn't settled closer to New York. That didn't make any sense at all; if it hadn't been for his father, he would never have gotten out of the city. In fact, he might not even have gotten away from the old neighborhood. His mother had wanted him to go to Brooklyn College and live at home like everyone else in Flatbush. But his father insisted that his only son should go out of town to college, like the rich kids.

His mother tried every tactic she knew. For weeks, tears streamed from her eyes, and she silently dabbed at them. When that didn't work, she had screaming fits, cornering her husband in the easy chair from which he watched television. She would grab Barry by the arm and drag him to his father. "Do you see this, you cold-hearted butcher?" she would yell. "This is my child, my only son. You want to send him 300 miles away. You want to break my heart. You don't get enough blood all day, go ahead, tear it out," she cried as she pounded her heart with one hand, the other still clutching Barry.

His father would say, "Ida, my mind is made up," and then return to his television.

"You want me to have a nervous breakdown, is that what you want? Okay, I'll have a nervous breakdown."

The fighting ended one night when his father yelled back, "Will you go ahead and do it already? Have your nervous break-down! Maybe then I can get some peace around here."

Barry and his father never talked about it, but Barry knew why his father had stuck to his guns and made sure that Barry got as far away as he could, without losing his state scholarship and in-state tuition. Underneath the bravado, that his son was going to get the best, like the rich people, was a fear that Barry was too quiet and shy, and that he would never be able to stand on his own.

Barry felt a warm glow as he thought of his father. He was a very special man, and Barry's mother had never fully appreciated her husband. Sometimes Barry suspected his mother had married his father only because he was a butcher and that way she could get the finest cuts. And since she had the best meats and free, all of the family holidays were celebrated in her house, so she got to control everything. It was Ida's dream. Barry remembered the large white sign painted in bold black letters: Mort's Meats — The Finest in Kosher Kuisine. All the new women in the neighborhood would come in just to tell him that his sign was spelled wrong. Once they were in, he'd sell them a piece of meat, and since his stock was top quality, he'd get a new customer.

He was a quiet man who read his newspaper regularly and loved the fights. Ida thought it was disgraceful that grown men needed to beat each other up, but better that two should do it and a thousand watch, than that all should have to do it. At least this way her scrawny husband would come home in one piece. "Disgusting," she would say when the fights came on. Barry agreed that boxing was pretty brutal, but he usually sat next to his father anyhow, just to be close to him. It became a father-son ritual that he looked forward to.

When he was in high school, his mother would tell him to ask a nice girl out, instead of staying at home with his *dumkopf* father who had no more sense than the men who beat their brains out for all the world to see. His father always defended him: "Ida, go back into the kitchen. You haven't scrubbed the sink in at least an hour. Leave my son to me." And his mother would retreat to the kitchen, mumbling that her son the doctor should not watch such brutality. Then she would find something to clean.

Ida was a fanatic about cleanliness, and the pots and pans, which hung from brass hooks over the whitest white stove, shone with a religious radiance. He and his father used to joke that she should do a Spic-and-Span commercial and show the world what cleanliness *really* was. She would say, "Stop being so stupid," but she loved their teasing.

On Friday nights they all went to *schul*, and afterwards Barry stood with the men and listened to them talk about politics, sports, and the situation in Israel. His mother went off to the other side of the steps, where the women gathered. Sometimes Barry overheard their conversations. There was a lot of boring stuff about specials at different markets, but every now and then he would hear some strands of gossip. Poor Mrs. Levine I hear her daughter is three months along. No. Yes. And did you hear about Mrs. Wasserman? Her son is dating a *shiksa*. No. And it's serious. And on top of that her husband is having an affair with you'll never guess.

Well, even though his parents were disappointed in him, they really didn't have anything to complain about. It could have been worse. He could have turned into a murderer or a thief, or a Jesus freak, or a homosexual. Barry stopped his thoughts and let that last one sink in. He had never really considered it before, but there couldn't be a worse way to hurt his parents than if he had been queer. They'd probably prefer for him to be an alcoholic or a philanderer. At least that would be normal.

He could just see his mother, frenzied, pulling on her hair, screaming, "What did we do wrong?" And his father, holding her back, his face stern and controlled, the blood vessels in his neck swollen, as he told Barry to get out and never come back again. Barry would stand in the doorway, listening to his father say *kaddish*, the prayer for the dead, while his mother sobbed, "No, Mort, he's our son!" Mort would reply without emotion, his face a frozen mask, "We have no son."

Barry stood up and walked slowly along the edge of the water, heading back in the direction of the courts. It wasn't unusual for him to imagine different situations or put himself in other people's lives, but the intensity of that little vignette surprised him. How could anybody gay ever tell their parents? Suicide or parricide seemed the more humane alternatives. Barry had often heard that homosexuality was no big deal; "live and let live" was the philosophy he learned from his father. But that philosophy applied to others, the *Goyim* and the assimilated Jews with their new names who lived crazy lives. It had nothing to do with your family. Barry was sure his father thought that homosexuality was a Gentile plot, with no Jews involved. There would be no way for him to understand if Barry told him he was homosexual. All he would feel would be the shame that Barry had brought to the family. He wouldn't say it, but he would think, "After all we gave to you, sacrificed for you, this is how you repay us." His father would let his mother say it out loud.

He wondered how gay people dealt with their families. Some obviously kept it a secret, but others seemed to be coming out of the closet, like Sandy. Did her parents know about her? They would be Jewish, also from New York, probably about the same age as his folks. Had they said *kaddish* over her? Maybe some parents handled it differently; and if they were more educated, they would be better informed about these things. But then again, Jenny's parents were educated and urbane, but he didn't think they'd be very accepting. They were upset enough that he and Jenny had been married almost ten years and not had any children yet. One time Jenny's mother pulled him aside and told him that she knew he wanted children and if Jenny was being stubborn and childish, she hoped he knew there were things he could do. He never told Jenny about that — there was no point getting her upset, and she would have been furious — her own mother telling him to trick her.

Barry started up the narrow dirt path to the courts. The morning sun was already warm on the back of his neck and shoulders. This definitely was not the right time to bring up the issue of children again. Running into Sandy had been unsettling for Jenny, and he would have to wait until she was back to normal.

For some reason, Jenny had been acting even more strangely since they ran into Sandy's lover, Shelly. She withdrew into herself and pretended to be engrossed in reading a novel, but she never turned the pages. It seemed a big effort for her to say even a few words to him. He was starting to get pissed. No, he had been pissed every since they first ran into Sandy, but he had done his best to be reasonable and not let it get out of hand. But this was ridiculous. She spent the whole time on Oahu saying she couldn't wait to get to Maui, and wasn't it a shame that they had made arrangements for so much time on the main island, and then when she arrived, all she wanted to do was sit by the pool or take long walks by herself. And at night she often locked herself in the bathroom and stayed there for hours.

Why was she shutting him out? Did she think he couldn't handle her feelings toward Sandy? So what if she was attracted to Sandy again, it was a natural thing when someone ran into an ex-lover. What was the big deal? Unless there *was* a big deal, Barry thought suddenly. Perhaps Jenny's feelings for Sandy were more intense than he had imagined. Could Jenny still be in love with Sandy? After all these years, it didn't seem possible.

Barry felt nauseated. There was a sickly sweet taste in his mouth, from the orange juice he had drunk at the cabin. The climb up the hill was fairly steep, and he stopped for a moment to rest. It just couldn't be. Jenny might feel love for Sandy, but there was no way she could be *in* love with her. So what could Jenny be hiding from him?

Maybe Jenny's attraction to Sandy wasn't a one-in-a-million thing, as she had claimed. Could it be that she had a more general and longstanding attraction to women? But Jenny didn't even have any female friends. Barry found himself growing suspicious. Why the hell didn't she have women friends? It was definitely strange, unless she didn't particularly like women. That was possible — Barry had heard some women say that they preferred the company of men — but then how to explain Sandy? Unless Sandy was more like a man in Jenny's mind, and that's why Jenny had been attracted to her, in the same way that she would have been attracted to some guy.

Barry felt a little relieved. If Jenny was attracted to Sandy because she was like a man, then he couldn't imagine her leaving him for something that wasn't even the real thing. But then, what about Shelly? She was pretty feminine-looking. In fact, she kind of resembled Jenny. A surge of panic swept through his body, blotting out his thoughts. Barry started walking up the hill quickly now, wanting to escape from this awful feeling that was choking him.

On the court he waved to John, who was readying for a serve.

"We're almost done," John called over.

Barry nodded hello to John's opponent. He was a short chubby man, in his sixties probably; Barry noticed sweat glistening on his chest and back. John served a fast ball into the right corner, and the small man moved swiftly to return it. He was surprisingly agile, and the ball shot back to the left side of John's court, forcing him to make an awkward backhand return.

Barry had met John and his wife at the pool yesterday, and they had discovered they both played tennis. John was a Golden Boy. It was an expression Barry used to describe the tall handsome blond Gentile men who grew up with silver jock straps, easy women, and fast sports cars. It was in college that he first encountered that type of men; they went out for tennis and fencing, and belonged to the best fraternities. They could have any woman they wanted, and they didn't want any woman they could have. Barry would watch them from a distance and hate them. It wasn't just that he was envious of them, which he was; nor was it just that he feared them, which he did; it was more that on some level he felt they were the enemy.

Now he watched as John finished off his opponent. The smaller man played well, but he was no match for John's long-legged grace and strength.

What was a lesbian, anyhow? Could Jenny be a lesbian? He had just assumed she wasn't because she told him she wasn't and because she married him. It never occurred to him that a lesbian would get married. But recently he read that many gay men were married and had families.

How could he have been so naive? Jenny had told him about her affair with Sandy; why hadn't he paid more attention to it at the time? Jenny acted like it was nothing important, and she was usually honest with him, but Barry knew that she kept certain things to herself.

Jolted, Barry realized that there might be things Jenny had told Sandy and had never told him. The idea of the two women being closer than he and Jenny was devastating. But then maybe there were also things Jenny was able to talk about with Barry and not with Sandy. There were ways he talked with the guys at the office, and he would never talk to Jenny like that. It was different. But that didn't mean he was closer to the guys, it was just different. In fact, he was much closer to Jenny; with the guys he had to bullshit some, put on a show. The more mature guys didn't take it very seriously, it was just a part of the game. But with Jenny, he could reveal himself as he really was.

Barry wondered what it was like among women. Did they brag to each other about their conquests? No, that didn't sound right. But maybe they showed off in different ways, like who had the bigger diamond or larger country home. What the hell was he thinking about? Jenny didn't have a diamond, and they didn't own a summer home or belong to a country club. So then how did women like Jenny talk with the women they were close to? Barry didn't know because he had never seen Jenny close to another woman. The only woman she had ever been close to was Sandy.

He was not thinking about this clearly. Barry remembered a conversation with Robert, one of the other accountants at work. Robert and his girlfriend had been going together for five years, living together for three, and Robert felt it was time for them to get married. But Jean didn't want marriage; she said it would ruin their relationship. "Women," Bob said in frustration. "Who understands them?" Barry had always thought he understood Jenny, just as he assumed he knew what made his mother tick. But maybe there was a whole other side to them, a secret part that no man ever got to see, and only they knew about it. Each woman guarded the secret, passing it down to her daughters when the men weren't at home.

He was getting paranoid. Before long he would be imagining a female conspiracy, with high priestesses in long flowing robes who wandered through silent stone temples, performing mysterious rituals. Where the hell was all this coming from? Then he remembered a late late movie he had watched a few weeks back when he was having trouble falling asleep. It was called "Cat Women on Mars," or something like that, and it was about a civilization where all the men had died off from some virus and only the women were left. Then a spaceship full of male astronauts from Earth landed. The women decided to kill the invaders, but were tricked and flattered out of it, so that by the end they were glad to have men back in their lives and were waiting for another shipload from Earth. It was a stupid movie, but he had been able to sleep afterwards.

Barry pondered over what strategy he should use with Jenny. Should he be more forceful, insisting that she tell him what was going on and that she not have any more contact with Sandy? Barry had been thinking a lot lately about his parents and how they handled things. Jenny was very different from his mother: she was educated, rational, and a liberated woman. Ida had never had a job; she married Mort when she was only seventeen. But Jenny was similar to his mother in that both were strong-willed women who were used to getting their way. His father rarely bucked Ida unless it was over something important, and Barry reacted the same way. He hated to hassle, to have negative feelings in the household or tension between him and Jenny. But maybe he shouldn't have let Jenny get away with so much. Maybe he had let her cut off his balls, and now she didn't respect him enough. He was tired of her taking him for granted, treating him like an old sofa, familiar and comfortable but boring. He deserved better than he was getting.

Of course if he set down an ultimatum he ran the risk that Jenny would get bullheaded and do just what he told her not to do. She had a very stubborn streak, and a tendency to fight prohibitions as if her life depended on it. His typical strategy was to act thoughtful and understanding. That way Jenny had to realize what a bargain he was, and there was nothing for her to rebel against. But he wasn't sure that this tactic would work now. Ever since Jenny had run into Sandy, she seemed dissatisfied with him; she appeared to want something else from him, but he wasn't sure what.

The short man walked over to the bench, breathing heavily. John collected the balls on his side of the net, then joined them.

"You ready for a set?" John asked, his bronzed body gleaming in the bright sunlight.

"Sure. Don't you want to take a few minutes' break first?"

"Nah. I'm in shape." John turned and walked back onto the court.

Barry felt angry. That guy really thought he was hot shit. "You played a nice game," he said, turning to the man next to him.

"Ah." The man shook his head as he wiped himself off with the towel.

"No, I mean it." Barry got up and positioned himself on the court. "You want to serve or should I?" he asked John.

"You can serve first." John waved his arm gallantly. He had already judged Barry as no threat. What he didn't know was that Barry played a pretty good game. It hadn't come easy for him, but he had worked hard. There was a court near the office, and he often played during his lunch hour and any other chance he got. Barry assessed his opponent: he had a good serve, was faster than Barry and stronger in his return. But he also seemed a bit sloppy, and he was walking into this overconfident. It just might balance out.

Barry served a low fast ball into the corner, forcing John to return it with his backhand. The ball came over the net, but without much power or control. John raced into the middle of the court just as Barry placed the ball again in the same spot. John had to turn in midstride, and he missed the ball by several feet.

In his second serve, Barry once again hit the ball into the weak corner. John was more prepared this time, but his return was still not up to par. They volleyed for a while, Barry holding back on power so that he could place the ball carefully. He saw the confidence leave John's face, which now showed a half-concealed confusion. Barry took the second point.

Readying for his third serve, Barry smiled to himself. He hadn't even realized it, but when he was watching before, he must have detected John's weak spot. The Golden Boy might not have a care in the world, but he was going to get his ass whipped today.

48

Jenny finished the last page and rested the book on her lap. She sat there soundlessly, trying to quiet the many voices that spoke simultaneously within her, until she felt quite dizzy. She turned the book over and stared at the lavender cover with the curly white letters: "Lesbian/Woman." She opened the book again, as she had first done four days ago in the drugstore. Then, her motions had been furtive; she made sure no one was looking in her direction before picking up the book and reading the inside cover page.

The question in bold caps jumped out at her again:

WHAT ARE LESBIANS?

And then the series of questions above that one, printed normally.

Are they women who think, act,
live and love as men?
Are they physiological freaks of nature?
Are they women so sexually driven
that they choose their
love partners indiscriminately?

Jenny's eyes dropped to the answer: "They are suburban house-wives and spinsters, career girls, show girls and cab drivers, society matrons, royalty, middle-class married women and mothers."

She had closed the book there. She knew she wanted to buy it; the question was, how was she going to do it? She looked quickly for a novel by a male author. Seeing John Updike's *Rabbit, Run*, she grabbed it off the shelf and put it on top of *Lesbian/Woman*.

As she waited at the counter, between a man paying for shaving cream and a woman with two youngsters, Jenny observed the way she held the books, covering up the titles by pressing them to her chest. She told herself that she just didn't want to give anyone the wrong impression. They might think she was gay, and it would be wrong to mislead them. But she immediately knew that was bullshit. She was frightened. She didn't want them to think there was something wrong with her. The man might glare at her instead of smile as he excused himself while passing. And the young mother might give her a dirty look or, God forbid, say something to the children like, "See that woman? You stay away from her kind." Then she would move the kids to the other side of the room, transmitting to them her hate and disgust as completely as the air they shared.

Jenny wasn't proud of herself for it, but she had hidden the book when she got back to the hotel. She put it in her cosmetic case. Barry never looked there. She didn't want to have to deal with Barry's questioning look, nor to share the book with him. The book was hers, and she wanted to read it in privacy.

She read it late at night after Barry was asleep, or early in the morning when she awakened with the first light. There were many things in the book that shocked her, and yet somehow they were also things she knew. It was a very strange experience — as if she were reading a book she had once read a very long time ago, and then forgotten entirely. There was a haunting quality of displaced time and space as she felt her life merge with the lives of the women in the book. In many of the women's stories Jenny saw Sandy and, amazingly, she saw herself.

She had often said that categories seemed meaningless and she didn't like labels, but suddenly the divisions in her mind were melting and she felt lost. She told herself that was ridiculous, but every night she was drawn back to the book, and she hungrily followed these women's hardships and triumphs. During the day, she would think about the book, and then time would slow down and she would find herself involved in some activity or other, without knowing quite where she was or how she had gotten there. Other days, she hated the distractions of the shopping, sightseeing, dinners; all she wanted was to get home and read some more from the book, which was burning words into her mind, etching a tale that somehow had something to do with her.

As she read, she found herself getting angry, then furious at the "double life" so many women had to live just to protect their jobs, their children, their reputation in the community. The injustices were overwhelming.

Other sections made her more anxious than angry. She would suddenly stop paying attention. At first she thought she had hit a boring passage, but when she went back and reread it, she felt frightened. Three times Jenny read over these lines: "Some never make it through this long and lonely journey. They can't face rejection, the concept of being 'queer' or different." Each time she put the book down, then picked it up again.

She had never wanted to see what she and Sandy had done as lesbian acts. And she had certainly never thought of herself as a lesbian. Was she fooling herself? Could she be one of the victims of an anti-lesbian society? She hated that word "victim." It wasn't at all how she saw herself. It might be appropriate to describe the suicides, the alcoholics, the ones who had ended up in mental hospitals. But she was a fully functioning person.

The book said that many women engage in lesbian relationships, even live together, but never discuss or admit their lesbianism to anyone. They tell themselves, "I fell in love with a person who just happened to be a woman, but I'm not really a lesbian." Jenny had told herself just that; she had always assumed that what happened between her and Sandy was unique. Now she was finding out that thousands of other women had had similar experiences. Many of those women later discovered that they were in fact lesbians. What did that make *her*?

With relief she read that many women who married had known all along about their true predilection but kept it a secret. That certainly wasn't true of her. She never kept secrets from Barry, and she really loved him and enjoyed sex with him. She never thought about women.

But later in the book she learned that women "came out" at different times and in different ways. Some already knew they were lesbians as little girls, others as teenagers, some had lesbian experiences when they were young, then got married, and then years later realized they were lesbians; some women never had any conscious feelings of attraction to women until they had married and raised a family, and then they discovered they were lesbians and probably always had been. It was incredible, the variety of paths women took to identifying and then accepting their lesbianism.

As a psychological issue Jenny found it fascinating; there were so many questions around denial and repression in response to conformity pressures. And as a personal issue it was mind-boggling; there were so many things she had never questioned, never really thought about. And the amazing thing was that she was an intelligent, educated, and psychologically astute person. It was hard to imagine that seeing Sandy could have created all this confusion. No, it must be that her turmoil had been right under the surface, ready to emerge, and Sandy was the catalyst. As she had been so many years before.

Jenny couldn't get Sandy out of her mind. She fantasied constantly about their making love. They were on the beach, the waves lapping against them as they pressed their bodies together, their mouths finding each other in secret places. Jenny kept thinking back to the life they had shared in the dorm. She imagined Sandy's body, her smell; she tried to remember what Sandy's skin had tasted like. When she thought about Sandy she felt light, exuberant and excited. Then at other times she was confused and agitated.

But it was not just Sandy. Jenny found herself staring at women in the streets of Honolulu and now down at the pool. Several days back, she had been sitting in front of the hotel,

232

looking at the breasts of women as they passed. She was watching one particularly attractive woman, in a tight summer shell, when she saw the woman was eyeing her too. The woman looked amused, not at all upset, but Jenny turned bright red. How could she be so out of control? And what was this sudden fascination with breasts? After that incident Jenny stopped staring; now she just glanced covertly.

It was as if seeing Sandy had opened up a dike, and a flood of lust was pouring out of her. Dike. Jesus. She really was free-associating. But there didn't seem to be any way of stopping. And Jenny wasn't sure that she wanted to stop. It was fun to teel alive and curious, and why shouldn't she have her fantasies?

She remembered the card games she and Sandy had played in college. That was such a carefree period: no serious worries, and plenty of time to enjoy themselves. In fact, she enjoyed herself so much that her grades suffered. But not Sandy. Somehow she pulled the grades, even though she never studied. So she was the lucky one to go to California.

Jenny wondered what would have happened if she had gone to California instead of Sandy. How would her life be different? She would have married someone else. Or would she ever have gotten married? California seemed such a swinging place, you could do whatever you wanted and nobody noticed. Any life style was acceptable. Even Sandy's. If Sandy had gone to Ohio and Jenny to UCLA, would Jenny now be the lesbian and Sandy married, perhaps to Barry? Jenny laughed at the thought of Sandy married to Barry. It was an impossible match. Sandy would eat him up alive. Just as I do, a small voice answered.

Why *did* she marry Barry? The usual answer — that she had fallen in love with him — didn't seem adequate today. Barry was a sweet, kind man. A loving man. Some of her friends had thought him a bit *nebbishy*, but that hadn't stopped her. A more assertive and handsome man would have been more independent. Then she would have had to compete with other women for him, and Jenny didn't want that. She wanted to know that her husband was someone she could count on, someone safe and reliable. That was more important than his being sexy.

She had to admit that she didn't find Barry very attractive. His body was too round and soft; she preferred men who were slim and taut and hairless. At least Barry wasn't particulary hairy. And they did have good sex. She came almost every time, and he loved to make love to her, and was tender and competent in his touches. But she never really enjoyed making love to his body. It was okay, she did it, but she didn't really get involved. She had given him some blow jobs when they were first together, but over the years she stopped doing that, and Barry didn't seem to mind. He never said anything about it, anyhow. Not that she ever gave blow jobs to the other men. No, she couldn't do that unless she really cared about a man, and the only one she had felt enough for was Roger.

Jenny remembered the last time they had made love, four years ago. She had wanted him to fuck her so much, she was half-crazy until he finally stuck it in. She was wiggling everywhere, and he in control, enjoying seeing her want him so much. But he was never serious about her. It was just a fling for him. Wasn't that typical! Barry was more involved with her than she with him, and she had been crazy about Roger, who was only playing with her. Relationships were never equal. And if that was the case, she wanted the winning hand. No way was she going to put herself in a marriage where the man had more power and used it to fuck her over.

She tried to think if there had ever been a man she wanted more than Barry. Roger had been a passionate affair, but looking back on it now, she knew she wouldn't have wanted to marry him. They were powerfully attracted to each other, but there wasn't much substance to their relationship; and he would have made a terrible husband. He was much too egocentric. No, Barry was the best man she had ever met. She couldn't imagine any man being a better mate for her. So what was the matter? She had been lucky enough to find a kind, sensitive, giving man and she still wasn't satisfied. What did she want?

Jenny didn't know what she wanted, but she felt a vague aching inside her gut. She had known this feeling before, but now it was more intense. It clamored for her attention, insisted that she translate the obscure body message, which spoke in yearnings rather than words. Her skin felt tightly stretched over small pockets of fluid that enlarged slowly, the pressure building under the surface until she could no longer contain the liquid and would burst.

But even more present than the fear that she would split wide open were the hot flashes of excitement which seemed to grab her body and catapult her into motion. At night she would toss feverishly, totally involved in dreams she could not remember upon awakening. And during the day, she vacillated between an almost catatonic stupor, in which she could sit for hours staring at nothing in particular, and a manic burst of energy, which would send her racing from one place to another.

It was as if something were incubating, not yet quite ready to be born. Sometimes she would lie quietly, letting the unknown unfold naturally, at its own pace. Other times, she felt pushed and pulled in conflicting directions. But always there was that undercurrent of excitement.

What made her think it would be any different with a woman? Lesbians were bound to get bored with each other, to settle into comfortable relationships like everyone else. And then there would be two of you getting cranky a few days before

234

your period. Jenny had read a study in some psychological bulletin showing that women who lived together often ended up getting their periods on the same day. She tried to remember how it was when she and Sandy roomed together; she didn't think they got their periods at the same time. She wondered whether Sandy and Shelly were on the same cycle.

Shelly was certainly not very pretty. She looked like a school teacher. I wonder if she's molested any little girls lately, Jenny thought, then stopped herself, shocked. What was the matter with her? It was one thing to act petty, but that was an evil thought and terribly unfair. Shelly seemed like a very nice woman. Neither fancy nor plain, just a regular woman. There was no call for Jenny to put her down like that.

Why had Shelly been in such a hurry to get away from her and Barry at the pool? She probably hadn't realized who Barry was, and then the pieces fell into place. Jenny couldn't blame her for not wanting to make conversation, but she was surprised that Shelly wasn't more curious about her. The way she was about Shelly.

Jenny wondered what type of relationship Sandy and Shelly had. She'd put her money on Sandy running the show; she seemed as bossy and opinionated as ever. Then did Shelly love Sandy more than Sandy loved Shelly? Jenny hadn't seen them together, but Sandy seemed crazy about Shelly; her expression got very soft whenever she mentioned her name. Jenny had ignored it at the time, but she remembered Sandy's face now and she felt a wave of jealousy.

It would be just like Sandy to end up being the happy one. In college all she did was bellow that life was miserable and suffering was the essence of existence, and now she was the one living the groovy life in Southern California. Sandy seemed to have everything she wanted. And there was something magical about California. Jenny had always hoped to live there some day, but it never happened. Instead, she had spent the last ten years in Ohio. What the hell was she doing there? Oh, she had a good job and some friends, but she felt like everything was passing her by. Maybe it was time to move. She had sworn she would never live in a big city again, but she no longer felt that way. She needed more stimulation. The job situation was tight, but maybe she and Barry could find work in California.

A half-formed thought was refusing to make itself clear. Jenny tried a trick that she often recommended to her clients when they were on the threshold of an insight but couldn't seem to make the necessary leap of imagination. She closed her eyes and took three deep breaths. In and out. In and out. In and out. There was nothing in her mind except a dark void. She told herself that she was unafraid. Then she rocked back and forth gently, losing herself in the slow rhythm of her body.

235

There was a woman behind a doorway. Jenny couldn't make out her face, but it was someone she knew. The woman entered the room, but it was dark and Jenny still couldn't see who she was. She moved swiftly in the dark; somehow she knew Jenny's room and was able to avoid the furniture. Now she was standing behind Jenny, her body only inches away from Jenny's. Jenny felt her closeness and was afraid. What did this woman want? She wasn't sure whether the woman would harm her. The woman rested her face on Jenny's shoulder. Surprisingly, her breath was cool. Jenny could smell the woman's skin; it was familiar and pleasant. She tried to turn her head to see who the woman was, but the woman evaded Jenny's maneuver, moving with her, anticipating what Jenny's next move would be. Jenny opened her eyes in frustration.

A woman who knew her, a woman who sneaked up from behind: obviously, someone from her past taking her by surprise Sandy. That fragrance lingered; Jenny remembered that Sandy had a strong body smell for a woman. She had always liked Sandy's smell, there was something comforting about it. It was less pungent than a man's smell, than Barry's smell. She hadn't liked Barry's smell in the beginning, but she got used to it with time. But it wasn't the kind of smell that made her want to nuzzle in an underarm, the way she had with Sandy.

So women smelled better than men. Was that the only difference? Jenny struggled to remember what it had been like with Sandy. But how could she make a comparison that was ten years old? She had been a different person then, just beginning to find out who she was and what she wanted. Sandy was a strange mystery, an unknown phenomenon. She was really quite charming when you got over the initial shock, and Jenny found her unconventionality attractive.

Come to think of it, her relationship with Sandy was pretty nearly equal. Sandy had had more power in a certain way: she was more naturally bossy and usually knew exactly what she wanted to do, and Jenny often went along with her. Sandy probably felt that Jenny had more power in that she insisted that they date. But that hadn't felt like power to Jenny; it seemed like necessity. Jenny had done them a favor in protecting their good name.

Of course, that didn't seem totally necessary anymore. At least not in California, where not only was Sandy a lesbian, but she even let everybody know. Jenny wondered what that was like. How did her colleagues treat her? Did they give her a hard time, or reserve the jokes for behind her back? Or did they maybe respect her honesty and courage? Or maybe there were a lot of gay psychologists in California, and they had their own little community.

And what about Sandy's parents? Jenny would have to ask

her more about how they were taking it. Sandy wasn't very close to them in college, so maybe she didn't care what they thought; maybe she had given up winning their approval years before. As Jenny should have. Her parents couldn't even understand why she and Barry hadn't had any children yet. What were they waiting for, her mother always said. Then her father made his pitch about the joys of parenthood and what a shame it would be if she missed out on it. What a bunch of bullshit. She saw what the joys of parenthood had done to her brothers' marriages. One was divorced, and the other staying with his wife because of the children. As if a phony, tension-filled relationship were good for children.

Her parents certainly hadn't had much *nachas* lately. Their children had caused them more grief than pleasure, but they still insisted that having children was the most wonderful experience in life. How could they live with such denial? It was really incredible, the lengths they went to fool themselves, to pretend that everything was okay and going according to plan.

And she had learned their lessons well. They had taught her that security was all she could hope for in life, and it would be obtained through money and family. Only family would take care of you when things got rough. No one else gave a damn. It was a philosophy they had forged in pain and fear. She couldn't blame them for what they believed. But she was born *after* the Holocaust, and it was still haunting her. Were her parents right that nothing had really changed, and she must be prepared for nightmares that might strike at any time? Or was the world really different now? Maybe she was living in unnecessary fear, holed up in her bomb shelter to wait for a disaster that would never come.

Given the chance, would she leave Barry for Sandy? Would Sandy leave Michelle for her? It didn't make sense that two people who hadn't seen each other in years could feel so intensely about each other. But then again, she and Sandy had been close, as close at two people can be, and although they had been through a lot, that basic understanding of one another was still there. Jenny just knew that was true. Sandy was no stranger. Even with all her lesbian rhetoric, she was not a stranger. It didn't matter what her words said. Jenny could see the girl she had known fifteen years ago in the smile and frown and stance of the woman she saw now. There was the same political fervor, the same intensity, the same vulnerability Sandy was still Sandy. But was Jenny still Jenny?

That question upset Jenny more than she wanted to recognize. She had changed a lot in the last ten years, but she wasn't sure she liked those changes. She seemed to have grown more conservative, more rigid. She had gained confidence but lost some of her curiosity. Her life had sanity and moderation, but she was less sure of its meaningfulness and rightness than she had been in a long time.

Rightness. That was the feeling she had with Sandy when they were roommates. When they were lovers. The time they spent together was complete. The hours would pass, and somehow they were never bored with one another. Each mind was fascinated by the other, eager to learn every corner and niche so that nothing would be left unknown. Yet there was still a deep mystery between them, with nothing to hold them together except the rightness of their feelings. It was strange that people said homosexuality was unnatural. If anything, it seemed too natural. Perhaps that was what was so scary about it. She had always been afraid that she would lose herself in Sandy, that they would become a self-contained unit separate from the world. And that was what made it unnatural. Being a homosexual in this world. But it was the only world around. Or so Jenny had always thought. Now she was wondering whether living in Ohio for the last ten years had distorted her world view. Maybe it was possible to live as a lesbian without daily horrors and traumas. If that was so, then one would have something more closely approximating a choice

---

49

Barry held a copy of *Newsweek* in front of himself and watched Jenny zip her slacks. She was humming softly as she dressed; usually Barry enjoyed this sound, a cross between a purr and a trill, but tonight he found her joviality irritating. She had given him little warning about her dinner date with Sandy, and he didn't like her sudden good humor. He got the impatience and grouchiness, and Sandy got the charm and the big smile. Well, he was tired of playing doormat to Jenny's delicate feet.

Jenny positioned herself in front of the bathroom mirror and began to rifle through her cosmetic case. If he was going to say anything to her, the time was now. Barry put the magazine down and tried to gather his thoughts. She was still humming. How dare she be so happy! She, the cause of all his misery, was completely untouched by it. He leaped out of bed and strode to the bathroom.

"There's just one thing before you go." Barry stood behind her, staring at her face reflected in the mirror. "You're never seeing her again."

"What on earth are you talking about?" Jenny put on the elegant gold hoop earrings that he had bought her for her birthday. She had no right to wear those earrings on a date with that dyke.

"You heard me the first time, Jenny." Barry could tell that his voice was threatening, but he didn't care. "I don't want you to have any contact with Sandy after tonight."

Jenny wheeled around and looked at him coldly. "Just who the hell do you think you're talking to?" Her tone was haughty. "I'm not your teenage daughter, who you can order around."

"No, you're my wife." Barry met her stare squarely. "And it's about time you started acting like one."

"And just what is that supposed to mean?"

"That means there's going to be some little changes around here." Barry stood between Jenny and the doorway. "Or else there's going to be some very big changes."

"Is that an ultimatum?" Jenny brushed past him and picked up her purse, which was on the bureau by the bed. Barry controlled an impulse to grab her by the shoulders and shake her. He forced his anger into abeyance. This was only the beginning. They had a long struggle before them.

"Call it what you like," he said quietly. "I love you, Jenny. But you've got to recognize that I have my limits."

"Well, this is one hell of a time for you to get indignant with me." Jenny took the offensive now, seeing that Barry had backed up a bit. "I'm not going to get sucked into a fight with you, Barry." She picked up her jacket and draped it across her shoulders. "I've got a dinner commitment, and I'm not willing to be late for it. We can talk about this later."

She walked briskly down the path to the front office. Damn that Barry. This was the one event she had been looking forward to all week, and he was trying to ruin it for her. She couldn't really blame him, though. He hadn't said a lot, but he was obviously threatened by Sandy. And Jenny knew she hadn't done much to reassure him that everything was okay. Because everythink wasn't okay. Of course, Barry probably sensed that something important was happening to her. No wonder he had started with that ultimatum business. That wasn't like him. He must be very frightened. Jenny felt guilty; she hadn't paid much attention to him during this trip. She had been all wrapped up in herself.

"Shit," Jenny mumbled under her breath as she tripped on a rock, losing her balance for a moment. This was the last thing she wanted to worry about now. There were so many questions to ask about Sandy's life and her relationship with Shelly. And this would be the last opportunity for a while — forever, if Barry had his way.

She was going to have to put all this out of her mind for now. There was no point getting all upset and guilty about Barry.

239

She would make it up to him later. But she wanted tonight just for her and Sandy.

The waiter brought the wine to the table and hesitated for a moment, trying to decide who should taste it.

"Let her do it," Sandy said gallantly. "I'm no connoisseur."

Jenny felt pleased. She sipped the wine, enjoying the warm texture in her mouth.

"It's lovely. Thank you." She waited for him to leave. "So what shall we toast to?" she said as she raised her glass.

"How about the class of '69?" Sandy said with an innocent smile. Jenny did not miss the double entendre. Sandy looked ravishing. She was wearing white linen pants and a black silk shirt that slashed downward between her breasts, tantalizingly revealing her newly acquired golden tan. Jenny smiled as Sandy raised her glass. "To the class of '69."

"To the class of '69," Jenny repeated as their glasses touched lightly.

After they had both taken a sip, Sandy said, "You remember when you asked me if I had stayed in touch with anyone from Buffalo, and I said no?" Jenny nodded. "I totally forgot about Mike."

"Mike Sandler?"

"Yeah. We've stayed in touch all these years."

"That's amazing," Jenny said, not the least bit interested. She was trying to think of a tactful way to ask Sandy about her relationship with Shelly. "Is he still living in Canada?"

"Yeah, he's in Vancouver now. We usually see each other once a year. He'll come down and visit us or we'll go up there for a week or so."

"Then he's met Michelle?" Jenny said cautiously, her interest kindled.

"Oh, yeah, they're the best of friends. They love girlwatching together. I can't get into it. I've always preferred older women."

The waiter brought their dinners: sauteed scallops for Sandy, and Lobster Thermidor for her. Sandy dug into her food with great relish, allowing the conversation to lapse. There were some ways she had definitely not changed.

"You want to taste this?" Sandy bounced in her seat with pleasure. "It's really good."

"Sure."

Sandy speared two scallops on her fork and swished them in the butter sauce before conveying the dripping fork to Jenny's plate. Jenny noticed Sandy eyeing her lobster.

"I assume you'd like to taste mine?" Jenny said with an amused smile.

"I'd love a taste."

"I wouldn't have thought you and Mike would have stayed

friends," Jenny blurted without thinking. Now why did she say that? She realized she was hurt and jealous that Sandy had stayed friends with Mike but never got in touch with her.

"Why?" Sandy looked puzzled. "Because he's a man?"

"Well, actually, I was thinking more of your history together." Why was Shelly willing to be friends with Mike and not her? They were both ex-lovers. Unless Shelly saw Jenny as more of a threat. Jenny felt excited.

"Oh, we worked that through years ago." Sandy swirled the last of her wine in her glass and then drank it in one swift gesture. "Besides, Mike is one of the least sexist men I know, and he has really good lesbian consciousness, so it's been okay."

Jenny felt uncomfortable with the lesbian talk, although she simultaneously wanted more information. The conversation wasn't going at all the way she'd planned, but she didn't seem able or willing to steer it in another direction.

"Did he every marry?" Jenny wanted to know if Sandy was happy. You couldn't come right out and ask someone that. Even Sandy. Maybe she should just ask what kind of friendship Sandy and Shelly had, and let Sandy structure it from there.

"No." Sandy seemed to withdraw a bit.

"Oh, that's too bad." Jenny phrased her question in her mind.

"Why?" Sandy's tone was unmistakably hostile. Jenny jerked back to the conversation they were having, rather than the one in her mind.

"I just meant that it was too bad he hadn't found anyone." Jenny heard how defensive her own voice was. "You know . . . that he was probably lonely."

"No, I don't know." Sandy was irritated with her. Jenny suddenly felt very anxious, the way she had felt years before when Sandy would get stern with her. "What makes you think that just because he's not married, he has to be lonely?"

"What are you getting so upset about?" Jenny didn't understand why Sandy was so touchy about Mike. What was the difference whether he had married or not? Jenny didn't want to be talking about Mike in the first place.

"I'm not upset, I'm annoyed," Sandy said, sounding upset. "The last conversation we had, you espoused the same crazy assumptions about marriage. Are you really that naive? Do you really think that marriage is such a wonderful institution?"

So, it was marriage that was the sore point. Well, Jenny didn't want to be talking about marriage either. Marriage was boring. And she certainly didn't think it was a wonderful institution. Necessary perhaps, but far from wonderful.

"No, I'm not that naive. I was simply . . ."

Sandy cut her off. "Then why did you talk that way about Doris and Bunny? I asked you what *they* were doing, and you told me first what their husbands were doing. The main message you communicated was how happy they were now that they had gotten married. The assumptions are that marriage is great, people get married for good reasons, and anyone who's married must be happy. And now you implied the same thing about Mike." Sandy stopped for a moment to get her breath.

Jenny felt her own anger swell in response to Sandy's. "Why are you picking at everything I say? Look, I haven't seen you in eight years. I'm nervous. I feel like I have to watch my words constantly. And instead I find myself saying things my mother could have said." Sandy was sitting quietly now; Jenny finally had her attention. She took a deep breath. "No, of course I don't believe marriage is all there is in life . . . but I don't think it's such a horrible thing either. I like being married. What's so terrible about that?"

Jenny realized that Sandy's comments had wounded her ego. She didn't think of herself as super-straight, but Sandy surely did and somehow Sandy seemed to elicit that type of response from her. She felt as if her whole life was under attack. Well, who was Sandy to pass judgment on her life anyhow? No one's life could pass the test of close scrutiny with flying colors, and if Sandy didn't know that, then she was still a baby.

"You're taking this personally, Jenny, when I'm talking politically." Sandy was obviously trying to be careful now. Perhaps she didn't want to fight either. "There's nothing so terrible about marriage, if you define it as a voluntary lifetime contract that two people negotiate. But that's an abstraction. In reality, when you look at the institution of marriage in a historical and cultural context, it's an entirely different story. . . . But what made me angry was that you acted as though married people were the only happy and successful people. That makes single people — a category which, by the way, includes most gay people — implicitly unhappy."

Sandy's voice got louder as she moved into her harangue. When she said the word "gay" she was almost shouting. Jenny noticed heads turn, then look away when their eyes met Jenny's. She felt embarrassed and conspicuous. Sandy didn't seem to have any judgment at all.

"Would you lower your voice?" Jenny hissed, leaning over the table. "Does everyone in the restaurant have to know our business?"

"No, of course not." Sandy looked abashed. "I'm sorry, Jenny. It's just that some of the things you say really piss me off." She picked up the check and looked it over. "Why don't we settle here and take a walk on the beach? It's on the way back to our cabins."

Jenny nodded. She was very much confused. Her feelings for Sandy seemed to change with every turn of their conversation

242

At some moments she wanted to be close to Sandy, to touch her and have her return the touch, but at other times she wanted to wring Sandy's cantankerous little neck. Why couldn't Sandy just be amiable? She was so damned likable when she wasn't acting difficult.

It was a beautiful evening, the cool breeze moist with ocean spray. A full moon lit up the sand in shades of gray and black. Sandy felt like howling into the wind but held herself back. She was sure Jenny wouldn't appreciate it, and Jenny seemed freaked out enough already.

Sandy didn't know what was the matter with herself. It seemed like she always ended up fighting about the wrong things. So Jenny had been unconsciously sexist; that didn't mean Sandy had to come to the rescue and correct the mistake. And her feminist analysis of marriage — Jesus, she could see that Jenny hadn't taken a word of it in. And what did she expect? "Happily married women" did not admit their private doubts to mouthy lesbian feminists. Besides, Sandy usually tried not to get involved in theoretical political discussions without a mutually agreed-upon subject.

There must be something else about this marriage business that was bothering her. She hadn't been to a wedding in years, so it wasn't that. Actually, the last time she went to a wedding was — the image was clear, passing before her at an incredible speed. It was so obvious now. Why hadn't she seen it before?

"Do you have any understanding of what it was like for me to go to your wedding, Jenny?" Sandy tried to keep her voice from trembling. "Let alone as the maid of honor? It was the ultimate invalidation of our relationship." *And one of the most difficult experiences of my life.*

"What are you talking about?" Jenny's tone was impatient. "You were my best friend. Asking you to be my maid of honor was a validation of that friendship."

Sandy stared closely at Jenny to see if she was trying to wiggle out of this one, but Jenny really didn't seem to understand what she had done wrong. It was amazing, but then again not really. At the time Sandy hadn't really known how outrageous the whole situation was either.

"Sure. And it was also an invalidation of the fact that we were lovers and that our affair did not end by mutual consent. I wanted you when you left, and I hadn't stopped loving you a year later." *I almost lost my mind, Jenny. I've never felt so lonely or so frightened as I did then. Do you have any idea of the pain I went through? No, I don't think you do. I doubt you've ever let yourself feel that kind of anguish over anyone.*

"Can you imagine inviting me to your wedding if I'd been a male lover?" Sandy continued in the logical vein. "And then having the *chutspa* to ask me to be the best man? But even that isn't a fair parallel." *Nothing about this whole damned thing was fair, Jenny. Doesn't that eat your guts up?* "If I'd been a man, your leaving me would have been for a different reason, like not loving me."

Sandy paused and waited for Jenny to respond. Jenny was walking with her head pointed straight in front of her; her gait was almost military in fashion. She looked like a candidate for the Junta Steering Committee.

"So what are you saying?" Jenny spit the words out from between tightly pressed lips. Sandy couldn't decipher what Jenny was feeling, but at least something was getting through.

"I'm saying it was one thing for you to choose not to recognize our relationship publicly. I'm angry about that, but I understand your fears. But it was an entirely different thing for you to invalidate our relationship *between us*, by asking me to your wedding. You must have known how painful that would be for me. Yet you asked it of me, in the name of our friendship." *For God's sake, Jenny, how could you have done that to me? Didn't you love me at all?* "That's what I don't understand. It was as if you wanted me to pretend that everything was okay. As if you wanted my blessing." *Do you understand what that put me through, Jenny? I hated your getting married, but I loved you. I loved you so much, Jenny.*

"And how do you think you would have felt if I hadn't invited you?" Jenny retorted defensively. "If I had just gotten married without telling you? Are you saying you would have preferred that I ignore you or make believe you didn't exist?"

Sandy was just about to answer when she stepped down on something slimy and soft. A burning sensation shot up her foot and calf. "Oh, fuck." She lifted her foot and hopped around the sand, trying to see what had happened, but there didn't seem to be anything on the sand or on her foot.

"What's the matter?"

"I stepped on something. It was smooth and mushy. Anyhow, it bit me." Sandy hopped around a bit more, trying to get her foot directly into the moonlight. "Damn it, that hurts."

"You want to go right back?" Jenny sounded relieved.

"Listen." Sandy still wanted to make her point and force Jenny to deal with it. "You make it sound like we were still best friends at the time of your wedding. We hadn't had any contact in almost a year when you called me up out of the blue to invite me. And if you had just wanted me to know, you could have sent me an invitation and left it up to me. But instead, you called to coerce me on the phone."

Sandy could still see that scene. She was sitting at her desk studying when the phone rang. It was late and she was tired. Just hearing Jenny's voice threw her into shock.

"You knew I wouldn't come unless you coerced me. I'm not denying it was my choice. I chose to do what you wanted. But you used my love for you." *How could you do that to me, Jenny? Wasn't it bad enough that you left me, without degrading me in that way? Without forcing me to pretend that what you were doing was okay with me? To this day, I am so ashamed of my lack of courage in that moment. How could I have let you do that to me?*

"And don't give me this caring-about-my-feelings bullshit." Sandy felt her anger now, her righteous indignation. "'Cause if you had cared, I would have heard from you after the wedding. But I never did." Sandy stopped walking and faced Jenny, pulling her arm so that Jenny faced her too. "No, you got me to play my part, and then you blithely walked down the aisle and out of my life. Why, Jenny? Why put me through that?"

There were tears streaming down Jenny's face. Her expression was that of an animal trapped, looking for a way to escape. Sandy felt no mercy, no compassion. There wasn't enough liquid in Jenny's body to make up for the thousands of tears Sandy had shed.

"Look, I don't have to listen to this." Jenny jerked her arm free. "I'm going home." She turned back to the lodge and started walking quickly.

Without a second thought, Sandy grabbed her arm and turned her back around. "You're not going anywhere!" she screamed, her rage exploding to the wind, the ocean, the moon. "You can't bullshit me or shut me up. Because I know. I know that you loved me, loved me in a way you could never love that *schlub* in there. You wanted me in a way you've never wanted any man. You know what we had. And you walked out on it. On me. On us. And dammit, on yourself. And I don't understand why. I've never understood it. I know it's got something to do with fear. But you're so fucking busy being normal that you've totally lost touch with anything real."

Jenny's entire body was shaking, her tightly clenched fists digging into her sides. The look she gave Sandy tore through her, shocking her with its savage anguish.

"What do you know?" Jenny whispered, her face eerie in the moonlight. She was breathing hard. "What do you know about me?" she demanded fiercely. "Shall I tell you what you know about me? What you know about me is what you know about life. Nothing." Jenny spit the word out as she moved menacingly closer, her face stopping a few inches from Sandy's. "Do you hear me, Sandy Stein?" She was screaming now. "Nothing," she shrieked. "Nothing. Nothing. Nothing." She pummeled her fists into Sandy's shoulders. Sandy stood there, at first too stunned to protect herself. Then she grabbed Jenny's fists and held them back.

"Jenny," she pleaded. "Jenny, please."

Jenny seemed dazed; she stared at Sandy without comprehension. Then she jerked away from Sandy and walked a few feet away. Her body bent over, and she breathed deeply. Sandy stood quite still; in some ways Jenny's outburst had been a release for her too. She waited. After a while Jenny's breathing became calmer. She turned slowly to face Sandy.

"You're a romantic, Sandy. You always were. You think the world is divided into good and evil, right and wrong, and if you're honest everything works out okay. Well, it doesn't." There was a weary bitterness in Jenny's voice that brought tears to Sandy's eyes. "People can be awful. Ugly and cruel. You used to armor yourself with a facade of cynicism, but I saw right through you. You're a softy, Sandy. Well, I'm not vulnerable like you. I never was. I don't want to be." Jenny sounded furious again, but this time Sandy knew the anger wasn't directed against her. It was a much deeper anger.

Jenny crouched down and ran the sand through her fingers. She seemed like a small frightened child, her delicate frame hunched over itself, no match for the expanse of beach and ocean. Sandy felt an urge to take her into her arms and hold her, to protect her from the ugliness that had injured her so badly. But her scars were on the inside, and Jenny had never really allowed her into that concealed place.

"Fear, you want to know about fear." Jenny's voice took on the universality of a chant now. She stood up angrily and threw a handful of sand toward the ocean. The wind blew it back to shore. "There were nights when you would drop off to sleep like a baby, and then I'd lie there near you and feel the terror creep into my soul, and I'd be paralyzed. I couldn't move. Sometimes I was too scared to breathe. And I knew as you slept peacefully that we could have no life together. They'd never let us be."

Jenny looked at Sandy with a strange expression: a combination of love and frustration. "Persecution was never real to you, Sandy. Oh, you knew about racism and anti-Semitism," Jenny added quickly in response to Sandy's skeptical look, "but it was never real. Love would conquer all. God, sometimes you talked like such a child. And other times you were so womanly. But I knew better. We could get away with it during college. Nobody pays attention to college kids. But once we got out there in the real world — well, that would be different. It would have meant total isolation." Jenny sighed deeply as she stared out at the ocean. "There was no point in even trying. I'd have given in to the pressures eventually."

Sandy's anger was gone now as she gazed at the woman who had once been her whole world. *I would have risked it all, Jenny; I would have died for you. I wouldn't have let them hurt you.*

246

Idiotic sentences, the ravings of a teenage romantic who had found her one true love and was sure she would never love again. Perhaps Jenny was right; maybe they never had a chance.

Sandy sighed. "There was no way for us to know that the Women's Movement was just around the corner, that there were others like us, that some day there would be sisters and support." She too looked into the ocean. The enormousness of the forces they had been up against was too great to grasp. What had happened to them seemed such a senseless waste, so monstrously unfair. Jenny was right about Sandy's childishness. Why did she still think that life was supposed to be fair?

"Jenny, my foot doesn't feel so good." The throbbing had gotten much worse, and the pain shot up her leg in a steady rhythm.

"Oh, God. What's the matter?" Jenny put her arm around Sandy's waist, allowing Sandy to lift her foot up and get a good look at it. It was very badly swollen.

"It's already doubled in size. At this rate I'll be able to pass for Big Foot in a couple of hours."

"This is no time for jokes," Jenny said impatiently. Sandy could tell Jenny was upset; that made her feel good. Jenny did care. "Can you walk on it?"

Sandy tried to put her foot down, but lifted it quickly, winching from the pain. "I don't think so. This is obviously a case for Wonder Woman." She pretended to look around the empty beach. "But you know those heroines — they're never around when you need them."

Jenny ignored Sandy's small talk. She stared at the lights from the lodge; she was a competent woman again. "You were always good at distances. . . . How far would you say we are from the hotel?"

Sandy squinted at the distant lights. "Half a mile, maybe three-quarters of a mile."

"Christ."

"You're going to have to leave me here. Get some help." Sandy tried to sound as matter-of-fact as she could.

"I don't want to leave you here alone, San." Jenny looked worried. She didn't seem to even notice that she had called Sandy by an intimate abbreviation. Suddenly, Sandy felt very peaceful.

"There's no choice. I'm not going to be able to hop it, not that distance in the sand. Run back and call an ambulance. You won't have any trouble finding me," Sandy said with a big smile. "I'm not going anywhere."

Jenny looked at Sandy closely. "Are you sure?"

"Yeah, I'm sure. Give me a hand."

Jenny helped Sandy sit down. Sandy stretched her injured foot in front of her. The pain was worse. Jenny stood around awkwardly, still reluctant to leave.

"You'd better get going." Sandy was brusque. "You were never famous for how fast you ran the 100."

"Don't worry, Sandy. I'll be right back." Taking off her beads and throwing them to the ground, she ran off in the direction of the hotel.

Sandy leaned back on her elbows and gazed contentedly at the stars. The bright pinpoints of light were mesmerizing in their beauty: an elegant succession of incandescent rocks, so spread out that the whole stretch of her imagination was lost in one small corner of the sky. She stared at the concentrations of light and the expanses of black. Awareness of her surroundings slipped away, and she was lulled into a hypnotic state.

Her lungs felt about to burst, but Jenny forced herself to place each foot in front of the other. The sound of her breathing was so loud that it drowned out the roar of the ocean; as she exhaled, she heard the rasp of a wheeze. This was it. She was going to stop smoking. Stumbling along the shoreline, she made a solemn vow: "If I don't have a heart attack or stroke now, God, I promise to quit smoking." It was a contract with a deity Jenny didn't intellectually believe in, but somehow having a second person involved seemed to make it more binding.

Jenny thought she saw a shadow in the distance. Lurching forward, she kept her eyes on the approaching blotch. Thank God, it was Sandy. She collapsed on the beach next to her.

"We're some crew," Sandy said with an ironic smile. "I can't walk, and you sound like you've got terminal emphysema. I guess the smog is pretty bad in rural Ohio."

Jenny was still too badly out of breath to get anything out except, "Shut up, Sandy." She felt the sweat trickle down her chest. When her breathing was more normal, she got up and wiped some of the sand off her clothes.

"I spoke with the manager. It sounds like you stepped on a jellyfish. She called an ambulance, and she'll show them where we are when they arrive. How are you doing?"

"Okay. Jellyfish. Why didn't they warn us at the hotel?"

"The manager said this wasn't the right season for them. Don't look at *me*. She said they usually come later in the year. She even acted surprised."

"Yeah, sure." Sandy still sounded very much like a New Yorker. Even when she was in pain, there was that sarcastic vitality about her. She was so damned alive.

"How come none of this information is ever in the tourist brochures? I can see it now. 'Welcome to Hawaii, land of jellyfish, sun poisoning, and the largest man-eating — excuse me, Great Goddess — people-eating mosquitos, this side of the equator.'"

Jenny laughed heartily as she looked into Sandy's dancing eyes. She had forgotten how good it felt to laugh.

"Is there something you can put under my head?" Sandy squirmed uncomfortably. Jenny saw that she was still leaning back on her elbows. "I hate the feel of sand in my hair."

Jenny moved over, lifted Sandy's head, and placed it in her lap. "How's this?"

"Great." Sandy twisted her head slightly to get more comfortable.

Jenny brushed some sand out of Sandy's hair, then smoothed the tousled hair back into place. "How's the pain?" she asked softly, continuing to caress Sandy's hair, feeling a longing in her body as she stared at Sandy's face, which was streaked with moonlight.

"What pain?" Sandy answered in a chivalrous tone. "I'm an old pro at this. You hardly feel a thing after the 251st accident."

Jenny chuckled. "This reminds me of all the times I took you to the emergency room." She rumpled Sandy's hair in mock frustration. "There was the time you went through a glass door — 30 stitches in your arm; the time you were poisoned by the cafeteria tuna — a week in the infirmary; then there was the time you jumped off a fence and broke your ankle — 4 weeks on crutches, and guess who carried your books all over campus and washed you in the shower; and let's not forget the time you jumped off a chair ir the closet and hit your head on the ceiling. I'll never figure out how you did that one."

Sandy seemed very contented lying there. Her head fit perfectly in Jenny's lap. Jenny ran her finger along Sandy's forehead, then down her nose, stopping at the cleft above her upper lip.

"I never could understand it," Jenny said. "You're one of the best-coordinated women I've ever known. You're so graceful and athletic, and yet you were always hurting yourself. It must have been attention-getting behavior." Sandy smiled at Jenny. Then, lifting her head a little, she nestled it against Jenny's breasts. Jenny slid her arm under Sandy's head and pressed Sandy's face against her. Sandy's cheek was smooth against her skin. Jenny felt very peaceful.

"It's good to be close to you again, Jen." Sandy nuzzled her face in Jenny's breast, then lifted it up to look at Jenny. "That's why I stopped writing and calling — it wasn't just the wedding. The contacts were so superficial. I couldn't stand it. Not after the way it had been." Sandy looked at her with such vulnerability that Jenny felt her insides knot, then relax.

"You ask so much, Sandy." Jenny controlled herself; she didn't want to hurt Sandy again. "Sometimes it's not good to be close. We would never have made the separation. You probably thought that it was easy for me, leaving and starting over. That I never thought about you. I tried not to. But I did. And then I started seeing Barry . . . he's a good man, Sandy." Jenny looked back at the twinkling lights from the lodge. "You have a certain kind of courage. You always did. I respect that in you . . . I loved that in you while we were together." Jenny stared off into the ocean again. She followed one wave as it crested, then dissipated against the shore. Each wave seemed so lonely, so ephemeral. It formed, rose, then died. "We really have gone our separate ways."

"Yeah." Sandy raised herself on her elbows and brought her face close to Jenny's. With a shock, Jenny realized that Sandy was beautiful. She felt something gather in her throat. She cleared her throat, but it refused to go away. Sandy started to say something, stopped, then started again. "Many years ago, you said, 'Sandy, I'd like to kiss you.' That was probably the most important thing any person has ever said to me. It changed my whole life. I wonder sometimes, if you hadn't, if we hadn't, whether I would have become a lesbian. I think eventually I would have, probably when the Women's Movement gained force. But God knows what shit I would have gone through first." Sandy's eyes searched Jenny's. "I owe you an awful lot, Jenny. If I hadn't known what it could be like to be with a woman, I might have settled for so much less."

Jenny swallowed several times. The lump got smaller, enabling her to talk. "I don't think so, Sandy. There's something in you . . . I don't think you've ever settled in your entire life, about anything."

"I'd like to kiss you," Sandy said softly. Jenny laughed, then saw that Sandy was serious. Jenny felt something in her stretch as she leaned forward, her lips meeting Sandy's. They kissed slowly, gingerly, and then with growing familiarity. It was like riding a bicycle. Once you've done it you never forget. Sandy's lips were soft and gentle; they surrendered when Jenny advanced and moved forward when Jenny wavered. There was a familiar rhythm to the give and take, the balance between them. Jenny felt her entire body focus its energy into that kiss, as though her lips were drawing her body's force up and out, to mingle with Sandy's.

Slowly, Sandy stopped the kiss, her lips forming a smile, then pulling away. Jenny watched as Sandy sank back into her lap, laying her head against Jenny's belly. Sandy seemed serene, self-contained. Jenny struggled to calm the pounding in her veins and hands and chest, but the hammering continued.

They had taken Sandy away, and nobody bothered to tell her anything. Jenny paced the empty waiting room, her eyes constantly returning to the two swinging doors, which were lifeless now but had been full of activity a few moments before when Sandy was wheeled in. Sandy waved a vaudeville goodbye, propped up on one elbow, before disappearing behind those doors.

She was good-humored all during the ambulance ride; she

cracked one joke after another, until the attendant was guffawing. And Jenny too. But now the laughter seemed to have happened a very long time ago, and Jenny felt the heaviness of those damned doors. That was the thing about hospitals: they could take someone away smiling, and then you never saw them again. What went on behind those doors was a carefully guarded secret; the white uniforms and spotless hallways were supposed to convince you that everything possible was being done for you, the patient, the loved ones. But no one believed that shit anymore. Everyone knew Medicine was an institution that had created its own rules and rituals to protect the interests of its members. You could bitch and scream, but there was little you could do; alternative systems had been systematically destroyed or forced underground. It was the only game in town, and you played it or you didn't play at all.

There was a sour taste in her mouth. Jenny walked to the water fountain and rinsed her mouth, but the taste refused to go away. All night her body had been revolting against her orders: responding when she didn't want it to, not reacting when it should. The others would be here shortly. She could not tolerate losing control in these circumstances.

Jenny looked at her body in an old mirror that hung by the bulletin board. "Okay," she whispered to the image that looked at her as mercilessly as she looked at it. "We'll strike a bargain. You leave me alone for the rest of tonight, and tomorrow if you want to take over, I won't put up a fight."

She stood there motionless, unaware of the time or her surroundings, her mind mercifully blank. From a distance she heard a car engine approach, then shut off. There was the sound of hurried footsteps, and then the main door swung open, clanging against the wall. Jenny turned hesitantly to face the intruder. It was Shelly.

"How is she?" Shelly ran up to Jenny. Her blouse was unbuttoned at the bottom, and her sandal straps were not clasped properly.

"I don't know. They've got her in there." Jenny motioned to the closed doors. "I don't think it's serious, though," she added automatically when she saw Shelly's concern. She felt very far away, as if she were watching the action of a play through a pair of binoculars; she could see the actors' expressions close up, but she wasn't there.

"Damn." Shelly started to walk toward the doors, then changed her mind and rejoined Jenny. "She's always hurting herself. I can't tell you how many times we've played this emergency room scene." Shelly looked closely at Jenny. "But then, you probably know all that."

"Yeah. She was the same way when I knew her." Jenny felt very awkward. She hadn't expected Shelly to be this nice;

she was even acknowledging that Jenny had known Sandy intimately, too.

"Thank you for taking care of her." Shelly seemed sincerely grateful.

"Oh, sure." Jenny could hear the casual distance in her voice. This was what she had thought she wanted, to get to know Shelly. So why was she acting so stilted and uncommunicative? There was a momentary quizzical look in Shelly's eyes, and then it was gone.

Jenny knew she was blowing this encounter, but she couldn't think of anything to say. Her bargain with her body had called for a suspension of feeling, but she hadn't realized that would include a lockout of her mind. She tried to force her brain to function, to find the words to reach out to Shelly and return that act of kindness. She stood there mute, her mind wandering through empty chambers, as she helplessly watched Shelly walk away from her and ring the bell at the admissions desk.

The front door slammed open again. This time it was Barry. He was wearing his striped pajama top that had been hastily tucked into his pants. Ten to one he still had his pajama bottoms on under the slacks.

"Hi. What's going on?" Barry saw Shelly at the desk and walked over to Jenny.

"It's Sandy. She stepped on a jellyfish. They're treating her now." Jenny's voice sounded mechanical to her, almost bored. At least all the characters had arrived, and she wouldn't have to describe the scene to anyone else. There was a TV soap opera called "Universal Hospital," or something like that. Maybe she should write up this scene and send it in; she was sure they hadn't done anything from this angle.

"You woke me up from a sound sleep. All I remembered was you telling me to get to the hospital quick." Barry loosened his belt and tucked in his shirt. "Whew." Jenny looked at the man standing next to her. She felt no connection to Barry; he was a stranger with a familiar face.

Shelly was talking to someone who had appeared before the sliding glass window. She listened intently, then said something, then listened again. Jenny tried to remember why she had thought Shelly unattractive. She certainly wasn't beautiful, but there was something very appealing about her. A sense of trustworthiness, honesty. Her face revealed character.

The swinging doors spun open, and an orderly entered the room and looked around. He approached Barry.

"You must be Mr. Stein. Your wife is fine." Just at that moment, a nurse rolled Sandy out in a wheelchair, her foot bandaged and extended in front of her.

"How does it feel to be my hubby, Barry?" Sandy said with a sly grin.

"Different," Barry said, getting into the spirit of it.

Jenny watched Sandy spot Shelly, who was standing in the corner, shaking her head and staring at Sandy's bandaged foot.

"Honey, don't be angry. It wasn't my fault, really." Sandy turned to Jenny for support. "Tell her, Jenny. We were just walking by the ocean . . ."

"It's always something, Sandy," Shelly chastised, but she was obviously relieved that Sandy was okay. She walked over to the wheelchair and placed her hand on Sandy's shoulder. Jenny winced as if she had been struck. "How is it?"

Sandy smiled as she looked up to Shelly. "Okay. Actually, not bad." Shelly laughed. Bending over, she hugged Sandy's head against her breast. Jenny felt like she was being smothered. She didn't seem able to breathe.

"God, I could kill you." Shelly tousled Sandy's hair, much as Jenny had done only an hour before. Jenny wanted to escape from the room, but her feet didn't move and her eyes continued to stare at the two women, who seemed oblivious to everyone else around them.

"If this is death, I'd like some more." Sandy stretched her body upward to kiss Shelly lightly on the lips. It was a tasteful kiss for a public setting, but Jenny sensed the intimacy behind it. She felt like a voyeur, gawking at a private interchange that she had no right to be privy to. She turned to face Barry. He was standing awkwardly, one foot resting on the other as he looked first at the two women hugging, then at his wife. It was time for them to leave.

"Well, we should go now," Jenny said as she turned back to the two women. Sandy looked up with surprise, as if she had forgotten Jenny was there.

"Oh, right. Listen, thanks again, Jenny. I'm sorry I was such a pain."

"That's okay." Jenny turned to Barry. "Ready?"

"Yeah." Barry turned to Sandy. "Well, I hope you feel better."

"Thanks."

"Bye."

"Goodbye," Sandy and Shelly answered in unison.

Jenny and Barry walked toward the door.

"You really are something, aren't you?" Shelly's voice said behind them. There was a loving quality to this teasing that almost made Jenny throw up her expensive Lobster Thermidor. She opened the door and held it for Barry.

As she left, she took one last look. Shelly was holding Sandy's hand against her breast, and Sandy was smiling up at her innocently. It was an image carved into her brain. Two dykes and a wheelchair.

50

Jenny stared at her reflection in the water. In the last twenty-four hours she had found herself drawn to mirrors, glass windows, things that duplicated her appearance. Again and again she studied her representation, as if close scrutiny would reveal the answers she sought. But her investigations disclosed only what she already knew; the face that peered back at her was no more willing or able to expose itself than she was. Frustrated, Jenny draped her leg over the side of the pool, her foot splashing the water.

Something had changed last night on the beach. She still didn't understand it completely, but she knew that a door had opened and it was now an issue of courage whether she stepped through to see what was on the other side. She regarded the man sitting next to her. She had always liked his profile: the sharp nose, the long forehead accentuated by bushy eyebrows. How could she explain to this man what was going on inside her? He had his own world of dreams and fears and desires; how could they both explore those worlds without hurting or destroying each other?

She didn't want to lose him. That was one of the few things she was sure of. But neither did she want to close the door she had just discovered. At one time, he probably would have let her go through, and he would wait in fear, hoping she would come back to him. But he had changed, and Jenny wasn't sure he would be there when she came back. If she came back. It seemed very unfair to have to choose between something you knew and loved and something unknown but beckoning you nonetheless.

Last night, after fighting for hours, they had made love. It was just about the best sex they had ever had. She had wanted him with a passion she hadn't felt for years. And he had been more present, more selfish in his needs, freeing her to be selfish too. What did it all mean?

At the same time, she couldn't forget what she had felt while she held Sandy in her arms last night. She had wanted to clutch her tightly and build a screen around them, so no one could tear them apart. They would sit on the beach, the moment of their reunion frozen forever under the cool light of the evening stars. They would be a unit unto themselves, the completion of a circle. When they kissed, she felt her body boundaries fade, and excited and frightened, she allowed it to happen. It was Sandy who cut it short. And then the ambulance, with its shrill screeching siren that pierced their magical world, jerking them back to reality. Or at least to this reality.

"Where are you, Jenny?" She looked up to see Barry gazing at her, his expression concerned, worried. He was being very mature. Whatever his limitations, he certainly had a way of coming through in a crunch.

"I don't know." Jenny wasn't going to lie to him, but she wasn't sure what the truth was. "I don't know what I'm feeling. I know it sounds silly, but it started when Sandy kissed me. Something happened. It was as if a capsule in my body burst and released a warm liquid."

She threw up her hands in exasperation. How could she expect Barry to understand what she was feeling when her explanations sounded like those of a stoned teeny-bopper on her first psychedelic trip. "It was just a strange experience."

Jenny looked away from Barry, pretending to be interested in a couple of children who were swimming and laughing at the other end of the pool. He was visibly disturbed; his hands cracked his knuckles compulsively, as they often did when he was nervous.

"Things are going to change now." Barry said it as half-question, half-statement. "It's funny. I've known about the different men over the years, and that's been okay. Not great, mind you," he said with a pained smile, "but okay. I never expected to meet all of your needs. I guess I knew your feelings for women would come up again some day, and I thought that would be the same for me. But it isn't. I know that when it comes to men, I'm a pretty good deal. I can compete with what other men could offer you. But this woman thing is different . . . it's got me scared." Barry was looking at her pleadingly, wanting her to guarantee that it would be all right. She wanted to reach out to him, to reassure him . . . but what was there to say? She said nothing.

"What happens now, Jen?" Barry had collected himself; his voice was steady. She let him see the tears in her eyes, hoping they would tell him something that her words could not.

"I don't know." She felt the tears spill over and trickle down her cheeks, splashing onto her thighs. Barry made no attempt to comfort her. That was right. For a while they would have to comfort themselves.

Jenny sensed that there was a flood of tears behind the few solitary ones that had found their way to her eyes. A deluge that would swell, surge, and overflow in a rush to find a new balance. She might be overwhelmed by that inundation, even engulfed; but she wouldn't drown. After all, she was a survivor.

51

Sandy leaned back against the soft upholstery and watched the two columns of fruit trees rush by. There was something special about riding in taxi cabs, particularly the older, more spacious ones whose interiors had been constructed with comfort in mind. Perhaps it was the feeling that you could just sit back and let someone else take charge for a while, secure in the knowledge that they would get you where you wanted to go. Taxis were somewhat like a magic carpet: you climbed aboard, gave the instructions, and then swoosh, you were off, free to relax and enjoy the scenery, which was always beautiful in the country-side and at least interesting in the cities.

It was very pleasant every once in a while to turn over your life to someone else, and escape for a moment from the awesome responsibility. Shelly often complained that Sandy had a problem with control. She was probably right; Sandy did have a hard time letting go. Just as she had a hard time accepting that there were many things she was powerless to affect, let alone direct.

Like Jenny. Maybe that was why she had found the end of that affair so difficult. No matter what she had said or done, she had been unable to change Jenny's mind. And if you can't get someone you love and who loves you to change her mind — well, that's about as helpless and powerless as you can get.

Sandy watched the graceful eucalyptus ripple in the wind. The seductiveness of that motion further lulled her into the serene contemplative state she was already in. There was more to it than control. The affair with Jenny had haunted her as relentlessly as a 24-hour ghost service. Sandy smiled to herself. Southern California was a mecca for astrology, occultism, ouija boards and other "esoteric phenomena." Maybe she should blame it on the supernatural. She and Jenny had been kindred spirits in a past life, and that was why she had so much trouble letting go. They had been sisters in medieval France, and Jenny had watched Sandy burned at the stake as a witch. The experience was harder on the sister who lived; that explained why Jenny now had so much difficulty committing herself to an unacceptable life style. And as they had once been sisters, there was also the incest taboo, which would have made Jenny even more uncom-fortable about staying in the relationship. By some people's standards it was a perfectly plausible explanation, but Sandy was dissatisfied. How come *she* was not freaked out by the taboos? And what made her able to choose an unacceptable life style when her sister couldn't?

Sandy suddenly remembered Marilyn's dream of being in a mental hospital with a man and coming upon a group of lesbians, from whom she fled in fear that her own lesbianism would be discovered. Marilyn was at an early stage of the coming-out process: an intense panic, which included both confusion about her identity and terror of being found out. But at least she had started the process. With all her fears and insecurities and con-fusions, she had taken the jump. Why? Perhaps that was an even more interesting question than why Jenny and the millions of women like her had not. What was it that enabled any woman to put so much on the line?

Sandy felt a light hand on her thigh. "How you doing?" a warm, familiar voice asked. She turned to face Shelly.

"Oh, the pain's not too bad." Sandy picked up Shelly's hand with her own and raised it to her lips, then put it back on her thigh again. "Nothing a few Midols won't cure."

"I didn't mean your foot."

"Oh . . . okay. A little spaced-out. Actually, better than okay." Shelly raised her eyebrows as she looked at Sandy questioningly.

"I feel relieved. As if I've freed myself from a burden I carried for a long time. I certainly let go of some of my anger," Sandy chuckled and shook her head, "and I think I'm more finished with that part of my past." She wrapped her fingers around Shelly's and felt the solidness of their interlocking. Shelly was so damned open and supportive; what had Sandy done to deserve such a fine woman?

"I know this hasn't been easy for you, Shelly, and on our romantic vacation, too." Sandy noticed the cab driver staring at them in his rear-view mirror. Well, he'd have one hell of a story for the gang at the station tonight.

Then she had an idea. "I'll tell you what. I owe you one, right?" Shelly nodded. "So how about we do something you've always wanted to do, but I never agreed to? . . . For our next vacation, we could go to that place in France and see the cave drawings. Shit, that wouldn't be so bad."

"Sandy."

"Huh?"

"If this is supposed to be for me, how about I get to choose what it is we do?"

"Oh. I'm sorry, I just thought . . ."

"That you were being helpful," Shelly interrupted. "What you were being was bossy."

"Sorry." Sandy hung her head.

"My choice," Shelly said, accentuating every word in regal fashion, "is that we order subscription tickets to the opera this season."

"The opera!" Sandy shrieked. "Oh, come on, Shelly, I haven't done anything that horrible." Shelly's look was firm. Sandy tried a different strategy. "Look, okay, let's buy tickets for one performance and see if we enjoy it. Who knows, maybe you won't like the stuff anymore, or the company in L.A. won't be any good?"

"I'll like it," Shelly said definitely.

Sandy knew she was losing. "Please, Shelly, have a heart," she whined. "Are you really going to make me listen to a bunch of shrill women and bullfrog men croaking in some weird language

I can't even understand, every Friday night for three months?"

"The weird language is Italian, Sandy."

"God, you're cruel."

"So, it's settled." Shelly was looking very pleased with herself.

Sandy groaned and collapsed onto Shelly's shoulder. Shelly wrapped her arms around Sandy. After a minute, Sandy melodramatically threw her arms out and cried, "What will happen to poor Sandy Stein? First there was the opera. Then she started carrying around a snuff case. And before long she was seen wearing taffeta dresses, Louis XIV style, of course." Shelly was holding her sides as she rolled around the cab in a fit of laughter. "And then one miserable day, she went into a ritzy neighborhood and signed up for ballet lessons. And before she had a chance to think twice, she married Prince Charming and lived unhappily ever after. Is that what you want to happen to me, Shelly?"

Shelly pulled out a tissue and wiped her eyes as she tried to stop laughing. "You're incredible! Do you really think that if you go to the opera you're going to end up straight?"

"Stranger things have happened." Shelly looked skeptical. "Well, shit, Shelly, ' don't know. It just seems like it's going to change me, I'm going to lose something."

Shelly was suddenly serious as she put her hand on Sandy's arm. "You've worked very hard to be the kind of person you are, Sandy. No one can take that away from you."

Sandy felt the warmth spread through her body. Shelly put an arm around her shoulders, and Sandy snuggled close, feeling protected equally by Shelly's brilliance and her softness. They sat there for a long time. Shelly broke the silence.

"What about Jenny? What's going to happen to her?"

"I'm not sure. She's always so damned cool, it's hard to read her. And she deals with stuff so differently from me. She must have mixed feelings about the choices she made. But I don't know that a lesbian choice would have been as right for her as it was for me. She genuinely seems comfortable, maybe even happy with him."

"Sure. Comfortable. Secure. Safe." Shelly rolled these words out as if she were citing items on a grocery list. "But she's paid a price in passion."

"Probably. But who's to say how important passion is?"

Shelly started to say something, then appeared to decide better of it and instead stared out the window. Sandy looked at her with affection. At the moment she was too tired to feel much passion, but she knew it would return.

Maybe Shelly was right. Maybe there were some things they couldn't take away from you.

About the Author

Nancy Toder is a clinical psychologist specializing in therapy with lesbians. *Choices* is her first novel. She has been active in the feminist and lesbian movements since the early '70s, and contributed chapters to *Our Right To Love* and *Positively Gay*.